Blackstone's Statutes on

PUBLIC LAW

Blackstone's Statutes on

PUBLIC LAW

Seventh Edition

Edited by

Peter Wallington MA, LLM, Barrister
11 King's Bench Walk Chambers

and

Robert G. Lee LLB
Professor of Law, Cardiff Law School

BLACKSTONE PRESS LIMITED

First published in Great Britain 1988 by Blackstone Press Limited,
Aldine Place, London W12 8AA. Telephone 0181-740 2277

First edition, 1988
Second edition, 1990
Third edition, 1992
Reprinted, 1993
Fourth edition, 1994
Fifth edition, 1995
Sixth edition, 1996
Seventh edition, 1997

ISBN: 1 85431 666 4

British Library in cataloguing in Publication Data
A CIP cataloguing record for this book is available from the British Library

Typeset by Montage Studios Limited, Tonbridge, Kent
Printed by Ashford Colour Press, Gosport, Hampshire

CONTENTS

EDITORS' PREFACE

The adage that Britain has no written constitution, while still technically true, is an increasingly unhelpful and unreal starting point for the study of Constitutional and Administrative Law. As in many other areas of the law, statute has assumed an increasingly pervasive role. And while there is no domestic constitutional document to use as a starting point for studying 'the British Constitution', international sources play an increasing part in the regulation of power in the UK, and the continuing controversy over Bills of Rights makes it important to look for comparison at the constitutional approach of some other jurisdictions. The volume of statutory and analogous material to which students in the field of Public Law now need to refer has become such that a separate set of materials is a necessary guide. Hence this book.

We have assembled here a collection of statutes on all aspects of Constitutional and Administrative Law and Civil Liberties. It is not intended to replace textbooks or cases and materials books, but to complement them and to provide necessary and quick reference to essential texts. Since it contains no commentary it is suitable — and we hope will be adopted — for reference in examinations in these subjects (but do check with your faculty or department whether this is so). We hope it will also encourage students to become more accustomed to reading and unravelling the language of Parliament — one of the most basic skills of a lawyer.

The selection of materials for a collection of statutes is a matter of sometimes arbitrary editorial judgment. Our selection is based on the knowledge that courses vary in content and an attempt to meet the major needs of a fairly broad range of undergraduate courses. This means the book will contain some material irrelevant to your particular course — but much that is central, or a valuable supplement, to any course in the Public Law area (including important parts of English Legal System courses). The book is designed to be used by English, Welsh and Scottish students; the territorial extent of each Act is indicated and where there is parallel English and Scottish legislation we have included both (with exceptions, especially in the field of Local Government). For reasons of space this approach was not possible for Northern Ireland, but we have included those parts of Northern Irish legislation of most interest to students elsewhere in the UK.

As well as statutes, we include the Bill of Rights amendments to the United States Constitution, the European Convention on Human Rights, parts of the Treaty of Rome as amended by the Single European Act and the (Maastricht) Treaty of European Union (and an example of a Regulation and a Directive made under it) and major extracts from the key Codes of Practice issued under the Police and Criminal Evidence Act 1984 (as reissued in 1995). We have also included Order 53 of the Rules of the Supreme Court, which lays down the procedures for applications for Judicial Review.

Because this is a text for students rather than practitioners we have been able to be more selective in cutting material down to a manageable length. Omissions are indicated by a row of asterisks. Provisions as to commencement, etc. have also been omitted. The text is printed, where appropriate, as subsequently amended; new materials are shown by square brackets and repeals by dots. Statutes are printed in chronological order; other material is gathered together in Part II.

This edition coincides with the first change in Government of the United Kingdom for 18 years. Significant legislation in the field of public law has been promised in the Queen's Speech for the first session of the Labour Government, and changes will be reflected in future editions of this book. This edition represents the significant provisions of public law as at the departure from office of the Conservatives on 2 May 1997. All legislative changes enacted up to that date have been incorporated, whether or not yet in force (it is quite possible some of the most recent Acts will not now be brought into force at all — this should be checked). The final new legislation now included covers familiar ground: police powers, criminal investigation, Northern Ireland, immigration, asylum and nationality, as well as one of the very few Acts affecting Parliamentary Privilege, the Defamation Act 1996. Of the changes the most sweeping and controversial in 1996–7 is the Police Act 1997, conferring significant new powers in support of the investigation of major crime, with novel procedures to protect individuals from their misuse. Whether this legislation will be retained remains to be seen.

We gratefully acknowledge the help we received from Clive Lewis, who advised on content and carefully checked the manuscript of the first edition, and Urfan Khaliq who checked the material on the ECHR. We are also indebted to Jeremy McBride of the University of Birmingham both for suggestions as to inclusions and for the benefits of collaboration over the years in the internal production of statutory materials for students at Cambridge, Birmingham and Lancaster. Finally our thanks are due to our publishers for their speed and efficiency in production. The responsibility for errors is the editors' alone.

Peter Wallington
Robert G. Lee
September 1997

PART I

STATUTES OF THE UK PARLIAMENT AND ITS PREDECESSORS

MAGNA CARTA
(Statute 25 Edw. 1, 1297)

Territorial extent England and Wales, Northern Ireland

The Great Charter of the Liberties of England, and of the Liberties of the Forest; confirmed by King Edward, in the Twenty-fifth Year of his Reign.
Edward by the grace of God King of England, Lord of Ireland, and Duke of Guyan, to all archbishops, bishops, &c. We have seen the Great Charter of the Lord Henry sometimes King of England, our father, of the liberties of England in these words:

Henry by the grace of God King of England, Lord of Ireland, Duke of Normandy and Guyan, and Earl of Anjou, to all archbishops, bishops, abbots, priors, earls, barons, sheriffs, provosts, officers, and to all bailiffs, and other our faithful subjects, which shall see this present charter, greeting: Know ye, that we, unto the honour of Almighty God, and for the salvation of the souls of our progenitors and successors Kings of England, to the advancement of holy church and amendment of our realm, of our meer and free will, have given and granted to all archbishops, bishops, abbots, priors, earls, barons, and to all freemen of this our realm, these liberties following, to be kept in our kingdom of England for ever.

Chapter 1 Confirmation of liberties
First, we have granted to God, and by this our present charter have confirmed, for us and our heirs for ever, that the church of England shall be free, and shall have all her whole rights and liberties inviolable. We have granted also, and given to all the freemen of our realm, for us and our heirs for ever, these liberties underwritten, to have and to hold to them and their heirs, of us and our heirs for ever.

Chapters 2-28 . . .

Chapter 29 Imprisonment, etc. contrary to law
No freeman shall be taken or imprisoned, or be disseised of his freehold, or liberties, or free customs, or be outlawed, or exiled, or any other wise destroyed; nor will we not pass upon him, nor condemn him, but by lawful judgment of his peers, or by the law of the land. We will sell to no man, we will not deny or defer to any man either justice or right.

Chapters 30-36 . . .
[Chapter 37 (Escuage) omitted]

TREASON ACT 1351
(25 Edw. 3 Stat 5, c. 2)

Territorial extent United Kingdom

Declaration what offences shall be adjudged treason

Item, whereas divers opinions have been before this time in what case treason shall be said, and in what not; the King, at the request of the lords and of the commons, hath made a declaration in the manner as hereafter followeth, that is to say; when a man doth compass or imagine the death of our lord the King, or of our lady his Queen or of their eldest son and heir; or if a man do violate the King's companion, or the King's eldest daughter unmarried, or the wife the King's eldest son and heir; or if a man do levy war against our lord the King in his realm, or be adherent to the King's enemies in his realm, giving to them aid and comfort in the realm, or elsewhere, and thereof be probably attainted of open deed by the people of their condition: . . . and if a man slea the chancellor, treasurer, or the King's justices of the one bench or the other, justices in eyre, or justices of assise, and all other justices assigned to hear and determine, being in their places, doing their offices: and it is to be understood, that in the cases above rehearsed, that ought to be judged treason which extends to our lord the King, and his royal majesty: . . .

JUSTICES OF THE PEACE ACT 1361
(34 Edw. 3, c. 1)

Who shall be justices of the peace — Their jurisdiction over offenders; rioters; barrators; and vagabonds — Commissions of general inquiries to end — Fines to be reasonable

Territorial extent England and Wales, Northern Ireland (in part — see Magistrates' Courts Act (Northern Ireland) 1964. Sch. 2).

First, that in every county of England shall be assigned for the keeping of the peace, one lord, and with him three or four of the most worthy in the county, with some learned in the law, and they shall have power to restrain the offenders, rioters, and all other barrators and to pursue, arrest, take, and chastise them according their trespass or offence; and to cause them to be imprisoned and duly punished according to the law and customs of the realm, and according to that which to them shall seem best to do by their discretions and good advisement; . . . and to take and arrest all those that they may find by indictment, or by suspicion, and to put them in prison; and to take of all them that be not of good fame, where they shall be found, sufficient surety and mainprise of their good behaviour towards the King and his people, and the other duly to punish; to the intent that the people be not by such rioters or rebels troubled nor endamaged, nor the peace blemished, nor merchants nor other passing by the highways of the realm disturbed, nor put in the peril which may happen of such offenders . . .

THE BILL OF RIGHTS (1688)
(1 Will. & Mar. sess 2, c. 2)

An Act declaring the Rights and Liberties of the Subject and Setleing the Succession of the Crowne

Territorial extent England and Wales, Northern Ireland (for Scotland see the equivalent Act of the Scottish Parliament, the Claim of Right 1689).

Whereas the lords spirituall and temporall and comons assembled at Westminster lawfully fully and freely representing all estates of the people of this realme did upon the thirteenth day of February in the yeare of our Lord one thousand six hundred eighty eight present unto their Majesties then called and known by the names and stile of William and Mary Prince and Princesse of Orange being present in their proper persons a certaine declaration in writeing made by the said lords and comons in the words following viz

The heads of declaration of lords and commons, recited — Whereas the late King James the Second by the assistance of diverse evill councillors judges and ministers imployed by him did endeavour to subvert and extirpate the Protestant religion and the lawes and liberties of this kingdome

Dispensing and suspending power — By assumeing and exerciseing a power of dispensing with and suspending of lawes and the execution of lawes without consent of Parlyament.

Committing prelates — By committing and prosecuting diverse worthy prelates for humbly petitioning to be excused from concurring to the said assumed power.

Ecclesiastical commission — By issueing and causeing to be executed a commission under the great seale for erecting a court called the court of commissioners for ecclesiasticall causes.

Levying money — By levying money for and to the use of the Crowne by pretence of prerogative for other time and in other manner then the same was granted by Parlyament.

Standing army — By raising and keeping a standing army within this kingdome in time of peace without consent of Parlyament and quartering soldiers contrary to law.

Disarming Protestants, etc. — By causing severall good subjects being protestants to be disarmed at the same time when papists were both armed and imployed contrary to law.

Violating elections — By violating the freedome of election of members to serve in Parlyament.

Illegal prosecutions — By prosecutions in the Court of King's Bench for matters and causes cognizable onely in Parlyament and by diverse other arbitrary and illegall courses.

Juries — And whereas of late yeares partiall corrupt and unqualifyed persons have beene returned and served on juryes in tryalls and particularly diverse jurors in tryalls for high treason which were not freeholders.

Excessive bail — And excessive baile hath beene required of persons committed in criminall cases to elude the benefitt of the lawes made for the liberty of the subjects.

Fines — And excessive fines have beene imposed.

Punishments — And illegall and cruell punishments inflicted.

Grants of fines, etc., before conviction, etc. — And severall grants and promises made of fines and forfeitures before any conviction or judgement against the persons upon whome the same were to be levyed.

All which are uterly and directly contrary to the knowne lawes and statutes and freedome of the realme.

And whereas the said late King James the Second haveing abdicated the government and the throne being thereby vacant his Highnesse the Prince of Orange (whome it hath pleased Almighty God to make the glorious instrument of delivering this kingdome from popery and arbitrary power) did (by the advice of the lords spirituall and temporall and diverse principall persons of the commons) cause letters to be written to the lords spirituall and temporall being protestants and other letters to the severall countyes cityes universities boroughss and cinque ports for the choosing of such persons to represent them as were of right to be sent to Parlyament to meete and sitt at Westminster upon the two and twentyeth day of January in this yeare one thousand six hundred eighty and eight in order to such an establishment as that their religion lawes and liberties might not againe be in danger of being subverted, upon which letters elections haveing beene accordingly made.

The subject's Rights — And thereupon the said lords spirituall and temporall and commons pursuant to their respective letters and elections being now assembled in a full and free representative of this nation takeing into their most serious consideration the best meanes for attaining the ends aforesaid doe in the first place (as their auncestors in like case have usually done) for the vindicating and asserting their auntient rights and liberties, declare

[1] Suspending power — That the pretended power of suspending of laws or the execution of laws by regall authority without consent of Parlyament is illegall.

Late dispensing power — That the pretended power of dispensing with laws or the execution of laws by regall authoritie as it hath beene assumed and exercised of late is illegall.

Ecclesiastical courts illegal — That the commission for erecting the late court of commissioners for ecclesiasticall causes and all other commissions and courts of like nature are illegal and pernicious.

Levying money — That levying money for or to the use of the Crowne by pretence of prerogative without grant of Parlyament for longer time or in other manner than the same is or shall be granted is illegal.

Right to petition — That it is the right of the subjects to petition the King and all commitments and prosecutions for such petitioning are illegal.

Standing army — That the raising or keeping a standing army within the kingdome in time of peace unlesse it be with consent of Parlyament is against law.

Subject's arms — That the subjects which are protestants may have arms for their defence suitable to their conditions and as allowed by law.

Freedom of election — That election of members of Parlyament ought to be free.

Freedom of speech — That the freedome of speech and debates or proceedings in Parlyament ought not to be impeached or questioned in any court or place out of Parlyament.

Excessive bail — That excessive baile ought not to be required nor excessive fines imposed nor cruell and unusuall punishments inflicted.

Juries — That jurors ought to be duly impannelled and returned . . .

Grants of forfeitures — That all grants and promises of fines and forfeitures of particular persons before conviction are illegal and void.

Frequent Parliaments — And that for redresse of all grievances and for the amending strengthening and preserving of the lawes Parlyaments ought to be held frequently.

The said right claimed, tender of the crown, regal power exercised, limitation of the crown, new oaths of allegiance, etc. — And they doe claime demand and insist upon all and singular the premises as their undoubted rights and liberties and that noe declarations judgements doeings or proceedings to the prejudice of the people in any of the said premisses ought in any wise to be drawne hereafter into consequence or example. To which demand of their rights they are particularly encouraged by the declaration of his Highnesse the Prince of Orange as being the only meanes for obtaining a full redresse and remedy therein. Haveing therefore an intire confidence that his said Highnesse the Prince of Orange will perfect the deliverance soe farr advanced by him and will still preserve them from the violation of their rights which they have here asserted and from all other attempts upon their religion rights and liberties. The said lords spirituall and temporall and commons assembled at Westminster doe resolve that William and Mary Prince and Princesse of Orange be and be declared King and Queene of England France and Ireland and the dominions thereunto belonging to hold the crowne and royall dignity of the said kingdomes and dominions to them the said prince and princesse dureing their lives and the life of the survivour of them. And that the sole and full exercise of the regall power be onely in and executed by the said Prince of Orange in the names of the said prince and princesse dureing their joynt lives and after their deceases the said crowne and royall dignitie of the said kingdoms and dominions to be to the heires of the body of the said princesse and for default of such issue to the Princesse Anne of Denmarke and the heires of her body and for default of such issue to the heires of the body of the said Prince of Orange. And the lords spirituall and temporall and commons doe pray the said prince and princesse to accept the same accordingly. And that the oathes hereafter mentioned be taken by all persons of whome the oathes of allegiance and supremacy might be required by law instead of them and that the said oathes of allegiance and supremacy be abrogated.

I A B doe sincerely promise and sweare that I will be faithfull and beare true allegiance to their Majestyes King William and Queen Mary

Soe helpe me God

I A B doe sweare that I doe from my heart abhorr, detest and abjure as impious and hereticall this damnable doctrine and position that princes excommunicated or deprived by the Pope or any authority of the see of Rome may be deposed or murdered by their subjects or any other whatsoever. And I doe declare that noe forreigne prince person prelate, state or potentate hath or ought to have any jurisdiction power superiority preeminence or authoritie ecclesiasticall or spirituall within this realme.

Soe help me God

[**Note** for the modern version of this effectively obsolete oath see the Accession Declaration Act 1910, Sch.]

Acceptance of the crown, the two Houses to sit, subjects' liberties to be allowed, and ministers hereafter to serve according to the same, William and Mary declared King and Queen, limitation of the crown, papists debarred the crown, every King, etc, shall make the declaration of 30 Car 2, if under 12 years old, to be done after attainment thereof, King's and Queen's assent. Upon which their said Majestyes did accept the crowne and royall dignitie of the kingdoms of England France and Ireland and the dominions thereunto belonging according to the resolution and desire of the said lords and commons contained in the said declaration. And thereupon their Majestyes were pleased that the said lords spirituall and temporall and commons being the two Houses of Parlyament should continue to sitt and with their Majesties royall concurrence make effectuall provision for the settlement of the religion lawes and liberties of this kingdome soe that the same for the future might not be in danger againe of being subverted, to which the said lords spirituall and temporall and commons did agree and proceede to act accordingly. Now in pursuance of the premises the said lords spirituall and temporall and commons in Parlyament assembled for the ratifying confirming and establishing the said declaration and the articles clauses matters and things therein contained by the force of a law made in due forme by authority of Parlyament doe pray that it may be declared and enacted that all and singular the rights and liberties asserted and claimed in the said declaration are the true auntient and indubitable rights and liberties of the people of this kingdome and soe shall be esteemed allowed adjudged deemed and taken to be and that all and every the paritculars aforesaid shall be firmly and strictly holden and observed as they are expressed in the said declaration. And all officers and ministers whatsoever shall serve their Majestyes and their successors according to the same in all times to come. And the said lords spirituall and temporall and commons seriously considering how it hath pleased Almighty God in his marvellous providence and mercifull goodness to this nation to provide and preserve their said Majestyes royall persons most happily to raigne over us upon the throne of their auncestors for which they render unto him from the bottome of their hearts their humblest thanks and praises doe truely firmely assuredly and in the sincerity of their hearts thinke and doe hereby recognize acknowledge and declare that King James the Second haveing abdicated the government and their Majestyes having accepted the crowne and royall dignity as aforesaid their said Majestyes did become were are and of right ought to be by the lawes of the realme our soveraigne liege lord and lady King and Queene of England France and Ireland and the dominions thereunto belonging in and to whose princely persons the royall state crowne and dignity of the said realmes with all honours stiles titles regalities prerogatives powers jurisdictions and authorities to the same belonging and appertaining are most fully and rightfully and intirely invested and incorporated united and annexed. And for preventing all questions and divisions in this realme by reason of any pretended titles to the crowne and for preserveing a certainty in the succession thereof in and upon which the unity peace tranquillity and safety of this nation doth under God wholly consist and depend the said lords spirituall and temporall and commons doe beseech their Majestyes that it may be enacted established and declared that the crowne and regall government of the said kingdoms and dominions with all and singular the premisses thereunto belonging and appertaining shall bee and continue to their said Majestyes and the survivour of them dureing their lives and the life of the survivour of them and that the entire perfect and full exercise of the regall power and government be onely in and executed by his Majestie in the names of both their Majestyes dureing their joynt lives and after their deceases the said crowne and premisses shall be and remaine to the heires of the body of her Majestie and for default of such issue to her royall Highnesse the Princess Anne of Denmarke and the heires of her body and for default of such issue to the heires of the body of his said Majestie And thereunto the said lords spirituall and temporall and commons doe in the name of all the people aforesaid most humbly and faithfully submitt themselves their heires and posterities for ever and doe faithfully promise that they will stand to maintaine and defend their said Majesties and alsoe the limitation and succession of the crowne herein specified and contained to the utmost of their powers with their lives and estates against all persons whatsoever that shall attempt any thing to the contrary. And whereas it hath beene found by experience that it is inconsistent with the safety and welfaire of this protestant kingdome to be governed by a popish prince or by any King or Queene marrying a papist the said lords spirtuall and temporall and commons doe further pray that it may be enacted that all and every person and persons that is are or shall be reconciled to or shall hold communion with the see or church of Rome or shall professe the popish religion or shall marry a papist shall be excluded and be for ever uncapeable to inherit possesse or enjoy the crowne and government of this realme and Ireland and the dominions thereunto belonging or any part of the same or to have use or exercise any regall power authoritie or jurisdiction within the same And in all and every such case or cases the people of these realmes shall be and are hereby absolved of their allegiance and the said crowne and government shall from time to time descend to and be enjoyed by such person or persons being protestants as should have inherited and enjoyed the same in case the said person or persons soe reconciled holding communion or professing or marrying as aforesaid were naturally dead And that every King and Queene of this realme who at any time hereafter shall come to and succeede in the imperiall crowne of this kingdome shall on the first day of the meeting of the first Parlyament next after his or her comeing to the crowne sitting in his or her throne in the House of Peeres in the presence of the lords and commons therein assembled or at his or her coronation before such person or persons who shall administer the coronation oath to him or her at the time of his or her takeing the said oath (which shall first happen) make subscribe and audibly repeate the declaration mentioned in the Statute made in the thirtyeth yeare of the raigne of King Charles the Second entituled An Act for the more effectuall preserveing the Kings person and government by disableing papists from sitting in either House of Parlyament But if it shall happen that such King or Queene upon his or her succession to the crowne of this realme shall be under the age of twelve yeares then every such King or Queene shall make subscribe and audibly repeate the said declaration at his or her coronation or the first day of the meeting of the first Parlyament as aforesaid which shall first happen after such King or Queene shall have attained the said age of twelve years. All which their Majestyes are contented and pleased shall be declared enacted and established by authoritie of this present Parliament and shall stand remaine and be the law of this realme for ever And the same are by their said Majesties by and with the advice and consent of the lords spirituall and temporall and commons in Parlyament assembled and by the authoritie of the same declared enacted and established accordingly

2 Non obstantes made void
... noe dispensation by non obstante of or to any statute or any part thereof shall be allowed but ... the same shall be held void and of noe effect except a dispensation be allowed of in such statute ...

3 ...

CROWN AND PARLIAMENT RECOGNITION ACT 1689
(2 Will. & Mar., c. 1)

An Act for Recognizing King William and Queene Mary and for avoiding all Questions touching the Acts made in the Parliament assembled at Westminster the thirteenth day of February one thousand six hundred eighty eight

Territorial extent England and Wales, Northern Ireland (effectively extended to Scotland by the Union with Scotland Act 1706, below).

Wee your Majestyes most humble and loyall subjects the lords spirituall and temporall and commons in this present Parlyament assembled doe beseech your most excellent Majestyes that it may be publisehd and declared in this High Court of Parlyament and enacted by authoritie of the same that we doe recognize and acknowledge your Majestyes were are and of right ought to be by the laws of this realme our soveraigne liege lord and lady King and Queene of England France and Ireland and the dominions thereunto belonging in and to whose princely persons the royall state crowne and dignity of the said realms with all honours stiles tiles regalities prerogatives powers jurisdictions and authorities to the same belonging and appertaining are most fully rightfully and intirely invested and incorporated united and annexed. And for the avoiding of all disputes and questions concerning the being and authority of the late Parliament assembled at Westminster the thirteenth day of February one thousand six hundred eighty eight wee doe most humbly beseech your Majestyes that it may be enacted and bee it enacted by the King and Queenes most excellent Majestyes by and with the advice and consent of the lords spirituall and temporall and commons in this present Parlyament assembled and by authoritie of the same that all and singular the Acts made and enacted in the said Parlyament were and are laws and statutes of this kingdome and as such ought to be reputed taken and obeyed by all the people of this kingdome.

THE ACT OF SETTLEMENT (1700)
(12 & 13 Will. 3, c. 2)

An Act for the further Limitation of the Crown and better securing the Rights and Liberties of the Subject

Territorial extent England and Wales, Northern Ireland; effectively extended to Scotland by the Union With Scotland Act 1706.

Whereas in the first year of the reign of your Majesty and of our late most gracious soverign lady Queen Mary (of blessed memory) an Act of Parliament was made intituled (An Act for declaring the rights and liberties of the subject and for setling the succession of the crown) wherein it was (amongst other things) enacted established and declared that the crown and regall government of the kingdoms of England France and Ireland and the dominions thereunto belonging should be and continue to your Majestie and the said late Queen during the joynt lives of your Majesty and the said Queen and to the survivor and that after the decease of your Majesty and of the said Queen the said crown and regall government should be and remain to the heirs of the body of the said late Queen and for default of such issue to her royall Highness the Princess Ann of Denmark and the heirs of her body and for default of such issue to the heirs of the body of your Majesty And it was thereby further enacted that all and every person and persons that then were or afterwards should be reconciled to or shall hold communion with the see or church of Rome or should professe the popish religion or marry a papist should be excluded and are by that Act made for ever incapable to inherit possess or enjoy the crown and government of this realm and Ireland and the dominions thereunto belonging or any part of the same or to have use or exercise any regall power authority or jurisdiction within the same and in all and every such case and cases the people of these realms shall be and are thereby absolved of their allegiance and that the said crown and government shall from time to time descend to and be enjoyed by such person or persons being protestants as should have inherited and enjoyed the same in case the said person or persons so reconciled holding communion professing or marrying as aforesaid were naturally dead After the making of which Statute and the settlement therein contained your Majesties good subjects who were restored to the full and free possession and enjoyment of their religion rights and liberties by the providence of God giving success to your Majesties just undertakings and unwearied endeavours for that purpose had no greater temporall felicity to hope or wish for than to see a royall progeny descending from your Majesty to whom (under God) they owe their tranquility and whose ancestors have for many years been principall assertors of the reformed religion and the liberties of Europe and from our said most gracious sovereign lady whose memory will always be precious to the subjects of these realms And it having since pleased Almighty God to take away our said sovereign lady and also the most hopefull Prince William Duke of Gloucester (the only surviving issue of her royall Highness the Princess Ann of Denmark) to the unspeakable grief and sorrow of your Majesty and your said good subjects who under such losses being sensibly put in mind that it standeth wholly in the pleasure of Almighty God to prolong the lives of your Majesty and of her royall Highness and to grant to your Majesty or to her royall Highness such issue as may be inheritable to the crown and regall government aforesaid by the respective limitations in the said recited Act contained doe constantly implore the divine mercy for those blessings And your Majesties said subjects having daily experience of your royall care and concern for the present and future welfare of these kingdoms and particularly recommending from your throne a further provision to be made for the succession of the crown in the protestant line for the happiness of the nation and the security of our religion and it being absolutely necessary for the safety peace and quiet of this realm to obviate all doubts and contentions in the same by reason of any pretended titles to the crown and to maintain a certainty in the succession thereof to which your subjects may safely have recourse for their protection in case the limitations in the said recited Act should determine Therefore for a further provision of the succession of the crown in the protestant line we your Majesties most dutifull and loyal subjects the lords spirituall and temporall and commons in this present Parliament assembled do beseech your Majesty that it may be enacted and declared and be it enacted and declared by the Kings most excellent Majesty by and with the advice and consent of the lords spirituall and temporall and commons in this present Parliament assembled and by the authority of the same that

1 The Princess Sophia, Electress and Duchess dowager of Hanover, daughter of the late Queen of Bohemia, daughter of King James the First, to inherit after the King and the Princess Anne, in default of issue of the said princess and his Majesty, respectively; and the heirs of her body, being protestants

the most excellent Princess Sophia Electress and Dutchess dowager of Hanover daughter of the most excellent Princess Elizabeth late Queen of Bohemia daughter of our late sovereign lord King James the First of happy memory be and is hereby declared to be the next in succession in the protestant line to the imperiall crown and dignity of the [said] realms of England France and Ireland with the dominions and territories thereunto belonging after his Majesty and the Princess Ann of Denmark and in default of issue of the said Princess Ann and of his Majesty respectively and that from and after the deceases of his said Majesty our own soveriegn lord and of her royall Highness the Princess Ann of Denmark and for default of issue of the said Princess Ann and of his Majesty respectively the crown and regall government of the said kingdoms of England France and Ireland and of the dominions thereunto belonging with the royall state and dignity of the said realms and all honours stiles titles regalities prerogatives powers jurisdictions and authorities to the same belonging and appertaining shall be remain and continue to the said most excellent Princess Sophia and the heirs of her body being protestants And thereunto the said lords spirituall and temporall and commons shall and will in the name of all the people of this realm most humbly and faithfully submitt themselves their heirs and posterities and do faithfully promise that after the deceases of his Majesty and her royall Highness and the failure of the heirs of their respective bodies to stand to maintain and defend the said Princess Sophia and the heirs of her body being protestants according to the limitation and succession of the crown in this Act specified and contained to the utmost of their powers with their lives and estates against all persons whatsoever that shall attempt any thing to the contrary.

2 The persons inheritable by this Act, holding communion with the church of Rome, incapacitated as by the former Act; to take the oath at their coronation, according to Stat 1 W & M c. 6

Provided always and it is hereby enacted that all and every person and persons who shall or may take or inherit the said crown by vertue of the limitation of this present Act and is are or shall be reconciled to or shall hold communion with the see or church of Rome or shall profess the popish religion or shall marry a papist shall be subject to such incapacities as in such case or cases are by the said recited Act provided enacted and established. And that every King and Queen of this realm who shall come to and succeed in the imperiall crown of this kingdom by vertue of this Act shall have the coronation oath administered to him her or them at their respective coronations according to the Act of Parliament made in the first year of the reign of his Majesty and the said late Queen Mary intituled An Act for establishing the coronation oath and shall make subscribe and repeat the declaration in the Act first above recited mentioned or referred to in the manner and form thereby prescribed.

3 Further provisions for securing the religions, laws, and liberties of these realms

And whereas it is requisite and necessary that some further provision be made for securing our religion laws and liberties from and after the death of his Majesty and the Princess Ann of Denmark and in default of issue of the body of the said princess and of his Majesty respectively Be it enacted by the Kings most excellent Majesty by and with the advice and consent of the lords spirituall and temporall and commons in Parliament and by the authority of the same

That whosoever shall hereafter come to the possession of this crown shall joyn in communion with the Church of England as by law established

That in case the crown and imperiall dignity of this realm shall hereafter come to any person not being a native of this kingdom of England this nation be not obliged to ingage in any warr for the defence of any dominions or territories which do not belong to the crown of England without the consent of Parliament

. . . . .

That after the said limitation shall take effect as aforesaid no person born out of the kingdoms of England Scotland or Ireland or the dominions thereunto belonging (although he be . . . made a denizen (except such as are born of English parents)) shall be capable to be of the privy councill or a member of either House of Parliament or to enjoy any office or place of trust either civill or military or to have any grant of lands tenements or hereditaments from the Crown to himself or to any other or others in trust for him.

. . . . .

That no pardon under the great seal of England be pleadable to an impeachment by the commons in Parliament.

4 The laws and statutes of the realm confirmed
And whereas the laws of England are the birthright of the people thereof and all the Kings and Queens who shall ascend the throne of this realm ought to administer the government of the same according to the said laws and all their officers and ministers ought to serve them respectively according to the same The said lords spirituall and temporall and commons do therefore further humbly pray that all the laws and statutes of this realm for securing the established religion and the rights and liberties of the people thereof and all other laws and statutes of the same now in force may be ratified and confirmed And the same are by his Majesty by and with the advice and consent of the said lords spirituall and temporall and commons and by authority of the same ratified and confirmed accordingly.

UNION WITH SCOTLAND ACT 1706
(6 Anne, c. 11)

An Act for an Union of the Two Kingdoms of England and Scotland

Territorial extent England, Wales and Scotland (by the combined effect of this Act and the equivalent Act of the Parliament of Scotland (APS, XI, 406)); subsequently applied to Northern Ireland.

Most Gracious Sovereign
Whereas articles of union were agreed on the twenty second day of July in the fifth year of your Majesties reign by the commissioners nominated on behalf of the kingdom of England under your Majesties great seal of England bearing date at Westminster the tenth day of April then last past in pursuance of an Act of Parliament made in England in the third year of your Majesties reign and the commissioners nominated on the behalf of the kingdom of Scotland under your Majesties great seal of Scotland bearing date the twenty-seventh day of February in the fourth year of your Majesties reign in pursuance of the fourth Act of the third session of the present Parliament of Scotland to treat of and concerning an union of the said kingdoms And whereas an Act hath passed in the Parliament of Scotland at Edinburgh the sixteenth day of January in the fifth year of your Majesties reign wherein "tis mentioned that the estates of Parliament considering the said articles of union of the two kingdoms had agreed to and approved of the said articles of union with some additions and explanations and that your Majesty with advice and consent of the estates of Parliament for establishing the Protestant religion and Presbyterian Church government within the kingdom of Scotland had passed in the same session of Parliament an Act intituled Act for securing of the Protestant religion

and Presbyterian Church government which by the tenor thereof was appointed to be inserted in any Act ratifying the treaty and expresly declared to be a fundamental and essential condition of the said treaty or union in all times coming the tenor of which articles as ratified and approved of with additions and explanations by the said Act of Parliament of Scotland follows.

Article I

The kingdoms united; ensigns armorial — That the two kingdoms of England and Scotland shall upon the first day of May which shall be in the year one thousand seven hundred and seven and for ever after be united into one kingdom by the name of Great Britain and that the ensigns armorial of the said United Kingdom be such as her Majesty shall appoint and the crosses of St. George and St. Andrew be conjoyned in such manner as Her Majesty shall think fit and used in all flags banners standards and ensigns both at sea and land.

Article II

Succession to the monarchy — That the succession to the monarchy of the United Kingdom of Great Britain and of the dominions thereto belonging after her most sacred Majesty and in default of issue of her Majesty be remain and continue to the most excellent Princess Sophia Electoress and Dutchess dowager of Hanover and the heirs of her body being protestants upon whom the crown of England is settled by an Act of Parliament made in England in the twelfth year of the reign of his late Majesty King William the Third intituled An Act for the further limitation of the crown and better securing the right and liberties of the subject And that all papists and persons marrying papists shall be excluded from and for ever incapable to inherit possess or enjoy the imperial crown of Great Britain and the dominions thereunto belonging or any part thereof and in every such case the crown and government shall from time to time descend to and be enjoyed by such person being a protestant as should have inherited and enjoyed the same in case such papist or person marrying a papist was naturally dead according to the provision for the descent of the crown of England made by another Act of Parliament in England in the first year of the reign of their late Majesties King William and Queen Mary intituled An Act declaring the rights and liberties of the subject and settling the succession of the crown.

Article III

Parliament — That the United Kingdom of Great Britain be represented by one and the same Parliament to be stiled the Parliament of Great Britain.

Article IIII

Trade and navigation and other rights — That all the subjects of the United Kingdom of Great Britain shall from and after the union have full freedom and intercourse of trade and navigation to and from any port or place within the said United Kingdom and the dominions and plantations thereunto belonging and that there be a communication of all other rights privileges and advantages which do or may belong to the subjects of either kingdom except where it is otherwise expressly agreed in these articles.

Article V . . .

Article VI

Regulations of trade, duties, etc. — That all parts of the United Kingdom for ever from and after the union shall have the same allowances encouragements and drawbacks and be under the same prohibitions restrictions and regulations of trade and liable to the same customs and duties on import and export and that the allowances encouragements and drawbacks prohibitions restrictions and regulations of trade and the customs and duties on import and export settled in England when the union commences shall from and after the union take place throughout the whole United Kingdom . . .

★★★★★

Article XVIII

Laws concerning public rights; private rights — That the laws concerning regulation of trade customs and such excises to which Scotland is by virtue of this treaty to be liable be the same in Scotland from and after the union as in England and that all other laws in use within the kingdom of Scotland do after the union and notwithstanding thereof remain in the same force as before (except such as are contrary to or inconsistent with this treaty) but alterable by the Parliament of Great Britain with this difference betwixt the laws concerning publick right policy and civil government and those which concern private right that the laws which concern publick right policy and civil government may be made the same throughout the whole United Kingdom. But that no alteration be made in laws which concern private right except for evident utility of the subjects within Scotland

★★★★★

Article XXV

Laws inconsistent with the articles, void — That all laws and statutes in either kingdom so far as they are contrary to or inconsistent with the terms of these articles or any of them shall from and after the union cease and become void and shall be so declared to be by the respective Parliaments of the said kingdoms.

As by the said articles of union ratified and approved by the said Act of Parliament of Scotland relation being thereunto had may appear.

★★★★★

5 Cap 8 ante, and the said Act of Parliament of Scotland to be observed as fundamental conditions of the said union; and the said articles and Acts of Parliament to continue the union

And it is hereby further enacted by the authority aforesaid that the said Act passed in this present session of Parliament intituled An Act for securing the Church of England as by law established and all and every the matters and things therein contained and also the said Act of Parliament of Scotland intituled Act for securing the Protestant religion and Presbyterian Church government with the establishment in the said Act contained be and shall for ever be held and adjudged to be and observed as fundamental and essential conditions of the said union and shall in all times coming be taken to be and are hereby declared to be essential and fundamental parts of the said articles and union and the said articles of union so as aforesaid ratified approved and confirmed by Act of Parliament of Scotland and by this present Act and the said Act passed in this present session of Parliament intituled an Act for securing the Church of England as by law established and also the said Act passed in the Parliament of Scotland intituled Act for securing the Protestant religion and Presbyterian Church government are hereby enacted and ordained to be and continue in all times coming the complete and intire union of the two kingdoms of England and Scotland.

★★★★★

METROPOLITAN POLICE ACT 1839
(2 & 3 Vict., c. 47)

An Act for further improving the Police in and near the Metropolis

Territorial extent Metropolitan Police Area and City of London

* * * * *

52 Commissioners may make regulations for the route of carriages, and persons, and for preventing obstruction of the streets during public processions, etc., or in the neighbourhood of public buildings, etc.

. . . It shall be lawful for the commissioners of police from time to time, and as occasion shall require, to make regulations for the route to be observed by all carts, carriages, horses, and persons, and for preventing obstruction of the streets and thoroughfares within the metropolitan police district, in all times of public processions, public rejoicings, or illuminations, and also to give directions to the constables for keeping order and for preventing any obstruction of the thoroughfares in the immediate neighbourhood of her Majesty's palaces and the public offices, the High Court of Parliament, the courts of law and equity, the police courts, the theatres, and other places of public resort, and in any case when the streets or thoroughfares may be thronged or may be liable to be obstructed.

* * * * *

PARLIAMENTARY PAPERS ACT 1840
(3 & 4 Vict., c. 9)

An Act to give summary Protection to Persons employed in the Publication of Parliamentary Papers

Territorial extent United Kingdom

[1] Proceedings, criminal or civil, against persons for publication of papers printed by order of Parliament to be stayed upon delivery of a certificte and affidavit to the effect that such publication is by order of either House of Parliament

. . . It shall and may be lawful for any person or persons who now is or are, or hereafter shall be, a defendant or defendants in any civil or criminal proceedings commenced or prosecuted in any manner soever, for or on account or in respect of the publication of any such report, paper, votes, or proceedings by such person or persons, or by his, her, or their servant or servants, by or under the authority of either House of Parliament, to bring before the court in which such proceeding shall have been or shall be so commenced or prosecuted, or before any judge of the same (if one of the superior courts at Westminster), first giving twenty-four hours notice of his intention so to do to the prosecutor or plaintiff in such proceeding, a certificate under the hand of the lord high chancellor of Great Britain, or the lord keeper of the great seal, or of the speaker of the House of Lords, for the time being, or of the clerk of the Parliaments, or of the speaker of the House of Commons, or of the clerk of the same house, stating that the report, paper, votes, or proceedings, as the case may be, in respect whereof such civil or criminal proceeding shall have been commenced or prosecuted, was published by such person or persons, or by his, her, or their servant or servants, by order or under the authority of the House of Lords or of the House of Commons, as the case may be, together with an affidavit verifying such certificate; and such court or judge shall thereupon immediately stay such civil or criminal proceeding, and the same, and every writ or process issued therein, shall be and shall be deemed and taken to be finally put an end to, determined, and superseded by virtue of this Act.

2 Proceedings to be stayed when commenced in respect of a copy of an authenticated report, etc.
... In case of any civil or criminal proceeding hereafter to be commenced or prosecuted for or on account or in respect of the publication of any copy of such report, paper, votes, or proceedings, it shall be lawful for the defendant or defendants at any stage of the proceedings to lay before the court or judge such report, paper, votes, or proceedings, and such copy, with an affidavit verifying such report, paper, votes, or proceedings, and the correctness of such copy, and the court or judge shall immediately stay such civil or criminal proceedings, and the same, and every writ or process issued therein, shall be and shall be deemed and taken to be finally put an end to, determined, and superseded by virtue of this Act.

3 In proceedings for printing any extract or abstract of a paper, it may be shown that such extract was bona fide made
... It shall be lawful in any civil or criminal proceeding to be commenced or prosecuted for printing any extract from or abstract of such report, paper, votes, or proceedings, to give in evidence ... such report, paper, votes or proceedings, and to show that such extract or abstract was published bona fide and without malice; and if such shall be the opinion of the jury, a verdict of not guilty shall be entered for the defendant or defendants.

4 Act not to affect the privileges of Parliament
Provided always ... that nothing herein contained shall be deemed or taken, or held or construed, directly or indirectly, by implication or otherwise, to affect the privileges of Parliament in any manner whatsoever.

Note Sch. 20, para. 1 to the Broadcasting Act 1990 provides that s. 3 above is to have effect as if the reference to printing included a reference to inclusion in a programme service (as defined in that Act).

TREASON FELONY ACT 1848
(11 & 12 Vict., c. 12)

An Act for the better Security of the Crown and Government of the United Kingdom

Territorial extent See section 3.

* * * * *

3 Offences herein mentioned declared to be felonies
... If any person whatsoever shall, within the United Kingdom or without, compass, imagine, invent, devise, or intend to deprive or depose our Most Gracious Lady the Queen, ... from the style, honour, or royal name of the imperial crown of the United Kingdom, or of any other of her Majesty's dominions and countries, or to levy war against her Majesty, ... within any part of the United Kingdom, in order by force or constraint to compel her ... to change her ... measures or counsels, or in order to put any force or constraint upon or in order to intimidate or overawe both Houses or either House of Parliament, or to move or stir any foreigner or stranger with force to invade the United Kingdom or any other of her Majesty's dominions or countries under the obeisance of her Majesty, ... and such compassings, imaginations, inventions, devices, or intentions, or any of them, shall express, utter, or declare, by publishing any printing or writing, ... or by any overt act or deed, every person so offending shall be guilty of

felony, and being convicted thereof shall be liable, . . . to be transported beyond the seas for the term of his or her natural life . . .

. . .

6 Saving as to 25 Edw 3 stat 5 c 2
Provided always, . . . that nothing herein contained shall lessen the force of or in any manner affect any thing enacted by the Treason Act 1351.

★ ★ ★ ★ ★

CUSTOMS CONSOLIDATION ACT 1876
(39 & 40 Vict., c. 36)

An Act to consolidate the Customs Laws

Territorial extent United Kingdom

AS TO THE IMPORTATION, PROHIBITION, ENTRY, EXAMINATION, LANDING, AND WAREHOUSING OF GOODS

. . .

42 Prohibitions and restrictions
The goods enumerated and described in the following table of prohibitions and restrictions inwards are hereby prohibited to be imported or brought into the United Kingdom . . .

A TABLE OF PROHIBITIONS AND RESTRICTIONS INWARDS

Goods prohibited to be imported

Indecent or obscene prints, paintings, photographs, books, cards, lithographic or other engravings, or any other indecent or obscene articles.

★ ★ ★ ★ ★

RIOT (DAMAGES) ACT 1886
(49 & 50 Vict., c. 38)

An Act to provide compensation for Losses by Riots

Territorial extent England and Wales. (For Scotland see the Riotous Assembly (Scotland) Act 1822.)

1 Short title
This act may be cited for all purposes as the Riot (Damages) Act 1886.

2 Compensation to persons for damage by riot
(1) Where a house, shop, or building in [a police area] has been injured or destroyed, or the property therein has been injured, stolen, or destroyed, by any persons riotously and tumultuously assembled together, such compensation as herein-after mentioned shall be paid out of [the police fund] of [the area] to any person who has sustained loss by such injury, stealing, or destruction; but in fixing the amount of such compensation regard shall be had to the conduct of the said person, whether as respects the precautions taken by him or as respects his being a party or accessory to such riotous or tumultuous assembly, or as regards any provocation offered to the persons assembled or otherwise.

(2) Where any person having sustained such loss as aforesaid has received, by way of insurance or otherwise, any sum to recoup him, in whole or in part, for such loss, the

compensation otherwise payable to him under this Act shall, if exceeding such sum, be reduced by the amount thereof, and in any other case shall not be paid to him, and the payer of such sum shall be entitled to compensation under this Act in respect of the sum so paid in like manner as if he had sustained the said loss, and any policy of insurance given by such payer shall continue in force as if he had made no such payment, and where such person was recouped as aforesaid otherwise than by payment of a sum, this enactment shall apply as if the value of such recoupment were a sum paid.

Note Section 10 of the Public Order Act 1986 provides that "riotous" and "riotously" are to be construed in accordance with the definition of "riot" in that Act.

PUBLIC MEETING ACT 1908
(8 Edw. 7, c. 66)

An Act to prevent disturbance of Public Meetings

Territorial extent England and Wales, Scotland

1 Penalty on endeavour to break up public meeting

(1) Any person who at a lawful public meeting acts in a disorderly manner for the purpose of preventing the transaction of the business for which the meeting was called together shall be guilty of an offence [and shall on summary conviction be liable to imprisonment for a term not exceeding six months or to a fine not exceeding [level 5 on the standard scale] or to both] . . .

(2) Any person who incites others to commit an offence under this section shall be guilty of a like offence.

[(3) If any constable reasonably suspects any person of committing an offence under the foregoing provisions of this section, he may if requested so to do by the chairman of the meeting require that person to declare to him immediately his name and address and, if that person refuses or fails so to declare his name and address or gives a false name and address he shall be guilty of an offence under this subsection and liable on summary conviction thereof to a fine not exceeding [level 1 on the standard scale], . . .

[(4) This section does not apply as respects meetings to which section 97 of the Representation of the People Act 1983 applies.]

OFFICIAL SECRETS ACT 1911
(1 & 2 Geo. 5, c. 28)

An Act to re-enact the Official Secrets Act 1889, with Amendments

Territorial extent United Kingdom. See also s. 10(1).

Note Printed as amended by the Official Secrets Act 1920; section 2 was repealed by the Official Secrets Act 1989 (below).

1 Penalties for spying

(1) If any person for any purpose prejudicial to the safety or interests of the State—

(a) approaches [inspects, passes over] or is in the neighbourhood of, or enters any prohibited place within the meaning of this Act; or

(b) makes any sketch, plan, model, or note which is calculated to be or might be or is intended to be directly or indirectly useful to an enemy; or

(c) obtains, [collects, records, or publishes,] or communicates to any other person [any secret official code word or pass word, or] any sketch, plan, model, article, or note, or other document or information which is calculated to be or might be or is intended to be directly or indirectly useful to an enemy;

he shall be guilty of felony . . .

(2) On a prosecution under this section, it shall not be necessary to show that the accused person was guilty of any particular act tending to show a purpose prejudicial to the safety or interests of the State, and, notwithstanding that no such act is proved against him, he may be convicted if, from the circumstances of the case, or his conduct, or his known character as proved, it appears that his purpose was a purpose prejudicial to the safety or interests of the State; and if any sketch, plan, model, article, note, document, or information relating to or used in any prohibited place within the meaning of this Act, or anything in such a place [or any secret official code word or pass word], is made, obtained, [collected, recorded, published], or communicated by any person other than a person acting under lawful authority, it shall be deemed to have been made, obtained, [collected, recorded, published] or communicated for a purpose prejudicial to the safety or interests of the State unless the contrary is proved.

2 ...

3 Definition of prohibited place

For the purposes of this Act, the expression "prohibited place" means—

(a) any work of defence, arsenal, naval or air force establishment or station, factory, dockyard, mine, minefield, camp, ship, or aircraft belonging to or occupied by or on behalf of His Majesty, or any telegraph, telephone, wireless or signal station, or office so belonging or occupied, and any place belonging to or occupied by or on behalf of His Majesty and used for the purpose of building, repairing, making, or storing any munitions of war, or any sketches, plans, models, or documents relating thereto, or for the purpose of getting any metals, oil, or minerals of use in time of war];

(b) any place not belonging to His Majesty where any [munitions of war], or any [sketches, models, plans] or documents relating thereto, are being made, repaired, [gotten] or stored under contract with, or with any person on behalf of, His Majesty, or otherwise on behalf of His Majesty; and

(c) any place belonging to [or used for the purposes of] His Majesty which is for the time being declared [by order of a Secretary of State] to be a prohibited place for the purposes of this section on the ground that information with respect thereto, or damage thereto, would be useful to an enemy; and

(d) any railway, road, way, or channel, or other means of communication by land or water (including any works or structures being part thereof or connected therewith), or any place used for gas, water, or electricity works or other works for purposes of a public character, or any place where any [munitions of war], or any [sketches, models, plans] or documents relating thereto, are being made, repaired, or stored otherwise than on behalf of His Majesty, which is for the time being declared [by order or a Secretary of State] to be a prohibited place for the purposes of this section, on the ground that information with respect thereto, or the destruction or obstruction thereof, or interference therewith, would be useful to an enemy.

4, 5 ...

6 Power of arrest

Any person who is found committing an offence under this Act ... or who is reasonably suspected of having committed, or having attempted to commit, or being about to commit, such an offence, may be apprehended and detained ...

7 * * * * *

8 Restriction on prosecution

A prosecution for an offence under this Act shall not be instituted except by or with the consent of the Attorney-General:

. . . . .

9 Search warrants

(1) If a justice of the peace is satisfied by information on oath that there is reasonable ground for suspecting that an offence under this Act has been or is about to be committed, he may grant a search warrant authorising any constable . . . to enter at any time any premises or place named in the warrant, if necessary, by force, and to search the premises or place and every person found therein, and to seize any sketch, plan, model, article, note, or document, or anything of a like nature or anything which is evidence of an offence under this Act having been or being about to be committed, which he may find on the premises or place or on any such person, and with regard to or in connexion with which he has reasonable ground for suspecting that an offence under this Act has been or is about to be committed.

(2) Where it appears to a superintendent of police that the case is one of great emergency and that in the interests of the State immediate action is necessary, he may by a written order under his hand give to any constable the like authority as may be given by the warrant of a justice under the section.

10 Extent of Act and place of trial of offence

(1) This Act shall apply to all acts which are offences under this Act when committed in any part of His Majesty's dominions, or when committed by British officers or subjects elsewhere.

* * * * *

PARLIAMENT ACT 1911
(1 & 2 Geo. 5, c. 13)

An Act to make provision with respect to the powers of the House of Lords in relation of the House of Commons, and to limit the duration of Parliament

Territorial extent United Kingdom

Note The words in square brackets in s. 2 were substituted by the Parliament Act 1949, and are included without prejudice to the suggestions of some writers that the 1949 Act (itself passed under the procedure of the 1911 Act) is not a valid Act of Parliament.

Preamble

Whereas it is expedient that provision should be made for regulating the relations between the two Houses of Parliament:

And whereas it is intended to substitute for the House of Lords as it at present exists a Second Chamber constituted on a popular instead of hereditary basis, but such substitution cannnot be immediately brought into operation:

And whereas provision will require hereafter to be made by Parliament in a measure effecting such substitution for limiting and defining the powers of the new Second Chamber, but it is expedient to make such provision as in this Act appears for restricting the existing powers of the House of Lords:

1 Powers of House of Lords as to Money Bills

(1) If a Money Bill, having been passed by the House of Commons, and sent up to the House of Lords at least one month before the end of the session, is not passed by the House of Lords without amendment within one month after it is so sent up to that House, the Bill shall, unless the House of Commons direct to the contrary, be presented to His Majesty and become an Act of Parliament on the Royal Assent being signified, notwithstanding that the House of Lords have not consented to the Bill.

(2) A Money Bill means a Public Bill which in the opinion of the Speaker of the House of Commons contains only provisions dealing with all or any of the following subjects, namely, the imposition, repeal, remission, alteration, or regulation of taxation;

the imposition for the payment of debt or other financial purposes of charges on the Consolidated Fund, [the National Loans Fund] or on money provided by Parliament, or the variation or repeal of any such charges; supply; the appropriation, receipt, custody, issue or audit of accounts of public money; the raising or guarantee of any loan or the repayment thereof; or subordinate matters incidental to those subjects or any of them. In this subsection the expressions "taxation", "public money" and "loan" respectively do not include any taxation, money, or loan raised by local authorities or bodies for local purposes.

(3) There shall be endorsed on every Money Bill when it is sent up to the House of Lords and when it is presented to His Majesty for assent the certificate of the Speaker of the House of Commons signed by him that it is a Money Bill. Before giving his certificate, the Speaker shall consult, if practicable, two members to be appointed from the Chairmen's Panel at the beginning of each Session by the Committee of Selection.

2 Restriction of the powers of the House of Lords as to Bills other than Money Bills

(1) If any Public Bill (other than a Money Bill or a Bill containing any provision to extend the maximum duration of Parliament beyond five years) is passed by the House of Commons [in two successive sessions] (whether of the same Parliament or not), and, having been sent up to the House of Lords at least one month before the end of the session, is rejected by the House of Lords in each of those sessions, that Bill shall, on its rejection [for the second time] by the House of Lords, unless the House of Commons direct to the contrary, be presented to His Majesty and become an Act of Parliament on the Royal Assent being signified thereto, notwithstanding that the House of Lords have not consented to the Bill: Provided that this provision shall not take effect unless [one year has elapsed] between the date of the second reading in the first of those sessions of the Bill in the House of Commons and the date on which it passes the House of Commons [in the second of those sessions].

(2) When a Bill is presented to His Majesty for assent in pursuance of the provisions of this section, there shall be endorsed on the Bill the certificate of the Speaker of the House of Commons signed by him that the provisions of this section have been duly complied with.

(3) A Bill shall be deemed to be rejected by the House of Lords if it is not passed by the House of Lords either without amendment or with such amendments only as may be agreed to by both Houses.

(4) A Bill shall be deemed to be the same Bill as a former Bill sent up to the House of Lords in the preceding session if, when it is sent up to the House of Lords, it is identical with the former Bill or contains only such alterations as are certified by the Speaker of the House of Commons to be necessary owing to the time which has elapsed since the date of the former Bill, or to represent any amendments which have been made by the House of Lords in the former Bill in the preceding sesion, and any amendments which are certified by the Speaker to have been made by the House of Lords [in the second session] and agreed to by the House of Commons shall be inserted in the Bill as presented for Royal Assent in pursuance of this section:

Provided that the House of Commons may, if they think fit, on the passage of such a Bill through the House [in the second session], suggest any further amendments without inserting the amendments in the Bill, and any such suggested amendments shall be considered by the House of Lords, and, if agreed to by that House, shall be treated as amendments made by the House of Lords and agreed to by the House of Commons; but the exercise of this power by the House of Commons shall not affect the operation of this section in the event of the Bill being rejected by the House of Lords.

3 Certificate of Speaker

Any certificate of the Speaker of the House of Commons given under this Act shall be conclusive for all purposes, and shall not be questioned in any court of law.

4 Enacting words

(1) In every Bill presented to His Majesty under the preceding provisions of this Act, the words of enactment shall be as follows, that is to say:—

"Be it enacted by the King's most Excellent Majesty, by and with the advice and consent of the Commons in this present Parliament assembled, in accordance with the provisions of [the Parliament Acts 1911 and 1949], and by authority of the same, as follows."

(2) Any alteration of a Bill necessary to give effect to this section shall not be deemed to be an amendment of the Bill.

5 Provisional Order Bills excluded

In this Act the expression "Public Bill" does not include any Bill for confirming a Provisional Order.

6 Saving for existing rights and privileges of the House of Commons

Nothing in this Act shall diminish or qualify the existing rights and privileges of the House of Commons.

7 Duration of Parliament

Five years shall be substituted for seven years as the time fixed for the maximum duration of Parliament under the Septennial Act, 1715.

EMERGENCY POWERS ACT 1920
(10 & 11 Geo. 5, c. 55)

An Act to make exceptional provision for the Protection of the Community in cases of Emergency

Territorial extent England and Wales, Scotland

Note Section 1 is printed as amended by the Emergency Powers Act 1964.

1 Issue of proclamations of emergency

(1) If at any time it appears to His Majesty that [there have occurred, or are about o occur, events of such a nature] as to be calculated, by interfering with the supply and distribution of food, water, fuel, or light, or with the means of locomotion, to deprive the community, or any substantial portion of the community, of the essentials of life, His Majesty may, by proclamation (hereinafter referred to as a proclamation of emergency), declare that a state of emergency exists.

No such proclamation shall be in force for more than one month, without prejudice to the issue of another proclamation at or before the end of that period.

(2) Where a proclamation of emergency has been made the occasion thereof shall forthwith be communicated to Parliament, and, if Parliament is then separated by such adjournment or prorogation as will not expire within five days, a proclamation shall be issued for the meeting of Parliament within five days, and Parliament shall accordingly meet and sit upon the day appointed by that proclamation, and shall continue to sit and act in like manner as if it had stood adjourned or prorogued to the same day.

2 Emergency regulations

(1) Where a proclamation of emergency has been made, and so long as the proclamation is in force, it shall be lawful for His Majesty in Council, by Order, to make regulations for securing the essentials of life to the community, and those regulations may confer or impose on a Secretary of State or other Government department, or any other persons in His Majesty's service or acting on His Majesty's behalf, such powers and duties as His Majesty may deem necessary for the preservation of the peace, for securing and regulating the supply and distribution of food, water, fuel, light, and other

necessities, for maintaining the means of transit or locomotion, and for any other purposes essential to the public safety and the life of the community, and may make such provisions incidental to the powers aforesaid as may appear to His Majesty to be required for making the exercise of those powers effective:

Provided that nothing in this Act shall be construed to authorise the making of any regulations imposing any form of compulsory military service or industrial conscription:

Provided also that no such regulation shall make it an offence for any person or persons to take part in a strike, or peacefully to persuade any other person or persons to take part in a strike.

(2) Any regulations so made shall be laid before Parliament as soon as may be after they are made, and shall not continue in force after the expiration of seven days from the time when they are so laid unless a resolution is passed by both Houses providing for the continuance thereof.

(3) The regulations may provide for the trial, by courts of summary jurisdiction, of persons guilty of offences against the regulations; so, however, that the maximum penalty which may be inflicted for any offence against any such regulations shall be imprisonment with or without hard labour for a term of three months, or a fine [not exceeding level 3 on the standard scale] or both such imprisonment and fine, together with the forfeiture of any goods or money in respect of which the offence has been committed: Provided that no such regulations shall alter any existing procedure in criminal cases, or confer any right to punish by fine or imprisonment without trial.

(4), (5) ★★★★★

GOVERNMENT OF IRELAND ACT 1920
(10 & 11 Geo. 5, c. 67)

An Act to provide for the better Government of Ireland

Territorial extent Northern Ireland ★★★★★

75 Saving for supreme authority of the Parliament of the United Kingdom

Notwithstanding ... anything contained in this Act, the supreme authority of the parliament of the United Kingdom shall remain unaffected and undiminished over all persons, matters, and things in Ireland and every part thereof.

★★★★★

OFFICIAL SECRETS ACT 1920
(10 & 11 Geo. 5, c. 75)

An Act to amend the Official Secrets Act 1911

Territorial extent United Kingdom

1 Unauthorised use of uniforms; falsification of reports, forgery, personation, and false documents

(1) If any person for the purpose of gaining admission, or of assisting any other person to gain admission, to a prohibited place, within the meaning of the Official Secrets Act 1911 (hereinafter referred to as "the principal Act"), or for any other purpose prejudicial to the safety or interests of the State within the meaning of the said Act—

(a) uses or wears, without lawful authority, any naval, military, air-force, police, or other official uniform, or any uniform so nearly resembling the same as to be calculated to deceive, or falsely represents himself to be a person who is or has been entitled to use or wear any such uniform; or

(b) orally, or in writing in any declaration or application, or in any document signed by him or on his behalf, knowingly makes or connives at the making of any false statement or any omission; or

(c) ... tampers with any passport or any naval, military, air-force, police, or official pass, permit, certificate, licence, or other document of a similar character (hereinafter in this section referred to as an official document), ... or has in his possession any ... forged, altered, or irregular official document; or

(d) personates, or falsely represents himself to be a person holding, or in the employment of a person holding office under His Majesty, or to be or not to be a person to whom an official document or secret official code word or pass word has been duly issued or communicated, or with intent to obtain an official document, secret official code word or pass word, whether for himself or any other person, knowingly makes any false statement; or

(e) uses, or has in his possession or under his control, without the authority of the Government Department or the authority concerned, any die, seal, or stamp of or belonging to, or used, made or provided by any Government Department, or by any diplomatic, naval, military, or air force authority appointed by or acting under the authority of His Majesty, or any die, seal or stamp so nearly resembling any such die, seal or stamp as to be calculated to deceive, or counterfeits any such die, seal or stamp, or uses, or has in his possession, or under his control, any such counterfeited die, seal or stamp;

he shall be guilty of a misdemeanour.

(2) If any person—

(a) retains for any purpose prejudicial to the safety or interests of the State any official document, whether or not completed or issued for use, when he has no right to retain it, or when it is contrary to his duty to retain it, or fails to comply with any directions issued by any Government Department or any person authorised by such department with regard to the return or disposal thereof; or

(b) allows any other person to have possession of any official document issued for his use alone, or communicates any secret official code word or pass word so issued, or, without lawful authority or excuse, has in his possession any official document or secret official code word or pass word issued for the use of some person other than himself, or on obtaining possession of any official document by finding or otherwise, neglects or fails to restore it to the person or authority by whom or for whose use it was issued, or to a police constable; or

(c) without lawful authority or excuse, manufactures or sells, or has in his possession for sale any such die, seal or stamp as aforesaid;

he shall be guilty of a misdemeanour.

(3) In the case of any prosecution under this section involving the proof of a purpose prejudicial to the safety or interests of the State, subsection (2) of section one of the principal Act shall apply in like manner as it applies to prosecutions under that section.

2-5 * * * * *

6 Duty of giving information as to commission of offences

[(1) Where a chief officer of police is satisfied that there is reasonable ground for suspecting that an offence under section one of the principal Act has been committed and for believing that any person is able to furnish information as to the offence or suspected offence, he may apply to a Secretary of State for permission to exercise the powers conferred by this subsection and, if such permission is granted, he may authorise a superintendent of police, or any police officer not below the rank of inspector, to require the person believed to be able to furnish information to give any information in his power relating to the offence or suspected offence, and, if so required and on tender of his reasonable expenses, to attend at such reasonable time and place as may be specified by the superintendent or other officer; and if a person required in pursuance of such an authorisation to give information, or to attend as aforesaid, fails to comply with any such requirement or knowingly gives false information, he shall be guilty of a misdemeanour.

(2) Where a chief officer of police has reasonable grounds to believe that the case is one of great emergency and that in the interest of the State immediate action is necessary, he may exercise the powers conferred by the last foregoing subsection without applying for or being granted the permission of a Secretary of State, but if he does so shall forthwith report the circumstances to the Secretary of State.

(3) References in this section to a chief officer of police shall be construed as including references to any other officer of police expressly authorised by a chief officer of police to act on his behalf for the purposes of this section when by reason of illness, absence or other cause he is unable to do so.]

7 * * * * *

8 Provisions as to trial and punishment of offences

(1) Any person who is guilty of a felony under the principal Act or this Act shall be liable to penal servitude for a term of not less than three years and not exceeding fourteen years.

(2) Any person who is guilty of a misdemeanour under the principal Act or this Act shall be liable on conviction on indictment to imprisonment with or without hard labour, for a term not exceeding two years, or, on conviction under the Summary Jurisdiction Acts, to imprisonment, with or without hard labour, for a term not exceeding three months or to a fine not exceeding [the prescribed sum], or both such imprisonment and fine:

Provided that no misdemeanour under the principal Act or this Act shall be dealt with summarily except with the consent of the Attorney General.

(3) For the purposes of the trial of a person for an offence under the principal Act or this Act, the offence shall be deemed to have been committed either at the place in which the same actually was committed, or at any place in the United Kingdom in which the offender may be found.

(4) In addition and without prejudice to any powers which a court may possess to order the exclusion of the public from any proceedings if, in the course of proceedings before a court against any person for an offence under the principal Act or this Act or the proceedings on appeal, or in the course of the trial of a person for felony or misdemeanour under the principal Act or this Act, application is made by the prosecution, on the ground that the publication of any evidence to be given or of any statement to be made in the course of the proceedings would be prejudicial to the national safety, that all or any portion of the public shall be excluded during any part of the hearing, the court may make an order to that effect, but the passing of sentence shall in any case take place in public.

(5) Where the person guilty of an offence under the principal Act or this Act is a company or corporation, every director and officer of the company or corporation shall be guilty of the like offence unless he proves that the act or omission constituting the offence took place without his knowledge or consent.

* * * * *

JUDICIAL PROCEEDINGS (REGULATION OF REPORTS) ACT 1926
(16 & 17 Geo. 5, c. 61)

An Act to regulate the publication of reports of judicial proceedings in such manner as to prevent injury to public morals

Territorial extent England and Wales, Scotland

1 Restriction on publication of reports of judicial proceedings

(1) It shall not be lawful to print or publish, or cause or procure to be printed or published—

(a) in relation to any judicial proceedings any indecent matter or indecent medical, surgical or physiological details being matter or details the publication of which would be calculated to injure public morals;

(b) in relation to [any proceedings under Part II of the Family Law Act 1996 or otherwise in relation to] any judicial proceedings for dissolution of marriage, for nullity of marriage, or for judicial separation, or for restitution of conjugal rights, any particulars other than the following, that is to say:—

(i) the names, addresses and occupations of the parties and witnesses;

(ii) a concise statement of the charges, defences and countercharges in support of which evidence has been given;

(iii) submissions on any point of law arising in the course of the proceedings, and the decision of the court thereon;

(iv) the summing-up of the judge and the finding of the jury (if any) and the judgment of the court and observations made by the judge in giving judgment:

Provided that nothing in this part of this subsection shall be held to permit the publication of anything contrary to the provisions of paragraph (a) of this subsection.

(2) If any person acts in contravention of the provisions of this Act, he shall in respect of each offence be liable, on summary conviction, to imprisonment for a term not exceeding four months, or to a fine not exceeding [level 5 on the standard scale], or to both such imprisonment and fine:

Provided that no person, other than a proprietor, editor, master printer or publisher, shall be liable to be convicted under this Act.

(3) No prosecution for an offence under this Act shall be commenced in England and Wales by any person without the sanction of the Attorney-General.

(4), (5) ★★★★★

THE STATUTE OF WESTMINSTER 1931
(22 & 23 Geo. 5, c. 4)

An Act to give effect to certain resolutions passed by Imperial Conferences held in the years 1926 and 1930

Territorial extent As indicated in the Act (and see note to section 4).

Whereas the delegates of His Majesty's Governments in the United Kingdom, the Dominion of Canada, the Commonwealth of Australia, the Dominion of New Zealand, the Union of South Africa, the Irish Free State and Newfoundland, at Imperial Conferences holden at Westminster in the years of our Lord nineteen hundred and twenty-six and nineteen hundred and thirty did concur in making the declarations and resolutions set forth in the Reports of the said Conferences:

And whereas it is meet and proper to set out by way of preamble to this Act that, inasmuch as the Crown is the symbol of the free association of the members of the British Commonwealth of Nations, and as they are united by a common allegiance to the Crown, it would be in accord with the established constitutional position of all the members of the Commonwealth in relation to one another that any alteration in the law touching the Succession to the Throne or the Royal Style and Titles shall hereafter require the assent as well of the Parliaments of all the Dominions as of the Parliament of the United Kingdom:

And whereas it is in accord with the established constitutional position that no law hereafter made by the Parliament of the United Kingdom shall extend to any of the said Dominions as part of the law of that Dominion otherwise than at the request and with the consent of that Dominion:

And whereas it is necessary for the ratifying, confirming and establishing of certain of the said declarations and resolutions of the said Conferences that a law be made and enacted in due form by authority of the Parliament of the United Kingdom:

And whereas the Dominion of Canada, the Commonwealth of Australia, the Dominion of New Zealand, the Union of South Africa, the Irish Free State and Newfoundland have severally requested and consented to the submission of a measure to the Parliament of the United Kingdom for making such provision with regard to the matters aforesaid as is hereafter in this Act contained:

1 Meaning of "Dominion" in this Act

In this Act the expression "Dominion" means any of the following Dominions, that is to say, the Dominion of Canada, the Commonwealth of Australia, the Dominion of New Zealand, . . . the Irish Free State and Newfoundland.

2 Validity of laws made by Parliament of a Dominion

(1) The Colonial Laws Validity Act 1865 shall not apply to any law made after the commencement of this Act by the Parliament of a Dominion.

(2) No law and no provision of any law made after the commencement of this Act by the Parliament of a Dominion shall be void or inoperative on the ground that it is repugnant to the law of England, or to the provisions of any existing or future Act of Parliament of the United Kingdom, or to any order, rule or regulation made under any such Act, and the powers of the Parliament of a Dominion shall include the power to repeal or amend any such Act, order, rule or regulation in so far as the same is part of the law of the Dominion.

3 Power of Parliament of Dominion to legislate extra-territorally

It is hereby declared and enacted that the Parliament of a Dominion has full power to make laws having extra-territorial operation.

4 Parliament of United Kingdom not to legislate for Dominion except by consent

No Act of Parliament of the United Kingdom passed after the commencement of this Act shall extend, or be deemed to extend, to a Dominion as part of the law of that Dominion unless it is expressly declared in that Act that that Dominion has requested, and consented to, the enactment thereof.

Note This section has been repealed in relation to Canada by the Canada Act 1982 s. 1, Sch B and in relation to Australia by the Australia Act 1986 s. 12.

INCITEMENT TO DISAFFECTION ACT 1934
(24 & 25 Geo. 5, c. 56)

An Act to make better provision for the prevention and punishment of endeavours to seduce members of His Majesty's forces from their duty or allegiance

Territorial extent United Kingdom

1 Penalty on persons endeavouring to seduce members of His Majesty's forces from their duty or allegiance

If any person maliciously and advisedly endeavours to seduce any member of His Majesty's forces from his duty or allegiance to His Majesty, he shall be guilty of an offence under this Act.

2 Provisions for the prevention and detection of offences under this Act

(1) If any person, with intent to commit or to aid, abet, counsel, or procure the commission of an offence under section one of this Act, has in his possession or under is control any document of such a nature that the dissemination of copies thereof among

members of His Majesty's forces would constitute such an offence, he shall be guilty of an offence under this Act.

(2) If a judge of the High Court is satisfied by information on oath that there is reasonable ground for suspecting that an offence under this Act has been committed, and that evidence of the commission thereof is to be found at any premises or place specified in the information, he may, on an application made by an officer of police of a rank not lower than that of inspector, grant a search warrant authorising any such officer as aforesaid named in the warrant together with any other persons named in the warrant and any other officers of police to enter the premises or place at any time within one month from the date of the warrant, if necessary by force, and to search the premises or place and every person found therein, and to seize anything found on the premises or place or on any such person which the officer has reasonable ground for suspecting to be evidence of the commission of such an offence as aforesaid:

Provided that—

(a) a search warrant shall only be issued in respect of an offence suspected to have been committed within the three months prior to the laying of the information thereof; and

(b) if a search warrant under this Act has been executed on any premises, it shall be the duty of the officer of police who has conducted or directed the search to notify the occupier that the search has taken place, and to supply him with a list of any documents or other objects which have been removed from the premises, and where any documents have been removed from any other person to supply that person with a list of such documents.

(3) No woman shall, in pursuance of a warrant issued under the last foregoing subsection, be searched except by a woman.

(4) * * * * *

3 Provisions as to punishment of offences

(1) A person guilty of an offence under this Act shall be liable, on conviction on indictment to imprisonment for a term not exceeding two years or to a fine . . . or on summary conviction to imprisonment for a term not exceeding four months or to a fine not exceeding [the prescribed sum], or (whether on conviction on indictment or on summary conviction) to both such imprisonment and fine.

(2) No prosecution in England under this Act shall take place without the consent of the Director of Public Prosecutions.

(3) Where a prosecution under this Act is being carried on by the Director of Public Prosecutions, a court of summary jurisdiction shall not deal with the case summarily without the consent of the Director.

(4) Where any person is convicted of an offence under this Act, the court dealing with the case may order any documents connected with the offence to be destroyed or dealt with in such other manner as may be specified in the order, but no documents shall be destroyed before the expiration of the period within which an appeal may be lodged, and if an appeal is lodged no document shall be destroyed until after the appeal has been heard and decided.

4 * * * * *

HIS MAJESTY'S DECLARATION OF ABDICATION ACT 1936
(1 Edw. 8 & 1 Geo. 6, c. 3)

An Act to give effect to His Majesty's declaration of abdication; and for purposes connected therewith

Territorial extent United Kingdom (and the Empire as in 1936; See Preamble as to application to named Dominions under the Statute of Westminster 1931).

Whereas His Majesty by His Royal Message of the tenth day of December in this present year has been pleased to declare that He is irrevocably determined to renounce the Throne for Himself and His descendants, and has for that purpose executed the Instrument of Abdication set out in the Schedule to this Act, and has signified His desire that effect thereto should be given immediately:

And whereas, following upon the communication to His Dominions of His Majesty's said declaration and desire, the Dominion of Canada pursuant to the provisions of section four of the Statute of Westminster 1931 has requested and consented to the enactment of this Act, and the Commonwealth of Australia, the Dominion of New Zealand, and the Union of South Africa have assented thereto:

1 Effect of His Majesty's declaration of abdication

(1) Immediately upon the Royal Assent being signified to this Act the Instrument of Abdication executed by His present Majesty on the tenth day of December, nineteen hundred and thirty-six, set out in the Schedule to this Act, shall have effect, and thereupon His Majesty shall cease to be King and there shall be a demise of the Crown, and accordingly the member of the Royal Family then next in succession to the Throne shall succeed thereto and to all the rights, privileges, and dignities thereunto belonging.

(2) His Majesty, His issue, if any, and the descendants of that issue, shall not after His Majesty's abdication have any right, title or interest in or to the succession to the Throne, and section one of the Act of Settlement shall be construed accordingly.

(3) The Royal Marriages Act 1772 shall not apply to His Majesty after His abdication nor to the issue, if any, of His Majesty or the descendants of that issue.

SCHEDULE

I, Edward the Eighth, of Great Britain, Ireland, and the British Dominions beyond the Seas, King, Emperor of India, do hereby declare My irrevocable determination to renounce the Throne for Myself and for My descendants, and My desire that effect should be given to this Instrument of Abdication immediately.

In token whereof I have hereunto set My hand this tenth day of December, nineteen hundred and thirty-six, in the presence of the witnesses whose signatures are subscribed.

EDWARD R.I.

Signed at Fort Belvedere
in the presence of
ALBERT.
HENRY.
GEORGE.

PUBLIC ORDER ACT 1936
(1 Edw. 8 & 1 Geo. 6, c. 6)

An Act to prohibit the wearing of uniforms in connection with political objects and the maintenance by private persons of associations of military or similar character; and to make further provision for the preservation of public order on the occasion of public processions and meetings and in public places

Territorial extent England and Wales, Scotland

1 Prohibition of uniforms in connection with political objects

(1) Subject as hereinafter provided, any person who in any public place or at any public meeting wears uniform signifying his association with any political organisation or with the promotion of any political object shall be guilty of an offence:

Provided that, if the chief officer of police is satisfied that the wearing of any such uniform as aforesaid on any ceremonial, anniversary, or other special occasion will not be likely to involve risk of public disorder, he may, with the consent of a Secretary of State, by order permit the wearing of such uniform on that occasion either absolutely or subject to such conditions as may be specified in the order.

(2) Where any person is charged before any court with an offence under this section, no further proceedings in respect thereof shall be taken against him without the consent of the Attorney-General [except such as are authorised by [section 6 of the Prosecution of Offences Act 1979]] so, however, that if that person is remanded in custody he shall, after the expiration of a period of eight days from the date on which he was so remanded, be entitled to be [released on bail] without sureties unless within that period the Attorney-General has consented to such further proceedings as aforesaid.

2 Prohibition of quasi-military organisations

(1) If the members or adherents of any association of persons, whether incorporated or not, are—

(a) organised or trained or equipped for the purpose of enabling them to be employed in usurping the functions of the police or of the armed forces of the Crown; or

(b) organised and trained or organised and equipped either for the purpose of enabling them to be employed for the use or display of physical force in promoting any political object, or in such manner as to arouse reasonable apprehension that they are organised and either trained or equipped for that purpose;

then any person who takes part in the control or management of the association, or in so organising or training as aforesaid any members or adherents thereof, shall be guilty of an offence under this section:

Provided that in any proceedings against a person charged with the offence of taking part in the control or management of such an association as aforesaid it shall be a defence to that charge to prove that he neither consented to nor connived at the organisation, training, or equipment of members or adherents of the association in contravention of the provisions of this section.

(2) No prosecution shall be instituted under this section without the consent of the Attorney-General.

(3), (4) * * * * *

(5) If a judge of the High Court is satisfied by information on oath that there is reasonable ground for suspecting that an offence under this section has been committed, and that evidence of the commission thereof is to be found at any premises or place specified in the information, he may, on an application made by an officer of police of a rank not lower than that of inspector, grant a search warrant authorising any such officer as aforesaid named in the warrant together with any other persons named in the warrant and any other officers of police to enter the premises or place at any time within one month from the date of the warrant, if necessary by force, and to search the premises or place and every person found therein, and to seize anything found on the premises or place or on any such person which the officer has reasonable ground for suspecting to be evidence of the commission of such an offence as aforesaid:

Provided that no woman shall, in pursuance of a warrant issued under this subsection, be searched except by a woman.

(6) Nothing in this section shall be construed as prohibiting the employment of a reasonable number of persons as stewards to assist in the preservation of order at any public meeting held upon private premises, or the making of arrangements for that purpose or the instruction of the persons to be so employed in their lawful duties as such stewards, or their being furnished with badges or other distinguishing signs.

3, 4, 5, 5A . . . (Repealed by the Public Order Act 1986, Sch. 3).

6 (Amends the Public Meeting Act 1908, printed above as amended).

7 Enforcement

(1) Any person who commits an offence under section two of this Act shall be liable on summary conviction to imprisonment for a term not exceeding six months or to a fine not exceeding [the prescribed sum], or to both such imprisonment and fine, or, on conviction on indictment, to imprisonment for a term not exceeding two years or to a fine . . . or to both such imprisonment and fine.

(2) Any person guilty of [any offence under this Act other than an offence under section 2 . . .] shall be liable on summary conviction to imprisonment for a term not exceeding three months or to a fine not exceeding [level 4 on the standard scale], or to both such imprisonment and fine.

(3) A constable may without warrant arrest any person reasonably suspected by him to be committing an offence under section one . . . of this Act.

8 Application to Scotland

This Act shall apply to Scotland subject to the following modifications:—

(1) Subsection (2) of section one and subsection (2) of section two of this Act shall not apply.

(2) In subsection (3) of section two the Lord Advocate shall be substituted for the Attorney-General and the Court of Session shall be substituted for the High Court.

(3) Subsection (5) of section two shall have effect as if for any reference to a judge of the High Court there were substituted a reference to the Sheriff and any application for a search warrant under the said subsection shall be made by the procurator fiscal instead of such officer as is therein mentioned.

(4) The power conferred on the sheriff by subsection (5) of section two, as modified by the last foregoing paragraph, shall not be exercisable by an honorary sheriff-substitute.

★ ★ ★ ★ ★

9 Interpretation, etc.

(1) In this Act the following expressions have the meanings hereby respectively assigned to them, that is to say:—

. . .

"Meeting" means a meeting held for the purpose of the discussion of matters of public interest or for the purpose of the expression of views on such matters;

"Private premises" means premises to which the public have access (whether on payment or otherwise) only by permission of the owner, occupier, or lessee of the premises;

"Public meeting" includes any meeting in a public place and any meeting which the public or any section thereof are permitted to attend, whether on payment or otherwise;

["Public place" includes any highway and any other premises or place to which at the material time the public have or are permitted to have access, whether on payment or otherwise;]

. . .

"Recognised corps" means a rifle club, miniature rifle club or cadet corps approved by a Secretary of State under the Firearms Acts 1920 to 1936, for the purposes of those Acts.

★ ★ ★ ★ ★

REGENCY ACT 1937
(1 Edw. 8 & 1 Geo. 6, c. 16)

An Act to make provision for a Regency in the event of the Sovereign being on His Accession under the age of eighteen years, and in the event of the incapacity of the Sovereign through illness, and for the performance of certain of the royal functions in the name and on behalf of the Sovereign in certain other events; to repeal the Lords Justice Act 1837; and for purposes connected with the matters aforesaid

Territorial extent United Kingdom

1 Regency while the Sovereign is under eighteen

(1) If the Sovereign is, at His Accession, under the age of eighteen years, then, until He attains that age, the royal functions shall be performed in the name and on behalf of the Sovereign by a Regent.

(2) * * * * *

2 Regency during total incapacity of the Sovereign

(1) If the following persons or any three or more of them, that is to say, the wife or husband of the Sovereign, the Lord Chancellor, the Speaker of the House of Commons, the Lord Chief Justice of England, and the Master of the Rolls, declare in writing that they are satisfied by evidence which shall include the evidence of physicians that the Sovereign is by reason of infirmity of mind or body incapable for the time being of performing the royal functions or that they are satisfied by evidence that the Sovereign is for some definite cause not available for the performance of those functions, then, until it is declared in like manner that His Majesty has so far recovered His health as to warrant His resumption of the royal functions or has become available for the performance thereof, as the case may be, those functions shall be performed in the name and on behalf of the Sovereign by a Regent.

(2) A declaration under this section shall be made to the Privy Council and communicated to the Governments of His Majesty's Dominions. . . .

3 The Regent

(1) If a Regency becomes necessary under this Act, the Regent shall be that person who, excluding any persons disqualified under this section, is next in the line of succession to the Crown.

(2) A person shall be disqualified from becoming or being Regent, if he is not a British subject of full age and domiciled in some part of the United Kingdom, or is a person who would, under section two of the Act of Settlement, be incapable of inheriting, possessing, and enjoying the Crown; and section three of the Act of Settlement shall apply in the case of a Regent as it applies in the case of a Sovereign.

(3) If any person who would at the commencement of a Regency have become Regent but for the fact that he was not then of full age becomes of full age during the Regency, he shall, if he is not otherwise disqualified under this section, thereupon become Regent instead of the person who has theretofore been Regent.

(4), (5) * * * * *

4 Oaths to be taken by, and limitations of power of, Regent

(1) The Regent shall, before he acts in or enters upon his office, take and subscribe before the Privy Council the oaths set out in the Schedule to this Act, and the Privy Council are empowered and required to administer those oaths and to enter them in the Council Books.

(2) The Regent shall not have power to assent to any Bill for changing the order of succession to the Crown or for repealing or altering an Act of the fifth year of the reign of Queen Anne made in Scotland entitled "An Act for Securing the Protestant Religion and Presbyterian Church Government".

5-8 ★★★★★

Section 4

SCHEDULE
OATHS TO BE TAKEN BY THE REGENT

1. I swear that I will be faithful and bear true allegiance to [*here insert the name of the Sovereign*] his heirs and successors according to law. So help me God.

2. I swear that I will truly and faithfully execute the office of Regent, and that I will govern according to law, and will, in all things, to the utmost of my power and ability, consult and maintain the safety, honour, and dignity of [*here insert the name of the Sovereign*] and the welfare of his people. So help me God.

3. I swear that I will inviolably maintain and preserve in England and in Scotland the Settlement of the true Protestant religion as established by law in England and as established in Scotland by the laws made in Scotland in prosecution of the Claim of Right, and particularly by an Act intituled "An Act for Securing the Protestant Religion and Presbyterian Church Government" and by the Acts passed in the Parliament of both Kingdoms for Union of the two Kingdoms, together with the Government, Worship, Discipline, Rights, and Privileges of the Church of Scotland. So help me God.

BANK OF ENGLAND ACT 1946
(9 & 10 Geo. 6, c. 27)

An Act to bring the capital stock of the Bank of England into public ownership and bring the Bank under public control, to make provision with respect to the relations between the Treasury, the Bank of England and other banks and for purposes connected with the matters aforesaid

[14 February 1946]

Territorial extent United Kingdom

1-3 ★★★★★

4 Treasury directions to the Bank and relations of the Bank with other banks

(1) The Treasury may from time to time give such directions to the Bank as, after consultation with the Governor of the Bank, they think necessary in the public interest.

(2) Subject to any such directions, the affairs of the Bank shall be managed by the court of directors in accordance with such provisions (if any) in that behalf as may be contained in any charter of the Bank for the time being in force and any byelaws made thereunder.

(3) The Bank, if they think it necessary in the public interest, may request information from and make recommendations to bankers, and may, if so authorised by the Treasury, issue directions to any banker for the purpose of securing that effect is given to any such request or recommendation:

Provided that:—

(a) no such request or recommendations shall be made with respect to the affairs of any particular customer of a banker; and

(b) before authorising the issue of any such directions the Treasury shall give the banker concerned, or such person as appears to them to represent him, an opportunity of making representations with respect thereto.

(4), (5) ...

(6), (7) ★★★★★

5, 6 ★★★★★

STATUTORY INSTRUMENTS ACT 1946
(9 & 10 Geo. 6, c. 36)

An Act to repeal the Rules Publication Act, 1893, and to make further provision as to the instruments by which statutory powers to make orders, rules, regulations and other subordinate legislation are exercised [26 March 1946]

Territorial extent United Kingdom

1 Definition of "Statutory Instrument"

(1) Where by this Act or any Act passed after the commencement of this Act power to make, confirm or approve orders, rules, regulations or other subordinate legislation is conferred on His Majesty in Council or on any Minister of the Crown then, if the power is expressed—

(a) in the case of a power conferred on His Majesty, to be exercisable by Order in Council;

(b) in the case of a power conferred on a Minister of the Crown, to be exercisable by statutory instrument,

any document by which that power is exercised shall be known as a "statutory instrument" and the provisions of this Act shall apply thereto accordingly.

(2) Whereby any Act passed before the commencement of this Act power to make statutory rules within the meaning of the Rules Publication Act, 1893, was conferred on any rule-making authority within the meaning of that Act, any document by which that power is exercised after the commencement of this Act shall, save as is otherwise provided by regulations made under this Act, be known as a "statutory instrument" and the provisions of this Act shall apply thereto accordingly.

2 Numbering, printing, publication and citation

(1) Immediately after the making of any statutory instrument, it shall be sent to the King's printer of Acts of Parliament and numbered in accordance with regulations made under this Act, and except in such cases as may be provided by any Act passed after the commencement of this Act or prescribed by regulations made under this Act, copies thereof shall as soon as possible be printed and sold by [or under the authority of] the King's printer of Acts of Parliament.

(2) Any statutory instrument may, without prejudice to any other mode of citation, be cited by the number given to it in accordance with the provisions of this section, and the calendar year.

3 Supplementary provisions as to publication

(1) Regulations made for the purposes of this Act shall make provision for the publication by His Majesty's Stationery Office of lists showing the date upon which every statutory instrument printed and sold by [or under the authority of] the King's printer of Acts of Parliament was first issued by [or under the authority of] that office; and in any legal proceedings a copy of any list so published . . . shall be received in evidence as a true copy, and an entry therein shall be conclusive evidence of the date on which any statutory instrument was first issued by [or under the authority of] His Majesty's Stationery Office.

(2) In any proceedings against any person for an offence consisting of a contravention of any such statutory instrument, it shall be a defence to prove that the instrument had not been issued by His Majesty's Stationery Office at the date of the alleged contravention unless it is proved that at that date reasonable steps had been taken for the purpose of bringing the purport of the instrument to the notice of the public, or of persons likely to be affected by it, or of the person charged.

(3) Save as therein otherwise expressly provided, nothing in this section shall affect any enactment or rule of law relating to the time at which any statutory instrument comes into operation.

4 Statutory instruments which are required to be laid before Parliament

(1) Where by this Act or any Act passed after the commencement of this Act any statutory instrument is required to be laid before Parliament after being made, a copy of the instrument shall be laid before each House of Parliament and, subject as hereinafter provided, shall be so laid before the instrument comes into operation:

Provided that if it is essential that any such instrument should come into operation before copies thereof can be so laid as aforesaid, the instrument may be made so as to come into operation before it has been so laid; and where any statutory instrument comes into operation before it is laid before Parliament, notification shall forthwith be sent to the Lord Chancellor and to the Speaker of the House of Commons drawing attention to the fact that copies of the instrument have yet to be laid before Parliament and explaining why such copies were not so laid before the instrument came into operation.

(2) Every copy of any such statutory instrument sold by [or under the authority of] the King's printer of Acts of Parliament shall bear on the face thereof—

(a) a statement showing the date on which the statutory instrument came or will come into operation; and

(b) either a statement showing the date on which copies thereof were laid before Parliament or a statement that such copies are to be laid before Parliament.

(3) ★★★★★

5 Statutory instruments which are subject to annulment by resolution of either House of Parliament

(1) Where by this Act or any Act passed after the commencement of this Act, it is provided that any statutory instrument shall be subject to annulment in pursuance of resolution of either House of Parliament, the instrument shall be laid before Parliament after being made and the provisions of the last foregoing section shall apply thereto accordingly, and if either House, within the period of forty days beginning with the day on which a copy thereof is laid before it, resolves that an Address be presented to His Majesty praying that the instrument be annulled, no further proceedings shall be taken thereunder after the date of the resolution, and His Majesty may by Order in Council revoke the instrument, so, however, that any such resolution and revocation shall be without prejudice to the validity of anything previously done under the instrument or to the making of a new statutory instrument.

(2) ★★★★★

6 Statutory instruments of which drafts are to be laid before Parliament

(1) Where by this Act or any Act passed after the commencement of this Act it is provided that a draft of any statutory instrument shall be laid before Parliament, but the Act does not prohibit the making of the instrument without the approval of Parliament, then, in the case of an Order in Council the draft shall not be submitted to His Majesty in Council, and in any other case the statutory instrument shall not be made, until after the expiration of a period of forty days beginning with the day on which a copy of the draft is laid before each House of Parliament, or, if such copies are laid on different days, with the later of the two days, and if within that period either House resolves that the draft be not submitted to His Majesty or that the statutory instrument be not made, as the case may be, no further proceedings shall be taken thereon, but without prejudice to the laying before Parliament of a new draft.

(2) ★★★★★

★★★★★

CROWN PROCEEDINGS ACT 1947
(10 & 11 Geo. 6, c. 44)

An Act to amend the law relating to the civil liabilities and rights of the Crown and to civil proceedings by and against the Crown, to amend the law relating to the civil liabilities of persons other than the Crown in certain cases involving the affairs or property of the Crown, and for purposes connected with the matters aforesaid [31 July 1947]

Territorial extent United Kingdom (ss. 2, 4, 11, 21, 40), England and Wales and Northern Ireland (ss. 1, 17, 25, 28), Scotland (ss. 41, 42, 43, 47).

PART I
SUBSTANTIVE LAW

1 Right to sue the Crown

Where any person has a claim against the Crown after the commencement of this Act, and, if this Act had not been passed, the claim might have been enforced, subject to the grant of His Majesty's fiat, by petition of right, or might have been enforced by a proceeding provided by any stautory provision repealed by this Act, then, subject to the provisions of this Act, the claim may be enforced as of right, and without the fiat of His Majesty, by proceedings taken against the Crown for that purpose in accordance with the provisions of this Act.

2 Liability of the Crown in tort

(1) Subject to the provisions of this Act, the Crown shall be subject to all those liabilities in tort to which, if it were a private person of full age and capacity, it would be subject—

(a) in respect of torts committed by its servants or agents;

(b) in respect of any breach of those duties which a person owes to his servants or agents at common law by reason of being their employer; and

(c) in respect of any breach of the duties attaching at common law to the ownership, occupation, possession or control of property:

Provided that no proceedings shall lie against the Crown by virtue of paragraph (a) of this subsection in respect of any act or omission of a servant or agent of the Crown unless the act or omission would apart from the provisions of this Act have given rise to a cause of action in tort against that servant or agent or his estate.

(2) Where the Crown is bound by a statutory duty which is binding also upon persons other than the Crown and its officers, then, subject to the provisions of this Act, the Crown shall, in respect of a failure to comply with that duty, be subject to all those liabilities in tort (if any) to which it would be so subject if it were a private person of full age and capacity.

(3) Where any functions are conferred or imposed upon an officer of the Crown as such either by any rule of the common law or by statute, and that officer commits a tort while performing or purporting to perform those functions, the liabilities of the Crown in respect of the tort shall be such as they would have been if those functions had been conferred or imposed solely by virtue of instructions lawfully given by the Crown.

(4) Any enactment which negatives or limits the amount of the liability of any Government department or officer of the Crown in respect of any tort committed by that department or officer shall, in the case of proceedings against the Crown under this section in respect of a tort committed by that department or officer, apply in relation to the Crown as it would have applied in relation to that department or officer if the proceedings against the Crown had been proceedings against that department or officer.

(5) No proceedings shall lie against the Crown by virtue of this section in respect of anything done or omitted to be done by any person while discharging or purporting to discharge any responsibilities of a judicial nature vested in him, or any responsibilities which he has in connection with the execution of judicial process.

(6) No proceedings shall lie against the Crown by virtue of this section in respect of any act, neglect or default of any officer of the Crown, unless that officer has been directly or indirectly appointed by the Crown and was at the material time paid in respect of his duties as an officer of the Crown wholly out of the Consolidated Fund of the United Kingdom, moneys provided by Parliament, . . ., or any other Fund certified by the Treasury for the purposes of this subsection or was at the material time holding an office in respect of which the Treasury certify that the holder thereof would normally be so paid.

3 ★★★★★

4 Application of law as to indemnity, contribution, joint and several tort-feasors, and contributory negligence

(1) Where the Crown is subject to any liability by virtue of this Part of this Act, the law relating to indemnity and contribution shall be enforceable by or against the Crown in respect of the liability to which it is so subject as if the Crown were a private person of full age and capacity.

(2) . . .

(3) Without prejudice to the general effect of section one of this Act, the Law Reform (Contributory Negligence) Act 1945 (which amends the law relating to contributory negligence) shall bind the Crown.

5-8 . . .

9 ★★★★★

10 (Repealed by the Crown Proceedings (Armed Forces) Act 1987) . . .

11 Saving in respect of acts done under prerogative and statutory powers

(1) Nothing in Part I of this Act shall extinguish or abridge any powers or authorities which, if this Act had not been passed, would have been exercisable by virtue of the prerogative of the Crown, or any powers or authorities conferred on the Crown by any statute, and, in particular, nothing in the said Part I shall extinguish or abridge any powers or authorities exercisable by the Crown, whether in time of peace or of war, for the purpose of the defence of the realm or of training, or maintaining the efficiency of, any of the armed forces of the Crown.

(2) Where in any proceedings under this Act it is material to determine whether anything was properly done or omitted to be done in the exercise of the prerogative of the Crown, . . . a Secretary of State may, if satisfied that the act or omission was necessary for any such purpose as is mentioned in the last preceding subsection, issue a certificate to the effect that the act or omission was necessary for that purpose; and the certificate shall, in those precedings, be conclusive as to the matter so certified.

12-16 ★★★★★

PART II
JURISDICTION AND PROCEDURE

17 Parties to proceedings

(1) [The Minister for the Civil Service] shall publish a list specifying the several Government departments which are authorised departments for the purposes of this Act, and the name and address for service of the person who is, or is acting for the purposes of this Act as, the solicitor for each such department, and may from time to time amend or vary the said list.

Any document purporting to be a copy of a list published under this section and purporting to be printed under the superintendence or the authority of His Majesty's Stationery Office shall in any legal proceedings be received as evidence for the purpose of establishing what departments are authorised departments for the purposes of this Act, and what person is, or is acting for the purposes of this Act as, the solicitor for any such department.

(2) Civil proceedings by the Crown may be instituted either by an authorised Government department in its own name, whether that department was or was not at the commencement of this Act authorised to sue, or by the Attorney General.

(3) Civil proceedings against the Crown shall be instituted against the appropriate authorised Government department, or, if none of the authorised Government departments is appropriate or the person instituting the proceedings has any reasonable doubt whether any and if so which of those departments is appropriate, against the Attorney General.

(4), (5) * * * * *

18-20 * * * * *

21 Nature of relief

(1) In any civil proceedings by or against the Crown the court shall, subject to the provisions of this Act, have power to make all such orders as it has power to make in proceedings between subjects, and otherwise to give such appropriate relief as the case may require:

Provided that:—

(a) where in any proceedings against the Crown any such relief is sought as might in proceedings between subjects be granted by way of injunction or specific performance, the court shall not grant an injunction or make an order for specific performance, but may in lieu thereof make an order declaratory of the rights of the parties; and

(b) in any proceedings against the Crown for the recovery of land or other property the court shall not make an order for the recovery of the land or the delivery of the property, but may in lieu thereof make an order declaring that the plaintiff is entitled as against the Crown to the land or property or to the possession thereof.

(2) The court shall not in any civil proceedings grant any injunction or make any order against an officer of the Crown if the effect of granting the injunction or making the order would be to give any relief against the Crown which could not have been obtained in proceedings against the Crown.

22-24 * * * * *

PART III
JUDGMENTS AND EXECUTION

25 Satisfaction of orders against the Crown

(1) Where in any civil proceedings by or against the Crown, or in any proceedings on the Crown side of the King's Bench Division, or in connection with any arbitration to which the Crown is a party, any order (including an order for costs) is made by any court in favour of any person against the Crown or against a Government department or against an officer of the Crown as such, the proper officer of the court shall, on an application in that behalf made by or on behalf of that person at any time after the expiration of twenty-one days from the date of the order or, in case the order provides for the payment of costs and the costs require to be taxed, at any time after the costs have been taxed, whichever is the later, issue to that person a certificate in the prescribed form containing particulars of the order:

Provided that, if the court so directs, a separate certificate shall be issued with respect to the costs (if any) ordered to be paid to the applicant.

(2) A copy of any certificate issued under this section may be served by the person in whose favour the order is made upon the person for the time being named in the record as the solicitor, or as the person acting as solicitor, for the Crown or for the Governmet department or officer concerned.

(3) If the order provides for the payment of any money by way of damages or otherwise, or of any costs, the certificate shall state the amount so payable, and the appropriate Government department shall, subject as hereinafter provided, pay to the person entitled or to his solicitor the amount appearing by the certificate to be due to him together with the interest, if any, lawfully due thereon:

Provided that the court by which any such order as aforesaid is made or any court to which an appeal against the order lies may direct that, pending an appeal or otherwise, payment of the whole of any amount so payable, or any part thereof, shall be suspended, and if the certificate has not been issued may order any such directions to be inserted therein.

(4) Save as aforesaid no execution or attachment or process in the nature thereof shall be issued out of any court for enforcing payment by the Crown of any such money or costs as aforesaid, and no person shall be individually liable under any order for the payment by the Crown, or any Government department, or any officer of the Crown as such, of any such money or costs.

(5) ...

26-27 * * * * *

PART IV
MISCELLANEOUS AND SUPPLEMENTAL

Miscellaneous

28 Discovery

(1) Subject to and in accordance with rules of court and county court rules:—

(a) in any civil proceedings in the High Court or a county court to which the Crown is a party, the Crown may be required by the court to make discovery of documents and produce documents for inspection; and

(b) in any such proceedings as aforesaid, the Crown may be required by the court to answer interrogatories:

Provided that this section shall be without prejudice to any rule of law which authorises or requires the withholding of any document or the refusal to answer any question on the ground that the disclosure of the document or the answering of the question would be injurious to the public interest.

Any order of the court made under the powers conferred by paragraph (b) of this subsection shall direct by what officer of the Crown the interrogatories are to be answered.

(2) Without prejudice to the proviso to the preceding subsection, any rules made for the purposes of this section shall be such as to secure that the existence of a document will not be disclosed if, in the opinion of a Minister of the Crown, it would be injurious to the public interest to disclose the existence thereof.

29, 31-33, 35, 37-8 * * * * *

30, 34, 36, 39 ...

40 Savings

(1) Nothing in this Act shall apply to proceedings by or against, or authorise proceedings in tort to be brought against, His Majesty in His private capacity.

(2)-(5) * * * * *

PART V
APPLICATION TO SCOTLAND

41 Application of Act to Scotland

The provisions of this Part of this Act shall have effect for the purpose of the application of this Act to Scotland.

42 Exclusion of certain provisions

Section one, Part II (except section thirteen so far as relating to proceedings mentioned in the First Schedule and section twenty-one), Part III (except section twenty-six) and section twenty-eight of this Act shall not apply to Scotland.

43 Interpretation for purposes of application to Scotland

In the application of this Act to Scotland:—

(a) for any reference to the High Court (except a reference to that Court as a prize court) there shall be substituted a reference to the Court of Session; for any reference to the county court there shall be substituted a reference to the sheriff court; the expression "plaintiff" means pursuer; the expression "defendant" means defender; the expression "county court rules" means Act of Sederunt applying to the sheriff court; and the expression "injunction" means interdict;

(b) the expression "tort" means any wrongful or negligent act or omission giving rise to liability in reparation, and any reference to liability or right or action or proceedings in tort shall be construed accordingly; and for any reference to Part II of the Law Reform (Married Women and Tortfeasors) Act, 1935, there shall be substituted a reference to section three of the Law Reform (Miscellaneous Provisions) (Scotland) Act, 1940.

44-46 * * * * *

47 Recovery of documents in possession of Crown

Subject to and in accordance with Acts of Sederunt applying to the Court of Session and the sheriff court, commission and diligence for the recovery of documents in the possession of the Crown may be granted in any action whether or not the Crown is a party thereto, in like manner in all respects as if the documents were in the possession of a subject:

Provided that—

(i) this subsection shall be without prejudice to any rule of law which authorises or requires the withholding of any document on the ground that its disclosure would be injurious to the public interest; and

(ii) the existence of a document shall not be disclosed if, in the opinion of a Minister of the Crown, it would be injurious to the public interest to disclose the existence thereof.

48-53 * * * * *

WIRELESS TELEGRAPHY ACT 1949
(12, 13 & 14 Geo. 6, c. 54)

An Act to amend the law relating to wireless telegraphy [30 July 1949]

Territorial extent United Kingdom

PART I

Regulation of Wireless Telegraphy

1 Licensing of wireless telegraphy

(1) No person shall establish or use any station for wireless telegraphy or instal or use any apparatus for wireless telegraphy except under the authority of a licence in that behalf [granted under this section—

(a) by the Secretary of State (unless it is a television licence); or

(b) if it is a television licence, by the BBC;

and any person] who establishes or uses any station for wireless telegraphy or instals or uses any apparatus for wireless telegraphy except under and in accordance with such a licence shall be guilty of an offence under this Act:

Provided that the [Secretary of State] may by regulations exempt from the provisions of this subsection the establishment, installation or use of stations for wireless telegraphy or wireless telegraphy apparatus of such classes or descriptions as may be specified in the regulations, either absolutely or subject to such terms, provisions and limitations as may be so specified.

(2) A licence granted under this section (hereafter in this Act referred to as a wireless telegraphy licence) may be issued subject to such terms, provisions and [limitations—

(a) as the Secretary of State may think fit; or

(b) in the case of a television licence, as the Secretary of State may direct or, (subject to any such direction) the BBC may think fit,

including] in particular in the case of a licence to establish a station, limitations as to the position and nature of the station, the purposes for which, the circumstances in which, and the persons by whom the station may be used, and the apparatus which may be installed or used therein, and, in the case of any other licence, limitations as to the apparatus which may be installed or used, and the places where, the purposes for which, the circumstances in which and the persons by whom the apparatus may be used.

(3) A wireless telegraphy licence shall, unless previously revoked by the [Secretary of State], [or (if it is a television licence), by the BBC] continue in force for such period as may be specified in the licence.

(4) A wireless telegraphy licence [(other than a television licence)] may be revoked, or the terms, provisions or limitations thereof varied, by a notice in writing of the [Secretary of State] served on the holder of the licence or by a general notice applicable to licences of the class to which the licence in question belongs published in such manner as may be specified in the licence [; and a television licence may be revoked, or the terms, provisions or limitations thereof varied, by the BBC (either of their own motion or to give effect to any direction of the Secretary of State under subsection (2)(b) of this section)—

(a) by a notice in writing served on the holder of the licence; or

(b) by a general notice published as mentioned above.]

(5) * * * * *

(6) Nothing in this section shall authorise the inclusion, in any wireless telegraphy licence relating solely to apparatus not designed or adapted for emission (as opposed to reception), of any term or provision requiring any person to concede any form of right of entry into any private dwelling-house.

(7) * * * * *

1A, 1B, 1C * * * * *

* * * * *

POST OFFICE ACT 1953
(1 & 2 Eliz. 2, c. 36)

An Act to consolidate certain enactments relating to the Post Office with corrections and improvements made under the Consolidation of Enactments (Procedure) Act 1949

[31 July 1953]

Territorial extent United Kingdom

1-7 . . .

General provisions as to transmission of postal packets

8 Conditions of transit of postal packets

(1), (2) . . .

(3) If any postal packet is posted or sent by post in contravention of this Act or of any . . . regulation made thereunder, the transmission thereof may be refused and the

packet may, if necessary, be detained and opened in the post office and may be returned to the sender thereof or forwarded to its destination, subject in either case to any ... regulations as to additional postage or other charges, or may be destroyed or otherwise disposed of as [the Post Office] may direct.

(4) ...

9 ...

10 ★★★★★

11 Prohibition on sending by post of certain articles

(1) A person shall not send or attempt to send or procure to be sent a postal packet which—

(a) save as [the Post Office] may either generally or in any particular case allow, encloses any explosive, dangerous, noxious or deleterious substance, any filth, any sharp instrument not properly protected, any noxious living creature, or any creature, article or thing whatsoever which is likely to injure either other postal packets in course of conveyance or [a person engaged in the business of the Post Office]; or

(b) encloses any indecent or obscene print, painting, photograph, lithograph, engraving, cinematograph film, book, card or written communication, or any indecent or obscene article whether similar to the above or not; or

(c) has on the packet, or on the cover thereof, any words, marks or designs which are grossly offensive or of an indecent or obscene character.

(2) If any person acts in contravention of the foregoing subsection, he shall be liable on summary conviction to a fine not exceeding [the prescribed sum] or on conviction on indictment to imprisonment for a term not exceeding twelve months.

★★★★★

58 Opening or delaying of postal packets by officers of the Post Office

(1) If any [person engaged in the business of the Post Office], contrary to his duty, opens, or procures or suffers to be opened, any postal packet in course of transmission by post, or wilfully detains or delays, or procures or suffers to be detained or delayed, any such postal packet, he shall be guilty of a misdemeanour and be liable to imprisonment [for a term not exceeding two years] or to a fine, or to both:

Provided that nothing in this section shall extend to the opening, detaining or delaying of a postal packet returned for want of a true direction, or returned by reason that the person to whom it is directed has refused it, or has refused or neglected to pay the postage thereof, or that the packet cannot for any other reason be delivered, or to the opening, detaining or delaying of a postal packet under the authority of this Act or in obedience to [a warrant issued by the Secretary of State under section 2 of the Interception of Communications Act 1985].

★★★★★

CHILDREN AND YOUNG PERSONS (HARMFUL PUBLICATIONS) ACT 1955 (3 & 4 Eliz. 2, c. 28)

An Act to prevent the dissemination of certain pictorial publications harmful to children and young persons [6 May 1955]

Territorial extent United Kingdom

1 Works to which this Act applies

This Act applies to any book, magazine or other like work which is of a kind likely to fall into the hands of children or young persons and consists wholly or mainly of stories told in pictures (with or without the addition of written matter), being stories portraying—

(a) the commission of crimes; or
(b) acts of violence or cruelty; or
(c) incidents of a repulsive or horrible nature;

in such a way that the work as a whole would tend to corrupt a child or young person into whose hands it might fall.

2 Penalty for printing, publishing, selling, &c, works to which this Act applies

(1) A person who prints, publishes, sells or lets on hire a work to which this Act applies, or has any such work in his possession for the purpose of selling it or letting it on hire, shall be guilty of an offence and liable, on summary conviction, to imprisonment for a term not exceeding four months or to a fine not exceeding [level 3 on the standard scale] or to both:

Provided that, in any proceedings taken under this subsection against a person in respect of selling or letting on hire a work or of having it in his possession for the purpose of selling it or letting it on hire, it shall be a defence for him to prove that he had not examined the contents of the work and had no reasonable cause to suspect that it was one to which this Act applies.

(2) A prosecution for an offence under this section shall not, in England or Wales, be instituted except by, or with the consent of, the Attorney General.

★ ★ ★ ★ ★

Note Section 3 (not reproduced) provides for the granting of search warrants and forfeiture of offending material on conviction; s. 4 prohibits importation of material subject to the Act.

LIFE PEERAGES ACT 1958
(6 & 7 Eliz. 2, c. 21)

An Act to make provision for the creation of life peerages carrying the right to sit and vote in the House of Lords [30 April 1958]

Territorial extent United Kingdom

1 Power to create life peerages carrying right to sit in the House of Lords

(1) Without prejudice to Her Majesty's powers as to the appointment of Lords of Appeal in Ordinary, Her Majesty shall have power by letters patent to confer on any person a peerage for life having the incidents specified in subsection (2) of this section.

(2) A peerage conferred under this section shall, during the life of the person on whom it is conferred, entitle him—

(a) to rank as a baron under such style as may be appointed by the letters patent; and

(b) subject to subsection (4) of this section, to receive writs of summons to attend the House of Lords and sit and vote therein accordingly,

and shall expire on his death.

(3) A life peerage may be conferred under this section on a woman.

(4) Nothing in this section shall enable any person to receive a writ of summons to attend the House of Lords, or to sit and vote in that House, at any time when disqualified therefor by law.

PUBLIC RECORDS ACT 1958
(6 & 7 Eliz. 2, c. 51)

An Act to make new provision with respect to public records and the Public Record Office, and for connected purposes [23 July 1958]

Territorial extent England and Wales, Scotland

1 General responsibility of the Lord Chancellor for public records

(1) The direction of the Public Record Office shall be transferred from the Master of the Rolls to the Lord Chancellor, and the Lord Chancellor shall be generally responsible for the execution of this Act and shall supervise the care and preservation of public records.

(2) There shall be an Advisory Council on Public Records to advise the Lord Chancellor on matters concerning public records in general and, in particular, on those aspects of the work of the Public Record Office which affect members of the public who make use of the facilities provided by the Public Record Office.

The Master of the Rolls shall be chairman of the said Council and the remaining members of the Council shall be appointed by the Lord Chancellor on such terms as he may specify.

(3) The Lord Chancellor shall in every year lay before both Houses of Parliament a report on the work of the Public Record Office, which shall include any report made to him by the Advisory Council on Public Records.

2 * * * * *

3 Selection and preservation of public records

(1) It shall be the duty of every person responsible for public records of any description which are not in the Public Record Office or a place of deposit appointed by the Lord Chancellor under this Act to make arrangements for the selection of those records which ought to be permanently preserved and for their safe-keeping.

(2) Every person shall perform his duties under this section under the guidance of the Keeper of Public Records and the said Keeper shall be responsible for co-ordinating and supervising all action taken under this section.

(3) All public records created before the year sixteen hundred and sixty shall be included among those selected for permanent preservation.

(4)-(8) * * * * *

4 * * * * *

5 Access to public records

(1) Public records in the Public Record Office, other than those to which members of the public had access before their transfer to the Public Record Office, shall not be available for public inspection [until the expiration of the period of thirty years beginning with the first day of January in the year next after that in which they were created, or such other period], either longer or shorter, as the Lord Chancellor may, with the approval, or at the request, of the Minister or other person, if any, who appears to him to be primarily concerned, for the time being prescribe as respects any particular class of public records.

(2) Without prejudice to the generality of the foregoing subsection, if it appears to the person responsible for any public records which have been selected by him under section three of this Act for permanent preservation that they contain information which was obtained from members of the public under such conditions that the opening of those records to the public after the period determined under the foregoing subsection would or might constitute a breach of good faith on the part of the Government or on the part of the persons who obtained the information, he shall inform the Lord

Chancellor accordingly and those records shall not be available in the Public Record Office for public inspection even after the expiration of the said period except in such circumstances and subject to such conditions, if any, as the Lord Chancellor and that person may approve, or, if the Lord Chancellor and that person think fit, after the expiration of such further period as they may approve.

(3)-(5) * * * * *

6-13 * * * * *

Section 10

FIRST SCHEDULE
DEFINITION OF PUBLIC RECORDS

1. The provisions of this Schedule shall have effect for determining what are public records for the purposes of this Act.

Departmental records

2.—(1) Subject to the provisions of this paragraph, administrative and departmental records belonging to Her Majesty, whether in the United Kingdom or elsewhere, in right of Her Majesty's Government in the United Kingdom and, in particular,—

(a) records, of, or held in, any department of her Majesty's Government in the United Kingdom, or

(b) records of any office, commission or other body or establishment whatsoever under Her Majesty's Government in the United Kingdom,

shall be public records.

(2) Sub-paragraph (1) of this paragaph shall not apply—

(a) to records of any government department or body which is wholly or mainly concerned with Scottish affairs, or which carries on its activities wholly or mainly in Scotland, or

(b) to registers, or certified copies of entries in registers, being registers or certified copies kept or deposited in the General Register Office under or in pursuance of any enactment, whether past or future, which provides for the registration of births, deaths, marriages or adoptions, or

(c) except so far as provided by paragraph 4 of this Schedule, to records of the Duchy of Lancaster, or

(d) to records of the office of the Public Trustee relating to individual trusts.

* * * * *

OBSCENE PUBLICATIONS ACT 1959
(7 & 8 Eliz. 2, c. 66)

An Act to amend the law relating to the publication of obscene matter; to provide for the protection of literature; and to strengthen the law concerning pornography [29 July 1959]

Territorial extent England and Wales

1 Test of obscenity

(1) For the purposes of this Act an article shall be deemed to be obscene if its effect or (where the article comprises two or more distinct items) the effect of any one of its items is, if taken as a whole, such as to tend to deprave and corrupt persons who are likely, having regard to all relevant circumstances, to read, see or hear the matter contained or embodied in it.

(2) In this Act "article" means any description of article containing or embodying matter to be read or looked at or both, any sound record, and any film or other record of a picture or pictures.

(3) For the purposes of this Act a person publishes an article who—

(a) distributes, circulates, sells, lets on hire, gives, or lends it, or who offers it for sale or for letting on hire; or

(b) in the case of an article containing or embodying matter to be looked at or a record, shows, plays or projects it [, or, where the matter is data stored electronically, transmits that data.]

. . .

[(4) For the purposes of this Act a person also publishes an article to the extent that any matter recorded on it is included by him in a programme included in a programme service.

(5) Where the inclusion of any matter in a programme so included would, if that matter were recorded matter, constitute the publication of an obscene article for the purposes of this Act by virtue of subsection (4) above, this Act shall have effect in relation to the inclusion of that matter in that programme as if it were recorded matter.

(6) In this section "programme" and "programme service" have the same meaning as in the Broadcasting Act 1990.]

2 Prohibition of publication of obscene matter

(1) Subject as hereinafter provided, any person who, whether for gain or not, publishes an obscene article [or who has an obscene article for publication for gain (whether gain to himself or gain to another)] shall be liable—

(a) on summary conviction to a fine not exceeding [the prescribed sum] or to imprisonment for a term not exceeding six months;

(b) on conviction on indictment to a fine or to imprisonment for a term not exceeding three years or both.

(2) . . .

(3) A prosecution . . . for an offence against this section shall not be commenced more than two years after the commission of the offence.

[(3A) Proceedings for an offence under this section shall not be instituted except by or with the consent of the Director of Public Prosecutions in any case where the article in question is a moving picture film of a width of not less than sixteen millimetres and the relevant publication or the only other publication which followed or could reasonably have been expected to follow from the relevant publication took place or (as the case may be) was to take place in the course of a [film exhibition]; and in this subsection "the relevant publication" means—

(a) in the case any proceedings under this section for publishing an obscene article, the publication in respect of which the defendant would be charged if the proceedings were brought; and

(b) in the case of any proceedings under this section for having an obscene article for publication for gain, the publication which, if the proceedings were brought, the defendant would be alleged to have had in contemplation.]

(4) A person publishing an article shall not be proceeded against for an offence at common law consisting of the publication of any matter contained or embodied in the article where it is of the essence of the offence that the matter is obscene.

[(4A) Without prejudice to subsection (4) above, a person shall not be proceeded against for an offence at common law—

(a) in respect of a [film exhibition] or anything said or done in the course of a [film exhibition], where it is of the essence of the common law offence that the exhibition or, as the case may be, what was said or done was obscene, indecent, offensive, disgusting or injurious to morality; or

(b) in respect of an agreement to give a [film exhibition] or to cause anything to be said or done in the course of such an exhibition where the common law offence consists of conspiring to corrupt public morals or to do any act contrary to public morals or decency.]

(5) A person shall not be convicted of an offence against this section if he proves that he had not examined the article in respect of which he is charged and had no reasonable cause to suspect that it was such that his publication of it would make him liable to be convicted of an offence against this section.

(6) In any proceedings against a person under this section the question whether an article is obscene shall be determined without regard to any publication by another person unless it could reasonably have been expected that the publication by the other person would follow from publication by the person charged.

[(7) In this section "film exhibition" has the same meaning as in the Cinemas Act 1985.]

3 Powers of search and seizure

(1) If a justice of the peace is satisfied by information on oath that there is reasonable ground for suspecting that, in any premises in the petty sessions area for which he acts, or on any stall or vehicle in that area, being premises or a stall or vehicle specified in the information, obscene articles are, or are from time to time, kept for publication for gain, the justice may issue a warrant under his hand empowering any constable to enter (if need be by force) and search the premises, or to search the stall or vehicle . . . and to seize and remove any articles found therein or thereon which the constable has reason to believe to be obscene articles and to be kept for publication for gain.

(2) A warrant under the foregoing subsection shall, if any obscene articles are seized under the warrant, also empower the seizure and removal of any documents found in the premises or, as the case may be, on the stall or vehicle which relate to a trade or business carried on at the premises or from the stall or vehicle.

(3) [Subject to subsection (3A) of this section] any articles seized under subsection (1) of this section shall be brought before a justice of the peace acting for the same petty sessions area as the justice who issued the warrant, and the justice before whom the articles are brought may thereupon issue a summons to the occupier of the premises or, as the case may be, the user of the stall or vehicle to appear on a day specified in the summons before a magistrates' court for that petty sessions area to show cause why the articles or any of them should not be forfeited; and if the court is satisfied, as respects any of the articles, that at the time when they were seized they were obscene articles kept for publication for gain, the court shall order those articles to be forfeited:

Provided that if the person summoned does not appear, the court shall not make an order unless service of the summons is proved.

[Provided also that this subsection does not apply in relation to any article seized under subsection (1) of this section which is returned to the occupier of the premises or, as the case may be, to the user of the stall or vehicle in or on which it was found.]

[(3A) Without prejudice to the duty of a court to make an order for the forfeiture of an article where section 1 (4) of the Obscene Publications Act 1964 applies (orders made on conviction), in a case where by virtue of subsection (3A) of section 2 of this Act proceedings under the said section 2 for having an article for publication for gain could not be instituted except by or with the consent of the Director of Public Prosecutions, no order for the forfeiture of the article shall be made under this section unless the warrant under which the article was seized was issued on an information laid by or on behalf of the Director of Public Prosecutions.]

(4) In addition to the person summoned, any other person being the owner, author or maker of any of the articles brought before the court, or any other person through whose hands they had passed before being seized, shall be entitled to appear before the court on the day specified in the summons to show cause why they should not be forfeited.

(5)-(8) * * * * *

4 Defence of public good

(1) [Subject to subsection (1A) of this section] a person shall not be convicted of an offence against section two of this Act, and an order for forfeiture shall not be made under the foregoing section, if it is proved that publication of the article in question is justified as being for the public good on the ground that it is in the interests of science, literature, art or learning, or of other objects of general concern.

[(1A) Subsection (1) of this section shall not apply where the article in question is a moving picture film or soundtrack, but—

(a) a person shall not be convicted of an offence against section 2 of this Act in relation to any such film or soundtrack, and

(b) an order for forfeiture of any such film or soundtrack shall not be made under section 3 of this Act,

if it is proved that publication of the film or soundtrack is justified as being for the public good on the ground that it is in the interests of drama, opera, ballet or any other art, or of literature or learning.]

(2) It is hereby declared that the opinion of experts as to the literary, artistic, scientific or other merits of an article may be admitted in any proceedings under this Act either to establish or to negative the said ground.

[(3) In this section "moving picture soundtrack" means any sound record designed for playing with a moving picture film, whether incorporated with the film or not.]

ADMINISTRATION OF JUSTICE ACT 1960
(8 & 9 Eliz. 2, c. 65)

An Act to make further provision for appeals to the House of Lords in criminal cases; to amend the law relating to contempt of court, habeas corpus and certiorari; and for purposes connected with the matters aforesaid [27 October 1960]

Territorial extent England and Wales

* * * * *

Contempt of Court, habeas corpus and certiorari

11 ... [Repealed by the Contempt of Court Act 1981, s. 3(4)]

12 Publication of information relating to proceedings in private

(1) The publication of information relating to proceedings before any court sitting in private shall not of itself be contempt of court except in the following cases, that is to say—

(a) where the proceedings—

(i) relate to the exercise of the inherent jurisdiction of the High Court with respect to minors;

(ii) [are brought under the Children Act 1989]; or

(iii) otherwise relate wholly or mainly to the maintenance or upbringing of a minor;

(b) where the proceedings are brought under Part VIII of the Mental Health Act 1959, or under any provision of that Act authorising an application or reference to be made to a Mental Health Review Tribunal or to a county court;

(c) where the court sits in private for reasons of national security during that part of the proceedings about which the information in question is published;

(d) where the information relates to a secret process, discovery or invention which is in issue in the proceedings;

(e) where the court (having power to do so) expressly prohibits the publication of all information relating to the proceedings or of information of the description which is published.

(2) Without prejudice to the foregoing subsection, the publication of the text or a summary of the whole or part of an order made by a court sitting in private shall not of

itself be contempt of court except where the court (having power to do so) expressly prohibits the publication.

(3) In this section references to a court include references to a judge and to a tribunal and to any person exercising the functions of a court, a judge or a tribunal; and references to a court sitting in private include references to a court sitting in camera or in chambers.

(4) Nothing in this section shall be construed as implying that any publication is punishable as contempt of court which would not be so punishable apart from this section.

13 Appeal in cases of contempt of court

(1) Subject to the provisions of this section, an appeal shall lie under this section from any order or decision of a court in the exercise of jurisdiction to punish for contempt of court (including criminal contempt); and in relation to any such order or decision the provisions of this section shall have effect in substitution for any other enactment relating to appeals in civil or criminal proceedings.

(2) An appeal under this section shall lie in any case at the instance of the defendant and, in the case of an application for committal or attachment, at the instance of the applicant; and the appeal shall lie—

(a) from an order or decision of any inferior court not referred to in the next following paragraph, to a Divisional court of the High Court;

(b) from an order or decision of a county court or any other inferior court from which appeals generally lie to the Court of Appeal, and from an order or decision . . ., of a single judge of the High Court or of a judge of that court, to the Court of Appeal;

[(bb) from an order or decision of the Crown Court to the Court of Appeal];

(c) from an order or decision of a Divisional Court or the Court of Appeal (including a decision of either of those courts on an appeal under this section), and from an order or decision of the Court of Criminal Appeal or the Courts-Martial Appeal Court, to the House of Lords.

(3) The court to which an appeal is brought under this section may reverse or vary the order or decision of the court below, and make such other order as may be just; and without prejudice to the inherent powers of any court referred to in subsection (2) of this section, provision may be made by rules of court for authorising the release on bail of an appellant under this section.

(4)-(6) * * * * *

PUBLIC BODIES (ADMISSION TO MEETINGS) ACT 1960
(8 & 9 Eliz. 2, c. 67)

An Act to provide for the admission of representatives of the press and other members of the public to the meetings of certain bodies exercising public functions [27 October 1960]

Territorial extent England and Wales, Scotland

1 Admission of public to meetings of local authorities and other bodies

(1) Subject to subsection (2) below, any meeting of a . . . body exercising public functions, being [a body] to which this Act applies, shall be open to the public.

(2) A body may, by resolution, exclude the public from a meeting (whether during the whole or part of the proceedings) whenever publicity would be prejudicial to the public interest by reason of the confidential nature of the business to be transacted or for other special reasons stated in the resolution and arising from the nature of that business or of the proceedings; and where such a resolution is passed, this Act shall not require the meeting to be open to the public during proceedings to which the resolution applies.

(3) A body may under subsection (2) above treat the need to receive or consider recommendations or advice from sources other than members, committees or sub-

committees of the body as a special reason why publicity would be prejudicial to the public interest, without regard to the subject or purport of the recommendations or advice; but the making by this subsection of express provision for that case shall not be taken to restrict the generality of subsection (2) above in relation to other cases (including in particular cases where the report of a committee or sub-committee of the body is of a confidential nature).

(4) Where a meeting of a body is required by this Act to be open to the public during the proceedings or any part of them, the following provisions shall apply, that is to say,—

(a) public notice of the time and place of the meeting shall be given by posting it at the offices of the body (or, if the body has no offices, then in some central and conspicuous place in the area with which it is concerned) three clear days at least before the meeting or, if the meeting is convened at shorter notice, then at the time it is convened;

(b) there shall, on request and on payment of postage or other necessary charge for transmission, be supplied for the benefit of any newspaper a copy of the agenda for the meeting as supplied to members of the body (but excluding, if thought fit, any item during which the meeting is likely not to be open to the public), together with such further statements or particulars, if any, as are necessary to indicate the nature of the items included or, if thought fit in the case of any item, with copies of any reports or other documents supplied to members of the body in connection with the item;

(c) while the meeting is open to the public, the body shall not have power to exclude members of the public from the meeting and duly accredited representatives of newspapers attending for the purpose of reporting the proceedings for those newspapers shall, so far as practicable, be afforded reasonable facilities for taking their report and, unless the meeting is held in premises not belonging to the body or not on the telephone, for telephoning the report at their own expense.

(5) Where a meeting of a body is required by this Act to be open to the public during the proceedings or any part of them, and there is supplied to a member of the public attending the meeting, or in pursuance of paragraph (b) of subsection (4) above there is supplied for the benefit of a newspaper, any such copy of the agenda as is mentioned in that paragraph, with or without further statements or particulars for the purpose of indicating the nature of any item included in the agenda, the publication thereby of any defamatory matter contained in the agenda or in the further statements or particulars shall be privileged, unless the publication is proved to be made with malice.

(6) When a body to which this Act applies resolves itself into committee, the proceedings in committee shall for the purposes of this Act be treated as forming part of the proceedings of the body at the meeting.

(7) Any reference in this section to a newspaper shall apply also to a news agency which systematically carries on the business of selling and supplying reports or information to newspapers, and to any organisation which is systematically engaged in collecting news for sound or television broadcasts [or for programme services (within the meaning of the Broadcasting Act 1990) other than sound or television broadcasting services]; but nothing in this section shall require a body to permit the taking of photographs of any proceedings, or the use of any means to enable persons not present to see or hear any proceedings (whether at the time or later), or the making of any oral report on any proceedings as they take place.

(8) The provisions of this section shall be without prejudice to any power of exclusion to suppress or prevent disorderly conduct or other misbehaviour at a meeting.

2, 3 * * * * *

OBSCENE PUBLICATIONS ACT 1964
(1964, c. 74)

An Act to strengthen the law for preventing the publication for gain of obscene matter and the publication of things intended for the production of obscene matter [31 July 1964]

Territorial extent England and Wales

1 Obscene articles intended for publication for gain

(1) ...

(2) For the purpose of any proceedings for an offence against the said section 2 a person shall be deemed to have an article for publication for gain if with a view to such publication he has the article in his ownership, possession or control.

(3) In proceedings brought against a person under the said section 2 for having an obscene article for publication for gain the following provisions shall apply in place of subsections (5) and (6) of that section, that is to say,—

(a) he shall not be convicted of that offence if he proves that he had not examined the article and had no reasonable cause to suspect that it was such that his having it would make him liable to be convicted of an offence against that section; and

(b) the question whether the article is obscene shall be determined by reference to such publication for gain of the article as in the circumstances it may reasonably be inferred he had in contemplation and to any further publication that could reasonably be expected to follow from it, but not to any other publication.

(4) Where articles are seized under section 3 of the Obscene Publications Act 1959 (which provides for the seizure and forfeiture of obscene articles kept for publication for gain), and a person is convicted under section 2 of the Act of having them for publication for gain, the court on his conviction shall order the forfeiture of those articles:

★ ★ ★ ★ ★

Note 'The said section 2' in subsections (2) and (3) is section 2 of the Obscene Publications Act 1959.

WAR DAMAGE ACT 1965
(1965, c. 18)

An Act to abolish rights at common law to compensation in respect of damage to, or destruction of, property effected by, or on the authority of, the Crown during, or in contemplation of the outbreak of, war [2 June 1965]

Territorial extent United Kingdom

1 Abolition of rights at common law to compensation for certain damage to, or destruction of, property

(1) No person shall be entitled at common law to receive from the Crown compensation in respect of damage to, or destruction of, property caused (whether before or after the passing of this Act, within or outside the United Kingdom) by acts lawfully done by, or on the authority of, the Crown during, or in contemplation of the outbreak of, a war in which the Sovereign was, or is, engaged.

(2) ...

CRIMINAL LAW ACT 1967
(1967, c. 58)

An Act to amend the law of England and Wales by abolishing the division of crimes into felonies and misdemeanours and to amend and simplify the law in respect of matters arising from or related to that division or the abolition of it; to do away (within or without England and Wales) with certain obsolete crimes together with the torts of maintenance and champerty; and for purposes connected therewith [21 July 1967]

Territorial extent England and Wales

PART I
FELONY AND MISDEMEANOUR

1 * * * * *

2 . . . (Repealed by the Police and Criminal Evidence Act 1984)

3 Use of force in making arrest, etc.

(1) A person may use such force as is reasonable in the circumstances in the prevention of crime, or in effecting or assisting in the lawful arrest of offenders or suspected offenders or of persons unlawfully at large.

(2) Subsection (1) above shall replace the rules of the common law on the question when force used for a purpose mentioned in the subsection is justified by that purpose.

* * * * *

PARLIAMENTARY COMMISSIONER ACT 1967
(1967, c. 13)

An Act to make provision for the appointment and functions of a Parliamentary Commissioner for the investigation of administrative action taken on behalf of the Crown, and for purposes connected therewith [22 March 1967]

Territorial extent United Kingdom

Note This Act is printed as extensively amended by the Parliamentary and Health Service Commissioners Act 1987.

The Parliamentary Commissioner for Administration

1 Appointment and tenure of office

(1) For the purpose of conducting investigations in accordance with the following provisions of this Act there shall be appointed a Commissioner, to be known as the Parliamentary Commissioner for Administration.

(2) Her Majesty may by Letters Patent from time to time appoint a person to be the Commissioner, and any person so appointed shall (subject to [subsections (3) and (3A)] of this section) hold office during good behaviour.

(3) A person appointed to be the Commissioner may be relieved of office by Her Majesty at his own request, or may be removed from office by Her Majesty in consequence of Addresses from both Houses of Parliament, and shall in any case vacate office on completing the year of service in which he attains the age of sixty-five years.

[(3A) Her Majesty may declare the office of Commissioner to have been vacated if satisfied that the person appointed to be the Commissioner is incapable for medical reasons—

(a) of performing the duties of his office; and
(b) of requesting to be relieved of it.]

(4), (5) . . .

2 ★★★★★

3 Administrative provisions

(1) The Commissioner may appoint such officers as he may determine with the approval of the Treasury as to numbers and conditions of service.

(2), (3) . . .

3A ★★★★★

4 Departments etc. subject to investigation

(1) Subject to the provisions of this section and to the notes contained in Schedule 2 to this Act, this Act applies to the government departments, corporations and unincorporated bodies listed in that Schedule; and references in this Act to an authority to which this Act applies are references to any such corporation or body.

(2) Her Majesty may by Order in Council amend Schedule 2 to this Act by the alteration of any entry or note, the removal of any entry or note or the insertion of any additional entry or note.

(3) An Order in Council may only insert an entry if—

(a) it relates—

(i) to a government department; or

(ii) to a corporation or body whose functions are exercised on behalf of the Crown; or

(b) it relates to a corporation or body—

(i) which is established by virtue of Her Majesty's prerogative or by an Act of Parliament or an Order in Council or order made under an Act of Parliament or which is established in any other way by a Minister of the Crown in his capacity as a Minister or by a government department;

(ii) at least half of whose revenues derive directly from money provided by Parliament, a levy authorised by an enactment, a fee or charge of any other description so authorised or more than one of those sources; and

(iii) which is wholly or partly constituted by appointment made by Her Majesty or a Minister of the Crown or government department.

(4) No entry shall be made in respect of a corporation or body whose sole activity is, or whose main activities are, included among the activities specified in subsection (5) below.

(5) The activities mentioned in subsection (4) above are—

(a) the provision of education, or the provision of training otherwise than under the Industrial Training Act 1982;

(b) the development of curricula, the conduct of examinations or the validation of educational courses;

(c) the control of entry to any profession or the regulation of the conduct of members of any profession;

(d) the investigation of complaints by members of the public regarding the actions of any person or body, or the supervision or review of such investigations or of steps taken following them.

(6) No entry shall be made in respect of a corporation or body operating in an exclusively or predominantly commercial manner or a corporation carrying on under national ownership an industry or undertaking or part of an industry or undertaking.

(7) Any statutory instrument made by virtue of this section shall be subject to annulment in pursuance of a resolution of either House of Parliament.

(8) ★★★★★

5 Matters subject to investigation

(1) Subject to the provisions of this section, the Commissioner may investigate any action taken by or on behalf of a government department or other authority to which this

Act applies, being action taken in the exercise of administrative functions of that department or authority, in any case where—

(a) a written complaint is duly made to a member of the House of Commons by a member of the public who claims to have sustained injustice in consequence of maladministration in connection with the action so taken; and

(b) the complaint is referred to the Commissioner, with the consent of the person who made it, by a member of that House with a request to conduct an investigation thereon.

(2) Except as hereinafter provided, the Commissioner shall not conduct an investigation under this Act in respect of any of the following matters, that is to say—

(a) any action in respect of which the person aggrieved has or had a right of appeal, reference or review to or before a tribunal constituted by or under any enactment or by virtue of Her Majesty's prerogative;

(b) any action in respect of which the person aggrieved has or had a remedy by way of proceedings in any court of law:

Provided that the Commissioner may conduct an investigation notwithstanding that the person aggrieved has or had such a right or remedy if satisfied that in the particular circumstances it is not reasonable to expect him to resort or have resorted to it.

(3) Without prejudice to subsection (2) of this section, the Commisioner shall not conduct an investigation under this Act in respect of any such action or matter as is described in Schedule 3 to this Act.

(4) Her Majesty may by Order in Council amend the said Schedule 3 so as to exclude from the provisions of that Schedule such actions or matters as may be described in the Order; and any statutory instrument made by virtue of this subsection shall be subject to annulment in pursuance of a resolution of either House of Parliament.

(5) In determining whether to initiate, continue or discontinue an investigation under this Act, the Commissioner shall, subject to the foregoing provisions of this section, act in accordance with his own discretion; and any question whether a complaint is duly made under this Act shall be determined by the Commissioner.

[(6) For the purposes of this section, administrative functions exercised by any person appointed by the Lord Chancellor as a member of the administrative staff of any court or tribunal shall be taken to be administrative functions of the Lord Chancellor's Department or, in Northern Ireland, of the Northern Ireland Court Service.]

(7)-(9) * * * * *

6 Provisions relating to complaints

(1) A complaint under this Act may be made by any individual, or by any body of persons whether incorporated or not, not being—

(a) a local authority or other authority or body constituted for purposes of the public service or of local government or for the purposes of carrying on under national ownership any industry or undertaking or part of an industry or undertaking;

(b) any other authority or body whose members are appointed by Her Majesty or any Minister of the Crown or government department, or whose revenues consist wholly or mainly of moneys provided by Parliament.

(2) Where the person by whom a complaint might have been made under the foregoing provisions of this Act has died or is for any reason unable to act for himself, the complaint may be made by his personal representative or by a member of his family or other individual suitable to represent him; but except as aforesaid a complaint shall not be entertained under this Act unless made by the person aggrieved himself.

(3) A complaint shall not be entertained under this Act unless it is made to a member of the House of Commons not later than twelve months from the day on which the person aggrieved first had notice of the matters alleged in the complaint; but the

Commissioner may conduct an investigation pursuant to a complaint not made within that period if he considers that there are special circumstances which make it proper to do so.

(4) [Except as provided in subsection (5) below] a complaint shall not be entertained under this Act unless the person aggrieved is resident in the United Kingdom (or, if he is dead, was so resident at the time of his death) or the complaint relates to action taken in relation to him while he was present in the United Kingdom or on an installation in a designated area within the meaning of the Continental Shelf Act 1964 or on a ship registered in the United Kingdom or an aircraft so registered, or in relation to rights or obligations which accrued or arose in the United Kingdom or on such an installation, ship or aircraft.

[(5) A complaint may be entertained under this Act in circumstances not falling within subsection (4) above where—

(a) the complaint relates to action taken in any country or territory outside the United Kingdom by an officer (not being an honorary consular officer) in the exercise of a consular function on behalf of the Government of the United Kingdom; and

(b) the person aggrieved is a citizen of the United Kingdom and Colonies who, under section 2 of the Immigration Act 1971, has the right of abode in the United Kingdom.]

7 Procedure in respect of investigations

(1) Where the Commissioner proposes to conduct an investigation pursuant to a complaint under this Act, he shall afford to the principal officer of the department or authority concerned, and to any person who is alleged in the complaint to have taken or authorised the action complained of, an opportunity to comment on any allegations contained in the complaint.

(2) Every such investigation shall be conducted in private, but except as aforesaid the procedure for conducting an investigation shall be such as the Commissioner considers appropriate in the circumstances of the case; and without prejudice to the generality of the foregoing provision the Commissioner may obtain information from such persons and in such manner, and make such inquiries, as he thinks fit, and may determine whether any person may be represented, by counsel or solicitor or otherwise, in the investigation.

(3), (4) * * * * *

8 Evidence

(1) For the purposes of an investigation under this Act the Commissioner may require any Minister, officer or member of the department or authority concerned or any other person who in his opinion is able to furnish information or produce documents relevant to the investigation to furnish any such information or produce any such document.

(2) For the purposes of any such investigation the Commissioner shall have the same powers as the Court in respect of the attendance and examination of witnesses (including the administration of oaths or affirmations and the examination of witnesses abroad) and in respect of the production of documents.

(3) No obligation to maintain secrecy or other restriction upon the disclosure of information obtained by or furnished to persons in Her Majesty's service, whether imposed by any enactment or by any rule of law, shall apply to the disclosure of information for the purposes of an investigation under this Act; and the Crown shall not be entitled in relation to any such investigation to any such privilege in respect of the production of documents or the giving of evidence as is allowed by law in legal proceedings.

(4) No person shall be required or authorised by virtue of this Act to furnish any information or answer any question relating to proceedings of the Cabinet or of any

committee of the Cabinet or to produce so much of any document as relates to such proceedings; and for the purposes of this subsection a certificate issued by the Secretary of the Cabinet with the approval of the Prime Minister and certifying that any information, question, document or part of a document so relates shall be conclusive.

(5) * * * * *

9 Obstruction and contempt

(1) If any person without lawful excuse obstructs the Commissioner or any officer of the Commissioner in the performance of his functions under this Act, or is guilty of any act or omission in relation to any investigation under this Act which, if that investigation were a proceeding in the Court, would constitute contempt of court, the Commissioner may certify the offence to the Court.

(2) Where an offence is certified under this section, the Court may inquire into the matter and, after hearing any witnesses who may be produced against or on behalf of the person charged with the offence, and after hearing any statement that may be offered in defence, deal with him in any manner in which the court could deal with him if he had committed the like offence in relation to the Court.

(3) * * * * *

10 Reports by Commissioner

(1) In any case where the Commissioner conducts an investigation under this Act or decides not to conduct such an investigation, he shall send to the member of the House of Commons by whom the request for investigation was made (or if he is no longer a member of that House, to such member of that House as the Commissioner thinks appropriate) a report of the results of the investigation or, as the case may be, a statement of his reasons for not conducting an investigation.

(2) In any case where the Commissioner conducts an investigation under this Act, he shall also send a report of the results of the investigation to the principal officer of the department or authority concerned and to any other person who is alleged in the relevant complaint to have taken or authorised the action complained of.

(3) If, after conducting an investigation under this Act, it appears to the Commissioner that injustice has been caused to the person aggrieved in consequence of maladministration and that the injustice has not been, or will not be, remedied, he may, if he thinks fit, lay before each House of Parliament a special report upon the case.

(4) The Commissioner shall annually lay before each House of Parliament a general report on the performance of his functions under this Act and may from time to time lay before each House of Parliament such other reports with respect to those functions as he thinks fit.

(5) For the purposes of the law of defamation, any such publication as is hereinafter mentioned shall be absolutely privileged, that is to say—

(a) the publication of any matter by the Commissioner in making a report to either House of Parliament for the purposes of this Act;

(b) the publication of any matter by a member of the House of Commons in communicating with the Commissioner or his officers for those purposes or by the Commissioner or his officers in communicating with such a member for those purposes;

(c) the publication by such a member to the person by whom a complaint was made under this Act of a report or statement sent to the member in respect of the complaint in pursuance of section (1) of this section;

(d) the publication by the Commissioner to such a person as is mentioned in subsection (2) of this section of a report to that person in pursuance of that subsection.

11 Provision for secrecy of information

(1) . . .

(2)-(4) * * * * *

11A, 11B ★★★★★

Supplemental

12 Interpretation

(1), (2) ★★★★★

(3) It is hereby declared that nothing in this Act authorises or requires the Commissioner to question the merits of a decision taken without maladministration by a government department or other authority in the exercise of a discretion vested in that department or authority.

13, 14 ★★★★★

Section 3

SCHEDULE 2

DEPARTMENTS ETC. SUBJECT TO INVESTIGATION

Advisory, Conciliation and Arbitration Service.
Agricultural Wages Committee.
Ministry of Agriculture, Fisheries and Food.
Arts Council of Great Britain.
British Council.
British Library Board.
Building Societies Commission.
[Coal Authority.]
Certification Officer.
Charity Commission.
Civil Service Commission.
[Office of the Commissioner for the Rights of Trade Union Members.]
Co-operative Development Agency.
Countryside Commission.
. . .
[Countryside Council for Wales.]
Craft Council.
Crofters Commission.
Crown Estate Office.
Customs and Excise.
Data Protection Registrar.
Ministry of Defence.
Development Commission.
. . .
Central Bureau for Educational Visits and Exchanges.
[Department for Education and Employment.]
. . .
Department of the Environment.
[Education Assets Board.]
Equal Opportunities Commission.
[Environment Agency.]
[Scottish Environment Protection Agency.]
Export Credits Guarantee Department.
Office of the Director General of Fair Trading.
British Film Institute.
Foreign and Commonwealth Office.
Forestry Commission.
Registry of Friendly Societies.
[Friendly Societies Commission.]

Office of the Director General of Gas Supply.
Health and Safety Commission.
Health and Safety Executive.
Department of Health and Social Security.
[Office of Her Majesty's Chief Inspector of Schools for England.]
[Office of Her Majesty's Chief Inspector of Schools for Wales.]
. . .
Historic Buildings and Monuments Commission for England.
Home Office.
Horserace Betting Levy Board.
Housing Corporation.
[Housing for Wales.]
Central Office of Information.
Inland Revenue.
Intervention Board for Agricultural Produce.
Land Registry.
[Legal Aid Board.]
The following general lighthouse authorities—
(a) the Corporation of the Trinity House of Deptford Strond;
(b) the Commissioners of Northern Lighthouses.
[Local Government Commission for England.]
The Lord Chancellor's Department.
Lord President of the Council's Office.
Management and Personnel Office.
. . .
Medical Practices Committee.
Scottish Medical Practices Committee.
Museums and Galleries Commission.
National Debt Office.
Trustees of the National Heritage Memorial Fund.
Department for National Savings.
[Nature Conservancy Council for England.]
[Nature Conservancy Council for Wales.]
Commission for the New Towns.
Development corporations for new towns.
Northern Ireland Court Service.
Northern Ireland Office.
[The Occupational Pensions Regulatory Authority.]
Ordnance Survey.
[The Office for National Statistics.]
Registrar of Public Lending Right.
[Office of Public Service . . .]
Public Record Office.
Scottish Record Office.
Commission for Racial Equality.
Department of the Registers of Scotland.
General Register Office, Scotland.
Agricultural and Food Research Council.
Economic and Social Research Council.
Medical Research Council.
Natural Environment Research Council.
Science and Engineering Research Council.
Residuary Bodies.

Royal Mint.
Scottish Courts Administration.
[Scottish Natural Heritage.]
Scottish Office.
Council for Small Industries in Rural Areas.
Central Council for Education and Training in Social Work.
[English] Sports Council.
Scottish Sports Council.
Sports Council for Wales.
[The Staff Commission for Wales (Comisiwn Staff Cymru).]
Stationery Office.
Office of the Director General of Telecommunications.
English Tourist Board.
Scottish Tourist Board.
Wales Tourist Board.
Board of Trade.
Department of Trade and Industry.
Agricultural Training Board.
Clothing and Allied Products Industry Training Board.
Construction Industry Training Board.
Engineering Industry Training Board.
Hotel and Catering Industry Training Board.
Plastics Processing Industry Training Board.
Road Transport Industry Training Board.
Department of Transport.
Treasury.
Treasury Solicitor.
[United Kingdom Sports Council.]
Urban development corporations.
[Urban Regeneration Agency.]
Development Board for Rural Wales.
Welsh Office.

Note Schedule printed as substituted by the Parliamentary and Health Service Commissioners Act 1987,Sch. 1 (as amended), with notes to the Schedule omitted. See *ibid.* for these notes.

Section 5

SCHEDULE 3
MATTERS NOT SUBJECT TO INVESTIGATION

1. Action taken in matters certified by a Secretary of State or other Minister of the Crown to affect relations or dealings between the Government of the United Kingdom and any other Government or any international organisation of States or Governments.

2. Action taken, in any country or territory outside the United Kingdom, by or on behalf of any officer representing or acting under the authority of Her Majesty in respect of the United Kingdom, or any other officer of the Government of the United Kingdom [other than action which is taken by an officer (not being an honorary consular officer) in the exercise of a consular function on behalf of the Government of the United Kingdom and which is so taken in relation to a citizen of the United Kingdom and Colonies who has the right of abode in the United Kingdom].

3. Action taken in connection with the administration of the goverment of any country or territory outside the United Kingdom which forms part of Her Majesty's dominions or in which Her Majesty has jurisdiction.

4. Action taken by the Secretary of State under the Extradition Act 1870 or the Fugitive Offenders Act 1881.

5. Action taken by or with the authority of the Secretary of State for the purposes of investigating crime or of protecting the security of the State, including action so taken with respect to passports.

6. The commencement or conduct of civil or criminal proceedings before any court of law in the United Kingdom, of proceedings at any place under the Naval Discipline Act 1957, the Army Act 1955 or the Air Force Act 1955, or of proceedings before any international court or tribunal.

[6A. Action taken by any person appointed by the Lord Chancellor as a member of the administrative staff of any court or tribunal, so far as that action is taken at the direction, or on the authority (whether express or implied) of any person acting in a judicial capacity or as a member of the tribunal.]

[6B. (1) Action taken by any member of the administrative staff of a relevant tribunal so far as that action is taken at the direction, or on the authority (whether express or implied), of any person acting in his capacity as a member of the tribunal.

(2) In this paragraph, "relevant tribunal" has the meaning given by section 5(8) of this Act.]

[6C. Action taken by any person appointed under section 5(3)(c) of the Criminal Injuries Compensation Act 1995, so far as that action is taken at the direction, or on the authority (whether express or implied) of any person acting as an adjudicator appointed under section 5 of that Act to determine appeals.]

7. Any exercise of the prerogative of mercy or of the power of a Secretary of State to make a reference in respect of any person to the High Court of Justiciary or the Courts-Martial Appeal Court.

8. Action taken on behalf of the Minister of Health or the Secretary of State by a [Health Authority, any Special Health Authority], [except the [Rampton Hospital board] [the Broadmoor Hospital Board and the Moss Side and Park Lane Hospitals 'Board]], ... [a Health Board or the Common Services Agency for the Scottish Health Service, [by the Dental Practice Board or the Scottish Dental Practice Board]], or by the Public Health Laboratory Service Board.

9. Action taken in matters relating to contractual or other commercial transactions, whether within the United Kingdom or elsewhere, being transactions of a government department or authority to which this Act applies or of any such authority or body as is mentioned in paragraph (a) or (b) of subsection (1) of section 6 of this Act and not being transactions for or relating to—

(a) the acquisition of land compulsorily or in circumstances in which it could be acquired compulsorily;

(b) the disposal as surplus of land acquired compulsorily or in such circumstances as aforesaid.

10. (1) Action taken in respect of appointments or removals, pay, discipline, superannuation or other personnel matters, in relation to—

(a) service in any of the armed forces of the Crown, including reserve and auxiliary and cadet forces;

(b) service in any office or employment under the Crown or under any authority [(to which this Act applies)]; or

(c) service in any office or employment, or under any contract for services, in respect of which power to take action, or to determine or approve the action to be taken, in such matters is vested in Her Majesty, any Minister of the Crown or any such authority as aforesaid.

[(2) Sub-paragraph (1)(c) above shall not apply to any action (not otherwise excluded from investigation by this Schedule) which is taken by the Secretary of State in connection with—

(a) the provision of information relating to the terms and conditions of any employment covered by an agreement entered into by him under section 12(1) of the Overseas Development and Cooperation Act 1980 or

(b) the provision of any allowance, grant or supplement or any benefit (other than those relating to superannuation) arising from the designation of any person in accordance with such an agreement.]

11. The grant of honours, awards or privileges within the gift of the Crown, including the grant of Royal Charters.

★ ★ ★ ★ ★

FIREARMS ACT 1968
(1968, c. 27)

An Act to consolidate the Firearms Acts 1937 and 1965, the Air Guns and Shot Guns, etc, Act 1962, Part V of the Criminal Justice Act 1967 and certain enactments amending the Firearms Act 1937 [30 May 1968]

Territorial extent England and Wales, Scotland

★ ★ ★ ★ ★

PART III
LAW ENFORCEMENT AND PUNISHMENT OF OFFENCES

[46 Power of search with warrant

(1) If a justice of the peace or, in Scotland, the sheriff, is satisfied by information on oath that there is reasonable ground for suspecting—

(a) that an offence relevant for the purposes of this section has been, is being, or is about to be committed; or

(b) that, in connection with a firearm or ammunition, there is a danger to the public safety or to the peace,

he may grant a warrant for any of the purposes mentioned in subsection (2) below.

(2) A warrant under this section may authorise a constable or civilian officer—

(a) to enter at any time any premises or place named in the warrant, if necessary by force, and to search the premises or place and every person found there;

(b) to seize and detain anything which he may find on the premises or place, or on any such person, in respect of which or in connection with which he has reasonable ground for suspecting—

(i) that an offence relevant for the purposes of this section has been, is being or is about to be committed; or

(ii) that in connection with a firearm, imitation firearm or ammunition there is a danger to the public safety or to the peace.

(3) The power of a constable or civilian officer under subsection (2)(b) above to seize and detain anything found on any premises or place shall include power to require any information which is kept by means of a computer and is accessible from the premises or place to be produced in a form in which it is visible and legible and can be taken away.

(4) The offences relevant for the purposes of this section are all offences under this Act except an offence under section 22(3) or an offence relating specifically to air weapons.

(5) It is an offence for any person intentionally to obstruct a constable or civilian officer in the exercise of his powers under this section.]

47 Powers of constables to stop and search

(1) A constable may require any person whom he has reasonable cause to suspect—

(a) of having a firearm, with or without ammunition, with him in a public place; or

(b) to be committing or about to commit, elsewhere than in a public place, an offence relevant for the purposes of this section,

to hand over the firearm or any ammunition for examination by the constable.

(2) It is an offence for a person having a firearm or ammunition with him to fail to hand it over when required to do so by a constable under subsection (1) of this section.

(3) If a constable has reasonable cause to suspect a person of having a firearm with him in a public place, or to be committing or about to commit, elsewhere than in a public place, an offence relevant for the purposes of this section, the constable may search that person and may detain him for the purpose of doing so.

(4) If a constable has reasonable cause to suspect that there is a firearm in a vehicle in a public place, or that a vehicle is being or is about to be used in connection with the commission of an offence relevant for the purposes of this section elsewhere than in a public place, he may search the vehicle and for that purpose require the person driving or in control of it to stop it.

(5) For the purpose of exercising the powers conferred by this section a constable may enter any place.

(6) The offences relevant for the purpose of his section are those under sections 18(1) and (2) and 20 of this Act.

48 Production of certificates

(1) A constable may demand, from any person whom he believes to be in possession of a firearm or ammunition to which section 1 of this Act applies, or of a shot gun, the production of his firearm certificate or, as the case may be, his shot gun certificate.

(2) If a person upon whom a demand is made under this section fails to produce the certificate or to permit the constable to read it, or to show that he is entitled by virtue of this Act to have the firearm, ammunition or shot gun in his possession without holding a certificate, the constable may seize and detain the firearm, ammunition or shot gun and may require the person to declare to him immediately his name and address.

(3) If under this section a person is required to declare to a constable his name and address, it is an offence for him to refuse to declare it or to fail to give his true name and address.

★ ★ ★ ★ ★

THEATRES ACT 1968
(1968, c. 54)

An Act to abolish censorship of the theatre and to amend the law in respect of theatres and theatrical performances [26 July 1968]

Territorial extent England and Wales, Scotland

Abolition of censorship of the theatre

1 Abolition of censorship of the theatre

(1) The Theatres Act 1843 is hereby repealed; and none of the powers which were exercisable thereunder by the Lord Chamberlain of Her Majesty's Household shall be exercisable by or on behalf of Her Majestyby virtue of Her royal prerogative.

(2) In granting, renewing or transferring any licence under this Act for the use of any premises for the public performance of plays or in varying any of the terms, conditions or restrictions on or subject to which any such licence is held, the licensing authority shall not have power to impose any term, condition or restriction as to the nature of the plays which may be performed under the licence or as to the manner of performing plays thereunder:

Provided that nothing in this subsection shall prevent a licensing authority from imposing any term, condition or restriction which they consider necessary in the interests of physical safety or health or any condition regulating or prohibiting the giving of an exhibition, demonstration or performance of hypnotism within the meaning of the Hypnotism Act 1952.

Provisions with respect to performances of plays

2 Prohibition of presentation of obscene performances of plays

(1) For the purposes of this section a performance of a play shall be deemed to be obscene if, taken as a whole, its effect was such as to tend to deprave and corrupt persons who were likely, having regard to all relevant circumstances, to attend it.

(2) Subject to sections 3 and 7 of this Act, if an obscene performance of a play is given, whether in public or private, any person who (whether for gain or not) presented or directed that performance shall be liable—

(a) on summary conviction, to a fine not exceeding [level 5 on the standard scale] or to imprisonment for a term not exceeding six months;

(b) on conviction on indictment, to a fine or to imprisonment for a term not exceeding three years, or both.

(3) A prosecution on indictment for an offence under this section shall not be commenced more than two years after the commission of the offence.

(4) No person shall be proceeded against in respect of a performance of a play or anything said or done in the course of such a performance—

(a) for an offence at common law where it is of the essence of the offence that the performance or, as the case may be, what was said or done was obscene, indecent, offensive, disgusting or injurious to morality;

. . .

and no person shall be proceeded against for an offence at common law of conspiring to corrupt public morals, or to do any act contrary to public morals or decency, in respect of an agreement to present or give a performance of a play, or to cause anything to be said or done in the course of such a performance.

3 Defence of public good

(1) A person shall not be convicted of an offence under section 2 of this Act if it is proved that the giving of the performance in question was justified as being for the public good on the ground that it was in the interests of drama, opera, ballet or any other art, or of literature or learning.

(2) It is hereby declared that the opinion of experts as to the artistic, literary or other merits of a performance of a play may be admitted in any proceedings for an offence under section 2 of this Act either to establish or negative the said ground.

4 Amendment of law of defamation

(1) For the purposes of the law of libel and slander (including the law of criminal libel so far as it relates to the publication of defamatory matter) the publication of words in the course of a performance of a play shall, subject to section 7 of this Act, be treated as publication in permanent form.

(2)-(4) * * * * *

5 . . . [Repealed by the Public Order Act 1986].

6 Provocation of breach of peace by means of public performance of a play

(1) Subject to section 7 of this Act, if there is given a public performance of a play involving the use of threatening, abusive or insulting words or behaviour, any person who (whether for gain or not) presented or directed that performance shall be guilty of an offence under this section if—

(a) he did so with intent to provoke a breach of the peace; or
(b) the performance, taken as a whole, was likely to occasion a breach of the peace.

(2) A person guilty of an offence under this section shall be liable [on summary conviction to a fine not exceeding [level 5 on the standard scale] or to imprisonment for a period not exceeding six months or both].

7 Exceptions for performances given in certain circumstances

(1) Nothing in sections 2 to 4 of this Act shall apply in relation to a performance of a play given on a domestic occasion in a private dwelling.

(2) Nothing in sections 2 to 6 of this Act shall apply in relation to a performance of a play given solely or primarily for one or more of the following purposes, that is to say—
(a) rehearsal; or
(b) to enable—
(i) a record or cinematograph film to be made from or by means of the performance; or
(ii) the performance to be broadcast; or
(iii) [the performance to be included in a programme service (within the meaning of the Broadcasting Act 1990)];

but in any proceedings for an offence under section 2 . . . or 6 of this Act alleged to have been committd in respect of a performance of a play or an offence at common law alleged to have been committed in England and Wales by the publication of defamatory matter in the course of a performance of a play, if it is proved that the performance was attended by persons other than persons directly connected with the giving of the performance or the doing in relation thereto of any of the things mentioned in paragraph (b) above, the performance shall be taken not to have been solely or primarily for one or more of the said purposes unless the contrary is shown.

(3) ★★★★★

8 Restriction on institution of proceedings

Proceedings for an offence under section 2 . . . or 6 of this Act or an offence at common law committed by the publication of defamatory matter in the course of a performance of a play shall not be instituted in England and Wales except by or with the consent of the Attorney-General.

9 Script as evidence of what was performed

(1) Where a performance of a play was based on a script, then, in any proceedings for an offence under section 2 . . . or 6 of this Act alleged to have been committed in respect of that performance—
(a) an actual script on which that performance was based shall be admissible as evidence of what was performed and of the manner in which the performance or any part of it was given; and
(b) if such a script is given in evidence on behalf of any party to the proceedings then, except in so far as the contrary is shown, whether by evidence given on behalf of the same or any other party, the performance shall be taken to have been given in accordance with that script.

(2) In this Act "script", in relation to a performance of a play, means the text of the play (whether expressed in words or in musical or other notation) together with any stage or other directions for its performance, whether contained in a single document or not.

★★★★★

FOREIGN COMPENSATION ACT 1969
(1969, c. 20)

An Act to make provision with respect to certain property (including the proceeds thereof and any income or other property accruing therefrom) of persons formerly resident or carrying on business in Estonia, Latvia, Lithuania or a part of Czechoslovakia, Finland, Poland or Rumania which has been ceded to the Union of Soviet Socialist Republics, and to amend the Foreign Compensation Act 1950 [16 May 1969]

Territorial extent United Kingdom

* * * * *

3 Determination of the Foreign Compensation Commission and appeals against such determinations

(1) The Foreign Compensation Commission shall have power to determine any question as to the construction or interpretation of any provision of an Order in Council under section 3 of the Foreign Compensation Act 1950 with respect to claims falling to be determined by them.

(2) Subject to subsection (4) below, the Commission shall, if so required by a person mentioned in subsection (6) below who is aggrieved by any determination of the Commission on any question of law relating to the jurisdiction of the Commission or on any question mentioned in subsection (1) above, state and sign a case for the decision of the Court of Appeal.

(3) In this section "determination" includes a determination which under rules under section 4(2) of the Foreign Compensation Act 1950 (rules of procedure) is a provisional determination, and anything which purports to be a determination.

(4) Where the Court of Appeal decide a question on a case stated and signed by the Commission on a provisional determination in any proceedings, subsection (2) above shall not require the Commission to state and sign a case on a final determination by them of that question in those proceedings.

(5) Any person mentioned in subsection (6) below may, with a view to requiring the Commission to state and sign a case under this section, request the Commission to furnish a written statement of the reasons for any determination of theirs, but the Commission shall not be obliged to state the reasons for any determination unless it is given on a claim in which a question mentioned in subsection (2) above arises.

(6) The person who may make a request under subsection (5) above or a requirement under subsection (2) above in relation to any claim are the claimant and any person appointed by the Commission to represent the interests of any fund out of which the claim would, if allowed, be met.

(7) * * * * *

(8) Notwithstanding anything in section 3 of the Appellate Jurisdiction Act 1876 (right of appeal to the House of Lords from decisions of the Court of Appeal), no appeal shall lie to the House of Lords from a decision of the Court of Appeal on an appeal under this section.

(9) Except as provided by subsection (2) above and subsection (10) below, no determination by the Commission on any claim made to them under the Foreign Compensation Act 1950 shall be called in question in any court of law.

(10) Subsection (9) above shall not affect any right of any person to bring proceedings questioning any determination of the Commission on the ground that it is contrary to natural justice.

(11) Subsection (2) to (10) above shall not apply to a determination of the Commission of which notice was sent by them before the passing of this Act.

(12) Section 4(4) of the Foreign Compensation Act 1950 (which makes provision corresponding to subsection (9) above) shall not apply to a determination of the Commission of which notice is sent by them after the passing of this Act.

★ ★ ★ ★ ★

GENOCIDE ACT 1969
(1969, c. 12)

An Act to give effect to the Convention on the Prevention and Punishment of the Crime of Genocide [27 March 1969]

Territorial extent United Kingdom

1 Genocide

(1) A person commits an offence of genocide if he commits any act falling within the definition of "genocide" in Article II of the Genocide Convention as set out in the Schedule to this Act.

(2) A person guilty of an offence of genocide shall on conviction on indictment—

(a) if the offence consists of the killing of any person, be sentenced to imprisonment for life;

(b) in any other case, be liable to imprisonment for a term not exceeding fourteen years.

(3) Proceedings for an offence of genocide shall not be instituted in England or Wales except by or with the consent of the Attorney General and shall not be instituted in Northern Ireland except by or with the consent of the Attorney General for Northern Ireland.

(4)-(7) . . .

2 Extradition and evidence for foreign courts

(1) . . .

(2) ★ ★ ★ ★ ★

(3) It shall not be an objection to any proceedings taken against a person by virtue of the preceding provisions of this section that under the law in force at the time when and in the place where he is alleged to have committed the act of which he is accused or of which he was convicted he could not have been punished therefor.

★ ★ ★ ★ ★

TAXES MANAGEMENT ACT 1970
(1970, c. 9)

An Act to consolidate certain of the enactments relating to income tax, capital gains tax and corporation tax, including certain enactments relating also to other taxes [12 March 1970]

Territorial extent United Kingdom

Note The sections printed here were added by the Finance Act 1976, Sch. 6.

★ ★ ★ ★ ★

20C Entry with warrant to obtain documents

(1) If the appropriate judicial authority is satisfied on information on oath given by an officer of the Board that—

(a) there is reasonable ground for suspecting that an offence involving any form of fraud in connection with, or in relation to, tax has been committed and that evidence of it is to be found on premises specified in the information; and

(b) in applying under this section, the officer acts with the approval of the Board given in relation to the particular case,
the authority may issue a warrant in writing authorising an officer of the Board to enter the premises, if necessary by force, at any time within 14 days from the time of issue of the warrant, and search them.

(2) Section 4A of the Inland Revenue Regulation Act 1890 (Board's functions to be exercisable by an officer acting under their authority) does not apply to the giving of Board approval under this section.

(3) On entering the premises with a warrant under this section, the officer may seize and remove any things whatsoever found there which he has reasonable cause to believe may be required as evidence for the purposes of proceedings in respect of such an offence as is mentioned in subsection (1) above.

But this does not authorise the seizure and removal of documents in the possession of a barrister, advocate or solicitor with respect to which a claim to professional privilege could be maintained.

(4) Where entry to premises has been made with a warrant under this section, and the officer making the entry has seized any things under the authority of the warrant, he shall, if so requested by a person showing himself either—

(a) to be the occupier of the premises; or

(b) to have had the possession or custody of those things immediately before the seizure,

provided that person with a list of them.

(5) Where documents are seized which relate to any business, and it is shown that access to them is required for the continued conduct of the business, the officer who has seized them shall afford reasonable access to the documents to the person carrying on the business.

20D Interpretation of ss. 20 to 20C

(1) For the purposes of section 20A and 20C above, "the appropriate judicial authority" is—

(a) in England and Wales, a Circuit judge;

(b) in Scotland, a Sheriff; and

(c) in Northern Ireland, a county court judge.

(2), (3) ★★★★★

★★★★★

COURTS ACT 1971
(1971, c. 23)

An Act to make further provision as respects the Supreme Court and county courts, judges and juries, to establish a Crown Court as part of the Supreme Court to try indictments and exercise certain other jurisdiction, to abolish courts of assize and certain other courts and to deal with their jurisdiction and other consequential matters, and to amend in other respects the law about courts and court proceedings [12 May 1971]

Teritorial extent England and Wales

1-15 ... [Repealed by the Supreme Court Act 1981].

PART III
JUDGES

16 Appointment of Circuit Judges

(1) Her Majesty may from time to time appoint as Circuit judges, to serve in the Crown Court and county courts and to carry out such other judicial functions as may

be conferred on them under this or any other enactment, such qualified persons as may be recommended to Her by the Lord Chancellor.

(2) The maximum number of Circuit judges shall be such as may be determined from time to time by the Lord Chancellor with the concurrence of the Minister for the Civil Service.

(3) No person shall be qualified to be appointed a Circuit judge unless he is a barrister of at least ten years' standing or a Recorder who has held that office for at least [three] years.

(4) Before recommending any person to Her Majesty for appointment as a Circuit judge, the Lord Chancellor shall take steps to satisfy himself that that person's health is satisfactory.

(5) ★ ★ ★ ★ ★

17 Retirement, removal and disqualifications of Circuit judges

[(1) Subject to subsection (4) below and to subsections (4) to (6) of Section 26 of the Judicial Pensions and Retirement Act 1993, a Circuit judge shall vacate his office on the day on which he attains the age of 70.]

(2), (3) ...

(4) The Lord Chancellor may, if he thinks fit, remove a Circuit judge from office on the ground of incapacity or misbehaviour.

(5), (6) ...

★ ★ ★ ★ ★

IMMIGRATION ACT 1971
(1971, c. 77)

An Act to amend and replace the present immigration laws, to make certain related changes in the citizenship law and enable help to be given to those wishing to return abroad, and for purposes connected therewith [28 October 1971]

Teritorial extent United Kingdom; Part II of the Act extends to the Isle of Man.

Note This Act is printed as extensively amended by the British Nationality Act 1981.

PART I
REGULATION OF ENTRY INTO AND STAY IN UNITED KINGDOM

1 General principles

(1) All those who are in this Act expressed to have the right of abode in the United Kingdom shall be free to live in, and to come and go into and from, the United Kingdom without let or hindrance except such as may be required under and in accordance with this Act to enable their right to be established or as may be otherwise lawfully imposed on any person.

(2) Those not having that right may live, work and settle in the United Kingdom by permission and subject to such regulation and control of their entry into, stay in and departure from the United Kingdom as is imposed by this Act; and indefinite leave to enter or remain in the United Kingdom shall, by virtue of this provision, be treated as having been given under this Act to those in the United Kingdom at its coming into force, if they are then settled there (and not exempt under this Act from the provisions relating to leave to enter or remain).

(3) Arrival in and departure from the United Kingdom on a local journey from or to any of the Islands (that is to say, the Channel Islands and Isle of Man) or the Republic of Ireland shall not be subject to control under this Act, nor shall a person require leave to enter the United Kingdom on so arriving, except in so far as any of those places is for

any purpose excluded from this subsection under the powers conferred by this Act; and in this Act the United Kingdom and those places, or such of them as are not so excluded, are collectively referred to as "the common travel area".

(4) The rules laid down by the Secretary of State as to the practice to be followed in the administration of this Act for regulating the entry into and stay in the United Kingdom of persons not having the right of abode shall include provision for admitting (in such cases and subject to such restrictions as may be provided by the rules, and subject or not to conditions as to length of stay or otherwise) persons coming for the purpose of taking employment, or for purposes of study, or as visitors, or as dependants of persons lawfully in or entering the United Kingdom.

(5) ...

[2 Statement of right of abode in United Kingdom

(1) A person is under this Act to have the right of abode in the United Kingdom if—

(a) he is a British citizen; or

(b) he is a Commonwealth citizen who—

(i) immediately before the commencement of the British Nationality Act 1981 was a Commonwealth citizen having the right of abode in the United Kingdom by virtue of section 2(1)(d) or section 2(2) of this Act as then in force; and

(ii) has not ceased to be a Commonwealth citizen in the meanwhile.

(2) In relation to Commonwealth citizens who have the right of abode in the United Kingdom by virtue of subsection (1)(b) above, this Act, except this section and section [(5(2)] shall apply as if they were British citizens; and in this Act (except as aforesaid) "British citizen" shall be construed accordingly.]

[**Note** Sections 2(1) and 2(2) as in force prior to the commencement of the 1981 Act provided as follows:

"(1) A person is under this Act to have the right of abode in the United Kingdom if—

(a) he is a citizen of the United Kingdom and Colonies who has that citizenship by his birth, adoption, naturalisation or (except as mentioned below) registration in the United Kingdom or in any of the Islands; or

(b) he is a citizen of the United Kingdom and Colonies born to or legally adopted by a parent who had that citizenship at the time of the birth or adoption, and the parent either—

(i) then had that citizenship by his birth, adoption, naturalisation or (except as mentioned below) registration in the United Kingdom or in any of the Islands; or

(ii) had been born to or legally adopted by a parent who at the time of that birth or adoption so had it; or

(c) he is a citizen of the United Kingdom and Colonies who has at any time been settled in the United Kingdom and Islands and had at that time (and while such a citizen) been ordinarily resident there for the last five years or more; or

(d) he is a Commonwealth citizen born to or legally adopted by a parent who at the time of the birth or adoption had citizenship of the United Kingdom and Colonies by his birth in the United Kingdom or in any of the Islands.

(2) A woman is under this Act also to have the right of abode in the United Kingdom if she is a Commonwealth citizen and either—

(a) is the wife of any such citizen of the United Kingdom and Colonies as is mentioned in subsection (1)(a), (b) or (c) above or any such Commonwealth citizen as is mentioned in subsection (1)(d); or

(b) has at any time been the wife—

(i) of a person then being such a citizen of the United Kingdom and Colonies or Commonwealth citizen; or

(ii) of a British subject who but for his death would on the date of commencement of the British Nationality Act 1948 have been such a citizen of the United Kingdom and Colonies as is mentioned in subsection (1)(a) or (b);
but in subsection (1)(a) and (b) above references to registration as a citizen of the United Kingdom and Colonies shall not, in the case of a woman, include registration after the passing of this Act under or by virtue of section 6(2) (wives) of the British Nationality Act 1948 unless she is so registered by virtue of her marriage to a citizen of the United Kingdom and Colonies before the passing of this Act."]

3 General provisions for regulation and control

(1) Except as otherwise provided by or under this Act, where a person is not [a British citizen]—

(a) he shall not enter the United Kingdom unless given leave to do so in accordance with this Act;

(b) he may be given leave to enter the United Kingdom (or, when already there, leave to remain in the United Kingdom) either for a limited or for an indefinite period;

[(c) if he is given limited leave to enter or remain in the United Kingdom, it may be given subject to all or any of the following conditions, namely—

(i) a condition restricting his employment or occupation in the United Kingdom;

(ii) a condition requiring him to maintain and accommodate himself, and any dependents of his, without recourse to public funds, and

(iii) a condition requiring him to register with the police.]

(2) The Secretary of State shall from time to time (and as soon as may be) lay before Parliament statements of the rules, or of any changes in the rules, laid down by him as to the practice to be followed in the administration of this Act for regulating the entry into and stay in the United Kingdom of persons required by this Act to have leave to enter, including any rules as to the period for which leave is to be given and the conditions to be attached in different circumstances; and section 1(4) above shall not be taken to require uniform provision to be made by the rules as regards admission of persons for a purpose or in a capacity specified in section 1(4) (and in particular, for this as well as other purposes of this Act, account may be taken of citizenship or nationality).

If a statement laid before either House of Parliament under this subsection is disapproved by a resolution of that House passed within the period of forty days beginning with the date of laying (and exclusive of any period during which Parliament is dissolved or prorogued or during which both Houses are adjourned for more than four days), then the Secretary of State shall as soon as may be make such changes or further changes in the rules as appear to him to be required in the circumstances, so that the statement of those changes be laid before Parliament at least by the end of the period of forty days beginning with the date of the resolution (but exclusive as aforesaid).

(3) In the case of a limited leave to enter or remain in the United Kingdom,—

(a) a person's leave may be varied, whether by restricting, enlarging or removing the limit on its duration, or by adding, varying or revoking conditions, but if the limit on its duration is removed, any conditions attached to the leave shall cease to apply; and

(b) the limitation on and any conditions attached to a person's leave [(whether imposed originally or on a variation) shall], if not superseded, apply also to any subsequent leave he may obtain after an absence from the United Kingdom within the period limited for the duration of the earlier leave.

(4) A person's leave to enter or remain in the United Kingdom shall lapse on his going to a country or territory outside the common travel area (whether or not he lands there), unless within the period for which he had leave he returns to the United Kingdom in circumstances in which he is not required to obtain leave to enter; but, if he

does so return, his previous leave (and any limitation on it or conditions attached to it) shall continue to apply.

[(4A) For the purposes of subsection (4) above a person seeking to leave the United Kingdom through the tunnel system who is refused admission to France shall be treated as having gone to a country outside the common travel area.]

(5) A person who is not [a British citizen] shall be liable to deportation from the United Kingdom—

(a) if, having only a limited leave to enter or remain, he does not observe a condition attached to the leave or remains beyond the time limited by the leave; or

[(aa) if he has obtained leave to remain by deception; or]

(b) if the Secretary of State deems his deportation to be conducive to the public good; or

(c) if another person to whose family he belongs is or has been ordered to be deported.

(6) Without prejudice to the operation of subsection (5) above, a person who is not [a British citizen] shall also be liable to deportation from the United Kingdom if, after he has attained the age of seventeen, he is convicted of an offence for which he is punishable with imprisonment and on his conviction is recommended for deportation by a court empowered by this Act to do so.

(7) Where it appears to Her Majesty proper so to do by reason of restrictions or conditions imposed on [British citizens, British Dependent Territories citizens or British Overseas citizens] when leaving or seeking to leave any country or the territory subject to the government of any country, Her Majesty may by Order in Council make provision for prohibiting persons who are nationals or citizens of the country and are not [British citizens] from embarking in the United Kingdom, or from doing so elsewhere than at a port of exit, or for imposing restrictions or conditions on them when embarking or about to embark in the United Kingdom; and Her Majesty may also make provision by Order in Council to enable those who are not [British citizens] to be, in such cases as may be prescribed by the Order, prohibited in the interests of safety from so embarking on a ship or aircraft specified or indicated in the prohibition.

Any Order in Council under this subsection shall be subject to annulment in pursuance of a resolution of either House of Parliament.

[(7A) Any reference in an Order in Council under subsection (7) above to embarking or being about to embark shall be construed as including a reference to leaving or seeking to leave the United Kingdom through the tunnel system.]

(8) When any question arises under this Act whether or not a person is [a British citizen], or is entitled to any exemption under this Act, it shall lie on the person asserting it to prove that he is.

[(9) A person seeking to enter the United Kingdom and claiming to have the right of abode there shall prove that he has that right by means of either—

(a) a United Kingdom passport describing him as a British citizen or as a citizen of the United Kingdom and Colonies having the right of abode in the United Kingdom; or

(b) a certificate of entitlement issued by or on behalf of the Government of the United Kingdom certifying that he has such a right of abode.]

4, 5 ★★★★★

6 Recommendations by court for deportation

(1) Where under section 3(6) above a person convicted of an offence is liable to deportation on the recommendation of a court, he may be recommended for deportation by any court having power to sentence him for the offence unless the court commits him to be sentenced or further dealt with for that offence by another court:

. . . . . .

(2)-(4) ★★★★★

(5) Where a court recommends or purports to recommend a person for deportation, the validity of the recommendation shall not be called in question except on an appeal against the recommendation or against the conviction on which it is made; but—

... the recommendation shall be treated as a sentence for the purpose of any ... enactment providing an appeal against sentence; ...

(6), (7) ★★★★★

7 Exemption from deportation for certain existing residents

(1) Notwithstanding anything in section 3(5) or (6) above but subject to the provisions of this section, a Commonwealth citizen or citizen of the Republic of Ireland who was such a citizen at the coming into force of this Act and was then ordinarily resident in the United Kingdom—

(a) shall not be liable to deportation under section 3(5)(b) if at the time of the Secretary of State's decision he had at all times since the coming into force of this Act been ordinarily resident in the United Kingdom and Islands; and

(b) shall not be liable to deportation under section 3(5)(a), (b) or (c) if at the time of the Secretary of State's decision he had for the last five years been ordinarily resident in the United Kingdom and Islands; and

(c) shall not on conviction of an offence be recommended for deportation under section 3(6) if at the time of the conviction he had for the last five years been ordinarily resident in the United Kingdom and Islands.

(2) A person who has at any time become ordinarily resident in the United Kingdom or in any of the Islands shall not be treated for the purposes of this section as having ceased to be so by reason only of his having remained there in breach of the immigration laws.

(3) The "last five years" before the material time under subsection (1)(b) or (c) above is to be taken as a period amounting in total to five years exclusive of any time during which the person claiming exemption under this section was undergoing imprisonment or detention by virtue of a sentence passed for an offence on a conviction in the United Kingdom and Islands, and the period for which he was imprisoned or detained by virtue of the sentence amounted to six months or more.

(4), (5) ★★★★★

★★★★★

PART II
APPEALS

The appellate authorities

12 Immigration Appeal Tribunal and adjudicators

The Immigration Appeal Tribunal and adjudicators provided for by the Immigration Appeals Act 1969 shall continue for purposes of this Act, and—

(a) members of the Tribunal shall continue to be appointed by the Lord Chancellor and adjudicators by the Secretary of State; and

(b) the provisions of Schedule 1 to that Act shall continue to apply, as set out in Schedule 5 to this Act with the required adaptation of references to that Act, but with the substitution also of references to the Minister for the Civil Service for references to the Treasury.

Appeals to adjudicator or Tribunal in first instance

13 Appeals against exclusion from United Kingdom

(1) Subject to the provisions of this Part of this Act, a person who is refused leave to enter the United Kingdom under this Act may appeal to an adjudicator against the decision that he requires leave or against the refusal.

(2) Subject to the provisions of this Part of this Act, a person who, on an application duly made, is refused a [certificate of entitlement] or an entry clearance may appeal to an adjudicator against the refusal.

[(3) A person shall not be entitled to appeal, on the ground that he has a right of abode in the United Kingdom, against a decision that he requires leave to enter the United Kingdom unless he holds such a passport or certificate as is mentioned in section 3(9) above;]
and a person shall not be entitled to appeal against a refusal of leave to enter so long as he is in the United Kingdom, unless he was refused leave . . . and at a time when he held a current entry clearance or was a person named in a current work permit.

[(3A) A person who seeks to enter the United Kingdom—

(a) as a visitor, or

(b) in order to follow a course of study of not more than six months duration for which he has been accepted, or

(c) with the intention of studying but without having been accepted for any course of study, or

(d) as a dependant of a person within paragraph (a), (b) or (c) above,

shall not be entitled to appeal against a refusal of an entry clearance and shall not be entitled to appeal against a refusal of leave to enter unless he held a current entry clearance at the time of the refusal.

(3AA) The Secretary of State shall appoint a person, not being an officer of his, to monitor, in such manner as the Secretary of State may determine, refusals of entry clearance in cases where there is, by virtue of subsection (3A) above, no right of appeal; and the person so appointed shall make an annual report on the discharge of his functions to the Secretary of State who shall lay a copy of it before each House of Parliament.

(3AB) The Secretary of State may pay to a person appointed under subsection (3AA) above such fees and allowances as he may with the approval of the Treasury determine.

(3B) A person shall not be entitled to appeal against a refusal of an entry clearance if the refusal is on the ground that—

(a) he or any person whose dependant he is does not hold a relevant document which is required by the immigration rules; or

(b) he or any person whose dependant he is does not satisfy a requirement of the immigration rules as to age or nationality or citizenship; or

(c) he or any person whose dependant he is seeks entry for a period exceeding that permitted by the immigration rules;

and a person shall not be entitled to appeal against a refusal of leave to enter if the refusal is on any of those grounds.

(3C) For the purposes of subsection (3B)(a) above, the following are "relevant documents"—

(a) entry clearances;

(b) passports or other identity documents; and

(c) work permits.]

(4) An appeal against a refusal of leave to enter shall be dismissed by the adjudicator if he is satisfied that the appellant was at the time of the refusal an illegal entrant, and an appeal against a refusal of an entry clearance shall be dismissed by the adjudicator if he is satisfied that a deportation order was at the time of the refusal in force in respect of the appellant.

(5) A person shall not be entitled to appeal against a refusal of leave to enter, or against a refusal of an entry clearance, if the Secretary of State certifies that directions have been given by the Secretary of State (and not by a person acting under his authority) for the appellant not to be given entry to the United Kingdom on the ground

that his exclusion is conducive to the public good, or if the leave to enter or entry clearance was refused in obedience to any such directions.

14 Appeals against conditions

(1) Subject to the provisions of this Part of this Act, a person who has a limited leave under this Act to enter or remain in the United Kingdom may appeal to an adjudicator against any variation of the leave (whether as regards duration or conditions), or against any refusal to vary it; and a variation shall not take effect so long as an appeal is pending under this subsection against the variation, nor shall an appellant be required to leave the United Kingdom by reason of the expiration of his leave so long as his appeal is pending under this subsection against a refusal to enlarge or remove the limit on the duration of the leave.

(2) * * * * *

[(2ZA) A person shall not be entitled to appeal under subsection (1) above against—

(a) a variation of his leave which adds such a condition as is mentioned in section 3(1)(c)(ii) above; or

(b) a refusal to vary his leave by revoking such a condition.]

[(2A) A person shall not be entitled to appeal under subsection (1) above against any refusal to vary his leave if the refusal is on the ground that—

(a) a relevant document which is required by the immigration rules has not been issued; or

(b) the person or a person whose dependant he is does not satisfy a requirement of the immigration rules as to age or nationality or citizenship; or

(c) the variation would result in the duration of the person's leave exceeding what is permitted by the immigration rules; or

(d) any fee required by or under any enactment has not been paid.

(2B) For the purposes of subsection (2A)(a) above, the following are relevant documents—

(a) entry clearances;

(b) passports or other identity documents; and

(c) [work permits or equivalent documents issued after entry.]]

(3) A person shall not be entitled to appeal under subsection (1) above against any variation of his leave which reduces its duration, or against any refusal to enlarge or remove the limit on its duration, if the Secretary of State certifies that the appellant's departure from the United Kingdom would be conducive to the public good, as being in the interest of national security or of the relations between the United Kingdom and any other country or for other reasons of a political nature, or the decision questioned by the appeal was taken on that ground by the Secretary of State (and not by a person acting under his authority).

(4) A person shall not be entitled to appeal under subsection (1) above against any variation made by statutory instrument, or against any refusal of the Secretary of State to make a statutory instrument.

[(5) Where a deportation order is made against a person any pending appeal by that person under subsection (1) above shall lapse.]

15 Appeals in respect of deportation orders

(1) Subject to the provisions of this Part of this Act, a person may appeal to an adjudicator against—

(a) a decision of the Secretary of State to make a deportation order against him by virtue of section 3(5) above; or

(b) a refusal by the Secretary of State to revoke a deportation order made against him.

(2) A deportation order shall not be made against a person by virtue of section 3(5) above so long as an appeal may be brought against the decision to make it nor, if such

an appeal is duly brought, so long as the appeal is pending; but, in calculating the period of eight weeks limited by section 5(3) above for making a deportation order against a person as belonging to the family of another person, there shall be disregarded any period during which there is pending an appeal against the decision to make it.

(3) A person shall not be entitled to appeal against a decision to make a deportation order against him if the ground of the decision was that his deportation is conducive to the public good as being in the interests of national security or of the relations between the United Kingdom and any other country or for other reasons of a political nature.

(4) A person shall not be entitled to appeal under this section against a refusal to revoke a deportation order, if the Secretary of State certifies that the appellant's exclusion from the United Kingdom is conducive to the public good or if revocation was refused on that ground by the Secretary of State (and not by a person acting under his authority).

(5) A person shall not be entitled to appeal under this section against a refusal to revoke a deportation order so long as he is in the United Kingdom, whether because he has not complied with the requirement to leave or because he has contravened the prohibition on entering.

(6) ⋆ ⋆ ⋆ ⋆ ⋆

(7) An appeal under this section shall be to the Appeal Tribunal in the first instance, instead of to an adjudicator, if—

(a) it is an appeal against a decision to make a deportation order and the ground of the decision was that the deportation of the appellant is conducive to the public good; or

(b) it is an appeal against a decision to make a deportation order against a person as belonging to the family of another person, or an appeal against a refusal to revoke a deportation order so made; or

(c) there is pending a related appeal to which paragraph (b) above applies.

(8), (9) ⋆ ⋆ ⋆ ⋆ ⋆

16 ⋆ ⋆ ⋆ ⋆ ⋆

17 Appeals against removal on objection to destination

(1) Subject to the provisions of this Part of this Act, where directions are given under this Act for a person's removal from the United Kingdom either—

(a) on his being refused leave to enter; or

(b) on a deportation order being made against him; or

(c) on his having entered the United Kingdom in breach of a deportation order;

he may appeal to an adjudicator against the directions on the ground that he ought to be removed (if at all) to a different contry or territory specified by him.

(2) Where a person appeals under section 13(1) above on being refused leave to enter the United Kingdom, and either—

(a) before he does so, directions have been given for his removal from the United Kingdom to any country or territory; or

(b) before or after he does so, the Secretary of State or an immigration officer serves on him notice that any directions which may be given for his removal by virtue of the refusal will be for his removal to a country or territory or one of several countries or territories specified in the notice;

then he may on that appeal object to the country or territory to which he would be removed in pursuance of the directions, or to that specified in the notice (or to one or more of those specified), and claim that he ought to be removed (if at all) to a different country or territory specified by him.

(3) Where a person appeals under section 15 above against a decision to make a deportation order against him, and before or after he does so the Secretary of State serves on him notice that any directions which may be given for his removal by virtue of

the deportation order will be for his removal to a country or territory or one of several countries or territories specified in the notice, then he may on the appeal object to the country or territory specified in the notice (or to one or more of those specified), and claim that he ought to be removed (if at all) to a different country or territory specified by him.

(4) Where by virtue of subsection (2) or (3) above a person is able to object to a country or territory on an appeal under section 13(1) or 15, and either he does not object to it on that appeal or his objection to it on that appeal is not sustained, then he shall not be entitled to appeal under this section against any directions subsequently given by virtue of the refusal or order in question, if their effect will be his removal to that country or territory.

(5) A person shall not be entitled to appeal under this section against any directions given on his being refused leave to enter the United Kingdom, unless either he is also appealing under section 13(1) against the decision that he requires leave to enter or he was refused leave at a port of entry and at a time when he held a current entry clearance or was a person named in a current work permit.

18 * * * * *

19 Determination of appeals by adjudicators

(1) Subject to sections 13(4) and 16(4) above, and to any restriction on the grounds of appeal, an adjudicator on an appeal to him under this Part of this Act—

(a) shall allow the appeal if he considers—

(i) that the decision or action against which the appeal is brought was not in accordance with the law or with any immigration rules applicable to the case; or

(ii) where the decision or action involved the exercise of a discretion by the Secretary of State or an officer, that the discretion should have been exercised differently; and

(b) in any other case, shall dismiss the appeal.

(2) For the purposes of subsection (1)(a) above the adjudicator may review any determination of a question of fact on which the decision or action was based; and for the purposes of subsection (1)(a)(ii) no decision or action which is in accordance with the immigration rules shall be treated as having involved the exercise of a discretion by the Secretary of State by reason only of the fact that he has been requested by or on behalf of the appellant to depart, or to authorise any officer to depart, from the rules and has refused to do so.

(3), (4) * * * * *

Appeals from adjudicator to Tribunal, and review of decisions

20 Appeal to Tribunal from determination of adjudicator

(1) Subject to any requirement of rules of procedure as to leave to appeal, any party to an appeal to an adjudicator may, if dissatisfied with his determination thereon, appeal to the Appeal Tribunal, and the Tribunal may affirm the determination or make any other determination which could have been made by the adjudicator.

(2), (3) * * * * *

21-23 * * * * *

PART III
CRIMINAL PROCEEDINGS

24 Illegal entry and similar offences

(1) A person who is not [a British citizen] shall be guilty of an offence punishable on summary conviction with a fine of not more than [level [5] on the standard scale] or with imprisonment for not more than six months, or with both, in any of the following cases:—

(a) if contrary to this Act he knowingly enters the United Kingdom in breach of a deportation order or without leave;

[(aa) if, by means which include deception by him, he obtains or seeks to obtain leave to enter or remain in the United Kingdom;]

(b) if, having only a limited leave to enter or remain in the United Kingdom, he knowingly either—

(i) remains beyond the time limited by the leave; or

(ii) fails to observe a condition of the leave;

(c) if, having lawfully entered the United Kingdom without leave by virtue of section 8(1) above, he remains without leave beyond the time allowed by section 8(1);

(d) if, without reasonable excuse, he fails to comply with any requirement imposed on him under Schedule 2 to this Act to report to a medical officer of health, or to attend, or submit to a test or examination, as required by such an officer;

(e) if, without reasonable excuse, he fails to observe any restriction imposed on him under Schedule 2 or 3 to this Act as to residence or as to reporting to the police or to an immigration officer;

(f) if he [leaves a train in the United Kingdom] after being placed on board under Schedule 2 or 3 to this Act with a view to his removal from the United Kingdom;

(g) if he [leaves or seeks to leave the United Kingdom through the tunnel system] in contravention of a restriction imposed by or under an Order in Council under section 3(7) of this Act.

[(1A) A person commits an offence under subsection (1)(b)(i) above on the day when he first knows that the time limited by his leave has expired and continues to commit it throughout any period during which he is in the United Kingdom thereafter; but a person shall not be prosecuted under that provision more than once in respect of the same limited leave.]

(2) A constable or immigration officer may arrest without warrant anyone who has, or whom he, with reasonable cause, suspects to have, committed or attempted to commit an offence under this section other than an offence under subsection (1)(d) above.

(3), (4) * * * * *

25-32 * * * * *

PART IV
SUPPLEMENTARY

33 Interpretation

(1) For purposes of this Act, except in so far as the context otherwise requires—

* * * * *

["entrant" means a person entering or seeking to enter the United Kingdom, and "illegal entrant" means a person—

[(a) unlawfuly entering or seeking to enter in breach of a deportation order or of the immigration laws, or

(b) entering or seeking to enter by means which include deception by another person,

and includes also a person who has entered as mentioned in paragraph (a) or (b) above;]

"entry clearance" means a visa, entry certificate or other document which, in accordance with the immigration rules, is to be taken as evidence [or the requisite evidence] of a person's eligibility, though not [a British citizen], for entry into the United Kingdom (but does not include a work permit);

"immigration laws" means this Act and any law for purposes similar to this Act which is for the time being or has (before or after the passing of this Act) been in force in any part of the United Kingdom and Islands;

"immigration rules" means the rules for the time being laid down as mentioned in section 3(2) above;

* * * * *

"limited leave" and "indefinite leave" mean respectively leave under this Act to enter or remain in the United Kingdom which is, and one which is not, limited as to duration;

"settled" shall be construed in accordance [with subsection (2A) below];

* * * * *

"work permit" means a permit indicating, in accordance with the immigration rules, that a person named in it is eligible, though not [a British citizen], for entry into the United Kingdom for the purpose of taking employment.

(2) It is hereby declared that, except as otherwise provided in this Act, a person is not to be treated for the purposes of any provision of this Act as ordinarily resident in the United Kingdom or in any of the Islands at a time when he is there in breach of the immigration laws.

[(2A) Subject to section 8(5) above, references to a person being settled in the United Kingdom are references to his being ordinarily resident there without being subject under the immigration laws to any restriction on the period for which he may remain.]

(3), (4) * * * * *

(5) This Act shall not be taken to supersede or impair any power exercisable by Her Majesty in relation to aliens by virtue of Her prerogative.

34-37 * * * * *

MISUSE OF DRUGS ACT 1971
(1971, c. 38)

An Act to make new provision with respect to dangerous or otherwise harmful drugs and related matters, and for purposes connected therewith [27 May 1971]

Territorial extent United Kingdom

* * * * *

Law enforcement and punishment of offences

23 Powers to search and obtain evidence

(1) A constable or other person authorised in that behalf by a general or special order of the Secretary of State (or in Northern Ireland either of the Secretary of State or the Ministry of Home Affairs for Northern Ireland) shall, for the purposes of the execution of this Act, have power to enter the premises of a person carrying on business as a producer or supplier of any controlled drugs and to demand the production of, and to inspect, any books or documents relating to dealings in any such drugs and to inspect any stocks of any such drugs.

(2) If a constable has reasonable grounds to suspect that any person is in possession of a controlled drug in contravention of this Act or of any regulations made thereunder, the constable may—

(a) search that person, and detain him for the purpose of searching him;

(b) search any vehicle or vessel in which the constable suspects that the drug may be found, and for that purpose require the person in control of the vehicle or vessel to stop it;

(c) seize and detain, for the purposes of proceedings under this Act, anything found in the course of the search which appears to the constable to be evidence of an offence under this Act.

In this subsection "vessel" includes a hovercraft within the meaning of the Hovercraft Act 1968; and nothing in this subsection shall prejudice any power of search or any power to seize or detain property which is exercisable by a constable apart from this subsection.

(3) If a justice of the peace (or in Scotland a justice of the peace, a magistrate or a sheriff) is satisfied by information on oath that there is reasonable ground for suspecting—

(a) that any controlled drugs are, in contravention of this Act or of any regulations made thereunder, in the possession of a person on any premises; or

(b) that a document directly or indirectly relating to, or connected with, a transaction or dealing which was, or an intended transaction or dealing which would if carried out be, an offence under this Act, or in the case of a transaction or dealing carried out or intended to be carried out in a place outside the United Kingdom, an offence against the provision of a corresponding law in force in that place, is in the possession of a person on any premises,

he may grant a warrant authorising any constable acting for the police area in which the premises are situated at any time or times within one month from the date of the warrant, to enter, if need be by force, the premises named in the warrant, and to search the premises and any person found therein and, if there is reasonable ground for suspecting that an offence under this Act has been committed in relation to any controlled drugs found on the premises or in the possession of any such persons, or that a document so found is such a document as is mentioned in paragraph (b) above, to seize and detain those drugs or that document, as the case may be.

(4) A person commits an offence if he—

(a) intentionally obstructs a person in the exercise of his powers under this section; or

(b) conceals from a person acting in the exercise of his powers under subsection (1) above any such books, documents, stocks or drugs as are mentioned in that subsection; or

(c) without reasonable excuse (proof of which shall lie on him) fails to produce any such books or documents as are so mentioned where their production is demanded by a person in the exercise of his powers under that subsection.

★★★★★

EUROPEAN COMMUNITIES ACT 1972
(1972, c. 68)

An Act to make provision in connection with the enlargement of the European Communities to include the United Kingdom, together with (for certain purposes) the Channel Islands, the Isle of Man and Gibraltar [17 October 1972]

Territorial extent United Kingdom

PART I
GENERAL PROVISIONS

1 Short title and interpretation

(1) This Act may be cited as the European Communities Act 1972.

(2) In this Act . . .

"the Communities" means the European Economic Community, the European Coal and Steel Community and the European Atomic Energy Community;

"the Treaties" or "the Community Treaties" means, subject to subsection (3) below, the pre-accession treaties, that is to say, those described in Part I of Schedule 1 to this Act, taken with—

★★★★★ [full list omitted]

and any expression defined in Schedule 1 to this Act has the meaning there given to it.

(3) If Her Majesty by Order in Council declares that a treaty specified in the Order is to be regarded as one of the Community Treaties as herein defined, the Order shall be conclusive that it is to be so regarded; but a treaty entered into by the United Kingdom after the 22nd January 1972, other than a pre-accession treaty to which the United Kingdom accedes on terms settled on or before that date, shall not be so regarded unless it is so specified, nor be so specified unless a draft of the Order in Council has been approved by resolution of each House of Parliament.

(4) For purposes of subsections (2) and (3) above, "treaty" includes any international agreement, and any protocol or annex to a treaty or international agreement.

Note The full list of Treaties in s. 1(2) includes those adopted and ratified by the UK since 1972 as well as the original treaties, so that major constitutional changes such as the incorporation of the Single European Act of 1986 and the Maastricht Treaty, 1992 are achieved by amendments to the subsection.

2 General implementation of Treaties

(1) All such rights, powers, liabilities, obligations and restrictions from time to time created or arising by or under the Treaties, and all such remedies and procedures from time to time provided for by or under the Treaties, as in accordance with the Treaties are without further enactment to be given legal effect or used in the United Kingdom shall be recognised and available in law, and be enforced, allowed and followed accordingly; and the expression "enforceable Community right" and similar expressions shall be read as referring to one to which this subsection applies.

(2) Subject to Schedule 2 to this Act, at any time after its passing Her Majesty may by Order in Council, and any designated Minister or department may by regulations, make provision—

(a) for the purpose of implementing any Community obligation of the United Kingdom, or enabling any such obligation to be implemented, or of enabling any rights enjoyed or to be enjoyed by the United Kingdom under or by virtue of the Treaties to be exercised; or

(b) for the purpose of dealing with matters arising out of or related to any such obligation or rights or the coming into force, or the operation from time to time, of subsection (1) above;

and in the exercise of any statutory power or duty, including any power to give directions or to legislate by means of orders, rules, regulations or other subordinate instrument, the person entrusted with the power or duty may have regard to the objects of the Communities and to any such obligation or rights as aforesaid.

In this subsection "designated Minister or Department" means such Minister of the Crown or government department as may from time to time be designated by Order in Council in relation to any matter or for any purpose, but subject to such restrictions or conditions (if any) as may be specified by the Order in Council.

(3) There shall be charged on and issued out of the Consolidated Fund or, if so determined by the Treasury, the National Loans Fund the amounts required to meet any Community obligation to make payments to any of the Communities or member States, or any Community obligation in respect of contributions to the capital or reserves of the European Investment Bank or in respect of loans to the Bank, or to redeem any notes or obligations issued or created in respect of any such Community obligation; and, except as otherwise provided by or under any enactment,—

(a) any other expenses incurred under or by virtue of the Treaties or this Act by any Minister of the Crown or government department may be paid out of moneys provided by Parliament; and

(b) any sums received under or by virtue of the Treaties or this Act by any Minister of the Crown or government department, save for such sums as may be required for disbursements permitted by any other enactment, shall be paid into the Consolidated Fund or, if so determined by the Treasury, the National Loans Fund.

(4) The provision that may be made under subsection (2) above includes, subject to Schedule 2 to this Act, any such provision (of any such extent) as might be made by Act of Parliament, and any enactment passed or to be passed, other than one contained in this Part of this Act, shall be construed and have effect subject to the foregoing provisions of this section; but, except as may be provided by any Act passed after this Act, Schedule 2 shall have effect in connection with the powers conferred by this and the following sections of this Act to make Orders in Council and regulations.

(5), (6) * * * * *

3 Decisions on, and proof of, Treaties and Community instruments, etc.

(1) For the purposes of all legal proceedings any question as to the meaning or effect of any of the Treaties, or as to the validity, meaning or effect of any Community instrument, shall be treated as a question of law (and, if not referred to the European Court, be for determination as such in accordance with the principles laid down by and any relevant decision of the European Court).

(2) Judicial notice shall be taken of the Treaties, of the Official Journal of the Communities and of any decision of, or expression of opinion by, the European Court on any such question as aforesaid; and the Official Journal shall be admissible as evidence of any instrument or other act thereby communicated of any of the Communities or of any Community institution.

(3), (4), (5) * * * * *

* * * * *

Section 2

SCHEDULE 2
PROVISIONS AS TO SUBORDINATE LEGISLATION

1.—(1) The powers conferred by section 2(2) of this Act to make provision for the purposes mentioned in section 2(2)(a) and (b) shall not include power—

(a) to make any provision imposing or increasing taxation; or

(b) to make any provision taking effect from a date earlier than that of the making of the instrument containing the provision; or

(c) to confer any power to legislate by means of orders, rules regulations or other subordinate instrument, other than rules of procedure for any court or tribunal; or

(d) to create any new criminal offence punishable with imprisonment for more than two years or punishable on summary conviction with imprisonment for more than three months or with a fine of more than [level 5 on the standard scale] (if not calculated on a daily basis) or with a fine of more than [£100 a day].

(2) Sub-paragraph (1)(c) above shall not be taken to preclude the modification of a power to legislate conferred otherwise than under section 2(2), or the extension of any such power to purposes of the like nature as those for which it was conferred; and a power to give directions as to matters of administration is not to be regarded as a power to legislate within the meaning of sub-paragraph (1)(c).

2.—(1) Subject to paragraph 3 below, where a provision contained in any section of this Act confers power to make regulations (otherwise than by modification or extension of an existing power), the power shall be exercisable by statutory instrument.

(2) Any statutory instrument containing an Order in Council or regulations made in the exercise of a power so conferred, if made without a draft having been approved by resolution of each House of Parliament, shall be subject to annulment in pursuance of a resolution of either House.

LOCAL GOVERNMENT ACT 1972
(1972, c. 70)

An Act to make provision with respect to local government and the functions of local authorities in England and Wales; to amend Part II of the Transport Act 1968; to confer rights of appeal in respect of decisions relating to licences under the Home Counties (Music and Dancing) Licensing Act 1926; to make further provision with respect to magistrates' courts committees; to abolish certain inferior courts of record; and for connected purposes [26 October 1972]

Territorial extent England and Wales

★★★★★

PART V
GENERAL PROVISIONS AS TO MEMBERS AND PROCEEDINGS OF LOCAL AUTHORITIES

Restrictions on voting

94 Disability of members of authorities for voting on account of interest in contracts, etc.

(1) Subject to the provisions of section 97 below, if a member of a local authority has any pecuniary interest, direct or indirect, in any contract, proposed contract or other matter, and is present at a meeting of the local authority at which the contract or other matter is the subject of consideration, he shall at the meeting and as soon as practicable after its commencement disclose the fact and shall not take part in the consideration or discussion of the contract or other matter or vote on any question with respect to it.

(2) If any person fails to comply with the provisions of subsection (1) above he shall for each offence be liable on summary conviction to a fine not exceeding [level 4 on the standard scale] unless he proves that he did not know that the contract, proposed contract or other matter in which he had a pecuniary interest was the subject of consideration at that meeting.

(3) A prosecution for an offence under this section shall not be instituted except by or on behalf of the Director of Public Prosecutions.

(4), (5) ★★★★★

95 Pecuniary interests for purposes of section 94

(1) For the purposes of section 94 above a person shall be treated, subject to the following provisions of this section and to section 97 below, as having indirectly a pecuniary interest in a contract, proposed contract or other matter, if—

(a) he or any nominee of his is a member of a company or other body with which the contract was made or is proposed to be made or which has a direct pecuniary interest in the other matter under consideration; or

(b) he is a partner, or is in the employment, of a person with whom the contract was made or is proposed to be made or who has a direct pecuniary interest in the other matter under consideration.

(2) Subsection (1) above does not apply to membership of or employment under any public body, and a member of a company or other body shall not by reason only of his membership be treated as having an interest in any contract, proposed contract or other matter if he has no beneficial interest in any securities of that company or other body.

(3) In the case of married persons living together the interest of one spouse shall, if known to the other, be deemed for the purpose of section 94 above to be also an interest of the other.

96 General notices and recording of disclosures for purposes of section 94

(1) A general notice given in writing to the proper officer of the authority by a member thereof to the effect that he or his spouse is a member or in the employment of a specified company or other body, or that he or his spouse is a partner or in the employment of a specified person, or that he or his spouse is the tenant of any premises owned by the authority, shall, unless and until the notice is withdrawn, be deemed to be a sufficient disclosure of his interest in any contract, proposed contract or other matter relating to that company or other body or to that person or to those premises which may be the subject of consideration after the date of the notice.

(2) The proper officer of the authority shall record in a book to be kept for the purpose particulars of any disclosure made under section 94 above and of any notice given under this section, and the book shall be open at all reasonable hours to the inspection of any member of the local authority.

97-100 ★★★★★

[PART VA
ACCESS TO MEETINGS AND DOCUMENTS OF CERTAIN AUTHORITIES, COMMITTEES AND SUB-COMMITEES

Note This Part was added by the Local Government (Access to Information) Act 1985. It now also applies to Community Health Councils: Community Health Councils (Access to Information) Act 1988.

100A Admission to meetings of principal councils

(1) A meeting of a principal council shall be open to the public except to the extent that they are excluded (whether during the whole or part of the proceedings) under subsection (2) below or by resolution under subsection (4) below.

(2) The public shall be excluded from a meeting of a principal council during an item of business whenever it is likely, in view of the nature of the business to be transacted or the nature of the proceedings, that, if members of the public were present during that item, confidential information would be disclosed to them in breach of the obligation of confidence; and nothing in this Part shall be taken to authorise or require the disclosure of confidential information in breach of the obligation of confidence.

(3) For the purposes of subsection (2) above, "confidential information" means—

(a) information furnished to the council by a Government department upon terms (however expressed) which forbid the disclosure of the information to the public; and

(b) information the disclosure of which to the public is prohibited by or under any enactment or by the order of a court;

and, in either case, the reference to the obligation of confidence is to be construed accordingly.

(4) A principal council may by resolution exclude the public from a meeting during an item of business whenever it is likely, in view of the nature of the business to be transacted or the nature of the proceedings, that if members of the public were present during that item there would be disclosure to them of exempt information, as defined in section 100I below.

(5), (6) ★★★★★

(7) Nothing in this section shall require a principal council to permit the taking of photographs of any proceedings, or the use of any means to enable persons not present to see or hear any proceedings (whether at the time or later), or the making of any oral report on any proceedings as they take place.

(8) This section is without prejudice to any power of exclusion to supress or prevent disorderly conduct or other misbehaviour at a meeting.

100B Access to agenda and connected reports

(1) Copies of the agenda for a meeting of a principal council and, subject to subsection (2) below, copies of any report for the meeting shall be open to inspection by members of the public at the offices of the council in accordance with subsection (3) below.

(2) If the proper officer thinks fit, there may be excluded from the copies of reports provided in pursuance of subsection (1) above the whole of any report which, or any part which, relates only to items during which, in his opinion, the meeting is likely not to be open to the public.

(3) Any document which is required by subsection (1) above to be open to inspection shall be so open at least three clear days before the meeting, except that—

(a) where the meeting is convened at shorter notice, the copies of the agenda and reports shall be open to inspection from the time the meeting is convened, and

(b) where an item is added to an agenda copies of which are open to inspection by the public, copies of the item (or of the revised agenda), and the copies of any report for the meeting relating to the item, shall be open to inspection from the time the item is added to the agenda;

but nothing in this subsection requires copies of any agenda, item or report to be open to inspection by the public until copies are available to members of the council.

(4) An item of business may not be considered at a meeting of a principal council unless either—

(a) a copy of the agenda including the item (or a copy of the item) is open to inspection by members of the public in pursuance of subsection (1) above for at least three clear days before the meeting or, where the meeting is convened at shorter notice, from the time the meeting is convened; or

(b) by reason of special circumstances, which shall be specified in the minutes, the chairman of the meeting is of the opinion that the item should be considered at the meeting as a matter of urgency.

(5)-(8) ★ ★ ★ ★ ★

100C Inspection of minutes and other documents after meetings

(1) After a meeting of a principal council the following documents shall be open to inspection by members of the public at the offices of the council until the expiration of the period of six years beginning with the date of the meeting, namely—

(a) the minutes, or a copy of the minutes, of the meeting, excluding so much of the minutes of proceedings during which the meeting was not open to the public as discloses exempt information;

(b) where applicable, a summary under subsection (2) below;

(c) a copy of the agenda for the meeting; and

(d) a copy of so much of any report for the meeting as relates to any item during which the meeting was open to the public.

(2) ★ ★ ★ ★ ★

100D Inspection of background papers

(1) Subject, in the case of section 100C(1), to subsection (2) below, if and so long as copies of the whole or part of a report for a meeting of a principal council are required by section 100B(1) or 100C(1) above to be open to inspection by members of the public—

(a) copies of a list, compiled by the proper officer, of the background papers for the report or the part of the report, and

(b) at least one copy of each of the documents included in that list,

shall also be open to their inspection at the offices of the council.

(2) Subsection (1) above does not require a copy of the list, or of any document included in the list, to be open to inspection after the expiration of the period of four years beginning with the date of the meeting.

(3)-(5) ★ ★ ★ ★ ★

100E Application to committees and sub-committees

(1) Sections 100A to 100D above shall apply in relation to a committee or sub-committee of a principal council as they apply in relation to a principal council.

(2)-(4) ★ ★ ★ ★ ★

100F ★ ★ ★ ★ ★

100G Principal councils to publish additional information

(1) A principal council shall maintain a register stating—

(a) the name and address of every member of the council for the time being and the ward or division which he represents; and

[(b) in respect of every committee or sub-committee of the council—

(i) the members of the council who are members of the committee or sub-committee or who are entitled, in accordance with any standing orders relating to the committee or sub-committee, to speak at its meetings or any of them;

(ii) the name and address of every other person who is a member of the committee or sub-committee or who is entitled, in accordance with any standing orders relating to the committee or sub-committee, to speak at its meetings or any of them otherwise than in the capacity of an officer of the council; and

(iii) the functions in relation to the committee or sub-committee of every person falling within sub-paragraph (i) above who is not a member of the committee or sub-committee and of every person falling within sub-paragraph (ii) above.

(2) A principal council shall maintain a list—

(a) specifying those powers of the council which, for the time being, are exercisable from time to time by officers of the council in pursuance of arrangements made under this Act or any other enactment for their discharge by those officers; and

(b) stating the title of the officer by whom each of the powers so specified is for the time being so exercisable;

but this subsection does not require a power to be specified in the list if the arrangements for its discharge by the officer are made for a specified period not exceeding six months.

(3), (4) ★ ★ ★ ★ ★]

PART VI
DISCHARGE OF FUNCTIONS

101 Arrangements for discharge of functions by local authorities

(1) Subject to any express provision contained in this Act or any Act passed after this Act, a local authority may arrange for the discharge of any of their functions—

(a) by a committee, a sub-committee or an officer of the authority; or

(b) by any other local authority.

(2) Where by virtue of this section any functions of a local authority may be discharged by a committee of theirs, then, unless the local authority otherwise direct, the committee may arrange for the discharge of any of those functions by a sub-committee or an officer of the authority and where by virtue of this section any functions of a local authority may be discharged by a sub-committee of the authority, then, unless the local authority or the committee otherwise direct, the sub-committee may arrange for the discharge of any of those functions by an officer of the authority.

(3) Where arrangements are in force under this section for the discharge of any functions of a local authority by another local authority, then, subject to the terms of the arrangements, that other authority may arrange for the discharge of those functions by a committee, sub-committee or officer of theirs and subsection (2) above shall apply in relation to those functions as it applies in relation to the functions of that other authority.

(4) Any arrangements made by a local authority or committee under this section for the discharge of any functions by a committee, sub-committee, officer or local authority shall not prevent the authority or committee by whom the arrangements are made from exercising those functions.

(5) Two or more local authorities may discharge any of their functions jointly and, where arrangements are in force for them to do so,—

(a) they may also arrange for the discharge of those functions by a joint committee of theirs or by an officer of one of them and subsection (2) above shall apply in relation to those functions as it applies in relation to the functions of the individual authorities; and

(b) any enactment relating to those functions or the authorities by whom or the areas in respect of which they are to be discharged shall have effect subject to all necessary modifications in its application in relation to those functions and the authorities by whom and the areas in respect of which (whether in pursuance of the arrangements or otherwise) they are to be discharged.

(6) A local authority's functions with respect to levying, or issuing a precept for, a rate . . . shall be discharged only by the authority.

★ ★ ★ ★ ★

PART XI
GENERAL PROVISIONS AS TO LOCAL AUTHORITIES

Legal proceedings

222 Power of local authorities to prosecute or defend legal proceedings

(1) Where a local authority consider it expedient for the promotion or protection of the interests of the inhabitants of their area—

(a) they may prosecute or defend or appear in any legal proceedings and, in the case of civil proceedings, may institute them in their own name, and

(b) they may, in their own name, make representations in the interests of the inhabitants at any public inquiry held by or on behalf of any Minister or public body under any enactment.

(2) In this section "local authority" includes the Common Council.

★ ★ ★ ★ ★

Byelaws

235 Power of councils to make byelaws for good rule and government and suppression of nuisances

(1) The council of a district [, the council of a principal area in Wales] and the council of a London borough may make byelaws for the good rule and government of the whole or any part of the district [principal area] or borough, as the case may be, and for the prevention and suppression of nuisances therein.

(2) The confirming authority in relation to byelaws made under this section shall be the Secretary of State.

(3) Byelaws shall not be made under this section for any purpose as respects any area if provision for that purpose as respects that area is made by, or is or may be made under, any other enactment.

236 Procedure, etc., for byelaws

(1) Subject to subsection (2) below, the following provisions of this section shall apply to byelaws to be made by a local authority under this Act [and to byelaws made by a local authority, a metropolitan county passenger transport authority or the Inner London Education Authority under any other enactment conferring on the authority] a power to make byelaws and for which specific provision is not otherwise made.

(2) This section shall not apply to byelaws made by statutory water undertakers under section 17 or 18 of the Water Act 1945 or by the Civil Aviation Authority under [section 29 of the Civil Aviation Act 1982].

(3) The byelaws shall be made under the common seal of the authority, or, in the case of byelaws made by a parish or community council not having a seal, under the hands and seals of two members of the council, and shall not have effect until they are confirmed by the confirming authority.

(4) At least one month before application for conformation of the byelaws is made, notice of the intention to apply for confirmation shall be given in one or more local newspapers circulating in the area to which the byelaws are to apply.

(5) For at least one month before application for confirmation is made, a copy of the byelaws shall be deposited at the offices of the authority by whom the byelaws are made, and shall at all reasonable hours be open to public inspection without payment.

(6) The authority by whom the byelaws are made shall, on application, furnish to any person a copy of the byelaws, or of any part thereof on payment of such sum, not exceeding 10p for every hundred words contained in the copy, as the authority may determine.

(7) The confirming authority may confirm, or refuse to confirm, any byelaw submitted under this section for confirmation, and may fix the date on which the byelaw is to come into operation and if no date is so fixed the byelaw shall come into operation at the expiration of one month from the date of its confirmation.

(8) A copy of the byelaws, when confirmed, shall be printed and deposited at the offices of the authority by whom the byelaws are made, and shall at all reasonable hours be open to public inspection without pyament, and a copy thereof shall, on application, be furnished to any person on payment of such sum, not exceeding 20p for every copy, as the authority may determine.

(9), (10), (10A) * * * * *

(11) In this section the expression "the confirming authority" means the authority or person, if any, specified in the enactment (including any enactment in this Act) under which the byelaws are made, or in any enactment incorporated therein or applied thereby, as the authority or person by whom the byelaws are to be confirmed, or if no authority or person is so specified, means the Secretary of State.

* * * * *

[SCHEDULE 12A
ACCESS TO INFORMATION: EXEMPT INFORMATION

PART I
DESCRIPTIONS OF EXEMPT INFORMATION

1. Information relating to a particular employee, former employee or applicant to become an employee of, or a particular office-holder, former office-holder or applicant to become an office-holder under, the authority.

2. Information relating to a particular employee, former employee or applicant to become an employee of, or a particular officer, former officer or applicant to become an officer appointed by—

(a) a magistrates' court committee, within the meaning of section 19 of the Justices of the Peace Act 1979; or

(b) a probation committee [within the meaning of the Probation Service Act 1993].

3. Information relating to any particular occupier or former occupier of, or applicant for accommodation provided by or at the expense of the authority.

4. Information relating to any particular applicant for, or recipient or former recipient of, any service provided by the authority.

5. Information relating to any particular applicant for, or recipient or former recipient of, any financial assistance provided by the authority.

6. Information relating to the adoption, care, fostering or education of any particular child.

7. Information relating to the financial or business affairs of any particular person (other than the authority).

8. The amount of any expenditure proposed to be incurred by the authority under any particular contract for the acquisition of property or the supply of goods or services.

9. Any terms proposed or to be proposed by or to the authority in the course of negotiations for a contract for the acquisition or disposal of property or the supply of goods or services.

10. The identity of the authority (as well as of any other person, by virtue of paragraph 7 above) as the person offering any particular tender for a contract for the supply of goods or services.

11. Information relating to any consultations or negotiations, or contemplated consultations or negotiations, in connection with any labour relations matter arising between the authority or a Minister of the Crown and employees of, or office-holders under, the authority.

12. Any instructions to counsel and any opinion of counsel (whether or not in connection with any proceedings) and any advice received, information obtained or action to be taken in connection with—

(a) any legal proceedings by or against the authority, or

(b) the determination of any matter affecting the authority,

(whether, in either case, proceedings have been commenced or are in contemplation).

13. Information which, if disclosed to the public, would reveal that the authority proposes—

(a) to give under any enactment a notice under or by virtue of which requirements are imposed on a person; or

(b) to make an order or direction under any enactment.

14. Any action taken or to be taken in connection with the prevention, investigation or prosecution of crime.

15. The identity of a protected informant.]

* * * * *

NORTHERN IRELAND CONSTITUTION ACT 1973
(1973, c. 36)

An Act to make new provision for the government of Northern Ireland [18 July 1973]

Territorial extent United Kingdom

PART I
PRELIMINARY

Status of Northern Ireland

1 Status of Northern Ireland as part of United Kingdom

It is hereby declared that Northern Ireland remains part of Her Majesty's dominions and of the United Kingdom, and it is hereby affirmed that in no event will Northern Ireland or any part of it cease to be part of Her Majesty's dominions and of the United Kingdom without the consent of the majority of the people of Northern Ireland voting in a poll held for the purposes of this section in accordance with Schedule 1 to this Act.

* * * * *

LOCAL GOVERNMENT ACT 1974
(1974, c. 7)

An Act to make further provision, in relation to England and Wales, with respect to the payment of grants to local authorities, rating and valuation, borrowing and lending by local authorities and the classification of highways; to extend the powers of the Countryside Commission to give financial assistance; to provide for the establishment of Commissions for the investigation of administrative action taken by or on behalf of local and other authorities; to restrict certain grants under the Transport Act 1968; to provide for the removal or relaxation of certain statutory controls affecting local government activities; to make provision in relation to the collection of sums by local authorities on behalf of water authorities; to amend section 259(3) of the Local Government Act 1972 and to make certain minor amendments of or consequential on that Act; and for connected purposes

[8 February 1974]

Territorial extent England and Wales

PART III
LOCAL GOVERNMENT ADMINISTRATION

23 The Commissions for Local Administration

(1) For the purpose of conducting investigations in accordance with this Part of this Act, there shall be—

(a) a body of commissioners to be known as the Commission for Local Administration in England, and

(b) a body consisting of two or more commissioners to be known as the Commission for Local Administration in Wales.

(2) The Parliamentary Commissioner shall be a member of each of the Commissions.

(3) In the following provisions of this Part of this Act the expression "Local Commissioner" means a person, other than the Parliamentary Commissioner, who is a member of one of the Commissions.

(4) Appointments to the office of . . . Commissioner shall be made by Her Majesty on the recommendation of the Secretary of State after consultation with the appropriate representative body, and a person so appointed shall, subject to subsection (6) below, hold office during good behaviour.

(5) . . . Commissioners may be appointed to serve either as full-time commissioners or as part-time commissioners.

(6) A Commissioner may be relieved of office by Her Majesty at his own request or may be removed from office by Her Majesty on grounds of incapacity or misbehaviour, and shall in any case vacate office on completing the year of service in which he attains the age of sixty-five years.

(7) The Secretary of State shall designate two of the Local Commissioners for England as chairman and vice-chairman respectively of the Commission for Local Administration in England and, in the event of there being more than one Local Commissioner for Wales, shall designate one of them as chairman of the Commission for Local Administration in Wales.

(8) The Commission for Local Administration in England shall divide England into areas and shall provide, in relation to each area, for one or more of the Local Commissioners to be responsible for the area; and where the Commission for Local Administration in Wales consist of more than one Local Commissioner they may, if they think fit, act in a similar way in Wales.

A Local Commissioner may, by virtue of this Subsection, be made responsible for more than one area.

(9)-(13) ★ ★ ★ ★ ★

24 ...

25 Authorities subject to investigation

(1) This Part of this Act applies to [the following authorities]—

(a) any local authority,

[(aa) the Land Authority for Wales ...],

[(ab) a National Park Authority;]

(b) any joint board the constituent authorities of which are all local authorities,

[(ba) the Commission for the New Towns;

(bb) any development corporation established for the purposes of a new town;

(bc) the Development Board for Rural Wales;

(bd) any urban development corporation established by an order under section 135 of the Local Government, Planning and Land Act 1980;]

[(be) any housing action trust established under Part III of the Housing Act 1988,]

[(bf) the Urban Regeneration Agency,]

[(c) any joint authority established by Part IV of the Local Government Act 1985;

(ca) [any police authority established under section 3 of the Police Act 1996]; ... and]

(d) [in relation to the flood defence functions of the Environment Agency, within the meaning of the Water Resources Act 1991, the Environment Agency and any regional flood defence committee].

(2) Her Majesty may by Order in Council provide that this Part of this Act shall also apply, subject to any modifications or exceptions specified in the Order, to any authority specified in the Order, being an authority which is established by or under an Act of Parliament, and which has power to levy a rate, or to issue a precept.

(3)-(5) ★ ★ ★ ★ ★

26 Matters subject to investigation

(1) Subject to the provisions of this Part of this Act where a written complaint is made by or on behalf of a member of the public who claims to have sustained injustice in consequence of maladministration in connection with action taken by or on behalf of an authority to which this Part of this Act applies, being action taken in the exercise of administrative functions of that authority, a Local Commissioner may investigate that complaint.

(2) A complaint shall not be entertained under this Part of this Act unless—

(a) [it is made in writing to the Local Commissioner, specifying the action alleged to constitute maladministration, or]

(b) it is referred to the Local Commissioner, with the consent of the person aggrieved, or of a person acting on his behalf, by that member, or by any other person who is a member of any authority concerned, with a request to investigate the complaint.

(3) If the Local Commissioner is satisfied that any member of any authority concerned has been requested to refer the complaint to a Local Commissioner, and has not done so, the Local Commissioner may, if he thinks fit, dispense with the requirements in subsection (2)(b) above.

(4) A complaint shall not be entertained unless it was made to [the Local Commissioner or] a member of any authority concerned within twelve months from the day on which the person aggrieved first had notice of the matters alleged in the complaint, but a Local Commissioner may conduct an investigation pursuant to a complaint not made within that period if he considers that [it is reasonable] to do so.

(5) Before proceeding to investigate a complaint, a Local Commissioner shall satisfy himself that the complaint has been brought, by or on behalf of the person

aggrieved, to the notice of the authority to which the complaint relates and that that authority has been afforded a reasonable opportunity to investigate, and reply to, the complaint.

(6) A Local Commissioner shall not conduct an investigation under this Part of this Act in respect of any of the following matters, that is to say,—

(a) any action in respect of which the person aggrieved has or had a right of appeal, reference or review to or before a tribunal constituted by or under any enactment;

(b) any action in respect of which in the person aggrieved has or had a right of appeal to a Minister of the Crown; or

(c) any action in respect of which the person aggrieved has or had a remedy by way of proceedings in any court of law:

Provided that a Local Commissioner may conduct an investigation notwithstanding the existence of such a right or remedy if satisfied that in the particular circumstances it is not reasonable to expect the person aggrieved to resort or have resorted to it.

(7) A Local Commissioner shall not conduct an investigation in respect of any action which in his opinion affects all or most of the inhabitants of the [following area:

[(aa) where the complaint relates to a National Park Authority, the area of the Park for which it is such an authority;]

(a) where the complaint relates to the Commission for the New Towns, the area of the new town or towns to which the complaint relates;

(b) where the complaint relates to the Development Board for Rural Wales, the area in Wales for which the Board is for the time being responsible;

[(ba) where the complaint relates to the Urban Regeneration Agency, any designated area within the meaning of Part III of the Leasehold Reform, Housing and Urban Development Act 1993;]

(c) in any other case, the area of the authority concerned.]

(8) Without prejudice to the preceding provisions of this section, a Local Commissioner shall not conduct an investigation under this Part of this Act in respect of any such action or matter as is described in Schedule 5 to this Act.

(9) Her Majesty may by Order in Council amend the said Schedule 5 so as [to add to or to exclude from the provisions of that Schedule (as it has effect for the time being)] such actions or matters as may be described in the Order; and any Order made by virtue of this subsection shall be subject to annulment in pursuance of a resolution of either House of Parliament.

(10) In determining whether to initiate, continue or discontinue an investigation, a Local Commissioner shall, subject to the proceeding provisions of this section, act at discretion; and any question whether a complaint is duly made under this Part of this Act shall be determined by the Local Commissioner.

(11), (12), (13) ★★★★★

27 Provisions relating to complaints

(1) A complaint under this Part of this Act may be made by any individual, or by any body of persons whether incorporated or not, not being—

(a) a local authority or other authority or body constituted for purposes of the public service or of local government, or for the purposes of carrying on under national ownership any industry or undertaking or part of an industry or undertaking;

(b) any other authority or body whose members are appointed by Her Majesty or any Minister of the Crown or government department, or whose revenues consist wholly or mainly of moneys provided by Parliament.

(2) ★★★★★

28 Procedure in respect of investigations

(1) Where a Local Commissioner proposes to conduct an investigation pursuant to a complaint, he shall afford to the authority concerned, and to any person who is alleged

in the complaint to have taken or authorised the action complained of, an opportunity to comment on any allegations contained in the complaint.

(2) Every such investigation shall be conducted in private, but except as aforesaid the procedure for conducting an investigation shall be such as the Local Commissioner considers appropriate in the circumstances of the case; and without prejudice to the generality of the preceding provision the Local Commissioner may obtain information from such persons and in such manner, and make such inquiries as he thinks fit, and may determine whether any person may be represented (by counsel or solicitor or otherwise) in the investigation.

(3) ★ ★ ★ ★ ★

(4) The conduct of an investigation under this Part of this Act shall not affect any action taken by the authority concerned, or any power or duty of that authority to take further action with respect to any matters subject to the investigation.

29 Investigations: further provisions

(1) For the purposes of an investigation under this Part of this Act a Local Commissioner may require any member or officer of the authority concerned, or any other person who in his opinion is able to furnish information or produce documents relevant to the investigation, to furnish any such information or produce any such documents.

(2) For the purposes of any such investigation a Local Commissioner shall have the same powers as the High Court in respect of the attendance and examination of witnesses, and in respect of the production of documents.

(3) A Local Commissioner may, under subsection (1) above, require any person to furnish information concerning communications between the authority concerned and any Government department, or to produce any correspondence or other documents forming part of any such written communications.

(4) No obligation to maintain secrecy or other restriction upon the disclosure of information obtained by or furnished to persons in Her Majesty's service, whether imposed by any enactment or by any rule of law, shall apply to the disclosure of information in accordance with subsection (3) above; and where that subsection applies the Crown shall not be entitled to any such privilege in respect of the production of documents or the giving of evidence as is allowed by law in legal proceedings.

(5)-(10) ★ ★ ★ ★ ★

30 Reports on investigations

(1) In any case where a Local Commissioner conducts an investigation, or decides not to conduct an investigation, he shall send a report of the results of the investigation, or as the case may be a statement of his reasons for not conducting an investigation—

(a) to the person, if any, who referred the complaint to the Local Commissioner in accordance with section 26(2) above, and

(b) to the complainant, and

(c) to the authority concerned, and to any other authority or person who is alleged in the complaint to have taken or authorised the action complained of.

(2), (2A) ★ ★ ★ ★ ★

(3) Apart from identifying the authority or authorities concerned the report shall not—

(a) mention the name of any person, or

(b) contain any particulars which, in the opinion of the Local Commissioner, are likely to identify any person and can be omitted without impairing the effectiveness of the report,

unless, after taking into account the public interest as well as the interests of the complainant and of persons other than the complainant, the Local Commissioner considers it necessary to mention the name of that person or to include in the report any such particulars.

(4) Subject to the provisions of subsection (7) below, the authority concerned shall for a period of three weeks make copies of the report available for inspection by the public without charge at all reasonable hours at one or more of their offices; and any person shall be entitled to take copies of, or extracts from, the report when so made available.

[(4A) Subject to subsection (7) below, the authority concerned shall supply a copy of the report to any person on request if he pays such charge as the authority may reasonably require.

(5) Not later than [two weeks] after the report is received by the authority concerned, the proper officer of the authority shall give public notice, by advertisement in the newspapers and such other ways as appear to him appropriate, that [copies of the report will be available as provided by subsections (4) and (4A)] above, and shall specify the date, being a date [not more than one week after the public notice is first given] from which the period of three weeks will begin.

(6) ★★★★★

(7) The Local Commissioner may, if he thinks fit after taking into account the public interest as well as the interests of the complainant and of persons other than the complainant, direct that a report specified in the direction shall not be subject to the provisions of subsections (4) [,(4A) and (5) above.]

31 Reports on investigations: further provisions

(1) If in the opinion of the Local Commissioner, as set out in the report, injustice has been caused to the person aggrieved in consequence of maladministration, the report shall be laid before the authority concerned, and it shall be the duty of that authority to consider the report, and to notify the Local Commissioner of the action which the authority have taken, or propose to take.

(2) If the Local Commissioner—

(a) does not receive any such notification within a reasonable time; or

(b) is not satisfied with the action which the authority concerned have taken; or

(c) does not within a reasonable time receive confirmation from the authority concerned that they have taken action, as proposed, to the satisfaction of the Local Commissioner,

he shall make a further report setting out those facts; and section 30 above shall apply, with any necessary modifications, to that further report.

[(2A) A report under subsection (2) above shall be laid before the authority concerned as it shall be the duty of the authority to consider the report and to notify the Local Commissioner of the action which the authority have taken, or propose to take.]

[(3) In any case where—

(a) a report is laid before an authority under subsection (1) [or (2A)] above, and

(b) on consideration of the report, it appears to the authority that a payment should be made to, or some other benefit should be provided for, a person who has suffered injustice in consequence of maladministration [to which the report relates,]

the authority may incur such expenditure as appears to them to be appropriate in making such a payment or providing such a benefit.]

32, 33 ★★★★★

34 Interpretation of Part III

(1), (2) ★★★★★

(3) It is hereby declared that nothing in this Part of this Act authorises or requires a Local Commissioner to question the merits of a decision taken without maladministration by an authority in the exercise of a discretion vested in that authority.

★★★★★

Section 26

SCHEDULE 5
MATTERS NOT SUBJECT TO INVESTIGATION

1. The commencement or conduct of civil or criminal proceedings before any court of law.

2. Action taken by any authority in connection with the investigation or prevention of crime.

3.—(1) Action taken in matters relating to contractual or other commercial transactions of any authority to which Part III of this Act applies, including transactions falling within sub-paragraph (2) below but excluding transactions falling within sub-paragraph (3) below.

(2) The transactions mentioned in sub-paragraph (1) above as included in the matters which, by virtue of that sub-paragraph, are not subject to investigation are all transactions of an authority to which Part III of this Act applies relating to the operation of public passenger transport, the carrying on of a dock or harbour undertaking, the provision of entertainment, or the provision and operation of industrial establishments and of markets, [other than transactions relating to the grant, renewal or revocation of a licence to occupy a pitch or stall in a fair or market, or the attachment of any condition to such a licence.]

(3) The transactions mentioned in sub-paragraph (1) above as not included in those matters are—

(a) transactions for or relating to the acquisition or disposal of land [or the provision of moorings (not being moorings provided in connection with a dock or harbour undertaking)]; and

(b) all transactions (not being transactions falling within sub-paragraph (2) above) in the discharge of functions exercisable under any public general Act, other than those required for the procurement of the goods and services necessary to discharge those functions.

4. Action taken in respect of appointments or removals, pay, discipline, superannuation or other personnel matters.

5.—(1) Any action taken by a local education authority in the exercise of functions under section 23 of the Education Act 1944 [or sections 17 to 19 of the Education (No 2) Act 1986] (secular instruction in county schools and in voluntary schools).

(2) Any action concerning—

(a) the giving of instruction, whether secular or religious, or

(b) conduct, curriculum, internal organisation, management or discipline, whether—

(i) in any school maintained by the authority, or

(ii) in any college of education or establishment of further education maintained by the authority.

[6. Any action taken by an authority mentioned in section 25(1)(ba), (bb) or (bc) or this Act which is not action in connection with functions in relation to housing.

7. Action taken by an authority mentioned in section 25(1)(bd) of this Act which is not action in connection with functions in relation to town and country planning.]

[8. Action taken by the Urban Regeneration Agency which is not action in connection with functions in relation to town and country planning.]

NORTHERN IRELAND ACT 1974
(1974, c. 28)

An Act to provide for the dissolution of the existing Northern Ireland Assembly and its prorogation until dissolution; to make temporary provision for the government of Northern

Ireland; to provide for the election and holding of a Constitutional Convention in Northern Ireland; and for purposes connected with those matters [17 July 1974]

Territorial extent Northern Ireland

1 Dissolution and prorogation of existing Assembly and temporary provision for government of Northern Ireland

(1) Her Majesty may by Order in Council dissolve the Assembly elected under the Northern Ireland Assembly Act 1973; and subsection (7) of section 27 of the Northern Ireland Constitution Act 1973 (power to appoint day for new elections etc) shall have effect on the dissolution of that Assembly under this section as if it had been dissolved by Her Majesty under subsection (5) of that section.

(2) . . .

(3) The provisions of Schedule 1 to this Act shall have effect with respect to the exercise of legislative, executive and other functions in relation to Northern Ireland during the interim period specified by or under subsection (4) below.

(4) The interim period shall be the period of one year beginning with the passing of this Act but the Secretary of State may by order direct that it shall continue until a date after, or end on a date earlier than, the date on which it would otherwise expire (whether by virtue of this subsection or of a previous order thereunder).

(5) No order under subsection (4) above shall provide for the interim period to continue until a date more than one year after the date on which it would otherwise expire.

(6) The power to make an order under subsection (4) above shall be exercisable by statutory instrument; and no order shall be made under that subsection unless a draft of it has been approved by resolution of each House of Parliament.

2 . . .

Section 1(3) SCHEDULE 1

TEMPORARY PROVISION FOR GOVERNMENT OF NORTHERN IRELAND

Legislative functions

1.—(1) During the interim period—

(a) no Measure shall be passed by the Assembly; and

(b) Her Majesty may by Order in Council make laws for Northern Ireland, and in particular, provision for any matter for which the Constitution Act authorises or requires provision to be made by Measure.

(2) No recommendation shall be made to Her Majesty to make any Order in Council under this paragraph containing a provision in relation to which the Secretary of State would be precluded by section 5(1) of the Constitution Act from giving his consent if it were contained in a proposed Measure.

(3) The power to make an Order in Council under this paragraph includes power to vary or revoke a previous Order made thereunder.

(4) No recommendation shall be made to Her Majesty to make an Order in Council under this paragraph unless either—

(a) a draft of the Order has been approved by resolution of each House of Parliament; or

(b) the Order declares that it has been made to appear to Her Majesty that by reason of urgency the Order requires to be made without a draft having been so approved.

(5) Any Order in Council under this paragraph, other than an Order of which a draft has been approved by resolution of each House of Parliament, shall be laid before Parliament after being made and, if at the end of the period of forty days after the date on which it is made the Order has not been approved by resolution of each House, shall

then cease to have effect (but without prejudice to anything previously done under the Order or to the making of a new Order).

(6) In reckoning the period mentioned in sub-paragraph (5) above no account shall be taken of any time during which Parliament is dissolved or prorogued or during which both Houses are adjourned for more than four days.

(7) References to Measures in any enactment or instrument (whether passed or made before or after the passing of this Act) shall, so far as the context permits, be deemed to include references to Orders in Council under this paragraph.

(8) Orders in Council under this paragraph may be omitted from any annual edition of statutory instruments required to be prepared under regulations made by virtue of section 8 of the Statutory Instruments Act 1946.

★ ★ ★ ★ ★

HOUSE OF COMMONS DISQUALIFICATION ACT 1975
(1975, c. 24)

An Act to consolidate certain enactments relating to disqualification for membership of the House of Commons [8 May 1975]

Territorial extent United Kingdom

1 Disqualification of holders of certain offices and places

(1) Subject to the provisions of this Act, a person is disqualified for membership of the House of Commons who for the time being—

(a) holds any of the judicial offices specified in Part I of Schedule 1 to this Act;

(b) is employed in the civil service of the Crown, whether in an established capacity or not, and whether for the whole or part of his time;

(c) is a member of any of the regular armed forces of the Crown or the Ulster Defence Regiment;

(d) is a member of any police force maintained by a police authority;

(e) is a member of the legislature of any country or territory outside the Commonwealth; or

(f) holds any office described in Part II or Part III of Schedule 1.

(2), (3) ★ ★ ★ ★ ★

(4) Except as provided by this Act, a person shall not be disqualified for membership of the House of Commons by reason of his holding an office or place of profit under the Crown or any other office or place; and a person shall not be disqualified for appointment to or for holding any office or place by reason of his being a member of that House.

2 Ministerial offices

(1) Not more than ninety-five persons being the holders of offices specified in Schedule 2 to this Act (in this sectin referred to as Ministerial offices) shall be entitled to sit and vote in the House of Commons at any one time.

(2) If at any time the number of members of the House of Commons who are holders of Ministerial offices exceeds the number entitled to sit and vote in that House under subsection (1) above, none except any who were both members of that House and holders of Ministerial offices before the excess occurred shall sit or vote therein until the number has been reduced, by death, resignation or otherwise, to the number entitled to sit and vote as aforesaid.

(3) A person holding a Ministerial office is not disqualified by this Act by reason of any office held by him ex officio as the holder of that Ministerial office.

3 Reserve and Auxiliary Forces etc. ★ ★ ★ ★ ★

4 Stewardship of Chiltern Hundreds, etc.
For the purposes of the provisions of this Act relating to the vacation of the seat of a member of the House of Commons who becomes disqualified by this Act for membership of that House, the office of steward or bailiff of Her Majesty's three Chiltern Hundreds of Stoke, Desborough and Burnham, or of the Manor of Northstead, shall be treated as included among the offices described in Part III of Schedule 1 to this Act.

5 Power to amend Schedule 1
(1) If at any time it is resolved by the House of Commons that Schedule 1 to this Act be amended, whether by the addition or omission of any office or the removal of any office from one Part of the Schedule to another, or by altering the description of any office specified therein, Her Majesty may by Order in Council amend that Schedule accordingly.
(2) ★ ★ ★ ★ ★

6 Effects of disqualification and provision for relief
(1) Subject to any order made by the House of Commons under this section,—
(a) if any person disqualified by this Act for membership of that House, or for membership for a particular constituency, is elected as a member of that House, or as a member for that constituency, as the case may be, his election shall be void; and
(b) if any person being a member of that House becomes disqualified by this Act for membership for the constituency for which he is sitting, his seat shall be vacated.
(2) If, in a case falling or alleged to fall within subsection (1) above, it appears to the House of Commons that the grounds of disqualification or alleged disqualification under this Act which subsisted or arose at the material time have been removed, and that it is otherwise proper so to do, that House may by order direct that any such disqualification incurred on those grounds at that time shall be disregarded for the purposes of this section.
(3), (4) ★ ★ ★ ★ ★

7 Jurisdiction of Privy Council as to disqualification
(1) Any person who claims that a person purporting to be a member of the House of Commons is disqualified by this Act, or has been so disqualified at any time since his (election, may apply to Her Majesty in Council, in accordance with such rules as Her Majesty in Council may prescribe, for a declaration to that effect.
(2) Section 3 of the Judicial Committee Act 1833 (reference to the Judicial Committee of the Privy Council of appeals to Her Majesty in Council) shall apply to any application under this section as it applies to an appeal to Her Majesty in Council from a court.
(3)-(5) ★ ★ ★ ★ ★

8, 9 ★ ★ ★ ★ ★

10 Savings as to disqualification of priests in holy orders etc.
Nothing in this Act shall be construed as affecting the enactments relating to the disqualification for membership of the House of Commons of priests in holy orders or ministers of any religious denomination.

★ ★ ★ ★ ★

Section 2

SCHEDULE 2
MINISTERIAL OFFICE

Prime Minister and First Lord of the Treasury.
Lord President of the Council.

Lord Privy Seal.
Chancellor of the Duchy of Lancaster.
Paymaster General.
President of the Board of Trade.
Secretary of State.
Chancellor of the Exchequer.
Minister of Agriculture, Fisheries and Food.
Minister of State.
Chief Secretary to the Treasury.
Minister in charge of a public department of Her Majesty's Government in the United Kingdom (if not within the other provisions of this Schedule).
Attorney General.
Lord Advocate.
Solicitor General.
Solicitor General for Scotland.
Parliamentary Secretary to the Treasury.
Financial Secretary to the Treasury.
Parliamentary Secretary in a Government Department other than the Treasury, or not in a department.
Junior Lord of the Treasury.
Treasurer of Her Majesty's Household.
Comptroller of Her Majesty's Household.
Vice-Chamberlain of Her Majesty's Household.
Assistant Government Whip.

MINISTERIAL AND OTHER SALARIES ACT 1975
(1975, c. 27)

An Act to consolidate the enactments relating to the salaries of Ministers and Opposition Leaders and Chief Whips and to other matters connected therewith [8 May 1975]

Territorial extent United Kingdom

1 Salaries

(1) Subject to the provisions of this Act—

(a) there shall be paid to the holder of any Ministerial office specified in Schedule 1 to this Act such salary as is provided for by that Schedule; and

(b) there shall be paid to the Leaders and Whips of the Opposition such salaries as are provided for by Schedule 2 to this Act.

(2) There shall be paid to the Lord Chancellor a salary (which shall be charged on and paid out of the Consolidated Fund of the United Kingdom) at such rate as together with the salary payable to him as Speaker of the House of Lords will amount to [[£2,500] a year more than the salary payable to the Lord Chief Justice], . . .

(3) There shall be paid to the Speaker of the House of Commons a salary (which shall be charged on and paid out of the Consolidated Fund of the United Kingdom) of [£60,000] a year; and on a dissolution of Parliament the Speaker of the House of Commons at the time of the dissolution shall for this purpose be deemed to remain Speaker until a Speaker is chosen by the New Parliament.

(4), (5) ★ ★ ★ ★ ★

2 Opposition Leaders and Whips

(1) In this Act "Leader of the Opposition" means, in relation to either House of Parliament, that Member of that House who is for the time being the Leader in that House of the party in opposition to Her Majesty's Government having the greatest

numerical strength in the House of Commons; and "Chief Opposition Whip" means, in relation to either House of Parliament, the person for the time being nominated as such by the Leader of the Opposition in that House; and "Assistant Opposition Whip", in relation to the House of Commons, means a person for the time being nominated as such, and to be paid as such, by the Leader of the Opposition in the House of Commons.

(2) If any doubt arises as to which is or was at any material time the party in opposition to Her Majesty's Government having the greatest numerical strength in the House of Commons, or as to who is or was at any material time the leader in that House of such a party, the question shall be decided for the purposes of this Act by the Speaker of the House of Commons, and his decision, certified in writing under his hand, shall be final and conclusive.

(3) If any doubt arises as to who is or was at any material time the Leader in the House of Lords of the said party, the question shall be decided for the purposes of this Act by the Lord Chancellor, and his decision, certified in writing under his hand, shall be final and conclusive.

3 ★★★★★

4 Interpretation

(1) In this Act—

"Junior Lord of the Treasury" means any Lord Commissioner of the Treasury other than the First Lord and the Chancellor of the Exchequer;

"Minister of State" and "Parliamentary Secretary" have the same meanings as in the House of Commons Disqualification Act 1975.

(2) ★★★★★

★★★★★

MINISTERS OF THE CROWN ACT 1975
(1975, c. 26)

An Act to consolidate the enactments relating to the redistribution of functions between Ministers of the Crown, the alteration of the style and title of such Ministers and certain other provisions about such Ministers [8 May 1975]

Territorial extent United Kingdom

1 Power by Order in Council to transfer functions of Ministers

(1) Her Majesty may by Order in Council—

(a) provide for the transfer to any Minister of the Crown of any functions previously exercisable by another Minister of the Crown;

(b) provide for the dissolution of the government department in the charge of any Minister of the Crown and the transfer to or distribution among such other Minister or Ministers of the Crown as may be specified in the Order of any functions previously exercisable by the Minister in charge of that department;

(c) direct that functions of any Minister of the Crown shall be exercisable concurrently with another Minister of the Crown, or shall cease to be so exercisable.

(2) An Order in Council under this section may contain such incidental, consequential and supplemental provisions as may be necessary or expedient for the purpose of giving full effect to the Order, including provisions—

(a) for the transfer of any property, rights and liabilities held, enjoyed or incurred by any Minister of the Crown in connection with any functions transferred or distributed;

(b) for the carrying on and completion by or under the authority of the Minister to whom any functions are transferred of anything commenced by or under the authority of a minister of the Crown before the date when the Order takes effect;

(c) for such adaptations of the enactments relating to any functions transferred as may be necessary to enable them to be exercised by the Minister to whom they are transfered and his officers;

(d) for making in the enactments regulating the number of offices in respect of which salaries may be paid or in section 2 of, and Schedule 2 to, the House of Commons Disqualification Act 1975 (which regulate the number of office holders who may be elected, and sit and vote, as members of the House of Commons), such modifications as may be expedient by reason of any transfer of functions or dissolution of a Department effected by the Order;

(e) for the substitution of the Minister to whom functions are transferred for any other Minister of the Crown in any instrument, contract, or legal proceedings made or commenced before the date when the Order takes effect.

(3) No modifications shall be made by virtue of paragraph (d) of subsection (2) above, in any of the enactments mentioned in that paragraph, so as to increase the amount of any salary which may be paid, or the aggregate number of persons to whom salaries may be paid, under those enactments or the aggregate number of persons capable thereunder of sitting and voting as Members of the House of Commons.

(4) Where by any Order made under this section provision is made for the transfer of functions in respect of which any Minister may sue or be sued by virtue of any enactment, the Order shall make any provision which may be required for enabling the Minister to whom those functions are transferred to sue or be sued in like manner.

2, 3 * * * * *

4 Change of title of Ministers

If Her Majesty is pleased by Order in Council to direct that any change shall be made in the style and title of a Minister of the Crown, the Order may contain provisions substituting the new style and title—

(a) in the enactments (including those mentioned in section 1(2)(d) above) relating to the Minister;

(b) in any instrument, contract, or legal proceedings made or commenced before the date when the Order takes effect.

5 Supplementary provisions as to Orders

(1) No Order in Council which provides for the dissolution of a government department shall be made under this Act unless, after copies of the draft thereof have been laid before Parliament, each House presents an Address to Her Majesty praying that the Order be made.

(2) An Order in Council under this Act, not being an Order made in pursuance of such an Address as aforesaid, shall be laid before Parliament and shall be subject to annulment in pursuance of a resolution of either House of Parliament.

(3), (4) * * * * *

(5) Nothing in this Act shall prejudice any power exercisable by virtue of the prerogative of the Crown in relation to the functions of Ministers of the Crown.

(6) * * * * *

* * * * *

SEX DISCRIMINATION ACT 1975
(1975, c. 65)

An Act to render unlawful certain kinds of sex discrimination and discrimination on the ground of marriage, and establish a Commission with the function of working towards the elimination of such discrimination and promoting equality of opportunity between men and women generally; and for related purposes [12 November 1975]

Territorial extent England and Wales, Scotland

* * * * *

PART V
GENERAL EXCEPTIONS FROM PARTS II TO IV

52 Acts safeguarding national security

(1) Nothing in Parts II to IV shall render unlawful an act done for the purpose of safeguarding national security.

(2) A certificate purporting to be signed by or on behalf of a Minister of the Crown and certifying that an act specified in the certificate was done for the purpose of safeguarding national security shall be conclusive evidence that it was done for that purpose.

(3) A document purporting to be a certificate such as is mentioned in subsection (2) shall be received in evidence and, unless the contrary is proved, shall be deemed to be such a certificate.

★★★★★

Note: Subsections (2) and (3) are disapplied in relation to Part II of the Act (employment) and to vocational training, by SI 1988 No. 249.

RACE RELATIONS ACT 1976
(1976, c. 74)

An Act to make fresh provision with respect to discrimination on racial grounds and relations between people of different racial groups; and to make in the Sex Discrimination Act 1975 amendments for bringing provisions in that Act relating to its administration and enforcement into conformity with the corresponding provisons in this Act [22 November 1976]

Territorial extent England and Wales, Scotland

★★★★★

PART VI
GENERAL EXEMPTIONS FROM PARTS II TO IV

42 Acts safeguarding national security

Nothing in Parts II to IV shall render unlawful an act done for the purpose of safeguarding national security.

PART VIII
ENFORCEMENT

Evidence

69 Evidence

(1) ★★★★★

(2) In any proceedings under this Act a certificate signed by or on behalf of a Minister of the Crown and certifying—

(a) that any arrangements or conditions specified in the certificate were made, approved or imposed by a Minister of the Crown and were in operation at a time or throughout a period so specified; or

(b) that an act specified in the certificate was done for the purpose of safeguarding national security,

shall be conclusive evidence of the matters certified.

(3) A document purporting to be a certificate such as is mentioned in subsection (2) shall be received in evidence and, unless the contrary is proved, shall be deemed to be such a certificate.

70 . . .

PART X
SUPPLEMENTAL

71 Local Authorities: general statutory duty

(1) Without prejudice to their obligation to comply with any other provision of this Act, it shall be the duty of every local authority to make appropriate arangements with a view to securing that their various functions are carried out with due regard to the need—

(a) to eliminate unlawful racial discrimination; and

(b) to promote equality of opportunity and good relations, between persons of different racial groups;

[and in this section "local authority" includes ... [a police authority established under section 3 of the Police Act 1996 and] a joint authority established by Part IV of the Local Government Act 1985.]

[The Broads Authority [and every National Park Authority] shall be treated as a local authority for the purposes of this section.]

[(2) In this section "local authority" in relation to Scotland means a council constituted under section 2 of the Local Government etc. (Scotland) Act 1994 ("the 1994 Act") and includes—

(a) a joint board and a joint committee within the meaning of the Local Government (Scotland) Act 1973;

(b) the staff commission established by virtue of section 12 of the 1994 Act;

(c) a water and sewerage authority within the meaning of the 1994 Act; and

(d) the Strathclyde Passenger Transport Authority.]

★ ★ ★ ★ ★

CRIMINAL LAW ACT 1977
(1977, c. 45)

An Act to amend the law of England and Wales with respect to criminal conspiracy; to make new provision in that law, in place of the provisions of the common law and the Statutes of Forcible Entry, for restricting the use or threat of violence for securing entry into any premises and for penalising unauthorised entry or remaining on premises in certain circumstances; otherwise to amend the criminal law, including the law with respect to the administration of criminal justice; to provide for the alteration of certain pecuniary and other limits; to amend section 9(4) of the Administration of Justice Act 1973, the Legal Aid Act 1974, the Rabies Act 1974 and the Diseases of Animals (Northern Ireland) Order 1975 and the law about juries and coroners' inquests; and for conencted purposes [29 July 1977]

Territorial extent England and Wales

PART I
CONSPIRACY

1 The offence of conspiracy

[(1) Subject to the following provisions of this Part of this Act, if a person agrees with any other person or persons that a course of conduct shall be pursued which, if the agreement is carried out in accordance with their intentions, either—

(a) will necessarily amount to or involve the commission of any offence or offences by one or more of the parties to the agreement, or

(b) would do so but for the existence of facts which render the commission of the offence or any of the offences impossible,

he is guilty of conspiracy to commit the offence in question.]

[(1A) ★ ★ ★ ★ ★]

(2) Where liability for any offence may be incurred without knowledge on the part of the person committing it of any particular fact or circumstances necessary for the commission of the offence, a person shall nevertheless not be guilty of conspiracy to commit that offence by virtue of subsection (1) above unless he and at least one other party to the agreement intend or know that the fact or circumstances shall or will exist at the time when the conduct constituting the offence is to take place.

(3) ...

(4), [(5), (6)] ★★★★★

5 Abolitions, savings, transitional provisions, consequential amendment and repeals

(1) Subject to the following provisions of this section, the offence of conspiracy at common law is hereby abolished.

(2) Subsection (1) above shall not affect the offence of conspiracy at common law so far as relates to conspiracy to defraud, ...

(3) Subsection (1) above shall not affect the offence of conspiracy at common law if and in so far as it may be committed by entering into an agreement to engage in conduct which—

(a) tends to corrupt public morals or outrages public decency; but

(b) would not amount to or involve the commission of an offence if carried out by a single person otherwise than in pursuance of an agreement.

(4)-(9) ★★★★★

(10), (11) ...

★★★★★

EUROPEAN PARLIAMENT ELECTIONS ACT 1978
(1978, c. 10)

An Act to make provision for and in connection with the election of representatives to the Parliament of the European Communities, and to prevent any treaty providing for any increase in the powers of the Parliament from being ratified by the United Kingdom unless approved by Act of Parliament [5 May 1978]

Territorial extent United Kingdom

Note This Act was originally entitled the European Assembly Elections Act. References to the Assembly should now be read as references to the Parliament: European Communities (Amendment) Act 1986, s. 3(1).

1 Election of representatives to the European Parliament

The representatives of the people of the United Kingdom in the Parliament of the European Communities ... shall be elected in accordance with this Act.

2 Number of representatives

The number of representatives to the Parliament to be elected in the United Kingdom shall be [87]; and of those representatives—

(a) [71] shall be elected in England;

(b) 8 shall be elected in Scotland;

(c) [5] shall be elected in Wales; and

(d) 3 shall be elected in Northern Ireland.

3 Method of election

Parliamentary elections shall be held and conducted in accordance with the provisions of Schedule 1 to this Act (with Schedule 2) under the simple majority system (for Great Britain) and the single transferable vote system (for Northern Ireland).

4, 5 ★★★★★

6 Parliamentary approval of treaties increasing Parliament's powers

(1) No treaty which provides for any increase in the powers of the Parliament shall be ratified by the United Kingdom unless it has been approved by an Act of Parliament.

(2) In this section "treaty" includes any international agreement, and any protocol or annex to a treaty or international agreement.

Note Section 3(4) of the European Communities (Amendment) Act 1986 provides that for the purposes of this section the Single European Act is approved. As to section 6(1) above see section 1 of the European Communities (Amendment) Act 1993. See also section 2 of the European Union (Accessions) Act 1994.

★★★★★

PROTECTION OF CHILDREN ACT 1978
(1978, c. 37)

An Act to prevent the exploitation of children by making indecent photographs of them; and to penalise the distribution, showing and advertisement of such indecent photographs

[20 July 1978]

Territorial extent England and Wales

1 Indecent photographs of children

(1) It is an offence for a person—

(a) to take, or permit to be taken [or to make any indecent photograph [or pseudo-photograph] of a child . . . or

(b) to distribute or show such indecent photograph [or pseudo-photograph]; or

(c) to have in his possession such indecent photographs [or pseudo-photographs], with a view to their being distributed or shown by himself or others; or

(d) to publish or cause to be published any advertisement likely to be understood as conveying that the advertiser distributes or shows such indecent photographs [or pseudo-photographs] or intends to do so.

(2) For purposes of this Act, a person is to be regarded as distributing an indecent photograph [or pseudo-photograph] if he parts with possession of it to, or exposes or offers it for acquisition by, another person.

(3) Proceedings for an offence under this Act shall not be instituted except by or with the consent of the Director of Public Prosecutions.

(4) Where a person is charged with an offence under subsection (1)(b) or (c), it shall be a defence for him to prove—

(a) that he had a legitimate reason for distributing or showing the photographs [or pseudo-photographs] or (as the case may be) having them in his possession; or

(b) that he had not himself seen the photographs [or pseudo-photographs] and did not know, nor had any cause to suspect, them to be indecent.

(5), (6) ★★★★★

2 Evidence

(1), (2) . . .

(3) In proceedings under this Act [relating to indecent photographs of children] a person is to be taken as having been a child at any material time if it appears from the evidence as a whole that he was then under the age of 16.

3 ★★★★★

4 Entry, search and seizure

(1) The following applies where a justice of the peace is satisfied by information on oath, laid by or on behalf of the Director of Public Prosecutions or by a constable, that

there is reasonable ground for suspecting that, in any premises in the petty sessions area for which he acts, there [is an indecent photograph [or pseudo-photograph] of a child].

(2) The justice may issue a warrant under his hand authorising any constable to enter (if need be by force) and search the premises ... and to seize and remove any articles which he believes (with reasonable cause) to be or include indecent photographs [or pseudo-photographs] of children ....

(3) Articles seized under the authority of the warrant, and not returned to the occupier of the premises, shall be brought before a justice of the peace acting for the same petty sessions area as the justice who issued the warrant.

(4) ★★★★★

5 ★★★★★

6 Punishments

(1) Offences under this Act shall be punishable either on conviction on indictment or on summary conviction.

(2) A person convicted on indictment of any offence under this Act shall be liable to imprisonment for a term of not more than three years, or to a fine or to both.

(3) A person convicted summarily of any offence under this Act shall be liable—

(a) to imprisonment for a term not exceeding six months; or

(b) to a fine not exceeding the prescribed sum for the purposes of [section 32 of the Magistrates' Courts Act 1980] (punishment on summary conviction of offences triable either way: £1,000 or other sum substituted by order under that Act), or to both.

7 Interpretation

(1)-(5) ★★★★★

[(6) "Child", subject to subsection (8), means a person under the age of 16.

(7) "Pseudo-photograph" means an image, whether made by computer-graphics or otherwise howsoever, which appears to be a photograph.

(8) If the impression conveyed by a pseudo-photograph is that the person shown is a child, the pseudo-photograph shall be treated for all purposes of this Act as showing a child and so shall a pseudo-photograph where the predominant impression conveyed is that the person shown is a child notwithstanding that some of the physical characteristics shown are those of an adult.

(9) References to an indecent pseudo-photograph include—

(a) a copy of an indecent pseudo-photograph; and

(b) data stored on a computer disc or by other electronic means which is capable of conversion into a pseudo-photograph.]

8, 9 ★★★★★

SUPPRESSION OF TERRORISM ACT 1978
(1978, c. 26)

An Act to give effect to the European Convention on the Suppression of Terrorism; to amend the law relating to the extradition of criminals and the obtaining of evidence for criminal proceedings outside the United Kingdom; to confer jurisdiction in respect of certain offences committed outside the United Kingdom; and for connected purposes [30 June 1978]

Territorial extent United Kingdom

1 Cases in which certain offences are not to be regarded as of a political character

(1) This section applies to any offence of which a person is accused or has been convicted outside the United Kingdom if the act constituting the offence, or the equivalent act, would, if it took place in any part of the United Kingdom or, in the case

of an extra-territorial offence, in corresponding circumstances outside the United Kingdom, constitute one of the offences listed in Schedule 1 to this Act.

(2) For the purposes mentioned in subsection (3) below—

(a) no offence to which this section applies shall be regarded as an offence of a political character; and

(b) no proceedings in respect of an offence to which this section applies shall be regarded as a criminal matter of a political character or as criminal proceedings of a political character.

(3) . . .

(a) . . .

(b) . . .

(c) the purposes of the Backing of Warrants (Republic of Ireland) Act 1965 in relation to any warrant issued in the Republic of Ireland to which this paragraph applies by virtue of an order under subsection (4) below; and

(d) the purposes of section 5 of the Extradition Act 1873 (evidence for foreign criminal matters) and section 5 of the Evidence (Proceedings in Other Jurisdictions) Act 1975 (evidence for criminal proceedings outside the United Kingdom) in relation to—

(i) any criminal proceedings instituted in a convention country (not being the Republic of Ireland) after the coming into force of this sub-paragraph; and

(ii) any criminal proceedings in the Republic of Ireland to which this sub-paragraph applies by virtue of an order under subsection (4) below.

(4), (5) ★★★★★

2 ★★★★★

3 . . .

4 Jurisdiction in respect of offences committed outside United Kingdom

(1) If a person, whether a citizen of the United Kingdom and Colonies or not, does in a convention country any act which, if he had done it in a part of the United Kingdom, would have made him guilty in that part of the United Kingdom of—

(a) an offence mentioned in paragraph 1, 2, 4, 5, 10, 11, [11B,] 12, 13, 14 or 15 of Schedule 1 to this Act; or

(b) an offence of attempting to commit any offence so mentioned,

he shall, in that part of the United Kingdom, be guilty of the offence or offences aforesaid of which the act would have made him guilty if he had done it there.

(2) ★★★★★

(3) If a person who is a national of a convention country but not a citizen of the United Kingdom and Colonies does outside the United Kingdom and that convention country any act which makes him in that convention country guilty of an offence and which, if he had been a citizen of the United Kingdom and Colonies, would have made him in any part of the United Kingdom guilty of an offence mentioned in paragraph 1, 2 or 13 of Schedule 1 to this Act, he shall, in any part of the United Kingdom, be guilty of the offence or offences aforesaid of which the act would have made him guilty if he had been such a citizen.

(4) Proceedings for an offence which [(disregarding the provisions of the Internationally Protected Persons Act 1978)] [, the Nuclear Material (Offences) Act 1983 and the United Nations Personnel Act 1997] would not be an offence apart from this section shall not be instituted—

(a) in Northern Ireland, except by or with the consent of the Attorney General for Northern Ireland; or

(b) in England and Wales, except by or with the consent of the Attorney General;

and references to a consent provision in Article 7(3) to (5) of the Prosecution of Offences (Northern Ireland) Order 1972 (which relates to consents to prosecutions) shall include so much of this subsection as precedes paragraph (b).

(5)-(7) ★★★★★

5 Power to apply provisions of Act to non-convention countries

(1) In the case of any country which, not being a convention country, is either—

(a) a designated Commonwealth country within the meaning of the Fugitive Offenders Act 1967; or

(b) a foreign state with which there is in force an arrangement of the kind described in section 2 of the Extradition Act 1870 [or Part I of the Criminal Justice Act 1988] with respect to the surrender to that state of fugitive criminals; or

(c) a United Kingdom dependency within the meaning of the Fugitive Offenders Act 1967,

the Secretary of State may by order direct—

(i) in the case of a country within paragraph (a) or (b) above, that all or any of the provisions of this Act which would, apart from this section, apply only in relation to convention countries shall apply in relation to that country (subject to such exceptions, if any, as may be specified in the order) as they apply in relation to a covention country; or

(ii) in the case of a country within paragraph (c) above, that the provisions of section 4 above shall so apply in relation to that country;

and while such an order is in force in the case of any country, the provisions in question shall apply in relation to it accordingly.

(2) The Secretary of State may, at any time when the Republic of Ireland is not a convention country, by order direct that section 4 above shall apply in relation to the Republic as if it were a convention country; and while such an order is in force, that section shall apply in relation to the Republic accordingly.

(3) An order under subsection (2) above shall, unless previously revoked, cease to have effect if the Republic of Ireland subsequently becomes a convention country.

★★★★★

Sections 1, 4

SCHEDULE 1
LIST OF OFFENCES

Common law offences

1. Murder.
2. Manslaughter or culpable homicide.
3. Rape.
4. Kidnapping, abduction or plagium.
5. False imprisonment.
6. Assault occasioning actual bodily harm or causing injury.
7. Wilful fire-raising.

Offences against the person

8. An offence under any of the following provisions of the Offences against the Person Act 1861—

(a) section 18 (wounding with intent to cause grievous bodily harm);

(b) section 20 (causing grievous bodily harm);

(c) section 21 (attempting to choke etc. in order to commit or assist in the committing of any indictable offence);

(d) section 22 (using chloroform etc. to commit or assist in the committing of any indictable offence);

(e) section 23 (maliciously administering poison etc. so as to endanger life or inflict grievous bodily harm);

(f) section 24 (maliciously administering poison etc. with intent to injure etc.);

(g) section 48 (rape).

9. An offence under section 1 of the Sexual Offences Act 1956 (rape).

Abduction

10. An offence under any of the following provisions of the Offences against the Person Act 1861—

(a) section 55 (abduction of unmarried girl under 16);

(b) section 56 (child-stealing or receiving stolen child).

11. An offence under section 20 of the Sexual Offences Act 1956 (abduction of unmarried girl under 16).

[*Taking of hostages*

11A. An offence under the Taking of Hostages Act 1982.]

[11B. An offence under section 2 of the Child Abduction Act 1984 (abduction of child by person other than parent etc.) or any corresponding provision in force in Northern Ireland.]

Explosives

12. An offence under any of the following provisions of the Offences against the Person Act 1861—

(a) section 28 (causing bodily injury by gunpowder);

(b) section 29 (causing gunpowder to explode etc. with intent to do grievous bodily harm).

(c) section 30 (placing gunpowder near a building etc. with intent to cause bodily injury).

13. An offence under any of the following provisions of the Explosive Substances Act 1883—

(a) section 2 (causing explosion likely to endanger life or property);

(b) section 3 (doing any act with intent to cause such an explosion, conspiring to cause such an explosion, or making or possessing explosive with intent to endanger life or property).

Firearms

14. The following offences under the Firearms Act 1968—

(a) an offence under section 16 (possession of firearm with intent to injure);

(b) an offence under subsection (1) of section 17 (use of firearm or imitation firearm to resist arrest) involving the use or attempted use of a firearm within the meaning of that section.

15. The following offences under the [Firearms (Northern Ireland) Order 1981]

(a) an offence under [Article 17] consisting of a person's having in his possession any firearm or ammunition (within the meaning of [that Article]) with intent by means thereof to endanger life, or to enable another person by means thereof to endanger life;

(b) an offence under [paragraph (1) of Article 18] (use of firearm or imitation firearm to resist arrest) involving the use or attempted use of a firearm within the meaning of [that Article].

Offences against property

16. An offence under section 1(2) of the Criminal Damage Act 1971 (destroying or damaging property intending to endanger life or being reckless as to danger to life).

17. An offence under Article 3(2) of the Criminal Damage (Northern Ireland) Order 1977 (destroying or damaging property intending to endanger life or being reckless as to danger to life).

Offences in relation to aircraft

[18. An offence under Part I of the Aviation Security Act 1982 (other than an offence under section 4 or 7 of that Act.]

[18A. An offence under section 1 of the Aviation and Maritime Security Act 1990.

Offences relating to ships and fixed platforms

18B. An offence under Part II of the Aviation and Maritime Security Act 1990 (other than an offence under section 15 of that Act).]

[Financing Terrorism

19. ...

19A. An offence under Part III of the Prevention of Terrorism (Temporary Provisions) Act 1989.]

Attempts

20. An offence of attempting to commit any offence mentioned in a preceding paragraph of this Schedule.

* * * * *

HIGHWAYS ACT 1980
(1980, c. 66)

An Act to consolidate the Highways Acts 1959 to 1971 and related enactments with amendments to give effect to recommendations of the Law Commission [13 November 1980]

Territorial extent England and Wales

* * * * *

Obstruction of highways and streets

137 Penalty for wilful obstruction

(1) If a person, without lawful authority or excuse, in any way wilfully obstructs the free passage along a highway he is guilty of an offence and liable to a fine not exceeding [level 3 on the standard scale].

(2) ...

* * * * *

MAGISTRATES' COURTS ACT 1980
(1980, c. 43)

An Act to consolidate certain enactments relating to the jurisdiction of, and the practice and procedure before, magistrates' courts and the functions of justices' clerks, and to matters connected therewith, with amendments to give effect to recommendations of the Law Commission [1 August 1980]

Territorial extent England and Wales

PART I
CRIMINAL JURISDICTION AND PROCEDURE

Jurisdiction to issue process and deal with charges

1 Issue of summons to accused or warrant for his arrest

(1) Upon an information being laid before a justice of the peace for an area to which this section applies that any person has, or is suspected of having, committed an offence,

the justice may, in any of the events mentioned in subsection (2) below, but subject to subsections (3) to (5) below,—

(a) issue a summons directed to that person requiring him to appear before a magistrates' court for the area to answer to the information, or

(b) issue a warrant to arrest that person and bring him before a magistrates' court for the area or such magistrates' court as is provided in subsection (5) below.

(2) * * * * *

(3) No warrant shall be issued under this section unless the information is in writing and substantiated on oath.

(4) No warrant shall be issued under this section for the arrest of any person who has attained the age of 18 years unless—

(a) the offence to which the warrant relates is an indictable offence or is punishable with imprisonment, or

(b) the person's address is not sufficiently established for a summons to be served on him.

(5)-(7) * * * * *

(8) The areas to which this section applies are [any commission area in England, or preserved county in Wales].

* * * * *

[6 Application for dismissal

(1) Where a notice of the prosecution case has been given in respect of proceedings before a magistrates' court, the accused, or any of them, may, within the prescribed period, or within such further period as the court may on application allow, make an application in writing to the court ("an application for dismissal") for the charge or, as the case may be, any of the charges to be dismissed.]

(2)-(14) * * * * *

* * * * *

[8A Reporting restrictions

(1) Except as provided in this section, it shall not be lawful—

(a) to publish in Great Britain a written report of an application for dismissal to a magistrates' court under section 6 above; or

(b) to include in a relevant programme for reception in Great Britain a report of such an application,

if (in either case) the report contains any matter other than matter permitted by this section.

(2) A magistrates' court may, on an application for the purpose made with reference to proceedings on an application for dismissal, order that subsection (1) above shall not apply to reports of those proceedings.

(3) Where in the case of two or more accused one of them objects to the making of an order under subsection (2) above, the magistrates' court shall make the order if, and only if, the court is satisfied, after hearing the representations of the accused, that it is in the interests of justice to do so.

(4) An order under subsection (2) above shall not apply to reports of proceedings under subsection (3) above, but any decision of the court to make or not to make such an order may be contained in reports published or included in a relevant programme before the time authorised by subsection (5) below.

(5) It shall not be unlawful under this section to publish or include in a relevant programme a report of an application for dismissal containing any matter other than matter permitted by subsection (9) below where the application is successful.

(6) Where—

(a) two or more persons are charged in the same proceedings; and

(b) applications for dismissal are made by more than one of them,
subsection (5) above shall have effect as if for the words "the application is" there were substituted the words "all the applications are".

(7) It shall not be unlawful under this section to publish or include in a relevant programme a report of an unsuccessful application for dismissal at the conclusion of the trial of the person charged, or of the last of the persons charged to be tried.

(8) Where, at any time during its consideration of an application for dismissal, the court proceeds to try summarily the case of one or more of the accused under section 25(3) or (7) below, while dismissing the application for dismissal of the other accused or one or more of the other accused, it shall not be unlawful under this section to publish or include in a relevant programme as part of a report of the summary trial, after the court determines to proceed as aforesaid, a report of so much of the application for dismissal containing any matter other than matter permitted by subsection (9) below as takes place before the determination.

(9) The following matters may be published or included in a relevant programme without an order under subsection (2) above before the time authorised by subsection (5) or (7) above, that is to say—

(a) the identity of the magistrates' court and the names of the justices composing it;

(b) the names, age, home address and occupation of the accused;

(c) the offence, or offences, or a summary of them, with which the accused is or are charged;

(d) the names of legal representatives engaged in the proceedings;

(e) where the proceedings are adjourned, the date and place to which they are adjourned;

(f) the arrangements as to bail;

(g) whether legal aid was granted to the accused or any of the accused.

(10) The addresses that may be published or included in a relevant programme under subsection (9) are addresses—

(a) at any relevant time; and

(b) at the time of their publication or inclusion in a relevant programme.

(11) If a report is published or included in a relevant programme in contravention of this section, the following persons, that is to say—

(a) in the case of a publication of a written report as part of a newspaper or periodical, any proprietor, editor or publisher of the newspaper or periodical;

(b) in the case of a publication of a written report otherwise than as part of a newspaper or periodical, the person who publishes it;

(c) in the case of the inclusion of a report in a relevant programme, any body corporate which is engaged in providing the service in which the programme is included and any person having functions in relation to the programme corresponding to those of the editor of a newspaper,

shall be liable on summary conviction to a fine not exceeding level 5 on the standard scale.

(12) Proceedings for an offence under this section shall not, in England and Wales, be instituted otherwise than by or with the consent of the Attorney General.

(13) Subsection (1) above shall be in addition to, and not in derogation from, the provisions of any other enactment with respect to the publication of reports of court proceedings.

(14) In this section—

"publish", in relation to a report, means publish the report, either by itself or as part of a newspaper or periodical, for distribution to the public;

"relevant programme" means a programme included in a programme service (within the meaning of the Broadcasting Act 1990); and "relevant time" means a time when events giving rise to the charges to which the proceedings relate occurred.]

★★★★★

PART VI
RECOGNIZANCES

Recognizances to keep the peace or be of good behaviour

115 Binding over to keep the peace or be of good behaviour

(1) The power of a magistrates' court on the complaint of any person to adjudge any other person to enter into a recognizance, with or without sureties, to keep the peace or to be of good behaviour towards the complaint shall be exercised by order on complaint.

(2) ★★★★★

(3) If any person ordered by a magistrates' court under subsection (1) above to enter into a recognizance, with or without sureties, to keep the peace or to be of good behaviour fails to comply with the order, the court may commit him to custody for a period not exceeding 6 months or until he sooner complies with the order.

★★★★★

BRITISH NATIONALITY ACT 1981
(1981, c. 61)

An Act to make fresh provision about citizenship and nationality, and to amend the Immigration Act 1971 as regards the right of abode in the United Kingdom

[30 October 1981]

Territorial extent United Kingdom

Note A new form of British Nationality, British National (Overseas), has been created by the Hong Kong (British Nationality) Order 1986 (SI 1986 No. 948) with effect from 1 July 1987. See the text of the Order for details. Amendments to this Act made by the Order consequent on this new category are incorporated in the text.

PART I
BRITISH CITIZENSHIP

Acquisition after commencement

1 Acquisition by birth or adoption

(1) A person born in the United Kingdom after commencement shall be a British citizen if at the time of the birth his father or mother is—

(a) a British citizen; or

(b) settled in the United Kingdom.

(2) A new-born infant who, after commencement, is found abandoned in the United Kingdom shall, unless the contrary is shown, be deemed for the purposes of subsection (1)—

(a) to have been born in the United Kingdom after commencement; and

(b) to have been born to a parent who at the time of the birth was a British citizen or settled in the United Kingdom.

(3) A person born in the United Kingdom after commencement who is not a British citizen by virtue of subsection (1) or (2) shall be entitled to be registered as a British citizen if, while he is a minor—

(a) his father or mother becomes a British citizen or becomes settled in the United Kingdom; and

(b) an application is made for his registration as a British citizen.

(4) A person born in the United Kingdom after commencement who is not a British citizen by virtue of subsection (1) or (2) shall be entitled, on an application for his registration as a British citizen made at any time after he has attained the age of ten years, to be registered as such a citizen if, as regards each of the first ten years of that person's life, the number of days on which he was absent from the United Kingdom in that year does not exceed 90.

(5) Where after commencement an order authorising the adoption of a minor who is not a British citizen is made by any court in the United Kingdom, he shall be a British citizen as from the date on which the order is made if the adopter or, in the case of a joint adoption, one of the adopters is a British citizen on that date.

(6) Where an order in consequence of which any person became a British citizen by virtue of subsection (5) ceases to have effect, whether on annulment or otherwise, the cesser shall not affect the status of that person as a British citizen.

(7) If in the special circumstances of any particular case the Secretary of State thinks fit, he may for the purposes of subsection (4) treat the person to whom the application relates as fulfilling the requirement specified in that subsection although, as regards any one or more of the first ten years of that person's life, the number of days on which he was absent from the United Kingdom in that year or each of the years in question exceeds 90.

(8) In this section and elsewhere in this Act "settled" has the meaning given by section 50.

2 Acquisition by descent

(1) A person born outside the United Kingdom after commencement shall be a British citizen if at the time of the birth his father or mother—

(a) is a British citizen otherwise than by descent; or

(b) is a British citizen and is serving outside the United Kingdom in service to which this paragraph applies, his or her recruitment for that service having taken place in the United Kingdom; or

(c) is a British citizen and is serving outside the United Kingdom in service under a Community institution, his or her recruitment for that service having taken place in a country which at the time of the recruitment was a member of the Communities.

(2) Paragraph (b) of subsection (1) applies to—

(a) Crown service under the government of the United Kingdom; and

(b) service of any description for the time being designated under subsection (3).

(3) For the purposes of this section the Secretary of State may by order made by statutory instrument designate any description of service which he considers to be closely associated with the activities outside the United Kingdom of Her Majesty's government in the United Kingdom.

(4) Any order made under subsection (3) shall be subject to annulment in pursuance of a resolution of either House of Parliament.

3 Acquisition by registration: minors

(1) If while a person is a minor an application is made for his registration as a British citizen, the Secretary of State may, if he thinks fit, cause him to be registered as such a citizen.

(2) A person born outside the United Kingdom shall be entitled, on an application for his registration as a British citizen made within the period of twelve months from the date of the birth, to be registered as such a citizen if the requirements specified in subsection (3) or, in the case of a person born stateless, the requirements specified in paragraphs (a) and (b) of that subsection, are fulfilled in the case of either that person's father or his mother ("the parent in question").

(3) The requirements referred to in subsection (2) are—

(a) that the parent in question was a British citizen by descent at the time of the birth; and

(b) that the father or mother of the parent in question—

(i) was a British citizen otherwise than by descent at the time of the birth of the parent in question; or

(ii) became a British citizen otherwise than by descent at commencement, or would have become such a citizen otherwise than by descent at commencement but for his or her death; and

(c) that, as regards some period of three years ending with a date not later than that date of the birth—

(i) the parent in question was in the United Kingdom at the beginning of that period; and

(ii) the number of days on which the parent in question was absent from the United Kingdom in the period does not exceed 270.

(4) If in the special circumstances of any particular case the Secretary of State thinks fit, he may treat subsection (2) as if the reference to twelve months were a reference to six years.

(5) A person born outside the United Kingdom shall be entitled, on an application for his registration as a British citizen made while he is a minor, to be registered as such a citizen if the following requirements are satisfied, namely—

(a) that at the time of that person's birth his father or mother was a British citizen by descent; and

(b) subject to subsection (6), that that person and his father and mother were in the United Kingdom at the beginning of the period of three years ending with the date of the application and that, in the case of each of them, the number of days on which the person in question was absent from the United Kingdom in that period does not exceed 270; and

(c) subject to subsection (6), that the consent of his father and mother to the registration has been signified in the prescribed manner.

(6) In the case of an application under subsection (5) of the registration of a person as a British citizen—

(a) if his father or mother died, or their marriage was terminated, on or before the date of the application, or his father and mother were legally separated on that date, the references to his father and mother in paragraph (b) of that subsection shall be read either as references to his father or as references to his mother;

(b) if his father or mother died on or before that date, the reference to his father and mother in paragraph (c) of that subsection shall be read as a reference to either of them; and

(c) if he was born illegitimate, all those references shall be read as references to his mother.

4 Acquisition by registration: British Dependent Territories citizens etc.

(1) This section applies to any person who is a British Dependent Territories citizen, [a British National [(Overseas),] a British Overseas citizen, a British subject under this Act or a British protected person.

(2) A person to whom this section applies shall be entitled, on an application for his registration as a British citizen, to be registered as such a citizen if the following requirements are satisfied in the case of that person, namely—

(a) subject to subsection (3), that he was in the United Kingdom at the beginning of the period of five years ending with the date of the application and that the number of days on which he was absent from the United Kingdom in that period does not exceed 450; and

(b) that the number of days on which he was absent from the United Kingdom in the period of twelve months so ending does not exceed 90; and

(c) that he was not at any time in the period of twelve months so ending subject under the immigration laws to any restriction on the period for which he might remain in the United Kingdom; and

(d) that he was not at any time in the period of five years so ending in the United Kingdom in breach of the immigration laws.

(3) So much of subsection (2)(a) as requires the person in question to have been in the United Kingdom at the beginning of the period there mentioned shall not apply in relation to a person who was settled in the United Kingdom immediately before commencement.

(4) If in the special circumstances of any particular case the Secretary of State thinks fit, he may for the purposes of subsection (2) do all or any of the following things, namely—

(a) treat the person to whom the application relates as fulfilling the requirement specified in subsection (2)(a) or subsection (2)(b), or both, although the number of days on which he was absent from the United Kingdom in the period there mentioned exceeds the number there mentioned;

(b) disregard any such restriction as is mentioned in subsection (2)(c), not being a restriction to which that person was subject on the date of the application;

(c) treat that person as fulfilling the requirement specified in subsection (2)(d) although he was in the United Kingdom in breach of the immigration laws in the period there mentioned.

(5) If, on an application for registration as a British citizen made by a person to whom this section applies, the Secretary of State is satisfied that the applicant has at any time served in service to which this subsection applies, he may, if he thinks fit in the special circumstances of the applicant's case, cause him to be registered as such a citizen.

(6) Subsection (5) applies to—

(a) Crown service under the government of a dependent territory; and

(b) paid or unpaid service (not falling within paragraph (a)) as a member of any body established by law in a dependent territory members of which are appointed by or on behalf of the Crown.

5 Acquisition by registration: nationals for purposes of the Community treaties

A British Dependent Territories citizen who falls to be treated as a national of the United Kingdom for the purposes of the Community Treaties shall be entitled to be registered as a British citizen if an application is made for his registration as such a citizen.

6 Acquisition by naturalisation

(1) If, on an application for naturalisation as a British citizen made by a person of full age and capacity, the Secretary of State is satisfied that the applicant fulfils the requirements of Schedule 1 for naturalisation as such a citizen under this subsection, he may, if he thinks fit, grant to him a certificate of naturalisation as such a citizen.

(2) If, on an application for naturalisation as a British citizen made by a person of full age and capacity who on the date of the application is married to a British citizen, the Secretary of State is satisfied that the applicant fulfils the requirements of Schedule 1 for naturalisation as such a citizen under this subsection, he may, if he thinks fit, grant to him a certificate of naturalisation as such a citizen.

Acquisition at commencement

11 Citizens of UK and Colonies who are to become British citizens at commencement

(1) Subject to subsection (2), a person who immediately before commencement—

(a) was a citizen of the United Kingdom and Colonies; and

(b) had the right of abode in the United Kingdom under the Immigration Act 1971 as then in force,

shall at commencement become a British citizen.

(2) A person who was registered as a citizen of the United Kingdom and Colonies under section 1 of the British Nationality (No 2) Act 1964 (stateless persons) on the ground mentioned in subsection (1)(a) of that section (namely that his mother was a citizen of the United Kingdom and Colonies at the time when he was born) shall not become a British citizen under subsection (1) unless—

(a) his mother becomes a British citizen under subsection (1) or would have done so but for her death; or

(b) immediately before commencement he had the right of abode in the United Kingdom by virtue of section 2(1)(c) of the Immigration Act 1971 as then in force (settlement in United Kingdom, combined with five or more years' ordinary residence there as a citizen of the United Kingdom and Colonies).

(3) * * * * *

Renunciation and resumption

12 Renunciation

(1) If any British citizen of full age and capacity makes in the prescribed manner a declaration of renunciation of British citizenship, then, subject to subsection (3) and (4), the Secretary of State shall cause the declaration to be registered.

(2) On the registration of a declaration made in pursuance of this section the person who made it shall cease to be a British citizen.

(3) A declaration made by a person in pursuance of this section shall not be registered unless the Secretary of State is satisfied that the person who made it will after the registration have or acquire some citizenship or nationality other than British citizenship; and if that person does not have any such citizenship or nationality on the date of registration and does not acquire some such citizenship or nationality within six months from that date, he shall be, and be deemed to have remained, a British citizen notwithstanding the registration.

(4) The Secretary of State may withhold registration of any declaration made in pursuance of this section if it is made during any war in which Her Majesty may be engaged in right of Her Majesty's government in the United Kingdom.

(5) For the purposes of this section any person who has been married shall be deemed to be of full age.

13, 14 * * * * *

PART II
BRITISH DEPENDENT TERRITORIES CITIZENSHIP

Acquisition after commencement

15 Acquisition by birth or adoption

(1) A person born in a dependent territory after commencement shall be a British Dependent Territories citizen if at the time of the birth his father or mother is—

(a) a British Dependent Territories citizen; or

(b) settled in a dependent territory.

(2) A new-born infant who, after commencement, is found abandoned in a dependent territory shall, unless the contrary is shown, be deemed for the purposes of subsection (1)—

(a) to have been born in that territory after commencement; and

(b) to have been born to a parent who at the time of the birth was a British Dependent Territories citizen or settled in a dependent territory.

(3) A person born in a dependent territory after commencement who is not a British Dependent Territories citizen by virtue of subsection (1) or (2) shall be entitled to be registered as such a citizen if, while he is a minor—

(a) his father or mother becomes such a citizen or becomes settled in a dependent territory; and

(b) an application is made for his registration as such a citizen.

(4) A person born in a dependent territory after commencement who is not a British Dependent Territories citizen by virtue of subsection (1) or (2) shall be entitled, on an application for registration as a British Dependent Territories citizen made at any time after he has attained the age of ten years, to be registered as such a citizen if, as regards each of the first ten years of that person's life, the number of days on which he was absent from the territory in that year does not exceed 90.

(5), (6) * * * * *

(7) If in the special circumstances of any particular case the Secretary of State thinks fit, he may for the purposes of subsection (4) treat the person to whom the application relates as fulfilling the requirements specified in that subsection although, as regards any one or more of the first ten years of that person's life, the number of days on which he was absent from the dependent territory there mentioned in that year or each of the years in question exceeds 90.

16 Acquisition by descent

(1) A person born outside the dependent territories after commencment shall be a British Dependent Territories citizen if at the time of the birth his father or mother—

(a) is such a citizen otherwise than by descent; or

(b) is such a citizen and is serving outside the dependent territories in service to which this paragraph applies, his or her recruitment for that service having taken place in a dependent territory.

(2) Paragraph (b) of subsection (1) applies to—

(a) Crown service under the government of a dependent territory; and

(b) service of any description for the time being designated under subsection (3).

(3) For the purposes of this section the Secretary of State may by order made by statutory instrument designate any description of service which he considers to be closely associated with the activities outside the dependent territories of the government of any dependent territory.

(4) Any order made under subsection (3) shall be subject to annulment in pursuance of a resolution of either House of Parliament.

17-25 * * * * *

PART III
BRITISH OVERSEAS CITIZENSHIP

26 Citizens of UK and Colonies who are to become British Overseas citizens at commencement

Any person who was a citizen of the United Kingdom and Colonies immediately before commencement and who does not at commencement become either a British citizen or a British Dependent Territories citizen shall at commencement become a British Overseas citizen.

27-35 * * * * *

PART V
MISCELLANEOUS AND SUPPLEMENTARY

36 * * * * *

37 Commonwealth citizenship

(1) Every person who—

(a) under [the British Nationality Acts 1981 and 1983] is a British citizen, a British Dependent Territories citizen, [a British National (Overseas),] a British Overseas citizen or a British subject; or

(b) under any enctment for the time being in force in any country mentioned in Schedule 3 is a citizen of that country,

shall have the status of a Commonwealth citizen.

(2) Her Majesty may by Order in Council amend Schedule 3 by the alteration of any entry, the removal of any entry, or the insertion of any additional entry.

(3) Any Order in Council made under this section shall be subject to annulment in pursuance of a resolution of either House of Parliament.

(4) After commencement no person shall have the status of a Commonwealth citizen or the status of a British subject otherwise than under this Act.

Note Schedule 3 (not printed) lists those countries currently members of the Commonwealth.

38-39 * * * * *

40 Deprivation of citizenship

(1) Subject to the provisions of this section, the Secretary of State may by order deprive any British citizen to whom the subsection applies of his British citizenship if the Secretary of State is satisfied that the registration or certificate of naturalisation by virtue of which he is such a citizen was obtained by means of fraud, false representation or the concealment of any material fact.

(2) Subsection (1) applies to any British citizen who—

(a) became a British citizen after commencement by virtue of—

(i) his registration as a British citizen under any provision of [the British Nationality Acts 1981 and 1983]; or

(ii) a certificate of naturalisation granted to him under section 6; or

(b) being immediately before commencement a citizen of the United Kingdom and Colonies by virtue of registration as such a citizen under any provision of the British Nationality Acts 1948 to 1964, became at commencement a British citizen; or

(c) at any time before commencement became a British subject (within the meaning of that expression at that time), or a citizen of Eire or of the Republic of Ireland, by virtue of a certificate of naturalisation granted to him or in which his name was included.

(3) Subject to the provisions of this section, the Secretary of State may by order deprive any British citizen to whom this subsection applies of his British citizenship if the Secretary of State is satisfied that that citizen—

(a) has shown himself by act or speech to be disloyal or disaffected towards Her Majesty; or

(b) has, during any war in which Her Majesty was engaged, unlawfully traded or communicated with an enemy or been engaged in or associated with any business that was to his knowledge carried on in such a manner as to assist an enemy in that war; or

(c) has, within the period of five years from the relevant date, been sentenced in any country to imprisonment for a term of not less than twelve months.

(4) Subsection (3) applies to any British citizen who falls within paragraph (a) or (c) of subsection (2); and in subsection (3) "the relevant date", in relation to a British

citizen to whom subsection (3) applies, means the date of the registration by virtue of which he is such a citizen or, as the case may be, the date of the grant of the certificate of naturalisation by virtue of which he is such a citizen.

(5) The Secretary of State—

(a) shall not deprive a person of British citizenship under this section unless he is satisfied that it is not conducive to the public good that that person should continue to be a British citizen; and

(b) shall not deprive a person of British citizenship under subsection (3) on the ground mentioned in paragraph (c) of that subsection if it appears to him that that person would thereupon become stateless.

(6) Before making an order under this section the Secretary of State shall give the person against whom the order is proposed to be made notice in writing informing him of the ground or grounds on which it is proposed to be made and of his right to an inquiry under this section.

(7) If the person against whom the order is proposed to be made applies in the prescribed manner for an inquiry, the Secretary of State shall, and in any other case the Secretary of State may, refer the case to a committee of inquiry consisting of a chairman, being a person possessing judicial experience, appointed by the Secretary of State and of such other members appointed by the Secrtetary of State as he thinks proper.

(8)-(10) * * * * *

41 * * * * *

42 Registration and naturalisation: general provisions

(1) Subject to subsection (2)—

(a) a person shall not be registered under any provision of this Act as a citizen of any description or as a British subject; and

(b) a certificate of naturalisation shall not be granted to a person under any provision of this Act,

unless—

(i) any fee payable by virtue of this Act in connection with the registration or as the case may be, the grant of the certificate has been paid; and

(ii) the person concerned has within the prescribed time taken an oath of allegiance in the form indicated in Schedule 5.

(2) So much of subsection (1) as requires the taking of an oath of allegiance shall not apply to a person who—

(a) is not of full age; or

(b) is already a British citizen, a British Dependent Territories citizen, [a British National (Overseas),] a British Overseas citizen, a British subject, or a citizen of any country of which Her Majesty is Queen.

(3) Any provision of this Act which provides for a person to be entitled to registration as a citizen of any description or as a British subject shall have effect subject to the preceding provisions of this section.

(4) A person registered under any provision of this Act as a British citizen, or as a British Dependent Territories citizen, [or as a British National (Overseas),] or as a British Overseas citizen, or as a British subject, shall be a citizen of that description or, as the case may be, [a British National (Overseas) or] a British subject as from the date on which he is so registered.

(5) A person to whom a certificate of naturalisation as a British citizen or as a British Dependent Territories citizen is granted under any provision of this Act shall be a citizen of that description as from the date on which the certificate is granted.

43 * * * * *

44 Decisions involving exercise of discretion

(1) Any discretion vested by or under this Act in the Secretary of State, a Governor or a Lieutenant-Governor shall be exercised without regard to the race, colour or religion of any person who may be affected by its exercise.

(2) The Secretary of State, a Governor or a Lieutenant-Governor, as the case may be, shall not be required to assign any reason for the grant or refusal of any application under this Act the decision on which is at his discretion; and the decision of the Secretary of State or a Governor or Lieutenant-Governor on any such application shall not be subject to appeal to, or review in, any court.

(3) Nothing in this section affects the jurisdiction of any court to entertain proceedings of any derscription concerning the rights of any person under any provision of this Act.

45-46 ★ ★ ★ ★ ★

47 Legitimated children

(1) A person born out of wedlock and legitimated by the subsequent marriage of his parents shall, as from the date of the marriage, be treated for the purposes of this Act as if he had been born legitimate.

(2) A person shall be deemed for the purposes of this section to have been legitimated by the subsequent marriage of his parents if by the law of the place in which his father was domiciled at the time of the marriage the marriage operated immediately or subsequently to legitimate him, and not otherwise.

48 Posthumous children

Any reference in this Act to the status or descriptions of the father or mother of a person at the time of that person's birth shall, in relation to a person born after the death of his father or mother, be construed as a reference to the status or description of the parent in question at the time of that parent's death; and where that death occurred before, and the birth occurs after, commencement, the status or description which would have been applicable to the father or mother had he or she died after commencement shall be deemed to be the status or description applicable to him or her at the time of his or her death.

49 . . .

50 Interpretation

(1) In this Act, unless the context otherwise requires—

"the 1948 Act" means the British Nationality Act 1948:

"alien" means a person who is neither a Commonwealth citizen nor a British protected person nor a citizen of the Republic of Ireland;

"association" means an unincorporated body of persons;

["British National (Overseas)" means a person who is a British National (Overseas) under the Hong Kong (British Nationality) Order 1986, and "status of a British National (Overseas)" shall be construed accordingly;

"British Overseas citizen" includes a person who is a British Overseas citizen under the Hong Kong (British Nationality) Order 1986;]

"British protected person" means a person who is a member of any class of person declared to be British protected persons by an Order in Council for the time being in force under section 38 or is a British protected person by virtue of the Solomon Islands Act 1978;

★ ★ ★ ★ ★

"Crown service" means the service of the Crown, whether within Her Majesty's dominions or elsewhere;

"Crown service under the government of the United Kingdom" means Crown service under Her Majesty's government in the United Kingdom or under Her Majesty's government in Northern Ireland;
"dependent territory" means a territory mentioned in Schedule 6;
"enactment" includes an enactment comprised in Northern Ireland legislation;
"foreign country" means a country other than the United Kingdom, a dependent territory, a country mentioned in Schedule 3 and the Republic of Ireland;
★★★★★
"immigration laws"—

(a) in relation to the United Kingdom, means the Immigration Act 1971 and any law for purposes similar to that Act which is for the time being or has at any time been in force in any part of the United Kingdom;

(b) in relation to a dependent territory, means any law for purposes similar to the Immigration Act 1971 which is for the time being or has at any time been in force in that territory;

"the Islands" means the Channel Islands and the Isle of Man;
"minor" means a person who has not attained the age of eighteen years;
"prescribed" means prescribed by regulations made under section 41;
"settled" shall be construed in accordance with subsections (2) to (4);
"ship" includes a hovercraft;
★★★★★
"United Kingdom consulate" means the office of a consular officer of Her Majesty's government in the United Kingdom where a register of births is kept or, where there is no such office, such office as may be prescribed.

(2) Subject to subsection (3), references in this Act to a person being settled in the United Kingdom or in a dependent territory are references to his being ordinarily resident in the United Kingdom or, as the case may be, in that territory without being subject under the immigration laws to any restriction on the period for which he may remain.

(3), (4) ★★★★★

(5) It is hereby declared that a person is not to be treated for the purpose of any provision of this Act as ordinarily resident in the United Kingdom or in a dependent territory at a time when he is in the United Kingdom or, as the case may be, in that territory in breach of the immigration laws.

(6)-(8) ★★★★★

(9) For the purposes of this Act—

(a) the relationship of mother and child shall be taken to exist between a woman and any child (legitimate or illegitimate) born to her; but

(b) subject to section 47, the relationship of father and child shall be taken to exist only between a man and any legitimate child born to him;

and the expressions "mother", "father", "parent", "child" and "descended" shall be construed accordingly.

(10)-(13) ★★★★★

51-53 ★★★★★

Sections 6, 18

SCHEDULE 1
REQUIREMENTS FOR NATURALISATION

Naturalisation as a British citizen under section 6(1)

1.—(1) Subject to paragraph 2, the requirements for naturalisation as a British citizen under section 6(1) are, in the case of any person who applies for it—

(a) the requirements specified in sub-paragraph (2) of this paragraph, or the alternative requirement specified in sub-paragraph (3) of this paragraph; and

(b) that he is of good character; and

(c) that he has a sufficient knowledge of the English, Welsh or Scottish Gaelic language; and

(d) that either—

(i) his intentions are such that, in the event of a certificate of naturalisation as a British citizen being granted to him, his home or (if he has more than one) his principal home will be in the United Kingdom; or

(ii) he intends, in the event of such a certificate being granted to him, to enter into, or continue in, Crown service under the government of the United Kingdom, or service under an international organisation of which the United Kingdom or Her Majesty's government therein is a member, or service in the employment of a company or association established in the United Kingdom.

(2) The requirements referred to in sub-paragraph (1)(a) of this paragraph are—

(a) that the applicant was in the United Kingdom at the beginning of the period of five years ending with the date of the application, and that the number of days on which he was absent from the United Kingdom in that period does not exceed 450; and

(b) that the number of days on which he was absent from the United Kingdom in the period of twelve months so ending does not exceed 90; and

(c) that he was not at any time in the period of twelve months so ending subject under the immigration laws to any restriction on the period for which he might remain in the United Kingdom; and

(d) that he was not at any time in the period of five years so ending in the United Kingdom in breach of the immigration laws.

(3) The alternative requirement referred to in sub-paragraph (1)(a) of this paragraph is that on the date of the application he is serving outside the United Kingdom in Crown service under the government of the United Kingdom.

2. ★ ★ ★ ★ ★

Naturalisation as a British citizen under section 6(2)

3. Subject to paragraph 4, the requirements for naturalisation as a British citizen under section 6(2) are, in the case of any person who applies for it—

(a) that he was in the United Kingdom at the beginning of the period of three years ending with the date of the application, and that the number of days on which he was absent from the United Kingdom in that period does not exceed 270; and

(b) that the number of days on which he was absent from the United Kingdom in the period of twelve months so ending does not exceed 90; and

(c) that on the date of the application he was not subject under the immigration laws to any restriction on the period for which he might remain in the United Kingdom; and

(d) that he was not at any time in the period of three years ending with the date of the application in the United Kingdom in breach of the immigration laws; and

(e) the requirement specified in paragraph 1(1)(b).

★ ★ ★ ★ ★

CONTEMPT OF COURT ACT 1981
(1981, c. 49)

An Act to amend the law relating to contempt of court and related matters [27 July 1981]

Territorial extent United Kingdom (ss. 1-6, 8-11, Sch. 1); England and Wales (ss. 12-14); Scotland (s. 15); England, Wales and Northern Ireland (s. 7). For additional provisions applying to Northern Ireland see Sch. 4.

Strict liability

1 The strict liability rule
In this Act "the strict liability rule" means the rule of law whereby conduct may be treated as a contempt of court as tending to interfere with the course of justice in particular legal proceedings regardless of intent to do so.

2 Limitation of scope of strict liability
(1) The strict liability rule applies only in relation to publications, and for this purpose "publication" includes any speech, writing, [programme included in a programme service] or other communication in whatever form, which is addressed to the public at large or any section of the public.
(2) The strict liability rule applies only to a publication which creates a substantial risk that the course of justice in the proceedings in question will be seriously impeded or prejudiced.
(3) The strict liability rule applies to a publication only if the proceedings in question are active within the meaning of this section at the time of the publication.
(4) Schedule 1 applies for determining the times at which proceedings are to be treated as active within the meaning of this section.
[(5) In this section, "programme service" has the same meaning as in the Broadcasting Act 1990.]

3 Defence of innocent publication or distribution
(1) A person is not guilty of contempt of court under the strict liability rule as the publisher of any matter to which that rule applies if at the time of publication (having taken all reasonable care) he does not know and has no reason to suspect that relevant proceedings are active.
(2) A person is not guilty of contempt of court under the strict liability rule as the distributor of a publication containing any such matter if at the time of distribution (having taken all reasonable care) he does not know that it contains such matter and has no reason to suspect that it is likely to do so.
(3) The burden of proof of any fact tending to establish a defence afforded by this section to any person lies upon that person.
(4) ...

4 Contemporary reports of proceedings
(1) Subject to this section a person is not guilty of contempt of court under the strict liability rule in respect of a fair and accurate report of legal proceedings held in public, published contemporaneously and in good faith.
(2) In any such proceedings the court may, where it appears to be necessary for avoiding a substantial risk of prejudice to the administration of justice in those proceedings, or in any other proceedings pending or imminent, order that the publication of any report of the proceedings, or any part of the proceedings, be postponed for such period as the court thinks necessary for that purpose.
[(2A) Where in proceedings for any offence which is an administration of justice offence for the purposes of section 54 of the Criminal Procedure and Investigations Act 1996 (acquittal tainted by administration of justice offence) it appears to the court that there is a possibility that (by virtue of that section) proceedings may be taken against a person for an offence of which he has been acquitted, subsection (2) of this section shall apply as if those proceedings were pending or imminent.]
(3) * * * * *
(4) ...

5 Discussion of public affairs

A publication made as or as part of a discussion in good faith of public affairs or other matters of general public interest is not to be treated as a contempt of court under the strict liability rule if the risk of impediment or prejudice to particular legal proceedings is merely incidental to the discussion.

6 Savings

Nothing in the foregoing provisions of this Act—

(a) prejudices any defence available at common law to a charge of contempt of court under the strict liability rule;

(b) implies that any publication is punishable as contempt of court under that rule which would not be so punishable apart from those provisions;

(c) restricts liability for contempt of court in respect of conduct intended to impede or prejudice the administration of justice.

7 Consent required for institution of proceedings

Proceedings for a contempt of court under the strict liability rule (other than Scottish proceedings) shall not be instituted except by or with the consent of the Attorney General or on the motion of a court having jurisdiction to deal with it.

Other aspects of law and procedure

8 Confidentiality of jury's deliberations

(1) Subject to subsection (2) below, it is a contempt of court to obtain, disclose or solicit any particulars of statements made, opinions expressed, arguments advanced or votes cast by members of a jury in the course of their deliberations in any legal proceedings.

(2) This section does not apply to any disclosure of any particulars—

(a) in the proceedings in question for the purpose of enabling the jury to arrive at their verdict, or in connection with the delivery of that verdict, or

(b) in evidence in any subsequent proceedings for an offence alleged to have been committed in relation to the jury in the first mentioned proceedings,

or to the publication of any particulars so disclosed.

(3) Proceedings for a contempt of court under this section (other than Scottish proceedings) shall not be instituted except by or with the consent of the attorney general or on the motion of a court having jurisdiction to deal with it.

9 Use of tape recorders

(1) Subject to subsection (4) below, it is a contempt of court—

(a) to use in court, or bring into court for use, any tape recorder or other instrument for recording sound, except with the leave of the court;

(b) to publish a recording of legal proceedings made by means of any such instrument, or any recording derived directly or indirectly from it, by playing it in the hearing of the public or any section of the public, or to dispose of it or any recording so derived, with a view to such publication;

(c) to use any such recording in contravention of any conditions of leave granted under paragraph (a).

(2) Leave under paragraph (a) of subsection (1) may be granted or refused at the discretion of the court, and if granted may be granted subject to such conditions as the court thinks proper with respect to the use of any recording made pursuant to the leave; and where leave has been granted the court may at the like discretion withdraw or amend it either generally or in relation to any particular part of the proceedings.

(3) Without prejudice to any other power to deal with an act of contempt under paragraph (a) of subsection (1), the court may order the instrument, or any recording

made with it, or both, to be forfeited; and any object so forfeited shall (unless the court otherwise determines on application by a person appearing to be the owner) be sold or otherwise disposed of in such manner as the court may direct.

(4) This section does not apply to the making or use of sound recordings for purposes of official transcripts of proceedings.

10 Sources of information

No court may require a person to disclose, nor is any person guilty of contempt of court for refusing to disclose, the source of information contained in a publication for which he is responsible, unless it be established to the satisfaction of the court that disclosure is necessary in the interests of justice or national security or for the prevention of disorder or crime.

11 Publication of matters exempted from disclosure in court

In any case where a court (having power to do so) allows a name or other matter to be withheld from the public in proceedings before the court, the court may give such directions prohibiting the publication of that name or matter in connection with the proceedings as appear to the court to be necessary for the purpose of which it was so withheld.

12 Offences of contempt of magistrates' courts

(1) A magistrates' court has jurisdiction under this section to deal with any person who—

(a) wilfully insults the justice or justices, any witness before or officer of the court or any solicitor or counsel having business in the court, during his or their sitting or attendance in court or in going to or returning from the court; or

(b) wilfully interrupts the proceedings of the court or otherwise misbehaves in court.

(2) In any such case the court may order any officer of the court, or any constable, to take the offender into custody and detain him until the rising of the court; and the court may, if it thinks fit, commit the offender to custody for a specified period not exceeding one month or impose on him a fine not exceeding [£2,500], or both.

(2A) * * * * *

(3) . . .

(4), (5) * * * * *

13 . . .

Penalties for contempt and kindred offences

14 Proceedings in England and Wales

(1) In any case where a court has power to commit a person to prison for contempt of court and (apart from this provision) no limitation applies to the period of committal, the committal shall (without prejudice to the power of the court to order his earlier discharge) be for a fixed term, and that term shall not on any occasion exceed two years in the case of committal by a superior court, or one month in the case of committal by an inferior court.

(2) In any case where an inferior court has power to fine a person for contempt of court and (apart from the provision) no limit applies to the amount of the fine, the fine shall not on any occasion exceed [£2,500].

(2A), (3), (4) * * * * *

[(4A) For the purposes of the preceding provisions of this section a county court shall be treated as a superior court and not as an inferior court.]

(5) * * * * *

15 Penalties for contempt of court in Scottish proceedings

(1) In Scottish proceedings, when a person is committed to prison for contempt of court the committal shall (without prejudice to the power of the court to order his earlier discharge) be for a fixed term.

(2) The maximum penalty which may be imposed by way of imprisonment or fine for contempt of court in Scottish proceedings shall be two years' imprisonment or a fine or both, except that—

(a) where the contempt is dealt with by the sheriff in the course of or in connection with proceedings other than criminal proceedings on indictment, such penalty shall not exceed three months' imprisonment or a fine [of level 4 on the standard scale] or both; and

(b) where the contempt is dealt with by the district court, such penalty shall not exceed sixty days' imprisonment or a fine of [level 4 on the standard scale] or both.

(3)-(5) ★★★★★

(6) ...

16-21 ★★★★★

Section 2 SCHEDULE 1

TIMES WHEN PROCEEDINGS ARE ACTIVE FOR PURPOSES OF SECTION 2

Preliminary

1. In this Schedule "criminal proceedings" means proceedings against a person in respect of an offence, not being appellate proceedings or proceedings commenced by motion for committal or attachment in England and Wales or Northern Ireland; and "appellate proceedings" means proceedings on appeal from or for the review of the decision of a court in any proceedings.

2. Criminal, appellate and other proceedings are active within the meaning of section 2 at the times respectively prescribed by the following paragraphs of this Schedule; and in relation to proceedings in which more than one of the steps described in any of those paragraphs is taken, the reference in that paragraph is a reference to the first of those steps.

Criminal proceedings

3. Subject to the following provisions of this Schedule, criminal proceedings are active from the relevant initial step specified in paragraph 4 [or 4A] until concluded as described in paragraph 5.

4. The initial steps of criminal proceedings are:—

(a) arrest without warrant;

(b) the issue, or in Scotland the grant, of a warrant for arrest;

(c) the issue of a summons to appear, or in Scotland the grant of a warrant to cite;

(d) the service of an indictment or other document specifying the charge;

(e) except in Scotland, oral charge.

[4A. Where as a result of an order under section 54 of the Criminal Procedure and Investigations Act 1996 (acquittal tainted by administration of justice offence) proceedings are brought against a person for an offence of which he has previously been acquitted, the initial step of the proceedings is a certification under subsection (2) of that section; and paragraph 4 has effect subject to this.]

5. Criminal proceedings are concluded—

(a) by acquittal or, as the case may be, by sentence;

(b) by any other verdict, finding, order or decision which puts an end to the proceedings;

(c) by discontinuance or by operation of law.

6. The reference in paragraph 5(a) to sentence includes any order or decision consequent on conviction or finding of guilt which disposes of the case, either absolutely or subject to future events, and a deferment of sentence under section 1 of the Power of Criminal Courts Act 1973, section 219 or 432 of the Criminal Procedure (Scotland) Act 1975 or Article 14 of the Treatment of Offenders (Northern Ireland) Order 1976.

7. Proceedings are discontinued within the meaning of paragraph 5(c)—

(a) in England and Wales or Northern Ireland, if the charge or summons is withdrawn or a *nolle prosequi* entered;

(b) in Scotland, if the proceedings are expressly abandoned by the prosecutor or are deserted *simpliciter*;

(c) in the case of proceedings in England and Wales or Northern Ireland commenced by arrest without warrant, if the person arrested is released, otherwise than on bail, without having been charged.

8.-10. ★★★★★

11. Criminal proceedings against a person which become active on the issue or the grant of a warrant for his arrest cease to be active at the end of the period of twelve months beginning with the date of the warrant unless he has been arrested within that period, but become active again if he is subsequently arrested.

Other proceedings at first instance

12. Proceedings other than criminal proceedings and appellate proceedings are active from the time when arrangements for the hearing are made or, if no such arrangements are previously made, from the time the hearing begins, until the proceedings are disposed of or discontinued or withdrawn; and for the purposes of this paragraph any motion or application made in or for the purposes of any proceedings, and any pre-trial review in the county court, is to be treated as a distinct proceeding.

13. In England and Wales or Northern Ireland arrangements for the hearing of proceedings to which paragraph 12 applies are made within the meaning of that paragraph—

(a) in the case of proceedings in the High Court for which provision is made by rules of court for setting down for trial, when the case is set down;

(b) in the case of any proceedings, when a date for the trial or hearing is fixed.

14. In Scotland arrangements for the hearing of proceedings to which paragraph 12 applies are made within the meaning of that paragraph—

(a) in the case of an ordinary action in the Court of Session or in the sheriff court, when the record is closed;

(b) in the case of a motion or application, when it is enrolled or made;

(c) in any other case, when the date for a hearing is fixed or a hearing is allowed.

Appellate proceedings

15. Appellate proceedings are active from the time when they are commenced—

(a) by application for leave to appeal or apply for review, or by notice of such an application;

(b) by notice of appeal or of application for review;

(c) by other originating process,

until disposed of or abandoned, discontinued or withdrawn.

16. Where, in appellate proceedings relating to criminal proceedings, the court—

(a) remits the case to the court below; or

(b) orders a new trial or a *venire de novo*, or in Scotland grants authority to bring a new prosecution,

any further or new proceedings which result shall be treated as active from the conclusion of the appellate proceedings.

★★★★★

INDECENT DISPLAYS (CONTROL) ACT 1981
(1981, c. 42)

An Act to make fresh provision with respect to the public display of indecent matter; and for purposes connected therewith [27 July 1981]

Territorial extent England and Wales, Scotland

1 Indecent displays

(1) If any indecent matter is publicly displayed the person making the display and any person causing or permitting the display to be made shall be guilty of an offence.

(2) Any matter which is displayed in or so as to be visible from any public place shall, for the purposes of this section, be deemed to be publicly displayed.

(3) In subsection (2) above, "public place", in relation to the display of any matter, means any place to which the public have or are permitted to have access (whether on payment or otherwise) while that matter is displayed except—

(a) a place to which the public are permitted to have access only on payment which is or includes payment for that display; or

(b) a shop or any part of a shop to which the public can only gain access by passing beyond an adequate warning notice;

but the exclusions contained in paragraphs (a) and (b) above shall only apply where persons under the age of 18 years are not permitted to enter while the display in question is continuing.

(4) Nothing in this section applies in relation to any matter—

[(a) included by any person in a television broadcasting service or other television programme service (within the meaning of Part I of the Broadcasting Act 1990);] or

(b) included in the display of an art gallery or museum and visible only from within the gallery or museum; or

(c) displayed by or with the authority of, and visible only from within a building occupied by, the Crown or any local authority; or

(d) included in a performance of a play (within the meaning of the Theatres Act 1968); or

[(e) included in a film exhibition as defined in the Cinemas Act 1985—

(i) given in a place which as regards that exhibition is required to be licensed under section 1 of the Act or by virtue only of section 5, 7 or 8 of that Act is not required to be so licensed; or

(ii) which is an exhibition to which section 6 of that Act applies given by an exempted organisation as defined by subsection (6) of that section.]

(5) In this section "matter" includes anything capable of being displayed, except that it does not include an actual human body or any part thereof; and in determining for the purpose of this section whether any displayed matter is indecent—

(a) there shall be disregarded any part of that matter which is not exposed to view; and

(b) account may be taken of the effect of juxtaposing one thing with another.

(6) A warning notice shall not be adequate for the purposes of this section unless it complies with the following requirements—

(a) The warning notice must contain the following words, and no others—

"WARNING

Persons passing beyond this notice will find material on display which they may consider indecent. No admittance to persons under 18 years of age."

(b) The word "WARNING" must appear as a heading.

(c) No pictures or other matter shall appear on the notice.

(d) The notice must be so situated that no one could reasonably gain access to the shop or part of the shop in question without being aware of the notice and it must be easily legible by any person gaining such access.

2 Power of arrest, seizure and entry

(1) . . .

(2) A constable may seize any article which he has reasonable grounds for believing to be or to contain indecent matter and to have been used in the commission of an offence under this Act.

(3) In England and Wales, a justice of the peace if satisfied on information on oath that there are reasonable grounds for suspecting that an offence under this Act has been or is being committed on any premises and, in Scotland, a sheriff or justice of the peace on being so satisfied on evidence on oath, may issue a warrant authorising any constable to enter the premises specified in the information or, as the case may be, evidence (if need be by force) . . . to seize any article which the constable has reaonable grounds for believing to be or to contain indecent matter and to have been used in the commission of an offence under this Act.

3 ★★★★★

4 Penalties

(1) In England and Wales, any person guilty of an offence under this Act shall be liable—

(a) on summary conviction, to a fine not exceeding the statutory maximum; or

(b) on conviction on indictment, to imprisonment for a term not exceeding two years or a fine or both.

(2) In Scotland, any person guilty of an offence under this Act shall be liable—

(a) on summary conviction—

(i) in the District Court, to a fine not exceeding [level 4 on the standard scale];

(ii) in the sheriff court, to a fine not exceeding the statutory maximum; or

(b) on conviction on indictment, to imprisonment for a term not exceeding two years or a fine or both.

(3) . . .

SUPREME COURT ACT 1981
(1981, c. 54)

An Act to consolidate with amendments the Supreme Court of Judicature (Consolidation) Act 1925 and other enactments relating to the Supreme Court in England and Wales and the administration of justice therein; to repeal certain obsolete or unnecessary enactments so relating; to amend Part VIII of the Mental Health Act 1959, the Courts-Martial (Appeals) Act 1968, the Arbitration Act 1979 and the law relating to county courts; and for connected purposes

[28 July 1981]

Territorial extent England and Wales

PART I
CONSTITUTION OF SUPREME COURT

The Supreme Court

1 The Supreme Court

(1) The Supreme Court of England and Wales shall consist of the Court of Appeal, the High Court of Justice and the Crown Court, each having such jurisdiction as is conferred on it by or under this or any other Act.

(2) The Lord Chancellor shall be president of the Supreme Court.

2, 3 ★★★★★

The High Court

4 The High Court

(1) The High Court shall consist of—

(a) the Lord Chancellor;

(b) the Lord Chief Justice;

(c) the President of the Family Division;

(d) the Vice-Chancellor; and

(e) not more than [98] puisne judges of that court.

(2) The puisne judges of the High Court shall be styled "Justices of the High Court".

(3) All the judges of the High Court shall, except where this Act expressly provides otherwise, have in all respects equal power, authority and jurisdiction.

(4)-(6) ★★★★★

5-9 ★★★★★

10 Appointment of judges of Supreme Court

(1) Whenever the office of Lord Chief Justice, Master of the Rolls, President of the Family Division or Vice-Chancellor is vacant, Her Majesty may by letters patent appoint a qualified person to that office.

(2) Subject to the limits on numbers for the time being imposed by sections 2(1) and 4(1), Her Majesty may from time to time by letters patent appoint qualified persons as Lords Justices of Appeal or as puisne judges of the High Court.

(3) No person shall be qualified for appointment—

(a) as Lord Chief Justice, Master of the Rolls, President of the Family Division or Vice-Chancellor, unless he is qualified for appointment as a Lord Justice of Appeal or is a judge of the Court of Appeal;

(b) as a Lord Justice of Appeal, [unless—

(i) he has a 10 year High Court qualification within the meaning of section 71 of the Courts and Legal Services Act 1990; or

(ii) he is a judge of the High Court;] or

(c) as a puisne judge of the High Court, [unless—

(i) he has a 10 year High Court qualification within the meaning of section 71 of the Courts and Legal Services Act 1990; or

(ii) he is a Circuit Judge who has held that office for at least 2 years.]

(4) Every person appointed to an office mentioned in subsection (1) or as a Lord Justice of Appeal or puisne judge of the High Court shall, as soon as may be after his acceptance of office, take the oath of allegiance and the judicial oath, as set out in the Promissory Oaths Act 1868, in the presence of the Lord Chancellor.

11 Tenure of office of judges of Supreme Court

(1) This section applies to the office of any judge of the Supreme Court except the Lord Chancellor.

(2) A person appointed to an office to which this section applies shall vacate it on the day on which he attains the age of [seventy] years unless by virtue of this section he has ceased to hold it before then.

(3) A person appointed to an office to which this section applies shall hold that office during good behaviour, subject to a power of removal by Her Majesty on an address presented to Her by both Houses of Parliament.

(4)-(6) ★★★★★

(7) A person who holds an office to which this section applies may at any time resign it by giving the Lord Chancellor notice in writing to that effect.

(8) The Lord Chancellor, if satisfied by means of a medical certificate that a person holding an office to which this section applies—

(a) is disabled by permanent infirmity from the performance of the duties of his office; and

(b) is for the time being incapacitated from resigning his office,

may, subject to subsection (9), by instrument under his hand declare that person's office to have been vacated; and the instrument shall have the like effect for all purposes as if that person had on the date of the instrument resigned his office.

(9) A declaration under subsection (8) with respect to a person shall be of no effect unless it is made—

(a) in the case of any of the Lord Chief Justice, the Master of the Rolls, the President of the Family Division and the Vice-Chancellor, with the concurrence of two others of them;

(b) in the case of a Lord Justice of Appeal, with the concurrence of the Master of the Rolls;

(c) in the case of a puisne judge of any Division of the High Court, with the concurrence of the senior judge of that Division.

(10) ★★★★★

12 Salaries etc of judges of Supreme Court

(1) Subject to subsections (2) and (3), there shall be paid to judges of the Supreme Court, other than the Lord Chancellor, such salaries as may be determined by the Lord Chancellor with the concurrence of the Minister for the Civil Service.

(2) Until otherwise determined under this section, there shall be paid to the judges mentioned in subsection (1) the same salaries as at the commencement of this Act.

(3) Any salary payable under this section may be increased, but not reduced, by a determination or further determination under this section.

(4) ...

(5)-(7) ★★★★★

13-18 ★★★★★

PART II
JURISDICTION
THE HIGH COURT

General jurisdiction

19 General jurisdiction

(1) The High Court shall be a superior court of record.

(2) Subject to the provisions of this Act, there shall be exercisable by the High Court—

(a) all such jurisdiction (whether civil or criminal) as is conferred on it by this or any other Act; and

(b) all such other jurisdiction (whether civil or criminal) as was exercisable by it immediately before the commencment of this Act (including jurisdiction conferred on a judge of the High Court by any statutory provision).

(3), (4) ★★★★★

★★★★★

Other particular fields of jurisdiction

29 Orders of mandamus, prohibition and certiorari

(1) The High Court shall have jurisdiction to make orders of mandamus, prohibition and certiorari in those classes of cases in which it had power to do so immediately before the commencement of this Act.

(2) Every such order shall be final, subject to any right of appeal therefrom.

(3) In relation to the jurisdiction of the Crown Court, other than its jurisdiction in matters relating to trial on indictment, the High Court shall have all such jurisdiction to make orders of mandamus, prohibition or certiorari as the High Court possesses in relation to the jurisdiction of an inferior court.

(4) The power of the High Court under any enactment to require justices of the peace or a judge or officer of a county court to do any act relating to the duties of their respective offices, or to require a magistrates' court to state a case for the opinion of the High Court, in any case where the High Court formerly had by virtue of any enactment jurisdiction to make a rule absolute, or an order, for any of those purposes, shall be exercisable by order of mandamus.

(5) In any enactment—

(a) references to a writ of mandamus, of prohibition or of certiorari shall be read as references to the corresponding order; and

(b) references to the issue or award of any such writ shall be read as references to the making of the corresponding order.

30 ★★★★★

31 Application for judicial review

(1) An application to the High Court for one or more of the following forms of relief, namely—

(a) an order of mandamus, prohibition or certiorari;

(b) a declaration or injunction under subsection (2); or

(c) an injunction under section 30 restraining a person not entitled to do so from acting in an office to which that section applies,

shall be made in accordance with rules of court by a procedure to be known as an application for judicial review.

(2) A declaration may be made or an injunction granted under this subsection in any case where an application for judicial review, seeking that relief, has been made and the High Court considers that, having regard to—

(a) the nature of the matters in respect of which relief may be granted by orders of mandamus, prohibition or certiorari;

(b) the nature of the persons and bodies against whom relief may be granted by such orders; and

(c) all the circumstances of the case,

it would be just and convenient for the declaration to be made or for the injunction to be granted, as the case may be.

(3) No application for judicial review shall be made unless the leave of the High Court has been obtained in accordance with rules of court; and the court shall not grant leave to make such an application unless it considers that the applicant has a sufficient interest in the matter to which the application relates.

(4) On an application for judicial review the High Court may award damages to the applicant if—

(a) he has joined with his application a claim for damages arising from any matter to which the application relates; and

(b) the court is satisfied that, if the claim had been made in an action begun by the applicant at the time of making his application, he would have been awarded damages.

(5) If, on an application for judicial review seeking an order of certiorari, the High Court quashes the decision to which the application relates, the High Court may remit the matter to the court, tribunal or authority concerned, with a direction to reconsider it and reach a decision in accordance with the findings of the High Court.

(6) Where the High Court considers that there has been undue delay in making an application for judicial review, the court may refuse to grant—

(a) leave for the making of the application; or
(b) any relief sought on the application,

if it considers that the granting of the relief sought would be likely to cause substantial hardship to, or substantially prejudice the rights of, any person or would be detrimental to good administration.

(7) Subsection (6) is without prejudice to any enactment or rule of court which has the effect of limiting the time within which an application for judicial review may be made.

Note The provisions of s. 31 are implemented by Order 53 of the Rules of the Supreme Court, printed below.

★★★★★

CANADA ACT 1982
(1982, c. 11)

An Act to give effect to a request by the Senate and House of Commons of Canada

[29 March 1982]

Territorial extent Canada

Whereas Canada has requested and consented to the enactment of an Act of the Parliament of the United Kingdom to give effect to the provisions hereinafter set forth and the Senate and the House of Commons of Canada in Parliament assembled have submitted an address to Her Majesty requesting that Her Majesty may graciously be pleased to cause a Bill to be laid before the Parliament of the United Kingdom for that purpose:

Be it therefore enacted by the Queen's Most Excellent Majesty, by and with the advice and consent of the Lords Spiritual and Temporal, and Commons, in this present Parliament assembled, and by the authority of the same, as follows:

1 Constitution Act, 1982 enacted

The Constitution Act, 1982 set out in Schedule B to this Act is hereby enacted for and shall have the force of law in Canada and shall come into force as provided in that Act.

2 Termination of power to legislate for Canada

No Act of the Parliament of the United Kingdom passed after the Constitution Act, 1982 comes into force shall extend to Canada as part of its law.

3 French version

So far as it is not contained in Schedule B, the French version of this Act is set out in Schedule A to this Act and has the same authority in Canada as the English version thereof.

4 Short title

This Act may be cited as the Canada Act 1982.

★★★★★

SCHEDULE B
CONSTITUTION ACT, 1982
PART I
CANADIAN CHARTER OF RIGHTS AND FREEDOMS

Whereas Canada is founded upon principles that recognize the supremacy of God and the rule of law:

Guarantee of Rights and Freedoms

1 Rights and freedoms in Canada

The *Canadian Charter of Rights and Freedoms* guarantees the rights and freedoms set out in it subject only to such reasonable limits prescribed by law as can be demonstrably justified in a free and democratic society.

Fundamental Freedoms

2 Fundamental freedoms

Everyone has the following fundamental freedoms:

(a) freedom of conscience and religion;

(b) freedom of thought, belief, opinion and expression, including freedom of the press and other media of communication;

(c) freedom of peaceful assembly; and

(d) freedom of association.

Democratic Rights

3 Democratic rights of citizens

Every citizen of Canada has the right to vote in an election of members of the House of Commons or of a legislative assembly and to be qualified for membership therein.

4 Maximum duration of legislative bodies

(1) No House of Commons and no legislative assembly shall continue for longer than five years from the date fixed for the return of the writs at a general election of its members.

Continuation in special circumstances

(2) In time of real or apprehended war, invasion or insurrection, a House of Commons may be continued by Parliament and a legislative assembly may be continued by the legislature beyond five years if such continuation is not opposed by the votes of more than one-third of the members of the House of Commons or the legislative assembly, as the case may be.

5 Annual sitting of legislative bodies

There shall be a sitting of Parliament and of each legislature at least once every twelve months.

Mobility Rights

6 Mobility of citizens

(1) Every citizen of Canada has the right to enter, remain in and leave Canada.

Rights to move and gain livelihood

(2) Every citizen of Canada and every person who has the status of a permanent resident of Canada has the right

(a) to move to and take up residence in any province; and

(b) to pursue the gaining of a livelihood in any province.

Limitation

(3) The rights specified in subsection (2) are subject to

(a) any laws or practices of general application in force in a province other than those that discriminate among persons primarily on the basis of province of present or previous residence; and

(b) any laws providing for reasonable residency requirements as a qualification for the receipt of publicly provided social services.

Affirmative action programs

(4) Subsections (2) and (3) do not preclude any law, program or activity that has as its object the amelioration in a province of conditions of individuals in that province who are socially or economically disadvantaged if the rate of employment in that province is below the rate of employment in Canada.

Legal Rights

7 Life, liberty and security of person

Everyone has the right to life, liberty and security of the person and the right not to be deprived thereof except in accordance with the principles of fundamental justice.

8 Search or seizure

Everyone has the right to be secure against unreasonable search or seizure.

9 Detention or imprisonment

Everyone has the right not to be arbitrarily detained or imprisoned.

10 Arrest or detention

Everyone has the right on arrest or detention

(a) to be informed promptly of the reasons therefor;

(b) to retain and instruct counsel without delay and to be informed of that right; and

(c) to have the validity of the detention determined by way of *habeas corpus* and to be released if the detention is not lawful.

11 Proceedings in criminal and penal matters

Any person charged with an offence has the right

(a) to be informed without unreasonable delay of the specific offence;

(b) to be tried within a reasonable time;

(c) not to be compelled to be a witness in proceedings against that person in respect of the offence;

(d) to be presumed innocent until proven guilty according to law in a fair and public hearing by an independent and impartial tribunal;

(e) not to be denied reasonable bail without just cause;

(f) except in the case of an offence under military law tried before a military tribunal, to the benefit of trial by jury where the maximum punishment for the offence is imprisonment for five years or a more severe punishment;

(g) not to be found guilty on account of any act or omission unless, at the time of the act or omission, it constituted an offence under Canadian or international law or was criminal according to the general principles of law recognized by the community of nations;

(h) if finally acquitted of the offence, not to be tried for it again and, if finally found guilty and punished for the offence, not to be tried or punished for it again; and

(i) if found guilty of the offence and if the punishment for the offence has been varied between the time of commission and the time of sentencing, to the benefit of the lesser punishment.

12 Treatment or punishment

Everyone has the right not to be subjected to any cruel and unusual treatment or punishment.

13 Self-crimination

A witness who testifies in any proceedings has the right not to have any incriminating evidence so given used to incriminate that witness in any other proceedings, except in a prosecution for perjury or for the giving of contradictory evidence.

14 Interpreter
A party or witness in any proceedings who does not understand or speak the language in which the proceedings are conducted or who is deaf has the right to the assistance of an interpreter.

Equality Rights

15 Equality before and under law and equal protection and benefit of law
(1) Every individual is equal before and under the law and has the right to the equal protection and equal benefit of the law without discrimination and, in particular, without discrimination based on race, national or ethnic origin, colour, religion, sex, age or mental or physical disability.

Affirmative action programs
(2) Subsection (1) does not preclude any law, program or activity that has as its object the amelioration of conditions of disadvantaged individuals or groups including those that are disadvantaged because of race, national or ethnic origin, colour, religion, sex, age or mental or physical disability.

Official Languages of Canada

16 Official languages of Canada
(1) English and French are the official languages of Canada and have equality of status and equal rights and privileges as to their use in all institutions of the Parliament and government of Canada.
(2), (3) ★★★★★

17-23 ★★★★★

Enforcement

24 Enforcement of guaranteed rights and freedoms
(1) Anyone whose rights or freedoms, as guaranteed by this Charter, have been infringed or denied may apply to a court of competent jurisdiction to obtain such remedy as the court considers appropriate and just in the circumstances.

Exclusion of evidence bringing administration of justice into disrepute
(2) Where, in proceedings under subsection (1), a court concludes that evidence was obtained in a manner that infringed or denied any rights or freedoms guaranteed by this Charter, the evidence shall be excluded if it is established that, having regard to all the circumstances, the admission of it in the proceedings would bring the administration of justice into disrepute.

General

25 Aboriginal rights and freedoms not affected by Charter
The guarantee in this Charter of certain rights and freedoms shall not be construed so as to abrogate or derogate from any aboriginal, treaty or other rights or freedoms that pertain to the aboriginal peoples of Canada including
(a) any rights or freedoms that have been recognised by the Royal Proclamation of October 7, 1763; and
(b) any rights or freedoms that may be acquired by the aboriginal peoples of Canada by way of land claims settlement.

26 Other rights and freedoms not affected by Charter
The guarantee in this Charter of certain rights and freedoms shall not be construed as denying the existence of any other rights or freedoms that exist in Canada.

27 Multicultural heritage
This Charter shall be interpreted in a manner consistent with the preservation and enhancement of the multicultural heritage of Canadians.

28 Rights guaranteed equally to both sexes
Notwithstanding anything in this Charter, the rights and freedoms referred to in it are guaranteed equally to male and female persons.

29 Rights respecting certain schools preserved
Nothing in this Charter abrogates or derogates from any rights or privileges guaranteed by or under the Constitution of Canada in respect of denominational, separate or dissentient schools.

30 ★ ★ ★ ★ ★

31 Legislative powers not extended
Nothing in this Charter extends the legislative powers of any body or authority.

Application of Charter

32 Application of Charter
(1) This Charter applies

(a) to the Parliament and government of Canada in respect of all matters within the authority of Parliament including all matters relating to the Yukon Territory and Northwest Territories; and

(b) to the legislature and government of each province in respect of all matters within the authority of the legislature of each province.

Exception
(2) Notwithstanding subsection (1), section 15 shall not have effect until three years after this section comes into force.

33 Exceptions where express declaration
(1) Parliament or the legislature of a province may expressly declare in an Act of Parliament or of the legislature, as the case may be, that the Act or a provision thereof shall operate notwithstanding a provision included in section 2 or sections 7 to 15 of this Charter.

Operation of exception
(2) An Act or a provision of an Act in respect of which a declaration made under this section is in effect shall have such operation as it would have but for the provision of this Charter referred to in the declaration.

Five year limitation
(3) A declaration made under subsection (1) shall cease to have effect five years after it comes into force or on such earlier date as may be specified in the declaration.

Re-enactment
(4) Parliament or the legislature of a province may re-enact a declaration made under subsection (1).

Five year limitation
(5) Subsection (3) applies in respect of a re-enactment made under subsection (4).

Citation

34 Citation
This Part may be cited as the *Canadian Charter of Rights and Freedoms.*

★ ★ ★ ★ ★

Note Schedule A to this Act is a French language version of the Act, and Schedule B is also printed in English and French. Both texts have equal status.

CIVIC GOVERNMENT (SCOTLAND) ACT 1982
(1982, c. 45)

An Act to make provision as regards Scotland for the licensing and regulation of certain activities; for the preservation of public order and safety and the prevention of crime; for prohibiting the taking of and dealing with indecent photographs of children; as to certain powers of constables and others; ★ ★ ★ ★ ★ [28 October 1982]

Territorial extent Scotland

51 Obscene material

(1) Subject to subsection (4) below, any person who displays any obscene material in any public place or in any other place where it can be seen by the public shall be guilty of an offence under this section.

(2) Subject to subsection (4) below, any person who publishes, sells or distributes or, with a view to its eventual sale or distribution, makes, prints, has or keeps any obscene material shall be guilty of an offence under this section.

[(2A) Subject to subsection (4) below, any person who—

(a) is responsible for the inclusion of any obscene material in a programme included in a programme service; or

(b) with a view to its eventual inclusion in a programme so included, makes, prints, has or keeps any obscene material,

shall be guilty of an offence under this section.]

(3) A person guilty of an offence under this section shall be liable, on summary conviction, to a fine not exceeding the prescribed sum or to imprisonment for a period not exceeding [6 months] or to both or, on conviction on indictment to a fine or to imprisonment for a period not exceeding [3 years] or to both.

(4) A person shall not be convicted of an offence under this section if he proves that he had used all due diligence to avoid committing the offence.

(5) Under an indictment for or on a complaint of a breach of subsection (1) above, the court may, if satisfied that the person accused is guilty of an offence under section 1(1) of the Indecent Displays (Control) Act 1981 (offence of public display of indecent matter), convict him of a breach of the said section 1(1).

(6) Nothing in this section applies in relation to any matter—

. . .

(b) included in a performance of a play (within the meaning of the Theatres Act 1968).

(7) For section 5(4)(b) of the Indecent Displays (Control) Act 1981 (saving) there shall be substituted the following—

"(b) section 51 of the Civic Government (Scotland) Act 1982".

(8) In this section—

"material" includes any book, magazine, bill, paper, print, film, tape, disk or other kind of recording (whether of sound or visual images or both), photograph, drawing, painting, representation, model or figure . . .

"photograph" includes the negative as well as the positive version;

"public place" has the same meaning as in section 133 of this Act except that it includes any place to which at the material time the public are permitted to have access, whether on payment or otherwise;

"prescribed sum" has the same meaning as in [section 225(8) of the Criminal Procedure (Scotland) Act 1995];

["programme" and "programme service" have the same meaning as in the Broadcasting Act 1990;]

and the reference to publishing includes a reference to . . . playing, projecting or otherwise reproducing [, or, where the material is data stored electronically, transmitting that data].

52-59 ★★★★★

Powers of constables, etc.

60 Powers of search and seizure

Subject to subsections (2) and (3) below, if a constable has reasonable grounds to suspect that a person is in possession of any stolen property, the constable may without warrant—

(a) search that person or anything in his possession, and detain him for as long as is necessary for the purpose of that search;

(b) enter and search any vehicle or vessel in which the constable suspects that that thing may be found, and for that purpose require the person in control of the vehicle or vessel to stop it and keep it stopped;

(c) enter and search any premises occupied by a second-hand dealer or a metal dealer for the purposes of his business;

(d) seize and detain anything found in the course of any such search which appears to the constable to have been stolen or to be evidence of the commission of the crime of theft,

and may, in doing so, use reasonable force.

In this subsection "second-hand dealer" and "metal dealer" have the meanings respectively assigned to them by sections 24(2) and 37(1) of this Act.

(2) The power under subsection (1)(b) above to require the person in charge of a vehicle or vessel to stop it shall be exercisable only by a constable in uniform.

(3) A constable who is not in uniform shall not be entitled to exercise the powers which he may exercise under subsections (1)(a) to (c) above until he has produced his identification—

(a) in relation to the exercise of powers under subsection (1)(a) above, to the person in respect of whom the powers are exercised;

(b) in relation to the exercise of powers under subsections (1)(b) or (c) above, to the person for the time being in charge of the vehicle, vessel or premises and to any other person in or on the vehicle, vessel or premises who, having reasonable cause to do so, requests to see it.

(4) In subsection (1) above "theft" includes any aggravation of theft including robbery.

(5) Nothing in this section prejudices any power of entry or search or any power to seize or detain property or any power to require any vehicle or vessel to be stopped which is exercisable by a constable apart from this section.

(6) Any person who, without reasonable excuse—

(a) fails to allow a constable in pursuance of subsection (1) above to enter and search any premises, vehicle or vessel, or seize and detain anything found in the course of such search;

(b) when required by a constable in pursuance of subsection (1) above to stop a vehicle or vessel and keep it stopped, fails to do so; or

(c) obstructs a constable in the exercise of his powers under subsection (1) above,

shall be guilty of an offence and liable, on summary conviction, to a fine not exceeding £200.

61 ★★★★★

PART V
PUBLIC PROCESSIONS

62 Notification of processions

(1) A person proposing to hold a procession in public shall give written notice of that proposal in accordance with subsections (2) and (3) below

(a) to the [local authority] in whose area the procession is to be held, or if it is to be held in the areas of more than one such [authority], to each such [authority] [and

(b) to the chief constable].

(2) Notice shall be given for the purposes of subsection (1) above by—

(a) its being posted to the main office of the [local authority] [and to the chief constable] so that in the normal course of post it might be expected to arrive not later than 7 days before the date when the procession is to be held; or

(b) its being delivered by hand to [those offices] not later than 7 days before that date.

(3) The notice to be given under subsection (1) above shall specify—

(a) the date and time when the procession is to be held;

(b) its route;

(c) the number of persons likely to take part in it;

(d) the arrangements for its control being made by the person proposing to hold it; and

(e) the name and address of that person.

(4) A [local authority] may, on application in accordance with subsection (5) below by a person proposing to hold a procession in public in their area

(a) made to them [and

(b) intimated to the chief constable,]

within the period of 7 days before the date when the procession is to be held, make an order dispensing with the requirements of subsection (2) above in relation to the time limits for the giving of notice of that proposal.

(5) An application under subsection (4) above shall specify the matters mentioned in subsection (3) above and, where an order has been made under the said subsection (4), the application for it shall be treated as notice duly given for the purposes of subsection (1) above.

(6)-(11) ★ ★ ★ ★ ★

(12) In this section and in sections 63 to 65 of this Act—

"procession in public" means a procession in a public place;

"chief constable" means, in relation to a [local authority], the chief constable of the police force for the area which comprises or includes the area of the [authority]; and

"public place" has the same meaning as in [Part II of the Public Order Act 1986].

63 Functions of [local authorities] in relation to processions

(1) The [local authority] may, after consulting the chief constable in respect of a procession notice of which has been given or falls to be treated as having been given in accordance with section 62(1) of this Act, make an order—

(i) prohibiting the holding of the procession; or

(ii) imposing conditions on the holding of it.

(1A) ★ ★ ★ ★ ★

(2) The conditions which may be imposed under subsection (1) [or (1A)] above on the holding of a procession may include conditions—

(a) as to the date, time and duration of the procession;

(b) as to the route to be taken by it;

(c) prohibiting its entry into any public place specified in the order.

(3) A [local authority] shall—

(a) where notice of a proposal to hold a procession has been given or falls to be treated as having been given in accordance with section 62(1) of this Act, deliver at least 2 days before the date when, in terms of the notice, the procession is to be held, to the person who gave the notice—

(i) where they have made an order under subsection (1) [or (1A)] above, a copy of it and a written statement of the reasons for it; . . .

(ii) where they decide not to make [an order under subsection (1) above or to revoke an order already made under subsection (1) or (1A) above], notification of that fact;

[(iii) where they have under subsection (1A) above varied such an order, a copy of the order as varied and a written statement of the reasons for the variation; and]

(b) where they have made an order under subsection (1) [or (1A)] above in relation to a proposal to hold a procession, make such arrangements as will ensure that persons who might take or are taking part in that procession are made aware of the fact that the order has been made [and, if the order has been varied under subsection (1A) above, that it has been so varied] and of its effect; [and

(c) where they have revoked an order made under subsection (1) or (1A) above in relation to a proposal to hold a procession, make such arrangements as will ensure that persons who might take or are taking part in that procession are made aware of the fact that the order has been revoked.]

(4) The [local authority] shall comply with subsection (3) above—

(a) as early as possible;

(b) only in so far as it is reasonably practicable for them to do so.

64 Appeals against orders under section 63

(1) An appeal to the sheriff shall lie at the instance of a person who, in accordance with section 62 of this Act, has or falls to be treated as having given notice of a proposal to hold a procession in public [against—

(a) an order made under section 63(1) or (1A) of this Act; or

(b) a variation under section 63(1A) of this Act of an order made under section 63(1) or (1A), in relation to the procession.

(2) An appeal under this section shall be made by way of summary application and shall be lodged with the sheriff clerk within 14 days from the date on which the copy of the order and statement of reasons were received by the appellant.

(3) On good cause being shown, the sheriff may hear an appeal under this section notwithstanding that it was not lodged within the time mentioned in subsection (2) above.

(4) The sheriff may uphold an appeal under this section only if he considers that the [local authority] in arriving at their decision to make [or, as the case may be, to vary] the order—

(a) erred in law;

(b) based their decision on any incorrect material fact;

(c) exercised their discretion in an unreasonable manner; or

(d) otherwise acted beyond their powers.

(5)-(9) * * * * *

65 Offences and enforcement

(1) Subject to subsection (3) below, a person who holds a procession in public—

(a) without—

(i) having given or being a person who is treated as having given notice in accordance with section 62 of this Act of his proposal to do so; and

(ii) there being in force in relation to the procession an exempting order under section 62(6) of this Act;

(b) in contravention of an order under section 63(1) [or (1A)] or 64(6)(a)(ii) of this Act prohibiting the holding of it;

(c) otherwise than in accordance with a condition imposed by an order under section 63(1) [or (1A)] or 64(6)(a)(ii) of this Act in relation to the procession; or

(d) otherwise than in accordance with the particulars of its date, time and route specified—

(i) in the notice given under section 62(1) to (3) of this Act; or

(ii) where an order has been made under subsection (4) of that section, in the application for the order,

except to the extent that a condition referred to in paragraph (c) above relates to its date, time or route, shall be guilty of an offence and liable, on summary conviction, to a fine not exceeding £500 or to imprisonment for a period not exceeding 3 months or to both.

(2) Subject to subsection (3) below, a person who takes part in a procession in public—

(a) in respect of which—

(i) notice has not been or is not treated as having been given in accordance with section 62 of this Act; and

(ii) there is not in force an exempting order under section 62(6) of this Act in relation to the procession;

(b) in relation to which an order has been made under section 63(1) [or (1A)] or 64(6)(a)(ii) of this Act prohibiting the holding of it;

(c) which is held otherwise than in accordance with a condition imposed by an order under section 63(1) [or (1A)] or 64(6)(a)(ii) of this Act in relation to the procession; or

(d) which is held otherwise than in accordance with the particulars of its date, time and route specified—

(i) in the notice given under section 62(1) to (3) of this Act; or

(ii) where an order has been made under subsection (4) of that section, in the application for the order

except to the extent that a condition referred to in paragraph (c) above relates to its date, time or route,

and refuses to desist when required to do so by a constable in uniform shall be guilty of an offence and liable, on summary conviction, to a fine not exceeding £200.

★ ★ ★ ★ ★

(4) Subject to subsection (5) below, a constable may arrest without warrant a person whom he reasonably suspects of committing or having committed an offence under this section.

(5) A constable who is not in uniform shall produce his identification if required to do so by any person whom he is arresting under subsection (4) above.

66 Relationship of sections 62 to 65 with Public Order Act 1936

Sections 62 to 65 of this Act are subject to [Part II of the Public Order Act 1986]; and, without prejudice to that generality—

(a) an order under those sections, so far as relating to the same matters as those to which any directions given under section 12 of that Act relate, shall be subject to those directions . . .; and

(b) anything done in conformity with any such directions ... or omitted, in conformity therewith, to be done shall not be an offence under section 65 of this Act.

★ ★ ★ ★ ★

LOCAL GOVERNMENT (MISCELLANEOUS PROVISIONS) ACT 1982
(1982, c. 30)

An Act to make amendments for England and Wales of provisions of that part of the law relating to local authorities or highways which is commonly amended by local Acts; to make provision for the control of sex establishments ★ ★ ★ ★ ★ [13 July 1982]

Territorial extent England and Wales

1 ★ ★ ★ ★ ★

PART II
CONTROL OF SEX ESTABLISHMENTS

2 Control of sex establishments

(1) A local authority may resolve that Schedule 3 to this Act is to apply to their area; and if a local authority do so resolve, that Schedule shall come into force in their area on the day specified in that behalf in the resolution (which must not be before the expiration of the period of one month beginning with the day on which the resolution is passed).

(2) A local authority shall publish notice that they have passed a resolution under this section in two consecutive weeks in a local newspaper circulating in their area.

(3) The first publication shall not be later than 28 days before the day specified in the resolution for the coming into force of Schedule 3 to this Act in the local authority's area.

(4) The notice shall state the general effect of that Schedule.

(5) In this Part of this Act "local authority" means—

(a) the council of a district;

(b) the council of a London borough; and

(c) the Common Council of the City of London.

★ ★ ★ ★ ★

Section 2

SCHEDULE 3
CONTROL OF SEX ESTABLISHMENTS

Saving for existing law

1. Nothing in this Schedule—

(a) shall afford a defence to a charge in respect of any offence at common law or under an enactment other than this Schedule; or

(b) shall be taken into account in any way—

(i) at a trial for such an offence; or

(ii) in proceedings for forfeiture under section 3 of the Obscene Publications Act 1959 or section 5 of the Protection of Children Act 1978; or

(iii) in proceedings for condemnation under Schedule 3 to the Customs and Excise Management Act 1979 of goods which section 42 of the Customs Consolidation Act 1876 prohibits to be imported or brought into the United Kingdom as being indecent or obscene; or

(c) shall in any way limit the other powers exercisable under any of those Acts.

Meaning of "sex establishment"

2. In this Schedule "sex establishment" means a sex cinema or a sex shop.

Meaning of "sex cinema"

3.—(1) In this Schedule "sex cinema" means any premises, vehicle, vessel or stall used to a significant degree for the exhibition of moving pictures, by whatever means produced, which—

(a) are concerned primarily with the portrayal of, or primarily deal with or relate to, or are intended to stimulate or encourage—

(i) sexual activity; or

(ii) acts of force or restraint which are associated with sexual activity; or

(b) are concerned primarily with the portrayal of, or primarily deal with or relate to, genital organs or urinary or excretory functions,

but does not include a dwelling-house to which the public is not admitted.

(2) No premises shall be treated as a sex cinema by reason only—

(a) if they are licensed under [section 1 of the Cinemas Act 1985], of their use for a purpose for which a licence under that section is required; or

(b) of their use for an exhibition to which [section 6 of that Act (certain non-commercial exhibitions) applies given by an exempted organisation within the meaning of section 6(6) of that Act.]

Meaning of "sex shop" and "sex article"

4.—(1) In this Schedule "sex shop" means any premises, vehicle, vessel or stall used for a business which consists to a significant degree of selling, hiring, exhanging, lending, displaying or demonstrating—

(a) sex articles; or

(b) other things intended for use in connection with, or for the purpose of stimulating or encouraging—

(i) sexual activity; or

(ii) acts of force or restraint which are associated with sexual activity.

(2) No premises shall be treated as a sex shop by reason only of their use for the exhibition of moving pictures by whatever means produced.

(3) In this Schedule "sex article" means—

(a) anything made for use in connection with, or for the purpose of stimulating or encouraging—

(i) sexual activity; or

(ii) acts or force or restraint which are associated with sexual activity; and

(b) anything to which sub-paragraph (4) below applies.

(4) This sub-paragraph applies—

(a) to any article containing or embodying matter to be read or looked at or anything intended to be used, either alone or as one of a set, for the reproduction or manufacture of any such article; and

(b) to any recording of vision or sound,

which—

(i) is concerned primarily with the portrayal of, or primarily deals with or relates to, or is intended to stimulate or encourage, sexual activity or acts of force or restraint which are associated with sexual activity; or

(ii) is concerned primarily with the portrayal of, or primarily deals with or relates to, genital organs, or urinary or excretory functions.

5. * * * * *

Requirement for licences for sex establishments

6.—(1) Subject to the provisions of this Schedule, no person shall in any area in which this Schedule is in force use any premises, vehicle, vessel or stall as a sex establishment except under and in accordance with the terms of a licence granted under this Schedule by the appropriate authority.

(2) Sub-paragraph (1) above does not apply to the sale, supply or demonstration of articles which—

(a) are manufactured for use primarily for the purposes of birth control; or

(b) primarily relate to birth control.

7.—(1) Any person who—

(a) uses any premises, vehicle, vessel or stall as a sex establishment; or

(b) proposes to do so,

may apply to the appropriate authority for them to waive the requirement of a licence.

(3)-(7) * * * * *

Grant, renewal and transfer of licences for sex establishments

8. Subject to paragraph 12(1) below, the appropriate authority may grant to any applicant, and from time to time renew, a licence under this Schedule for the use of any

premises, vehicle, vessel or stall specified in it for a sex establishment on such terms and conditions and subject to such restrictions as may be so specified.

9.—(1) Subject to paragraphs 11 and 27 below, any licence under this Schedule shall, unless previously cancelled under paragraph 16 or revoked under paragraph 17(1) below, remain in force for one year or for such shorter period specified in the licence as the appropriate authority may think fit.

(2) Where a licence under this Schedule has been granted to any person, the appropriate authority may, if they think fit, transfer that licence to any other person on the application of that other person.

10., 11. ★★★★★

Refusal of licences

12.—(1) A licence under this Schedule shall not be granted—

(a) to a person under the age of 18; or

(b) to a person who is for the time being disqualified under paragraph 17(3) below; or

(c) to a person, other than a body corporate, who is not resident in the United Kingdom or was not so resident throughout the period of six months immediately preceding the date when the application was made; or

(d) to a body corporate which is not incorporated in the United Kingdom; or

(e) to a person who has, within a period of 12 months imediately preceding the date when the application was made, been refused the grant or renewal of a licence for the premises, vehicle, vessel or stall in respect of which the application is made, unless the refusal has been reversed on appeal.

(2) Subject to paragraph 27 below, the appropriate authority may refuse—

(a) an application for the grant or renewal of a licence on one or more of the grounds specified in sub-paragraph (3) below;

(b) an application for the transfer of a licence on either or both of the grounds specified in paragraphs (a) and (b) of that sub-paragraph.

(3) The grounds mentioned in sub-paragraph (2) above are—

(a) that the applicant is unsuitable to hold the licence by reason of having been convicted of an offence or for any other reason;

(b) that if the licence were to be granted, renewed or transferred the business to which it relates would be managed by or carried on for the benefit of a person, other than the applicant, who would be refused the grant, renewal or transfer of such a licence if he made the application himself;

(c) that the number of sex establishments in the relevant locality at the time the application is made is equal to or exceeds the number which the authority consider is appropriate for that locality;

(d) that the grant or renewal of the licence would be inappropriate, having regard—

(i) to the character of the relevant locality; or

(ii) to the use to which any premises in the vicinity are put; or

(iii) to the layout, character or condition of the premises, vehicle, vessel or stall in respect of which the application is made.

(4) Nil may be an appropriate number of the purposes of sub-paragraph (3)(c) above.

(5) In this paragraph "the relevant locality" means—

(a) in relation to premises, the locality where they are situated; and

(b) in relation to a vehicle, vessel or stall, any locality where it is desired to use it as a sex establishment.

13.-16. ★★★★★

Revocation of licences

17.—(1) The appropriate authority may, after giving the holder of a licence under this Schedule an opportunity of appearing before and being heard by them, at any time revoke the licence—

(a) on any ground specified in sub-paragraph (1) of paragraph 12 above; or

(b) on either of the grounds specified in sub-paragraph (3)(a) and (b) of that paragraph.

(2) Where a licence is revoked, the appropriate authority shall, if required to do so by the person who held it, give him a statement in writing of the reasons for their decision within 7 days of his requiring them to do so.

(3) Where a licence is revoked, its holder shall be disqualified from holding or obtaining a licence in the area of the appropriate authority for a period of 12 months beginning with the date of revocation.

18. * * * * *

Fees

19. An applicant for the grant, renewal or transfer of a licence under this Schedule shall pay a reasonable fee determined by the appropriate authority.

Enforcement

20.—(1) A person who—

(a) knowingly uses, or knowingly causes or permits the use of, any premises, vehicle, vessel or stall contrary to paragraph 6 above; or

(b) being the holder of a licence for a sex establishment, employs in the business of the establishment any person known to him to be disqualified from holding such a licence; or

(c) being the holder of a licence under this Schedule, without reasonable excuse knowingly contravenes, or without reasonable excuse knowingly permits the contravention of, a term, condition or restriction specified in the licence; or

(d) being the servant or agent of the holder of a licence under this Schedule, without reasonable excuse knowingly contravenes, or without reasonable excuse knowingly permits the contravention of, a term, condition or restriction specified in the licence,

shall be guilty of an offence.

21. Any person who, in connection with an application for the grant, renewal or transfer of a licence under this Schedule, makes a false statement which he knows to be false in any material respect or which he does not believe to be true, shall be guilty of an offence.

22.—(1) A person guilty of an offence under paragraph 20 or 21 above shall be liable on summary conviction to a fine not exceeding £10,000.

(2) A person who, being the holder of a licence under this Schedule, fails without reasonable excuse to comply with paragraph 14(1) above shall be guilty of an offence and liable on summary conviction to a fine not exceeding £200.

Offences relating to persons under 18

23.—(1) A person who, being the holder of a licence for a sex establishment—

(a) without reasonable excuse knowingly permits a person under 18 years of age to enter the establishment; or

(b) employs a person known to him to be under 18 years of age in the business of the establishment,

shall be guilty of an offence.

(2) A person guilty of an offence under this paragraph shall be liable on summary conviction to a fine not exceeding £10,000.

Powers of constables and local authority officers

24. If a constable has reasonable cause to suspect that a person has committed an offence under paragraph 20 or 23 above, he may require him to give his name and address, and if that person refuses or fails to do so, or gives a name or address which the constable reasonably suspects to be false, the constable may arrest him without warrant.

25., 26. * * * * *

Appeals

27.—(1) Subject to sub-paragraphs (2) and (3) below, any of the following persons, that is to say—

(a) an applicant for the grant, renewal or transfer of a licence under this Schedule whose application is refused;

(b) an applicant for the variation of the terms, conditions or restrictions on or subject to which any such licence is held whose application is refused;

(c) a holder of any such licence who is aggrieved by any term, condition or restrictions on or subject to which the licence is held; or

(d) a holder of any such licence whose licence is revoked,

may at any time before the expiration of the period of 21 days beginning with the relevant date appeal to the magistrates' court acting for the relevant area.

(2) An applicant whose application for the grant or renewal of a licence is refused, or whose licence is revoked, on any ground specified in paragraph 12(1) above shall not have a right to appeal under this paragraph unless the applicant seeks to show that the ground did not apply to him.

(3) An applicant whose application for the grant or renewal of a licence is refused on either ground specified in paragraph 12(3)(c) or (d) above shall not have the right to appeal under this paragraph.

(4)-(12) * * * * *

28.-30. * * * * *

BRITISH NATIONALITY (FALKLAND ISLANDS) ACT 1983
(1983, c. 6)

An Act to provide for the acquisition of British citizenship by persons having connections with the Falkland Islands [28 March 1983]

Territorial extent United Kingdom

1 Acquisition of British citizenship at commencement of 1981 Act or by birth or adoption

(1) A person shall at commencement become a British citizen if—

(a) that person becomes a British Dependent Territories citizen at commencement under section 23 of the 1981 Act (persons becoming British Dependent Territories citizens at commencement); and

(b) immediately before commencement either—

(i) that person was a citizen of the United Kingdom and Colonies who had that citizenship by his birth, naturalisation or registration in the Falkland Islands; or

(ii) one of that person's parents, or a parent of one of that person's parents, was, or but for his death would have been, a citizen of the United Kingdom and Colonies who so had that citizenship; or

(iii) that person, being a woman, was, or had at any time been, the wife of a man who by virtue of sub-paragraph (i) or (ii) becomes a British citizen at commencement or would have done so but for his death.

(2) A person born in the Falkland Islands after commencement shall be a British citizen if at the time of the birth his father or mother is—

(a) a British citizen; or

(b) settled in the Falkland Islands.

(3)-(5) * * * * *

2, 3 * * * * *

4 Supplementary provisions

(1) In this Act—

"the 1981 Act" means the British Nationality Act 1981;

"commencement" has the same meaning as in the 1981 Act, that is to say the beginning of 1st January 1983 (that being the day appointed under section 53(2) of that Act for the commencment of all except sections 49 and 53 of that Act);

"the Falkland Islands" means the Colony of the Falkland Islands.

(2), (3) * * * * *

5 Citation, provision for retrospective effect, and extent

(1) This Act may be cited as the British Nationality (Falkland Islands) Act 1983; and this Act and the British Nationality Act 1981 may be cited together as the British Nationality Acts 1981 and 1983.

(2) This Act shall be deemed to have come into force on 1st January 1983 (that is to say at commencement as defined in section 4(1)); and accordingly, subject to subsection (3), where the requirements of any provision of section 1 for the acquisition of British citizenship were satisfied in relation to any person at commencement or at any time between commencement and the passing of this Act, that person shall be treated as having acquired that citizenship at that time.

(3)-(5) * * * * *

NATIONAL AUDIT ACT 1983
(1983, c. 44)

An Act to strengthen Parliamentary control and supervision of expenditure of public money by making new provision for the appointment and status of the Comptroller and Auditor General, establishing a Public Accounts Commission and a National Audit Office and making new provision for promoting economy, efficiency and effectiveness in the use of such money by government departments and other authorities and bodies; to amend or repeal certain provisions of the Exchequer and Audit Departments Acts 1866 and 1921; and for connected purposes

[13 May 1983]

Territorial extent United Kingdom

* * * * *

PART II
ECONOMY, EFFICIENCY AND EFFECTIVENESS EXAMINATIONS

6 Public departments etc.

(1) The Comptroller and Auditor General may carry out examinations into the economy, efficiency and effectiveness with which any department, authority or other body to which this section applies has used its resources in discharging its functions.

(2) Subsection (1) above shall not be construed as entitling the Comptroller and Auditor General to question the merits of the policy objectives of any department, authority or body in respect of which an examination is carried out.

(3) Subject to subsections (4) and (5) below, this section applies to—

(a) any department in respect of which appropriation accounts are required to be prepared under the Exchequer and Audit Departments Act 1866;

(b) any body required to keep accounts under section 98 of the National Health Service Act 1977 or section 86 of the National Health Service (Scotland) Act 1978;

(c) any other authority or body whose accounts are required to be examined and certified by, or are open to the inspection of, the Comptroller and Auditor General by virtue of any enactment, including an enactment passed after this Act; and

(d) any authority or body which does not fall within section 7 below and whose accounts are required to be examined and certified by, or are open to the inspection of, the Comptroller and Auditor General by virtue of any agreement made, whether before or after the passing of this Act, between that authority or body and a Minister of the Crown.

(4)-(6) ★★★★★

(7) In this section—

"authority" includes any person holding a public office;

"Minister" or "Minister of the Crown" includes any department falling within subsection (3)(a) above;

"policy", in relation to any such department, includes any policy of the government so far as relating to the functions of that department;

and references to an agreement made by a Minister include references to conditions imposed by him in pursuance of any statutory power in that behalf, whether in connection with the provision of financial assistance or otherwise.

7 Other bodies mainly supported by public funds

(1) If the Comptroller and Auditor General has reasonable cause to believe that any authority or body to which this section applies has in any of its financial years received more than half its income from public funds he may carry out an examination into the economy, efficiency and effctiveness with which it has in that year used its resources in discharging its functions.

(2) Subsection (1) above shall not be construed as entitling the Comptroller and Auditor General to question the merits of the policy objectives or any authority or body in respect of which an examination is carried out.

(3) In determining for the purposes of subsection (1) above whether the income of an authority or body is such as to bring it within that subsection the Comptroller and Auditor General shall consult that authority or body and the Treasury.

(4) This section applies to any authority or body appointed, or whose members are required to be appointed, by or on behalf of the Crown except a body specified in Schedule 4 to this Act.

(5), (6) ★★★★★

8 Right to obtain documents and information

(1) Subject to subsection (2) below, the Comptroller and Auditor General shall have a right of access at all reasonable times to all such documents as he may reasonably require for carrying out any examination under section 6 or 7 above and shall be entitled to require from any person holding or accountable for any such document such information and explanation as are reasonably necessary for that purpose.

(2) Subsection (1) above applies only to documents in the custody or under the control of the department, authority or body to which the examination relates.

9 Reports to House of Commons

The Comptroller and Auditor General may report to the House of Commons the results of any examination carried out by him under section 6 or 7 above.

★★★★★

REPRESENTATION OF THE PEOPLE ACT 1983
(1983, c. 2)

An Act to consolidate the Representation of the People Acts of 1949, 1969, 1977, 1978 and 1980, The Electoral Registers Acts of 1949 and 1953, the Elections (Welsh Forms) Act 1964, Part III of the Local Government Act 1972, sections 6 to 10 of the Local Government (Scotland) Act 1973, the Representation of the People (Armed Forces) Act 1976, the Returning Officers (Scotland) Act 1977, section 3 of the Representation of the People Act 1981, section 62 of and Schedule 2 to the Mental Health (Amendment) Act 1982, and connected provisions; and to repeal as obsolete the Representation of the People Act 1979 and other enactments related to the Representation of the People Acts [8 February 1983]

PART I
PARLIAMENTARY AND LOCAL GOVERNMENT FRANCHISE AND ITS EXERCISE

Parliamentary and local government franchise

1 Parliamentary electors

(1) A person entitled to vote as an elector at a parliamentary election in any constituency is one who—

(a) is resident there on the qualifying date (subject to subsection (2) below in relation to Northern Ireland); and

(b) on that date and on the date of the poll—

(i) is not subject to any legal incapacity to vote (age apart); and

(ii) is either a Commonwealth citizen or a citizen of the Republic of Ireland; and

(c) is of voting age (that is, 18 years or over) on the date of the poll.

(2) A person is not entitled to vote as an elector at a parliamentary election in any constituency in Northern Ireland unless he was resident in Northern Ireland during the whole of the period of three months ending on the qualifying date for that election.

(3) A person is not entitled to vote as an elector in any constituency unless registered there in the register of parliamentary electors to be used at the election.

(4) A person is not entitled to vote as an elector—

(a) more than once in the same constituency at any parliamentary election;

(b) in more than one constituency at a general election.

★ ★ ★ ★ ★

75 Prohibition of expenses not authorised by election agent

(1) No expenses shall, with a view to promoting or procuring the election of a candidate at an election, be incurred by any person other than the candidate, his election agent and persons authorised in writing by the election agent on account—

(a) of holding public meetings or organising any public display; or

(b) of issuing advertisements, circulars or publications; or

(c) of otherwise presenting to the electors the candidate or his views or the extent or nature of his backing or disparaging another candidate,

but paragraph (c) of this subsection shall not—

(i) restrict the publication of any matter relating to the election in a newspaper or other periodical or in a broadcast made by the British Broadcasting Corporation or [by Sianel Pedwar Cymru or in a programme included in any service licensed under Part I or III of the Broadcasting Act 1990 [or Part I or II of the Broadcasting Act 1996];] or

(ii) apply to any expenses not exceeding in the aggregate the sum of [£5] which may be incurred by an individual and are not incurred in pursuance of a plan suggested by or concerted with others, or to expenses incurred by any person in travelling or in living away from home or similar personal expenses.

(2) Where a person incurs any expenses required by this section to be authorised by the election agent—

(a) that person shall [within 21 days after the day on which the result of the election is declared deliver] to the appropriate officer a return of the amount of those expenses, stating the election at which and the candidate in whose support they were incurred, and

(b) the return shall be accompanied by a declaration made by that person (or in the case of an association or body of persons, by a director, general manager, secretary or other similar officer of the association or body) verifying the return and giving particulars of the matters for which the expenses were incurred,

but this subsection does not apply to any person engaged or employed for payment or promise of payment by the candidate or his election agent.

(3) * * * * *

(4) A copy of every return and declaration made under subsection (2) above in relation to a parliamentary election in England, Wales or Northern Ireland shall be sent to the Clerk of the Crown within [21 days after the day on which the result of the election is declared] by the person making the return or declaration, and rule 57 of the parliamentary elections rules applies to any documents sent to the Clerk of the Crown under this subsection.

In this subsection references to the Clerk of the Crown in relation to an election in Northern Ireland are references to the Clerk of the Crown for Northern Ireland.

(5) If a person—

(a) incurs, or aids, abets, counsels or procures any other person to incur, any expenses in contravention of this section, or

(b) knowingly makes the declaration required by subsection (2) falsely,

he shall be guilty of a corrupt practice; and if a person fails to [deliver] or send any declaration or return or a copy of it as required by this section he shall be guilty of an illegal practice, but—

(i) the court before whom a person is convicted under this subsection may, if they think it just in the special circumstances of the case, mitigate or entirely remit any incapacity imposed by virtue of section 173 below; and

(ii) a candidate shall not be liable, nor shall his election be avoided, for a corrupt or illegal practice under this subsection committed by an agent without his consent or connivance.

(6) * * * * *

* * * * *

92 Broadcasting from outside United Kingdom

[(1) No person shall, with intent to influence persons to give or refrain from giving their votes at a parliamentary or local government election, include, or aid, abet, counsel or procure the inclusion of, any matter relating to the election in any programme service (within the meaning of the Broadcasting Act 1990) provided from a place outside the United Kingdom otherwise than in pursuance of arrangements made with—

(a) the British Broadcasting Corporation;

(b) Sianel Pedwar Cymru; or

(c) the holder of any licence granted by the Independent Television Commission or the Radio Authority,

for the reception and re-transmission of that matter by that body or the holder of that licence.]

(2) An offence under this section shall be an illegal practice, but the court before whom a person is convicted of an offence under this section may, if they think it just in the special circumstances of the case, mitigate or entirely remit any incapacity imposed by virtue of section 173 below.

(3) * * * * *

93 Broadcasting during elections

(1) In relation to a parliamentary or local government election—

(a) pending such an election it shall not be lawful for any item about the constituency or electoral area to be

[(i) broadcast by the British Broadcasting Corporation or Sianel Pedwar Cymru; or

(ii) included in any service licensed under Part I or III of the Broadcasting Act 1990 or Part I or II of the Broadcasting Act 1996]

if any of the persons who are for the time being candidates at the election takes part in the item and the broadcast is not made with his consent; and

(b) where an item about a constituency or electoral area is so broadcast pending such an election there, then if the broadcast either is made before the latest time for delivery of nomination papers, or is made after that time but without the consent of any candidate remaining validly nominated, any person taking part in the item for the purpose of promoting or procuring his election shall be guilty of an illegal practice, unless the broadcast is so made without his consent.

(2) For the purposes of subsection (1) above—

(a) a parliamentary election shall be deemed to be pending during the period ending with the close of the poll and beginning—

(i) at a general election, with the date of the dissolution of Parliament or any earlier time at which Her Majesty's intention to dissolve Parliament is announced; or

(ii) at a by-election, with the date of the issue of the writ for the election or any earlier date on which a certificate of the vacancy is notified in the London Gazette in accordance with the Recess Elections Act 1975; and

(b) a local government election shall be deemed to be pending during the period ending with the close of the poll and beginning [with the last date on which notice of the election may be published in accordance with rules made under section 36 or, in Scotland, section 42 above].

(3) ...

94 ★★★★★

Election meetings

95 Schools and rooms for parliamentary election meetings

(1) Subject to the provisions of this section, a candidate at a parliamentary election is entitled for the purpose of holding public meetings in furtherance of his candidature to the use [free of charge] at reasonable times between the receipt of the writ and [the day preceding] the date of the poll of—

(a) a suitable room in the premises of a school to which this section applies;

(b) any meeting room to which this section applies.

(2) This section applies—

(a) in England and Wales, to county schools and voluntary schools of which the premises are situated in the constituency or an adjoining constituency, and

(b) in Scotland, to any school of which the premises are so situated, not being an independent school within the meaning of the Education (Scotland) Act 1980,

but a candidate is not entitled under this section to the use of a room in school premises outside the constituency if there is a suitable room in other premises in the constituency which are reasonably accessible from the same parts of the constituency as those outside and are premises of a school to which this section applies.

(3) This section applies to meeting rooms situated in the constituency, the expense of maintaining which is payable wholly or mainly out of public funds or out of any rate, or by a body whose expenses are so payable.

(4)-(8) ★★★★★

[96 Schools and rooms for local election meetings

(1) Subject to the provisions of this section, a candidate at a local government election is entitled for the purpose of holding public meetings in furtherance of his candidature to the use free of charge at reasonable times between the last day on which notice of the election may be published in accordance with rules made under section 36 or, in Scotland, section 42 above and the day preceding the day of election of—

(a) a suitable room in the premises of a school to which this section applies; or

(b) a meeting room to which this section applies.

(2) This section applies—

(a) in England and Wales, to a county or voluntary school situated in the electoral area for which the candidate is standing (or, if there is no such school in the area, in any such school in an adjacent electoral area) or in a parish or community, as the case may be, in part comprised in that electoral area) and

(b) in Scotland, to any school (not being an independent school within the meaning of the Education (Scotland) Act 1980) situated in the electoral area for which the candidate is standing (or, if there is no such school in the area, any such school in an adjacent electoral area).

(3) This section applies—

(a) in England and Wales, to any meeting room situated in the electoral area for which the candidate is standing or in a parish or community, as the case may be, in part comprised in that electoral area, the expense of maintaining which is payable wholly or mainly out of public funds or out of any rate, or by a body whose expenses are so payable;

(b) in Scotland, to any meeting room the expense of maintaining which is payable by [a local authority].

(4) ★★★★★]

97 Disturbances at election meetings

(1) A person who at a lawful public meeting to which this section applies acts, or incites others to act, in a disorderly manner for the purpose of preventing the transaction of the business for which the meeting was called together shall be guilty of an illegal practice.

(2) This section applies to—

(a) a political meeting held in any constituency between the date of the issue of a writ for the return of a member of Parliament for the constituency and the date at which a return to the writ is made;

(b) a meeting held with reference to a local government election in the electoral area for that election [in the period beginning with the last date on which notice of the election may be published in accordance with rules made under section 36 or, in Scotland, section 42 above and ending with] the day of election.

(3) If a constable reasonably suspects any person of committing an offence under subsection (1) above, he may if requested so to do by the chairman of the meeting require that person to declare to him immediately his name and address and, if that person refuses or fails so to declare his name and address or gives a false name and address, he shall be liable on summary conviction to a fine not exceeding [level 1 on the standard scale,] . . .

This subsection does not apply in Northern Ireland.

98, 99 ★★★★★

100 Illegal canvassing by police officers

(1) No member of a police force shall by word, message, writing or in any other manner, endeavour to persuade any person to give, or dissuade any person from giving, his vote, whether as an elector or as proxy—

(a) at any parliamentary election for a constituency, or
(b) at any local government election for any electoral area,
wholly or partly within the police area.

(2) A person acting in contravention of subsection (1) above shall be liable [on summary conviction to a fine not exceeding level 3 on the standard scale, but] nothing in that subsection shall subject a member of a police force to any penalty for anything done in the discharge of his duty as a member of the force.

(3) In this section references to a member of a police force and to a police area are to be taken in relation to Northern Ireland as references to a member of the Royal Ulster Constabulary and to Northern Ireland.

* * * * *

POLICE AND CRIMINAL EVIDENCE ACT 1984
(1984, c. 60)

An Act to make further provision in relation to the powers and duties of the police, persons in police detention, criminal evidence, police discipline and complaints against the police; to provide for arrangements for obtaining the views of the community on policing and for a rank of deputy chief constable; to amend the law relating to the Police Federations and Police Forces and Police Cadets in Scotland; and for connected purposes [31 October 1984]

Territorial extent England and Wales.

Note For the application of this Act to investigating officers of the Customs and Excise see the Police and Criminal Evidence Act 1984 (Application to Customs and Excise) Order 1985 (SI 1985 No 1800).

PART I
POWERS TO STOP AND SEARCH

1 Power of constable to stop and search persons, vehicles etc

(1) A constable may exercise any power conferred by this section—

(a) in any place to which at the time when he proposes to exercise the power the public or any section of the public has access, on payment or otherwise, as of right or by virtue of express or implied permission; or

(b) in any other place to which people have ready access at the time when he proposes to exercise the power but which is not a dwelling.

(2) Subject to subsection (3) to (5) below, a constable—
(a) may search—
(i) any person or vehicle;
(ii) anything which is in or on a vehicle,
for stolen or prohibited articles [or any article to which subsection (8A) below applies]; and
(b) may detain a person or vehicle for the purpose of such a search.

(3) This section does not give a constable power to search a person or vehicle or anything in or on a vehicle unless he has reasonable grounds for suspecting that he will find stolen or prohibited articles [or any article to which subsection (8A) below applies].

(4) If a person is in a garden or yard occupied with and used for the purposes of a dwelling or on other land so occupied and used, a constable may not search him in the exercise of the power conferred by this section unless the constable has reasonable grounds for believing—
(a) that he does not reside in the dwelling; and
(b) that he is not in the place in question with the express or implied permission of a person who resides in the dwelling.

(5) If a vehicle is in a garden or yard occupied with and used for the purposes of a dwelling or on other land so occupied and used, a constable may not search the vehicle or anything in or on it in the exercise of the power conferred by this section unless he has reasonable grounds for believing—

(a) that the person in charge of the vehicle does not reside in the dwelling; and

(b) that the vehicle is not in the place in question with the express or implied permission of a person who resides in the dwelling.

(6) If in the course of such a search a constable discovers an article which he has reasonable grounds for suspecting to be a stolen or prohibited article [or an article to which subsection (8A) applies], he may seize it.

(7) An article is prohibited for the purposes of this Part of this Act if it is—

(a) an offensive weapon; or

(b) an article—

(i) made or adapted for use in the course of or in connection with an offence to which this sub-paragraph applies; or

(ii) intended by the person having it with him for such use by him or by some other person.

(8) The offences to which subsection (7)(b)(i) above applies are—

(a) burglary;

(b) theft;

(c) offences under section 12 of the Theft Act 1968 (taking motor vehicle or other conveyance without authority); and

(d) offences under section 15 of that Act (obtaining property by deception).

[(8A) This subsection applies to any article in relation to which a person has committed, or is committing or is going to commit an offence under section 139 of the Criminal Justice Act 1988.]

(9) In this Part of this Act "offensive weapon" means any article—

(a) made or adapted for use for causing injury to persons; or

(b) intended by the person having it with him for such use by him or by some other person.

2 Provisions relating to search under section 1 and other powers

(1) A constable who detains a person or vehicle in the exercise—

(a) of the power conferred by section 1 above; or

(b) of any other power—

(i) to search a person without first arresting him; or

(ii) to search a vehicle without making an arrest,

need not conduct a search if it appears to him subsequently—

(i) that no search is required; or

(ii) that a search is impracticable.

(2) If a constable contemplates a search, other than a search of an unattended vehicle, in the exercise—

(a) of the power conferred by section 1 above; or

(b) of any other power, except the power conferred by section 6 below and the power conferred by section 27(2) of the Aviation Security Act 1982—

(i) to search a person without first arresting him; or

(ii) to search a vehicle without making an arrest,

it shall be his duty, subject to subsection (4) below, to take reasonable steps before he commences the search to bring to the attention of the appropriate person—

(i) if the constable is not in uniform, documentary evidence that he is a constable; and

(ii) whether he is in uniform or not, the matters specified in subsection (3) below;

and the constable shall not commence the search until he has performed that duty.

(3) The matters referred to in subsection (2)(ii) above are—

(a) the constable's name and the name of the police station to which he is attached;

(b) the object of the proposed search;

(c) the constable's grounds for proposing to make it; and

(d) the effect of section 3(7) or (8) below, as may be appropriate.

(4) A constable need not bring the effect of section 3(7) or (8) below to the attention of the appropriate person if it appears to the constable that it will not be practicable to make the record in section 3(1) below.

(5) In this section "the appropriate person" means—

(a) if the constable proposes to search a person, that person; and

(b) if he proposes to search a vehicle, or anything in or on a vehicle, the person in charge of the vehicle.

(6) On completing a search of an unattended vehicle or anything in or on such a vehicle in the exercise of any such power as is mentioned in subsection (2) above a constable shall leave a notice—

(a) stating that he has searched it;

(b) giving the name of the police station to which he is attached;

(c) stating that an application for compensation for any damage caused by the search may be made to that police station; and

(d) stating the effect of section 3(8) below.

(7) ★ ★ ★ ★ ★

(8) The time for which a person or vehicle may be detained for the purposes of such a search is such time as is reasonably required to permit a search to be carried out either at the place where the person or vehicle was first detained or nearby.

(9) Neither the power conferred by section 1 above nor any other power to detain and search a person without first arresting him or to detain and search a vehicle without making an arrest is to be construed—

(a) as authorising a constable to require a person to remove any of his clothing in public other than an outer coat, jacket or gloves; or

(b) as authorising a constable not in uniform to stop a vehicle.

(10) ★ ★ ★ ★ ★

3 Duty to make records concerning searches

(1) Where a constable has carried out a search in the exercise of any such power as is mentioned in section 2(1) above, other than a search—

(a) under section 6 below; or

(b) under section 27(2) of the Aviation Security Act 1982,

he shall make a record of it in writing unless it is not practicable to do so.

(2) If—

(a) a constable is required by subsection (1) above to make a record of a search; but

(b) it is not practicable to make the record on the spot,

he shall make it as soon as practicable after the completion of the search.

(3) The record of a search of a person shall include a note of his name, if the constable knows it, but a constable may not detain a person to find out his name.

(4) If a constable does not know the name of the person whom he has searched, the record of the search shall include a note otherwise describing that person.

(5) The record of a search of a vehicle shall include a note describing the vehicle.

(6) The record of a search of a person or a vehicle—

(a) shall state—

(i) the object of the search;

(ii) the grounds for making it;

(iii) the date and time when it was made;
(iv) the place where it was made;
(v) whether anything, and if so what, was found;
(vi) whether any, and if so what, injury to a person or damage to property appears to the constable to have resulted from the search; and
(b) shall identify the constable making it.

(7) If a constable who conducted a search of a person made a record of it, the person who was searched shall be entitled to a copy of the record if he asks for one before the end of the period specified in subsection (9) below.

(8) If—
(a) the owner of a vehicle which has been searched or the person who was in charge of the vehicle at the time when it was searched asks for a copy of the record of the search before the end of the period specified in subsection (9) below; and
(b) the constable who conducted the search made a record of it,
the person who made the request shall be entitled to a copy.

(9) The period mentioned in subsections (7) and (8) above is the period of 12 months beginning with the date on which the search was made.

(10) ★★★★★

4 Road checks

(1) This section shall have effect in relation to the conduct of road checks by police officers for the purpose of ascertaining whether a vehicle is carrying—
(a) a person who has committed an offence other than a road traffic offence or a [vehicle] excise offence;
(b) a person who is a witness to such an offence;
(c) a person intending to commit such an offence; or
(d) a person who is unlawfully at large.

(2) For the purposes of this section a road check consists of the exercise in a locality of the power conferred by section [163 of the Road Traffic Act 1988] in such a way as to stop during the period for which its exercise in that way in that locality continues all vehicles or vehicles selected by any criterion.

(3) Subject to subsection (5) below, there may only be such a road check if a police officer of the rank of superintendent or above authorises it in writing.

(4) An officer may only authorise a road check under subsection (3) above—
(a) for the purpose specified in subsection (1)(a) above, if he has reasonable grounds—
(i) for believing that the offence is a serious arrestable offence; and
(ii) for suspecting that the person is, or is about to be, in the locality in which vehicles would be stopped if the road check were authorised;
(b) for the purpose specified in subsection (1)(b) above, if he has reasonable grounds for believing that the offence is a serious arrestable offence;
(c) for the purpose specified in subsection (1)(c) above, if he has reasonable grounds—
(i) for believing that the offence would be a serious arrestable offence; and
(ii) for suspecting that the person is, or is about to be, in the locality in which vehicles would be stopped if the road check were authorised;
(d) for the purpose specified in subsection (1)(d) above, if he has reasonable grounds for suspecting that the person is, or is about to be, in that locality.

(5) An officer below the rank of superintendent may authorise such a road check if it appears to him that it is required as a matter of urgency for one of the purposes specified in subsection (1) above.

(6) If an authorisation is given under subsection (5) above, it shall be the duty of the officer who gives it—

(a) to make a written record of the time at which he gives it; and

(b) to cause an officer of the rank of superintendent or above to be informed that it has been given.

(7)-(14) ★★★★★

(15) Where a vehicle is stopped in a road check, the person in charge of the vehicle at the time when it is stopped shall be entitled to obtain a written statement of the purpose of the road check if he applies for such a statement not later than the end of the period of twelve months from the day on which the vehicle was stopped.

(16) Nothing in this section affects the exercise by police officers of any power to stop vehicles for purposes other than those specified in subsection (1) above.

5-7 ★★★★★

PART II
POWERS OF ENTRY, SEARCH AND SEIZURE

Search warrants

8 Power of justice of the peace to authorise entry and search of premises

(1) If on an application made by a constable a justice of the peace is satisfied that there are reasonable grounds for believing—

(a) that a serious arrestable offence has been committed; and

(b) that there is material on premises specified in the application which is likely to be of substantial value (whether by itself or together with other material) to the investigation of the offence; and

(c) that the material is likely to be relevant evidence; and

(d) that it does not consist of or include items subject to legal privilege, excluded material or special procedure material; and

(e) that any of the conditions specified in subsection (3) below applies,

he may issue a warrant authorising a constable to enter and search the premises.

(2) A constable may seize and retain anything for which a search has been authorised under subsection (1) above.

(3) The conditions mentioned in subsection (1)(e) above are—

(a) that it is not practicable to communicate with any person entitled to grant entry to the premises;

(b) that it is practicable to communicate with a person entitled to grant entry to the premises but it is not practicable to communicate with any person entitled to grant access to the evidence;

(c) that entry to the premises will not be granted unless a warrant is produced;

(d) that the purpose of a search may be frustrated or seriously prejudiced unless a constable arriving at the premises can secure immediate entry to them.

(4) In this Act "relevant evidence", in relation to an offence, means anything that would be admissible in evidence at a trial for the offence.

(5) The power to issue a warrant conferred by this section is in addition to any such power otherwise conferred.

9 Special provisions as to access

(1) A constable may obtain access to excluded material or special procedure material for the purposes of a criminal investigation by making an application under Schedule 1 below and in accordance with that Schedule.

(2) Any Act (including a local Act) passed before this Act under which a search of premises for the purposes of a criminal investigation could be authorised by the issue of a warrant to a constable shall cease to have effect so far as it relates to the authorisation of searches—

(a) for items subject to legal privilege; or

(b) for excluded material; or

(c) for special procedure material consisting of documents or records other than documents.

10 Meaning of "items subject to legal privilege"

(1) Subject to subsection (2) below, in this Act "items subject to legal privilege" means—

(a) communications between a professional legal adviser and his client or any person representing his client made in connection with the giving of legal advice to the client;

(b) communications between a professional legal adviser and his client or any person representing his client or between such an adviser or his client or any such representative and any other person made in connection with or in contemplation of legal proceedings and for the purposes of such proceedings; and

(c) items enclosed with or referred to in such communications and made—

(i) in connection with the giving of legal advice; or

(ii) in connection with or in contemplation of legal proceedings and for the purposes of such proceedings,

when they are in the possession of a person who is entitled to possesion of them.

(2) Items held with the intention of furthering a criminal purpose are not items subject to legal privilege.

11 Meaning of "excluded material"

(1) Subject to the following provisions of this section, in this Act "excluded material" means—

(a) personal records which a person has acquired or created in the course of any trade, business, profession or other occupation or for the purposes of any paid or unpaid office and which he holds in confidence;

(b) human tissue or tissue fluid which has been taken for the purposes of diagnosis or medical treatment and which a person holds in confidence;

(c) journalistic material which a person holds in confidence and which consists—

(i) of documents; or

(ii) of records other than documents.

(2) A person holds material other than journalistic material in confidence for the purposes of this section if he holds it subject—

(a) to an express or implied undertaking to hold it in confidence; or

(b) to a restriction on disclosure or an obligation of secrecy contained in any enactment, including an enactment contained in an Act passed after this Act.

(3) A person holds journalistic material in confidence for the purposes of this section if—

(a) he holds it subject to such an undertaking, restriction or obligation; and

(b) it has been continuously held (by one or more persons) subject to such an undertaking, restriction or obligation since it was first acquired or created for the purposes of journalism.

12 Meaning of "personal records"

In this Part of this Act "personal records" means documentary and other records concerning an individual (whether living or dead) who can be identified from them and relating—

(a) to his physical or mental health;

(b) to spiritual counselling or assistance given or to be given to him; or

(c) to counselling or assistance given or to be given to him, for the purposes of his personal welfare, by any voluntary organisation or by any individual who—

(i) by reason of his office or occupation has responsibilities for his personal welfare; or

(ii) by reason of an order of a court has responsibilities for his supervision.

13 Meaning of "journalistic material"

(1) Subject to subsection (2) below, in this Act "journalistic material" means material acquired or created for the purposes of journalism.

(2) Material is only journalistic material for the purposes of this Act if it is in the possession of a person who acquired or created it for the purposes of journalism.

(3) A person who receives material from someone who intends that the recipient shall use it for the purposes of journalism is to be taken to have acquired it for those purposes.

14 Meaning of "special procedure material"

(1) In this Act "special procedure material" means—

(a) material to which subsection (2) below applies; and

(b) journalistic material, other than excluded material.

(2) Subject to the following provisions of this section, this subsection applies to material, other than items subject to legal privilege and excluded material, in the possession of a person who—

(a) acquired or created it in the course of any trade, business, profession or other occupation or for the purposes of any paid or unpaid office; and

(b) holds it subject—

(i) to an express or implied undertaking to hold it in confidence; or

(ii) to a restriction or obligation such as is mentioned in section 11(2)(b) above.

(3)-(6) ★★★★★

15 Search warrants — safeguards

(1) This section and section 16 below have effect in relation to the issue to constables under any enactment, including an enactment contained in an Act passed after this Act, of warrants to enter and search premises; and an entry on or search of premises under a warrant is unlawful unless it complies with this section and section 16 below.

(2) Where a constable applies for any such warrant, it shall be his duty—

(a) to state—

(i) the ground on which he makes the application; and

(ii) the enactment under which the warrant would be issued;

(b) to specify the premises which it is desired to enter and search; and

(c) to identify, so far as is practicable, the articles or persons to be sought.

(3) An application for such a warrant shall be made ex parte and supported by an information in writing.

(4) The constable shall answer on oath any question that the justice of the peace or judge hearing the application asks him.

(5) A warrant shall authorise an entry on one occasion only.

(6) A warrant—

(a) shall specify—

(i) the name of the person who applies for it;

(ii) the date on which it is issued;

(iii) the enactment under which it is issued; and

(iv) the premises to be searched; and

(b) shall identify, so far as is practicable, the articles or persons to be sought.

(7), (8) ★★★★★

16 Execution of warrants

(1) A warrant to enter and search premises may be executed by any constable.

(2) Such a warrant may authorise persons to accompany any constable who is executing it.

(3) Entry and search under a warrant must be within one month from the date of its issue.

(4) Entry and search under a warrant must be at a reasonable hour unless it appears to the constable executing it that the purpose of a search may be frustrated on an entry at a reasonable hour.

(5) Where the occupier of premises which are to be entered and searched is present at the time when a constable seeks to execute a warrant to enter and search them, the constable—

(a) shall identify himself to the occupier and, if not in uniform, shall produce to him documentary evidence that he is a constable;

(b) shall produce the warrant to him; and

(c) shall supply him with a copy of it.

(6) Where—

(a) the occupier of such premises is not present at the time when a constable seeks to execute such a warrant; but

(b) some other person who appears to the constable to be in charge of the premises is present,

subsection (5) above shall have effect as if any reference to the occupier were a reference to that other person.

(7) If there is no person present who appears to the constable to be in charge of the premises, he shall leave a copy of the warrant in a prominent place on the premises.

(8) A search under a warrant may only be a search to the extent required for the purpose for which the warrant was issued.

(9) A constable executing a warrant shall make an endorsement on it stating—

(a) whether the articles or persons sought were found; and

(b) whether any articles were seized, other than articles which were sought.

(10)-(12) ★★★★★

Entry and search without search warrant

17 Entry for purpose of arrest etc.

(1) Subject to the following provisions of this section, and without prejudice to any other enactment, a constable may enter and search any premises for the purpose—

(a) of executing—

(i) a warrant of arrest issued in connection with or arising out of criminal proceedings; or

(ii) a warrant of commitment issued under section 76 of the Magistrates' Courts Act 1980;

(b) of arresting a person for an arrestable offence;

(c) of arresting a person for an offence under—

(i) section 1 (prohibition of uniforms in connection with political objects) . . . of the Public Order Act 1936;

(ii) any enactment contained in sections 6 to 8 or 10 of the Criminal Law Act 1977 (offences relating to entering and remaining on property);

[(iii) section 4 of the Public Order Act 1986 (fear or provocation of violence)] [; or

(iv) section 76 of the Criminal Justice and Public Order Act 1994 (failure to comply with an interim possession order);]

[(ca) of arresting, in pursuance of section 32(1A) of the Children and Young Persons Act 1969, any child or young person who has been remanded or committed to local authority accommodation under section 23(1) of that Act;

(cb) of recapturing any person who is, or is deemed for any purpose to be, unlawfully at large while liable to be detained—

(i) in a prison, remand centre, young offender institution or secure training centre, or

(ii) in pursuance of section 53 of the Children and Young Persons Act 1933 (dealing with children and young persons guilty of grave crimes), in any other place;]

(d) of recapturing [any person whatever] who is unlawfully at large and whom he is pursuing; or

(e) of saving life or limb or preventing serious damage to property.

(2) Except for the purpose specified in paragraph (e) of subsection (1) above, the powers of entry and search conferred by this section—

(a) are only exercisable if the constable has reasonable grounds for believing that the person whom he is seeking is on the premises; and

(b) are limited, in relation to premises consisting of two or more separate dwellings, to powers to enter and search—

(i) any parts of the premises which the occupiers of any dwelling comprised in the premises use in common with the occupiers of any other such dwelling; and

(ii) any such dwelling in which the constable has reasonable grounds for believing that the person whom he is seeking may be.

(3) The powers of entry and search conferred by this section are only exercisable for the purposes specified in subsection (1)(c)(ii) [or (iv)] above by a constable in uniform.

(4) The power of search conferred by this section is only a power to search to the extent that is reasonably required for the purpose for which the power of entry is exercised.

(5) Subject to subsection (6) below, all the rules of common law under which a constable has power to enter premises without a warrant are hereby abolished.

(6) Nothing in subsection (5) above affects any power of entry to deal with or prevent a breach of the peace.

18 Entry and search after arrest

(1) Subject to the following provisions of this section, a constable may enter and search any premises occupied or controlled by a person who is under arrest for an arrestable offence, if he has reasonable grounds for suspecting that there is on the premises evidence, other than items subject to legal privilege, that relates—

(a) to that offence; or

(b) to some other arrestable offence which is connected with or similar to that offence.

(2) A constable may seize and retain anything for which he may search under subsection (1) above.

(3) The power to search conferred by subsection (1) above is only a power to search to the extent that is reasonably required for the purpose of discovering such evidence.

(4) Subject to subsection (5) below, the powers conferred by this section may not be exercised unless an officer of the rank of inspector or above has authorised them in writing.

(5) A constable may conduct a search under subsection (1) above—

(a) before taking the person to a police station; and

(b) without obtaining an authorisation under subsection (4) above,

if the presence of that person at a place other than a police station is necssary for the effective investigation of the offence.

(6) If a constable conducts a search by virtue of subsection (5) above, he shall inform an officer of the rank of inspector or above that he has made the search as soon as practicable after he has made it.

(7) An officer who—

(a) authorises a search; or

(b) is informed of a search under subsection (6) above, shall make a record in writing—

(i) of the ground for the search; and

(ii) of the nature of the evidence that was sought.

(8) If the person who was in occupation or control of the premises at the time of the search is in police detention at the time the record is to be made, the officer shall make the record as part of his custody record.

Seizure etc.

19 General power of seizure etc.

(1) The powers conferred by subsections (2), (3) and (4) below are exercisable by a constable who is lawfully on any premises.

(2) The constable may seize anything which is on the premises if he has reasonable grounds for believing—

(a) that it has been obtained in consequence of the commission of an offence; and

(b) that it is necessary to seize it in order to prevent it being concealed, lost, damaged, altered or destroyed.

(3) The constable may seize anything which is on the premises if he has reasonable grounds for believing—

(a) that it is evidence in relation to an offence which he is investigating or any other offence; and

(b) that it is necessary to seize it in order to prevent the evidence being concealed, lost, altered or destroyed.

(4) The constable may require any information which is contained in a computer and is accessible from the premises to be produced in a form in which it can be taken away and in which it is visible and legible if he has reasonable grounds for believing—

(a) that—

(i) it is evidence in relation to an offence which he is investigating or any other offence; or

(ii) it has been obtained in consequence of the commission of an offence; and

(b) that it is necessary to do so in order to prevent it being concealed, lost, tampered with or destroyed.

(5) The powers conferred by this section are in addition to any power otherwise conferred.

(6) No power of seizure conferred on a constable under any enactment (including an enactment contained in an Act passed after this Act) is to be taken to authorise the seizure of an item which the constable exercising the power has reasonable grounds for believing to be subject to legal privilege.

20 Extension of powers of seizure to computerised information

(1) Every power of seizure which is conferred by an enactment to which this section applies on a constable who has entered premises in the exercise of a power conferred by an enactment shall be construed as including a power to require any information contained in a computer and accessible from the premises to be produced in a form in which it can be taken away and in which it is visible and legible.

(2) This section applies—

(a) to any enactment contained in an Act passed before this Act;

(b) to sections 8 and 18 above;

(c) to paragraph 13 of Schedule 1 to this Act; and

(d) to any enactment contained in an Act passed after this Act.

21 Access and copying

(1) A constable who seizes anything in the exercise of a power conferred by any enactment, including an enactment contained in an Act passed after this Act, shall, if so requested by a person showing himself—

(a) to be the occupier of premises on which it was seized; or

(b) to have had custody or control of it immediately before the seizure,

provide that person with a record of what he seized.

(2) The officer shall provide the record within a reasonable time from the making of the request for it.

(3) Subject to subsection (8) below, if a request for permission to be granted access to anything which—

(a) has been seized by a constable; and

(b) is retained by the police for the purpose of investigating an offence,

is made to the officer in charge of the investigation by a person who had custody or control of the thing immediately before it was so seized or by someone acting on behalf of such a person the officer shall allow the person who made the request access to it under the supervision of a constable.

(4) Subject to subsection (8) below, if a request for a photograph or copy of any such thing is made to the officer in charge of the investigation by a person who had custody or control of the thing immediately before it was so seized, or by someone acting on behalf of such a person, the officer shall—

(a) allow the person who made the rquest access to it under the supervision of a constable for the purpose of photographing or copying it; or

(b) photograph or copy it, or cause it to be photographed or copied.

(5) A constable may also photograph or copy, or have photographed or copied, anything which he has power to seize, without a request being made under subsection (4) above.

(6) Where anything is photographed or copied under subsection (4)(b) above, the photograph or copy shall be supplied to the person who made the request.

(7) The photograph or copy shall be so supplied within a reasonable time from the making of the request.

(8) There is no duty under this section to grant access to, or to supply a photograph or copy of, anything if the officer in charge of the investigation for the purposes of which it was seized has reasonable grounds for believing that to do so would prejudice—

(a) that investigation;

(b) the investigation of an offence other than the offence for the purposes of investigating which the thing was seized; or

(c) any criminal proceedings which may be brought as a result of—

(i) the investigation of which he is in charge; or

(ii) any such investigation as is mentioned in paragraph (b) above.

22 Retention

(1) Subject to subsection (4) below, anything which has been seized by a constable or taken away by a constable following a requirement made by virtue of section 19 or 20 above may be retained so long as is necessary in all the circumstances.

(2) Without prejudice to the generality of subsection (1) above—

(a) anything seized for the purposes of a criminal investigation may be retained, except as provided by subsection (4) below—

(i) for use as evidence at a trial for an offence; or

(ii) for forensic examination or for investigation in connection with an offence;

and

(b) anything may be retained in order to establish its lawful owner, where there are reasonable grounds for believing that it has been obtained in consequence of the commission of an offence.

(3) Nothing seized on the ground that it may be used—

(a) to cause physical injury to any person;

(b) to damage property;

(c) to interfere with evidence; or

(d) to assist in escape from police detention or lawful custody, may be retained when the person from whom it was seized is no longer in police detention or the custody of a court or is in the custody of a court but has been released on bail.

(4) Nothing may be retained for either of the purposes mentioned in subsection (2)(a) above if a photograph or copy would be sufficient for that purpose.

(5) Nothing in this section affects any power of a court to make an order under section 1 of the Police (Property) Act 1897

23 * * * * *

PART III
ARREST

24 Arrest without warrant for arrestable offences

(1) The powers of summary arrest conferred by the following subsections shall apply—

(a) to offences for which the sentence is fixed by law;

(b) to offences for which a person of 21 years of age or over (not previously convicted) may be sentenced to imprisonment for a term of five years (or might be so sentenced but for the restrictions imposed by section 33 of the Magistrates' Courts Act 1980); and

(c) to the offences to which subsection (2) below applies,

and in this Act "arrestable offence" means any such offence.

(2) The offences to which this subsection applies are—

(a) offences for which a person may be arrested under the customs and excise Acts, as defined in section 1(1) of the Customs and Excise Management Act 1979;

(b) offences under [the Official Secrets Act 1920] that are not arrestable offences by virtue of the term of imprisonment for which a person may be sentenced in respect of them;

[(bb) offences under any provision of the Official Secrets Act 1989 except section 8(1), (4) or (5);]

(c) offences under section ... 22 (causing prostitution of women) or 23 (procuration of girl under 21) of the Sexual Offences Act 1956;

(d) offences under section 12(1) (taking motor vehicle or other conveyance without authority etc.) or 25(1) (going equipped for stealing, etc.) of the Theft Act 1968; ....

[(e) any offence under the Football (Offences) Act 1991];

[(f) an offence under section 2 of the Obscene Publications Act 1959 (publication of obscene matter);

(g) an offence under section 1 of the Protection of Children Act 1978 (indecent photographs and pseudo-photographs of children);]

[(h) an offence under section 166 of the Criminal Justice and Public Order Act 1994 (sale of tickets by unauthorised persons);

(i) an offence under section 19 of the Public Order Act 1986 (publishing etc., material intended or likely to stir up racial hatred);

(j) an offence under section 167 of the Criminal Justice and Public Order Act 1994 (touting for hire car services)];

[(k) an offence under section 1(1) of the Prevention of Crime Act 1953 (prohibition of the carrying of offensive weapons without lawful authority or reasonable excuse);

(l) an offence under section 139(1) of the Criminal Justice Act 1988 (offence of having article with blade or point in public place);]

[(m) an offence under section 139A(1) or (2) of the Criminal Justice Act 1988 (offence of having article with blade or point (or offensive weapon) on school premises);]

[(n) an offence under the Protection from Harassment Act 1997 (harassment)].

(3) Without prejudice to section 2 of the Criminal Attempts Act 1981, the powers of summary arrest conferred by the following subsections shall also apply to the offences of—

(a) conspiring to commit any of the offences mentioned in subsection (2) above;

(b) attempting to commit any such offence [other than an offence under section 12(1) of the Theft Act 1968];

(c) inciting, aiding, abetting, counselling or procuring the commission of any such offence;

and such offences are also arrestable offences for the purposes of this Act.

(4) Any person may arrest without a warrant—

(a) anyone who is in the act of committing an arrestable offence;

(b) anyone whom he has reasonable grounds for suspecting to be committing such an offence.

(5) Where an arrestable offence has been committed, any person may arrest without a warrant—

(a) anyone who is guilty of the offence;

(b) anyone whom he has reasonable grounds for suspecting to be guilty of it.

(6) Where a constable has reasonable grounds for suspecting that an arrestable offence has been committed, he may arrest without a warrant anyone whom he has reasonable grounds for suspecting to be guilty of the offence.

(7) A constable may arrest without a warrant—

(a) anyone who is about to commit an arrestable offence;

(b) anyone whom he has reasonable grounds for suspecting to be about to commit an arrestable offence.

25 General arrest conditions

(1) Where a constable has reasonable grounds for suspecting that any offence which is not an arrestable offence has been committed or attempted, or is being committed or attempted, he may arrest the relevant person if it appears to him that service of a summons is impracticable or inappropriate because any of the general arrest conditions is satisfied.

(2) In this section "the relevant person" means any person whom the constable has reasonable grounds to suspect of having committed or having attempted to commit the offence or of being in the course of committing or attempting to commit it.

(3) The general arrest conditions are—

(a) that the name of the relevant person is unknown to, and cannot be readily ascertained by, the constable;

(b) that the constable has reasonable grounds for doubting whether a name furnished by the relevant person as his name is his real name;

(c) that—

(i) the relevant person has failed to furnish a satisfactory address for service; or

(ii) the constable has reasonable grounds for doubting whether an address furnished by the relevant person is a satisfactory address for service;

(d) that the constable has reasonable grounds for believing that arrest is necessary to prevent the relevant person—

(i) causing physical injury to himself or any other person;

(ii) suffering physical injury;

(iii) causing loss of or damage to property;

(iv) committing an offence against public decency; or

(v) causing an unlawful obstruction of the highway;

(e) that the constable has reasonable grounds for believing that arrest is necessary to protect a child or other vulnerable person from the relevant person.

(4) For the purposes of subsection (3) above an address is a satisfactory address for service if it appears to the constable—

(a) that the relevant person will be at it for a sufficiently long period for it to be possible to serve him with a summons; or

(b) that some other person specified by the relevant person will accept service of a summons for the relevant person at it.

(5) Nothing in subsection (3)(d) above authorises the arrest of a person under sub-paragraph (iv) of that paragraph except where members of the public going about their normal business cannot reasonably be expected to avoid the person to be arrested.

(6) This section shall not prejudice any power of arrest conferred apart from this section.

26 Repeal of statutory powers of arrest without warrant or order

(1) Subject to subsection (2) below, so much of any Act (including a local Act) passed before this Act as enables a constable—

(a) to arrest a person for an offence without a warrant; or

(b) to arrest a person otherwise than for an offence without a warrant or an order of a court,

shall cease to have effect.

(2) Nothing in subsection (1) above affects the enactments specified in Schedule 2 to this Act.

27 ★★★★★

28 Information to be given on arrest

(1) Subject to subsection (5) below, where a person is arrested, otherwise than by being informed that he is under arrest, the arrest is not lawful unless the person arrested is informed that he is under arrest as soon as is practicable after his arrest.

(2) Where a person is arrested by a constable, subsection (1) above applies regardless of whether the fact of the arrest is obvious.

(3) Subject to subsection (5) below, no arrest is lawful unless the person arrested is informed of the ground for the arrest at the time of, or as soon as is practicable after, the arrest.

(4) Where a person is arrested by a constable, subsection (3) above applies regardless of whether the ground for the arrest is obvious.

(5) Nothing in this section is to be taken to require a person to be informed—

(a) that he is under arrest; or

(b) of the ground for the arrest,

if it was not reasonably practicable for him to be so informed by reason of his having escaped from arrest before the information could be given.

29 Voluntary attendance at police station etc.

Where for the purpose of assisting with an investigation a person attends voluntarily at a police station or at any other place where a constable is present or accompanies a constable to a police station or any such other place without having been arrested—

(a) he shall be entitled to leave at will unless he is placed under arrest;

(b) he shall be informed at once that he is under arrest if a decision is taken by a constable to prevent him from leaving at will.

30 Arrest elsewhere than at police station

(1) Subject to the following provisions of this section, where a person—

(a) is arrested by a constable for an offence; or

(b) is taken into custody by a constable after being arrested for an offence by a person other than a constable, at any place other than a police station, he shall be taken to a police station by a constable as soon as practicable after the arrest.

(2) Subject to subsections (3) and (5) below, the police station to which an arrested person is taken under subsection (1) above shall be a designated police station.

(3)-(5) ★★★★★

(6) If the first police station to which an arrested person is taken after his arrest is not a designated police station, he shall be taken to a designated police station not more than six hours after his arrival at the first police station unless he is released previously.

(7) A person arrested by a constable at a place other than a police station shall be released if a constable is satisfied, before the person arrested reaches a police station, that there are no grounds for keeping him under arrest.

(8), (9) ★★★★★

(10) Nothing in subsection (1) above shall prevent a constable delaying taking a person who has been arrested to a police station if the presence of that person elsewhere is necessary in order to carry out such investigations as it is reasonable to carry out immediately.

(11)-(13) ★★★★★

31 Arrest for further offence

Where—

(a) a person—

(i) has been arrested for an offence; and

(ii) is at a police station in consequence of that arrest; and

(b) it appears to a constable that, if he were released from that arrest, he would be liable to arrest for some other offence,

he shall be arrested for that other offence.

32 Search upon arrest

(1) A constable may search an arrested person, in any case where the person to be searched has been arrested at a place other than a police station, if the constable has reasonable grounds for believing that the arrested person may present a danger to himself or others.

(2) Subject to subsections (3) to (5) below, a constable shall also have power in any such case—

(a) to search the arrested person for anything—

(i) which he might use to assist him to escape from lawful custody; or

(ii) which might be evidence relating to an offence; and

(b) to enter and search any premises in which he was when arrested or immediately before he was arrested for evidence relating to the offence for which he has been arrested.

(3) The power to search conferred by subsection (2) above is only a power to search to the extent that is reasonably required for the purpose of discovering any such thing or any such evidence.

(4) The powers conferred by this section to search a person are not to be construed as authorising a constable to require a person to remove any of his clothing in public other than an outer coat, jacket or gloves [but they do authorise a search of a person's mouth].

(5) A constable may not search a person in the exercise of the power conferred by subsection (2)(a) above unless he has reasonable grounds for believing that the person to be searched may have concealed on him anything for which a search is permitted under that paragraph.

(6) A constable may not search premises in the exercise of the power conferred by subsection (2)(b) above unless he has reasonable grounds for believing that there is evidence for which a search is permitted under that paragraph on the premises.

(7) In so far as the power of search conferred by subsection (2)(b) above relates to premises consisting of two or more separate dwellings, it is limited to a power to search—

(a) any dwelling in which the arrest took place or in which the person arrested was immediately before his arrest; and

(b) any parts of the premises which the occupier of any such dwelling uses in common with the occupiers of any other dwellings comprised in the premises.

(8) A constable searching a person in the exercise of the power conferred by subsection (1) above may seize and retain anything he finds, if he has reasonable grounds for believing that the person searched might use it to cause physical injury to himself or to any other person.

(9) A constable searching a person in the exercise of the power conferred by subsection (2)(a) above may seize and retain anything he finds, other than an item subject to legal privilege, if he has reasonable grounds for believing—

(a) that he might use it to assist him to escape from lawful custody; or

(b) that it is evidence of an offence or has been obtained in consequence of the commission of an offence.

(10) Nothing in this section shall be taken to affect the power conferred by [section 15(3), (4) and (5) of the Prevention of Terrorism (Temporary Provisions) Act 1989].

33 ★★★★★

PART IV
DETENTION

Detention — conditions and duration

34 Limitations on police detention

(1) A person arrested for an offence shall not be kept in police detention except in accordance with the provisions of this Part of this Act.

(2) Subject to subsection (3) below, if at any time a custody officer—

(a) becomes aware, in relation to any person in police detention, that the grounds for the detention of that person have ceased to apply; and

(b) is not aware of any other grounds on which the continued detention of that person could be justified under the provisions of this Part of this Act,

it shall be the duty of the custody officer, subject to subsection (4) below, to order his immediate release from custody.

(3) No person in police detention shall be released except on the authority of a custody officer at the police station where his detention was authorised or, if it was authorised at more than one station, a custody officer at the station where it was last authorised.

(4) A person who appears to the custody officer to have been unlawfully at large when he was arrested is not to be released under subsection (2) above.

(5)-(7) ★★★★★

35 Designated police stations

(1) The chief officer of police for each police area shall designate the police stations in his area which, subject to sections 30(3) and (5) above, are to be the stations in that area to be used for the purpose of detention arrested persons.

(2) A chief officer's duty under subsection (1) above is to designate police stations appearing to him to provide enough accommodation for that purpose.

(3), (4) ★★★★★

36 Custody officers at police stations

(1) One or more custody officers shall be appointed for each designated police station.

(2) A custody officer for a designated police station shall be appointed—

(a) by the chief officer of police for the area in which the designated police station is situated; or

(b) by such other police officer as the chief officer of police for that area may direct.

(3) No officer may be appointed a custody officer unless he is of at least the rank of sergeant.

(4) An officer of any rank may perform the functions of a custody officer at a designated police station if a custody officer is not readily available to perform them.

(5) Subject to the following provisions of this section and to section 39(2) below, none of the functions of a custody officer in relation to a person shall be performed by an officer who at the time when the function falls to be performed is involved in the investigation of an offence for which that person is in police detention at that time.

(6)-(10) * * * * *

37 Duties of custody officer before charge

(1) Where—

(a) a person is arrested for an offence—

(i) without a warrant; or

(ii) under a warrant not endorsed for bail,

the custody officer at each police station where he is detained after his arrest shall determine whether he has before him sufficient evidence to charge that person with the offence for which he was arrested and may detain him at the police station for such period as is necessary to enable him to do so.

(2) If the custody officer determines that he does not have such evidence before him, the person arrested shall be released either on bail or without bail, unless the custody officer has reasonable grounds for believing that his detention without being charged is necessary to secure or preserve evidence relating to an offence for which he is under arrest or to obtain such evidence by questioning him.

(3) If the custody officer has reasonable grounds for so believing, he may authorise the person arrested to be kept in police detention.

(4) Where a custody officer authorises a person who has not been charged to be kept in police detention, he shall, as soon as is practicable, make a written record of the grounds for the detention.

(5) Subject to subsection (6) below, the written record shall be made in the presence of the person arrested who shall at that time be informed by the custody officer of the grounds for his detention.

(6) Subsection (5) above shall not apply where the person arrested is, at the time when the written record is made—

(a) incapable of understanding what is said to him;

(b) violent or likely to become violent; or

(c) in urgent need of medical attention.

(7) Subject to section 41(7) below, if the custody officer determines that he has before him sufficient evidence to charge the person arrested with the offence for which he was arrested, the person arrested—

(a) shall be charged; or

(b) shall be released without charge, either on bail or without bail.

(8) * * * * *

(9) If the person arrested is not in a fit state to be dealt with under subsection (7) above, he may be kept in police detention until he is.

(10) The duty imposed on the custody officer under subsection (1) above shall be carried out by him as soon as practicable after the person arrested arrives at the police station or, in the case of a person arrested at the police station, as soon as practicable after the arrest.

(11)-(14) ...
(15) ★★★★★

38 Duties of custody officer after charge

(1) Where a person arrested for an offence otherwise than under a warrant endorsed for bail is charged with an offence, the custody officer shall order his release from police detention, either on bail or without bail, unless—

(a) if the person arrested is not an arrested juvenile—

(i) his name or address cannot be ascertained or the custody officer has reasonable grounds for doubting whether a name or address furnished by him as his name or address is his real name or address;

[(ii) the custody officer has reasonable grounds for believing that the person arrested will fail to appear in court to answer to bail;

(iii) in the case of a person arrested for an imprisonable offence, the custody officer has reasonable grounds for believing that the detention of the person arrested is necessary to prevent him from committing an offence;

(iv) in the case of a person arrested for an offence which is not an imprisonable offence, the custody officer has reasonable grounds for believing that the detention of the person arrested is necessary to prevent him from causing physical injury to any other person or from causing loss of or damage to property;

(v) the custody officer has reasonable grounds for believing that the detention of the person arrested is necessary to prevent him from interfering with the administration of justice or with the investigation of offences or of a particular offence; or

(vi) the custody officer has reasonable grounds for believing that the detention of the person arrested is necessary for his own protection;]

(b) if he is an arrested juvenile—

(i) any of the requirements of paragraph (a) above is satisfied; or

(ii) the custody officer has reasonable grounds for believing that he ought to be detained in his own interests.

(2) If the release of a person arrested is not required by subsection (1) above, the custody officer may authorise him to be kept in police detention.

(2A) ★★★★★

(3) Where a custody officer authorises a person who has been charged to be kept in police detention, he shall, as soon as practicable, make a written record of the grounds for the detention.

(4) Subject to subsection (5) below, the written record shall be made in the presence of the person charged who shall at that time be informed by the custody officer of the grounds for his detention.

(5) Subsection (4) above shall not apply where the person charged is, at the time when the written record is made—

(a) incapable of understanding what is said to him;

(b) violent or likely to become violent; or

(c) in urgent need of medical attention.

[(6) Where a custody officer authorises an arrested juvenile to be kept in police detention under subsection (1) above, the custody officer shall, unless he certifies—

(a) that by reason of such circumstances as are specified in the certificate, it is impracticable for him to do so; or

(b) in the case of an arrested juvenile who has attained the [age of 12 years], that no secure accommodation is available and that keeping him in other local authority accommodation would not be adequate to protect the public from serious harm from him, secure that the arrested juvenile is moved to local authority accommodation.]

(6A) ★★★★★

[(6B) Where an arrested juvenile is moved to local authority accommodation under subsection 6 above, it shall be lawful for any person acting on behalf of the authority to detain him.]

(7), (7A), (8) ★★★★★

39 Responsibilities in relation to persons detained

(1) Subject to subsection (2) and (4) below, it shall be the duty of the custody officer at a police station to ensure—

(a) that all persons in police detention at that station are treated in accordance with this Act and any code of practice issued under it and relating to the treatment of persons in police detention; and

(b) that all matters relating to such persons which are required by this Act or by such codes of practice to be recorded are recorded in the custody records relating to such persons.

(2)-(5) ★★★★★

(6) Where—

(a) an officer of higher rank than the custody officer gives directions relating to a person in police detention; and

(b) the directions are at variance—

(i) with any decision made or action taken by the custody officer in the performance of a duty imposed on him under this Part of this Act; or

(ii) with any decision or action which would be for the directions have been made or taken by him in the performance of such a duty,

the custody officer shall refer the matter at once to an officer of the rank of superintendent or above who is responsible for the police station for which the custody officer is acting as custody officer.

40 Review of police detention

(1) Reviews of the detention of each person in police detention in connection with the investigation of an offence shall be carried out periodically in accordance with the following provisions of this section—

(a) in the case of a person who has been arrested and charged, by the custody officer; and

(b) in the case of a person who has been arrested but not charged, by an officer of at least the rank of inspector who has not been directly involved in the investigation.

(2) The officer to whom it falls to carry out a review is referred to in this section as a "review officer".

(3) Subject to subsection (4) below—

(a) the first review shall be not later than six hours after the detention was first authorised;

(b) the second review shall be not later than nine hours after the first;

(c) subsequent reviews shall be at intervals of not more than nine hours.

(4) A review may be postponed—

(a) if, having regard to all the circumstances prevailing at the latest time for it specified in subsection (3) above, it is not practicable to carry out the review at that time;

(b) without prejudice to the generality of paragraph (a) above—

(i) if at that time the person in detention is being questioned by a police officer and the review officer is satisfied that an interruption of the questioning for the purpose of carrying out the review would prejudice the investigation in connection with which he is being questioned; or

(ii) if at that time no review officer is readily available.

(5) If a review is postponed under subsection (4) above it shall be carried out as soon as practicable after the latest time specified for it in subsection (3) above.

(6) If a review is carried out after postponement under subsection (4) above, the fact that it was so carried out shall not affect any requirement of this section as to the time at which any subsequent review is to be carried out.

(7) The review officer shall record the reasons for any postponement of a review in the custody record.

(8) Subject to subsection (9) below, where the person whose detention is under review has not been charged before the time of the review, section 37(1) to (6) above shall have effect in relation to him, but with the substitution—

(a) of references to the person whose detention is under review for references to the person arrested; and

(b) of references to the review officer for references to the custody officer.

(9) Where a person has been kept in police detention by virtue of section 37(9) above, section 37(1) to (6) shall not have effect in relation to him but it shall be the duty of the review officer to determine whether he is yet in a fit state.

(10) Where the person whose detention is under review has been charged before the time of the review, section 38(1) to (6) above shall have effect in relation to him, with the sutstitution of references to the person whose detention is under review for references to the person arrested.

(11) Where—

(a) an officer of higher rank than the review officer gives directions relating to a person in police detention; and

(b) the directions are at variance—

(i) with any decision made or action taken by the review officer in the performance of a duty imposed on him under this Part of this Act; or

(ii) with any decision or action which would but for the directions have been made or taken by him in the performance of such a duty,

the review officer shall refer the matter at once to an officer of the rank of superintendent or above who is responsible for the police station for which the review officer is acting as review officer in connection with the detention.

(12) Before determining whether to authorise a person's continued detention the review officer shall give—

(a) that person (unless he is asleep); or

(b) any solicitor representing him who is available at the time of the review,

an opportunity to make representations to him abut the detention.

(13), (14) * * * * *

41 Limits on period of detention without charge

(1) Subject to the following provisions of this section and to sections 42 and 43 below, a person shall not be kept in police detention for more than 24 hours without being charged.

(2) The time from which the period of detention of a person is to be calculated (in this Act referred to as "the relevant time")—

(a) in the case of a person to whom this paragraph applies, shall be—

(i) the time at which that person arrives at the relevant police station; or

(ii) the time 24 hours after the time of that person's arrest,

whichever is the earlier;

(b) in the case of a person arrested outside England and Wales, shall be—

(i) the time at which that person arrives at the first police station to which he is taken in the police area in England or Wales in which the offence for which he was arrested is being investigated; or

(ii) the time 24 hours after the time of that person's entry into England and Wales,

whichever is the earlier;

(c) in the case of a person who—
(i) attends voluntarily at a police station; or
(ii) accompanies a constable to a police station without having been arrested,
and is arrested at the police station, the time of his arrest;
(d) in any other case, except where subsection (5) below applies, shall be the time at which the person arrested arrives at the first police station to which he is taken after his arrest.
(3)-(6) ★★★★★
(7) Subject to subsection (8) below, a person who at the expiry of 24 hours after the relevant time is in police detention and has not been charged shall be released at that time either on bail or without bail.
(8) Subsection (7) above does not apply to a person whose detention for more than 24 hours after the relevant time has been authorised or is otherwise permitted in accordance with section 42 or 43 below.
(9) ★★★★★

42 Authorisation of continued detention
(1) Where a police officer of the rank of superintendent or above who is responsible for the police station at which a person is detained has reasonable grounds for believing that—
(a) the detention of that person without charge is necessary to secure or preserve evidence relating to an offence for which he is under arrest or to obtain such evidence by questioning him;
(b) an offence for which he is under arrest is a serious arrestable offence; and
(c) the investigation is being conducted diligently and expeditiously,
he may authorise the keeping of that person in police detention for a period expiring at or before 36 hours after the relevant time.
(2) Where an officer such as is mentioned in subsection (1) above has authorised the keeping of a person in police detention for a period expiring less than 36 hours after the relevant time, such an officer may authorise the keeping of that person in police detention for a further period expiring not more than 36 hours after that time if the conditions specified in subsection (1) above are still satisfied when he gives the authorisation.
(3) If it is proposed to transfer a person in police detention to another police area, the officer determining whether or not to authorise keeping him in detention under subsection (1) above shall have regard to the distance and the time the journey would take.
(4) No authorisation under subsection (1) above shall be given in respect of any person—
(a) more than 24 hours after the relevant time; or
(b) before the second review of his detention under section 40 above has been carried out.
(5) Where an officer authorises the keeping of a person in police detention under subsection (1) above, it shall be his duty—
(a) to inform that person of the grounds for his continued detention; and
(b) to record the grounds in that person's custody record.
(6) Before determining whether to authorise the keeping of a person in detention under subsection (1) or (2) above, an officer shall give—
(a) that person; or
(b) any solicitor representing him who is available at the time when it falls to the officer to determine whether to give the authorisation,
an opportunity to make representations to him about the detention.
(7), (8) ★★★★★

(9) Where—

(a) an officer authorises the keeping of a person in detention under subsection (1) above; and

(b) at the time of the authorisation he has not yet exercised a right conferred on him by section 56 or 58 below,

the officer—

(i) shall inform him of that right;

(ii) shall decide whether he should be permitted to exercise it;

(iii) shall record the decision in his custody record; and

(iv) if the decision is to refuse to permit the exercise of the right, shall also record the grounds for the decision in that record.

(10) Where an officer has authorised the keeping of a person who has not been charged in detention under subsection (1) or (2) above, he shall be released from detention, either on bail or without bail, not later than 36 hours after the relevant time, unless—

(a) he has been charged with an offence; or

(b) his continued detention is authorised or otherwise permitted in accordance with section 43 below.

(11) A person released under subsection (10) above shall not be re-arrested without a warrant for the offence for which he was previously arrested unless new evidence justifying a further arrest has come to light since his release [; but this subsection does not prevent an arrest under section 46A below].

43 Warrants of further detention

(1) Where, on an application on oath made by a constable and supported by an information, a magistrate's court is satisfied that there are reasonable grounds for believing that the further detention of the person to whom the application relates is justified, it may issue a warrant of further detention authorising the keeping of that person in police detention.

(2) A court may not hear an application for a warrant of further detention unless the person to whom the application relates—

(a) has been furnished with a copy of the information; and

(b) has been brought before the court for the hearing.

(3) The person to whom the application relates shall be entitled to be legally represented at the hearing and, if he is not so represented but wishes to be so represented—

(a) the court shall adjourn the hearing to enable him to obtain representation; and

(b) he may be kept in police detention during the adjournment.

(4) A person's further detention is only justified for the purposes of this section or section 44 below if—

(a) his detention without charge is necessary to secure or preserve evidence relating to an offence for which he is under arrest or to obtain such evidence by questioning him;

(b) an offence for which he is under arrest is a serious arrestable offence; and

(c) the investigation is being conducted diligently and expeditiously.

(5) Subject to subsection (7) below, an application for a warrant of further detention may be made—

(a) at any time before the expiry of 36 hours after the relevant time; or

(b) in a case where—

(i) it is not practicable for the magistrates' court to which the application will be made to sit at the expiry of 36 hours after the relevant time; but

(ii) the court will sit during the 6 hours following the end of that period, at any time before the expiry of the said 6 hours.

(6) In a case to which subsection (5)(b) above applies—

(a) the person to whom the application relates may be kept in police detention until the application is heard; and

(b) the custody officer shall make a note in that person's custody record—

(i) of the fact that he was kept in police detention for more than 36 hours after the relevant time; and

(ii) of the reason why he was so kept.

(7) If—

(a) an application for a warrant of further detention is made after the expiry of 36 hours after the relevant time; and

(b) it appears to the magistrates' court that it would have been reasonable for the police to make it before the expiry of that period,

the court shall dismiss the application.

(8) Where on an application such as is mentioned in subsection (1) above a magistrates' court is not satisfied that there are reasonable grounds for believing that the further detention of the person to whom the application relates is justified, it shall be its duty—

(a) to refuse the application; or

(b) to adjourn the hearing of it until a time not later than 36 hours after the relevant time.

(9) The person to whom the application relates may be kept in police detention during the adjournment.

(10) A warrant of further detention shall—

(a) state the time at which it is issued;

(b) authorise the keeping in police detention of the person to whom it relates for the period stated in it.

(11) Subject to subsection (12) below, the period stated in a warrant of further detention shall be such period as the magistrates' court thinks fit, having regard to the evidence before it.

(12) The period shall not be longer than 36 hours.

(13) ★ ★ ★ ★ ★

(14) Any information submitted in support of an application under this section shall state—

(a) the nature of the offence for which the person to whom the application relates has been arrested;

(b) the general nature of the evidence on which that person was arrested;

(c) what inquiries relating to the offence have been made by the police and what further inquiries are proposed by them;

(d) the reasons for believing the continued detention of that person to be necessary for the purposes of such further inquiries.

(15) Where an application under this section is refused, the person to whom the application relates shall forthwith be charged or, subject to subsection (16) below, released, either on bail or without bail.

(16) A person need not be released under subsection (15) above—

(a) before the expiry of 24 hours after the relevant time; or

(b) before the expiry of any longer period for which his continued detention is or has been authorised under section 42 above.

(17) Where an application under this section is refused, no further application shall be made under this section in repect of the person to whom the refusal relates, unless supported by evidence which has come to light since the refusal.

(18) Where a warrant of further detention is issued, the person to whom it relates shall be released from police detention, either on bail or without bail, upon or before the expiry of the warrant unless he is charged.

(19) A person released under subsection (18) above shall not be re-arrested without a warrant for the offence for which he was previously arrested unless new evidence justifying a further arrest has come to light since his release [; but this subsection does not prevent an arrest under section 46A below].

44 Extension of warrants of further detention

(1) On an application on oath made by a constable and supported by an information a magistrates' court may extend a warrant of further detention issued under section 43 above if it is satisfied that there are reasonable grounds for believing that the further detention of the person to whom the application relates is justified.

(2) Subject to subsection (3) below, the period for which a warrant of further detention may be extended shall be such period as the court thinks fit, having regard to the evidence before it.

(3) The period shall not—

(a) be longer than 36 hours; or

(b) end later than 96 hours after the relevant time.

(4) Where a warrant of further detention has been extended under subsection (1) above, or further extended under this subsection, for a period ending before 96 hours after the relevant time, on an application such as is mentioned in that subsection a magistrates' court may further extend the warrant if it is satisfied as there mentioned; and subsections (2) and (3) above apply to such further extensions as they apply to extensions under subsection (1) above.

(5) A warrant of further detention shall, if extended or further extended under this section, be endorsed with a note of the period of the extension.

(6) Subsections (2), (3), and (14) of section 43 above shall apply to an application made under this section as they apply to an application made under that section.

(7), (8) * * * * *

45 Detention before charge — supplementary

(1) In sections 43 and 44 of this Act "magistrates' court" means a court consisting of two or more justices of the peace sitting otherwise than in open court.

(2) Any reference in this Part of this Act to a period of time or a time of day is to be treated as approximate only.

Detention — miscellaneous

46 Detention after charge

(1) Where a person—

(a) is charged with an offence; and

(b) after being charged—

(i) is kept in police detention; or

(ii) is detained by a local authority in pursuance of arrangements made under section 38(6) above,

he shall be brought before a magistrates' court in accordance with the provisions of this section.

(2) If he is to be brought before a magistrates' court for the petty sessions area in which the police station at which he was charged is situated, he shall be brought before such a court as soon as is practicable and in any event not later than the first sitting after he is charged with the offence.

(3) If no magistrates' court for that area is due to sit either on the day on which he is charged or on the next day, the custody officer for the police station at which he was charged shall inform the clerk to the justices for the area that there is a person in the area to whom subsection (2) above applies.

(4) If the person charged is to be brought before a magistrates' court for a petty sessions area other than that in which the police station at which he was charged is

situated, he shall be removed to that area as soon as is practicable and brought before such a court as soon as is practicable after this arrival in the area and in any event not later than the first sitting of a magistrates' court for that area after this arrival in the area.

(5) If no magistrates' court for that area is due to sit either on the day on which he arrives in the area or on the next day—

(a) he shall be taken to a police station in the area; and

(b) the custody officer at that station shall inform the clerk to the justices for the for the area that there is a person in the area to whom subsection (4) applies.

(6) Subject to subsection (8) below, where a clerk to the justices for a petty sessions area has been informed—

(a) under subsection (3) above that there is a person in the area to whom subsection (2) above applies; or

(b) under subsection (5) above that there is a person in the area to whom subsection (4) above applies,

the clerk shall arrange for a magistrates' court to sit not later than the day next following the relevant day.

(7) In this section "the relevant day"—

(a) in relation to a person who is to be brought before a magistrates' court for the petty sessions area in which the police station at which he was charged is situated, means the day on which he was charged; and

(b) in relation to a person who is to be brought before a magistrates' court for any other petty sessions area, means the day on which he arrives in the area.

(8) Where the day next following the relevant day is Christmas Day, Good Friday or a Sunday, the duty of the clerk under subsection (6) above is a duty to arrange for a magistrates' court to sit not later than the first day after the relevant day which is not one of those days.

(9) ★ ★ ★ ★ ★

[46A Power of arrest for failure to answer to police bail

(1) A constable may arrest without a warrant any person who, having been released on bail under this Part of this Act subject to a duty to attend at a police station, fails to attend at that police station at the time appointed for him to do so.

(2) A person who is arrested under this section shall be taken to the police station appointed as the place at which he is to surrender to custody as soon as practicable after the arrest.

(3) For the purpose of—

(a) section 30 above (subject to the obligation in subsection (2) above), and

(b) section 31 above,

an arrest under the section shall be treated as an arrest for an offence.]

47 Bail after arrest

(1) Subject to subsection (2) below, a release on bail of a person under this Part of this Act shall be a release on bail granted in accordance with [sections 3, 3A, 5 and 5A of the Bail Act 1976 as they apply to bail granted by a constable].

[(1A) The normal powers to impose conditions of bail shall be available to him where a custody officer releases a person on bail under section 38(1) above (including that subsection as applied by section 40(10) above) but not in any other cases.

In this subsection "the normal powers to impose conditions of bail" has the meaning given in section 3(6) of the Bail Act 1976.]

(2) Nothing in the Bail Act 1976 shall prevent the re-arrest without warrant of a person released on bail subject to a duty to attend at a police station if new evidence justifying a further arrest has come to light since his release.

(3), (4) ★ ★ ★ ★ ★

(5) . . .

(6)-(8) * * * * *

48-52 * * * * *

PART V
QUESTIONING AND TREATMENT OF PERSONS BY POLICE

53 Abolition of certain powers of constables to search persons

(1) Subject to subsection (2) below, there shall cease to have effect any Act (including a local Act) passed before this Act in so far as it authorises—

(a) any search by a constable of a person in police detention at a police station; or

(b) an intimate search of a person by a constable;

and any rule of common law which authorises a search such as is mentioned in paragraph (a) or (b) above is abolished.

(2) Nothing in subsection (1)(a) above shall affect paragraph 6(2) of Schedule 3 to the Prevention of Terrorism (Temporary Provisions) Act 1984.

54 Search of detained persons

(1) The custody officer at a police station shall ascertain and record or cause to be recorded everything which a person has with him when he is—

(a) brought to the station after being arrested elsewhere or after being committed to custody by an order or sentence of a court; or

(b) [arrested at the station or detained there [as a person falling within section 34(7), under section 37 above].]

(2) In the case of an arrested person the record shall be made as part of his custody record.

(3) Subject to subsection (4) below, a custody officer may seize and retain any such thing or cause any such thing to be seized and retained.

(4) Clothes and personal effects may only be seized if the custody officer—

(a) believes that the person from whom they are seized may use them—

(i) to cause physical injury to himself or any other person;

(ii) to damage property;

(iii) to interfere with evidence; or

(iv) to assist him to escape; or

(b) has reasonable grounds for believing that they may be evidence relating to an offence.

(5) Where anything is seized, the person from whom it is seized shall be told the reason for the seizure unless he is—

(a) violent or likely to become violent; or

(b) incapable of understanding what is said to him.

(6) Subject to subsection (7) below, a person may be searched if the custody officer considers it necessary to enable him to carry out his duty under subsection (1) above and to the extent that the custody officer considers necessary for that purpose.

[(6A) A person who is in custody at a police station or is in police detention otherwise than at a police station may at any time be searched in order to ascertain whether he has with him anything which he could use for any of the purposes specified in subsection (4)(a) above.

(6B) Subject to subsection (6C) below, a constable may seize and retain, or cause to be seized and retained, anything found on such a search.

(6C) A constable may only seize clothes and personal effects in the circumstances specified in subsection (4) above.]

(7) An intimate search may not be conducted under this section.

(8) A search under this section shall be carried out by a constable.

(9) The constable carrying out a search shall be of the same sex as the person searched.

55 Intimate searches

(1) Subject to the following provisions of this section, if an officer of at least the rank of superintendent has reasonable grounds for believing—

(a) that a person who has been arrested and is in police detention may have concealed on him anything which—

(i) he could use to cause physical injury to himself or others; and

(ii) he might so use while he is in police detention or in the custody of a court;

or

(b) that such a person—

(i) may have a Class A drug concealed on him; and

(ii) was in possession of it with the appropriate criminal intention before his arrest,

he may authorise [an intimate] search of that person.

(3) ⋆ ⋆ ⋆ ⋆ ⋆

(4) An intimate search which is only a drug offence search shall be by way of examination by a suitably qualified person.

(5) Except as provided by subsection (4) above, an intimate search shall be by way of examination by a suitably qualified person unless an officer of at least the rank of superintendent considers that this is not practicable.

(6) An intimate search which is not carried out as mentioned in subsection (5) above shall be carried out by a constable.

(7) A constable may not carry out an intimate search of a person of the opposite sex.

(8) No intimate search may be carried out except—

(a) at a police station;

(b) at a hospital;

(c) at a registered medical practitioner's surgery; or

(d) at some other place used for medical purposes.

(9) An intimate search which is only a drug offence search may not be carried out at a police station.

(10) If an intimate search of a person is carried out, the custody record relating to him shall state—

(a) which parts of his body were searched; and

(b) why they were searched.

(11) ⋆ ⋆ ⋆ ⋆ ⋆

(12) This custody officer at a police station may seize and retain anything which is found on an intimate search of a person, or cause any such thing to be seized and retained—

(a) if he believes that the person from whom it is seized may use it—

(i) to cause physical injury to himself or any other person;

(ii) to damage property;

(iii) to interfere with evidence; or

(iv) to assist him to escape; or

(b) if he has reasonable grounds for believing that it may be evidence relating to an offence.

(13) Where anything is seized under this section, the person from whom it is seized shall be told the reason for the seizure unless he is—

(a) violent or likely to become violent; or

(b) incapable of understanding what is said to him.

(14)-(16) ⋆ ⋆ ⋆ ⋆ ⋆

(17) In this section—

⋆ ⋆ ⋆ ⋆ ⋆

"Class A drug" has the meaning assigned to it by section 2(1)(b) of the Misuse of Drugs Act 1971;

"drug offence search" means an intimate search for a Class A drug which an officer has authorised by virtue of subsection (1)(b) above; and

"suitably qualified person" means—

(a) a registered medical practitioner; or

(b) a registered nurse.

56 Right to have someone informed when arrested

(1) Where a person has been arrested and is being held in custody in a police station or other premises, he shall be entitled, if he so requests, to have one friend or relative or other person who is known to him or who is likely to take an interest in his welfare told, as soon as is practicable except to the extent that delay is permitted by this section, that he has been arrested and is being detained there.

(2) Delay is only permitted—

(a) in the case of a person who is in police detention for a serious arrestable offence; and

(b) if an officer of at least the rank of superintendent authorises it.

(3) In any case the person in custody must be permitted to exercise the right conferred by subsection (1) above within 36 hours from the relevant time as defined in section 41(2) above.

(4) ★ ★ ★ ★ ★

(5) [Subject to subsection (5A) below] an officer may only authorise delay where he has reasonable grounds for believing that telling the named person of the arrest—

(a) will lead to interference with or harm to evidence connected with a serious arrestable offence or interference with or physical injury to other persons; or

(b) will lead to the alerting of other persons suspected of having committed such an offence but not yet arrested for it; or

(c) will hinder the recovery of any property obtained as a result of such an offence.

[(5A) An officer may also authorise delay where the serious arrestable offence is a drug trafficking offence and the officer has reasonable grounds for believing—

(a) that the detained person has benefited from drug trafficking, and

(b) that the recovery of the value of that person's proceeds of drug trafficking will be hindered by telling the named person of the arrest.]

(6) If a delay is authorised—

(a) the detained person shall be told the reason for it; and

(b) the reason shall be noted on his custody record.

(7) The duties imposed by subsection (6) above shall be performed as soon as is practicable.

(8) The rights conferred by this section on a person detained at a police station or other premises are exercisable whenever he is transferred from one place to another; and this section applies to each subsequent occasion on which they are exercisable as it applies to the first such occasion.

(9) There may be no further delay in permitting the exercise of the right conferred by subsection (1) above once the reason for authorising delay ceases to subsist.

(10) In the foregoing provisions of this section references to a person who has been arrested include references to a person who has been detained under the terrorism provisions and "arrest" includes detention under those provisions.

(11) In its application to a person who has been arrested or detained under the terrorism provisions—

(a) subsection (2)(a) above shall have effect as if for the words "for a serious arrestable offence" there were substituted the words "under the terrorism provisions";

(b) subsection (3) above shall have effect as if for the words from "within" onwards there were substituted the words "before the end of the period beyond which he may no longer be detained without the authority of the Secretary of State"; and

(c) subsection (5) above shall have effect as if at the end there were added "or

(d) will lead to interference with the gathering of information about the commission, preparation or instigation of an act of terrorism; or

(e) by alerting any person, will make it more difficult—

(i) to prevent an act of terrorism; or

(ii) to secure the apprehension, prosecution or conviction of any person in connection with the commission, preparation or instigation of an act of terrorism."

57 * * * * *

58 Access to legal advice

(1) A person arrested and held in custody in a police station or other premises shall be entitled, if he so requests, to consult a solicitor privately at any time.

(2) Subject to subsection (3) below, a request under subsection (1) above and the time at which it was made shall be recorded in the custody record.

(3) Such a request need not be recorded in the custody record of a person who makes it at a time while he is at a court after being charged with an offence.

(4) If a person makes such a request, he must be permitted to consult a solicitor as soon as is practicable except to the extent that delay is permitted by this section.

(5) In any case he must be permitted to consult a solicitor within 36 hours from the relevant time, as defined in section 41(2) above.

(6) Delay in compliance with a request is only permitted—

(a) in the case of a person who is in police detention for a serious arrestable offence; and

(b) if an officer of at least the rank of superintendent authorises it.

(7) An officer may give an authorisation under subsection (6) above orally or in writing but, if he gives it orally, he shall confirm it in writing as soon as is practicable.

(8) [Subject to subsection (8A) below] an officer may only authorise delay where he has reasonable grounds for believing that the exercise of the right conferred by subsection (1) above at the time when the person detained desires to exercise it—

(a) will lead to interference with or harm to evidence connected with a serious arrestable offence or interference with or physical injury to other persons; or

(b) will lead to the alerting of other persons suspected of having committed such an offence but not yet arrested for it; or

(c) will hinder the recovery of any property obtained as a result of such an offence.

[(8A) An officer may also authorise delay where the serious arrestable offence is a drug trafficking offence and the officer has reasonable grounds for believing—

(a) that the detained person has benefited from drug trafficking, and

(b) that the recovery of the value of that person's proceeds of drug trafficking will be hindered by the exercise of the right conferred by subsection (1) above.]

(9) If delay is authorised—

(a) the detained person shall be told the reason for it; and

(b) the reason shall be noted on his custody record.

(10) The duties imposed by subsection (9) above shall be performed as soon as is practicable.

(11) There may be no further delay in permitting the exercise of the right conferred by subsection (1) above once the reason for authorising delay ceases to subsist.

(12) The reference in subsection (1) above to a person arrested includes a reference to a person who has been detained under the terrorism provisions.

(13) In the application of this section to a person who has been arrested or detained under the terrorism provisions—

(a) subsection (5) above shall have effect as if for the words from "within" onwards there were substituted the words "before the end of the period beyond which he may no longer be detained without the authority of the Secretary of State";

(b) subsection (6)(a) above shall have effect as if for the words "for a serious arrestable offence" there were substituted the words "under the terrorism provisions"; and

(c) subsection (8) above shall have effect as if at the end there were added "or

(d) will lead to interference with the gathering of information about the commission, preparation or instigation of acts of terrorism; or

(e) by alerting any person, will make it more difficult—

(i) to prevent an act of terrorism; or

(ii) to secure the apprehension, prosecution or conviction of any person in connection with the commission, preparation or instigation of an act of terrorism."

(14) If an officer of appropriate rank has reasonable grounds for believing that, unless he gives a direction under subsection (15) below, the exercise by a person arrested or detained under the terrorism provisions of the right conferred by subsection (1) above will have any of the consequences specified in subsection (8) above (as it has effect by virtue of subsection (13) above), he may give a direction under that subsection.

(15) A direction under this subsection is a direction that a person desiring to exercise the right conferred by subsection (1) above may only consult a solicitor in the sight and hearing of a qualified officer of the uniformed branch of the force of which the officer giving the direction is a member.

(16) An officer is qualified for the purpose of subsection (15) above if—

(a) he is of at least the rank of inspector; and

(b) in the opinion of the officer giving the direction he has no connection with the case.

(17) An officer is of appropriate rank to give a direction under subsection (15) above if he is of at least the rank of Commander or Assistant Chief Constable.

(18) A direction under subsection (15) above shall cease to have effect once the reason for giving it ceases to subsist.

59 . . .

60 Tape-recording of interviews

(1) It shall be the duty of the Secretary of State—

(a) to issue a code of practice in connection with the tape-recording of interviews of persons suspected of the commission of criminal offences which are held by police officers at police stations; and

(b) to make an order requiring the tape-recording of interviews of persons suspected of the commission of criminal offences, or of such descriptions of criminal offences as may be specified in the order, which are so held, in accordance with the code as it has effect for the time being.

(2) An order under subsection (1) above shall be made by statutory instrument and shall be subject to annulment in pursuance of a resolution of either House of Parliament.

61 Fingerprinting

(1) Except as provided by this section no person's fingerprints may be taken without the appropriate consent.

(2) Consent to the taking of a person's fingerprints must be in writing if it is given at a time when he is at a police station.

(3) The fingerprints of a person detained at a police station may be taken without the appropriate consent—

(a) if an officer of at least the rank of superintendent authorises then to be taken; or

(b) if—

(i) he has been charged with a recordable offence or informed that he will be reported for such an offence; and

(ii) he has not had his fingerprints taken in the course of the investigation of the offence by the police.

(4) An officer may only give an authorisation under subsection (3)(a) above if he has reasonable grounds—

(a) for suspecting the involvement of the person whose fingerprints are to be taken in a criminal offence; and

(b) for believing that his fingerprints will tend to confirm or disprove his involvement.

(5) An officer may give an authorisation under subsection (3)(a) above orally or in writing but, if he gives it orally, he will confirm it in writing as soon as is practicable.

(6) Any person's fingerprints may be taken without the appropriate consent if he has been convicted of a recordable offence.

(7) In a case where by virtue of subsection (3) or (6) above a person's fingerprints are taken without the appropriate consent—

(a) he shall be told the reason before his fingerprints are taken; and

(b) the reason shall be recorded as soon as is practicable after the fingerprints are taken.

[(7A) If a person's fingerprints are taken at a police station, whether with or without the appropriate consent—

(a) before the fingerprints are taken, an officer shall inform him that they may be the subject of a speculative search; and

(b) the fact that the person has been informed of this possibility shall be recorded as soon as is practicable after the fingerprints have been taken.]

(8) If he is detained at a police station when the fingerprints are taken, the reason for taking them shall be recorded on his custody record [and, in the case falling within subsection (7A) above, the fact referred to in paragraph (b) of that subsection.]

(9) Nothing in this section—

(a) affects any power conferred by paragraph 18(2) of Schedule 2 to the Immigration Act 1971; or

(b) [except as provided in section 15(10) of, and paragraph 7(6) of Schedule 5 to, the Prevention of Terrorism (Temporary Provisions) Act 1989,] applies to a person arrested or detained under the terrorism provisions.

62 Intimate samples

(1) An intimate sample may be taken from a person in police detention only—

(a) if a police officer of at least the rank of superintendent authorises it to be taken; and

(b) if the appropriate consent is given.

[(1A) An intimate sample may be taken from a person who is not in police detention but from whom, in the course of the investigation of an offence, two or more non-intimate samples suitable for the same means of analysis have been taken which have proved insufficient—

(a) if a police officer of at least the rank of superintendent authorises it to be taken; and

(b) if the appropriate consent is given.]

(2) An officer may only give an authorisation [under subsection (1) or (1A) above] if he has reasonable grounds—

(a) for suspecting the involvement of the person from whom the sample is to be taken in a [recordable offence]; and

(b) for believing that the sample will tend to confirm or disprove his involvement.

(3) An officer may give an authorisation under subsection (1) above orally or in writing but, if he gives it orally, he shall confirm it in writing as soon as is practicable.

(4) The appropriate consent must be given in writing.

(5) Where—

(a) an authorisation has been given; and

(b) it is proposed that an intimate sample shall be taken in pursuance of the authorisation,

an officer shall inform the person from whom the sample is to be taken—

(i) of the giving of the authorisation; and

(ii) of the grounds for giving it.

(6) The duty imposed by subsection (5)(ii) above includes a duty to state the nature of the offence in which it is suspected that the person from whom the sample is to be taken has been involved.

(7) If an intimate sample is taken from a person—

(a) the authorisation by virtue of which it was taken;

(b) the grounds for giving the authorisation; and

(c) the fact that the appropriate consent was given,

shall be recorded as soon as is practicable after the sample is taken.

[(7A) If an intimate sample is taken from a person at a police station—

(a) before the sample is taken, an officer shall inform him that it may be the subject of a speculative search; and

(b) the fact that the person has been informed of this possibility shall be recorded as soon as practicable after the sample has been taken.]

(8) If an intimate sample is taken from a person detained at a police station, the matters required to be recorded by subsection (7) [or (7A)] above shall be recorded in his custody record.

(9) An intimate sample, other than a sample of urine [or a dental impression] may only be taken from a person by a registered medical practitioner [and a dental impression may only be taken by a registered dentist.]

(10) Where the appropriate consent to the taking of an intimate sample from a person was refused without good cause, in any proceedings against that person for an offence—

(a) the court, in determining—

(i) [whether to grant an application for dismissal made by that person under section 6 of the Magistrates' Courts Act 1980 (application for dismissal of charge in course of proceedings with a view to transfer for trial);] or

(ii) whether there is a case to answer;

(aa) * * * * *; and

(b) the court or jury, in determining whether that person is guilty of the offence charged,

may draw such inferences from the refusal as appear proper; and the refusal may, on the basis of such inferences, be treated as, or as capable of amounting to corroboration of any evidence against the person in relation to which the refusal is material.

(11) Nothing in this section affects sections [4 to 11 of the Road Traffic Act 1988].

(12) * * * * *

63 Other samples

(1) Except as provided by this section, a non-intimate sample may not be taken from a person without the appropriate consent.

(2) Consent to the taking of a non-intimate sample must be given in writing.

(3) A non-intimate sample may be taken from a person without the appropriate consent if—

(a) he is in police detention or is being held in custody by the police on the authority of a court; and

(b) an officer of at least the rank of superintendent authorises it to be taken without the appropriate consent.

[(3A) A non-intimate sample may be taken from a person (whether or not he falls within subsection (3)(a) above) without the appropriate consent if—

(a) he has been charged with a recordable offence or informed that he will be reported for such an offence; and

(b) either he has not had a non-intimate sample taken from him in the course of the investigation of the offence by the police or he has had a non-intimate sample taken from him but either it was not suitable for the same means of analysis or, though so suitable, the sample proved insufficient.

(3B) A non-intimate sample may be taken from a person without the appropriate consent if he has been convicted of a recordable offence.]

[(3C) A non-intimate sample may also be taken without the appropriate consent if he is a person to whom section 2 of the Criminal Evidence (Amendment) Act 1997 applies (persons detained following acquittal on grounds of insanity or finding of unfitness to plead).]

(4) An officer may only give an authorisation under subsection (3) above if he has reasonable grounds—

(a) for suspecting the involvement of the person from whom the sample is to be taken in a serious arrestable offence; and

(b) for believing that the sample will tend to confirm or disprove his involvement.

(5) An officer may give an authorisation under subsection (3) above orally or in writing but, if he gives it orally, he shall confirm it in writing as soon as is practicable.

(6) Where—

(a) an authorisation has been given; and

(b) it is proposed that a non-intimate sample shall be taken in pursuance of the authorisation,

an officer shall inform the person from whom the sample is to be taken—

(i) of the giving of the authorisation; and

(ii) of the grounds for giving it.

(7) the duty imposed by subsection (6)(ii) above includes a duty to state the nature of the offence in which it is suspected that the person from whom the sample is to be taken has been involved.

(8) If a non-intimate sample is taken from a person by virtue of subsection (3) above—

(a) the authorisation by virtue of which it was taken; and

(b) the grounds for giving the authorisation,

shall be recorded as soon as is practicable after the sample is taken.

[(8A) In a case where by virtue of subsection (3A), [(3B) or (3C) above] a sample is taken from a person without the appropriate consent—

(a) he shall be told the reason before the sample is taken; and

(b) the reason shall be recorded as soon as practicable after the sample is taken.]

[(8B) If a non-intimate sample is taken from a person at a police station, whether with or without the appropriate consent—

(a) before the sample is taken, an officer shall inform him that it may be the subject of a speculative search; and

(b) the fact that the person has been informed of this possibility shall be recorded as soon as practicable after the sample has been taken.]

(9) If a non-intimate sample is taken from a person detained at a police station, the matters required to be recorded by subsection (8) [or (8A) or (8B)] above shall be recorded in his custody record.

(9A), (10) ★★★★★

63A ★★★★★

64 Destruction of fingerprints and samples

(1) If—

(a) fingerprints or samples are taken from a person in connection with the investigation of an offence; and

(b) he is cleared of that offence,

they must [except as provided in subsection (3A) below] be destroyed as soon as is practicable after the conclusion of the proceedings.

(2) If—

(a) fingerprints or samples are taken from a person in connection with such an investigation; and

(b) it is decided that he shall not be prosecuted for the offence and he has not admitted it and been dealt with by way of being cautioned by a constable,

they must [except as provided in subsection (3A) below] be destroyed as soon as is practicable after that decision is taken.

(3) If—

(a) fingerprints or samples are taken from a person in connection with the investigation of an offence; and

(b) that person is not suspected of having committed the offence,

they must [except as provided in subsection (3A) below] be destroyed as soon as they have fulfilled the purpose for which they were taken.

[(3A) Samples which are required to be destroyed under subsection (1), (2) or (3) above need not be destroyed if they were taken for the purpose of the same investigation of an offence of which a person from whom one was taken has been convicted, but the information derived from the sample of any person entitled (apart from this subsection) to its destruction under subsection (1), (2) or (3) above shall not be used—

(a) in evidence against the person so entitled; or

(b) for the purposes of any investigation of an offence.

(3B) Where samples are required to be destroyed under subsections (1), (2) or (3) above, and subsection (3A) above does not apply, information derived from the sample of any person entitled to its destruction under subsection (1), (2) or (3) above shall not be used—

(a) in evidence against the person so entitled; or

(b) for the purposes of any investigation of an offence.]

(4)-(7) ★ ★ ★ ★ ★

65 Part V — supplementary

In this Part of this Act—

"appropriate consent" means—

(a) in relation to a person who has attained the age of 17 years, the consent of that person;

(b) in relation to a person who has not attained that age but has attained the age of 14 years, the consent of that person and his parent or guardian; and

(c) in relation to a person who has not attained the age of 14 years, the consent of his parent or guardian;

["drug trafficking" and "drug trafficking offence" have the same meaning as in the [Drug Trafficking Act 1994];]

"fingerprints" includes palm prints;

["intimate sample" means—

(a) a sample of blood, semen or any other tissue fluid, urine or pubic hair;

(b) a dental impression;

(c) a swab taken from a person's body orifice other than the mouth;

"intimate search" means a search which consists of the physical examination of a person's body orifices other than the mouth;

"non-intimate sample" means—

(a) a sample of hair other than pubic hair;

(b) a sample taken from a nail or from under a nail;

(c) a swab taken from any part of a person's body including the mouth but not any other body orifice;

(d) saliva;

(e) a footprint or a similar impression of any part of a person's body other than a part of his hand;

"registered dentist" has the same meaning as in the Dentists Act 1984;

"speculative search", in relation to a person's fingerprints or samples, means such a check against other fingerprints or samples or against information derived from other samples as is referred to in section 63A(1) above;

"sufficient" and "insufficient" in relation to a sample, means sufficient or insufficient (in point of quantity or quality) for the purpose of enabling information to be produced by the means of analysis used or to be used in relation to the sample;]

["the terrorism provisions" means section 14(1) of the Prevention of Terrorism (Temporary Provisions) Act 1989 and any provision of Schedule 2 or 5 to that Act conferring a power of arrest or detention; and

"terrorism" has the meaning assigned to it by section 20(1) of that Act];

[and references in this Part to any person's proceeds of drug trafficking are to be construed in accordance with the [Drug Trafficking Act 1994].]

PART VI
CODES OF PRACTICE — GENERAL

66 Codes of practice

The Secretary of State shall issue codes of practice in connection with—

(a) the exercise by police officers of statutory powers—

(i) to search a person without first arresting him; or

(ii) to search a vehicle without making an arrest;

(b) the detention, treatment, questioning and indication of persons by police officers;

(c) searches of premises by police officers; and

(d) the seizure of property found by police officers on persons or premises.

67 Codes of practice — supplementary

(1) When the Secretary of State proposes to issue a code of practice to which this section applies, he shall prepare and publish a draft of that code, shall consider any representations made to him about the draft and may modify the draft accordingly.

(2) This section applies to a code of practice under section 60 or 66 above.

(3) The Secretary of State shall lay before both Houses of Parliament a draft of any code of practice prepared by him under this section.

(4) When the Secretary of State has laid the draft of a code before Parliament, he may bring the code into operation by order made by statutory instrument.

(5) No order under subsection (4) above shall have effect until approved by a resolution of each House of Parliament.

(6) An order bringing a code of practice into operation may contain such transitional provisions or savings as appear to the Secretary of State to be necessary or expedient in connection with the code of practice thereby brought into operation.

(7) The Secretary of State may from time to time revise the whole or any part of a code of practice to which this section applies and issue that revised code; and the foregoing provisions of this section shall apply (with appropriate modifications) to such a revised code as they apply to the first issue of a code.

(8) . . .

(9) Persons other than police officers who are charged with the duty of investigating offences or charging offenders shall in the discharge of that duty have regard to any relevant provision of such a code.

(10) A failure on the part—

(a) of a police officer to comply with any provision of such a code; or

(b) of any person other than a police officer who is charged with the duty of investigating offences or charging offenders to have regard to any relevant provision of such a code in the discharge of the duty,

shall not of itself render him liable to any criminal or civil proceedings.

(11) In all criminal and civil proceedings any such code shall be admissible in evidence; and if any provision of such a code appears to the court or tribunal conducting the proceedings to be relevant to any question arising in the proceedings it shall be taken into account in determining that question.

(12) ★★★★★

Note Extracts from the Codes of Practice issued under this section (as revised in 1995) are printed at the end of this book.

PART VIII
EVIDENCE IN CRIMINAL PROCEEDINGS — GENERAL

68-75 ★★★★★

Confessions

76 Confessions

(1) In any proceedings a confession made by an accused person may be given in evidence against him in so far as it is relevant to any matter in issue in the proceedings and is not excluded by the court in pursuance of this section.

(2) If, in any proceedings where the prosecution proposes to give in evidence a confession made by an accused person, it is represented to the court that the confession was or may have been obtained—

(a) by oppression of the person who made it; or

(b) in consequence of anything said or done which was likely, in the circumstances existing at the time, to render unreliable any confession which might be made by him in consequence thereof,

the court shall not allow the confession to be given in evidence against him except in so far as the prosecution proves to the court beyond reasonable doubt that the confession (notwithstanding that it may be true) was not obtained as aforesaid.

(3) In any proceedings where the prosecution proposes to give in evidence a confession made by an accused person, the court may of its own motion require the prosecution, as a condition of allowing it to do so, to prove that the confession was not obtained as mentioned in subsection (2) above.

(4) The fact that a confession is wholly or partly excluded in pursuance of this section shall not affect the admissibility in evidence—

(a) of any facts discovered as a result of the confession; or

(b) where the confession is relevant as showing that the accused speaks, writes or expresses himself in a particular way, of so much of the confession as is necessary to show that he does so.

(5) Evidence that a fact to which this subsection applies was discovered as a result of a statement made by an accused person shall not be admissible unless evidence of how it was discovered is given by him or on his behalf.

(6) Subsection (5) above applies—

(a) to any fact discovered as a result of a confession which is wholly excluded in pursuance of this section; and

(b) to any fact discovered as a result of a confession which is partly so excluded, if that fact is discovered as a result of the excluded part of the confession.

(7) Nothing in Part VII of this Act shall prejudice the admissibility of a confession made by an accused person.

(8) In this section "oppression" includes torture, inhuman or degrading treatment, and the use or threat of violence (whether or not amounting to torture).

(9) ★★★★★

77 Confessions by mentally handicapped persons

(1) Without prejudice to the general duty of the court at a trial on indictment to direct the jury on any matter on which it appears to the court appropriate to do so, where at such a trial—

(a) the case against the accused depends wholly or substantially on a confession by him; and

(b) the court is satisfied—

(i) that he is mentally handicapped; and

(ii) that the confession was not made in the presence of an independent person,

the court shall warn the jury that there is special need for caution before convicting the accused in reliance on the confession, and shall explain that the need arises because of the circumstances mentioned in paragraphs (a) and (b) above, but in doing so shall not be required to use any particular form of words.

(2) In any case where at the summary trial of a person for an offence it appears to the court that a warning under subsection (1) above would be required if the trial were on indictment, the court shall treat the case as one in which there is a special need for caution before convicting the accused on his confession.

(3) In this section—

"independent person" does not include a police officer or a person employed for, or engaged on police purposes;

"mentally handicapped", in relation to a person, means that he is in a state of arrested or incomplete development of mind which includes significant impairment of intelligence and social functioning; and

"police purposes" has the meaning assigned to it by [section 101(2) of the Police Act 1996.]

Note The Police and Criminal Evidence Act 1984 (Application to Customs and Excise) Order 1985 (SI 1985 No. 1800), Art. 10, provides that subsection (3) above "shall be modified to the extent that the definition of 'independent person' shall, in addition to the persons mentioned therein, also include an officer or any other person acting under the authority of the Commissioners of Customs and Excise".

Miscellaneous

78 Exclusion of unfair evidence

(1) In any proceedings the court may refuse to allow evidence on which the prosecution proposes to rely to be given if it appears to the court that, having regard to all the circumstances, including the circumstances in which the evidence was obtained, the admission of the evidence would have such an adverse effect on the fairness of the proceedings that the court ought not to admit it.

(2) Nothing in this section shall prejudice any rule of law requiring a court to exclude evidence.

(3) ★★★★★

79-81 ★★★★★

Part VIII — supplementary

82 Part VIII — interpretation

(1) In this Part of this Act—

"confession" includes any statement wholly or partly adverse to the person who made it, whether made to a person in authority or not and whether made in words or otherwise;

★ ★ ★ ★ ★

(2) ★ ★ ★ ★ ★

(3) Nothing in this Part of this Act shall prejudice any power of a court to exclude evidence (whether by preventing questions from being put or otherwise) at its discretion.

83-106 (Repealed and re-enacted by the Police Act 1996, see below.) . . .

PART XI
MISCELLANEOUS AND SUPPLEMENTARY

107-8, 110-1, 113-5 ★ ★ ★ ★ ★

109, 112 . . .

116 Meaning of "serious arrestable offence"

(1) This section has effect for determining whether an offence is a serious arrestable offence for the purposes of this Act.

(2) The following arrestable offences are always serious—

(a) an offence (whether at common law or under any enactment) specified in Part I of Schedule 5 to this Act; and

(b) an offence under an enactment specified in Part II of that Schedule [;and

(c) any of the offences mentioned in paragraphs (a) to (f) of section 1(3) of the Drug Trafficking Act 1994.]

(3) Subject to subsections (4) and (5) below, any other arrestable offence is serious only if its commission—

(a) has led to any of the consequences specified in subsection (6) below; or

(b) is intended or is likely to lead to any of those consequences.

(4) An arrestable offence which consists of making a threat is serious if carrying out the threat would be likely to lead to any of the consequences specified in subsection (6) below.

(5) An offence under [section 2, 8, 9, 10 or 11 of the Prevention of Terrorism (Temporary Provisions) Act 1989] is always a serious arrestable offence for the purposes of section 56 or 58 above, and an attempt or conspiracy to commit any such offence is also always a serious arrestable offence for those purposes.

(6) The consequences mentioned in subsections (3) and (4) above are

(a) serious harm to the security of the State or to public order;

(b) serious interference with the administration of justice or with the investigation of offences or of a particular offence;

(c) the death of any person;

(d) serious injury to any person;

(e) substantial financial gain to any person; and

(f) serious financial loss to any person.

(7) Loss is serious for the purposes of this section if, having regard to all the circumstances, it is serious for the person who suffers it.

(8) In this section "injury" includes any disease and any impairment of a person's physical or mental condition.

117 Power of constable to use reasonable force

Where any provision of this Act—

(a) confers a power on a constable; and

(b) does not provide that the power may only be exercised with the consent of some person, other than a police officer,

the officer may use reasonable force, if necessary, in the exercise of the power.

118 General interpretation

(1) ★★★★★

(2) A person is in police detention for the purposes of this Act if—

(a) he has been taken to a police station after being arrested for an offence [or after being arrested under section 14 of the Prevention of Terrorism (Temporary Provisions) Act 1989 or under paragraph 6 of Schedule 5 to that Act by an examining officer who is a constable]; or

(b) he is arrested at a police station after attending voluntarily at the station or accompanying a constable to it,

and is detained there or is detained elsewhere in the charge of a constable, except that a person who is at a court after being charged is not in police detention for those purposes.

★★★★★

Section 9

SCHEDULE 1
SPECIAL PROCEDURE

Making of orders by circuit judge

1. If on an application made by a constable a circuit judge is satisfied that one or other of the sets of access conditions is fulfilled, he may make an order under paragraph 4 below.

2. The first set of access conditions is fulfilled if—

(a) there are reasonable grounds for believing—

(i) that a serious arrestable offence has been committed;

(ii) that there is material which consists of special procedure material or includes special procedure material and does not also include excluded material on premises specified in the application;

(iii) that the material is likely to be of substantial value (whether by itself or together with other material) to the investigation in connection with which the application is made; and

(iv) that the material is likely to be relevant evidence;

(b) other methods of obtaining the material—

(i) have been tried without success; or

(ii) have not been tried because it appeared that they were bound to fail; and

(c) it is in the public interest, having regard—

(i) to the benefit likely to accrue to the investigation if the material is obtained; and

(ii) to the circumstances under which the person in possession of the material holds it,

that the material should be produced or that access to it should be given.

3. The second set of access conditions is fulfilled if—

(a) there are reasonable grounds for believing that there is material which consists of or includes excluded material or special procedure material on premises specified in the application;

(b) but for section 9(2) above a search of the premises for that material could have been authorised by the issue of a warrant to a constable under an enactment other than this Schedule; and

(c) the issue of such a warrant would have been appropriate.

4. An order under this paragraph is an order that the person who appears to the circuit judge to be in possession of the material to which the application relates shall—

(a) produce it to a constable for him to take away; or

(b) give a constable access to it,

not later than the end of the period of seven days from the date of the order or the end of such longer period as the order may specify.

5. Where the material consists of information contained in a computer—

(a) an order under paragraph 4(a) above shall have effect as an order to produce the material in a form in which it can be taken away and in which it is visible and legible; and

(b) an order under paragraph 4(b) above shall have effect as an order to give a constable access to the material in a form in which it is visible and legible.

6. For the purposes of sections 21 and 22 above material produced in pursuance of an order under paragraph 4(a) above shall be treated as if it were material seized by a constable.

Notices of applications for orders

7. An application for an order under paragraph 4 above shall be made inter partes.

8. Notice of an application for such an order may be served on a person either by delivering it to him or by leaving it at his proper address or by sending it by post to him in a registered letter or by the recorded delivery service.

9. Such a notice may be served—

(a) on a body corporate, by serving it on the body's secretary or clerk or other similar officer; and

(b) on a partnership, by serving it on one of the partners.

10. For the purposes of this Schedule, and of section 7 of the Interpretation Act 1978 in its application to this Schedule, the proper address of a person, in the case of secretary or clerk or other similar officer of a body corporate, shall be that of the registered or principal office of that body, in the case of a partner of a firm shall be that of the principal office of the firm, and in any other case shall be the last known address of the person to be served.

11. Where notice of an application for an order under paragraph 4 above has been served on a person, he shall not conceal, destroy, alter or dispose of the material to which the application relates except—

(a) with the leave of a judge; or

(b) with the written permission of a constable,

until—

(i) the application is dismissed or abandoned; or

(ii) he has complied with an order under paragraph 4 above made on the application.

Issue of warrants by circuit judge

12. If on an application made by a constable a circuit judge—

(a) is satisfied—

(i) that either set of access conditions is fulfilled; and

(ii) that any of the further conditions set out in paragraph 14 below is also fulfilled; or

(b) is satisfied—

(i) that the second set of access conditions is fufilled; and

(ii) that an order under paragraph 4 above relating to the material has not been complied with,

he may issue a warrant authorising a constable to enter and search the premises.

13. A constable may seize and retain anything for which a search has been authorised under paragraph 12 above.

14. The further conditions mentioned in paragraph 12(a)(ii) above are—

(a) that it is not practicable to communicate with any person entitled to grant entry to the premises to which the application relates;

(b) that it is practicable to communicate with a person entitled to grant entry to the premises but it is not practicable to communicate with any person entitled to grant access to the material;

(c) that the material contains information which—

(i) is subject to a restriction or obligation such as is mentioned in section 11(2)(b) above; and

(ii) is likely to be disclosed in breach of it if a warrant is not issued;

(d) that service of notice of an application for an order under paragraph 4 above may seriously prejudice the investigation.

15.—(1) If a person fails to comply with an order under paragraph 4 above, a circuit judge may deal with him as if he had committed a contempt of the Crown Court.

(2) Any enactment relating to contempt of the Crown Court shall have effect in relation to such a failure as if it were such a contempt.

16. ★★★★★

★★★★★

Section 116

SCHEDULE 5
SERIOUS ARRESTABLE OFFENCES

PART I
OFFENCES MENTIONED IN SECTION 116(2)(a)

1. Treason.
2. Murder.
3. Manslaughter.
4. Rape.
5. Kidnapping.
6. Incest with a girl under the age of 13.
[7. Buggery with a person under the age of 16.]
8. Indecent assault which constitutes an act of gross indecency.

PART II
OFFENCES MENTIONED IN SECTION 116(2)(b)

Explosive Substances Act 1883 (c. 3)

1. Section 2 (causing explosion likely to endanger life or property).

Sexual Offences Act 1956 (c. 69)

2. Section 5 (intercourse with a girl under the age of 13).

Firearms Act 1968 (c. 27)

3. Section 16 (possession of firearms with intent to injure).
4. Section 17(1) (use of firearms and imitation firearms to resist arrest).
5. Section 18 (carrying firearms with criminal intent).
6. . . .

Taking of Hostages Act 1982 (c. 28)

7. Section 1 (hostage-taking).

Aviation Security Act 1982 (c. 36)

8. Section 1 (hi-jacking).

[*Criminal Justice Act 1988 (c. 33)*

9. Section 134 (torture).]

[*The Road Traffic Act 1988 (c. 52)*

10. Section 1 (causing death by reckless driving).]

[*Aviation and Maritime Security Act 1990 (c. 31)*

11. Section 1 (endangering safety at aerodromes).
12. Section 9 (hijacking of ships).
13. Section 10 (seizing or exercising control of fixed platforms).]

[*Protection of Children Act 1978 (c. 37)*

14. Section 1 (indecent photographs and pseudo-photographs of children).]

Obscene Publications Act 1959 (c. 66)

15. Section 2 (publication of obscene matter).]

* * * * *

VIDEO RECORDINGS ACT 1984
(1984, c. 39)

An Act to make provision for regulating the distribution of video recordings and for connected purposes [12 July 1984]

Territorial extent United Kingdom

Preliminary

1 Interpretation of terms

(1) The provisions of this section shall have effect for the interpretation of terms used in this Act.

(2) "Video work" means any series of visual images (with or without sound)—

(a) produced electronically by the use of information contained on any disc . . . magnetic tape [or any other device capable of storing data electronically], and

(b) shown as a moving picture.

(3) "Video recording" means any disc . . . magnetic tape [or any other device capable of storing data electronically] containing information by the use of which the whole or a part of a video work may be produced.

(4) "Supply" means supply in any manner, whether or not for reward, and, therefore, includes supply by way of sale, letting on hire, exchange or loan; and references to a supply are to be interpreted accordingly.

2 Exempted works

(1) Subject to subsection (2) [or (3)] below, a video work is for the purposes of this Act an exempted work if, taken as a whole—

(a) it is designed to inform, educate or instruct;

(b) it is concerned with sport, religion or music; or

(c) it is a video game.

(2) A video work is not an exempted work for those purposes if, to any significant extent, it depicts—

(a) human sexual activity of acts of force or restraint associated with such activity;

(b) mutilation or torture of, or other acts of gross violence towards, humans or animals;

(c) human genital organs or human urinary or excretory functions;

[(d) techniques likely to be useful in the commission of offences;]

or is [likely] to any significant extent to stimulate or encourage anything falling within paragraph (a) or, in the case of anything falling within paragraph (b), is [likely] to any extent to do so.

[(3) A video work is not an exempted work for those purposes if, to any significant extent, it depicts criminal activity which is likely to any significant extent to stimulate or encourage the commission of offences.]

3 Exempted supplies

(1) The provisions of this section apply to determine whether or not a supply of a video recording is an exempted supply for the purposes of this Act.

(2) The supply of a video recording by any person is an exempted supply if it is neither—

(a) a supply for reward, nor

(b) a supply in the course or furtherance of a business.

(3) Where on any premises facilities are provided in the course or furtherance of a business for supplying video recordings, the supply by any person of a video recording on those premises is to be treated for the purposes of subsection (2) above as a supply in the course or furtherance of a business.

(4) Where a person (in this subsection referred to as the "original supplier") supplies a video recording to a person who, in the course of a business, makes video works or supplies video recordings, the supply is an exempted supply—

(a) if it is not made with a view to any further supply of that recording, or

(b) if it is so made, but is not made with a view to the eventual supply of that recording to the original supplier.

(5)-(12) * * * * *

Designated authority

4 Authority to determine suitability of video works for classification

(1) The Secretary of State may by notice under this section designate any person as the authority responsible for making arrangements—

(a) for determining for the purposes of this Act whether or not video works are suitable for classification certificates to be issued in respect of them, having special regard to the likelihood of video works in respect of which such certificates have been issued being viewed in the home,

(b) in the case of works which are determined in accordance with the arrangements to be so suitable—

[(ia) for assigning a unique title to each video work in respect of which a classification certificate is to be issued,]

(i) for making such other determinations as are required for the issue of classification certificates, and

(ii) for issuing such certificates, and

(c) for maintaining a record of such determinations (whether determinations made in pursuance of arrangements made by that person or by any person previously designated under this section), . .

(1A), (1B) * * * * *

(2) The power to designate any person by notice under this section includes power—

(a) to designate two or more persons jointly as the authority responsible for making those arrangements, and

(b) to provide that any person holding an office or employment specified in the notice is to be treated as designated while holding that office or employment.

(3) The Secretary of State shall not make any designation under this section unless he is satisfied that adequate arrangements will be made for an appeal by any person against a determination that a video work submitted by him for the issue of a classification certificate—

(a) is not suitable for a classification certificate to be issued in respect of it, or

(b) is not suitable for viewing by persons who have not attained a particular age,

or against a determination that no video recording containing the work is to be supplied other than in a licensed sex shop.

(4) The Secretary of State may at any time designate another person in place of any person designated under this section and, if he does so, may give directions as to the transfer of any record kept in pursuance of the arrangements referred to in subsection (1) above; and it shall be the duty of any person having control of any such record or any part of it to comply with the directions.

(5)-(8) * * * * *

4A Criteria for suitability to which special regard to be had

(1) The designated authority shall, in making any determination as to the suitability of a video work, have special regard (among the other relevant factors) to any harm that may be caused to potential viewers or, through their behaviour, to society by the manner in which the work deals with—

(a) criminal behaviour;

(b) illegal drugs;

(c) violent behaviour or incidents;

(d) horrific behaviour or incidents; or

(e) human sexual activity.

(2) For the purposes of this section—

"potential viewer" means any person (including a child or young person) who is likely to view the video work in question if a classification certificate or a classification certificate of a particular description were issued;

"suitability" means suitability for the issue of a classification certificate or suitability for the issue of a certificate of a particular description;

"violent behaviour" includes any act inflicting or likely to result in the infliction of injury;

and any behaviour or activity referred to in subsection (1)(a) to (e) above shall be taken to include behaviour or activity likely to stimulate or encourage it.

4B Review of determinations as to suitability

(1) The Secretary of State may by order make provision enabling the designated authority to review any determination made by them, before the coming into force of section 4A of this Act, as to the suitability of a video work.

(2) The order may in particular provide—

(a) for the authority's power of review to be exercisable in relation to such determinations as the authority think fit;

(b) for the authority to determine, on any review, whether, if they were then determining the suitability of the video work to which the determination under review relates, they—

(i) would issue a classification certificate, or

(ii) would issue a different classification certificate;

(c) for the cancellation of a classification certificate, where they determine that they would not issue a classification certificate;

(d) for the cancellation of a classification certificate and issue of a new classification certificate, where they determine that they would issue a different classification certificate;

(e) for any such cancellation or issue not to take effect until the end of such period as may be determined in accordance with the order;

(f) for such persons as may appear to the authority to fall within a specified category of person to be notified of any such cancellation or issue in such manner as may be specified;

(g) for treating a classification certificate, in relation to any act or omission occurring after its cancellation, as if it had not been issued;

(h) for specified provisions of this Act to apply to determinations made on a review subject to such modifications (if any) as may be specified;

(i) for specified regulations made under section 8 of this Act to apply to a video work in respect of which a new classification certificate has been issued subject to such modifications (if any) as may be specified.]

(3)-(6) ★★★★★

5 Parliamentary procedure for designation

(1) Where the Secretary of State proposes to make a designation under section 4 of this Act, he shall lay particulars of his proposal before both Houses of Parliament and shall not make the proposed designation until after the end of the period of forty days beginning with the day on which the particulars of his proposal were so laid.

(2), (3) ★★★★★

6 Annual report

(1) The designated authority shall, as soon as it is reasonably practicable to do so after 31st December, make a report to the Secretary of State on the carrying out in the year ending with that date of the arrangements referred to in section 4(1) and (3) of this Act (together with a statement of accounts) and on such other matters (if any) as the designated authority consider appropriate or the Secretary of State may require.

(2) The Secretary of State shall lay a copy of any report made to him under this section before each House of Parliament.

Classification and labelling

7 Classification certificates

(1) In this Act "classification certificate" means a certificate—

(a) issued in respect of a video work in pursuance of arrangements made by the designated authority; and

(b) satisfying the requirements of subsection (2) below.

(2) Those requirements are that the certificate must contain [the title assigned to the video work in accordance with section 4(1)(b)(ia) of this Act and]—

(a) a statement that the video work concerned is suitable for general viewing and unrestricted supply (with or without any advice as to the desirability of parental guidance with regard to the viewing of the work by young children or as to the particular suitability of the work for viewing by children [or young children]); or

(b) a statement that the video work concerned is suitable for viewing only by persons who have attained the age (not being more than eighteen years) specified in the certificate and that no video recording containing that work is to be supplied to any person who has not attained the age so specified; or

(c) the statement mentioned in paragraph (b) above together with a statement that no video recording containing that work is to be supplied other than in a licensed sex shop.

8 Requirements as to labelling, etc.

(1) The Secretary of State may, in relation to video works in respect of which classification certificates have been issued, by regulations require such indication as may be specified by the regulations of any of the contents of any classification certificate to

be shown in such a manner as may be so specified on any video recording containing the video work in respect of which the certificate was issued or any spool, case or other thing on or in which such a video recording is kept.

(2), (3) * * * * *

Offences and penalties

9 Supplying video recording of unclassified work

(1) A person who supplies or offers to supply a video recording containing a video work in respect of which no classification certificate has been issued is guilty of an offence unless—

(a) the supply is, or would if it took place be, an exempted supply, or

(b) the video work is an exempted work.

(2) It is a defence to a charge of committing an offence under this section to prove that the accused believed on reasonable grounds—

(a) that the video work concerned or, if the video recording contained more than one work to which the charge relates, each of those works was either an exempted work or a work in respect of which a classification certificate had been issued, or

(b) that the supply was, or would if it took place be, an exempted supply by vitrue of section 3(4) or (5) of this Act.

[(3) A person guilty of an offence under this section shall be liable—

(a) on conviction on indictment, to imprisonment for a term not exceeding two years, or a fine or both,

(b) on summary conviction, to imprisonment for a term not exceeding six months or a fine not exceeding £20,000 or both.]

10 Possession of video recording or unclassified work for the purposes of supply

(1) Where a video recording contains a video work in respect of which no classification certificate has been issued, a person who has the recording in his possession for the purpose of supplying it is guilty of an offence unless—

(a) he has it in his possession for the purpose only of a supply which, if it took place, would be an exempted supply, or

(b) the video work is an exempted work.

(2) It is a defence to a charge of committing an offence under this section to prove—

(a) that the accused believed on reasonable grounds that the video work concerned or, if the video recording contained more than one work to which the charge relates, each of those works was either an exempted work or a work in respect of which a classification certificate had been issued,

(b) that the accused had the video recording in his possession for the purpose only of a supply which he believed on reasonable grounds would, if it took place, be an exempted supply by virtue of section 3(4) or (5) of the Act, or

(c) that the accused did not intend to supply the video recording until a classification certificate had been issued in respect of the video work concerned.

[(3) A person guilty of an offence under this section shall be liable—

(a) on conviction on indictment, to imprisonment for a term not exceeding two years, or a fine or both,

(b) on summary conviction, to imprisonment for a term not exceeding six months or a fine not exceeding £20,000 or both.]

11 Supplying video recording of classified work in breach of classification

(1) Where a classification certificate issued in respect of a video work states that no video recording containing that work is to be supplied to any person who has not attained the age specified in the certificate, a person who supplies or offers to supply a video recording containing that work to a person who has not attained the age so

specified is guilty of an offence unless the supply is, or would if it took place be, an exempted supply.

(2) It is a defence to a charge of committing an offence under this section to prove—

(a) that the accused neither knew nor had reasonable grounds to believe that the classification certificate contained the statement concerned,

(b) that the accused neither knew nor had reasonable grounds to believe that the person concerned had not attained that age, or

(c) that the accused believed on reasonable grounds that the supply was, or would if it took place be, an exempted supply by virtue of section 3(4) or (5) of this Act.

[(3) A person guilty of an offence under this section shall be liable, on summary conviction, to imprisonment for a term not exceeding six months, or a fine not exceeding level 5 on the standard scale or both.]

12 Certain video recordings only to be supplied in licensed sex shops

(1) Where a classification certificate issued in respect of a video work states that no video recording containing that work is to be supplied other than in a licensed sex shop, a person who at any place other than in a sex shop for which a licence is in force under the relevant enactment—

(a) supplies a video recording containing the work, or

(b) offers to do so,

is guilty of an offence unless the supply is, or would if it took place be, an exempted supply.

(2)-(6) ★★★★★

13-16, 16A-C ★★★★★

17 Entry, search and seizure

(1) If a justice of the peace is satisfied by information on oath that there are reasonable grounds for suspecting—

(a) that an offence under this Act has been or is being committed on any premises, and

(b) that evidence that the offence has been or is being committed is on those premises,

he may issue a warrant under his hand authorising any constable to enter and search the premises . . .

(2) A constable entering or searching any premises in pursuance of a warrant under subsection (1) above may use reasonable force if necessary and may seize anything found there which he has reasonable grounds to believe may be required to be used in evidence in any proceedings for an offence under this Act.

(3) In subsection (1) above—

(a) the reference to a justice of the peace is, in Scotland, a reference to the sheriff or a justice of the peace and, in Northern Ireland, a reference to a resident magistrate, and

(b) the reference to information is, in Scotland, a reference to evidence and, in Northern Ireland, a reference to a complaint.

18 Arrest

(1) If a constable has reasonable grounds for suspecting that a person has committed an offence under this Act, he may require him to give his name and address and, if that person refuses or fails to do so or gives a name and address which the constable reasonably suspects to be false, the constable may arrest him without warrant.

(2) This section does not extend to Scotland.

19 ★★★★★

20 . . .

21 Forfeiture

(1) Where a person is convicted of any offence under this Act, the court may order any video recording—

(a) produced to the court, and

(b) shown to the satisfaction of the court to relate to the offence,

to be forfeited.

(2) The court shall not order any video recording to be forfeited under subsection (1) above if a person claiming to be the owner of it or otherwise interested in it applies to be heard by the court, unless an opportunity has been given to him to show cause why the order should not be made.

(3) References in this section to a video recording include a reference to any spool, case or other thing on or in which the recording is kept.

(4), (5) ★★★★★

★★★★★

CINEMAS ACT 1985
(1985, c. 13)

An Act to consolidate the Cinematograph Acts 1909 to 1982 and certain related enactments, with an amendment to give effect to a recommendation of the Law Commission

[27 March 1985]

Territorial extent England and Wales, Scotland

Control of exhibitions

1 Licence required for exhibitions

(1) Subject to sections 5 to 8 below, no premises shall be used for a film exhibition unless they are licensed for the purpose under this section.

(2) A licensing authority may grant a licence under this section to such a person as they think fit to use any premises specified in the licence for the purpose of film exhibitions on such terms and conditions and subject to such restrictions as, subject to regulations under section 4 below, they may determine.

(3) Without prejudice to the generality of subsection (2) above, it shall be the duty of a licensing authority, in granting a licence under this section as respects any premises,—

(a) to impose conditions or restrictions prohibiting the admission of children to film exhibitions involving the showing of works designated, by the authority or by such other body as may be specified in the licence, as works unsuitable for children; and

(b) to consider what (if any) conditions or restrictions should be imposed as to the admission of children to other film exhibitions involving the showing of works designated, by the authority or by such other body as may be specified in the licence, as works of such other description as may be so specified.

2 Consent required for exhibitions for children

(1) Subject to sections 5 and 6 below, no premises shall be used, except with the consent of the licensing authority, for a film exhibition organised wholly or mainly as an exhibition for children.

(2) ★★★★★

3, 4 ★★★★★

Exempted exhibitions

5 Exhibitions in private dwelling-houses

(1) This section applies to any film exhibition which—

(a) is given in a private dwelling-house,
(b) is one to which the public are not admitted, and
(c) satisfies the condition mentioned in subsection (2) below.

(2) The condition referred to in subsection (1)(c) above is that either—
(a) the exhibition is not promoted for private gain, or
(b) the sole or main purpose of the exhibition is to demonstrate any product, to advertise any goods or services or to provide information, education or instruction.

(3) The following exemptions have effect in relation to any film exhibition to which this section applies, that is to say—
(a) a licence shall not be required by reason only of the giving of the exhibition;
(b) where the exhibition is given in premises in respect of which a licence is in force, no condition or restriction on or subject to which the licence was granted shall apply to the exhibition;
(c) regulations under section 4 above shall not apply to the exhibition.

6 Other non-commercial exhibitions

(1) Subject to subsections (4) and (5) below, this section applies to any film exhibition (other than one to which section 5 above applies) which—
(a) is one to which the public are not admitted or are admitted without payment, or
(b) does not fall within paragraph (a) above but is given by an exempted organisation,
and (in either case) satisfies the condition mentioned in subsection (2) below.

(2) The condition referred to in subsection (1) above is that either—
(a) the exhibition is not promoted for private gain, or
(b) the sole or main purpose of the exhibition is to demonstrate any product, to advertise any goods or services or to provide information, education or instruction.

(3) The following exemptions have effect in relation to any film exhibition to which this section applies, that is to say—
(a) a licence under section 1 above shall not be required by reason only of the giving of the exhibition unless the pictures are produced by means specified in regulations under section 4 above as means involving such risk that it is inexpedient that this paragraph should have effect;
(b) where the exhibition is given in premises in respect of which a licence under section 1 above is in force, no condition or restriction on or subject to which the licence was granted shall apply to the exhibition except so far as it relates to the matters specified in section 4(2)(a) above;
(c) a consent under section 2 above shall not be required by reason only of the giving of the exhibition;
(d) where the exhibition is given in premises in respect of which a consent under section 2 above is in force, no condition or restriction on or subject to which the consent was granted shall apply to the exhibition;
(e) regulations under section 4 above making such provision as is mentioned in subsection (2)(b) of that section shall not apply to the exhibition and regulations under that section making such provision as is mentioned in subsection (2)(a) of that section shall not apply to the exhibition unless it is given in premises in respect of which a licence under section 1 above is in force.

(4) A film exhibition is excluded from being one to which this section applies if it is organised solely or mainly as an exhibition for children who are members of a club, society or association the principal object of which is attendance at film exhibitions, unless the exhibition is given in a private dwelling-house or as part of the activities of an educational or religious institution.

(5) A film exhibition is excluded from being one to which this section applies by virtue of paragraph (b) of subsection (1) above if on more than three out of the last

preceding seven days the premises in question were used for the giving of a film exhibition to which this section applied by virtue of that paragraph.

(6) In this section "exempted organisation" means a society, institution, committee or other organisation with respect to which there is in force at the time of the exhibition in question a certificate given by the Secretary of State certifying that he is satisfied that the organisation is not conducted or established for profit; and there shall be paid to the Secretary of State in respect of the giving of such a certificate such reasonable fee as he may determine.

(7), (8) * * * * *

7 Exhibitions in premises used occasionally

(1) Where the premises in which it is proposed to give a film exhibition are premises used occasionally and exceptionally only, and not on more than six days in any one calendar year, for the purposes of such an exhibition, it shall not be necessary to obtain a licence under section 1 above if—

(a) the occupier of the premises has given to the licensing authority, to the fire authority and to the chief officer of police, not less than seven days' notice in writing of his intention so to use the premises; and

(b) he complies with any regulations under section 4 above and, subject to any such regulations, with any conditions imposed by the licensing authority and notified to him in writing.

(2) For the purposes of subsection (1) above, the giving in any premises of an exhibition to which section 5 or 6 above applies shall be disregarded.

8-20 * * * * *

21 Interpretation

(1) In this Act, except where the contrary intention appears,—

* * * * *

"child" means a person under the age of sixteen;

"film exhibition" means any exhibition of moving pictures which is produced otherwise than by the simultaneous reception and exhibition of [programmes included in a programme service (within the meaning of the Broadcasting Act 1990];

* * * * *

(2) Any reference in this Act to an exhibition which requires a licence under section 1 above is a reference to an exhibition to which that section applies; and any reference in this Act to an exhibition which requires a consent under section 2 above is a reference to an exhibition to which that section applies.

* * * * *

INTERCEPTION OF COMMUNICATIONS ACT 1985
(1985, c. 56)

An Act to make new provision for and in connection with the interception of communications sent by post or by means of public telecommunication systems and to amend section 45 of the Telecommunications Act 1984 [25 July 1985]

Territorial extent United Kingdom

1 Prohibition on interception

(1) Subject to the following provisions of this section, a person who intentionally intercepts a communication in the course of its transmission by post or by means of a public telecommunication system shall be guilty of an offence and liable—

(a) on summary conviction, to a fine not exceeding the statutory maximum;

(b) on conviction on indictment, to imprisonment for a term not exceeding two years or to a fine or to both.

(2) A person shall not be guilty of an offence under this section if—

(a) the communication is intercepted in obedience to a warrant issued by the Secretary of State under section 2 below; or

(b) that person has reasonable grounds for believing that the person to whom, or the person by whom, the communication is sent has consented to the interception.

(3) A person shall not be guilty of an offence under this section if—

(a) the communication is intercepted for purposes connected with the provision of postal or public telecommunication services or with the enforcement of any enactment relating to the user of those services; or

(b) the communication is being transmitted by wireless telegraphy and is intercepted, with the authority of the Secretary of State, for purposes connected with the issue of licences under the Wireless Telegraphy Act 1949 or the prevention or detection of interference with wireless telegraphy.

(4) No proceedings in respect of an offence under this section shall be instituted—

(a) in England and Wales, except by or with the consent of the Director of Public Prosecutions;

(b) In Northern Ireland, except by or with the consent of the Director of Public Prosecutions for Northern Ireland.

2 Warrants for interception

(1) Subject to the provisions of this section and section 3 below, the Secretary of State may issue a warrant requiring the person to whom it is addressed to intercept, in the course of their transmission by post or by means of public telecommunication system, such communications as are described in the warrant; and such a warrant may also require the person to whom it is addressed to disclose the intercepted material to such persons and in such manner as are described in the warrant.

(2) The Secretary of State shall not issue a warrant under this section unless he considers that the warrant is necessary—

(a) in the interests of national security;

(b) for the purpose of preventing or detecting serious crime or;

(c) for the purpose of safeguarding the economic well-being of the United Kingdom.

(3) The matters to be taken into account in considering whether a warrant is necessary as mentioned in subsection (2) above shall include whether the information which it is considered necessary to acquire could reasonably be acquired by other means.

(4) A warrant shall not be considered necessary as mentioned in subsection (2)(c) above unless the information which it is considered necessary to acquire is information relating to the acts or intentions of persons outside the British Islands.

(5) References in the following provisions of this Act to a warrant are references to a warrant under this section.

3 Scope of warrants

(1) Subject to subsection (2) below, the interception required by a warrant shall be the interception of—

(a) such communications as are sent to or from one or more addresses specified in the warrant, being an address or addresses likely to be used for the transmission of communications to or from—

(i) one particular person specified or described in the warrant; or

(ii) one particular set of premises so specified or described; and

(b) such other communications (if any) as it is necessary to intercept in order to intercept communications falling within paragraph (a) above.

(2) Subsection (1) above shall not apply to a warrant if—

(a) the interception required by the warrant is the interception, in the course of their transmission by means of a public telecommunication system, of—

(i) such external communications as are described in the warrant; and

(ii) such other communications (if any) as it is necessary to intercept in order to intercept such external communications as are so described; and

(b) at the time when the warrant is issued, the Secretary of State issues a certificate certifying the descriptions of intercepted material the examination of which he considers necessary as mentioned in section 2(2) above.

(3) A certificate such as is mentioned in subsection (2) above shall not specify an address in the British Islands for the purpose of including communications sent to or from that address in the certified material unless—

(a) the Secretary of State considers that the examination of communications sent to or from that address is necessary for the purpose of preventing or detecting acts of terrorism; and

(b) communications sent to or from that address are included in the certified material only in so far as they are sent within such a period, not exceeding three months, as is specified in the certificate.

(4) A certificate such as is mentioned in subsection (2) above shall not be issued except under the hand of the Secretary of State.

(5) References in the following provisions of this Act to a certificate are references to a certificate such as is mentioned in subsection (2) above.

4 Issue and duration of warrants

(1) A warrant shall not be issued except—

(a) under the hand of the Secretary of State; or

(b) in an urgent case where the Secretary of State has expressly authorised its issue and a statement of that fact is endorsed thereon, under the hand of an official of his department of or above the rank of Assistant Under Secretary of State.

(2) A warrant shall, unless renewed under subsection (3) below, cease to have effect at the end of the relevant period.

(3) The Secretary of State may, at any time before the end of the relevant period, renew a warrant if he considers that the warrant continues to be necessary as mentioned in section 2(2) above.

(4) If, at any time before the end of the relevant period, the Secretary of State considers that a warrant is no longer necessary as mentioned in section 2(2) above, he shall cancel the warrant.

(5) A warrant shall not be renewed except by an instrument under the hand of the Secretary of State.

(6) In this section "the relevant period"—

(a) in relation to a warrant which has not been renewed, means—

(i) if the warrant was issued under subsection (1)(a) above, the period of two months beginning with the day on which it was issued; and

(ii) if the warrant was issued under subsection (1)(b) above, the period ending with the second working day following that day;

(b) in relation to a warrant which was last renewed within the period mentioned in paragraph (a)(ii) above, means the period of two months beginning with the day on which it was so renewed; and

(c) in relation to a warrant which was last renewed at any other time, means—

(i) if the instrument by which it was so renewed is endorsed with a statement that the renewal is considered necessary as mentioned in section 2(2)(a) or (c) above, the period of six months beginning with the day on which it was so renewed; and

(ii) if that instrument is not so endorsed, the period of one month beginning with that day.

5 *****

6 Safeguards

(1) Where the Secretary of State issues a warrant he shall, unless such arrangements have already been made, make such arrangements as he considers necessary for the purpose of securing—

(a) that the requirements of subsections (2) and (3) below are satisfied in relation to the intercepted material; and

(b) where a certificate is issued in relation to the warrant, that so much of the intercepted material as is not certified by the certificate is not read, looked at or listened to by any person.

(2) The requirements of this subsection are satisfied in relation to any intercepted material if each of the following, namely—

(a) the extent to which the material is disclosed;

(b) the number of persons to whom any of the material is disclosed;

(c) the extent to which the material is copied; and

(d) the number of copies made of any of the material,

is limited to the minimum that is necessary as mentioned in section 2(2) above.

(3) The requirements of this subsection are satisfied in relation to any intercepted material if each copy made of any of that material is destroyed as soon as its retention is no longer necessary as mentioned in section 2(2) above.

7 The Tribunal

(1) There shall be a tribunal (in this Act referred to as "the Tribunal") in relation to which the provisions of Schedule 1 to this Act shall apply.

(2) Any person who believes that communications sent to or by him have been intercepted in the course of their transmission by post or by means of a public telecommunication system may apply to the Tribunal for an investigation under this section.

(3) On such an application (other than one appearing to the Tribunal to be frivolous or vexatious), the Tribunal shall investigate—

(a) whether there is or has been a relevant warrant or a relevant certificate; and

(b) where there is or has been such a warrant or certificate, whether there has been any contravention of sections 2 to 5 above in relation to that warrant or certificate.

(4) If, on an investigation, the Tribunal, applying the principles applicable by a court on an application for judicial review, conclude that there has been a contravention of sections 2 to 5 above in relation to a relevant warrant or a relevant certificate, they shall—

(a) give notice to the applicant stating that conclusion;

(b) make a report of their findings to the Prime Minister; and

(c) if they think fit, make an order under subsection (5) below.

(5) An order under this subsection may do one or more of the following, namely—

(a) quash the relevant warrant or the relevant certificate;

(b) direct the destruction of copies of the intercepted material or, as the case may be, so much of it as is certified by the relevant certificate;

(c) direct the Secretary of State to pay to the applicant such sum by way of compensation as may be specified in the order.

(6), (7) *****

(8) The decisions of the Tribunal (including any decisions as to their jurisdiction) shall not be subject to appeal or liable to be questioned in any court.

(9) *****

8 The Commissioner

(1) The Prime Minister shall appoint a person who holds or has held a high judicial office (in this section referred to as "the Commissioner") to carry out the following functions, namely—

(a) to keep under review the carrying out by the Secretary of State of the functions conferred on him by sections 2 to 5 above and the adequacy of any arrangements made for the purposes of section 6 above; and

(b) to give to the Tribunal all such assistance as the Tribunal may require for the purpose of enabling them to carry out their functions under this Act.

(2) The Commissioner shall hold office in accordance with the terms of his appointment and there shall be paid to him out of money provided by Parliament such allowances as the Treasury may determine.

(3) It shall be the duty of every person holding office under the Crown or engaged in the business of the Post Office or in the running of a public telecommunication system to disclose or give to the Commissioner such documents or information as he may require for the purpose of enabling him to carry out his functions under this section.

(4) It shall be the duty of the Tribunal to send to the Commissioner a copy of every report made by them under section 7(4) above.

(5) If at any time it appears to the Commissioner—

(a) that there has been a contravention of sections 2 to 5 above which has not been the subject of a report made by the Tribunal under section 7(4) above; or

(b) that any arrangements made for the purposes of section 6 above have proved inadequate,

he shall make a report to the Prime Minister with respect to that contravention or those arrangements.

(6) As soon as practicable after the end of each calendar year, the Commissioner shall make a report to the Prime Minister with respect to the carrying out of his functions under this section.

(7) The Prime Minister shall lay before each House of Parliament a copy of every annual report made by the Commissioner under subsection (6) above together with a statement as to whether any matter has been excluded from that copy in pursuance of subsection (8) below.

(8) If it appears to the Prime Minister, after consultation with the Commissioner, that the publication of any matter in an annual report would be prejudicial to national security, to the prevention or detection of serious crime or to the economic well-being of the United Kingdom, the Prime Minister may exclude that matter from the copy of the report as laid before each House of Parliament.

9 Exclusion of evidence

(1) In any proceedings before any court or tribunal no evidence shall be adduced and no question in cross-examination shall be asked which (in either case) tends to suggest—

(a) that an offence under section 1 above has been or is to be committed by any of the persons mentioned in subsection (2) below; or

(b) that a warrant has been or is to be issued to any of those persons.

(2) The persons referred to in subsection (1) above are—

(a) any person holding office under the Crown;

(b) the Post Office and any person engaged in the business of the Post Office; and

(c) any public telecommunications operator and any person engaged in the running of a public telecommunication system.

(3) Subsection (1) above does not apply—

(a) in relation to proceedings for a relevant offence or proceedings before the Tribunal; or

(b) where the evidence is adduced or the question in cross-examination is asked for the purpose of establishing the fairness or unfairness of a dismissal on grounds of an offence under section 1 above or of conduct from which such an offence might be inferred; and paragraph (a) of that subsection does not apply where a person has been convicted of the offence under that section.

(4) * * * * *

10 Interpretation

(1), (2) * * * * *

(3) For the purposes of this Act conduct which constitutes or, if it took place in the United Kingdom, would constitute one or more offences shall be regarded as serious crime if, and only if—

(a) it involves the use of violence, results in substantial financial gain or is conduct by a large number of persons in pursuit of a common purpose; or

(b) the offence or one of the offences is an offence for which a person who has attained the age of twenty-one and has no previous convictions could reasonably be expected to be sentenced to imprisonment for a term of three years or more.

* * * * *

PROSECUTION OF OFFENCES ACT 1985
(1985, c. 23)

An Act to provide for the establishment of a Crown Prosecution Service for England and Wales; to make provision as to costs in criminal cases; to provide for the imposition of time limits in relation to preliminary stages of criminal proceedings; to amend section 42 of the Supreme Court Act 1981 and section 3 of the Children and Young Persons Act 1969; to make provision with respect to consents to prosecutions; to repeal section 9 of the Perjury Act 1911; and for connected purposes [23 May 1985]

Territorial extent England and Wales

PART I
THE CROWN PROSECUTION SERVICE

Constitution and functions of Service

1 The Crown Prosecution Service

(1) There shall be a prosecuting service for England and Wales (to be known as the "Crown Prosecution Service") consisting of—

(a) the Director of Public Prosecutions, who shall be head of the Service;

(b) the Chief Crown Prosecutors, designated under subsection (4) below, each of whom shall be the member of the Service responsible to the Director for supervising the operation of the service in his area; and

(c) the other staff appointed by the Director under this section.

(2) The Director shall appoint such staff for the Service as, with the approval of the Treasury as to numbers, remuneration and other terms and conditions of service, he considers necessary for the discharge of his functions.

(3) The Director may designate any member of the Service who is a barrister or solicitor for the purposes of this subsection, and any person so designated shall be known as a Crown Prosecutor.

(4) The Director shall divide England and Wales into areas and, for each of those areas, designate a Crown Prosecutor for the purposes of this subsection and any person so designated shall be known as a Chief Crown Prosecutor.

(5) The Director may, from time to time, vary the division of England and Wales made for the purpose of subsection (4) above.

(6) Without prejudice to any functions which may have been assigned to him in his capacity as a member of the Service, every Crown Prosecutor shall have all the powers of the Director as to the institution and conduct of proceedings but shall exercise those powers under the direction of the Director.

(7) Where any enactment (whenever passed)—

(a) prevents any step from being taken without the consent of the Director or without his consent or the consent of another; or

(b) requires any step to be taken by or in relation to the Director;

any consent given by or, as the case may be, step taken by or in relation to, a Crown Prosecutor shall be treated, for the purposes of that enactment, as given by or, as the case may be, taken by or in relation to the Director.

2 The Director of Public Prosecutions

(1) The Director of Public Prosecutions shall be appointed by the Attorney General.

(2) The Director must be a [person who has a 10 year general qualification, within the meaning of section 71 of the Courts and Legal Services Act 1990.]

(3) * * * * *

3 Functions of the Director

(1) The Director shall discharge his functions under this or any other enactment under the superintendence of the Attorney General.

(2) It shall be the duty of the Director—

(a) to take over the conduct of all criminal proceedings, other than specified proceedings, instituted on behalf of a police force (whether by a member of that force or by any other person);

(b) to institute and have the conduct of criminal proceedings in any case where it appears to him that—

(i) the importance or difficulty of the case makes it appropriate that proceedings should be instituted by him; or

(ii) it is otherwise appropriate for proceedings to be instituted by him;

(c) to take over the conduct of all binding over proceedings instituted on behalf of a police force (whether by a member of that force or by any other person);

* * * * * and

(g) to discharge such other functions as may from time to time be assigned to him by the Attorney General in pursuance of this paragraph.

(3), (4) * * * * *

4 Crown Prosecutors

[(1) Crown Prosecutors shall continue to have the same rights of audience, in any court, as they had immediately before the coming into force of the Courts and Legal Services Act 1990.

(2) Subsection (1) is not to be taken as preventing those rights being varied or added to in accordance with the provisions of that Act.

(3) The Lord Chancellor may at any time direct, as respects one or more specified places where the Crown Court sits, that Crown Prosecutors, or such category of Crown Prosecutors as may be specified in the direction, may have rights of audience in the Crown Court.

(3A) Any such direction may be limited to apply only in relation to proceedings of a description specified in the direction.

(3B) In considering whether to exercise his powers under this section the Lord Chancellor shall have regard, in particular, to the need to secure the availability of persons with rights of audience in the court or proceedings in question.

(3C) Any direction under this section may be revoked by direction of the Lord Chancellor.

(3D) Any direction under this section may be subject to such conditions and restrictions as appear to the Lord Chancellor to be necessary or expedient.

(3E) Any exercise by the Lord Chancellor of his powers to give a direction under this section shall be with the concurrence of the Lord Chief Justice, the Master of the Rolls, the President of the Family Division and the Vice-Chancellor.]

(4)-(6) ★ ★ ★ ★ ★

5 ★ ★ ★ ★ ★

6 Prosecutions instituted and conducted otherwise than by the Service

(1) Subject to subsection (2) below, nothing in this Part shall preclude any person from instituting any criminal proceedings or conducting any criminal proceedings to which the Director's duty to take over the conduct of proceedings does not apply.

(2) Where criminal proceedings are instituted in circumstances in which the Director is not under a duty to take over their conduct, he may nevertheless do so at any stage.

7-9 ★ ★ ★ ★ ★

Guidelines

10 Guidelines for Crown Prosecutors

(1) The Director shall issue a Code for Crown Prosecutors giving guidance on general principles to be applied by them—

(a) in determining, in any case—

(i) whether proceedings for an offence should be instituted or, where proceedings have been instituted, whether they should be discontinued; or

(ii) what charges should be preferred; and

(b) in considering, in any case, representations to be made by them to any magistrates' court about the mode of trial suitable for that case.

(2) The Director may from time to time make alterations in the Code.

(3) The provisions of the Code shall be set out in the Director's report under section 9 of this Act for the year in which the Code is issued; and any alteration in the Code shall be set out in his report under that section for the year in which the alteration is made.

11-21 ★ ★ ★ ★ ★

PART III
MISCELLANEOUS

22 Power of Secretary of State to set time limits in relation to preliminary stages of criminal proceedings

(1) The Secretary of State may by regulations make provision, with respect to any specified preliminary stage of proceedings for an offence, as to the maximum period—

(a) to be allowed to the prosecution to complete that stage;

(b) during which the accused may, while awaiting completion of that stage, be—

(i) in the custody of a magistrates' court; or

(ii) in the custody of the Crown Court;

in relation to that offence.

(2) The regulations may, in particular—

(a) be made so as to apply only in relation to proceedings instituted in specified areas;

(b) make different provision with respect to proceedings instituted in different areas;

(c) make such provision with respect to the procedure to be followed in criminal proceedings as the Secretary of State considers appropriate in consequence of any other provision of the regulations;

(d) provide for the Magistrates' Courts Act 1980 and the Bail Act 1976 to apply in relation to cases to which custody or overall time limits apply subject to such modifications as may be specified (being modifications which the Secretary of State considers necessary in consequence of any provision made by the regulations); and

(e) make such transitional provision in relation to proceedings instituted before the commencement of any provision of the regulations as the Secretary of State considers appropriate.

(3) The appropriate court may, at any time before the expiry of a time limit imposed by the regulations, extend, or further extend, that limit if it is satisfied—

(a) that there is good and sufficient cause for doing so; and

(b) that the prosecution has acted with all due expedition.

(4) Where, in relation to any proceedings for an offence, an overall time limit has expired before the completion of the stage of the proceedings to which the limit applies, the accused shall be treated, for all purposes, as having been acquitted of that offence.

(5)-(13) ★★★★★

★★★★★

REPRESENTATION OF THE PEOPLE ACT 1985
(1985, c. 50)

An Act to amend the law relating to parliamentary elections in the United Kingdom and local government elections in Great Britain, to provide for combining polls taken on the same date at such elections and elections to the Assembly of the European Communities, to extend the franchise at elections to that Assembly, to amend the law relating to the effect of the demise of the Crown on the summoning and duration of a new Parliament and to repeal section 21(3) of the Representation of the People Act 1918 [16 July 1985]

Territorial extent United Kingdom (ss. 1, 2)

Extension of franchise to British citizens overseas

1 Extension of parliamentary franchise

(1) Subject to section 1(3) of the principal Act, a person is entitled (notwithstanding anything in section 1(2) of that Act) to vote as an elector at a parliamentary election in any constituency if—

(a) he qualifies as an overseas elector in respect of that constituency on the qualifying date, and

(b) on that date and on the date of the poll he is not subject to any legal incapacity to vote and is a British citizen.

(2) For the purposes of this and the principal Act, a person qualifies as an overseas elector in respect of a constituency on the qualifying date if—

(a) on that date he is not resident in the United Kingdom, and

(b) he satisfies [one of the following sets of conditions].

(3) [The first set of conditions is that]—

(a) he was included in a register of parliamentary electors in respect of an address at a place that is situated within the constituency concerned,

(b) on the date by reference to which the register was prepared, he was resident or treated for the purposes of registration as resident at that address,

(c) that date fell within the period of 20 years ending immediately before the qualifying date, and

(d) if he was included in any register of parliamentary electors prepared by reference to a date later than the date referred to in paragraph (b) above, he was not resident or treated for the purposes of registration as resident at an address in the United Kingdom on that later date.

[(3A) The second set of conditions is that—

(a) he was last resident in the United Kingdom within the period of 20 years ending immediately before the qualifying date,

(b) he was by reason only of his age incapable of being included in any register of parliamentary electors prepared by reference to the last date within that period by reference to which such registers were prepared on which he was so resident, and

(c) the address at which he was resident on the date referred to in paragraph (b) above was at a place that is situated within the constituency concerned and a parent or guardian of his was included, in respect of that address, in a register of parliamentary electors or a register of local government electors prepared by reference to that date.]

(4) The reference in subsection (1) above to a person being subject to a legal incapacity to vote on the qualifying date does not include a reference to his being below the age of 18 on that date [and the reference in subsection (3A) above to a register of local government electors includes a register of electors prepared for the purposes of local elections (within the meaning of the Electoral Law Act (Northern Ireland) 1962)].

★★★★★

Note The "principal Act" is the Representation of the People Act 1983.

AUSTRALIA ACT 1986
(1986, c. 2)

An Act to give effect to a request by the Parliament and Government of the Commonwealth of Australia [17 February 1986]

Territorial extent Australia

1 Termination of power of Parliament of United Kingdom to legislate for Australia
No Act of the Parliament of the United Kingdom passed after the commencement of this Act shall extend, or be deemed to extend, to the Commonwealth, to a State or to a Territory as part of the law of the Commonwealth, of the State or of the Territory.

2, 3, 5-11 ★★★★★

4 . . .

12 Amendment of Statute of Westminster
Sections 4, 9(2) and (3) and 10(2) of the Statute of Westminster 1931, in so far as they are part of the law of the Commonwealth, of a State or of a Territory, are hereby repealed.

13, 14 ★★★★★

15 Method of repeal or amendment of this Act or Statute of Westminster
(1) This Act or the Statute of Westminster 1931, as amended and in force from time to time, in so far as it is part of the law of the Commonwealth, of a State or of a Territory, may be repealed or amended by an Act of the Parliament of the Commonwealth passed at the request or with the concurrence of the Parliaments of all the States and, subject to subsection (3) below, only in the manner.

(2) For the purposes of subsection (1) above, an Act of the Parliament of the Commonwealth that is repugnant to this Act or the Statute of Westminster 1931, as amended and in force from time to time, or to any provision of this Act or of that Satute as so amended and in force, shall, to the extent of the repugnancy, be deemed an Act to repeal or amend the Act, Statute or provision to which it is repugnant.

(3) Nothing in subsection (1) above limits or prevents the exercise by the Parliament of the Commonwealth of any powers that may be conferred upon that Parliament by any alteration to the Constitution of the Commonwealth made in accordance with section 128 of the Constitution of the Commonwealth after the commencement of this Act.

★★★★★

EDUCATION (NO. 2) ACT 1986
(1986, c. 61)

An Act to amend the law relating to education [7 November 1986]

Territorial extent England and Wales. The section below is the only relevant provision not repealed by the consolidating Education Act 1996.

PART IV
MISCELLANEOUS

43 Freedom of speech in universities, polytechnics and colleges

(1) Every individual and body of persons concerned in the government of any establishment to which this section applies shall take such steps as are reasonably practicable to ensure that freedom of speech within the law is secured for members, students and employees of the establishment and for visiting speakers.

(2) The duty imposed by subsection (1) above includes (in particular) the duty to ensure, so far as is reasonably practicable, that the use of any premises of the establishment is not denied to any individual or body of persons on any ground connected with—

(a) the beliefs or views of that individual or of any member of that body; or

(b) the policy or objectives of that body.

(3) The governing body of every such establishment shall, with a view to facilitating the discharge of the duty imposed by subsection (1) above in relation to that establishment, issue and keep up to date a code of practice setting out—

(a) the procedures to be followed by members, students and employees of the establishment in connection with the organisation—

(i) of meetings which are to be held on premises of the establishment and which fall within any class of meeting specified in the code; and

(ii) of other activities which are to take place on those premises and which fall within any class of activity so specified; and

(b) the conduct required of such persons in connection with any such meeting or activity;

and dealing with such other matters as the governing body consider appropriate.

(4) Every individual and body of persons concerned in the government of any such establishment shall take such steps as are reasonably practicable (including where appropriate the initiation of disciplinary measures) to secure that the requirements of the code of practice for that establishment, issued under subsection (3) above, are complied with.

(5) The establishments to which this section applies are—

(a) any university;

[(aa) any institution other than a university within the higher education sector;]

[(b) any establishment of higher or further education which is maintained by a local education authority;] [and

(ba) any institution within the further education sector.]

. . .

(6) ★★★★★

(7) Where any establishment—

(a) falls within subsection (5)(b) above;

. . .

the local education authority . . . shall, for the purposes of this section, be taken to be concerned in its government.

(8) Where a students' union occupies premises which are not premises of the establishment in connection with which the union is constituted, any reference in this section to the premises of the establishment shall be taken to include a reference to the premises occupied by the students' union.

LOCAL GOVERNMENT ACT 1986
(1986, c. 10)

An Act to require rating authorities to set a rate on or before 1st April; to prohibit political publicity and otherwise restrain local authority publicity; to require the mortgagor's consent and make other provision in connection with the disposal of local authority mortgages; to amend the law as to the effect of retirement and re-election of, and the allowances payable to, members of certain authorities; and for connected purposes [26 March 1986]

Territorial extent England and Wales; Scotland

* * * * *

PART II
LOCAL AUTHORITY PUBLICITY

2 Prohibition of political publicity

(1) A local authority shall not publish any material which, in whole or in part, appears to be designed to affect public support for a political party.

[(2) In determining whether material falls within the prohibition regard shall be had to the content and style of the material, the time and other circumstances of publication and the likely effect on those to whom it is directed and, in particular, to the following matters—

(a) whether the material refers to a political party or to persons identified with a political party or promotes or opposes a point of view on a question of political controversy which is identifiable as the view of one political party and not of another;

(b) where the material is part of a campaign, the effect which the campaign appears to be designed to achieve.]

(3) A local authority shall not give financial or other assistance to a person for the publication of material which the authority are prohibited by this section from publishing themselves.

[2A Prohibition on promoting homosexuality by teaching or by publishing material

(1) A local authority shall not—

(a) intentionally promote homosexuality or publish material with the intention of promoting homosexuality;

(b) promote the teaching in any maintained school of the acceptability of homosexuality as a pretended family relationship.

(2) Nothing in subsection (1) above shall be taken to prohibit the doing of anything for the purpose of treating or preventing the spread of disease.

(3) In any proceedings in connection with the application of this section a court shall draw such inferences as to the intention of the local authority as may reasonably be drawn from the evidence before it.

(4) In subsection (1)(b) above "maintained school" means,—

(a) in England and Wales, a county school, voluntary school, nursery school or special school, within the meaning of [the Education Act 1996]; and

(b) in Scotland, a public school, nursery school or special school, within the meaning of the Education (Scotland) Act 1980.]

PARLIAMENTARY CONSTITUENCIES ACT 1986
(1986, c. 56)

An Act to consolidate the House of Commons (Redistribution of Seats) Acts 1949 to 1979 and certain related enactments [7 November 1986]

Territorial extent United Kingdom

Note The Boundary Commissions Act 1992, s. 2(2), requires that the first report to be made by each Boundary Commission under Section 3 below must be submitted to the Secretary of State not later than 31st December 1994.

1 Parliamentary constituencies

(1) There shall for the purpose of parliamentary elections be the county and borough constituencies (or in Scotland the county and burgh constituencies), each returning a single member, which are described in Orders in Council made under this Act.

(2) In this Act and, except where the context otherwise requires, in any Act passed after the Representation of the People Act 1948, "constituency" means an area having separate representation in the House of Commons.

2 The Boundary Commissions

(1) For the purposes of the continuous review of the distribution of seats at parliamentary elections, there shall continue to be four permanent Boundary Commissions, namely a Boundary Commission for England, a Boundary Commission for Scotland, a Boundary Commission for Wales and a Boundary Commission for Northern Ireland.

(2) Schedule 1 to this Act shall have effect with respect to the constitution of, and other matters relating to, the Boundary Commissions.

3 Reports of the Commissions

(1) Each Boundary Commission shall keep under review the representation in the House of Commons of the part of the United Kingdom with which they are concerned and shall, in accordance with subsection (2) below, submit to the Secretary of State reports with respect to the whole of that part of the United Kingdom, either—

(a) showing the constituencies into which they recommend that it should be divided in order to give effect to the rules set out in paragraphs 1 to 6 of Schedule 2 to this Act (read with paragraph 7 of that Schedule), or

(b) stating that, in the opinion of the Commission, no alteration is required to be made in respect of that part of the United Kingdom in order to give effect to the said rules (read with paragraph 7).

(2) Reports under subsection (1) above shall be submitted by a Boundary Commission [not less than eight or more than twelve years] from the date of the submission of their last report under that subsection.

[(2A) A failure by a Boundary Commission to submit a report within the time limit which is appropriate to that report shall not be regarded as invalidating the report for the purpose of any enactment.]

(3) Any Boundary Commission may also from time to time submit to the Secretary of State reports with respect to the area comprised in any particular constituency or

constituencies in the part of the United Kingdom with which they are concerned, showing the constituencies into which they recommend that that area should be divided in order to give effect to the rules set out in paragraphs 1 to 6 of Schedule 2 to this Act (read with paragraph 7 of that Schedule).

(4) A report of a Boundary Commission under this Act showing the constituencies into which they recommend that any area should be divided shall state, as respects each constituency, the name by which they recommend that it should be known, and whether they recommend that it should be a county constituency or a borough constituency (or in Scotland a county constituency or a burgh constituency).

(5) As soon as may be after a Boundary Commission have submitted a report to the Secretary of State under this Act, he shall lay the report before Parliament together, except in a case where the report states that no alteration is required to be made in respect of the part of the United Kingdom with which the Commission are concerned, with the draft of an Order in Council for giving effect, whether with or without modifications, to the recommendations contained in the report.

(6) Schedule 2 to this Act which contains the rules referred to above and related provisions shall have effect.

(7), (8) ★ ★ ★ ★ ★

4 Orders in Council

(1) The draft of any Order in Council laid before Parliament by the Secretary of State under this Act for giving effect, whether with or without modifications, to the recommendations contained in the report of a Boundary Commission may make provision for any matters which appear to him to be incidental to, or consequential on, the recommendations.

(2) Where any such draft gives effect to any such recommendations with modifications, the Secretary of State shall lay before Parliament together with the draft a statement of the reasons for the modifications.

(3) If any such draft is approved by resolution of each House of Parliament, the Secretary of State shall submit it to Her Majesty in Council.

(4) If a motion for the approval of any such draft is rejected by either House of Parliament or withdrawn by leave of the House, the Secretary of State may amend the draft and lay the amended draft before Parliament, and if the draft as so amended is approved by resolution of each House of Parliament, the Secretary of State shall submit it to Her Majesty in Council.

(5) ★ ★ ★ ★ ★

(6) The coming into force of any such Order shall not affect any parliamentary election until a proclamation is issued by Her Majesty summoning a new Parliament, or affect the constitution of the House of Commons until the dissolution of the Parliament then in being.

(7) The validity of any Order in Council purporting to be made under this Act and reciting that a draft of the Order has been approved by resolution of each House of Parliament shall not be called in question in any legal proceedings whatsoever.

5 Notices

(1) Where a Boundary Commission intend to consider making a report under this Act they shall, by notice in writing, inform the Secretary of State accordingly, and a copy of the notice shall be published—

(a) in a case where it was given by the Boundary Commission for England or the Boundary Commission for Wales, in the London Gazette,

(b) in a case where it was given by the Boundary Commission for Scotland, in the Edinburgh Gazette, and

(c) in a case where it was given by the Boundary Commission for Northern Ireland, in the Belfast Gazette.

(2) Where a Boundary Commission have provisionally determined to make recommendations affecting any constituency, they shall publish in at least one newspaper circulating in the constituency a notice stating—

(a) the effect of the proposed recommendations and (except in a case where they propose to recommend that no alteration be made in respect of the constituency) that a copy of the recommendations is open to inspection at a specified place within the constituency, and

(b) that representations with respect to the proposed recommendations may be made to the Commission within one month after the publication of the notice;

and the Commission shall take into consideration any representations duly made in accordance with any such notice.

(3) Where a Boundary Commission revise any proposed recommendations after publishing a notice of them under subsection (2) above, the Commission shall comply again with that subsection in relation to the revised recommendations, as if no earlier notice had been published.

6 Local inquiries

(1) A Boundary Commission may, if they think fit, cause a local inquiry to be held in respect of any constituency or constituencies.

(2) Where, on the publication of the notice under section 5(2) above of a recommendation of a Boundary Commission for the alteration of any constituencies, the Commission receive any representation objecting to the proposed recommendation from an interested authority or from a body of electors numbering one hundred or more, the Commission shall not make the recommendation unless, since the publication of the notice, a local inquiry has been held in respect of the constituencies.

(3) Where a local inquiry was held in respect of the constituencies before the publication of the notice mentioned in subsection (2) above, that subsection shall not apply if the Commission, after considering the matters discussed at the local inquiry, the nature of the representations received on the publication of the notice and any other relevant circumstances, are of opinion that a further local inquiry would not be justified.

(4)-(7) ★★★★★

★★★★★

Section 2

SCHEDULE 1
THE BOUNDARY COMMISSIONS

Constitution

1. The Speaker of the House of Commons shall be the chairman of each of the four Commissions.

2. Each of the four Commissions shall consist of the chairman, a deputy chairman and two other members appointed by the Secretary of State.

3. The deputy chairman—

(a) in the case of the Commission for England shall be a judge of the High Court appointed by the Lord Chancellor,

(b) in the case of the Commission for Scotland shall be a judge of the Court of Session appointed by the Lord President of the Court of Session,

(c) in the case of the Commission for Wales shall be a judge of the High Court appointed by the Lord Chancellor,

(d) in the case of the Commission for Northern Ireland shall be a judge of the High Court in Northern Ireland appointed by the Lord Chief Justice of Northern Ireland.

4. A member of any Commission (other than the chairman) shall hold his appointment for such term and on such conditions as may be determined before his appointment by the person appointing him.

4A.-12. ★★★★★

Section 3

SCHEDULE 2
RULES FOR REDISTRIBUTION OF SEATS

The rules

1.—(1) The number of constituencies in Great Britain shall not be substantially greater or less than 613.

(2) The number of constituencies in Scotland shall not be less than 71.

(3) The number of constituencies in Wales shall not be less than 35.

(4) The number of constituencies in Northern Ireland shall not be greater than 18 or less than 16, and shall be 17 unless it appears to the Boundary Commission for Northern Ireland that Northern Ireland should for the time being be divided into 16 or (as the case may be) into 18 constituencies.

2. Every constituency shall return a single member.

3. There shall continue to be a constituency which shall include the whole of the City of London and the name of which shall refer to the City of London.

4.—(1) So far as is practicable having regard to rules 1 to 3—

(a) in England and Wales,—

(i) no county or part of a county shall be included in a constituency which includes the whole or part of any other county or the whole or part of a London borough,

(ii) no London borough or any part of a London borough shall be included in a constituency which includes the whole or part of any other London borough,

(b) in Scotland, regard shall be had to the boundaries of local authority areas,

(c) in Northern Ireland, no ward shall be included partly in one constituency and partly in another.

[(1A) In sub-paragraph (1)(a) above "county" means in relation to Wales, a preserved county (as defined by section 64 of the Local Government (Wales) Act 1994).]

(2) In sub-paragraph (1)(b) above "area" and "local authority" have the same meanings as in the Local Government (Scotland) Act 1973.

5. The electorate of any constituency shall be as near the electoral quota as is practicable having regard to rules 1 to 4; and a Boundary Commission may depart from the strict application of rule 4 if it appears to them that a departure is desirable to avoid an excessive disparity between the electorate of any constituency and the electoral quota, or between the electorate of any constituency and that of neighbouring constituencies in the part of the United Kingdom with which they are concerned.

6. A Boundary Commission may depart from the strict application of rules 4 and 5 if special geographical considerations, including in particular the size, shape and accessibility of a constituency, appear to them to render a departure desirable.

General and supplementary

7. It shall not be the duty of a Boundary Commission to aim at giving full effect in all circumstances to the above rules, but they shall take account, so far as they reasonably can—

(a) of the inconveniences attendant on alterations of constituencies other than alterations made for the purposes of rule 4, and

(b) of any local ties which would be broken by such alterations.

8., 9. ★ ★ ★ ★ ★

PUBLIC ORDER ACT 1986
(1986, c. 64)

An Act to abolish the common law offences of riot, rout, unlawful assembly and affray and certain statutory offences relating to public order; to create new offences relating to public order; to control public processions and assemblies; to control the stirring up of racial hatred; to provide for the exclusion of certain offenders from sporting events; to create a new offence relating to the contamination of or interference with goods; to confer power to direct certain trespassers to leave land; to amend section 7 of the Conspiracy and Protection of Property Act 1875, section 1 of the Prevention of Crime Act 1953, Part V of the Criminal Justice (Scotland) Act 1980 and the Sporting Events (Control of Alcohol etc.) Act 1985; to repeal certain obsolete or unnecessary enactments; and for connected purposes [7 November 1986]

Territorial extent England and Wales (ss. 1-9, 13, 39, 40(4)); England and Wales, Scotland (remainder)

PART I
NEW OFFENCES

1 Riot

(1) Where 12 or more persons who are present together use or threaten unlawful violence for a common purpose and the conduct of them (taken together) is such as would cause a person of reasonable firmness present at the scene to fear for his personal safety, each of the persons using unlawful violence for the common purpose is guilty of riot.

(2) It is immaterial whether or not the 12 or more use or threaten unlawful violence simultaneously.

(3) The common purpose may be inferred from conduct.

(4) No person of reasonable firmness need actually be, or be likely to be, present at the scene.

(5) Riot may be committed in private as well as in public places.

(6) A person guilty of riot is liable on conviction on indictment to imprisonment for a term not exceeding ten years or a fine or both.

2 Violent disorder

(1) Where 3 or more persons who are present together use or threaten unlawful violence and the conduct of them (taken together) is such as would cause a person of reasonable firmness present at the scene to fear for his personal safety, each of the persons using or threatening unlawful violence is guilty of violent disorder.

(2) It is immaterial whether or not the 3 or more use or threaten unlawful violence simultaneously.

(3) No person of reasonable firmness need actually be, or be likely to be, present at the scene.

(4) Violent disorder may be committed in private as well as in public places.

(5) A person guilty of violent disorder is liable on conviction on indictment to imprisonment for a term not exceeding 5 years or a fine or both, or on summary conviction to imprisonment for a term not exceeding 6 months or a fine not exceeding the statutory maximum or both.

3 Affray

(1) A person is guilty of affray if he uses or threatens unlawful violence towards another and his conduct is such as would cause a person of reasonable firmness present at the scene to fear for his personal safety.

(2) Where 2 or more persons use or threaten the unlawful violence, it is the conduct of them taken together that must be considered for the purposes of subsection (1).

(3) For the purposes of this section a threat cannot be made by the use of words alone.

(4) No person of reasonable firmness need actually be, or be likely to be, present at the scene.

(5) Affray may be committed in private as well as in public places.

(6) A constable may arrest without warrant anyone he reasonably suspects is committing affray.

(7) A person guilty of affray is liable on conviction on indictment to imprisonment for a term not exceeding 3 years or a fine or both, or on summary conviction to imprisonment for a term not exceeding 6 months or a fine not exceeding the statutory maximum or both.

4 Fear or provocation of violence

(1) A person is guilty of an offence if he—

(a) uses towards another person threatening, abusive or insulting words or behaviour, or

(b) distributes or displays to another person any writing, sign or other visible representation which is threatening, abusive or insulting,

with intent to cause that person to believe that immediate unlawful violence will be used against him or another by any person, or to provoke the immediate use of unlawful violence by that person or another, or whereby that person is likely to believe that such violence will be used or it is likely that such violence will be provoked.

(2) An offence under this section may be committed in a public or a private place, except that no offence is committed where the words or behaviour are used, or the writing, sign or other visible representation is distributed or displayed, by a person inside a dwelling and the other person is also inside that or another dwelling.

(3) A constable may arrest without warrant anyone he reasonably suspects is committing an offence under this section.

(4) A person guilty of an offence under this section is liable on summary conviction to imprisonment for a term not exceeding 6 months or a fine not exceeding level 5 on the standard scale or both.

[4A Intentional harassment, alarm or distress

(1) A person is guilty of an offence if, with intent to cause a person harassment, alarm or distress, he—

(a) uses threatening, abusive or insulting words or behaviour, or disorderly behaviour, or

(b) displays any writing, sign or other visible representation which is threatening, abusive or insulting,

thereby causing that or another person harassment, alarm or distress.

(2) An offence under this section may be committed in a public or a private place, except that no offence is committed where the words or behaviour are used, or the writing, sign or other visible representation is displayed, by a person inside a dwelling and the person who is harassed, alarmed or distressed is also inside that or another dwelling.

(3) It is a defence for the accused to prove—

(a) that he was inside a dwelling and had no reason to believe that the words or behaviour used, or the writing, sign or other visible representation displayed, would be heard or seen by a person outside that or any other dwelling, or

(b) that his conduct was reasonable.

(4) A constable may arrest without warrant anyone he reasonably suspects is committing an offence under this section.

(5) A person guilty of an offence under this section is liable on summary conviction to imprisonment for a term not exceeding 6 months or a fine not exceeding level 5 on the standard scale or both.]

5 Harassment, alarm or distress

(1) A person is guilty of an offence if he—

(a) uses threatening, abusive or insulting words or behaviour, or disorderly behaviour, or

(b) displays any writing, sign or other visible representation which is threatening, abusive or insulting,

within the hearing or sight of a person likely to be caused harassment, alarm or distress thereby.

(2) An offence under this section may be committed in a public or a private place, except that no offence is committed where the words or behaviour are used, or the writing, sign or other visible representation is displayed, by a person inside a dwelling and the other person is also inside that or another dwelling.

(3) It is a defence for the accused to prove—

(a) that he had no reason to believe that there was any person within hearing or sight who was likely to be caused harassment, alarm or distress, or

(b) that he was inside a dwelling and had no reason to believe that the words or behaviour used, or the writing, sign or other visible representation displayed, would be heard or seen by a person outside that or any other dwelling, or

(c) that his conduct was reasonable.

(4) A constable may arrest a person without warrant if—

(a) he engages in offensive conduct which [a] constable warns him to stop, and

(b) he engages in further offensive conduct immediately or shortly after the warning.

(5) In subsection (4) "offensive conduct" means conduct the constable reasonably suspects to constitute an offence under this section, and the conduct mentioned in paragraph (a) and the further conduct need not be of the same nature.

(6) A person guilty of an offence under this section is liable on summary conviction to a fine not exceeding level 3 on the standard scale.

6 Mental element: miscellaneous

(1) A person is guilty of riot only if he intends to use violence or is aware that his conduct may be violent.

(2) A person is guilty of violent disorder or affray only if he intends to use or threaten violence or is aware that his conduct may be violent or threaten violence.

(3) A person is guilty of an offence under section 4 only if he intends his words or behaviour, or the writing, sign or other visible representation, to be threatening, abusive or insulting, or is aware that it may be threatening, abusive or insulting.

(4) A person is guilty of an offence under section 5 only if he intends his words or behaviour, or the writing, sign or other visible representation, to be threatening, abusive or insulting, or is aware that it may be threatening, abusive or insulting or (as the case may be) he intends his behaviour to be or is aware that it may be disorderly.

(5) For the purposes of this section a person whose awareness is impaired by intoxication shall be taken to be aware of that of which he would be aware if not intoxicated, unless he shows either that his intoxication was not self-induced or that it was caused solely by the taking or administration of a substance in the course of medical treatment.

(6) In subsection (5) "intoxication" means any intoxication, whether caused by drink, drugs or other means, or by a combination of means.

(7) Subsections (1) and (2) do not affect the determination for the purposes of riot or violent disorder of the number of persons who use or threaten violence.

7 Procedure: miscellaneous

(1) No prosecution for an offence of riot or incitement to riot may be instituted except by or with the consent of the Director of Public Prosecutions.

(2)-(4) ★ ★ ★ ★ ★

8 Interpretation

In this Part—

"dwelling" means any structure or part of a structure occupied as a person's home or as other living accommodation (whether the occupation is separate or shared with others) but does not include any part not so occupied, and for this purpose "structure" includes a tent, caravan, vehicle, vessel or other temporary or movable structure;

"violence" means any violent conduct, so that—

(a) except in the context of affray, it includes violent conduct towards property as well as violent conduct towards persons, and

(b) it is not restricted to conduct causing or intended to cause injury or damage but includes any other violent conduct (for example, throwing at or towards a person a missile of a kind capable of causing injury which does not hit or falls short).

9 Offences abolished

(1) The Common Law offences of riot, rout, unlawful assembly and affray are abolished.

(2) * * * * *

10 * * * * *

PART II
PROCESSIONS AND ASSEMBLIES

11 Advance notice of public processions

(1) Written notice shall be given in accordance with this section of any proposal to hold a public procession intended—

(a) to demonstrate support for or opposition to the views or actions of any person or body of persons,

(b) to publicise a cause or campaign, or

(c) to mark or commemorate an event,

unless it is not reasonably practicable to give any advance notice of the procession.

(2) Subsection (1) does not apply where the procession is one commonly or customarily held in the police area (or areas) in which it is proposed to be held or is a funeral procession organised by a funeral director acting in the normal course of his business.

(3) The notice must specify the date when it is intended to hold the procession, the time when it is intended to start it, its proposed route, and the name and address of the person (or of one of the persons) proposing to organise it.

(4) Notice must be delivered to a police station—

(a) in the police area in which it is proposed the procession will start, or

(b) where it is proposed the procession will start in Scotland and cross into England, in the first police area in England on the proposed route.

(5) If delivered not less than 6 clear days before the date when the procession is intended to be held, the notice may be deliverd by post by the recorded delivery service; but section 7 of the Interpretation Act 1978 (under which a document sent by post is deemed to have been served when posted and to have been delivered in the ordinary course of post) does not apply.

(6) If not delivered in accordance with subsection (5), the notice must be delivered by hand not less than 6 clear days before the date when the procession is intended to be held or, if that is not reasonably practicable, as soon as delivery is reasonably practicable.

(7) Where a public procession is held, each of the persons organising it is guilty of an offence if—

(a) the requirements of this section as to notice have not been satisfied, or

(b) the date when it is held, the time when it starts, or its route, differs from the date, time or route specified in the notice.

(8) It is a defence for the accused to prove that he did not know of, and neither suspected nor had reason to suspect, the failure to satisfy the requirements or (as the case may be) the difference of date, time or route.

(9) To the extent that an alleged offence turns on a difference of date, time or route, it is a defence for the accused to prove that the difference arose from circumstances beyond his control or from something done with the agreement of a police officer or by his direction.

(10) A person guilty of an offence under subsection (7) is liable on summary conviction to a fine not exceeding level 3 on the standard scale.

12 Imposing conditions on public processions

(1) If the senior police officer, having regard to the time or place at which and the circumstances in which any public procession is being held or is intended to be held and to its route or proposed route, reasonably believes that—

(a) it may result in serious public disorder, serious damage to property or serious disruption to the life of the community, or

(b) the purpose of the persons organising it is the intimidation of others with a view to compelling them not to do an act they have a right to do, or to do an act they have a right not to do,

he may give directions imposing on the persons organising or taking part in the procession such conditions as appear to him necessary to prevent such disorder, damage, disruption or intimidation, including conditions as to the route of the procession or prohibiting it from entering any public place specified in the directions.

(2) In subsection (1) "the senior police officer" means—

(a) in relation to a procession being held, or to a procession intended to be held in a case where persons are assembling with a view to taking part in it, the most senior in rank of the police officers present at the scene, and

(b) in relation to a procession intended to be held in a case where paragraph (a) does not apply, the chief officer of police.

(3) A direction given by a chief officer of police by virtue of subsection (2)(b) shall be given in writing.

(4) A person who organises a public procession and knowingly fails to comply with a condition imposed under this section is guilty of an offence, but it is a defence for him to prove that the failure arose from circumstances beyond his control.

(5) A person who takes part in a public procession and knowingly fails to comply with a condition imposed under this section is guilty of an offence, but it is a defence for him to prove that the failure arose from circumstances beyond his control.

(6) a person who incites another to commit an offence under subsection (5) is guilty of an offence.

(7) A constable in uniform may arrest without warrant anyone he reasonably suspects is committing an offence under subsection (4), (5) or (6).

(8) A person guilty of an offence under subsection (4) is liable on summary conviction to imprisonment for a term not exceeding 3 months or a fine not exceeding level 4 on the standard scale or both.

(9) A person guilty of an offence under subsection (5) is liable on summary conviction to a fine not exceeding level 3 on the standard scale.

(10) A person guilty of an offence under subsection (6) is liable on summary conviction to imprisonment for a term not exceeding 3 months or a fine not exceeding level 4 on the standard scale or both, notwithstanding section 45(3) of the Magistrates' Courts Act 1980 (inciter liable to same penalty as incited).

(11) In Scotland this section applies only in relation to a procession being held, and to a procession intended to be held in a case where persons are assembling with a view to taking part in it.

13 Prohibiting public processions

(1) If at any time the chief officer of police reasonably believes that, because of particular circumstances existing in any district or part of a district, the powers under section 12 will not be sufficient to prevent the holding of public processions in that district or part from resulting in serious public disorder, he shall apply to the council of the district for an order prohibiting for such period not exceeding 3 months as may be specified in the application the holding of all public processions (or of any class of public procession so specified) in the district or part concerned.

(2) On receiving such an application, a council may with the consent of the Secretary of State make an order either in the terms of the application or with such modifications as may be approved by the Secretary of State.

(3) Subsection (1) does not apply in the City of London or the metropolitan police district.

(4) If at any time the Commissioner of Police for the City of London or the Commissioner of Police of the Metropolis reasonably believes that, because of particular circumstances existing in his police area or part of it, the powers under section 12 will not be sufficient to prevent the holding of public processions in that area or part from resulting in serious public disorder, he may with the consent of the Secretary of State make an order prohibiting for such period not exceeding 3 months as may be specified in the order the holding of all public processions (or of any class of public procession so specified) in the area or part concerned.

(5) An order made under this section may be revoked or varied by a subsequent order made in the same way, that is, in accordance with subsections (1) and (2) or subsection (4), as the case may be.

(6) An order under this section shall, if not made in writing, be recorded in writing as soon as practicable after being made.

(7) A person who organises a public procession the holding of which he knows is prohibited by virtue of an order under this section is guilty of an offence.

(8) A person who takes part in a public procession the holding of which he knows is prohibited by virtue of an order under this section is guilty of an offence.

(9) A person who incites another to commit an offence under subsection (8) is guilty of an offence.

(10) A constable in uniform may arrest without warrant anyone he reasonably suspects is committing an offence under subsection (7), (8) or (9).

(11) A person guilty of an offence under subsection (7) is liable on summary conviction to imprisonment for a term not exceeding 3 months or a fine not exceeding level 4 on the standard scale or both.

(12) A person guilty of an offence under subsection (8) is liable on summary conviction to a fine not exceeding level 3 on the standard scale.

(13) A person guilty of an offence under subsection (9) is liable on summary conviction to imprisonment for a term not exceeding 3 months or a fine not exceeding level 4 on the standard scale or both, notwithstanding section 45(3) of the Magistrates' Courts Act 1980.

14 Imposing conditions on public assemblies

(1) If the senior police officer, having regard to the time or place at which and the circumstances in which any public assembly is being held or is intended to be held, reasonably believes that—

(a) it may result in serious public disorder, serious damage to property or serious disruption to the life of the community, or

(b) the purpose of the persons organising it is the intimidation of others with a view to compelling them not to do an act they have a right to do, or to do an act they have a right not to do, he may give directions imposing on the persons organising or taking part in the assembly such conditions as to the place at which the assembly may be (or continue to be) held, its maximum duration, or the maximum number of persons who may constitute it, as appear to him necessary to prevent such disorder, damage, disruption or intimidation.

(2) In subsection (1) "the senior police officer" means—

(a) in relation to an assembly being held, the most senior in rank of the police officers present at the scene, and

(b) in relation to an assembly intended to be held, the chief officer of police.

(3) A direction given by a chief officer of police by virtue of subsection (2)(b) shall be given in writing.

(4) A person who organises a public assembly and knowingly fails to comply with a condition imposed under this section is guilty of an offence, but it is a defence for him to prove that the failure arose from circumstances beyond his control.

(5) A person who takes part in a public assembly and knowingly fails to comply with a condition imposed under this section is guilty of an offence, but it is a defence for him to prove that the failure arose from circumstances beyond his control.

(6) A person who incites another to commit an offence under subsection (5) is guilty of an offence.

(7) A constable in uniform may arrest without warrant anyone he reasonably suspects is committing an offence under subsection (4), (5) or (6).

(8) A person guilty of an offence under subsection (4) is liable on summary conviction to imprisonment for a term not exceeding 3 months or a fine not exceeding level 4 on the standard scale or both.

(9) A person guilty of an offence under subsection (5) is liable on summary conviction to a fine not exceeding level 3 on the standard scale.

(10) A person guilty of an offence under subsection (6) is liable on summary conviction to imprisonment for a term not exceeding 3 months or a fine not exceeding level 4 on the standard scale or both, notwithstanding section 45(3) of the Magistrates' Courts Act 1980.

[14A Prohibiting trespassory assemblies

(1) If at any time the chief officer of police reasonably believes that an assembly is intended to be held in any district at a place on land to which the public has no right of access or only a limited right of access and that the assembly—

(a) is likely to be held without the permission of the occupier of the land or to conduct itself in such a way as to exceed the limits of any permission of his or the limits of the public's right of access, and

(b) may result—

(i) in serious disruption to the life of the community, or

(ii) where the land, or a building or monument on it, is of historical, architectural, archaeological or scientific importance, in significant damage to the land, building or monument,

he may apply to the council of the district for an order prohibiting for a specified period the holding of all trespassory assemblies in the district or a part of it, as specified.

(2) On receiving such an application, a council may—

(a) in England and Wales, with the consent of the Secretary of State make an order either in the terms of the application or with such modifications as may be approved by the Secretary of State; or

(b) in Scotland, make an order in the terms of the application.

(3) Subsection (1) does not apply in the City of London or the metropolitan police district.

(4) If at any time the Commissioner of Police for the City of London or the Commissioner of Police of the Metropolis reasonably believes that an assembly is

intended to be held at a place on land to which the public has no right of access or only a limited right of access in his police area and that the assembly—

(a) is likely to be held without the permission of the occupier of the land or to conduct itself in such a way as to exceed the limits of any permission of his or the limits of the public's right of access, and

(b) may result—

(i) in serious disruption to the life of the community, or

(ii) where the land, or a building or monument on it, is of historical, architectural, archaeological or scientific importance, in significant damage to the land, building or monument,

he may with the consent of the Secretary of State make an order prohibiting for a specified period the holding of all trespassory assemblies in this area or a part of it, as specified.

(5) An order prohibiting the holding of trespassory assemblies operates to prohibit any assembly which—

(a) is held on land to which the public has no right of access or only a limited right of access, and

(b) takes place in the prohibited circumstances, that is to say, without the permission of the occupier of the land or so as to exceed the limits of any permission of his or the limits of the public as right of access.

(6) No order under this section shall prohibit the holding of assemblies for a period exceeding 4 days or in an area exceeding an area represented by a circle with a radius of 5 miles from a specified centre.

(7) An order made under this section may be revoked or varied by a subsequent order made in the same way, that is, in accordance with subsection (1) and (2) or subsection (4), as the case may be.

(8) Any order under this section shall, if not made in writing, be recorded in writing as soon as practicable after being made.

(9) In this section and sections 14B and 14C—

"assembly" means an assembly of 20 or more persons;

"land", means land in the open air;

"limited", in relation to a right of access by the public to land, means that their use of it is restricted to use for a particular purpose (as in the case of a highway or road) or is subject to other restrictions;

"occupier" means—

(a) in England and Wales, the person entitled to possession of the land by virtue of an estate or interest held by him; or

(b) in Scotland, the person lawfully entitled to natural possession of the land, and in subsection (1) and (4) includes the person reasonably believed by the authority applying for or making the order to be the occupier;

"public" includes a section of the public; and

"specified" means specified in an order under this section.

(10), (11) ★★★★★

14B Offences in connection with trespassory assemblies and arrest therefor

(1) A person who organises an assembly the holding of which he knows is prohibited by an order under section 14A is guilty of an offence.

(2) A person who takes part in an assembly which he knows is prohibited by an order under section 14A is guilty of an offence.

(3) In England and Wales, a person who incites another to commit an offence under subsection (2) is guilty of an offence.

(4) A constable in uniform may arrest without a warrant anyone he reasonably suspects to be committing an offence under this section.

(5)-(8) ★★★★★

14C Stopping persons from proceeding to trespassory assemblies

(1) If a constable in uniform reasonably believes that a person is on his way to an assembly within the area to which an order under section 14A applies which the constable reasonably believes is likely to be an assembly which is prohibited by that order, he may, subject to subsection (2) below—

(a) stop that person, and

(b) direct him not to proceed in the direction of the assembly.

(2) The power conferred by subsection (1) may only be exercised within the area to which the order applies.

(3) A person who fails to comply with a direction under subsection (1) which he knows has been given to him is guilty of an offence.

(4) A constable in uniform may arrest without a warrant anyone he reasonably suspects to be committing an offence under this section.

(5) A person guilty of an offence under subsection (3) is liable on summary conviction to a fine not exceeding level 3 on the standard scale.]

15 Delegation

(1) The chief officer of police may delegate, to such extent and subject to such conditions as he may specify, any of his functions under sections 12 to [14A] to [an] assistant chief constable; and references in those subsections to the person delegating shall be construed accordingly.

(2) Subsection (1) shall have effect in the City of London and the metropolitan police district as if "[an] assistant chief constable" read "an assistant commissioner of police".

16 Interpretation

In this Part—

★★★★★

"public assembly" means an assembly of 20 or more persons in a public place which is wholly or partly open to the air;

"public place" means—

(a) any highway, or in Scotland any road within the meaning of the Roads (Scotland) Act 1984, and

(b) any place to which at the material time the public or any section of the public has access, on payment or otherwise, as of right or by virtue of express or implied permission;

"public procession" means a procession in a public place.

PART III
RACIAL HATRED

Meaning of "racial hatred"

17 Meaning of "racial hatred"

In this Part "racial hatred" means hatred against a group of persons in Great Britain defined by reference to colour, race, nationality (including citizenship) or ethnic or national origins.

Acts intended or likely to stir up racial hatred

18 Use of words or behaviour or display of written material

(1) A person who uses threatening, abusive or insulting words or behaviour, or displays any written material which is threatening, abusive or insulting, is guilty of an offence if—

(a) he intends thereby to stir up racial hatred, or

(b) having regard to all the circumstances racial hatred is likely to be stirred up thereby.

(2) An offence under this section may be committed in a public or a private place, except that no offence is committed where the words or behaviour are used, or the written material is displayed, by a person inside a dwelling and are not heard or seen except by other persons in that or another dwelling.

(3) A constable may arrest without warrant anyone he reasonably suspects is committing an offence under this section.

(4) In proceedings for an offence under this section it is a defence for the accused to prove that he was inside a dwelling and had no reason to believe that the words or behaviour used, or the written material displayed, would be heard or seen by a person outside that or any other dwelling.

(5) A person who is not shown to have intended to stir up racial hatred is not guilty of an offence under this section if he did not intend his words or behaviour, or the written material, to be, and was not aware that it might be, threatening, abusive or insulting.

(6) This section does not apply to words or behaviour used, or written material displayed, solely for the purpose of being [included in a programme service].

19 Publishing or distributing written material

(1) A person who publishes or distributes written material which is threatening, abusive or insulting is guilty of an offence if—

(a) he intends thereby to stir up racial hatred, or

(b) having regard to all the circumstances racial hatred is likely to be stirred up thereby.

(2) In proceedings for an offence under this section it is a defence for an accused who is not shown to have intended to stir up racial hatred to prove that he was not aware of the content of the material and did not suspect, and had no reason to suspect, that it was threatening, abusive or insulting.

(3) References in this Part to the publication or distribution of written material are to its publication or distribution to the public or a section of the public.

20 Public performance of play

(1) If a public performance of a play is given which involves the use of threatening, abusive or insulting words or behaviour, any person who presents or directs the performance is guilty of an offence if—

(a) he intends thereby to stir up racial hatred, or

(b) having regard to all the circumstances (and, in particular, taking the performance as a whole) racial hatred is likely to be stirred up thereby.

(2)-(6) * * * * *

21 Distributing, showing or playing a recording

(1) A person who distributes, or shows or plays, a recording of visual images or sounds which are threatening, abusive or insulting is guilty of an offence if—

(a) he intends thereby to stir up racial hatred, or

(b) having regard to all the circumstances racial hatred is likely to be stirred up thereby.

(2) In this Part "recording" means any record from which visual images or sounds may, by any means, be reproduced; and references to the distribution, showing or playing of a recording are to its distribution, showing or playing to the public or a section of the public.

(3) In proceedings for an offence under this section it is a defence for an accused who is not shown to have intended to stir up racial hatred to prove that he was not aware of the content of the recording and did not suspect, and had no reason to suspect, that it was threatening, abusive or insulting.

(4) This section does not apply to the showing or playing of a recording solely for the purpose of enabling the recording to be [included in a programme service.]

22 Broadcasting or including programme in cable programme service

(1) If a programme involving threatening, abusive or insulting visual images or sounds is [included in a programme service], each of the persons mentioned in subsection (2) is guilty of an offence if—

(a) he intends thereby to stir up racial hatred, or

(b) having regard to all the circumstances racial hatred is likely to be stirred up thereby.

(2) The persons are—

(a) the person providing the ... programme service,

(a) any person by whom the programme is produced or directed, and

(c) any person by whom offending words or behaviour are used.

(3)-(6) * * * * *

(7), (8) ...

Racially inflammatory material

23 Possession of racially inflammatory material

(1) A person who has in his possession written material which is threatening, abusive or insulting, or a recording of visual images or sounds which are threatening, abusive or insulting, with a view to—

(a) in the case of written material, its being displayed, published, distributed, broadcast or included in a cable programme service, whether by himself or another, or

(b) in the case of a recording, its being distributed, shown, played, [or included in a programme service], whether by himself or another,

is guilty of an offence if he intends racial hatred to be stirred up thereby or, having regard to all the circumstances, racial hatred is likely to be stirred up thereby.

(2) For this purpose regard shall be had to such display, publication, distribution, showing, playing, [or inclusion in a programme service] as he has, or it may reasonably be inferred that he has, in view.

(3) In proceedings for an offence under this section it is a defence for an accused who is not shown to have intended to stir up racial hatred to prove that he was not aware of the content of the written material or recording and did not suspect, and had no reason to suspect, that it was threatening, abusive or insulting.

(4) ...

24 Powers of entry and search

(1) If in England and Wales a justice of the peace is satisfied by information on oath laid by a constable that there are reasonable grounds for suspecting that a person has possession of written material or a recording in contravention of section 23, the justice may issue a warrant under his hand authorising any constable to enter and search the premises where it is suspected the material or recording is situated.

(2) If in Scotland a sheriff or justice of the peace is satisfied by evidence on oath that there are reasonable grounds for suspecting that a person has possession of written material or a recording in contravention of section 23, the sheriff or justice may issue a warrant authorising any constable to enter and search the premises where it is suspected the material or recording is situated.

(3) A constable entering or searching premises in pursuance of a warrant issued under this section may use reasonable force if necessary.

(4) * * * * *

25 * * * * *

Supplementary provisions

26 Savings for reports of parliamentary or judicial proceedings

(1) Nothing in this Part applies to a fair and accurate report of proceedings in Parliament.

(2) Nothing in this Part applies to a fair and accurate report of proceedings publicly heard before a court or tribunal exercising judicial authority where the report is published contemporaneously with the proceedings or, if it is not reasonably practicable or would be unlawful to publish a report of them contemporaneously, as soon as publication is reasonably practicable and lawful.

27 Procedure and punishment

(1) No proceedings for an offence under this Part may be instituted in England and Wales except by or with the consent of the Attorney General.

(2) For the purposes of the rules in England and Wales against charging more than one offence in the same count or information, each of sections 18 to 23 creates one offence.

(3) A person guilty of an offence under this Part is liable—

(a) on conviction on indictment to imprisonment for a term not exceeding two years or a fine or both;

(b) on summary conviction to imprisonment for a term not exceeding six months or a fine not exceeding the statutory maximum or both.

28-38 ★★★★★

Note Section 29 provides that "programme service" has the same meaning as in the Broadcasting Act 1990.

39 . . .

40 Amendments repeals and savings

(1)-(3) ★★★★★

(4) Nothing in this Act affects the common law powers in England and Wales to deal with or prevent a breach of the peace.

(5) As respects Scotland, nothing in this Act affects any power of a constable under any rule of law.

★★★★★

CROWN PROCEEDINGS (ARMED FORCES) ACT 1987
(1987, c. 25)

An Act to repeal section 10 of the Crown Proceedings Act 1947 and to provide for the revival of that section in certain circumstances [15 May 1987]

Territorial extent United Kingdom

1 Repeal of s. 10 of the Crown Proceedings Act 1947

Subject to section 2 below, section 10 of the Crown Proceedings Act 1947 (exclusions from liability in tort in cases involving the armed forces) shall cease to have effect except in relation to anything suffered by a person in consequence of an act or omission committed before the date on which this Act is passed.

2 Revival of s. 10

(1) Subject to the following provisions of this section, the Secretary of State may, at any time after the coming into force of section 1 above, by order—

(a) revive the effect of section 10 of the Crown Proceedings Act 1947 either for all purposes or for such purposes as may be described in the order; or

(b) where that section has effect for the time being in pursuance of an order made by virtue of paragraph (a) above, provide for that section to cease to have effect either for all of the purposes for which it so has effect or for such of them as may be so described.

(2) The Secretary of State shall not make an order reviving the effect of the said section 10 for any purposes unless it appears to him necessary or expedient to do so—

(a) by reason of any imminent national danger or of any great emergency that has arisen; or

(b) for the purposes of any warlike operations in any part of the world outside the United Kingdom or of any other operations which are or are to be carried out in connection with the warlike activity of any persons in any such part of the world.

(3) Subject to subsection (4) below, an order under this section describing purposes for which the effect of the said section 10 is to be revived, or for which that section is to cease to have effect, may describe those purposes by reference to any matter whatever and may make different provision for different cases, circumstances or persons.

(4) Nothing in any order under this section shall revive the effect of the said section 10, or provide for that section to cease to have effect, in relation to anything suffered by a person in consequence of an act or omission committed before the date on which the order comes into force.

(5) The power to make an order under this section shall be exercisable by statutory instrument subject to annulment in pursuance of a resolution of either House of Parliament.

IMMIGRATION (CARRIERS' LIABILITY) ACT 1987
(1987, c. 24)

An Act to require carriers to make payments to the Secretary of State in respect of passengers brought by them to the United Kingdom without proper documents [15 May 1987]

Territorial extent United Kingdom

1 Liability of carriers for passengers without proper documents

(1) Where a person requiring leave to enter the United Kingdom arrives in the United Kingdom by ship or aircraft and, on being required to do so by an immigration officer, fails to produce—

(a) either a valid passport with photograph or some other document satisfactorily establishing his identity and nationality or citizenship; and

(b) if he is a person who under the immigration rules requires a visa for entry into the United Kingdom, [or by virtue of section 1A below requires a visa for passing through the United Kingdom, a valid visa for the purpose of entering or (as the case may be) passing through the United Kingdom,],

the owners or agents of the ship or aircraft shall, in respect of that person, be liable to pay the Secretary of State on demand the sum of £1,000 or such other sum as may be prescribed.

(2) No liability shall be incurred under subsection (1) above in respect of any person who is shown by the owners or agents to have produced to them or an employee of theirs the document or documents specified in that subsection when embarking on the ship or aircraft for the voyage or flight to the United Kingdom.

(3) In subsection (1) above "prescribed" means prescribed by an order made by the Secretary of State by statutory instrument subject to annulment in pursuance of a resolution of either House of Parliament.

(4), (5) * * * * *

1A Visas for transit passengers

(1) The Secretary of State may by order require persons of any description specified in the order who on arrival in the United Kingdom pass through to another country or territory without entering the United Kingdom to hold a visa for that purpose.

(2) An order under this section—

(a) may specify a description of persons by reference to nationality, citizenship, origin or other connection with any particular country or territory, but not by reference to race, colour or religion;

(b) shall not provide for the requirement imposed by the order to apply to any person who under the Immigration Act 1971 has the right of abode in the United Kingdom and may provide for any category of persons of a description specified in the order to be exempted from the requirement imposed by the order; and

(c) may make provision about the method of application for visas required by the order.

(3) An order under this section shall be made by statutory instrument which shall be subject to annulment in pursuance of a resolution of either House of Parliament.

MINISTRY OF DEFENCE POLICE ACT 1987
(1987, c. 4)

An Act to make fresh provision for the Ministry of Defence Police [5 March 1987]

Territorial extent United Kingdom

1 The Ministry of Defence Police

(1) There shall be a police force to be known as the Ministry of Defence Police and consisting—

(a) of persons nominated by the Secretary of State; and

(b) of persons who at the coming into force of this Act are special constables by virtue of appointment under section 3 of the Special Constables Act 1923 on the Nomination of the Defence Council.

(2) A person nominated under subsection (1) above shall—

(a) in England and Wales be attested as a constable by making the declaration required of a member of a police force maintained under [the Police Act 1996] before a justice of the peace;

(b) in Scotland make the declaration required of a person on appointment to the office of constable of a police force maintained under the Police (Scotland) Act 1967 before a person before whom such a declaration may be made by a person appointed to that office; and

(c) in Northern Ireland be attested as a constable by taking and subscribing the oath required of a member of the Royal Ulster Constabulary before a justice of the peace.

(3) The Secretary of State shall appoint a chief constable for the Ministry of Defence Police, and they shall operate under the chief constable's direction and control.

(4) The Secretary of State shall have power—

(a) to suspend a member of the Ministry of Defence Police from duty; and

(b) to terminate a person's membership.

(5), (6) * * * * *

2 Jurisdiction

(1) In any place in the United Kingdom to which subsection (2) below for the time being applies, members of the Ministry of Defence Police shall have the powers and privileges of constables.

(2) The places to which this subsection applies are—

(a) land, vehicles, vessels, aircraft and hovercraft in the possession, under the control or used for the purposes of—

(i) the Secretary of State for Defence;

(ii) the Defence Council;

(iii) a headquarters or defence organisation; or

(iv) the service authorities of a visiting force;

(b) land, vehicles, vessels, aircraft and hovercraft which are—

(i) in the possession, under the control or used for the purposes of an ordnance company; and

(ii) used for the purpose of, or for purposes which include, the making or development of ordnance or otherwise for naval, military or air force purposes;

(c) land, vehicles, vessels, aircraft and hovercraft which are—

(i) in the possession, under the control or used for the purposes of a dockyard contractor; and

(ii) used for the purpose of, or for purposes which include, providing designated services or otherwise for naval, military or air force purposes;

(d) land which is in the vicinity of land mentioned in any of paragraphs (a) to (c) above and on which a constable of the police force for the police area in which the first-mentioned land is situated, or, in Northern Ireland, of the Royal Ulster Constabulary, has asked the Ministry of Defence Police to assist him in the execution of his duties; and

(e) land where the Secretary of State has agreed to provide the services of the Ministry of Defence Police under an agreement notice of which has been published in the appropriate Gazette.

(3) Members of the Ministry of Defence Police shall also have the powers and privileges of constables in any place in the United Kingdom to which subsection (2) above does not for the time being apply, but only—

(a) in relation to Crown property, international defence property, ordnance property and dockyard property;

(b) in relation to persons—

(i) subject to the control of the Defence Council;

(ii) employed under or for the purposes of the Ministry of Defence or the Defence Council; or

(iii) in respect of whom the service courts and service authorities of any country may exercise powers by virtue of section 2 of the Visiting Forces Act 1952;

(c) in relation to matters connected with anything done under a contract entered into by the Secretary of State for Defence for the purposes of his Department or the Defence Council; and

(d) for the purpose of securing the unimpeded passage of any such property as is mentioned in paragraph (a) above.

(4), (5) *****

Note See the Atomic Weapons Establishment Act 1991, s. 4 (for extension of powers to certain contractors' property and premises).

3-5 *****

6 Causing disaffection

Any person who causes, or attempts to cause, or does any act calculated to cause, disaffection amongst the members of the Ministry of Defence Police, or induces or attempts to induce, or does any act calculated to induce, any member of the Ministry of Defence Police to withhold his services or to commit breaches of discipline, shall be guilty of an offence and liable—

(a) on summary conviction, to imprisonment for a term not exceeding six months or to a fine not exceeding the statutory maximum, or to both;

(b) on conviction on indictment, to imprisonment for a term not exceeding two years or to a fine or to both.

* * * * *

COPYRIGHT, DESIGNS AND PATENTS ACT 1988
(1988, c. 48)

An Act to restate the law of copyright, with amendments; to make fresh provision as to the rights of performers and others in performances; to confer a design right in original designs; to amend the Registered Designs Act 1949; to make provision with respect to patent agents and trade mark agents; to confer patents and designs jurisdiction on certain county courts; to amend the law of patents; to make provision with respect to devices designed to circumvent copy-protection of works in electronic form; to make fresh provision penalising the fraudulent reception of transmissions; to make the fraudulent application or use of a trade mark an offence; to make provision for the benefit of the Hospital for Sick Children, Great Ormond Street, London; to enable financial assistance to be given to certain international bodies; and for connected purposes [15 November 1988]

Territorial extent United Kingdom

CHAPTER III
ACTS PERMITTED IN RELATION TO COPYRIGHT WORKS

* * * * *

Public administration

45 Parliamentary and judicial proceedings

(1) Copyright is not infringed by anything done for the purposes of parliamentary or judicial proceedings.

(2) Copyright is not infringed by anything done for the purposes of reporting such proceedings; but this shall not be construed as authorising the copying of a work which is itself a published report of the proceedings.

* * * * *

49 Public records

Material which is comprised in public records within the meaning of the Public Records Act 1958, the Public Records (Scotland) Act 1937 or the Public Records Act (Northern Ireland) 1923 which are open to public inspection in pursuance of that Act, may be copied, and a copy may be supplied to any person, by or with the authority of any officer appointed under that Act, without infringement of copyright.

* * * * *

CHAPTER X
MISCELLANEOUS AND GENERAL

Crown and Parliamentary copyright

163 Crown copyright

(1) Where a work is made by Her Majesty or by an officer or servant of the Crown in the course of his duties—

(a) the work qualifies for copyright protection notwithstanding section 153(1) (ordinary requirement as to qualification for copyright protection), and

(b) Her Majesty is the first owner of any copyright in the work.

(2) Copyright in such a work is referred to in this Part as "Crown copyright", notwithstanding that it may be, or have been, assigned to another person.

(3) Crown copyright in a literary, dramatic, musical or artistic work continues to subsist—

(a) until the end of the period of 125 years from the end of the calendar year in which the work was made, or

(b) if the work is published commercially before the end of the period of 75 years from the end of the calendar year in which it was made, until the end of the period of 50 years from the end of the calendar year in which it was first so published.

(4) In the case of a work of joint authorship where one or more but not all of the authors are persons falling within subsection (1), this section applies only in relation to those authors and the copyright subsisting by virtue of their contribution to the work.

(5) Except as mentioned above, and subject to any express exclusion elsewhere in this Part, the provisions of this Part apply in relation to Crown copyright as to other copyright.

(6) This section does not apply to a work if, or to the extent that, Parliamentary copyright subsists in the work (see sections 165 and 166).

164 Copyright in Acts and Measures

(1) Her Majesty is entitled to copyright in every Act of Parliament or Measure of the General Synod of the Church of England.

(2) The copyright subsists from Royal Assent until the end of the period of 50 years from the end of the calendar year in which Royal Assent was given.

(3) References in this Part to Crown copyright (except in section 163) include copyright under this section; and, except as mentioned above, the provisions of this Part apply in relation to copyright under this section as to other Crown copyright.

(4) No other copyright, or right in the nature of copyright, subsists in an Act or Measure.

165 Parliamentary copyright

(1) Where a work is made by or under the direction or control of the House of Commons or the House of Lords—

(a) the work qualifies for copyright protection notwithstanding section 153(1) (ordinary requirement as to qualification for copyright protection), and

(b) the House by whom, or under whose direction or control, the work is made is the first owner of any copyright in the work, and if the work is made by or under the direction or control of both Houses, the two Houses are joint first owners of copyright.

(2) Copyright in such a work is referred to in this Part as "Parliamentary copyright", notwithstanding that it may be, or have been, assigned to another person.

(3) Parliamentary copyright in a literary, dramatic, musical or artistic work continues to subsist until the end of the period of 50 years from the end of the calendar year in which the work was made.

(4) For the purposes of this section, works made by or under the direction or control of the House of Commons or the House of Lords include—

(a) any work made by an officer or employee of that House in the course of his duties, and

(b) any sound recording, film, live broadcast or live cable programme of the proceedings of that House;

but a work shall not be regarded as made by or under the direction or control of either House by reason only of its being commissioned by or on behalf of that House.

(5)-(8) ★★★★★

166 Copyright in Parliamentary Bills

(1) Copyright in every Bill introduced into Parliament belongs, in accordance with the following provisions, to one or both of the Houses of Parliament.

(2) Copyright in a public Bill belongs in the first instance to the House into which the Bill is introduced, and after the Bill has been carried to the second House to both Houses jointly, and subsists from the time when the text of the Bill is handed in to the House in which it is introduced.

(3) Copyright in a private Bill belongs to both Houses jointly and subsists from the time when a copy of the Bill is first deposited in either House.

(4) Copyright in a personal Bill belongs in the first instance to the House of Lords, and after the Bill has been carried to the House of Commons to both Houses jointly, and subsists from the time when it is given a First Reading in the House of Lords.

(5) Copyright under this section ceases—

(a) on Royal Assent, or

(b) if the Bill does not receive Royal Assent, on the withdrawal or rejection of the Bill or the end of the Session:

Provided that, copyright in a Bill continues to subsist notwithstanding its rejection in any Session by the House of Lords if, by virtue of the Parliament Acts 1911 and 1949, it remains possible for it to be presented for Royal Assent in that Session.

(6) References in this Part to Parliamentary copyright (except in section 165) include copyright under this section; and, except as mentioned above, the provisions of this Part apply in relation to copyright under this section as to other Parliamentary copyright.

(7) No other copyright, or right in the nature of copyright, subsists in a Bill after copyright has once subsisted under this section; but without prejudice to the subsequent operation of this section in relation to a Bill which, not having passed in one Session, is reintroduced in a subsequent Session.

★ ★ ★ ★ ★

CRIMINAL JUSTICE ACT 1988
(1988, c. 33)

An Act to make fresh provision for extradition; to amend the rules of evidence in criminal proceedings; to provide for the reference by the Attorney General of certain questions relating to sentencing to the Court of Appeal; to amend the law with regard to the jurisdiction and powers of criminal courts, the collection, enforcement and remission of fines imposed by coroners, juries, supervision orders, the detention of children and young persons, probation and the probation service, criminal appeals, anonymity in cases of rape and similar cases, orders under sections 4 and 11 of the Contempt of Court Act 1981 relating to trials on indictment, orders restricting the access of the public to the whole or any part of a trial on indictment or to any proceedings ancillary to such a trial and orders restricting the publication of any report of the whole or any part of a trial on indictment or any such ancillary proceedings, the alteration of names of petty sessions areas, officers of inner London magistrates' courts and the costs and expenses of prosecution witnesses and certain other persons; to make fresh provision for the payment of compensation by the Criminal Injuries Compensation Board; to make provision for the payment of compensation for a miscarriage of justice which has resulted in a wrongful conviction; to create an offence of torture and an offence of having an article with a blade or point in a public place; to create further offences relating to weapons; to create a summary offence of possession of an indecent photograph of a child; to amend the Police and Criminal Evidence Act 1984 in relation to searches, computer data about fingerprints and bail for persons in customs detention; to make provision in relation to the taking of body samples by the police in Northern Ireland; to amend the Bail Act 1976; to give a justice of the peace power to authorise entry and search of premises for offensive weapons; to provide for the enforcement of the Video Recordings Act 1984 by officers of a weights and measures authority and in Northern Ireland by Officers of the Department of Economic Development; to extend to the purchase of easements and other rights over land the power to purchase land conferred on the Secretary of State by section 36 of the Prison Act 1952; and for connected purposes [29 July 1988]

Territorial extent England and Wales; Northern Ireland (except section 160)

PART XI
MISCELLANEOUS

Miscarriages of justice

133 Compensation for miscarriages of justice

(1) Subject to subsection (2) below, when a person has been convicted of a criminal offence and when subsequently his conviction has been reversed or he has been pardoned on the ground that a new or newly discovered fact shows beyond reasonable doubt that there has been a miscarriage of justice, the Secretary of State shall pay compensation for the miscarriage of justice to the person who has suffered punishment as a result of such conviction or, if he is dead, to his personal representatives, unless the non-disclosure of the unknown fact was wholly or partly attributable to the person convicted.

(2) No payment of compensation under this section shall be made unless an application for such compensation has been made to the Secretary of State.

(3) The question whether there is a right to compensation under this section shall be determined by the Secretary of State.

(4) If the Secretary of State determines that there is a right to such compensation, the amount of the compensation shall be assessed by an assessor appointed by the Secretary of State.

[(4A) In assessing so much of any compensation payable under this section to or in respect of a person as is attributable to suffering, harm to reputation or similar damage, the assessor shall have regard in particular to—

(a) the seriousness of the offence of which the person was convicted and the severity of the punishment resulting from the conviction;

(b) the conduct of the investigation and prosecution of the offence; and

(c) any other convictions of the person and any punishment resulting from them.]

(5)-(7) * * * * *

Torture

134 Torture

(1) A public official or person acting in an official capacity, whatever his nationality, commits the offence of torture if in the United Kingdom or elsewhere he intentionally inflicts severe pain or suffering on another in the performance or purported performance of his official duties.

(2) A person not falling within subsection (1) above commits the offence of torture, whatever his nationality, if—

(a) in the United Kingdom or elsewhere he intentionally inflicts severe pain or suffering on another at the instigation or with the consent of acquiescence—

(i) of a public official; or

(ii) of a person acting in an official capacity; and

(b) the official or other person is performing or purporting to perform his official duties when he instigates the commission of the offence or consents to or acquiesces in it.

(3) It is immaterial whether the pain or suffering is physical or mental and whether it is caused by an act or an omission.

(4) It shall be a defence for a person charged with an offence under this section in respect of any conduct of his to prove that he had lawful authority, justification or excuse for that conduct.

(5), (6) * * * * *

135 Requirement of Attorney General's consent for prosecutions

Proceedings for an offence under section 134 above shall not be begun—

(a) in England and Wales, except by, or with the consent of, the Attorney General; or

(b) in Northern Ireland, except by, or with the consent of, the Attorney General for Northern Ireland.

136-141 * * * * *

142 Power of justice of the peace to authorise entry and search of premises for offensive weapons

(1) If on an application made by a constable a justice of the peace (including, in Scotland, the sheriff) is satisfied that there are reasonable grounds for believing—

(a) that there are on premises specified in the application—

(i) knives such as are mentioned in section 1(1) of the Restriction of Offensive Weapons Act 1959; or

(ii) weapons to which section 141 above applies; and

(b) that an offence under section 1 of the Restriction of Offensive Weapons Act 1959 or section 141 above has been or is being committed in relation to them; and

(c) that any of the conditions specified in subsection (3) below applies, he may issue a warrant authorising a constable to enter and search the premises.

(2) A constable may seize and retain anything for which a search has been authorised under subsection (1) above.

(3) The conditions mentioned in subsection (1)(b) above are—

(a) that it is not practicable to communicate with any person entitled to grant entry to the premises;

(b) that it is practicable to communicate with a person entitled to grant entry to the premises but it is not practicable to communicate with any person entitled to grant access to the knives or weapons to which the application relates;

(c) that entry to the premises will not be granted unless a warrant is produced;

(d) that the purpose of a search may be frustrated or seriously prejudiced unless a constable arriving at the premises can secure immediate entry to them.

143-158 * * * * *

159 Crown Court proceedings—orders restricting or preventing reports or restricting public access

(1) A person aggrieved may appeal to the Court of Appeal, if that court grants leave, against—

(a) an order under section 4 or 11 of the Contempt of Court Act 1981 made in relation to a trial on indictment;

[(aa) An order made by the Crown Court under section 58(7) or (8) of the Criminal Procedure and Investigation 1996 in a case where the court has convicted a person on a trial on indictment;]

(b) any order restricting the access of the public to the whole or any part of a trial on indictment or to any proceedings ancillary to such a trial; and

(c) any order restricting the publication of any report of the whole or any part of a trial on indictment or any such ancillary proceedings;

and the decision of the Court of Appeal shall be final.

(2) Subject to Rules of Court, the jurisdiction of the Court of Appeal under this section shall be exercised by the criminal division of the Court, and references to the Court of Appeal in this section shall be construed as references to that division.

(3)-(7) ★★★★★

Possession of indecent photograph of child

160 Summary offence of possession of indecent photograph of child

(1) It is an offence for a person to have any indecent photograph [or pseudo-photograph] of a child . . . in his possession.

(2) Where a person is charged with an offence under subsection (1) above, it shall be a defence for him to prove—

(a) that he had a legitimate reason for having the photograph [or pseudo-photograph] in his possession; or

(b) that he had not himself seen the photograph [or pseudo-photograph] and did not know, nor had any cause to suspect, it to be indecent; or

(c) that the photograph [or pseudo-photograph] was sent to him without any prior request made by him or on his behalf and that he did not keep it for an unreasonable time.

(3) A person shall be liable on summary conviction of an offence under this section to [imprisonment for a term not exceeding six months or] a fine not exceeding level 5 on the standard scale [or both].

(4) Sections 1(3), 2(3), 3 and 7 of the Protection of Children Act 1978 shall have effect as if any reference in them to that Act included a reference to this section.

(5) . . .

★★★★★

IMMIGRATION ACT 1988
(1988, c. 14)

An Act to make further provision for the regulation of immigration into the United Kingdom; and for connected purposes [10 May 1988]

Territorial extent United Kingdom

1 ★★★★★

2 Restriction on exercise of right of abode in cases of polygamy

(1) This section applies to any woman who—

(a) has the right of abode in the United Kingdom under section 2(1)(b) of the principal Act as, or as having been, the wife of a man ("the husband")—

(i) to whom she is or was polygamously married; and

(ii) who is or was such a citizen of the United Kingdom and Colonies, Commonwealth citizen or British subject as is mentioned in section 2(2)(a) or (b) of that Act as in force immediately before the commencement of the British Nationality Act 1981; and

(b) has not before the coming into force of this section and since her marriage to the husband been in the United Kingdom.

(2) A woman to whom this section applies shall not be entitled to enter the United Kingdom in the exercise of the right of abode mentioned in subsection (1)(a) above or to be granted a certificate of entitlement in respect of that right if there is another woman living (whether or not one to whom this section applies) who is the wife or widow of the husband and who—

(a) is, or at any time since her marriage to the husband has been, in the United Kingdom; or

(b) has been granted a certificate of entitlement in respect of the right of abode mentioned in subsection (1)(a) above or an entry clearance to enter the United Kingdom as the wife of the husband.

(3) So long as a woman is precluded by subsection (2) above from entering the United Kingdom in the exercise of her right of abode or being granted a certificate of entitlement in respect of that right the principal Act shall apply to her as it applies to a person not having a right of abode.

(4) Subsection (2) above shall not preclude a woman from re-entering the United Kingdom if since her marriage to the husband she has at any time previously been in the United Kingdom and there was at that time no such other woman living as is mentioned in that subsection.

(5) Where a woman claims that this section does not apply to her because she had been in the United Kingdom before the coming into force of this section and since her marriage to the husband it shall be for her to prove that fact.

(6) For the purposes of this section a marriage may be polygamous although at its inception neither party has any spouse additional to the other.

(7)-(10) ★ ★ ★ ★ ★

3, 4 ★ ★ ★ ★ ★

5 Restricted right of appeal against deportation in cases of breach of limited leave

(1) A person to whom this subsection applies shall not be entitled to appeal under section 15 of the principal Act against a decision to make a deportation order against him—

(a) by virtue of section 3(5)(a) of that Act (breach of limited leave); or

[(aa) by virtue of section 3(5)(aa) of that Act (leave obtained by deception); or]

(b) by virtue of section 3(5)(c) of that Act as belonging to the family of a person who is or has been ordered to be deported by virtue of section 3(5)(a),

except on the ground that on the facts of his case there is in law no power to make the deportation order for the reasons stated in the notice of that decision.

(2) Subsection (1) above applies to any person who was last given leave to enter the United Kingdom less than seven years before the date of the decision in question but the Secretary of State may by order exempt any such persons from that subsection in such circumstances and to such extent as may be specified in the order.

(3) The power to make an order under subsection (2) above shall be exercisable by statutory instrument subject to annulment in pursuance of a resolution of either House of Parliament.

(4) It shall be presumed for the purposes of this section that a person was last given leave as mentioned in subsection (2) above unless he proves the contrary.

(5) Subsection (1) above shall not affect the grounds on which a person may appeal where written notice of the decision in question was given to him before the coming into force of this section.

6 ★ ★ ★ ★ ★

7 Persons exercising community rights and nationals of member States

(1) A person shall not under the principal Act require leave to enter or remain in the United Kingdom in any case in which he is entitled to do so by virtue of an enforceable Community right or of any provision made under section 2(2) of the European Communities Act 1972.

(2) The Secretary of State may by order made by statutory instrument give leave to enter the United Kingdom for a limited period to any class of persons who are nationals of member States but who are not entitled to enter the United Kingdom as mentioned in subsection (1) above; and any such order may give leave subject to such conditions as may be imposed by the order.

(3) References in the principal Act to limited leave shall include references to leave given by an order under subsection (2) above and a person having leave by virtue of such an order shall be treated and having been given that leave by a notice given to him by an immigration officer within the period specified in paragraph 6(1) of Schedule 2 to that Act.

8 Examination of passengers prior to arrival

(1) This section applies to a person who arrives in the United Kingdom with a passport or other travel document bearing a stamp which—

(a) has been placed there by an immigration officer before that person's departure on his journey to the United Kingdom or in the course of that journey; and

(b) states that the person may enter the United Kingdom either for an indefinite or a limited period and, if for a limited period, subject to specified conditions.

(2) A person to whom this section applies shall for the purposes of the principal Act be deemed to have been given on arrival in the United Kingdom indefinite or, as the case may be, limited leave in terms corresponding to those of the stamp.

(3) A person who is deemed to have leave by virtue of this section shall be treated as having been given it by a notice given to him by an immigration officer within the period specified in paragraph 6(1) of Schedule 2 to the principal Act.

(4) A person deemed to have leave by virtue of this section shall not on his arrival in the United Kingdom be subject to examination under paragraph 2 of Schedule 2 to the principal Act but may be examined by an immigration officer for the purpose of establishing that he is such a person.

(5) The leave which a person is deemed to have by virtue of this section may, at any time before the end of the period of twenty-four hours from his arrival at the port at which he seeks to enter the United Kingdom or if he has been examined under subsection (4) above, from the conclusion of that examination, be cancelled by an immigration officer by giving him a notice in writing refusing him leave to enter.

(6)-(7) ★★★★★

(8) ...

★★★★★

ROAD TRAFFIC ACT 1988
(1988, c. 52)

An Act to consolidate certain enactments relating to road traffic with amendments to give effect to recommendations of the Law Commission and the Scottish Law Commission

[15 November 1988]

Territorial extent England and Wales; Scotland

PART VII
MISCELLANEOUS AND GENERAL

Powers of constables and other authorised persons

163 Power of police to stop vehicles

(1) A person driving a [mechanically propelled vehicle] on a road must stop the vehicle on being required to do so by a constable in uniform.

(2) A person riding a cycle on a road must stop the cycle on being required to do so by a constable in uniform.

(3) If a person fails to comply with this section he is guilty of an offence.

164 Power of constables to require production of driving licence and in certain cases statement of date of birth

(1) Any of the following persons—

(a) a person driving a motor vehicle on a road,

(b) a person whom a constable [or vehicle examiner] has reasonable cause to believe to have been the driver of a motor vehicle at a time when an accident occurred owing to its presence on a road,

(c) a person whom a constable [or vehicle examiner] has reasonable cause to believe to have committed an offence in relation to the use of a motor vehicle on a road, or

(d) a person—

(i) who supervises the holder of a provisional licence while the holder is driving a motor vehicle on a road, or

(ii) whom a constable [or vehicle examiner] has reasonable cause to believe was supervising the holder of a provisional licence while driving, at a time when an accident occurred owing to the presence of the vehicle on a road or at a time when an offence is suspected of having been committed by the holder of the provisional licence in relation to the use of the vehicle on a road,

must, on being so required by a constable [or vehicle examiner], produce his licence for examination, so as to enable the constable [or vehicle examiner] to ascertain the name and address of the holder of the licence, the date of issue, and the authority by which it was issued.

(2) [A person required by a constable under subsection (1) above to produce his licence] must in prescribed circumstances, on being so required by the constable, state his date of birth.

(3)-(11) * * * * *

165 Power of constables to obtain names and addresses of drivers and others, and to require production of evidence of insurance or security and test certificates

(1) Any of the following persons—

(a) a person driving a motor vehicle (other than an invalid carriage) on a road, or

(b) a person whom a constable [or vehicle examiner] has reasonable cause to believe to have been the driver of a motor vehicle (other than an invalid carriage) at a time when an accident occurred owing to its presence on a road, or

(c) a person whom a constable [or vehicle examiner] has reasonable cause to believe to have committed an offence in relation to the use on a road of a motor vehicle (other than an invalid carriage),

must, on being so required by a constable [or vehicle examiner], give his name and address and the name and address of the owner of the vehicle and produce the following documents for examination.

(2) Those documents are—

(a) the relevant certificate of insurance or certificate of security (within the meaning of Part VI of this Act), or such other evidence that the vehicle is not or was not being driven in contravention of section 143 of this Act as may be prescribed by regulations made by the Secretary of State,

(b) in relation to a vehicle to which section 47 of this Act applies, a test certificate issued in respect of the vehicle as mentioned in subsection (1) of that section, and

(c) in relation to a goods vehicle the use of which on a road without a plating certificate or goods vehicle test certificate is an offence under section 53(1) or (2) of this Act, any such certificate issued in respect of that vehicle or any trailer drawn by it.

(3) Subject to subsection (4) below, a person who fails to comply with a requirement under subsection (1) is guilty of an offence.

(4) A person shall not be convicted of an offence under subsection (1) above by reason only of failure to produce any certificate or other evidence ... if in proceedings against him for the offence he shows that—

(a) within seven days after the date on which the production of the certificate or other evidence was required it was produced at a police station that was specified by him at the time when its production was required, or

(b) it was produced there as soon as was reasonably practicable, or

(c) it was not reasonably practicable for it to be produced there before the day on which the proceedings were commenced,

and for the purposes of this subsection the laying of the information or, in Scotland, the service of the complaint on the accused shall be treated as the commencement of the proceedings.

(5)-(7) * * * * *

166 * * * * *

167 Power of arrest in Scotland for reckless or careless driving or cycling

A constable—

(a) may arrest without warrant the driver of a motor vehicle who within his view commits an offence under section 2 or 3 of this Act unless the driver either gives his name and address or produces for examination his licence to drive a motor vehicle granted under Part III of this Act, and

(b) may arrest without warrant the rider of a cycle who within his view commits an offence under section 28 or 29 of this Act unless the rider gives his name and address.

This section extends only to Scotland.

Duty to give name and address

168 Failure to give, or giving false, name and address in case of reckless or careless or inconsiderate driving or cycling

Any of the following persons—

(a) the driver of a [mechanically propelled vehicle] who is alleged to have committed an offence under section 2 or 3 of this Act, or

(b) the rider of a cycle who is alleged to have committed an offence under section 28 or 29 of this Act,

who refuses, on being so required by any person having reasonable ground for so requiring, to give his name or address, or gives a false name or address, is guilty of an offence.

ELECTED AUTHORITIES (NORTHERN IRELAND) ACT 1989
(1989, c. 3)

An Act to amend the law relating to the franchise at elections to district councils in Northern Ireland, to make provision in relation to a declaration against terrorism to be made by candidates at such elections and at elections to the Northern Ireland Assembly and by persons co-opted as members of district councils, to amend sections 3 and 4 of the Local Government Act (Northern Ireland) 1972, and for connected purposes [15 March 1989]

1, 2 * * * * *

Disqualification for breach of declaration against terrorism or in consequence of imprisonment or detention

3 Declaration against terrorism: local elections

(1) A person is not validly nominated as a candidate at a local election unless his consent to nomination includes a declaration in the form set out in Part I of Schedule 2 to this Act.

(2) * * * * *

4 Declaration against terrorism: councillors co-opted to fill casual vacancies

(1) A person is not eligible to be chosen by a district council to fill a casual vacancy in the council unless he has made, and served on the clerk of the council, a declaration in the form set out in Part II of Schedule 2 to this Act.

(2) * * * * *

5 Declaration against terrorism: Assembly elections

A person is not validly nominated as a candidate at an election to the Northern Ireland Assembly unless his consent to nomination includes a declaration in the form set out in Part I of Schedule 2 to this Act.

6 Breach of terms of declaration

(1) A person who has made a declaration required for the purposes of section 3, 4 or 5 of this Act in connection with a local election, an election to the Northern Ireland Assembly or the filling of a casual vacancy in a district council acts in breach of the terms of the declaration if at any time after he is declared to be elected at that election or is chosen to fill that vacancy and while he remains a member of the district council or of the Assembly—

(a) he expresses support for or approval of—

(i) a proscribed organisation, or

(ii) acts of terrorism (that is to say, violence for political ends) connected with the affairs of Northern Ireland, and

(b) he does so—

(i) at a public meeting, or

(ii) knowing, or in such circumstances that he can reasonably be expected to know, that the fact that he has made that expression of support or approval is likely to become known to the public.

(2) For the purposes of subsection (1) above a person shall be taken to express support for, or approval of, any matter if his words or actions could reasonably be understood as expressing support for, or approval of, it.

(3) It is immaterial for the purposes of subsection (1) above—

(a) whether the expression of support or approval is made by spoken or written words, by the display of written matter or by other behaviour, and

(b) whether it is made in the United Kingdom or elsewhere.

(4) This section has effect notwithstanding section 26(1) of the Northern Ireland Constitution Act 1973 (privileges of the Northern Ireland Assembly).

(5) In this section—

"proscribed organisation" has the same meaning as in [section 30 of the Northern Ireland (Emergency Provisions) Act 1996],

"public meeting" includes—

(a) any meeting in a public place,

(b) any meeting which the public or any section of the public is permitted to attend, whether on payment or otherwise, and

(c) any meeting of the Northern Ireland Assembly, a district council or any committee or sub-committee of the Assembly or such a council (whether or not a meeting which the public is permitted to attend), and "public place" means—

(a) any highway, and

(b) any place to which at the material time the public or any section of the public has access, on payment or otherwise, as of right or by virtue of express or implied permission.

7 Application to the High Court

(1) Any one or more of the persons specified in subsection (2) below may apply to the High Court for a determination that a person has acted in breach of the terms of a declaration against terrorism made by him.

(2) The persons referred to in subsection (1) above are—

(a) in relation to a member of a district council—

(i) the district council,

(ii) any person who would be entitled to vote at an election to that council held on the date of the application, and

(iii) any other member of that council, and

(b) in relation to a member of the Northern Ireland Assembly—

(i) any person who would be entitled to vote at an election to the Assembly held in the member's constituency on the date of the application, and

(iii) any other member of the Assembly.

(3) For the purposes of this section, a person who was nominated—

(a) after the passing of this Act as a candidate for election to the office of member of a district council, or

(b) after the coming into force of section 5 of this Act as a candidate for election to the office of member of the Northern Ireland Assembly,

shall be conclusively presumed to have made a declaration in the form set out in Part I of Schedule 2 to this Act at the time of the nomination.

(4) For the purposes of this section, a person who was chosen by a district council after the passing of this Act to fill a casual vacancy in the council shall be conclusively presumed to have made a declaration in the form set out in Part II of Schedule 2 of this Act in relation to that vacancy before he was so chosen.

(5) Where on an appliction under this section the High Court is satisfied that the person to whom the application relates has acted in breach of the terms of a declaration against terrorism made by him, the court may make a determination accordingly.

(6) In this section—

(a) "declaration against terrorism" means a declaration required for the purposes of section 3, 4 or 5 of this Act, and

(b) references to acting in breach of the terms of such a declaration shall be construed in accordance with section 6 of this Act.

8 ★ ★ ★ ★ ★ (allows disqualification for breach of declaration)

9-13 ★ ★ ★ ★ ★

SCHEDULE 1

★ ★ ★ ★ ★

SCHEDULE 2

DECLARATION AGAINST TERRORISM

PART I

FORM FOR INCLUSION IN CONSENT TO NOMINATION

I declare that, if elected, I will not by word or deed express support for or approval of—

(a) any organisation that is for the time being a proscribed organisation specified in [Schedule 2 to the Northern Ireland (Emergency Provisions) Act 1996]; or

(b) acts of terrorism (that is to say, violence for political ends) connected with the affairs of Northern Ireland.

PART II
FORM FOR USE IN CASE OF DISTRICT COUNCILLOR CHOSEN TO FILL CASUAL VACANCY

I, (*name in full*), of (*home address in full*) declare that, if I am chosen to be a councillor for the District of (*name of district*), I will not by word or deed express support for or approval of—

(a) any organisation that is for the time being a proscribed organisation specified in Schedule 2 to the Northern Ireland (Emergency Provisions) Act 1978; or

(b) acts of terrorism (that is to say, violence for political ends) connected with the affairs of Northern Ireland.

Signed
Date

EXTRADITION ACT 1989
(1989, c. 33)

An Act to consolidate enactments relating to extradition under the Criminal Justice Act 1988, the Fugitive Offenders Act 1967 and the Extradition Acts 1870 to 1935, with amendments to give effect to recommendations of the Law Commission and the Scottish Law Commission

[27 July 1989]

Territorial extent United Kingdom

PART I
INTRODUCTORY

General

1 Liability to extradition

(1) Where extradition procedures under Part III of this Act are available as between the United Kingdom and a foreign state, a person in the United Kingdom who—

(a) is accused in that state of the commission of an extradition crime; or

(b) is alleged to be unlawfully at large after conviction of an extradition crime by a court in that state,

may be arrested and returned to that state in accordance with those procedures.

(2) Subject to the provisions of this Act, a person in the United Kingdom who is accused of an extradition crime—

(a) in a Commonwealth country designated for the purposes of this subsection under section 5(1) below; or

(b) in a colony,

or who is alleged to be unlawfully at large after conviction of such an offence in any such country or in a colony, may be arrested and returned to that country or colony in accordance with extradition procedures under Part III of this Act.

(3) Where an Order in Council under section 2 of the Extradition Act 1870 is in force in relation to a foreign state, Schedule 1 to this Act (the provisions of which derive from that Act and certain associated enactments) shall have effect in relation to that state, but subject to the limitations, restrictions, conditions, exceptions and qualifications, if any, contained in the Order.

Extradition crime

2 Meaning of "extradition crime"

(1) In this Act, except in Schedule 1, "extradition crime" means—

(a) conduct in the territory of a foreign state, a designated Commonwealth country or a colony which, if it occurred in the United Kingdom, would constitute an offence punishable with imprisonment for a term of 12 months, or any greater punishment, and which, however described in the law of the foreign state, Commonwealth country or colony, is so punishable under that law;

(b) an extra-territorial offence against the law of a foreign state, designated Commonwealth country or colony which is punishable under that law with imprisonment for a term of 12 months, or any greater punishment, and which satisfies—

(i) the condition specified in subsection (2) below; or

(ii) all the conditions specified in subsection (3) below.

(2) The condition mentioned in subsection (1)(b)(i) above is that in corresponding circumstances equivalent conduct would constitute an extra-territorial offence against the law of the United Kingdom punishable with imprisonment for a term of 12 months, or any greater punishment.

(3) The conditions mentioned in subsection (1)(b)(ii) above are—

(a) that the foreign state, Commonwealth country or colony bases its jurisdiction on the nationality of the offender;

(b) that the conduct constituting the offence occurred outside the United Kingdom; and

(c) that, if it occurred in the United Kingdom, it would constitute an offence under the law of the United Kingdom punishable with imprisonment for a term of 12 months, or any greater punishment.

(4) For the purposes of [this Act except Schedule 1]—

(a) the law of a foreign state, designated Commonwealth country or colony includes the law of any part of it and the law of the United Kingdom includes the law of any part of the United Kingdom;

(b) conduct in a colony or dependency of a foreign state or of a designated Commonwealth country, or a vessel, aircraft or hovercraft of a foreign state or of such a country, shall be treated as if it were conduct in the territory of that state or country;

(c) conduct in a vessel, aircraft or hovercraft of a colony of the United Kingdom shall be treated as if it were conduct in that colony; and

(d) reference shall be made to the law of the colony or dependency of a foreign state or of a designated Commonwealth country, and not (where different) to the law of the foreign state or Commonwealth country, to determine the level of punishment applicable to conduct in that colony or dependency].

Return to foreign states

3 Arrangements for availability of Part III procedure

(1) In this Act "extradition arrangements" means arrangements made with a foreign state under which extradition procedures under Part III of this Act will be available as between the United Kingdom and that state.

(2) For this purpose "foreign state" means any state other than—

(i) the United Kingdom;

(ii) a country mentioned in Schedule 3 to the British Nationality Act 1981 (countries whose citizens are Commonwealth citizens);

(iii) a colony; or

(iv) the Republic of Ireland,

but a state which is a party to the European Convention on Extradition done at Paris on 13th December 1957 may be treated as a foreign state.

(3) Extradition arrangements may be—

(a) arrangements of a general nature made with one or more states and relating to the operation of extradition procedures under Part III of this Act (in this Act referred to as "general extradition arrangements"); or

(b) arrangements relating to the operation of those procedures in particular cases (in this Act referred to as "special extradition arrangements") made with a state with which there are no general extradition arrangements.

4 Orders in Council as to extradition

(1) Where general extradition arrangements have been made, Her Majesty may, by Order in Council reciting or embodying their terms, direct that this Act, so far as it relates to extradition procedures under Part III of this Act, shall apply as between the United Kingdom and the foreign state, or any foreign state, with which they have been made, subject to the limitations, restrictions, exceptions and qualifications, if any, contained in the Order.

(2) An Order in Council under this section shall not be made unless the general extradition arrangements to which it relates—

(a) provide for their determination after the expiration of a notice given by a party to them and not exceeding one year or for their denunciation by means of such a notice; and

(b) are in conformity with the provisions of this Act, and in particular with the restrictions on return contained in Part II of this Act.

(3) An Order in Council under this section shall be conclusive evidence that the arrangements therein referred to comply with this Act and that this Act, so far as it relates to extradition procedures under Part III of this Act, applies in the case of the foreign state, or any foreign state, mentioned in the Order.

(4) An Order in Council under this section shall be laid before Parliament after being made.

(5) An Order in Council under this section which does not provide that a person may only be returned to the foreign state requesting his return if the court of committal is satisfied that the evidence would be sufficient to [make a case requiring an answer by that person if the proceedings were a summary trial of any information against him, and] the extradition crime had taken place within the jurisdiction of the court shall be subject to annulment in pursuance of a resolution of either House of Parliament.

Return to Commonwealth countries and colonies

5 Procedure for designation etc.

(1) Her Majesty may by Order in Council designate for the purposes of section 1(2) above any country for the time being mentioned in Schedule 3 to the British Nationality Act 1981 (countries whose citizens are Commonwealth citizens); and any country so designated is in this Act referred to as a "designated Commonwealth country".

(2) This Act has effect in relation to all colonies.

(3) Her Majesty may by Order in Council direct that this Act shall have effect in relation to the return of persons to, or in relation to persons returned from, any designated Commonwealth country or any colony subject to such exceptions, adaptations or modifications as may be specified in the Order.

(4) Any Order under this section may contain such transitional or other incidental and supplementary provisions as may appear to Her Majesty to be necessary or expedient.

(5) For the purposes of any Order in Council under subsection (1) above, any territory for the external relations of which a Commonwealth country is responsible may be treated as part of that country or, if the Government of that country so requests, as a separate country.

(6) Any Order in Council under this section, other than an Order to which subsection (7) below applies, shall be subject to annulment in pursuance of a resolution of either House of Parliament.

(7) No recommendation shall be made to Her Majesty in Council to make an Order containing any such direction as is authorised by subsection (3) above unless a draft of the Order has been laid before Parliament and approved by resolution of each House of Parliament.

PART II
RESTRICTIONS ON RETURN

6 General restrictions on return

(1) A person shall not be returned under Part III of this Act, or committed or kept in custody for the purposes of return, if it appears to an appropriate authority—

(a) that the offence of which that person is accused or was convicted is an offence of a political character;

(b) that it is an offence under military law which is not also an offence under the general criminal law;

(c) that the request for his return (though purporting to be made on account of an extradition crime) is in fact made for the purpose of prosecuting or punishing him on account of his race, religion, nationality or political opinions; or

(d) that he might, if returned, be prejudiced at his trial or punished, detained or restricted in his personal liberty by reason of his race, religion, nationality or political opinions.

(2) A person who is alleged to be unlawfully at large after conviction of an extradition crime shall not be returned to a foreign state, or committed or kept in custody for the purposes of return to a foreign state, if it appears to an appropriate authority—

(a) that the conviction was obtained in his absence; and

(b) that it would not be in the interest of justice to return him on the grounds of that conviction.

(3) A person accused of an offence shall not be returned, or committed or kept in custody for the purposes of return, if it appears to an appropriate authority that if charged with that offence in the United Kingdom he would be entitled to be discharged under any rule of law relating to previous acquittal or conviction.

(4) A person shall not be returned, or committed or kept in custody for the purposes of such return, unless provision is made by the relevant law, or by an arrangement made with the relevant foreign state, Commonwealth country or colony, for securing that he will not, unless he has first had an opportunity to leave it, be dealt with there for or in respect of any offence committed before his return to it other than—

(a) the offence in respect of which his return is ordered;

(b) an offence, other than an offence excluded by subsection (5) below, which is disclosed by the facts in respect of which his return was ordered; or

(c) subject to subsection (6) below, any other offence being an extradition crime in respect of which the Secretary of State may consent to his being dealt with.

(5) The offences excluded from paragraph (b) of subsection (4) above are offences in relation to which an order for the return of the person concerned could not lawfully be made.

(6) The Secretary of State may not give consent under paragraph (c) of that subsection in respect of an offence in relation to which it appears to him that an order for the return of the person concerned could not lawfully be made, or would not in fact be made.

(7) Any such arrangement as is mentioned in subsection (4) above which is made with a designated Commonwealth country or a colony may be an arrangement made for the particular case or an arrangement of a more general nature; and for the purposes of that subsection a certificate issued by or under the authority of the Secretary of State confirming the existence of an arrangement with a Commonwealth country or a colony

and stating its terms shall be conclusive evidence of the matters contained in the certificate.

(8) In relation to a Commonwealth country or a colony the reference in subsection (1) above to an offence of a political character does not include an offence against the life or person of the Head of the Commonwealth or attempting or conspiring to commit, or assisting, counselling or procuring the commission of or being accessory before or after the fact to such an offence, or of impeding the apprehension or prosecution of persons guilty of such an offence.

(9) In this Act "appropriate authority" means—

(a) the Secretary of State;

(b) the court of committal;

(c) the High Court or High Court of Justiciary on an application for habeas corpus or for review of the order of committal.

(10) In this section, in relation to Commonwealth countries and colonies, "race" includes tribe.

PART III
PROCEDURE

General

7 Extradition request and authority to proceed

(1) Subject to the provisions of this Act relating to provisional warrants, a person shall not be dealt with under this Part of this Act except in pursuance of an order of the Secretary of State (in this Act referred to as an "authority to proceed") issued in pursuance of a request (in this Act referred to as an "extradition request") for the surrender of a person under this Act made [to the Secretary of State]—

[(a) by—

(i) an authority in a foreign state which appears to the Secretary of State to have the function of making extradition requests in that foreign state, or

(ii) some person recognised by the Secretary of State as a diplomatic or consular representative of a foreign state; or]

(b) by or on behalf of the Government of a designated Commonwealth country, or the Governor of a Colony [and an extradition request may be made by facsimile transmission and an authority to proceed issued without waiting to receive the original.]

(2) There shall be furnished with any such request—

(a) particulars of the person whose return is requested;

(b) particulars of the offence of which he is accused or was convicted (including evidence [or, in a case falling within subsection (2A) below, information] sufficient to justify the issue of a warrant for his arrest under this Act);

(c) in the case of a person accused of an offence, a warrant [or a duly authenticated copy of a warrant] for his arrest issued in the foreign state, Commonwealth country or colony; and

(d) in the case of a person unlawfully at large after conviction of an offence, a certificate [or a duly authenticated copy of a certificate] of the conviction and sentence, and copies of them shall be served on the person whose return is requested before he is brought before the court of committal.

[(2A) Where—

(a) the extradition request is made by a foreign state; and

(b) an Order in Council falling within section 4(5) above is in force in relation to that state,

it shall be a sufficient compliance with subsection (2)(b) above to furnish information sufficient to justify the issue of a warrant for his arrest under this Act.]

(3) Rules under section 144 of the Magistrates' Courts Act 1980 may make provision as to the procedure for service under subsection (2) above in England and Wales and the High Court of Justiciary may, by Act of Adjournal, make rules as to such procedure in Scotland.

(4) On receipt of any such request the Secretary of State may issue an authority to proceed unless it appears to him that an order for the return of the person concerned could not lawfully be made, or would not in fact be made, in accordance with the provisons of this Act.

(5) An authority to proceed shall specify the offence or offences under the law of the United Kingdom which it appears to the Secretary of State would be constituted by equivalent conduct in the United Kingdom.

(6) In this section "warrant", in the case of any foreign state, includes any judicial document authorising the arrest of a person accused of a crime.

(7) * * * * *

8 Arrest for purposes of committal

(1) For the purposes of this Part of this Act a warrant for the arrest of a person may be issued—

(a) on receipt of an authority to proceed—

(i) by the chief metropolitan stipendiary magistrate or a designated metropolitan magistrate;

(ii) by the sheriff of Lothian and Borders;

(b) without such an authority—

(i) by a metropolitan magistrate;

(ii) by a justice of the peace in any part of the United Kingdom; and

(iii) in Scotland, by a sheriff,

upon information that the said person is or is believed to be in or on his way to the United Kingdom;

and any warrant issued by virtue of paragraph (b) above is in this Act referred to as a "provisional warrant".

(2) In this Act—

"designated metropolitan magistrate" means a metropolitan stipendiary magistrate designated for the purposes of this Act by the Lord Chancellor; and

"metropolitan magistrate" means the chief metropolitan stipendiary magistrate or a designated metropolitan magistrate.

(3) A person empowered to issue warrants of arrest under this section may issue such a warrant if he is supplied with such evidence [or, in a case falling within subsection (3A) below, information] as would in his opinion justify the issue of a warrant for the arrest of a person accused or, as the case may be, convicted within his jurisdiction and it appears to him that the conduct alleged would constitute an extradition crime.

[(3A) Where—

(a) the extradition request or, where a provisional warrant is applied for, the request for the person's arrest is made by a foreign state; and

(b) an Order in Council falling within section 4(5) above is in force in relation to that state,

it shall be sufficient for the purposes of subsection (3) above to supply such information as would, in the opinion of the person so empowered, justify the issue of a warrant of arrest.]

(4) Where a provisional warrant is issued under this section, the authority by whom it is issued shall forthwith give notice to the Secretary of State, and transmit to him the information and evidence, or certified copies of the information and evidence, upon which it was issued; and the Secretary of State may in any case, and shall if he decides not to issue an authority to proceed in respect of the person to whom the warrant relates,

by order cancel the warrant and, if that person has been arrested under it, discharge him from custody.

(5) A warrant of arrest issued under this section may, without being backed, be executed in any part of the United Kingdom and may be so executed by any person to whom it is directed or by any constable.

(6) Where a warrant is issued under this section for the arrest of a person accused of an offence of stealing or receiving stolen property in a designated Commonwealth country or colony or any other offence committed in such a country or in a colony in respect of property, a justice of the peace in any part of the United Kingdom and in Scotland a sheriff shall have the like power to issue a warrant to search for the property as if the offence had been committed within his jurisdiction.

9 Proceedings for committal

(1) A person arrested in pursuance of a warrant under section 8 above shall (unless previously discharged under subsection (4) of that section) be brought as soon as practicable before a court (in this Act referred to as "the court of committal") consisting of a metropolitan magistrate or the sheriff of Lothian and Borders, as may be directed by the warrant.

(2) For the purposes of proceedings under this section a court of committal in England and Wales shall have the like [powers, as nearly as may be, including powers to adjourn the case and meanwhile to remand the person arrested under the warrant either in custody or on bail, as if the proceedings were the summary trial of an information against him; and section 16(1)(c) of the Prosecution of Offences Act 1985 (costs on dismissal) shall apply accordingly reading the reference to the dismissal of the information as a reference to the discharge of the person arrested.]

[(2A) If a court of committal in England and Wales exercises its power to adjourn the case it shall on so doing remand the person arrested in custody or on bail.]

(3) For the purposes of proceedings under this section a court of committal in Scotland shall have the like powers, including power to adjourn the case and meanwhile to remand the person arrested under the warrant either in custody or on bail, and the proceedings shall be conducted as nearly as may be in the like manner, as if the proceedings were summary proceedings in respect of an offence alleged to have been committed by that person; and the provisions of the Legal Aid (Scotland) Act 1986 relating to such proceedings or any appellate proceedings following thereon shall apply accordingly to that person.

(4) Where—

(a) the extradition request is made by a foreign state; and

(b) an Order in Council such as is mentioned in subsection (8) below is in force in relation to that state,

there is no need to furnish the court of committal with evidence sufficient to [make a case requiring an answer by the arrested person if the proceedings were the summary trial of an information against him.]

(5) Where the person arrested is in custody by virtue of a provisional warrant and no authority to proceed has been received in respect of him, the court of committal may fix a period (of which the court shall give notice to the Secretary of State) after which he will be discharged from custody unless such an authority has been received.

(6) In exercising the power conferred by subsection (5) above in a case where the extradition request is made under general extradition arrangements the court shall have regard to any period specified for the purpose in the Order in Council relating to the arrangements.

(7) Where—

(a) the extradition request is made under general extradition arrangements but no period is so specified; or

(b) the application is made under special extradition arrangements,

the court of committal may fix a reasonable period.

(8) Where an authority to proceed has been issued in respect of the person arrested and the court of committal is satisfied, after hearing any representations made in support of the extradition request or on behalf of that person, that the offence to which the authority relates is an extradition crime, and is further satisfied—

(a) where that person is accused of the offence, unless an Order in Council giving effect to general extradition arrangements under which the extradition request was made otherwise provides, that the evidence would be sufficient to [make a case requiring an answer by that person if the proceedings were the summary trial of an information against him.]

(b) where that person is alleged to be unlawfully at large after conviction of the offence, that he has been so convicted and appears to be so at large,

the court, unless his committal is prohibited by any other provision of this Act, shall commit him to custody or on bail—

(i) to await the Secretary of State's decision as to his return; and

(ii) if the Secretary of State decides that he shall be returned, to await his return.

(9) If the court commits a person under subsection (8) above, it shall issue a certificate of the offence against the law of the United Kingdom which would be constituted by his conduct.

(10) If the court commits a person to custody in the exercise of that power, it may subsequently grant bail if it considers it appropriate to do so.

(11) If—

(a) the court is not satisfied as mentioned in subsection (8) above in relation to the person arrested; or

(b) his committal is prohibited by a provision of this Act,

it shall discharge him.

10 Statement of case by court

(1) If the court of committal refuses to make an order in relation to a person under section 9 above in respect of the offence or, as the case may be, any of the offences to which the authority to proceed relates, the foreign state, Commonwealth country or colony seeking the surrender of that person to it may question the proceeding on the ground that it is wrong in law by applying to the court to state a case for the opinion of the High Court or, in Scotland, the High Court of Justiciary on the question of law involved.

(2) If the state, country or colony seeking return immediately informs the court of committal that it intended to make such an application, the court shall make an order providing for the detention of the person to whom the authority to proceed relates, or directing that he shall not be released except on bail.

(3) Rules of Court may specify—

(a) a period within which such an application must be made unless the court grants a longer period; and

(b) a period within which the court of committal must comply with such an application.

(4) Where the court of committal fails to comply with an application under subsection (1) above within the period specified by Rules of Court, the High Court or, in Scotland, the High Court of Justiciary may, on the application of the state, country or colony that applied for the case to be stated, make an order requiring the court to state a case.

(5) The High Court or High Court of Justiciary shall have power—

(a) to remit the case to the court of committal to decide it according to the opinion of the High Court or High Court of Justiciary on the question of law; or

(b) to dismiss the appeal.

(6) Where the court dismisses an appeal relating to an offence, it shall by order declare that that offence is not an offence in respect of which the Secretary of State has power to make an order for return in respect of the person whose return was requested.

(7) An order made by a metropolitan magistrate under subsection (2) above shall cease to have effect if—

(a) the court dismisses the appeal in respect of the offence or all the offences to which it relates; and

(b) the foreign state, Commonwealth country or colony does not immediately—

(i) apply for leave to appeal to the House of Lords; or

(ii) inform the court that it intends to apply for leave.

(8) An order made by the sheriff of Lothian and Borders under subsection (2) above shall cease to have effect if the court dismisses the appeal in respect of the offence or all the offences to which it relates.

(9) In relation to a decision of a court on an appeal under this section, section 1 of the Administration of Justice Act 1960 (right of appeal to House of Lords) shall have effect as if so much of subsection (2) as restricts the grant of leave to appeal were omitted.

(10) The House of Lords may exercise any powers of the High Court under subsection (5) above and subsection (6) above shall apply to them as it applies to that Court.

(11)-(13) * * * * *

11 Application for habeas corpus etc.

(1) Where a person is committed under section 9 above, the court shall inform him in ordinary language of his right to make an application for habeas corpus, and shall forthwith give notice of the committal to the Secretary of State.

(2) A person committed shall not be returned—

(a) in any case, until the expiration of the period of 15 days beginning with the day on which the order for his committal is made;

(b) if an application for habeas corpus is made in his case, so long as proceedings on that application are pending.

(3) Without prejudice to any jurisdiction of the High Court apart from this section, the court shall order the applicant's discharge if it appears to the court in relation to the offence, or each of the offences, in respect of which the applicant's return is sought, that—

(a) by reason of the trivial nature of the offence; or

(b) by reason of the passage of time since he is alleged to have committed it or to have become unlawfully at large, as the case may be; or

(c) because the accusation against him is not made in good faith in the interests of justice,

it would, having regard to all the circumstances, be unjust or oppressive to return him.

(4) On any such application the court may receive additional evidence relevant to the exercise of its jurisdiction under section 6 above or subsection (3) above.

(5) Proceedings on an application for habeas corpus shall be treated for the purposes of this section as pending (unless they are discontinued) until (disregarding any power of a court to grant leave to appeal out of time) there is no further possibility of an appeal.

(6) In the application of this section to Scotland references to an application for habeas corpus shall be construed as references to an application for review of the order

of committal and references to the High Court shall be construed as references to the High Court of Justiciary.

12 Order for return

(1) Where a person is committed under section 9 above and is not discharged by order of the High Court or the High Court of Justiciary, the Secretary of State may by warrant order him to be returned unless his return is prohibited, or prohibited for the time being, by this Act, or the Secretary of State decides under this section to make no such order in his case.

(2) Without prejudice to his general discretion as to the making of an order for the return of a person to a foreign state, Commonwealth country or colony—

(a) the Secretary of State shall not make an order in the case of any person if it appears to the Secretary of State in relation to the offence, or each of the offences, in respect of which his return is sought, that—

(i) by reason of its trivial nature; or

(ii) by reason of the passage of time since he is alleged to have committed it or to have become unlawfully at large, as the case may be; or

(iii) because the accusation against him is not made in good faith in the interests of justice,

it would, having regard to all the circumstances, be unjust or oppressive to return him; and

(b) the Secretary of State may decide to make no order for the return of a person accused or convicted of an offence not punishable with death in Great Britain if that person could be or has been sentenced to death for that offence in the country by which the request for his return is made.

(3) An order for return shall not be made in the case of a person who is serving a sentence of imprisonment or detention, or is charged with an offence, in the United Kingdom—

(a) in the case of a person serving such a sentence, until the sentence has been served;

(b) in the case of a person charged with an offence, until the charge is disposed of or withdrawn or unless an order is made for it to lie on the file and, if it results in his serving a term of imprisonment or detention, until the sentence has been served.

(4) In the application of this section to Scotland, the reference in subsection (3) above to an order being made for the charge to lie on the file shall be construed as a reference to the diet being deserted pro loco et tempore.

(5) The Secretary of State may decide to make no order under this section for the return of a person committed in consequence of an extradition request if another extradition request or a requisition under Schedule 1 to this Act has been made in respect of him and it appears to the Secretary of State, having regard to all the circumstances of the case and in particular—

(a) the relative seriousness of the offences in question;

(b) the date on which each such request was made; and

(c) the nationality or citizenship of the person concerned and his ordinary residence,

that preference should be given to that other request or requisition.

(6) Notice of the issue of a warrant under this section for the return of a person to a Commonwealth country or colony shall forthwith be given to the person to be returned.

13 Return to foreign states — supplementary

(1) The Secretary of State shall give the person to whom an order under section 12(1) above for return to a foreign state would relate notice in writing that he is contemplating making such an order.

(2) The person to whom such an order would relate shall have a right to make representations, at any time before the expiration of the period of 15 days commencing

with the date on which the notice is given, as to why he should not be returned to the foreign state, and unless he waives that right, no such order shall be made in relation to him before the end of that period.

(3) A notice under subsection (1) above shall explain in ordinary language the right conferred by subsection (2) above.

(4) It shall be the duty of the Secretary of State to consider any representations made in the exercise of that right.

(5) Unless the person to whom it relates waives the right conferred on him by subsection (6) below, he shall not be returned to the foreign state until the expiration of the period of 7 days commencing with the date on which the warrant is issued or such longer period as—

(a) in England and Wales, rules under section 84 of the Supreme Court Act 1981 may provide; or

(b) in Scotland, the High Court of Justiciary may provide by Act of Adjournal.

(6) At any time within that period he may apply for leave to seek judicial review of the Secretary of State's decision to make the order.

(7) If he applies for judicial review, he may not be returned so long as the proceedings for judicial review are pending.

(8) Proceedings for judicial review shall be treated for the purposes of this section as pending (unless they are discontinued) until (disregarding any power of a court to grant leave to appeal out of time) there is no further possibility of an appeal.

(9) A warrant under section 12 above—

(a) shall state in ordinary language that the Secretary of State has considered any representations made in the exercise of the right conferred by subsection (2) above; and

(b) shall explain in ordinary language the rights conferred by this section on a person whose return to a foreign state has been ordered under section 12 above,

and a copy shall be given to the person to whom it relates as soon as the order for his return is made.

14 Simplified procedure

(1) A person may give notice that he waives the rights conferred on him by section 11 above.

(2) A notice under this section shall be given in England and Wales in the manner prescribed by rules under section 144 of the Magistrates' Courts Act 1980, and without prejudice to the generality of subsection (1) of that section, the power to make such rules shall include power to make provision for a magistrate to order the committal for return of a person with his consent at any time after his arrest.

(3) A notice under this section shall be given in Scotland in the manner prescribed by the High Court of Justiciary by Act of Adjournal and the sheriff may order the committal for return of a person with his consent at any time after his arrest.

(4) Where an order is made by virtue of this section, this Act shall cease to apply to the person in respect of whom it is made, except that, if he is not surrendered within one month after the order is made, the High Court or, in Scotland, the High Court of Justiciary, upon application by or on behalf of that person, may, unless reasonable cause is shown for the delay, order him to be discharged.

Special extradition arrangements

15 Special extradition arrangements

(1) Where special extradition arrangements have been made in respect of a person, extradition procedures shall be available in the case of that person, as between the United Kingdom and the foreign state with which the arrangements have been made,

subject to the limitations, restrictions, exceptions and qualifications, if any, contained in the arrangements.

(2) If the Secretary of State issues a certificate of special extradition arrangements, it shall be conclusive evidence of all matters stated in it.

(3) In subsection (2) above "certificate of special extradition arrangements" means a certificate—

(a) that special extradition arrangements have been made in respect of a person as between the United Kingdom and a foreign state specified in the certificte; and

(b) that extradition procedures are available in the case of that person as between the United Kingdom and the foreign state to the extent specified in the certificate.

Effect of delay

16 Discharge in case of delay

(1) If a person committed under section 9 above is still in the United Kingdom after he expiration of the relevant period, he may apply to the High Court or High Court of Justiciary for his discharge.

(2) Unless he has instituted proceedings for judicial review of the Secretary of State's decision to order his return, the relevant period is—

(a) the period of two months beginning with the first day on which, having regard to section 11(2) above, he could have been returned;

(b) where a warrant for his return has been issued under section 12 above, the period of one month beginning with the day on which that warrant was issued.

(3) If he has instituted such proceedings, the relevant period is the period expiring one month after they end.

(4) Proceedings for judicial review end for the purposes of this section—

(a) if they are discontinued, on the day of discontinuance; and

(b) if they are determined, on the day on which (disregarding any power of a court to grant leave to appeal out of time) there is no further possibility of an appeal.

(5) If upon an application under this section the court is satisfied that reasonable notice of the proposed application has been given to the Secretary of State, the court may, unless sufficient cause is shown to the contrary, by order direct the applicant to be discharged and, if a warrant for his return has been issued under section 12 above, quash that warrant.

17 Custody

(1) Any person remanded or committed to custody under this Part of this Act shall be committed to the like institution as a person charged with an offence before the court of committal.

(2) If any person who is in custody by virtue of a warrant under this Act escapes out of custody, he may be retaken in any part of the United Kingdom in like manner as a person escaping from custody under a warrant for his arrest issued in that part in respect of an offence committed in that part.

(3) Where a person, being in custody in any part of the United Kingdom whether under this Part of this Act or otherwise, is required to be removed in custody under this Act to another part of the United Kingdom and is so removed by sea or by air, he shall be deemed to continue in legal custody until he reaches the place to which he is required to be removed.

(4) A warrant for the return of any person shall be sufficient authority for all persons to whom it is directed and all constables to receive that person, keep him in custody and convey him into the jurisdiction to which he is to be returned.

★ ★ ★ ★ ★

OFFICIAL SECRETS ACT 1989
(1989, c. 6)

An Act to replace section 2 of the Official Secrets Act 1911 by provisions protecting more limited classes of official information [11 May 1989]

Territorial extent United Kingdom

1 Security and intelligence

(1) A person who is or has been—

(a) a member of the security and intelligence services; or

(b) a person notified that he is subject to the provisions of this subsection,

is guilty of an offence if without lawful authority he discloses any information, document or other article relating to security or intelligence which is or has been in his possession by virtue of his position as a member of any of those services or in the course of his work while the notification is or was in force.

(2) The reference in subsection (1) above to disclosing information relating to security or intelligence includes a reference to making any statement which purports to be a disclosure of such information or is intended to be taken by those to whom it is addressed as being such a disclosure.

(3) A person who is or has been a Crown Servant or government contractor is guilty of an offence if without lawful authority he makes a damaging disclosure of any information, document or other article relating to security or intelligence which is or has been in his possession by virtue of his position as such but otherwise than as mentioned in subsection (1) above.

(4) For the purposes of subsection (3) above a disclosure is damaging if—

(a) it causes damage to the work of, or of any part of, the security and intelligence service; or

(b) it is of information or a document or other article which is such that its unauthorised disclosure would be likely to cause such damage or which falls within a class or description of information, documents or articles the unauthorised disclosure of which would be likely to have that effect.

(5) It is a defence for a person charged with an offence under this section to prove that at the time of the alleged offence he did not know, and had no reasonable cause to believe, that the information, document or article in question related to security or intelligence or, in the case of an offence under subsection (3), that the disclosure would be damaging within the meaning of that subsection.

(6) Notification that a person is subject to subsection (1) above shall be effected by a notice in writing served on him by a Minister of the Crown; and such a notice may be served if, in the Minister's opinion, the work undertaken by the person in question is or includes work connected with the security and intelligence services and its nature is such that the interests of national security require that he should be subject to the provisions of that subsection.

(7) Subject to subsection (8) below, a notification for the purposes of subsection (1) above shall be in force for the period of five years beginning with the day on which it is served but may be renewed by further notices under subsection (6) above for periods of five years at a time.

(8) A notification for the purposes of subsection (1) above may at any time be revoked by a further notice in writing served by the Minister on the person concerned; and the Minister shall serve such a further notice as soon as, in his opinion, the work undertaken by that person ceases to be such as is mentioned in subsection (6) above.

(9) In this section "security or intelligence" means the work of, or in support of, the security and intelligence services or any part of them, and references to information

relating to security or intelligence include references to information held or transmitted by those services or by persons in support of, or of any part of, them.

2 Defence

(1) A person who is or has been a Crown servant or government contractor is guilty of an offence if without lawful authority he makes a damaging disclosure of any information, document or other article relating to defence which is or has been in his possession by virtue of his position as such.

(2) For the purposes of subsection (1) above a disclosure is damaging if—

(a) it damages the capability of, or of any part of, the armed forces of the Crown to carry out their tasks or leads to loss of life or injury to members of those forces or serious damage to the equipment or installations of those forces; or

(b) otherwise than as mentioned in paragraph (a) above, it endangers the interests of the United Kingdom abroad, seriously obstructs the promotion or protection by the United Kingdom of those interests or endangers the safety of British citizens abroad; or

(c) it is of information or of a document or article which is such that its unauthorised disclosure would be likely to have any of those effects.

(3) It is a defence for a person charged with an offence under this section to prove that at the time of the alleged offence he did not know, and had no reasonable cause to believe, that the information, document or article in question related to defence or that its disclosure would be damaging within the meaning of subsection (1) above.

(4) In this section "defence" means—

(a) the size, shape, organisation, logistics, order of battle, deployment, operations, state of readiness and training of the armed forces of the Crown;

(b) the weapons, stores or other equipment of those forces and the invention, development, production and operation of such equipment and research relating to it;

(c) defence policy and strategy and military planning and intelligence;

(d) plans and measures for the maintenance of essential supplies and services that are or would be needed in time of war.

3 International relations

(1) A person who is or has been a Crown servant or government contractor is guilty of an offence if without lawful authority he makes a damaging disclosure of—

(a) any information, document or other article relating to international relations; or

(b) any confidential information, document or other article which was obtained from a State other than the United Kingdom or an international organisation,

being information or a document or article which is or has been in his possession by virtue of his position as a Crown servant or government contractor.

(2) For the purposes of subsection (1) above a disclosure is damaging if—

(a) it endangers the interests of the United Kingdom abroad, seriously obstructs the promotion or protection by the United Kingdom of those interests or endangers the safety of British citizens abroad; or

(b) it is of information or of a document or article which is such that its unauthorised disclosure would be likely to have any of those effects.

(3) In the case of information or a document or article within subsection (1)(b) above—

(a) the fact that it is confidential, or

(b) its nature or contents,

may be sufficient to establish for the purposes of subsection (2)(b) above that the information, document or article is such that its unauthorised disclosure would be likely to have any of the effects there mentioned.

(4) It is a defence for a person charged with an offence under this section to prove that at the time of the alleged offence he did not know, and had no reasonable cause to

believe, that the information, document or article in question was such as is mentioned in subsection (1) above or that its disclosure would be damaging within the meaning of that subsection.

(5) In this section "international relations" means the relations between States, between international organisations or between one or more States and one or more such organisations and includes any matter relating to a State other than the United Kingdom or to an international organisation which is capable of affecting the relations of the United Kingdom with another State or with an international organisation.

(6) For the purposes of this section any information, document or article obtained from a State or organisation is confidential at any time while the terms on which it was obtained require it to be held in confidence or while the circumstances in which it was obtained make it reasonable for the State or organisation to expect that it would be so held.

4 Crime and special investigation powers

(1) A person who is or has been a Crown servant or government contractor is guilty of an offence if without lawful authority he discloses any information, document or other article to which this section applies and which is or has been in his possession by virtue of his position as such.

(2) This section applies to any information, document or other article—

(a) the disclosure of which—

(i) results in the commission of an offence; or

(ii) facilitates an escape from legal custody or the doing of any other act prejudicial to the safekeeping of persons in legal custody; or

(iii) impedes the prevention or detection of offences or the apprehension or prosecution of suspected offenders; or

(b) which is such that its unauthorised disclosure would be likely to have any of those effects.

(3) This section also applies to—

(a) any information obtained by reason of the interception of any communication in obedience to a warrant issued under section 2 of the Interception of Communications Act 1985, any information relating to the obtaining of information by reason of any such interception and any document or other article which is or has been used or held for use in, or has been obtained by reason of, any such interception; and

(b) any information obtained by reason of action authorised by a warrant issued under section 3 of the Security Services Act 1989 [or under section 5 of the Intelligence Services Act 1994 or by an authorisation given under section 7 of that Act,] any information relating to the obtaining of information by reason of any such action and any document or other article which is or has been used or held for use in, or has been obtained by reason of, any such action.

(4) It is a defence for a person charged with an offence under this section in respect of a disclosure falling within subsection (2)(a) above to prove that at the time of the alleged offence he did not know, and had no reasonable cause to believe, that the disclosure would have any of the effects there mentioned.

(5) It is a defence for a person charged with an offence under this section in respect of any other disclosure to prove that at the time of the alleged offence he did not know, and had no reasonable cause to believe, that the information, document or article in question was information or a document or article to which this section applies.

(6) In this section "legal custody" includes detention in pursuance of any enactment or any instrument made under an enactment.

5 Information resulting from unauthorised disclosures or entrusted in confidence

(1) Subsection (2) below applies where—

(a) any information, document or other article protected against disclosure by the foregoing provisions of this Act has come into a person's possession as a result of having been—

(i) disclosed (whether to him or another) by a Crown servant or government contractor without lawful authority; or

(ii) entrusted to him by a Crown servant or government contractor on terms requiring it to be held in confidence or in circumstances in which the Crown servant or government contractor could reasonably expect that it would be so held; or

(iii) disclosed (whether to him or another) without lawful authority by a person to whom it was entrusted as mentioned in sub-paragraph (ii) above; and

(b) the disclosure without lawful authority of the information, document or article by the person into whose possession it has come is not an offence under any of those provisions.

(2) Subject to subsections (3) and (4) below, the person into whose possession the information, document or article has come is guilty of an offence if he discloses it without lawful authority knowing, or having reasonable cause to believe, that it is protected against disclosure by the foregoing provisions of this Act and that it has come into his possession as mentioned in subsection (1) above.

(3) In the case of information or a document or article protected against disclosure by sections 1 to 3 above, a person does not commit an offence under subsection (2) above unless—

(a) the disclosure by him is damaging; and

(b) he makes it knowing, or having reasonable cause to believe, that it would be damaging;

and the question whether a disclosure is damaging shall be determined for the purposes of this subsection as it would be in relation to a disclosure of that information, document or article by a Crown servant in contravention of section 1(3), 2(1) or 3(1) above.

(4) A person does not commit an offence under subsection (2) above in respect of information or a document or other article which has come into his possession as a result of having been disclosed—

(a) as mentioned in subsection (1)(a)(i) above by a government contractor; or

(b) as mentioned in subsection (1)(a)(ii) above,

unless that disclosure was by a British citizen or took place in the United Kingdom, in any of the Channel Islands or in the Isle of Man or a colony.

(5) For the purposes of this section information or a document or article is protected against disclosure by the foregoing provisions of this Act if—

(a) it relates to security or intelligence, defence or international relations within the meaning of section 1, 2 or 3 above or is such as is mentioned in section 3(1)(b) above; or

(b) it is information or a document or article to which section 4 above applies;

and information or a document or article is protected against disclosure by sections 1 to 3 above if it falls within paragraph (a) above.

(6) A person is guilty of an offence if without lawful authority he discloses any information, document or other article which he knows, or has reasonable cause to believe, to have come into his possession as a result of a contravention of section 1 of the Official Secrets Act 1911.

6 Information entrusted in confidence to other States or international organisations

(1) This section applies where—

(a) any information, document or other article which—
(i) relates to security or intelligence, defence or international relations; and
(ii) has been communicated in confidence by or on behalf of the United Kingdom to another State or to an international organisation,
has come into a person's possession as a result of having been disclosed (whether to him or another) without the authority of that State or organisation or, in the case of an organisation, of a member of it; and
(b) the disclosure without lawful authority of the information, document or article by the person into whose possession it has come is not an offence under any of the foregoing provisions of this Act.

(2) Subject to subsection (3) below, the person into whose possession the information, document or article has come is guilty of an offence if he makes a damaging disclosure of it knowing, or having reasonable cause to believe, that it is such as is mentioned in subsection (1) above, that it has come into his possession as there mentioned and that its disclosure would be damaging.

(3) A person does not commit an offence under subsection (2) above if the information, document or article is disclosed by him wih lawful authority or has previously been made available to the public with the authority of the State or organisation concerned or, in the case of an organisation, of a member of it.

(4) For the purposes of this section "security or intelligence", "defence" and "international relations" have the same meaning as in sections 1, 2 and 3 above and the question whether a disclosure is damaging shall be determined as it would be in relation to a disclosure of the information, document or article in question by a Crown servant in contravention of sections 1(3), 2(1) and 3(1) above.

(5) For the purposes of this section information or a document or article is communicated in confidence if it is communicated on terms requiring it to be held in confidence or in circumstances in which the person communicating it could reasonably expect that it would be so held.

7 Authorised disclosures

(1) For the purposes of this Act a disclosure by—
(a) a Crown servant; or
(b) a person, not being a Crown servant or government contractor, in whose case a notification for the purposes of section 1(1) above is in force,
is made with lawful authority if, and only if, it is made in accordance with his official duty.

(2) For the purposes of this Act a disclosure by a government contractor is made with lawful authority if, and only if, it is made—
(a) in accordance with an official authorisation; or
(b) for the purposes of the functions by virtue of which he is a government contractor and without contravening an official restriction.

(3) For the purposes of this Act a disclosure made by any other person is made with lawful authority if, and only if, it is made—
(a) to a Crown servant for the purposes of his functions as such; or
(b) in accordance with an official authorisation.

(4) It is a defence for a person charged with an offence under any of the foregoing provisions of this Act to prove that at the time of the alleged offence he believed that he had lawful authority to make the disclosure in question and had no reasonable cause to believe otherwise.

(5) In this section "official authorisation" and "official restriction" mean, subject to subsection (6) below, an authorisation or restriction duly given or imposed by a Crown servant or government contractor or by or on behalf of a prescribed body or a body of a prescribed class.

(6) In relation to section 6 above "official authorisation" includes an authorisation duly given by or on behalf of the State or organisation concerned or, in the case of an organisation, a member of it.

8 Safeguarding of information

(1) Where a Crown servant or government contractor, by virtue of his position as such, has in his possession or under his control any document or other article which it would be an offence under any of the foregoing provisions of this Act for him to disclose without lawful authority he is guilty of an offence if—

(a) being a Crown servant, he retains the document or article contrary to his official duty; or

(b) being a government contractor, he fails to comply with an official direction for the return or disposal of the document or article,

or if he fails to take such care to prevent the unauthorised disclosure of the document or article as a person in his position may reasonably be expected to take.

(2) It is a defence for a Crown servant charged with an offence under subsection (1)(a) above to prove that at the time of the alleged offence he believed that he was acting in accordance with his official duty and had no reasonable cause to believe otherwise.

(3) In subsections (1) and (2) above references to a Crown servant include any person, not being a Crown servant or government contractor, in whose case a notification for the purposes of section 1(1) above is in force.

(4) Where a person has in his possession or under his control any document or other article which it would be an offence under section 5 above for him to disclose without lawful authority, he is guilty of an offence if—

(a) he fails to comply with an official direction for its return or disposal; or

(b) where he obtained it from a Crown servant or government contractor on terms requiring it to be held in confidence or in circumstances in which that servant or contractor could reasonably expect that it would be so held, he fails to take such care to prevent its unauthorised disclosure as a person in his position may reasonably be expected to take.

(5) Where a person has in his possession or under his control any document or other article which it would be an offence under section 6 above for him to disclose without lawful authority, he is guilty of an offence if he fails to comply with an official direction for its return or disposal.

(6) A person is guilty of an offence if he discloses any official information, document or other article which can be used for the purpose of obtaining access to any information, document or other article protected against disclosure by the foregoing provisions of this Act and the circumstances in which it is disclosed are such that it would be reasonable to expect that it might be used for that purpose without authority.

(7) For the purposes of subsection (6) above a person discloses information or a document or article which is official if—

(a) he has or has had it in his possession by virtue of his position as a Crown servant or government contractor; or

(b) he knows or has reasonable cause to believe that a Crown servant or government contractor has or has had it in his possession by virtue of his position as such.

(8) Subsection (5) of section 5 above applies for the purposes of subsection (6) above as it applies for the purposes of that section.

(9) In this section "official direction" means a direction duly given by a Crown servant or government contractor or by or on behalf of a prescribed body or a body of a prescribed class.

9 Prosecutions

(1) Subject to subsection (2) below, no prosecution for an offence under this Act shall be instituted in England and Wales or in Northern Ireland except by or with the

consent of the Attorney General or, as the case may be, the Attorney General for Northern Ireland.

(2) Subsection (1) above does not apply to an offence in respect of any such information, document or article as is mentioned in section 4(2) above but no prosecution for such an offence shall be instituted in England and Wales or in Northern Ireland except by or with the consent of the Director of Public Prosecutions or, as the case may be, the Director of Public Prosecutions for Northern Ireland.

10 Penalties

(1) A person guilty of an offence under any provision of this Act other than section 8(1), (4) or (5) shall be liable—

(a) on conviction on indictment, to imprisonment for a term not exceeding two years or a fine or both;

(b) on summary conviction, to imprisonment for a term not exceeding six months or a fine not exceeding the statutory maximum or both.

(2) A person guilty of an offence under section 8(1), (4) or (5) above shall be liable on summary conviction to imprisonment for a term not exceeding three months or a fine not exceeding level 5 on the standard scale or both.

11 Arrest, search and trial

(1), (2) ★ ★ ★ ★ ★

(3) Section 9(1) of the Official Secrets Act 1911 (search warrants) shall have effect as if references to offences under that Act included references to offences under any provision of this Act other than section 8(1), (4) or (5); and the following provisions of the Police and Criminal Evidence Act 1984, that is to say—

(a) section 9(2) (which excludes items subject to legal privilege and certain other material from powers of search conferred by previous enactments); and

(b) paragraph 3(b) of Schedule 1 (which prescribes access conditions for the special procedure laid down in that Schedule),

shall apply to section 9(1) of the said Act of 1911 as extended by this subsection as they apply to that section as originally enacted.

(4) Section 8(4) of the Official Secrets Act 1920 (exclusion of public from hearing on grounds of national safety) shall have effect as if references to offences under that Act included references to offences under any provision of this Act other than section 8(1), (4) or (5).

(5) Proceedings for an offence under this Act may be taken in any place in the United Kingdom.

12 "Crown servant" and "government contractor"

(1) In this Act "Crown servant" means—

(a) a Minister of the Crown;

(b) a person appointed under section 8 of the Northern Ireland Constitution Act 1973 (the Northern Ireland Executive etc.);

(c) any person employed in the civil service of the Crown, including Her Majesty's Diplomatic Service, Her Majesty's Overseas Civil Service, the civil service of Northern Ireland and the Northern Ireland Court Service;

(d) any member of the naval, military or air forces of the Crown, including any person employed by an association established for the purposes of [Part XI the Reserve Forces Act 1996];

(e) any constable and any other person employed or appointed in or for the purposes of any police force (including a police force within the meaning of the Police Act (Northern Ireland) 1970);

(f) any person who is member or employee of a prescribed body or a body of a prescribed class and either is prescribed for the purposes of this paragraph or belongs to a prescribed class of members or employees of any such body;

(g) any person who is the holder of a prescribed office or who is an employee of such a holder and either is prescribed for the purposes of this paragraph or belongs to a prescribed class of such employees.

(2) In this Act "government contractor" means, subject to subsection (3) below, any person who is not a Crown servant but who provides, or is employed in the provision of, goods or services—

(a) for the purposes of any Minister or person mentioned in paragraph (a) or (b) of subsection (1) above, of any of the services, forces or bodies mentioned in that subsection or of the holder of any office prescribed under that subsection; or

(b) under an agreement or arrangement certified by the Secretary of State as being one to which the government of a State other than the United Kingdom or an international organisation is a party or which is subordinate to, or made for the purposes of implementing, any such agreement or arrangement.

(3) Where an employee or class of employees of any body, or of any holder of an office, is prescribed by an order made for the purposes of subsection (1) above—

(a) any employee of that body, or of the holder of that office, who is not prescribed or is not within the prescribed class; and

(b) any person who does not provide, or is not employed in the provision of, goods or services for the purposes of the performance of those functions of the body or the holder of the office in connection with which the employee or prescribed class of employees is engaged,

shall not be a government contractor for the purposes of this Act.

13 Other interpretation provisions

(1) In this Act—

"disclose" and "disclosure", in relation to a document or other article, include parting with possession of it;

"international organisation" means, subject to subsections (2) and (3) below, an organisation of which only States are members and includes a reference to any organ of such an organisation;

"prescribed" means prescribed by an order made by the Secretary of State;

"State" includes the government of a State and any organ of its government and references to a State other than the United Kingdom include references to any territory outside the United Kingdom.

(2) In section 12(2)(b) above the reference to an international organisation includes a reference to any such organisation whether or not one of which only States are members and includes a commercial organisation.

(3) In determining for the purposes of subsection (1) above whether only States are members of an organisation, any member which is itself an organisation of which only States are members, or which is an organ of such an organisation, shall be treated as a State.

★ ★ ★ ★ ★

PREVENTION OF TERRORISM (TEMPORARY PROVISIONS) ACT 1989 (1989, c. 4)

An Act to make provision in place of the Prevention of Terrorism (Temporary Provisions) Act 1984; to make further provision in relation to powers of search under, and persons convicted of scheduled offences within the meaning of, the Northern Ireland (Emergency Provisions) Act

1978); and to enable the Secretary of State to prevent the establishment of new explosives factories, magazines and stores in Northern Ireland [15 March 1989]

Territorial extent United Kingdom

PART I
PROSCRIBED ORGANISATIONS

1 Proscribed organisations

(1) Any organisation for the time being specified in Schedule 1 to this Act is a proscribed organisation for the purposes of this Act; and any organisation which passes under a name mentioned in that Schedule shall be treated as proscribed whatever relationship (if any) it has to any other organisation of the same name.

(2) The Secretary of State may by order made by statutory instrument—

(a) add to Schedule 1 to this Act any organisation that appears to him to be concerned in, or in promoting or encouraging, terrorism occurring in the United Kingdom and connected with the affairs of Northern Ireland;

(b) remove an organisation from that Schedule.

(3) No order shall be made under this section unless—

(a) a draft of the order has been laid before and approved by a resolution of each House of Parliament; or

(b) it is declared in the order that it appears to the Secretary of State that by reason of urgency it is necessary to make the order without a draft having been so approved.

(4) An order under this section of which a draft has not been approved under subsection (3) above—

(a) shall be laid before Parliament; and

(b) shall cease to have effect at the end of the period of forty days beginning with the day on which it was made unless, before the end of that period, the order has been approved by a resolution of each House of Parliament, but without prejudice to anything previously done or to the making of a new order.

2 Membership, support and meetings

(1) Subject to subsection (3) below, a person is guilty of an offence if he—

(a) belongs or professes to belong to a proscribed organisation;

(b) solicits or invites support for a proscribed organisation other than support with money or other property; or

(c) arranges or assists in the arrangement or management of, or addresses, any meeting of three or more persons (whether or not it is a meeting to which the public are admitted) knowing that the meeting is—

(i) to support a proscribed organisation;

(ii) to further the activities of such an organisation; or

(iii) to be addressed by a person belonging or professing to belong to such an organisation.

(2) A person guilty of an offence under subsection (1) above is liable—

(a) on conviction on indictment, to imprisonment for a term not exceeding ten years or a fine or both;

(b) on summary conviction, to imprisonment for a term not exceeding six months or a fine not exceeding the statutory maximum or both.

(3) A person belonging to a proscribed organisation is not guilty of an offence under this section by reason of belonging to the organisation if he shows—

(a) that he became a member when it was not a poscribed organisation under the current legislation; and

(b) that he has not since he became a member taken part in any of its activities at any time while it was a proscribed organisation under that legislation.

(4), (5) * * * * *

3 Display of support in public

(1) Any person who in a public place—

(a) wears any item of dress; or

(b) wears, carries or displays any article,

in such a way or in such circumstances as to arouse reasonable apprehension that he is a member or supporter of a proscribed organisation, is guilty of an offence and liable on summary conviction to imprisonment for a term not exceeding six months or a fine not exceeding level 5 on the standard scale or both.

(2) In Scotland a constable may arrest without warrant anyone whom he has reasonable grounds to suspect of being a person guilty of an offence under this section.

(3) In this section "public place" includes any highway or, in Scotland, any road within the meaning of the Roads (Scotland) Act 1984 and any premises to which at the material time the public have, or are permitted to have, access, whether on payment or otherwise.

PART II
EXCLUSION ORDERS

4 Exclusion orders: general

(1) The Secretary of State may exercise the powers conferred on him by this Part of this Act in such a way as appears to him expedient to prevent acts of terrorism to which this Part of this Act applies.

(2) The acts of terrorism to which this Part of this Act applies are acts of terrorism connected with the affairs of Northern Ireland.

(3) An order under section 5, 6 or 7 below is referred to in this Act as an "exclusion order".

(4) Schedule 2 to this Act shall have effect with respect to the duration of exclusion orders, the giving of notices, the right to make representations, powers of removal and detention and other supplementary matters for this Part of this Act.

(5) The exercise of the detention powers conferred by that Schedule shall be subject to supervision in accordance with Schedule 3 to this Act.

5 Orders excluding persons from Great Britain

(1) If the Secretary of State is satisfied that any person—

(a) is or has been concerned in the commission, preparation or instigation of acts of terrorism to which this Part of this Act applies; or

(b) is attempting or may attempt to enter Great Britain with a view to being concerned in the commission, preparation or instigation of such acts of terrorism,

the Secretary of State may make an exclusion order against him.

(2) An exclusion order under this section is an order prohibiting a person from being in, or entering, Great Britain.

(3) In deciding whether to make an exclusion order under this section against a person who is ordinarily resident in Great Britain, the Secretary of State shall have regard to the question whether that person's connection with any country or territory outside Great Britain is such as to make it appropriate that such an order should be made.

(4) An exclusion order shall not be made under this section against a person who is a British citizen and who—

(a) is at the time ordinarily resident in Great Britain and has then been ordinarily resident in Great Britain throughout the last three years; or

(b) is at the time subject to an order under section 6 below.

6 Orders excluding persons from Northern Ireland

(1) If the Secretary of State is satisfied that any person—

(a) is or has been concerned in the commission, preparation or instigation of acts of terrorism to which this Part of this Act applies; or

(b) is attempting or may attempt to enter Northern Ireland with a view to being concerned in the commission, preparation or instigation of such acts of terrorism,
the Secretary of State may make an exclusion order against him.

(2) An exclusion order under this section is an order prohibiting a person from being in, or entering, Northern Ireland.

(3) In deciding whether to make an exclusion order under this section against a person who is ordinarily resident in Northern Ireland, the Secretary of State shall have regard to the question whether that person's connection with any country or territory outside Northern Ireland is such as to make it appropriate that such an order should be made.

(4) An exclusion order shall not be made under this section against a person who is a British citizen and who—

(a) is at the time ordinarily resident in Northern Ireland and has then been ordinarily resident in Northern Ireland throughout the last three years; or

(b) is at the time subject to an order under section 5 above.

7 Orders excluding persons from the United Kingdom

(1) If the Secretary of State is satisfied that any person—

(a) is or has been concerned in the commission, preparation or instigation of acts of terrorism to which this Part of this Act applies; or

(b) is attempting or may attempt to enter Great Britain or Northern Ireland with a view to being concerned in the commission, preparation or instigation of such acts of terrorism,
the Secretary of State may make an exclusion order against him.

(2) An exclusion order under this section is an order prohibiting a person from being in, or entering, the United Kingdom.

(3) In deciding whether to make an exclusion order under this section against a person who is ordinarily resident in the United Kingdom, the Secretary of State shall have regard to the question whether that person's connection with any country or territory outside the United Kingdom is such as to make it appropriate that such an order should be made.

(4) An exclusion order shall not be made under this section against a person who is a British citizen.

8 Offences in respect of exclusion orders

(1) A person who is subject to an exclusion order is guilty of an offence if he fails to comply with the order at a time after he has been, or has become liable to be, removed under Schedule 2 to this Act.

(2) A person is guilty of an offence—

(a) if he is knowingly concerned in arrangements for securing or facilitating the entry into Great Britain, Northern Ireland or the United Kingdom of a person whom he knows, or has reasonable grounds for believing, to be an excluded person; or

(b) if he knowingly harbours such a person in Great Britain, Northern Ireland or the United Kingdom.

(3) In subsection (2) above "excluded person" means—

(a) in relation to Great Britain, a person subject to an exclusion order made under section 5 above who has been, or has become liable to be, removed from Great Britain under Schedule 2 to this Act;

(b) in relation to Northern Ireland, a person subject to an exclusion order made under section 6 above who has been, or has become liable to be, removed from Northern Ireland under that Schedule; and

(c) in relation to the United Kingdom, a person subject to an exclusion order made under section 7 above who has been, or has become liable to be, removed from the United Kingdom under that Schedule.

(4) A person guilty of an offence under this section is liable—

(a) on conviction on indictment, to imprisonment for a term not exceeding five years or a fine or both;

(b) on summary conviction, to imprisonment for a term not exceeding six months or a fine not exceeding the statutory maximum or both.

PART III
FINANCIAL ASSISTANCE FOR TERRORISM

9 Contributions towards acts of terrorism

(1) A person is guilty of an offence if he—

(a) solicits or invites any other person to give, lend or otherwise make available, whether for consideration or not, any money or other property; . . .

(b) receives or accepts from any other person, whether for consideration or not, any money or other property, [or

(c) uses or has possession of, whether for consideration or not, any money or other property,]

intending that it shall be applied or used for the commission of, or in furtherance of or in connection with, acts of terrorism to which this section applies or having reasonable cause to suspect that it may be so used or applied.

(2) A person is guilty of an offence if he—

(a) gives, lends or otherwise makes available to any other person, whether for consideration or not, any money or other property; or

(b) enters into or is otherwise concerned in an arrangement whereby money or other property is or is to be made available to another person,

knowing or having reasonable cause to suspect that it will or may be applied or used as mentioned in subsection (1) above.

(3) The acts of terrorism to which this section applies are—

(a) acts of terrorism connected with the affairs of Northern Ireland; and

(b) subject to subsection (4) below, acts of terrorism of any other description except acts connected solely with the affairs of the United Kingdom or any part of the United Kingdom other than Northern Ireland.

(4) Subsection (3)(b) above does not apply to an act done or to be done outside the United Kingdom unless it constitutes or would constitute an offence triable in the United Kingdom.

(5) In proceedings against a person for an offence under this section in relation to an act within subsection (3)(b) above done or to be done outside the United Kingdom—

(a) the prosecution need not prove that that person knew or had reasonable cause to suspect that the act constituted or would constitute such an offence as is mentioned in subsection (4) above; but

(b) it shall be a defence to prove that he did not know and had no reasonable cause to suspect that the facts were such that the act constituted or would constitute such an offence.

10 Contributions to resources of proscribed organisations

(1) A person is guilty of an offence if he—

(a) solicits or invites any other person to give, lend or otherwise make available, whether for consideration or not, any money or other property for the benefit of a proscribed organisation;

(b) gives, lends or otherwise makes available or receives or accepts [or uses or has possession of], whether for consideration or not, any money or other property for the benefit of such an organisation; or

(c) enters into or is otherwise concerned in an arrangement whereby money or other property is or is to be made available for the benefit of such an organisation.

(2) In proceedings against a person for an offence under subsection (1)(b) above it is a defence to prove that he did not know and had no reasonable cause to suspect that the money or property was for the benefit of a proscribed organisation; and in proceedings against a person for an offence under subsection (1)(c) above it is a defence to prove that he did not know and had no reasonable cause to suspect that the arrangement related to a prosribed organisation.

(3) In this section and sections 11 and 13 below "proscribed organisation" includes a proscribed organisation for the purposes of [section 30 of the Northern Ireland (Emergency Provisions) Act 1996].

11 Assisting in retention or control of terrorist funds

(1) A person is guilty of an offence if he enters into or is otherwise concerned in an arrangement whereby the retention or control by or on behalf of another person of terrorist funds is facilitated, whether by concealment, removal from the jurisdiction, transfer to nominees or otherwise.

(2) In proceedings against a person for an offence under this section it is a defence to prove that he did not know and had no reasonable cause to suspect that the arrangement related to terrorist funds.

(3) In this section and section 12 below "terrorist funds" means—

(a) funds which may be applied or used for the commission of, or in furtherance of or in connection with, acts of terrorism to which section 9 above applies;

(b) the proceeds of the commission of such acts of terrorism or of activities engaged in in furtherance of or in connection with such acts; and

(c) the resources of a proscribed organisation.

(4) Paragraph (b) of subsection (3) includes any property which in whole or in part directly or indirectly represents such proceeds as are mentioned in that paragraph; and paragraph (c) of that subsection includes any money or other property which is or is to be applied or made available for the benefit of a proscribed organisation.

12 Disclosure of information about terrorist funds

(1) A person may notwithstanding any restriction on the disclosure of information imposed by [statute or otherwise] disclose to a constable a suspicion or belief that any money or other property is or is derived from terrorist funds or any matter on which such a suspicion or belief is based.

(2) A person who enters into or is otherwise concerned in any such transaction or arrangement as is mentioned in section 9, 10 or 11 above does not commit an offence under that section if he is acting with the express consent of a constable or if—

(a) he discloses to a constable his suspicion or belief that the money or other property concerned is or is derived from terrorist funds or any matter on which such a suspicion or belief is based; and

(b) the disclosure is made after he enters into or otherwise becomes concerned in the transaction or arrangement in question but is made on his own initiative and as soon as it is reasonable for him to make it,

but paragraphs (a) and (b) above do not apply in a case where, having disclosed any such suspicion, belief or matter to a constable and having been forbidden by a constable to enter into or otherwise be concerned in the transaction or arrangement in question, he nevertheless does so.

[(2A) For the purposes of subsection (2) above a person who uses or has possession of money or other property shall be taken to be concerned in a transaction or arrangement.]

(3) In proceedings against a person for an offence under section 9(1)(b) [or (c)] or (2), 10(1)(b) or (c) or 11 above it is a defence to prove—

(a) that he intended to disclose to a constable such a suspicion, belief or matter as is mentioned in paragraph (a) of subsection (2) above; and

(b) that there is a reasonable excuse for his failure to make the disclosure as mentioned in paragraph (b) of that subsection.

(4)-(6) ★★★★★

13 Penalties and forfeiture

(1) A person guilty of an offence under section 9, 10 or 11 above is liable—

(a) on conviction on indictment, to imprisonment for a term not exceeding fourteen years or a fine or both;

(b) on summary conviction, to imprisonment for a term not exceeding six months or a fine not exceeding the statutory maximum or both.

(2) Subject to the provisions of this section, the court by or before which a person is convicted of an offence under section 9(1) or (2)(a) above may order the forfeiture of any money or other property—

(a) which, at the time of the offence, he had in his possession or under his control; and

(b) which, at that time—

(i) in the case of an offence under subsection (1) of section 9, he intended should be applied or used, or had reasonable cause to suspect might be applied or used, as mentioned in that subsection;

(ii) in the case of an offence under subsection (2)(a) of that section, he knew or had reasonable cause to suspect would or might be applied or used as mentioned in subsection (1) of that section.

(3) Subject to the provisions of this section, the court by or before which a person is convicted of an offence under section 9(2)(b), 10(1)(c) or 11 above may order the forfeiture of the money or other property to which the arrangement in question related and which, in the case of an offence under section 9(2)(b), he knew or had reasonable cause to suspect would or might be applied or used as mentioned in section 9(1) above.

(4) Subject to the provisions of this section, the court by or before which a person is convicted of an offence under section 10(1)(a) or (b) above may order the forfeiture of any money or other property which, at the time of the offence, he had in his possession or under his control for the use or benefit of a proscribed organisation.

(5) The court shall not under this section make an order forfeiting any money or other property unless the court considers that the money or property may, unless forfeited, be applied or used as mentioned in section 9(1) above but the court may, in the absence of evidence to the contrary, assume that any money or property may be applied or used as there mentioned.

(6) Where a person other than the convicted person claims to be the owner of or otherwise interested in anything which can be forfeited by an order under this section, the court shall, before making such an order in respect of it, give him an opportunity to be heard.

(7) A court in Scotland shall not make an order under subsection (2), (3) or (4) above except on the application of the prosecutor when he moves for sentence; and for the purposes of any appeal or review an order under any of those subsections made by a court in Scotland is a sentence.

(8) Schedule 4 to this Act shall have effect in relation to orders under this section.

PART IV
[POWERS OF ARREST, STOP AND SEARCH, DETENTION AND CONTROL OF ENTRY]

[13A Powers to stop and search vehicles etc. and persons

(1) Where it appears to—

(a) any officer of police of or above the rank of commander of the metropolitan police, as respects the metropolitan police [district];

(b) any officer of police of or above the rank of commander of the City of London police, as respects the City of London; or

(c) any officer of police of or above the rank of assistant chief constable for any other police area,

that it is expedient to do so in order to prevent acts of terrorism to which this section applies he may give an authorisation that the powers to stop and search vehicles and persons conferred by this section shall be exercisable at any place within his area or a specified locality in his area for a specified period not exceeding twenty eight days.

(2) The acts of terrorism to which this section applies are—

(a) acts of terrorism connected with the affairs of Northern Ireland; and

(b) acts of terrorism of any other description except acts connected solely with the affairs of the United Kingdom or any part of the United Kingdom other than Northern Ireland.

(3) This section confers on any constable in uniform power—

(a) to stop any vehicle;

(b) to search any vehicle, its driver or any passenger for articles of a kind which could be used for a purpose connected with the commission, preparation or instigation of acts of terrorism to which this section applies;

(c) . . .

[(4) A constable may exercise his powers under this section whether or not he has any grounds for suspecting the presence of articles of that kind.

(4A) Nothing in this section authorises a constable to require a person to remove any of his clothing in public other than any headgear, footwear, outer coat, jacket or gloves.]

(5) This section applies (with the necessary modifications) to ships and aircraft as it applies to vehicles.

(6) A person is gulity of an offence if he—

(a) fails to stop . . . the vehicle when required to do so by a constable in the exercise of his powers under this section; or

(b) wilfully obstructs a constable in the exercise of those powers.

(7) A person guilty of a offence under subsection (6) above shall be liable on summary conviction to imprisonment for a term not exceeding six months or a fine not exceeding level 5 on the standard scale or both.

(8) If it appears to a police officer of the rank [mentioned] in subsection (1)(a), (b) or (c) (as the case may be) that the exercise of the powers conferred by this section ought to continue beyond the period for which their exercise has been authorised under this section he may, from time to time, authorise the exercise of those powers for a further period, not exceeding twenty eight days.

(9) Where a vehicle is stopped by a constable under this section, the driver shall be entitled to obtain a written statement that the vehicle was stopped under the powers conferred by this section if he applies for such a statement not later than the end of the period of twelve months from the day on which the vehicle was stopped. . . .

[(10) An authorisation under this section may be given in writing or orally but if given orally must be confirmed in writing by the person giving it as soon as is reasonably practicable.

(10A) In this section "specified" means specified in an authorisation under this section.]

(11) Nothing in this section affects the exercise by constables of any power to stop vehicles for purposes other than those specified in subsection (1) above.]

[13B Power to stop and search pedestrians

(1) Where it appears to a police officer of the rank mentioned in subsection (1)(a), (b) or (as the case may be) (c) of section 13A above that it is expedient to do so in order

to prevent acts of terrorism to which that section applies, he may give an authorisation that the powers to stop and search persons conferred by this section shall be exercisable at any place within his area or a locality in his area which is specified in the authorisation.

(2) This section confers on any constable in uniform power to stop any pedestrian and search him, or anything carried by him, for articles of a kind which could be used for a purpose connected with the commission, preparation or instigation of such acts of terrorism.

(3) A constable may exercise his powers under this section whether or not he has any grounds for suspecting the presence of articles of that kind.

(4) Nothing in this section authorises a constable to require a person to remove any of his clothing in public other than any headgear, foot-wear, outer coat, jacket or gloves.

(5) A person is guilty of an offence if he—

(a) fails to stop when required to do so by a constable in the exercise of his powers under this section; or

(b) wilfully obstructs a constable in the exercise of those powers.

(6) A person guilty of an offence under subsection (5) above shall be liable on summary conviction to imprisonment for a term not exceeding six months or a fine not exceeding level 5 on the standard scale or both.

(7) An authorisation under this section may be given in writing or orally but if given orally must be confirmed in writing by the person giving it as soon as is reasonably practicable.

(8) A person giving an authorisation under this section must cause the Secretary of State to be informed, as soon as is reasonably practicable, that it was given.

(9) An authorisation under this section—

(a) may be cancelled by the Secretary of State with effect from such time as he may direct;

(b) ceases to have effect if it is not confirmed by the Secretary of State before the end of the period of 48 hours beginning with the time when it was given; but

(c) if confirmed, continues in force—

(i) for such period, not exceeding 28 days beginning with the day on which it was given, as may be specified in the authorisation; or

(ii) for such shorter period as the Secretary of State may direct.

(10) If a person is stopped by a constable under this section, he shall be entitled to obtain a written statement that he was stopped under the powers conferred by this section if he applies for such a statement not later than the end of the period of twelve months from the day on which he was stopped.].

14 Arrest and detention of suspected persons

(1) Subject to subsection (2) below, a constable may arrest without warrant a person whom he has reasonable grounds for suspecting to be—

(a) a person guilty of an offence under section 2, 8, 9, 10 or 11 above;

(b) a person who is or has been concerned in the commission, preparation or instigation of acts of terrorism to which this section applies; or

(c) a person subject to an exclusion order.

(2) The acts of terrorism to which this section applies are—

(a) acts of terrorism connected with the affairs of Northern Ireland; and

(b) acts of terrorism of any other description except acts connected solely with the affairs of the United Kingdom or any part of the United Kingdom other than Northern Ireland.

(3) The power of arrest conferred by subsection (1)(c) above is exercisable only—

(a) in Great Britain if the exclusion order was made under section 5 above; and

(b) in Northern Ireland if it was made under section 6 above.

(4) Subject to subsection (5) below, a person arrested under this section shall not be detained in right of the arrest for more than forty-eight hours after his arrest.

(5) The Secretary of State may, in any particular case, extend the period of forty-eight hours mentioned in subsection (4) above by a period or periods specified by him, but any such further period or periods shall not exceed five days in all and if an application for such an extension is made the person detained shall as soon as practicable be given written notice of that fact and of the time when the application was made.

(6) The exercise of the detention powers conferred by this section shall be subject to supervision in accordance with Schedule 3 to this Act.

(7) The provisions of this section are without prejudice to any power of arrest exercisable apart from this section.

15 Provisions supplementary to s. 14

(1) If a justice of the peace is satisfied that there are reasonable grounds for suspecting that a person whom a constable believes to be liable to arrest under section 14(1)(b) above is to be found on any premises he may grant a search warrant authorising any constable to enter those premises for the purposes of searching for and arresting that person.

(2) In Scotland the power to issue a warrant under subsection (1) above shall be exercised by a sheriff or a justice of the peace, an application for such a warrant shall be supported by evidence on oath and a warrant shall not authorise a constable to enter any premises unless he is a constable for the police area in which they are situated.

(3) In any circumstances in which a constable has power under section 14 above to arrest a person, he may also, for the purpose of ascertaining whether he has in his possession any document or other article which may constitute evidence that he is a person liable to arrest, stop that person and search him.

(4) Where a constable has arrested a person under that section for any reason other than the commission of a criminal offence, he, or any other constable, may search him for the purpose of ascertaining whether he has in his possession any document or other article which may constitute evidence that he is a person liable to arrest.

(5) A search of a person under subsection (3) or (4) above may only be carried out by a person of the same sex.

(6)-(14) * * * * *

16-16D * * * * *

PART V
INFORMATION, PROCEEDINGS AND INTERPRETATION

17 Investigation of terrorist activities

(1) Schedule 7 to this Act shall have effect for conferring powers to obtain information for the purposes of terrorist investigations, that is to say—

(a) investigations into—

(i) the commission, preparation or instigation of acts of terrorism to which section 14 above applies; or

(ii) any other act which appears to have been done in furtherance of or in connection with such acts of terrorism, including any act which appears to constitute an offence under section 2, 9, 10 [, 11, 18 or 18A of this Act] or [section 29 or 30 of the Northern Ireland (Emergency Provisions) Act 1996]; or

(iii) without prejudice to sub-paragraph (ii) above, the resources of a proscribed organisation within the meaning of this Act or a proscribed organisation for the purposes of [section 30 of the said Act of 1996]; and

(b) investigations into whether there are grounds justifying the making of an order under section 1(2)(a) above or [section 30(3) of the Act of 1996].

[(2) A person is guilty of an offence if, knowing or having reasonable cause to suspect that a constable is acting, or is proposing to act, in connection with a terrorist investigation which is being, or is about to be, conducted, he—

(a) discloses to any other person information or any other matter which is likely to prejudice the investigation or proposed investigation, or

(b) falsifies, conceals or destroys or otherwise disposes of, or causes or permits the falsification, concealment, destruction or disposal of, material which is or is likely to be relevant to the investigation, or proposed investigation.

(2A) A person is guilty of an offence if, knowing or having reasonable cause to suspect that a disclosure ("the disclosure") has been made to a constable under section 12, 18 or 18A of this Act . . ., he—

(a) discloses to any other person information or any other matter which is likely to prejudice any investigation which might be conducted following the disclosure; or

(b) falsifies, conceals or destroys or otherwise disposes of, or causes or permits the falsification, concealment, destruction or disposal of, material which is or is likely to be relevant to any such investigation.

(2B) A person is guilty or an offence if, knowing or having reasonable cause to suspect that a disclosure ("the disclosure") of a kind mentioned in section 12(4) or 18A(5) of this Act . . . has been made, he—

(a) discloses to any person information or any other matter which is likely to prejudice any investigation which might be conducted following the disclosure; or

(b) falsifies, conceals or destroys or otherwise disposes of, or causes or permits the falsification, concealment, destruction or disposal of, material which is or is likely to be relevant to any such investigation.

(2C) Nothing in subsections (2) to (2B) above makes it an offence for a professional legal adviser to disclose any information or other matter—

(a) to, or to a representative of, a client of his in connection with the giving by the adviser of legal advice to the client; or

(b) to any person—

(i) in contemplation of, or in connection with, legal proceedings; and

(ii) for the purpose of those proceedings.

(2D) Subsection (2C) above does not apply in relation to any information or other matter which is disclosed with a view to furthering any criminal purpose.

(2E) No constable or other person shall be guilty of an offence under this section in respect of anything done by him in the course of acting in connection with the enforcement, or intended enforcement, of any provision of this Act or of any other enactment relating to terrorism or the proceeds or resources of terrorism.]

(3) In proceedings against a person for an offence under subsection (2)(a) above it is a defence to prove—

(a) that he did not know and had no reasonable cause to suspect that the disclosure was likely to prejudice the investigation [or proposed investigation]; or

(b) that he had lawful authority or reasonable excuse for making the disclosure.

[(3A) In proceedings against a person for an offence under subsection (2A)(a) or (2B)(a) above it is a defence to prove—

(a) that he did not know and had no reasonable cause to suspect that his disclosure was likely to prejudice the investigation in question; or

(b) that he had lawful authority or reasonable excuse for making his disclosure.]

(4) In proceedings against a person for an offence under subsection (2)(b) above it is a defence to prove that he had no intention of concealing any information contained in the material in question from [any person conducting, or likely to be conducting, the investigation or proposed investigation].

[(4A) In proceedings against a person for an offence under subsection (2A)(b) or (2B)(b) above, it is a defence to prove that he had no intention of concealing any information contained in the material in question from any person who might carry out the investigation in question.]

(5) A person guilty of an offence under subsection (2) [(2A) or (2B)] above is liable—

(a) on conviction on indictment, to imprisonment for a term not exceeding five years or a fine or both;

(b) on summary conviction, to imprisonment for a term not exceeding six months or a fine not exceeding the statutory maximum or both.

[(6) For the purposes of subsection (1) above, as it applies in relation to any offence under section 18 or 18A below . . ., "act" includes omission.]

18 * * * * *

18A Failure to disclose knowledge or suspicion of offences under sections 9 to 11

(1) A person is guilty of an offence if—

(a) he knows, or suspects, that another person is providing financial assistance for terrorism;

(b) the information, or other matter, on which that knowledge or suspicion is based came to his attention in the course of his trade, profession, business or employment; and

(c) he does not disclose the information or other matter to a constable as soon as is reasonably practicable after it comes to his attention.

(2) Subsection (1) above does not make it an offence for a professional legal adviser to fail to disclose any information or other matter which has come to him in privileged circumstances.

(3) It is a defence to a charge of committing an offence under this section that the person charged had a reasonable excuse for not disclosing the information or other matter in question.

(4) Where a person discloses to a constable—

(a) his suspicion or belief that another person is providing financial assistance for terrorism; or

(b) any information or other matter on which that suspicion or belief is based;

the disclosure shall not be treated as a breach of any restriction imposed by statute or otherwise.

(5) Without prejudice to subsection (3) or (4) above, in the case of a person who was in employment at the relevant time, it is a defence to a charge of committing an offence under this section that he disclosed the information or other matter in question to the appropriate person in accordance with the procedure established by his employer for the making of such disclosures.

(6) A disclosure to which subsection (5) above applies shall not be treated as a breach of any restriction imposed by statute or otherwise.

(7) In this section "providing financial assistance for terrorism" means doing any act which constitutes an offence under section 9, 10 or 11 above or, in the case of an act done otherwise than in the United Kingdom, which would constitute such an offence if done in the United Kingdom.

(8) For the purposes of subsection (7) above, having possession of any property shall be taken to be doing an act in relation to it.

(9) For the purposes of this section, any information or other matter comes to a professional legal adviser in privileged circumstances if it is communicated, or given, to him—

(a) by, or by a representative of, a client of his in connection with the giving by the adviser of legal advice to the client;

(b) by, or by a representative of, a person seeking legal advice from the adviser; or

(c) by any person—
(i) in contemplation of, or in connection with, legal proceedings; and
(ii) for the purpose of those proceedings.

(10) No information or other matter shall be treated as coming to a professional legal adviser in privileged circumstances if it is communicated or given with a view to furthering any criminal purpose.

(11) A person guilty of an offence under this section shall be liable—

(a) on summary conviction, to imprisonment for a term not exceeding six months or a fine not exceeding the statutory maximum or to both; or

(b) on conviction on indictment, to imprisonment for a term not exceeding five years or a fine or to both.]

19-28 * * * * *

SCHEDULES

Section 1

SCHEDULE 1
PROSCRIBED ORGANISATIONS

Irish Republican Army
Irish National Liberation Army

Section 4(4)

SCHEDULE 2
EXCLUSION ORDERS

Duration

1.—(1) An exclusion order may be revoked at any time by a further order made by the Secretary of State.

(2) An exclusion order shall, unless revoked earlier, expire at the end of the period of three years beginning with the day on which it is made.

(3) The fact that an exclusion order against a person has been revoked or has expired shall not prevent the making of a further exclusion order against him.

[(4) The fact that the Secretary of State has decided at any time not to make an exclusion order against a person on whom a notice has been served under paragraph 2(1) below shall not prevent the Secretary of State from making an exclusion order against him after a further notice has been served on him under that provision.]

[*Notice that exclusion order is being considered*

2.—(1) Where the Secretary of State is considering whether to make an exclusion order against a person—

(a) if the person is in the United Kingdom, notice in writing shall be served on him that the Secretary of State is considering that question; and

(b) if the person is not in the United Kingdom, notice in writing may be served on him that the Secretary of State is considering that question.

(2) A notice under sub-paragraph (1) above shall—

(a) specify whether the order under consideration is an order under section 5, 6 or 7 of this Act; and

(b) set out the rights afforded by paragraph 4 below and specify the manner in which those rights are to be exercised.

(3) Where a person on whom notice is served under sub-paragraph (1) above is not for the time being detained by virtue of this Act, the notice may be served on him by posting it to him at his last known address.

Advice

3. Where notice is served on a person under paragraph 2(1) above, the matter shall be referred for the advice of one or more persons nominated by the Secretary of State.

Representations and interview

4.—(1) Where a person on whom notice is served under paragraph 2(1) above objects to the making against him of the exclusion order under consideration, he may—

(a) make representations in writing to the Secretary of State setting out the grounds of his objections; and

(b) include in those representations a request for a personal interview with the person or persons nominated by the Secretary of State under paragraph 3 above.

(2) The person on whom the notice is served may exercise the rights conferred by sub-paragraph (1) above—

(a) if he is outside the relevant territory when the notice is served, within fourteen days of the service of the notice;

(b) if he is inside the relevant territory when the notice is served but departs with the Secretary of State's approval within seven days of the service of the notice, within fourteen days of his departure; and

(c) in any other case, within seven days of the service of the notice.

(3) In sub-paragraph (2) above "the relevant territory" means—

(a) Great Britain if the notice relates to the making of an order under section 5 of this Act;

(b) Northern Ireland if it relates to the making of an order under section 6 of this Act; and

(c) the United Kingdom if it relates to the making of an order under section 7 of this Act.

(4) A person who requests a personal interview under sub-paragraph (1)(b) above shall be granted one unless—

(a) sub-paragraph (2)(a) or (b) above applies to him; and

(b) it appears to the Secretary of State that it is not reasonably practicable to grant him such an interview in an appropriate country or territory within a reasonable period from the date on which he made his representations.

(5) Where, in the case of a person to whom sub-paragraph (2)(a) or (b) above applies, it appears to the Secretary of State that it is reasonably practicable to grant him a personal interview in more than one appropriate country or territory, the Secretary of State may grant him the personal interview in whichever of them he thinks fit.

(6) In sub-paragraphs (4) and (5) above "appropriate country or territory" means—

(a) Northern Ireland or the Republic of Ireland if the notice served on the person under paragraph 2(1) above relates to the making of an order under section 5 of this Act;

(b) Great Britain or the Republic of Ireland if it relates to the making of an order under section 6 of this Act; and

(c) the Republic of Ireland if it relates to the making of an order under section 7 of this Act.

(7) It is for the Secretary of State to determine the place in any country or territory at which a personal interview is to be granted under this paragraph.

Making of exclusion order

5.—(1) In deciding whether to make an exclusion order against any person, the Secretary of State shall take into account everything which appears to him to be relevant; and where a notice has been served on the person concerned under paragraph 2(1) above the Secretary of State shall in particular take account of—

(a) the advice of the person or persons to whom the matter was referred under paragraph 3 above;

(b) any representations made by the person under paragraph 4 above; and

(c) the report of any personal interview granted under that paragraph.

(2) The question whether to make an exclusion order against a person on whom notice has been served under paragraph 2(1) above shall be decided as soon as is reasonably practicable after—

(a) the Secretary of Sate has received the advice of the person or persons to whom the matter was referred under paragraph 3 above; and

(b) sub-paragraph (3) below is satisfied.

(3) This sub-paragraph is satisfied if—

(a) the Secretary of State has received representations made by the person under paragraph 4 above and the report of any personal interview granted under that paragraph;

(b) the Secretary of State has received from the person a statement in writing that he does not intend to make representations under that paragraph; or

(c) the period during which the person may make representations under that paragraph has expired.

(4) If the Secretary of State—

(a) makes an exclusion order against a person; or

(b) decides not to make an exclusion order against a person on whom notice has been served under paragraph 2(1) above,

notice in writing of the making of the order or the decision not to make an order shall be served on him if it is reasonably practicable to do so.

Detention pending decision whether to make exclusion order

5A.—(1) A person on whom notice has been served under paragraph 2(1) above may be detained under the authority of the Secretary of State until the Secretary of State has either made an exclusion order against him or decided not to make an exclusion order against him.

(2) A person liable to be detained under sub-paragraph (1) above may be arrested without warrant by an examining officer.

(3) The power of detention and the power of arrest conferred by sub-paragraphs (1) and (2) above are exercisable only—

(a) in Great Britain if the notice relates to the making of an order under section 5 of this Act; and

(b) in Northern Ireland if it relates to the making of an order under section 6 of this Act.

(4) A person may be removed from a vehicle for detention under this paragraph.]

6.-9. ★ ★ ★ ★ ★

SCHEDULES 3-6

★ ★ ★ ★ ★

Section 17

SCHEDULE 7
TERRORIST INVESTIGATIONS

PART I
ENGLAND, WALES AND NORTHERN IRELAND

Interpretation

1. In this Part of this Schedule a "terrorist investigation" means any investigation to which section 17(1) of this Act applies and "items subject to legal privilege", "excluded material" and "special procedure material" have the meanings given in sections 10 to 14 of the Police and Criminal Evidence Act 1984.

Search for material other than excluded or special procedure material

2.—(1) A justice of the peace may, on an application made by a constable, issue a warrant under this paragraph if satisfied that a terrorist investigation is being carried out and that there are reasonable grounds for believing—

(a) that there is material on premises specified in the application which is likely to be of substantial value (whether by itself or together with other material) to the investigation;

(b) that the material does not consist of or include items subject to legal privilege, excluded material or special procedure material; and

(c) that any of the conditions in sub-paragraph (2) below are fulfilled.

(2) The conditions referred to in sub-paragraph (1)(c) above are—

(a) that it is not practicable to communicate with any person entitled to grant entry to the premises;

(b) that it is practicable to communicate with a person entitled to grant entry to the premises but it is not practicable to communicate with any person entitled to grant access to the material;

(c) that entry to the premises will not be granted unless a warrant is produced;

(d) that the purpose of a search may be frustrated or seriously prejudiced unless a constable arriving at the premises can secure immediate entry to them.

(3) A warrant under this paragraph shall authorise a constable to enter the premises specified in the warrant and to search the premises and any person found there and to seize and retain anything found there or on any such person, other than items subject to legal privilege, if he has reasonable grounds for believing—

(a) that it is likely to be of substantial value (whether by itself or together with other material) to the investigation; and

(b) that it is necessary to seize it in order to prevent it being concealed, lost, damaged, altered or destroyed.

(4) In Northern Ireland an application for a warrant under this paragraph shall be made by a complaint on oath.

[*Search of non-residential premises*

2A.—(1) A justice of the peace may, on an application made by a police officer of at least the rank of superintendent, issue a warrant under this paragraph if satisfied that a terrorist investigation is being carried out and that there are reasonable grounds for believing—

(a) that there is material which is likely to be of substantial value (whether by itself or together with other material) to the investigation to be found on one or more of the premises specified in the application; and

(b) that the material does not consist of or include items subject to legal privilege, excluded material or special procedure material.

(2) The officer making an application under this paragraph may not include in the premises specified in the application any which he has reasonable cause to believe are used wholly or mainly as a dwelling.

(3) A warrant under this paragraph shall authorise a constable to enter any of the premises specified in the warrant and to search the premises and any person found there and to seize and retain anything found there or on any such person, other than an item subject to legal privilege, if he has reasonable grounds for believing—

(a) that it is likely to be of substantial value (whether by itself or together with other material) to the investigation; and

(b) that it is necessary to seize it in order to prevent it from being concealed, lost, damaged, altered or destroyed.

(4) Entry and search under a warrant issued under this paragraph must be within 24 hours from the time when the warrant is issued.]

3., 4. * * * * *

Search for excluded or special procedure material

5.—(1) A constable may apply to a Circuit judge for a warrant under this paragraph in relation to specified premises.

(2) On such an application the judge may issue a warrant under this paragraph if satisfied—

(a) that an order made under paragraph 3 above in relation to material on the premises has not been complied with; or

(b) that there are reasonable grounds for believing that there is on the premises material consisting of or including excluded material or special procedure material, that it does not include items subject to legal privilege and that the conditions in sub-paragraph (5) of that paragraph and the condition in sub-paragraph (3) below are fulfilled in respect of that material.

(3) The condition referred to in sub-paragraph (2)(b) above is that it would not be appropriate to make an order under paragraph 3 above in relation to the material because—

(a) it is not practicable to communicate with any person entitled to produce the material; or

(b) it is not practicable to communicate with any person entitled to grant access to the material or entitled to grant entry to the premises on which the material is situated; or

(c) the investigation for the purposes of which the application is made might be seriously prejudiced unless a constable could secure immediate access to the material.

(4) A warrant under this paragraph shall authorise a constable to enter the premises specified in the warrant and to search the premises and any person found there and to seize and retain anything found there or on any such person, other than items subject to legal privilege, if he has reasonable grounds for believing that it is likely to be of substantial value (whether by itself or together with other material) to the investigation for the purposes of which the application was made.

(5) In Northern Ireland the power to issue a warrant under this paragraph shall be exercised by a county court judge.

6. * * * * *

Urgent cases

7.—(1) If a police officer of at least the rank of superintendent has reasonable grounds for believing that the case is one of great emergency and that in the interests of the State immediate action is necessary, he may by a written order signed by him give to any constable the authority which may be given by a search warrant under paragraph 2 [, 2A] or 5 above.

(2) Where an authority is given under this paragraph particulars of the case shall be notified as soon as may be to the Secretary of State.

(3) An order under this paragraph may not authorise a search for items subject to legal privilege.

(4) If such a police officer as is mentioned in sub-paragraph (1) above has reasonable grounds for believing that the case is such as is there mentioned he may by a notice in writing signed by him require any person specified in the notice to provide an explanation of any material seized in pursuance of an order under the paragraph.

(5) Any person who without reasonable excuse fails to comply with a notice under sub-paragraph (4) above is guilty of an offence and liable on summary conviction to

imprisonment for a term not exceeding six months or a fine not exceeding level 5 on the standard scale or both.

(6) Sub-paragraphs (2) to (5) of paragraph 6 above shall apply to a requirement imposed under sub-paragraph (4) above as they apply to a requirement under that paragraph.

★★★★★

SECURITY SERVICE ACT 1989
(1989, c. 5)

An Act to place the Security Service on a statutory basis; to enable certain actions to be taken on the authority of warrants issued by the Secretary of State, with provision for the issue of such warrants to be kept under review by a Commissioner; to establish a procedure for the investigation by a Tribunal or, in some cases, by the Commissioner of complaints about the Service; and for connected purposes. [27 April 1989]

Territorial extent United Kingdom

1 The Security Service

(1) There shall continue to be a Security Service (in this Act referred to as "the Service") under the authority of the Secretary of State.

(2) The function of the Service shall be the protection of national security and, in particular, its protection against threats from espionage, terrorism and sabotage, from the activities of agents of foreign powers and from actions intended to overthrow or undermine parliamentary democracy by political, industrial or violent means.

(3) It shall also be the function of the Service to safeguard the economic well-being of the United Kingdom against threats posed by the actions or intentions of persons outside the British Islands.

[(4) It shall also be the function of the Service to act in support of the activities of police forces and other law enforcement agencies in the prevention and detection of serious crime.]

2 The Director-General

(1) The operations of the Service shall continue to be under the control of a Director-General appointed by the Secretary of State.

(2) The Director-General shall be responsible for the efficiency of the Service and it shall be his duty to ensure—

(a) that there are arrangements for securing that no information is obtained by the Service except so far as necessary for the proper discharge of its functions or disclosed by it except so far as necessary for that purpose or for the purpose of preventing or detecting serious crime [or for the purpose of any criminal proceedings]; and

(b) that the Service does not take any action to further the interests of any political party]; and

(c) that there are arrangements, agreed with a person designated by the Secretary of State, for co-ordinating the activities of the Service in pursuance of section 1 (4) of this Act with the activities of police forces and other law enforcement agencies.]

(3) The arrangements mentioned in subsection (2)(a) above shall be such as to ensure that information in the possession of the Service is not disclosed for use in determining whether a person should be employed, or continue to be employed, by any person, or in any office or capacity, except in accordance with provisions in that behalf approved by the Secretary of State.

(3A), (3B) ★★★★★

(4) The Director-General shall make an annual report on the work of the Service to the Prime Minister and the Secretary of State and may at any time report to either of them on any matter relating to its work.

3 . . .

4 The Security Service Commissioner

(1) The Prime Minister shall appoint as a Commissioner for the purposes of this Act a person who holds or has held high judicial office within the meaning of the Appellate Jurisdiction Act 1876.

(2) The Commissioner shall hold office in accordance with the terms of his appointment and there shall be paid to him by the Secretary of State such allowances as the Treasury may determine.

(3) In addition to his functions under the subsequent provisions of this Act the Commissioner shall keep under review the exercise by the Secretary of State of his [powers, so far as they relate to applications made by the Service, under sections 5 and 6 of the Intelligence Services Act 1994.]

(4) It shall be the duty of every member of the Service and of every official of the department of the Secretary of State to disclose or give to the Commissioner such documents or information as he may require for the purpose of enabling him to discharge his functions.

(5) The Commissioner shall make an annual report on the discharge of his functions to the Prime Minister and may at any time report to him on any matter relating to his discharge of those functions.

(6) The Prime Minister shall lay before each House of Parliament a copy of each annual report made by the Commissioner under subsection (5) above together with a statement as to whether any matter has been excluded from that copy in pursuance of subsection (7) below.

(7), (8) ★★★★★

5 Investigation of complaints

(1) There shall be a Tribunal for the purpose of investigating complaints about the Service in the manner specified in Schedule 2 to this Act.

(2) ★★★★★

(3) The Commissioner shall have the functions conferred on him by Schedule 1 to this Act and give the Tribunal all such assistance in discharging their functions under that Schedule as they may require.

(4) The decisions of the Tribunal and the Commissioner under that Schedule (including decisions as to their jurisdictions) shall not be subject to appeal or liable to be questioned in any court.

★★★★★

SCHEDULES

Section 5(1)

SCHEDULE 1
INVESTIGATION OF COMPLAINTS

Preliminary

1. Any person may complain to the Tribunal if he is aggrieved by anything which he believes the Service has done in relation to him or to any property of his; and, unless the Tribunal consider that the complaint is frivolous or vexatious, they shall investigate it in accordance with this Schedule.

Investigations and determinations

2.—(1) The Tribunal shall investigate whether the complainant has been the subject of inquiries by the Service.

(2) If the Tribunal find that the Service has made inquiries about the complainant but that those inquiries had ceased at the time when the complaint was made, they shall

determine whether, at the time when the inquiries were instituted, the Service had reasonable grounds for deciding to institute inquiries about the complainant in the discharge of its functions.

(3) If the Tribunal find that inquiries by the Service about the complainant were continuing at the time when the complaint was made, they shall determine whether, at that time, the Service had reasonable grounds for deciding to continue inquiries about the complainant in the discharge of its functions.

(4) Where it appears to the Tribunal that the inquiries had been or were being made about the complainant on the ground of his membership of a category of persons regarded by the Service as requiring investigation in the discharge of its functions, the Tribunal shall regard the Service as having reasonable grounds for deciding to institute or continue inquiries about the complainant if the Tribunal consider that the Service had reasonable grounds for believing him to be a member of that category.

3. If and so far as the complainant alleges that the Service has disclosed information for use in determining whether he should be employed, or continue to be employed, by any person or in any office or capacity specified by him, the Tribunal shall investigate whether the Service has disclosed information for that purpose and, if the Tribunal find that it has done so, they shall determine whether the Service had reasonable grounds for believing the information to be true.

4.—(1) If and so far as the complainant alleges that anything has been done by the Service in relation to any property of his, the Tribunal shall refer the complaint to the Commissioner who shall investigate whether a warrant has been issued under section 3 of this Act [or section 5 of the Intelligence Services Act 1994] in respect of that property and if he finds that such a warrant has been issued he shall, applying the principles applied by a court on an application for judicial review, determine whether the Secretary of State was acting properly in issuing or renewing the warrant.

(2) The Commissioner shall inform the Tribunal of his conclusion on any complaint so far as referred to him under this paragraph.

Report of conclusions

5.—(1) Where the Tribunal determine under paragraph 2 or 3 above that the Service did not have reasonable grounds for the decision or belief in question, they shall—

(a) give notice to the complainant that they have made a determination in his favour under that paragraph; and

(b) make a report of their findings to the secretary of State and to the Commissioner.

(2) The Tribunal shall also give notice to the complainant of any determination in his favour by the Commissioner under paragraph 4 above.

(3) Where in the case of any complaint no such determination as is mentioned in sub-paragraph (1) or (2) above is made by the Tribunal or the Commissioner the Tribunal shall give notice to the complainant that no determination in his favour has been made on his complaint.

6., 7. ★ ★ ★ ★ ★

Supplementary

8.—(1) The persons who may complain to the Tribunal under this Schedule include any organisation and any association or combination of persons.

(2) References in this Schedule to a complainant's property include references to any place where the complainant resides or works.

9. ★ ★ ★ ★ ★

SCHEDULE 2

★ ★ ★ ★ ★

BRITISH NATIONALITY (HONG KONG) ACT 1990
(1990, c. 34)

An Act to provide for the acquisition of British citizenship by selected Hong Kong residents, their spouses and minor children. [26 July 1990]

1 Acquisition of British citizenship

(1) Subject to the provisions of this section, the Secretary of State shall register as British citizens up to 50,000 persons recommended to him for that purpose by the Governor of Hong Kong under a scheme or schemes made and approved in accordance with Schedule 1 to this Act.

(2) No person shall be registered under subsection (1) above after 30th June 1997.

(3) The Secretary of State may direct the Governor to make not more than a specified proportion of his recommendations in a period or periods specified in the direction; and any such direction may make different provision in relation to recommendations in respect of persons of different classes or descriptions.

(4) Schedule 2 to this Act shall have effect for enabling the spouse and minor children of a person registered under subsection (1) above to acquire British citizenship by registration; and no spouse or minor child to whom Schedule 2 to this Act applies shall be registered under subsection (1) above.

(5) Neither the Secretary of State nor the Governor shall be required to give any reason for any decision made by him in the exercise of a discretion vested in him by or under this Act and no such decision shall be subject to appeal or liable to be questioned in any court.

2 Consequential nationality provisions

(1) A person who is registered as a British citizen by virtue of section 1(1) above shall be treated for the purposes of the British Nationality Act 1981 (in this Act referred to as "the principal Act") as a British citizen otherwise than by descent; and a person who is registered as a British citizen by virtue of Schedule 2 to this Act shall be treated for the purposes of that Act as a British citizen by descent.

(2), (3) ★ ★ ★ ★ ★

3-5 ★ ★ ★ ★ ★

6 Short title, savings, commencement and extent

(1) This Act may be cited as the British Nationality (Hong Kong) Act 1990.

(2) A person shall not under this Act be recommended for registration as a British citizen by the Governor of Hong Kong or registered as such a citizen by the Secretary of State if the Governor or, as the case may be, the Secretary of State has reason to believe that he is not of good character.

Schedules ★ ★ ★ ★ ★

BROADCASTING ACT 1990
(1990, c. 42)

An Act to make new provision with respect to the provision and regulation of independent television and sound programme services and of other services provided on television or radio frequencies; to make provision with respect to the provision and regulation of local delivery services; to amend in other respects the law relating to broadcasting and the provision of television and sound programme services and to make provision with respect to the supply and use of information about programmes; to make provision with respect to the transfer of the property, rights and liabilities of the Independent Broadcasting Authority and the Cable Authority and the dissolution of those bodies; to make new provision relating to the Broadcasting Complaints Commission; to provide for the establishment and functions of a Broadcasting Standards Council; to amend the Wireless Telegraphy Acts 1949 to 1967 and the Marine, &c., Broadcasting (Offences) Act 1967; to revoke a class licence granted under the Telecommunications Act 1984 to run broadcast relay systems; and for connected purposes.

[1 November 1990]

Territorial extent United Kingdom (in the case of materials reproduced here).

PART I
INDEPENDENT TELEVISION SERVICES

CHAPTER I
REGULATION BY COMMISSION OF TELEVISION SERVICES GENERALLY

Establishment of Independent Television Commission

1 The Independent Television Commission

(1) There shall be a commission to be called the Independent Television Commission (in this Part referred to as "the Commission").

(2) The Commission shall consist of—

(a) a chairman and a deputy chairman appointed by the Secretary of State; and

(b) such number of other members appointed by the Secretary of State, not being less than eight nor more than ten, as he may from time to time determine.

(3) * * * * *

Function of Commission

2 Regulation by Commission of provision of television services

(1) It shall be the function of the Commission to regulate, in accordance with this Part [and Part I of the Broadcasting Act 1996], the provision of the following services, namely—

(a) television programme services which are provided from places in the United Kingdom by persons other than the BBC and the Welsh Authority, . . .

(b) additional services which are provided from places in the United Kingdom, and to regulate, in accordance with Part II, the provision of local delivery services (within the meaning of that Part) which are so provided,

[(c) multiplex services (as defined by section 1(1) of the Broadcasting Act 1996) which are provided from places in the United Kingdom by persons other than the BBC, and

(d) digital additional services (as defined by section 24(1) of the Broadcasting Act 1996) which are provided from places in the United Kingdom by persons other than the BBC.]

(2) It shall be the duty of the Commission—

(a) to discharge their functions under this Part and Part II [and under Part I of the Broadcasting Act 1996] as respects the licensing of the services referred to in subsection (1) in the manner in which they consider is best calculated—

(i) to ensure that a wide range of such services is available throughout the United Kingdom, and

(ii) to ensure fair and effective competition in the provision of such services and services connected with them; and

(b) to discharge their functions under this Part [and Part I of the Broadcasting Act 1996] as respects the licensing of television programme services [and multiplex services (as defined by section 1(1) of that Act)] in the manner in which they consider is best calculated to ensure the provision of such services which (taken as a whole) are of high quality and offer a wide range of programmes calculated to appeal to a variety of tastes and interests.

(3)-(6) * * * * *

3-5 * * * * *

General provisions about licensed services

6 General requirements as to licensed services

(1) The Commission shall do all that they can to secure that every licensed service complies with the following requirements, namely—

(a) that nothing is included in its programmes which offends against good taste or decency or is likely to encourage or incite to crime or to lead to disorder or to be offensive to public feeling;

(b) that any news given (in whatever form) in its programmes is presented with due accuracy and impartiality;

(c) that due impartiality is preserved on the part of the person providing the service as respects matters of political or industrial controversy or relating to current public policy;

(d) that due responsibility is exercised with respect to the content of any of its programmes which are religious programmes, and that in particular any such programmes do not involve—

(i) any improper exploitation of any susceptibilities of those watching the programmes, or

(ii) any abusive treatment of the religious views and beliefs of those belonging to a particular religion or religious denomination; and

(e) that its programmes do not include any technical device which, by using images of very brief duration or by any other means, exploits the possibility of conveying a message to, or otherwise influencing the minds of, persons watching the programmes without their being aware, or fully aware, of what has occurred.

(2)-(8) * * * * *

7 General code for programmes

(1) The Commission shall draw up, and from time to time review, a code giving guidance—

(a) as to the rules to be observed with respect to the showing of violence, or the inclusion of sounds suggestive of violence, in programmes included in licensed services, particularly when large numbers of children and young persons may be expected to be watching the programmes;

(b) as to the rules to be observed with respect to the inclusion in such programmes of appeals for donations; and

(c) as to such other matters concerning standards and practice for such programmes as the Commission may consider suitable for inclusion in the code;

and the Commission shall do all that they can to secure that the provisions of the code are observed in the provision of licensed services.

(2) In considering what other matters ought to be included in the code in pursuance of subsection (1)(c), the Commission shall have special regard to programmes included in licensed services in circumstances such that large numbers of children and young persons may be expected to be watching the programmes.

(3) The Commission shall, in drawing up or revising the code under this section, take account of such of the international obligations of the United Kingdom as the Secretary of State may notify to them for the purposes of this subsection.

(4) The Commission shall publish the code drawn up under this section, and every revision of it, in such manner as they consider appropriate.

8 General provisions as to advertisements

(1) The Commission shall do all that they can to secure that the rules specified in subsection (2) are complied with in relation to licensed services.

(2) Those rules are as follows—

(a) a licensed service must not include—

(i) any advertisement which is inserted by or on behalf of any body whose objects are wholly or mainly of a political nature,

(ii) any advertisement which is directed towards any political end, or

(iii) any advertisement which has any relation to any industrial dispute (other than an advertisement of a public service nature inserted by, or on behalf of, a government department);

(b) in the acceptance of advertisements for inclusion in a licensed service there must be no unreasonable discrimination either against or in favour of any particular advertiser; and

(c) a licensed service must not, without the previous approval of the Commission, include a programme which is sponsored by any person whose business consists, wholly or mainly, in the manufacture or supply of a product, or in the provision of a service, which the licence holder is prohibited from advertising by virtue of any provision of section 9.

(3) Nothing in subsection (2) shall be construed as prohibiting the inclusion in a licensed service of any party political broadcast which complies with the rules (so far as applicable) made by the Commission for the purposes of section 36.

(4) After consultation with the Commission the Secretary of State may make regulations amending, repealing, or adding to the rules specified in subsection (2); but no such regulations shall be made unless a draft of the regulations has been laid before and approved by a resolution of each House of Parliament.

(5) The Commission shall not act as an advertising agent.

9 Control of advertisements

(1) It shall be the duty of the Commission—

(a) after the appropriate consultation, to draw up, and from time to time review, a code—

(i) governing standards and practice in advertising and in the sponsoring of programmes, and

(ii) prescribing the advertisements and methods of advertising or sponsorship to be prohibited, or to be prohibited in particular circumstances; and

(b) to do all that they can to secure that the provisions of the code are observed in the provision of licensed services;

and the Commission may make different provision in the code for different kinds of licensed services.

(2)-(6) ★ ★ ★ ★ ★

(7) The Commission may give directions to persons holding any class of licences with respect to the times when advertisements are to be allowed.

(8) Directions under this section may be, to any degree, either general or specific and qualified or unqualified; and directions under subsection (7) may, in particular, relate to—

(a) the maximum amount of time to be given to advertisements in any hour or other period,

(b) the minimum interval which must elapse between any two periods given over to advertisements and the number of such periods to be allowed in any programme or in any hour or day,

(c) the exclusion of advertisements from a specified part of a licensed service,

and may make different provision for different parts of the day, different days of the week, different types of programmes or for other differing circumstances.

(9) The Commission shall—

(a) in drawing up or revising the code, or

(b) in giving any directions under subsection (7),

take account of such of the international obligations of the United Kingdom as the Secretary of State may notify to them for the purposes of this subsection.

10 Government control over licensed services

(1) If it appears to him to be necessary or expedient to do so in connection with his functions as such, the Secretary of State or any other Minister of the Crown may at any time by notice require the Commission to direct the holders of any licences specified in the notice to publish in their licensed services, at such times as may be specified in the notice, such announcement as is so specified, with or without visual images of any picture, scene or object mentioned in the announcement; and it shall be the duty of the Commission to comply with the notice.

(2) Where the holder of a licence publishes any announcement in pursuance of a direction under subsection (1), he may announce that he is doing so in pursuance of such a direction.

(3) The Secretary of State may at any time by notice require the Commission to direct the holders of any licences specified in the notice to refrain from including in the programmes included in their licensed services any matter or classes of matter specified in the notice; and it shall be the duty of the Commission to comply with the notice.

(4) Where the Commission—

(a) have given the holder of any licence a direction in accordance with a notice under subsection (3), or

(b) in consequence of the revocation by the Secretary of State of such a notice, have revoked such a direction,

or where such a notice has expired, the holder of the licence in question may publish in the licensed service an announcement of the giving or revocation of the direction or of the expiration of the notice, as the case may be.

(5), (6) * * * * *

11, 12 * * * * *

Prohibition on providing unlicensed television services

13 Prohibition on providing television services without a licence

(1) Subject to subsection (2), any person who provides any service falling within section 2(1)(a) or (b) without being authorised to do so by or under a licence under this Part shall be guilty of an offence.

(2) The Secretary of State may, after consultation with the Commission, by order provide that subsection (1) shall not apply to such services or descriptions of services as are specified in the order.

(3) A person guilty of an offence under this section shall be liable—

(a) on summary conviction, to a fine not exceeding the statutory maximum;

(b) on conviction on indictment, to a fine.

(4) No proceedings in respect of an offence under this section shall be instituted—

(a) in England and Wales, except by or with the consent of the Director of Public Prosecutions;

(b) in Northern Ireland, except by or with the consent of the Director of Public Prosecutions for Northern Ireland.

(5) Without prejudice to subsection (3), compliance with this section shall be enforceable by civil proceedings by the Crown for an injunction or interdict or for any other appropriate relief.

(6) Any order under this section shall be subject to annulment in pursuance of a resolution of either House of Parliament.

14-35 ★★★★★

36 Party political broadcasts

(1) Subject to subsection (2), any regional Channel 3 licence or licence to provide Channel 4 or 5 shall include—

(a) conditions requiring the licence holder to include party political broadcasts in the licensed service; and

(b) conditions requiring the licence holder to observe such rules with respect to party political broadcasts as the Commission may determine.

(2) Where any determination under section 28(3), is in force, a licence to provide Channel 5 may (but need not) include any such conditions as are mentioned in subsection (1)(a) and (b).

(3) Without prejudice to the generality of paragraph (b) of subsection (1), the Commission may determine for the purposes of that subsection—

(a) the political parties on whose behalf party political broadcasts may be made; and

(b) in relation to any political party on whose behalf such broadcasts may be made, the length and frequency of such broadcasts.

(4) Any rules made by the Commission for the purposes of this section may make different provision for different cases or circumstances.

37-141 ★★★★★

142-161 ...

162-165 ★★★★★

COURTS AND LEGAL SERVICES ACT 1990
(1990, c. 41)

An Act to make provision with respect to the procedure in, and allocation of business between, the High Court and other courts; to make provision with respect to legal services; to establish a body to be known as the Lord Chancellor's Advisory Committee on Legal Education and Conduct and a body to be known as the Authorised Conveyancing Practitioners Board; to provide for the appointment of a Legal Services Ombudsman; to make provision for the establishment of a Conveyancing Ombudsman Scheme; to provide for the establishment of Conveyancing Appeal Tribunals; to amend the law relating to judicial and related pensions and judicial and other appointments; to make provision with respect to certain officers of the Supreme Court; to amend the Solicitors Act 1974; to amend the Arbitration Act 1950; to make provision with respect to certain loans in respect of residential property; to make provision with repect to the jurisdiction of the Parliamentary Commissioner for Administration in connection with the functions of court staff; to amend the Children Act 1989 and make further provision in connection with that Act; and for connected purposes. [1 November 1990]

Territorial extent England and Wales only in the case of sections reproduced here. (Certain other provisions apply additionally to Scotland and to Northern Ireland.)

★★★★★

PART II
LEGAL SERVICES

Introductory

17 The statutory objective and the general principle

(1) The general objective of this Part is the development of legal services in England and Wales (and in particular the development of advocacy, litigation, conveyancing and

probate services) by making provision for new or better ways of providing such services and a wider choice of persons providing them, while maintaining the proper and efficient administration of justice.

(2) In this Act that objective is referred to as "the statutory objective".

(3) As a general principle the question whether a person should be granted a right of audience, or be granted a right to conduct litigation in relation to any court or proceedings, should be determined only by reference to—

(a) whether he is qualified in accordance with the educational and training requirements appropriate to the court or proceedings;

(b) whether he is a member of a professional or other body which—

(i) has rules of conduct (however described) governing the conduct of its members;

(ii) has an effective mechanism for enforcing the rules of conduct; and

(iii) is likely to enforce them;

(c) whether, in the case of a body whose members are or will be providing advocacy services, the rules of conduct make satisfactory provision in relation to the court or proceedings in question requiring any such member not to withhold those services—

(i) on the ground that the nature of the case is objectionable to him or to any section of the public;

(ii) on the ground that the conduct, opinions or beliefs of the prospective client are unacceptable to him or to any section of the public;

(iii) on any ground relating to the source of any financial support which may properly be given to the prospective client for the proceedings in question (for example, on the ground that such support will be available under the Legal Aid Act 1988); and

(d) whether the rules of conduct are, in relation to the court or proceedings, appropriate in the interests of the proper and efficient administration of justice.

(4) In this Act that principle is referred to as "the general principle".

(5) Rules of conduct which allow a member of the body in question to withhold his services if there are reasonable grounds for him to consider that, having regard to—

(a) the circumstances of the case;

(b) the nature of his practice; or

(c) his experience and standing,

he is not being offered a proper fee, are not on that account to be taken as being incompatible with the general principle.

18 The statutory duty

(1) Where any person is called upon to exercise any functions which are conferred by this Part with respect to—

(a) the granting of rights of audience;

(b) the granting of rights to conduct litigation;

(c) the approval of qualification regulations or rules of conduct; or

(d) the giving of advice with respect to any matter mentioned in paragraphs (a) to (c),

it shall be the duty of that person to exercise those functions as soon as is reasonably practicable and consistent with the provisions of this Part.

(2) A person exercising any such functions shall act in accordance with the general principle and, subject to that, shall—

(a) so far as it is possible to do so in the circumstances of the case, act to further the statutory objective; and

(b) not act in any way which would be incompatible with the statutory objective.

The Advisory Committee

19 The Lord Chancellor's Advisory Committee on Legal Education and Conduct

(1) There shall be a body corporate to be known as the Lord Chancellor's Advisory Committee on Legal Education and Conduct (in this Act referred to as "the Advisory Committee").

(2) The Advisory Committee shall consist of a Chairman, and 16 other members, appointed by the Lord Chancellor.

(3) The Chairman shall be a Lord of Appeal in Ordinary or a judge of the Supreme Court of England and Wales.

(4) Of the 16 other members of the Advisory Committee—

(a) one shall be a judge who is or has been a Circuit judge;

(b) 2 shall be practising barristers appointed after consultation with the General Council of the Bar;

(c) 2 shall be practising solicitors appointed after consultation with the Law Society;

(d) 2 shall be persons with experience in the teaching of law, appointed after consultation with such institutions concerned with the teaching of law and such persons representing teachers of law as the Lord Chancellor considers appropriate; and

(e) 9 shall be persons other than—

(i) salaried judges of any court;

(ii) practising barristers;

(iii) practising solicitors; or

(iv) teachers of law,

appointed after consultation with such organisations as the Lord Chancellor considers appropriate.

(5) In appointing any member who falls within subsection (4)(e), the Lord Chancellor shall have regard to the desirability of appointing persons who have experience in, or knowledge of—

(a) the provision of legal services;

(b) civil or criminal proceedings and the working of the courts;

(c) the maintenance of professional standards among barristers or solicitors;

(d) social conditions;

(e) consumer affairs;

(f) commercial affairs; or

(g) the maintenance of professional standards in professions other than the legal profession.

(6) The Advisory Committee shall not be regarded as the servant or agent of the Crown, or as enjoying any status, immunity or privilege of the Crown.

(7)-(9) * * * * *

20 Duties of the Advisory Committee

(1) The Advisory Committee shall have the general duty of assisting in the maintenance and development of standards in the education, training and conduct of those offering legal services.

(2), (3) * * * * *

The Legal Services Ombudsman

21 The Legal Services Ombudsman

(1) The Lord Chancellor shall appoint a person for the purpose of conducting investigations under this Act.

(2) The person appointed shall be known as "the Legal Services Ombudsman".

(3) The Legal Services Ombudsman—

(a) shall be appointed for a period of not more than three years; and

(b) shall hold and vacate office in accordance with the terms of his appointment.

(4) At the end of his term of appointment the Legal Services Ombudsman shall be eligible for re-appointment.

(5) The Legal Services Ombudsman shall not be an authorised advocate, authorised litigator, licensed conveyancer, authorised practitioner or notary.

(6) * * * * *

22 Ombudsman's functions

(1) Subject to the provisions of this Act, the Legal Services Ombudsman may investigate any allegation which is properly made to him and which relates to the manner in which a complaint made to a professional body with respect to—

(a) a person who is or was an authorised advocate, authorised litigator, licensed conveyancer, registered foreign lawyer, recognised body or duly certificated notary public and a member of that professional body; or

(b) any employee of such a person,

has been dealt with by that professional body.

(2)-(6) * * * * *

(7) The Ombudsman shall not investigate—

(a) any issue which is being or has been determined by—

(i) a court;

(ii) the Solicitors Disciplinary Tribunal;

(iii) the Disciplinary Tribunal of the Council of the Inns of Court; or

(iv) any tribunal specified in an order made by the Lord Chancellor for the purposes of this subsection; or

(b) any allegation relating to a complaint against any person which concerns an aspect of his conduct in relation to which he has immunity from any action in negligence or contract.

(8)-(11) * * * * *

23 * * * * *

24 Advisory functions

(1) The Legal Services Ombudsman may make recommendations to any professional body about the arrangements which that body has in force for the investigation of complaints made with respect to persons who are subject to that body's control.

(2) It shall be the duty of any professional body to whom a recommendation is made under this section to have regard to it.

(3) The Ombudsman may refer to the Advisory Committee any matters which come to his notice in the exercise of his functions and which appear to him to be relevant to the Committee's functions.

25-61 * * * * *

62 Immunity of advocates from actions in negligence and for breach of contract

(1) A person—

(a) who is not a barrister; but

(b) who lawfully provides any legal services in relation to any proceedings,

shall have the same immunity from liability for negligence in respect of his acts or omissions as he would have if he were a barrister lawfully providing those services.

(2) No act or omission on the part of any barrister or other person which is accorded immunity from liability for negligence shall give rise to an action for breach of any contract relating to the provision by him of the legal services in question.

63 Legal professional privilege

(1) This section applies to any communication made to or by a person who is not a barrister or solicitor at any time when that person is—

(a) providing advocacy or litigation services as an authorised advocate or authorised litigator;

(b) providing conveyancing services as an authorised practitioner; or

(c) providing probate services as a probate practitioner.

(2) Any such communication shall in any legal proceedings be privileged from disclosure in like manner as if the person in question had at all material times been acting as his client's solicitor.

(3) In subsection (1), "probate practitioner" means a person to whom section 23(1) of the Solicitors Act 1974 (unqualified person not to prepare probate papers etc.) does not apply.

★ ★ ★ ★ ★

ARMS CONTROL AND DISARMAMENT (INSPECTIONS) ACT 1991
(1991, c. 41)

An Act to facilitate the carrying out in the United Kingdom of inspections under the Protocol of Inspection incorporated in the Treaty on Conventional Armed Forces in Europe signed in Paris on 19 November 1990; and for connected purposes. [25 July 1991]

Territorial extent United Kingdom

1 Interpretation etc

(1) In this Act "the Protocol" means the Protocol on Inspection incorporated in the Treaty on Conventional Armed Forces in Europe signed in Paris on November 19, 1990.

(2) In this Act—

(a) "challenge inspection" means an inspection conducted pursuant to Section VIII of the Protocol (challenge inspections within specified areas);

(b) "inspector" has the meaning given by Section I of the Protocol (definitions); and

(c) (subject to subsection (3) below) "escort team", "inspection team" and "specified area" shall be construed, in relation to any challenge inspection, in accordance with that Section.

(3), (4) ★ ★ ★ ★ ★

2 Rights of entry etc. for purposes of challenge inspections under the Protocol

(1) Where a request to conduct a challenge inspection within any specified area in the United Kingdom—

(a) has been made under the Protocol, and

(b) has been granted by Her Majesty's Government in the United Kingdom,

the Secretary of State may issue an authorisation under this section in respect of that inspection.

(2) An authorisation under this section shall contain a description of the specified area and state the names of the members of the inspection team by whom the inspection is to be carried out.

(3) Such an authorisation shall have the effect of authorising the inspection team—

(a) to exercise within the specified area such rights of access, entry and unobstructed inspection as are conferred on them by Section VI of the Protocol, and

(b) to do such other things within that area in connection with the conduct of the inspection as they are entitled to do by virtue of that Section.

(4) Such an authorisation shall in addition have the effect of—

(a) authorising an escort team to accompany the inspection team at all times, and

(b) authorising any constable to give such assistance as the person in command of the escort team may request for the purpose of facilitating the conduct of the inspection in accordance with Section VI of the Protocol;

and the name of the person in command of the escort team shall be stated in the authorisation.

(5) * * * * *

(6) Any constable giving assistance in accordance with subsection (4)(b) may use such reasonable force as he considers necessary for the purpose mentioned in that provision.

(7) The occupier of any premises—

(a) in relation to which it is proposed to exercise a right of entry in reliance on an authorisation under this section, or

(b) on which an inspection is being carried out in reliance on such an authorisation, or a person acting on behalf of the occupier of any such premises, shall be entitled to require a copy of the authorisation to be shown to him by a member of the escort team.

(8) The validity of any authorisation purporting to be issued under this section in respect of any challenge inspection shall not be called in question in any court of law at any time before the conclusion of that inspection; and accordingly no proceedings (of whatever nature) shall be brought at any time before the conclusion of any challenge inspection if they would, if successful, have the effect of preventing, delaying or otherwise affecting the carrying out of any such inspection.

(9) If in any proceedings any question arises whether a person at any time was or was not, in relation to any challenge inspection, a member of the inspection team or (as the case may be) a member of the escort team, a certificate issued by or under the authority of the Secretary of State stating any fact relating to that question shall be conclusive evidence of that fact.

3 Offences

(1) Where an authorisation has been issued under section 2 in respect of any challenge inspection, any person who—

(a) refuses to comply with any request made by any constable for the purpose of facilitating the conduct of that inspection in accordance with Section VI of the Protocol, or

(b) wilfully obstructs any member of the inspection team or of the escort team in the conduct of that inspection in accordance with that Section,

shall be guilty of an offence and liable on summary conviction to a fine not exceeding the third level on the standard scale.

(2), (3) * * * * *

4 Exercise of powers in relation to Crown land in private occupation

(1) The powers exercisable in the case of any authorisation by virtue of section 2 shall be exercisable in relation to any Crown land only to the extent that it is land which any person is entitled to occupy by virtue of a private interest (whether it is an interest in land or arises under a licence).

(2) In subsection (1)—

"Crown land" means land in which there is a Crown interest or a Duchy interest;

"private interest" means an interest which is neither a Crown interest nor a Duchy interest;

and for this purpose—

"Crown interest" means an interest—

(a) belonging to Her Majesty in right of the Crown (including the Crown in right of Her Majesty's Government in Northern Ireland), or

(b) belonging to a government department or Northern Ireland department, or an interest held in trust for Her Majesty for the purposes of any such department; and

"Duchy interest" means an interest belonging to Her Majesty in right of the Duchy of Lancaster or belonging to the Duchy of Cornwall.

★ ★ ★ ★ ★

WAR CRIMES ACT 1991
(1991, c. 13)

An Act to confer jurisdiction on United Kingdom courts in respect of certain grave violations of the laws and customs of war committed in German-held territory during the Second World War; and for connected purposes. [9 May 1991]

Territorial extent United Kingdom

1 Jurisdiction over certain war crimes

(1) Subject to the provisions of this section, proceedings for murder, manslaughter or culpable homicide may be brought against a person in the United Kingdom irrespective of his nationality at the time of the alleged offence if that offence—

(a) was committed during the period beginning with 1st September 1939 and ending with 5th June 1945 in a place which at the time was part of Germany or under German occupation; and

(b) constituted a violation of the laws and customs of war.

(2) No proceedings shall by virtue of this section be brought against any person unless he was on 8th March 1990, or has subsequently become, a British citizen or resident in the United Kingdom, the Isle of Man or any of the Channel Islands.

(3) No proceedings shall by virtue of this section be brought in England and Wales or in Northern Ireland except by or with the consent of the Attorney General or, as the case may be, the Attorney General for Northern Ireland.

(4) ★ ★ ★ ★ ★

★ ★ ★ ★ ★

LOCAL GOVERNMENT ACT 1992
(1992, c. 19)

An Act to make new provision, by giving effect to proposals in Cm. 1599 (The Citizen's Charter) relating to publicity and competition, for securing economy, efficiency and effectiveness in the manner in which local authorities carry on certain activities; and to make new provision in relation to local government in England for effecting structural, boundary and electoral changes. [6 March 1992]

Territorial extent: England (provisions reproduced here)

★ ★ ★ ★ ★

PART II
LOCAL GOVERNMENT CHANGES FOR ENGLAND

The Local Government Commission

12 The Local Government Commission for England

(1) There shall be a body corporate to be known as the Local Government Commission for England (in this Part referred to as "the Local Government Commission") for the purpose of carrying out the functions assigned to it by section 13 below.

(2) Schedule 2 to this Act shall have effect with respect to the Local Government Commission.

Functions of the Local Government Commission

13 Duty to conduct reviews and make recommendations

(1) If the Secretary of State so directs, the Local Government Commission shall, in accordance with this Part and any directions given under it—

(a) conduct a review of such areas in England as are specified in the direction or are of a description so specified; and

(b) recommend to the Secretary of State as respects each of those areas either—

(i) that he should make such structural, boundary or electoral changes as are specified in the recommendations; or

(ii) that he should make no such changes.

(2) It shall also be the duty of the Local Government Commission—

(a) independently of any reviews under subsection (1) above, to conduct periodic reviews of every principal area in England for the purpose of determining whether recommendations should be made for electoral changes in that area; and

(b) as respects any area reviewed, to recommend to the Secretary of State either—

(i) that he should make such electoral changes as are specified in the recommendations; or

(ii) that he should make no such changes.

(3) So far as reasonably practicable, the first periodic review of any area under subsection (2) above shall be conducted not less than ten or more than fifteen years after the report of the Local Government Boundary Commission for England on a review under Schedule 9 to the 1972 Act (initial review of counties) was submitted to the Secretary of State in relation to the county in which that area, or the greater part of it, was comprised.

(4) So far as reasonably practicable, subsequent reviews under subsection (2) above shall be conducted within the period of not less than ten or more than fifteen years from the submission to the Secretary of State of the last report on a review under that subsection of any area comprising the whole or a substantial part of that area.

(5) Any structural, boundary or electoral changes recommended to the Secretary of State under this section shall be such as appear to the Local Government Commission desirable having regard to the need—

(a) to reflect the identities and interests of local communities; and

(b) to secure effective and convenient local government.

(6) The Secretary of State may give directions as to the exercise by the Local Government Commission of any functions under this section; and such directions may require that Commission to have regard to any guidance given by the Secretary of State as respects matters to be taken into account.

14 Changes that may be recommended

(1) For the purposes of this Part—

(a) a structural change is the replacement, in any non-metropolitan area, of the two principal tiers of local government with a single tier;

(b) a boundary change is any of the changes specified in subsection (3) below, whether made for the purpose of facilitating a structural change or independently of any such change; and

(c) an electoral change is a change of electoral arrangements for any local government area, whether made in consequence of any structural or boundary change or independently of any such change;

and recommendations by the Local Government Commission for any structural or boundary changes shall include such recommendations as to the matters mentioned in subsection (5) below as the Commission thinks appropriate in connection with the recommended changes.

(2)-(7) * * * * *

15 Procedure on a review

(1) As soon as reasonably practicable after being directed to conduct a review, the Local Government Commission shall take such steps as it considers sufficient to secure that persons who may be interested in the review are informed of—

(a) the direction requiring that review to be conducted;

(b) any other directions under this Part which are relevant to the review; and

(c) the period within which representations with respect to the subject-matter of the review may be made.

(2) As soon as reasonably practicable after deciding to conduct a periodic review of any area under section 13(2) above, the Local Government Commission shall take such steps as it considers sufficient to secure that persons who may be interested in the review are informed of—

(a) the fact that the Commission is to conduct a periodic review of that area;

(b) any directions under this Part which are relevant to the review; and

(c) the period within which representations with respect to the subject-matter of the review may be made.

(3) In conducting a review, the Local Government Commission shall—

(a) take into consideration any representations made to it within the period mentioned in subsection (1)(c) or (2)(c) above;

(b) prepare draft recommendations and take such steps as it considers sufficient to secure that persons who may be interested in the recommendations are informed of them and of the period within which representations with respect to them may be made;

(c) deposit copies of the draft recommendations at the principal office of any principal council [or police authority] appearing to that Commission to be likely to be affected by them; and

(d) take into consideration any representations made to that Commission within that period.

(4) As soon as the Local Government Commission is in a position to submit to the Secretary of State a report on a review, it shall—

(a) submit such a report to him together with its recommendations;

(b) take such steps as it considers sufficient to secure that persons who may be interested in the recommendations are informed of them and of the period within which they may be inspected; and

(c) deposit copies of the recommendations at the principal office of any principal council [or police authority] appearing to that Commission to be likely to be affected by them.

(5)-(8) * * * * *

16 * * * * *

Implementation of recommendations

17 Implementation of recommendations by order

(1) Where the Local Government Commission submit to the Secretary of State a report on a review together with its recommendations, he may, if he thinks fit, by order give effect to all or any of the recommendations, with or without modifications.

(2) No order under this section shall be made before the end of the period of six weeks beginning with the submission of the report; and before making such an order, the Secretary of State may by a direction require the Local Government Commission to supply him with such additional information as may be described in the direction.

(3) An order under this section may, in particular, include provision which, for the purpose of giving effect (with or without modifications) to recommendations of the Local Government Commission, makes provision with respect to—

(a) the area of any authority and the name of any such area;

(b) the name of any authority;

(c) the establishment of any new authority for any county or district or the winding up and dissolution of any existing authority;

(d) the total number of councillors of any authority, the apportionment of councillors among electoral areas, the assignment of existing councillors to new or altered electoral areas, and the first election of councillors for any new or altered electoral area;

(e) without prejudice to paragraph (d) above, the holding of a fresh election of councillors for all electoral areas in a local government area where substantial changes have been made to some of those areas, or the order of retirement of councillors for any electoral areas in the local government area in question;

(f) in the case of an order relating to the system of election of district councillors, the ordinary year of election and the order of retirement of parish councillors for any parish situated in the district;

(g) the constitution [election and membership] of public bodies in any area affected by the order;

(h) the abolition or establishment, or the restriction or extension, of the jurisdiction of any public body in or over any part of any area affected by the order.

(4), (5) ★ ★ ★ ★ ★

SOCIAL SECURITY ADMINISTRATION ACT 1992
(1992 c. 5)

An Act to consolidate certain enactments relating to the administration of social security and related matters with amendments to give effect to recommendations of the Law Commission and the Scottish Law Commission. [13 February 1992]

Territorial extent: England and Wales, Scotland.

Note: The provisions of this Act printed here were inserted by the Social Security Administration (Fraud) Act 1997.

★ ★ ★ ★ ★

INFORMATION

Information held by tax authorities

[122 Supply of information held by tax authorities for fraud prevention and verification

(1) This section applies to information which is held—

(a) by the Commissioners of Inland Revenue or the Commissioners of Customs and Excise; or

(b) by a person providing services to the Commissioners of Inland Revenue or the Commissioners of Customs and Excise in connection with the provision of those services.

(2) Information to which this section applies may, with the authority of the Commissioners concerned, be supplied to, or to a person providing services to, the Secretary of State or the Northern Ireland Department—

(a) for use in the prevention, detection, investigation or prosecution of offences relating to social security; or

(b) for use in checking the accuracy of information relating to benefits, contributions or national insurance numbers or to any other matter relating to social security and (where appropriate) amending or supplementing such information.

(3) Information supplied under subsection (2) above shall not be supplied by the recipient to any other person or body unless—

(a) it could be supplied to that person or body under that subsection;

(b) it is supplied for the purposes of any civil or criminal proceedings relating to the Contributions and Benefits Act, the Jobseekers Act 1995 or this Act or to any provision of Northern Ireland legislation corresponding to any of them; or

(c) it is supplied under section 122C below;

and shall not be so supplied in those circumstances without the authority of the Commissioners concerned.

(4) But where information supplied under subsection (2) above has been used (in accordance with paragraph (b) of that subsection) in amending or supplementing other information, it is lawful for it to be—

(a) supplied to any person or body to whom that other information could be supplied; or

(b) used for any purpose for which that other information could be used.

(5) This section does not limit the circumstances in which information may be supplied apart from this section.]

[122A Supply of information by Inland Revenue for purposes of contributions

(1) This section applies to information which is held—

(a) by the Commissioners of Inland Revenue; or

(b) by a person providing services to the Commissioners of Inland Revenue in connection with the provision of those services.

(2) Information to which this section applies may, with the authority of the Commissioners, be supplied to, or to a person providing services to, the Secretary of State or the Northern Ireland Department for use for any purpose relating to contributions.

(3) Information supplied under subsection (2) above shall not be supplied by the recipient to any other person or body unless—

(a) it could be supplied to that person or body under that subsection; or

(b) it is supplied for the purposes of any civil or criminal proceedings relating to the Contributions and Benefits Act, the Jobseekers Act 1995 or this Act or to any provision of Northern Ireland legislation corresponding to any of them;

and shall not be so supplied in those circumstances without the authority of the Commissioners.

(4) But where information supplied under subsection (2) above has been used in amending or supplementing other information, it is lawful for it to be—

(a) supplied to any person or body to whom that other information could be supplied; or

(b) used for any purpose for which that other information could be used.

(5) This section does not limit the circumstances in which information may be supplied apart from this section.]

Other government information

[122B Supply of other government information for fraud prevention and verification

(1) This section applies to information which is held by, or by a person providing services to, a Minister of the Crown or a government department (including a Northern Ireland department) and which relates to—

(a) passports, immigration and emigration, nationality or prisoners; or

(b) any other matter which is prescribed.

(2) Information to which this section applies may be supplied to, or to a person providing services to, the Secretary of State or the Northern Ireland Department—

(a) for use in the prevention, detection, investigation or prosecution of offences relating to social security; or

(b) for use in checking the accuracy of information relating to benefits, contributions or national insurance numbers or to any other matter relating to social security and (where appropriate) amending or supplementing such information.

(3) Information supplied under subsection (2) above shall not be supplied by the recipient to any other person or body unless—

(a) it could be supplied to that person or body under that subsection;

(b) it is supplied for the purposes of any civil or criminal proceedings relating to the Contributions and Benefits Act, the Jobseekers Act 1995 or this Act or to any provision of Northern Ireland legislation corresponding to any of them; or

(c) it is supplied under section 122C below.

(4) But where information supplied under subsection (2) above has been used (in accordance with paragraph (b) of that subsection) in amending or supplementing other information, it is lawful for it to be—

(a) supplied to any person or body to whom that other information could be supplied; or

(b) used for any purpose for which that other information could be used.

(5) This section does not limit the circumstances in which information may be supplied apart from this section.]

★ ★ ★ ★ ★

TRADE UNION AND LABOUR RELATIONS (CONSOLIDATION) ACT 1992 (1992, c. 52)

An Act to consolidate the enactments relating to collective labour relations, that is to say, to trade unions, employers' associations, industrial relations and industrial action. [16 July 1992]

Territorial extent Great Britain (but see section 242 below)

CHAPTER III
CODES OF PRACTICE

Codes of Practice issued by the Secretary of State

203 Issue of Codes of Practice by the Secretary of State

(1) The Secretary of State may issue Codes of Practice containing such practical guidance as he thinks fit for the purpose—

(a) of promoting the improvement of industrial relations, or

(b) of promoting what appear to him to be desirable practices in relation to the conduct by trade unions of ballots and elections.

(2) The Secretary of State may from time to time revise the whole or any part of a Code of Practice issued by him and issue that revised Code.

204 Procedure for issue of Code by Secretary of State

(1) When the Secretary of State proposes to issue a Code of Practice, cr a revised Code, he shall after consultation with ACAS prepare and publish a draft of the Code, shall consider any representations made to him about the draft and may modify the draft accordingly.

(2) If he determines to proceed with the draft, he shall lay it before both Houses of Parliament and, if it is approved by resolution of each House, shall issue the Code in the form of the draft.

(3) A Code issued under this section shall come into effect on such day as the Secretary of State may by order appoint.

The order may contain such transitional provisions or savings as appear to him to be necessary or expedient.

(4) An order under subsection (3) shall be made by statutory instrument, which shall be subject to annulment in pursuance of a resolution of either House of Parliament.

205 * * * * *

206 Revocation of Code issued by Secretary of State

(1) A Code of Practice issued by the Secretary of State may be revoked by him by order made by statutory instrument.

The order may contain such transitional provisions and savings as appear to him to be appropriate.

(2) An order shall not be made under this section unless a draft of it has been laid before and approved by resolution of each House of Parliament.

Supplementary provisions

207 Effect of failure to comply with Code

(1) A failure on the part of any person to observe any provision of a Code of Practice issued under this Chapter shall not of itself render him liable to any proceedings.

(2) In any proceedings before an industrial tribunal or the Central Arbitration Committee any Code of Practice issued under this Chapter by ACAS shall be admissible in evidence, and any provision of the Code which appears to the tribunal or Committee to be relevant to any question arising in the proceedings shall be taken into account in determining that question.

(3) In any proceedings before a court or industrial tribunal or the Central Arbitration Committee any Code of Practice issued under this Chapter by the Secretary of State shall be admissible in evidence, and any provision of the Code which appears to the court, tribunal or Committee to be relevant to any question arising in the proceedings shall be taken into account in determining that question.

208-219 * * * * *

PART V
INDUSTRIAL ACTION

220 Peaceful picketing

(1) It is lawful for a person in contemplation or furtherance of a trade dispute to attend—

(a) at or near his own place of work, or

(b) if he is an official of a trade union, at or near the place of work of a member of the union whom he is accompanying and whom he represents,

for the purpose only of peacefully obtaining or communicating information, or peacefully persuading any person to work or abstain from working.

(2) If a person works or normally works—

(a) otherwise than at any one place, or

(b) at a place the location of which is such that attendance there for a purpose mentioned in subsection (1) is impracticable,

his place of work for the purposes of that subsection shall be any premises of his employer from which he works or from which his work is administered.

(3) In the case of a worker not in employment where—

(a) his last employment was terminated in connection with a trade dispute, or

(b) the termination of his employment was one of the circumstances giving rise to a trade dispute, in relation to that dispute his former place of work shall be treated for the purposes of subsection (1) as being his place of work.

(4) A person who is an official of a trade union by virtue only of having been elected or appointed to be a representative of some of the members of the union shall be regarded for the purposes of subsection (1) as representing only those members; but otherwise an official of a union shall be regarded for those purposes as representing all its members.

221-239 ⋆ ⋆ ⋆ ⋆ ⋆

Criminal offences

240 Breach of contract involving injury to persons or property

(1) A person commits an offence who wilfully and maliciously breaks a contract of service or hiring, knowing or having reasonable cause to believe that the probable consequences of his so doing, either alone or in combination with others, will be—

(a) to endanger human life or cause serious bodily injury, or

(b) to expose valuable property, whether real or personal, to destruction or serious injury.

(2) Subsection (1) applies equally whether the offence is committed from malice conceived against the person endangered or injured or, as the case may be, the owner of the property destroyed or injured, or otherwise.

(3) A person guilty of an offence under this section is liable on summary conviction to imprisonment for a term not exceeding three months or to a fine not exceeding level 2 on the standard scale or both.

(4) This section does not apply to seamen.

241 Intimidation or annoyance by violence or otherwise

(1) A person commits an offence who, with a view to compelling another person to abstain from doing or to do any act which that person has a legal right to do or abstain from doing, wrongfully and without legal authority—

(a) uses violence to or intimidates that person or his wife or children, or injures his property,

(b) persistently follows that person about from place to place,

(c) hides any tools, clothes or other property owned or used by that person, or deprives him of or hinders him in the use thereof,

(d) watch or besets the house or other place where the person resides, works, carries on business or happens to be, or the approach to any such house or place, or

(e) follows that person with two or more other persons in a disorderly manner in or through any street or road.

(2) A person guilty of an offence under this section is liable on summary conviction to imprisonment for a term not exceeding six months or a fine not exceeding level 5 on the standard scale, or both.

(3) A constable may arrest without warrant anyone he reasonably suspects is committing an offence under this section.

242 Restriction of offence of conspiracy: England and Wales

(1) Where in pursuance of any such agreement as is mentioned in section 1(1) of the Criminal Law Act 1977 (which provides for the offence of conspiracy) the acts in question in relation to an offence are to be done in contemplation or furtherance of a trade dispute, the offence shall be disregarded for the purposes of that subsection if it is a summary offence which is not punishable with imprisonment.

(2) This section extends to England and Wales only.

⋆ ⋆ ⋆ ⋆ ⋆

TRIBUNALS AND INQUIRIES ACT 1992
(1992, c. 53)

An Act to consolidate the Tribunals and Inquiries Act 1971 and certain other enactments relating to tribunals and inquiries. [16 July 1992]

Territorial extent United Kingdom

The Council on Tribunals and their functions

1 The Council on Tribunals

(1) There shall continue to be a council entitled the Council on Tribunals (in this Act referred to as "the Council")—

(a) to keep under review the constitution and working of the tribunals specified in Schedule 1 (being the tribunals constituted under or for the purposes of the statutory provisions specified in that Schedule) and, from time to time, to report on their constitution and working;

(b) to consider and report on such particular matters as may be referred to the Council under this Act with respect to tribunals other than the ordinary courts of law, whether or not specified in Schedule 1, or any such tribunal; and

(c) to consider and report on such matters as may be referred to the Council under this Act, or as the council may determine to be of special importance, with respect to administrative procedures involving, or which may involve, the holding by or on behalf of a Minister of a statutory inquiry, or any such procedure.

(2) Nothing in this section authorises or requires the Council to deal with any matter with respect to which the Parliament of Northern Ireland had power to make laws.

2 Composition of the Council and the Scottish Committee

(1) Subject to subsection (3), the Council shall consist of not more than fifteen nor less than ten members appointed by the Lord Chancellor and the Lord Advocate, and one of the members shall be so appointed to be chairman of the Council.

(2) There shall be a Scottish Committee of the Council (in this Act referred to as "the Scottish Committee") which, subject to subsection (3), shall consist of—

(a) either two or three members of the Council designated by the Lord Advocate, and

(b) either three or four persons, not being members of the Council, appointed by the Lord Advocate;

and the Lord Advocate shall appoint one of the members of the Scottish Committee (being a member of the Council) to be chairman of the Scottish Committee.

(3) In addition to the persons appointed or designated under subsection (1) or (2), the Parliamentary Commissioner for Administration shall, by virtue of his office, be a member of the Council and of the Scottish Committee.

(4) In appointing members of the Council regard shall be had to the need for representation of the interests of persons in Wales.

3, 4 ★★★★★

Composition and procedure of tribunals and inquiries

5 Recommendations of Council as to appointment of members of tribunals

(1) Subject to section 6 but without prejudice to the generality of section 1(1)(a), the Council may make to the appropriate Minister general recommendations as to the making of appointments to membership of any tribunals mentioned in Schedule 1 or of panels constituted for the purposes of any such tribunals; and (without prejudice to any

statutory provisions having effect with respect to such appointments) the appropriate Minister shall have regard to recommendations under this section.

(2) In this section "the appropriate Minister", in relation to appointments of any description, means the Minister making the appointments or, if they are not made by a Minister, the Minister in charge of the government department concerned with the tribunals in question.

(3) * * * * *

6 Appointment of chairmen of certain tribunals

(1) The chairman, or any person appointed to act as chairman, of any of the tribunals to which this subsection applies shall (without prejudice to any statutory provisions as to qualifications) be selected by the appropriate authority from a panel of persons appointed by the Lord Chancellor.

(2) Members of panels constituted under this section shall hold and vacate office under the terms of the instruments under which they are appointed, but may resign office by notice in writing to the Lord Chancellor; and any such member who ceases to hold office shall be eligible for re-appointment.

(3)-(9) * * * * *

7 Concurrence required for removal of members of certain tribunals

(1) Subject to subsection (2), the power of a Minister, other than the Lord Chancellor, to terminate a person's membership of any tribunal specified in Schedule 1, or of a panel constituted for the purposes of any such tribunal, shall be exercisable only with the consent of—

(a) the Lord Chancellor, the Lord President of the Court of Session and the Lord Chief Justice of Northern Ireland, if the tribunal sits in all parts of the United Kingdom;

(b) the Lord Chancellor and the Lord President of the Court of Session, if the tribunal sits in all parts of Great Britain;

(c) the Lord Chancellor and the Lord Chief Justice of Northern Ireland, if the tribunal sits both in England and Wales and in Northern Ireland;

(d) the Lord Chancellor, if the tribunal does not sit outside England and Wales;

(e) the Lord President of the Court of Session, if the tribunal sits only in Scotland;

(f) the Lord Chief Justice of Northern Ireland, if the tribunal sits only in Northern Ireland.

(2), (3) * * * * *

8 Procedural rules for tribunals

(1) The power of a Minister, the Lord President of the Court of Session, the Commissioners of Inland Revenue or the Foreign Compensation Commission to make, approve, confirm or concur in procedural rules for any tribunal specified in Schedule 1 shall be exercisable only after consultation with the Council.

(2)-(4) * * * * *

9 Procedure in connection with statutory inquiries

(1) The Lord Chancellor, after consultation with the Council, may make rules regulating the procedure to be followed in connection with statutory inquiries held by or on behalf of Ministers; and different provision may be made by any such rules in relation to different classes of such inquiries.

(2), (3) * * * * *

(4) In the application of this section to inquiries held in Scotland—

(a) for any reference to the Lord Chancellor there shall be substituted a reference to the Lord Advocate, and

(b) the Council, in exercising their functions under this section in relation to rules to be made by the Lord Advocate, shall consult with the Scottish Committee.

Judicial control of tribunals etc.

10 Reasons to be given for decisions of tribunals and Ministers

(1) Subject to the provisions of this section and of section 14, where—

(a) any tribunal specified in Schedule 1 gives any decision, or

(b) any Minister notifies any decision taken by him—

(i) after a statutory inquiry has been held by him or on his behalf, or

(ii) in a case in which a person concerned could (whether by objecting or otherwise) have required a statutory inquiry to be so held,

it shall be the duty of the tribunal or Minister to furnish a statement, either written or oral, of the reasons for the decision if requested, on or before the giving or notification of the decision, to state the reasons.

(2) The statement referred to in subsection (1) may be refused, or the specification of the reasons restricted, on grounds of national security.

(3), (4) ★ ★ ★ ★ ★

(5) Subsection (1) does not apply—

(a) to decisions in respect of which any statutory provision has effect, apart from this section, as to the giving of reasons,

(b) to decisions of a Minister in connection with the preparation, making, approval, confirmation, or concurrence in regulations, rules or bye-laws, or orders or schemes of a legislative and not executive character . . .

(6) Any statement of the reasons for a decision referred to in paragraph (a) or (b) of subsection (1), whether given in pursuance of that subsection or of any other statutory provision, shall be taken to form part of the decision and accordingly to be incorporated in the record.

(7), (8) ★ ★ ★ ★ ★

11 ★ ★ ★ ★ ★

12 Supervisory functions of superior courts not excluded by Acts passed before 1st August 1958

(1) As respects England and Wales—

(a) any provision in an Act passed before 1st August 1958 that any order or determination shall not be called into question in any court, or

(b) any provision in such an Act which by similar words excludes any of the powers of the High Court,

shall not have effect so as to prevent the removal of the proceedings into the High Court by order of certiorari or to prejudice the powers of the High Court to make orders of mandamus.

(2) As respects Scotland—

(a) any provision in an Act passed before 1st August 1958 that any order or determination shall not be called into question in any court, or

(b) any provision in such an Act which by similar words excludes any jurisdiction which the Court of Session would otherwise have to entertain an application for reduction or suspension of any order or determination, or otherwise to consider the validity of any order or determination,

shall not have effect so as to prevent the exercise of any such jurisdiction.

(3) Nothing in this section shall apply—

(a) to any order or determination of a court of law, or

(b) where an Act makes special provision for application to the High Court or the Court of Session within a time limited by the Act.

13-19, Schedules ★ ★ ★ ★ ★

ASYLUM AND IMMIGRATION APPEALS ACT 1993
(1993, c. 23)

An Act to make provision about persons who claim asylum in the United Kingdom and their dependants; to amend the law with respect to certain rights of appeal under the Immigration Act 1971; and to extend the provisions of the Immigration (Carriers' Liability) Act 1987 to transit passengers. [1 July 1993]

Territorial extent United Kingdom

Introductory

1 Interpretation
In this Act—

"the 1971 Act" means the Immigration Act 1971;

"claim for asylum" means a claim made by a person (whether before or after the coming into force of this section) that it would be contrary to the United Kingdom's obligations under the Convention for him to be removed from, or required to leave, the United Kingdom; and

"the Convention" means the Convention relating to the Status of Refugees done at Geneva on 28th July 1951 and the Protocol to that Convention.

2 Primacy of Convention
Nothing in the immigration rules (within the meaning of the 1971 Act) shall lay down any practice which would be contrary to the Convention.

Treatment of persons who claim asylum

3 Fingerprinting
(1) Where a person ("the claimant") has made a claim for asylum, an immigration officer, constable, prison officer or officer of the Secretary of State authorised for the purposes of this section may—

(a) take such steps as may be reasonably necessary for taking the claimant's fingerprints; or

(b) by notice in writing require the claimant to attend at a place specified in the notice in order that such steps may be taken.

(2) The powers conferred by subsection (1) above may be exercised not only in relation to the claimant but also in relation to any dependant of his; but in the exercise of the power conferred by paragraph (a) of that subsection, fingerprints shall not be taken from a person under the age of sixteen ("the child") except in the presence of a person of full age who is—

(a) the child's parent or guardian; or

(b) a person who for the time being takes responsibility for the child and is not an immigration officer, constable, prison officer or officer of the Secretary of State.

(3) Where the claimant's claim for asylum has been finally determined or abandoned—

(a) the powers conferred by subsection (1) above shall not be exercisable in relation to him or any dependant of his; and

(b) any requirement imposed on him or any dependant of his by a notice under subsection (1)(b) above shall no longer have effect.

(4) A notice given to any person under paragraph (b) of subsection (1) above—

(a) shall give him a period of at least seven days within which he is to attend as mentioned in that paragraph; and

(b) may require him so to attend at a specified time of day or between specified times of day.

(5) Any immigration officer or constable may arrest without warrant a person who has failed to comply with a requirement imposed on him by a notice under subsection (1)(b) above (unless the requirement no longer has effect) and, where a person is arrested under this subsection,—

(a) he may be removed to a place where his fingerprints may conveniently be taken, and

(b) (whether or not he is so removed) there may be taken such steps as may be reasonably necessary for taking his fingerprints,

before he is released.

(6) Fingerprints of a person which are taken by virtue of this section must be destroyed not later than the earlier of—

(a) the end of the period of one month beginning with any day on which he is given indefinite leave under the 1971 Act to enter or remain in the United Kingdom; and

(b) the end of the period of ten years beginning with the day on which the fingerprints are taken.

(7) Where fingerprints taken by virtue of this section are destroyed—

(a) any copies of the fingerprints shall also be destroyed; and

(b) if there are any computer data relating to the fingerprints, the Secretary of State shall, as soon as it is practicable to do so, make it impossible for access to be gained to the data.

(8) If—

(a) subsection (7)(b) above falls to be complied with, and

(b) the person to whose fingerprints the data relate asks for a certificate that it has been complied with,

such a certificate shall be issued to him by the Secretary of State not later than the end of the period of three months beginning with the day on which he asks for it.

(9) In this section—

(a) "immigration officer" means an immigration officer appointed for the purposes of the 1971 Act; and

(b) "dependant", in relation to the claimant, means a person—

(i) who is his spouse or a child of his under the age of eighteen; and

(ii) who has neither a right of abode in the United Kingdom nor indefinite leave under the 1971 Act to enter or remain in the United Kingdom.

(10) ★★★★★

4, 5 ★★★★★

6 Protection of claimants from deportation etc.

During the period beginning when a person makes a claim for asylum and ending when the Secretary of State gives him notice of the decision on the claim, he may not be removed from, or required to leave, the United Kingdom.

7 Curtailment of leave to enter or remain

(1) Where—

(a) a person who has limited leave under the 1971 Act to enter or remain in the United Kingdom claims that it would be contrary to the United Kingdom's obligations under the Convention for him to be required to leave the United Kingdom after the time limited by the leave, and

(b) the Secretary of State has considered the claim and given to the person notice in writing of his rejection of it,

the Secretary of State may by notice in writing, given to the person concurrently with the notice under paragraph (b) above, curtail the duration of the leave.

[(1A) Where the Secretary of State by notice under subsection (1) above curtails the duration of any person's leave to enter or remain in the United Kingdom, he may also by notice in writing given to any dependant of that person curtail to the same extent the duration of that dependant's leave so to enter or remain.]

(2) No appeal may be brought under section 14 of the 1971 Act or section 8(2) below against the curtailment of leave under subsection (1) [or 1A] above.

(3), (4) ★★★★★

Rights of appeal

8 Appeals to special adjudicator

(1) A person who is refused leave to enter the United Kingdom under the 1971 Act may appeal against the refusal to a special adjudicator on the ground that his removal in consequence of the refusal would be contrary to the United Kingdom's obligations under the Convention.

(2) A person who has limited leave under the 1971 Act to enter or remain in the United Kingdom may appeal to a special adjudicator against any variation of, or refusal to vary, the leave on the ground that it would be contrary to the United Kingdom's obligations under the Convention for him to be required to leave the United Kingdom after the time limited by the leave.

(3) Where the Secretary of State—

(a) has decided to make a deportation order against a person by virtue of section 3(5) of the 1971 Act, or

(b) has refused to revoke a deportation order made against a person by virtue of section 3(5) or (6) of that Act,

the person may appeal to a special adjudicator against the decision or refusal on the ground that his removal in pursuance of the order would be contrary to the United Kingdom's obligations under the Convention; . . .

[(3A) A person may not appeal under paragraph (b) of subsection (3) above if he has had the right to appeal under paragraph (a) of that subsection, whether or not he has exercised it.]

(4) ★★★★★

(5) The Lord Chancellor shall designate such number of the adjudicators appointed for the purposes of Part II of the 1971 Act as he thinks necessary to act as special adjudicators for the purposes of this section and may from time to time vary that number and the persons who are so designated.

(6) ★★★★★

9 Appeals from Immigration Appeal Tribunal

(1) Where the Immigration Appeal Tribunal has made a final determination of an appeal brought under Part II of the 1971 Act (including that Part as it applies by virtue of Schedule 2 to this Act) any party to the appeal may bring a further appeal to the appropriate appeal court on any question of law material to that determination.

(2) An appeal under this section may be brought only with the leave of the Immigration Appeal Tribunal or, if such leave is refused, with the leave of the appropriate appeal court.

(3) In this section "the appropriate appeal court" means—

(a) if the appeal is from the determination of an adjudicator or special adjudicator and that determination was made in Scotland, the Court of Session; and

(b) in any other case, the Court of Appeal.

(4), (5) ★★★★★

9A-16 ★★★★★

EUROPEAN COMMUNITIES (AMENDMENT) ACT 1993
(1993, c. 32)

An Act to make provision consequential on the Treaty on European Union signed at Maastricht on 7th February 1992. [20 July 1993]

Territorial extent United Kingdom

1 Treaty on European Union

(1) In section 1(2) of the European Communities Act 1972, in the definition of "the Treaties" and "the Community Treaties", after paragraph (j) (inserted by the European Communities (Amendment) Act 1986) there shall be inserted the words

"and

(k) Titles II, III and IV of the Treaty on European Union signed at Maastricht on 7th February 1992, together with the other provisions of the Treaty so far as they relate to those Titles, and the Protocols adopted at Maastricht on that date and annexed to the Treaty establishing the European Community with the exception of the Protocol on Social Policy on page 117 of Cm 1934".

(2) For the purpose of section 6 of the European Parliamentary Elections Act 1978 (approval of treaties increasing the Parliament's powers) the Treaty on European Union signed at Maastricht on 7th February 1992 is approved.

2 Economic and monetary union

No notification shall be given to the Council of the European Communities that the United Kingdom intends to move to the third stage of economic and monetary union (in accordance with the Protocol on certain provisions relating to the United Kingdom adopted at Maastricht on 7th February 1992) unless a draft of the notification has first been approved by Act of Parliament and unless Her Majesty's Government has reported to Parliament on its proposals for the co-ordination of economic policies, its role in the European Council of Finance Ministers (ECOFIN) in pursuit of the objectives of Article 2 of the Treaty establishing the European Community as provided for in Articles 103 and 102a, and the work of the European Monetary Institute in preparation for economic and monetary union.

3 * * * * *

4 Information for Commission

In implementing the provisions of Article 103(3) of the Treaty establishing the European Community, information shall be submitted to the Commission from the United Kingdom indicating performance on economic growth, industrial investment, employment and balance of trade, together with comparisons with those items of performance from other member States.

5 Convergence criteria: assessment of deficits

Before submitting the information required in implementing Article 103(3) of the Treaty establishing the European Community, Her Majesty's Government shall report to Parliament for its approval an assessment of the medium term economic and budgetary position in relation to public investment expenditure and to the social, economic and environmental goals set out in Article 2, which report shall form the basis of any submission to the Council and Commission in pursuit of their responsibilities under Articles 103 and 104c.

6 * * * * *

7 Commencement (Protocol on Social Policy)

This Act shall come into force only when each House of Parliament has come to a Resolution on a motion tabled by a Minister of the Crown concerning the question of adopting the Protocol on Social Policy.

8 * * * * *

EUROPEAN ECONOMIC AREA ACT 1993
(1993, c. 51)

An Act to make provision in relation to the European Economic Area established under the Agreement signed at Oporto on 2nd May 1992 as adjusted by the Protocol signed at Brussels on 17th March 1993. [5 November 1993]

Territorial extent United Kingdom

1 Agreement on European Economic Area

In section 1(2) of the 1972 Act, in the list in the definition of "the Treaties" and "the Community Treaties", there shall be added at the end the words "and

(m) the Agreement on the European Economic Area signed at Oporto on 2nd May 1992 together with the Protocol adjusting that Agreement signed at Brussels on 17th March 1993".

2 Consistent application of law to whole of EEA

(1) Where—

(a) the operation of any relevant enactment is limited (expressly or by implication) by reference to the Communities or by reference to some connection with the Communities, and

(b) the enactment relates to a matter to which the Agreement (as it has effect on the date on which it comes into force) relates,

then, unless the context otherwise requires, the enactment shall have effect on and after that date in relation to that matter with the substitution of a corresponding limitation relating to the European Economic Area (or, where appropriate, to both the Communities and the European Economic Area).

(2) Subsection (1) above shall have effect—

(a) subject to the Schedule to this Act, and

(b) subject to such exceptions and modifications as may be prescribed by regulations made by a Minister of the Crown.

(3) Subsection (1) above shall not be regarded—

(a) as having an effect which is inconsistent with the operation, by virtue of the Agreement, of section 2(1) of the 1972 Act, or

(b) as prejudicing any power to make provision for the purpose of implementing any obligation of the United Kingdom created or arising by or under the Agreement, or for any other purpose mentioned in section 2(2)(a) or (b) of the 1972 Act relating to the Agreement;

and any instrument made for such a purpose under section 2(2) of the 1972 Act or under any other enactment may exclude the operation of subsection (1) above.

(4) In relation to matters to which the Agreement (as it has effect on the date on which it comes into force or subsequently) relates, the powers conferred by section 2(2) of the 1972 Act shall include power to make provision for the elimination or reduction of any difference between—

(a) the application of any relevant enactment in cases having a connection with member States, and

(b) its application in cases having a connection with other States within the European Economic Area;

and paragraph 1(1)(a), (c) and (d) of Schedule 2 to the 1972 Act shall not apply to the powers conferred by section 2(2) of that Act so far as they are exercisable by virtue of this subsection.

(5) In relation to matters to which the Agreement (as it has effect on the date on which it comes into force or subsequently) relates, the powers conferred by section 2(2) of the 1972 Act shall include power to make provision for the avoidance, elimination or reduction of any difference between—

(a) the application of an instrument made under that section on or after the date on which the Agreement comes into force in cases having a connection with member States, and

(b) its application in cases having a connection with other States within the European Economic Area.

(6) The provision that may be made by virtue of subsection (4) above includes provision amending the Schedule to this Act.

(7) In this section (and in the Schedule to this Act) "relevant enactment" means a provision of an Act passed, or of any subordinate legislation made, before the date on which the Agreement comes into force.

3 General implementation of Agreement

(1) Subject to section 2 above, where by virtue of the Agreement (as it has effect on the date on which it comes into force) it is necessary for a purpose mentioned in section 2(2)(a) or (b) of the 1972 Act that any relevant provision should have effect with modifications which can be ascertained from the Agreement, then on and after that date the provision shall have effect with those modifications.

(2) A Minister of the Crown may be regulations modify or exclude the operation of subsection (1) above in relation to a relevant provision where it appears to him appropriate to do so because of the suspension of any part of the Agreement in accordance with the terms of the Agreement.

(3) Subsection (1) above shall not be regarded—

(a) as providing for modifications the effect of which is achieved through the operation, by virtue of the Agreement, of section 2(1) of the 1972 Act, or

(b) as prejudicing any power to make provision for the purpose of implementing any obligation of the United Kingdom created or arising by or under the Agreement, or for any other purpose mentioned in section 2(2)(a) or (b) of the 1972 Act relating to the Agreement;

and any instrument made for such a purpose under section 2(2) of the 1972 Act or under any other enactment may exclude the operation of subsection (1) above.

(4) Subsection (1) above shall not apply so as to require a modification if that modification, or a corresponding modification limited so as to relate only to the Communities,—

(a) could have been made, by Act passed before the date on which the Agreement comes into force, for a purpose mentioned in section 2(2)(a) or (b) of the 1972 Act, but

(b) was not made (by that or other means).

(5) In this section "relevant provision" means—

(a) a provision of an Act passed, or of any subordinate legislation made, before the date on which the Agreement comes into force;

(b) a provision of any other instrument made before that date by a person as against whom the effect of a directive issued by a Community institution (if such a directive were relevant) might be relied upon in proceedings to which he was a party.

4 * * * * *

5 Regulations

The power to make regulations under section 2(2) or section 3(2) above shall be exercisable by statutory instrument; and any statutory instrument containing such regulations, if made without a draft having been approved by resolution of each House of Parliament, shall be subject to annulment in pursuance of a resolution of either House.

6 Interpretation

(1) In this Act, except where the context otherwise requires,—

"the 1972 Act" means the European Communities Act 1972;

"Act" includes an Act of the Parliament of Northern Ireland and a Measure of the Northern Ireland Assembly;

"the Agreement" means the Agreement on the European Economic Area signed at Oporto on 2nd May 1992 as adjusted by the Protocol signed at Brussels on 17th March 1993;

"Minister of the Crown" includes the Treasury;

"subordinate legislation" means Orders in Council, orders, rules, regulations, schemes, warrants, byelaws and other instruments made under any Act.

(2) References in this Act to the date on which the Agreement comes into force are references to the date on which (in accordance with the Protocol signed at Brussels on 17th March 1993) it comes into force otherwise than as regards Liechtenstein.

7 * * * * *

COAL INDUSTRY ACT 1994
(1994, c. 21)

An Act to provide for the establishment and functions of a body to be known as the Coal Authority; to provide for the restructuring of the coal industry, for transfers of the property, rights and liabilities of the British Coal Corporation and its wholly-owned subsidiaries to other persons and for the dissolution of that Corporation; to abolish the Domestic Coal Consumer's Council; to make provision for the licensing of coal-mining operations and provision otherwise in relation to the carrying on of such operations; to amend the Coal Mining Subsidence Act 1991 and the Opencast Coal Act 1958; and for connected purposes. [5 July 1994]

Territorial extent England and Wales, Scotland

PART I
RE-ORGANISATION OF COAL INDUSTRY

The Coal Authority

1 Establishment of the Coal Authority

(1) There shall be a body corporate to be known as the Coal Authority (in this Act referred to as "the Authority") for the purpose of—

(a) holding, managing and disposing of interests and rights in or in relation to the unworked coal and other property which is transferred to or otherwise acquired by it by or under this Act;

(b) carrying out functions with respect to the licensing of coal-mining operations;

(c) carrying out functions with respect to coal-mining subsidence and in connection with other matters incidental to the carrying on of any opencast or other coal-mining operations;

(d) facilitating the establishment and maintenance of arrangements for the information to which persons are to be entitled under this Act to be made available to them; and

(e) carrying out the other functions conferred on it by virtue of this Act.

(2) The authority shall consist of not less than two nor more than eight members appointed by the Secretary of State.

(3) The Secretary of State shall designate one of the members appointed under this section as the chairman of the Authority and may, if he thinks fit, designate another such member as its deputy chairman.

(4) In appointing a person to be a member of the Authority, the Secretary of State shall have regard to the desirability of appointing a person who has experience of, and has shown capacity in, some matter relevant to its functions.

(5) The Authority shall not be regarded—

(a) as the servant or agent of the Crown, or as enjoying any status, immunity or privilege of the Crown; or

(b) by virtue of any connection with the Crown, as exempt from any tax, duty, rate, levy or other charge whatsoever, whether general or local;

and the Authority's property shall not be regarded as property of, or property held on behalf of, the Crown.

(6) * * * * *

2–56 * * * * *

PART IV
GENERAL AND SUPPLEMENTAL

Information provisions

57 Public access to information held by the Authority

(1) This section applies to the information contained in any register maintained by the Authority under section 35 or 56 above and to any of the following information which is for the time being in the possession of the Authority, that is to say—

(a) information about the geological or physiographical features or characteristics of any land in which any unworked coal or any coal mine is situated or of any other land;

(b) information about the identity of the persons in whom interests and rights in or in relation to any unworked coal or any coal mine have been vested;

(c) the contents of the plans of any coal mines or coal workings;

(d) any other information about proposals for the carrying on by any person of any coal-mining operations;

(e) information about any subsidence or subsidence damage or about claims made under the 1991 Act; and

(f) information about such other matters as the Secretary of State may by regulations prescribe for the purposes of this section.

(2) Subject to subsections (3) and (4) below, it shall be the duty of the Authority to establish and maintain arrangements under which every person is entitled, in such cases, on payment to the Authority of such fee and subject to such other conditions as the Authority may consider appropriate—

(a) to be furnished with any information to which this section applies;

(b) to have the contents of so much of the records maintained by the Authority as contains any information to which this section applies made available to him, at such office of the Authority as it may determine, for inspection at such times as may be reasonable; and

(c) to make or be supplied with copies of, or of extracts from, so much of the records maintained by the Authority as contains any information to which the section applies.

(3) Subject to subsection (5) below, nothing in this section shall require or authorise the disclosure by the Authority of any information which—

(a) relates to the affairs of an individual or specifically to the affairs of any body of persons (whether corporate or unincorporate), including the Authority itself, and

(b) is not contained in a register maintained under section 35 or 56 above,

if the disclosure of that information would or might, in the opinion of the Authority, seriously and prejudicially affect the interests of that individual or, as the case may be, of that body.

(4) Subject to subsection (5) below, nothing in this section shall require or authorise the disclosure by the Authority, without the consent of the person to whom the Authority owes the obligation of confidence, of any information which—

(a) has been furnished to the Authority—

(i) in pursuance of the provisions of a licence under Part II of this Act;

(ii) in pursuance of any provisions of an agreement entered into in connection with, or with any proposals for, the carrying on of any activities in the course of any exploration for coal or of any activities for which a licence under section 2 of the Petroleum (Production) Act 1934 is required; or

(iii) for the purposes of any application to the Authority for the grant of a licence under Part II of this Act, for the making of such an agreement or for the transfer or creation of any interest or rights in or in relation to any land;

and

(b) under the provisions of the licence under Part II of this Act, of that agreement or of any undertaking given by the Authority to the applicant for the purposes of that application, is to be treated as subject to an obligation of confidence owed by the Authority to any other person.

(5) The information that is to be excluded by virtue of subsections (3) and (4) above from the information which is to be made available to any person in pursuance of arrangements under this section shall not include any information of a description that appears to the Authority to comprise information relating to matters which are or may be relevant to the safety of members of the public or of any particular individual or individuals other than the person whose consent is required for its disclosure.

(6) For the purposes of this section it shall be the duty of the Authority to maintain such records as it considers appropriate of any information which comes into its possession and is information to which this section applies.

(7) The power to make regulations for the purposes of this section shall be exercisable by statutory instrument subject to annulment in pursuance of a resolution of either House of Parliament.

(8) In this section "records" includes registers, maps, plans and accounts, as well as computer records and other records kept otherwise than in documentary form.

58 * * * * *

59 Information to be kept confidential by the Authority

(1) Subject to the following provisions of this section, it shall be the duty of the Authority to establish and maintain such arrangements as it considers best calculated to secure that information which—

(a) is in the Authority's possession in consequence of either the carrying out of any of its functions or the transfer to the Authority, in accordance with a restructuring scheme, of any records, and

(b) relates to the affairs of any individual or to any particular business, is not during the lifetime of that individual or so long as that business continues to be carried on, disclosed to any person without the consent of that individual or, as the case may be, of the person for the time being carrying on that business.

(2) Nothing in subsection (1) above shall authorise or require the making of arrangements which prevent the disclosure of information—

(a) for the purpose of facilitating the carrying out by the Secretary of State, the Treasury or the Authority of any of his, their or, as the case may be, its functions under this Act;

(b) in pursuance of arrangements made under section 57 above;

(c) for the purpose of facilitating the carrying out by any relevant authority of any of the functions in relation to which it is such an authority;

(d) in connection with the investigation of any criminal offence or for the purposes of criminal proceedings;

(e) for the purposes of any civil proceedings brought under this Act or any relevant enactment, of any proceedings before the Lands Tribunal or the Lands Tribunal for Scotland under the 1991 Act or of any arbitration for which provision is made by regulations under section 47(2) above; or

(f) in pursuance of any Community obligation.

(3) For the purposes of this section—

(a) every Minister of the Crown and local weights and measures authority in Great Britain is a relevant authority in relation to his or, as the case may be, their functions under any relevant enactment;

(b) the Secretary of State and the Treasury are relevant authorities in relation to their functions under the Financial Services Act 1986 and the enactments relating to companies, insurance companies and insolvency;

(c) an inspector appointed under the enactments relating to companies, an official receiver and any recognised professional body for the purposes of section 391 of the Insolvency Act 1986 are relevant authorities in relation to their functions as such;

(d) every enforcing authority, within the meaning of Part I of the Health and Safety at Work etc. Act 1974, is a relevant authority in relation to its functions under any relevant statutory provision, within the meaning of that Act; and

(e) the following are relevant authorities in relation to all of their functions, that is to say—

(i) the Comptroller and Auditor General;

(ii) the Health and Safety Executive and the Health and Safety Commission;

(iii) the National Rivers Authority;

(iv) the Monopolies Commission;

(v) the Director General of Fair Trading and the Director General of Electricity Supply;

(vi) the river purification authorities referred to in the Rivers (Prevention of Pollution) (Scotland) Act 1951 and for the time being specified in subsection (2) of section 17 of the Act.

(4)-(9) * * * * *

* * * * *

CRIMINAL JUSTICE AND PUBLIC ORDER ACT 1994
(1994, c. 33)

An Act to make further provision in relation to criminal justice (including employment in the prison service); to amend or extend the criminal law and powers for preventing crime and enforcing that law; to amend the Video Recordings Act 1984; and for purposes connected with those purposes. [3 November 1994]

Territorial extent England and Wales, Scotland (ss. 61-66, 163), United Kingdom (ss. 68, 69), England and Wales (remaining provisions printed here). Sections 34-38 (below) have been applied, with modifications, to the armed forces by the Criminal Justice and Public Order Act 1994 (Application to the Armed Forces) Order 1997 (SI 1997/16).

Inferences from accused's silence

34 Effect of accused's failure to mention facts when questioned or charged

(1) Where, in any proceedings against a person for an offence, evidence is given that the accused—

(a) at any time before he was charged with the offence, on being questioned under caution by a constable trying to discover whether or by whom the offence had been committed, failed to mention any fact relied on in his defence in those proceedings; or

(b) on being charged with the offence or officially informed that he might be prosecuted for it, failed to mention any such fact,

being a fact which in the circumstances existing at the time the accused could reasonably have been expected to mention when so questioned, charged or informed, as the case may be, subsection (2) below applies.

(2) Where this subsection applies—

[(a) a magistrates' court inquiring into the case as examining justices;]

(b) a judge, in deciding whether to grant an application made by the accused under—

(i) section 6 of the Criminal Justice Act 1987 (application for dismissal of charge of serious fraud in respect of which notice of transfer has been given under section 4 of that Act); or

(ii) paragraph 5 of Schedule 6 to the Criminal Justice Act 1991 (application for dismissal of charge of violent or sexual offence involving child in respect of which notice of transfer has been given under section 53 of that Act);

(c) the court, in determining whether there is a case to answer; and

(d) the court or jury, in determining whether the accused is guilty of the offence charged,

may draw such inferences from the failure as appear proper.

(3) Subject to any directions by the court, evidence tending to establish the failure may be given before or after evidence tending to establish the fact which the accused is alleged to have failed to mention.

(4) This section applies in relation to questioning by persons (other than constables) charged with the duty of investigating offences or charging offenders as it applies in relation to questioning by constables; and in subsection (1) above "officially informed" means informed by a constable or any such person.

(5) This section does not—

(a) prejudice the admissibility in evidence of the silence or other reaction of the accused in the face of anything said in his presence relating to the conduct in respect of which he is charged, in so far as evidence thereof would be admissible apart from this section; or

(b) preclude the drawing of any inference from any such silence or other reaction of the accused which could properly be drawn apart from this section.

(6), (7) ★★★★★

35 Effect of accused's silence at trial

(1) At the trial of any person who has attained the age of fourteen years for an offence, subsections (2) and (3) below apply unless—

(a) the accused's guilt is not in issue; or

(b) it appears to the court that the physical or mental condition of the accused makes it undesirable for him to give evidence;

but subsection (2) below does not apply if, at the conclusion of the evidence for the prosecution, his legal representative informs the court that the accused will give evidence or, where he is unrepresented, the court ascertains from him that he will give evidence.

(2) Where this subsection applies, the court shall, at the conclusion of the evidence for the prosecution, satisfy itself (in the case of proceedings on indictment, in the presence of the jury) that the accused is aware that the stage has been reached at which evidence can be given for the defence and that he can, if he wishes, give evidence and that, if he chooses not to give evidence, or having been sworn, without good cause

refuses to answer any question, it will be permissible for the court or jury to draw such inferences as appear proper from his failure to give evidence or his refusal, without good cause, to answer any question.

(3) Where this subsection applies, the court or jury, in determining whether the accused is guilty of the offence charged, may draw such inferences as appear proper from the failure of the accused to give evidence or his refusal, without good cause, to answer any question.

(4) This section does not render the accused compellable to give evidence on his own behalf, and he shall accordingly not be guilty of contempt of court by reason of a failure to do so.

(5) For the purposes of this section a person who, having been sworn, refuses to answer any question shall be taken to do so without good cause unless—

(a) he is entitled to refuse to answer the question by virtue of any enactment, whenever passed or made, or on the ground of privilege; or

(b) the court in the exercise of its general discretion excuses him from answering it.

(6) ★ ★ ★ ★ ★

36 Effect of accused's failure or refusal to account for objects, substances or marks

(1) Where—

(a) a person is arrested by a constable, and there is—

(i) on his person; or

(ii) in or on his clothing or footwear; or

(iii) otherwise in his possession; or

(iv) in any place in which he is at the time of his arrest,

any object, substance or mark, or there is any mark on any such object; and

(b) that or another constable investigating the case reasonably believes that the presence of the object, substance or mark may be attributable to the participation of the person arrested in the commission of an offence specified by the constable; and

(c) the constable informs the person arrested that he so believes, and requests him to account for the presence of the object, substance or mark; and

(d) the person fails or refuses to do so,

then if, in any proceedings against the person for the offence so specified, evidence of those matters is given, subsection (2) below applies.

(2) Where this subsection applies—

[(a) a magistrates' court inquiring into the offence as examining justices;]

(b) a judge, in deciding whether to grant an application made by the accused under—

(i) section 6 of the Criminal Justice Act 1987 (application for dismissal of charge of serious fraud in respect of which notice of transfer has been given under section 4 of that Act); or

(ii) paragraph 5 of Schedule 6 to the Criminal Justice Act 1991 (application for dismissal of charge of violent or sexual offence involving child in respect of which notice of transfer has been given under section 53 of that Act);

(c) the court or jury, in determining whether the accused is guilty of the offence charged,

may draw such inferences from the failure or refusal as appear proper.

(3) Subsections (1) and (2) above apply to the condition of clothing or footwear as they apply to a substance or mark thereon.

(4) Subsections (1) and (2) above do not apply unless the accused was told in ordinary language by the constable when making the request mentioned in subsection (1)(c) above what the effect of this section would be if he failed or refused to comply with the request.

(5) *****

(6) This section does not preclude the drawing of any inference from a failure or refusal of the accused to account for the presence of an object, substance or mark or from the condition of clothing or footwear which could properly be drawn apart from this section.

(7) *****

37 Effect of accused's failure or refusal to account for presence at a particular place

(1) Where—

(a) a person arrested by a constable was found by him at a place at or about the time the offence for which he was arrested is alleged to have been committed; and

(b) that or another constable investigating the offence reasonably believes that the presence of the person at that place and at that time may be attributable to his participation in the commission of the offence; and

(c) the constable informs the person that he so believes, and requests him to account for that presence; and

(d) the person fails or refuses to do so,

then if, in any proceedings against the person for the offence, evidence of those matters is given, subsection (2) below applies.

(2) Where this subsection applies—

[(a) a magistrates' court inquiring into the offence as examining justices;]

(b) a judge, in deciding whether to grant an application made by the accused under—

(i) section 6 of the Criminal Justice Act 1987 (application for dismissal of charge of serious fraud in respect of which notice of transfer has been given under section 4 of that Act); or

(ii) paragraph 5 of Schedule 6 to the Criminal Justice Act 1991 (application for dismissal of charge of violent or sexual offence involving child in respect of which notice of transfer has been given under section 53 of that Act);

(c) the court, in determining whether there is a case to answer; and

(d) the court or jury, in determining whether the accused is guilty of the offence charged,

may draw such inferences from the failure or refusal as appear proper.

(3) Subsections (1) and (2) do not apply unless the accused was told in ordinary language by the constable when making the request mentioned in subsection (1)(c) above what the effect of this section would be if he failed or refused to comply with the request.

(4) *****

(5) This section does not preclude the drawing of any inference from a failure or refusal of the accused to account for his presence at a place which could properly be drawn apart from this section.

(6) *****

38 Interpretation and savings for sections 34, 35, 36 and 37

(1) In sections 34, 35, 36 and 37 of this Act—

"legal representative" means an authorised advocate or authorised litigator, as defined by section 119(1) of the Courts and Legal Services Act 1990; and

"place" includes any building or part of a building, any vehicle, vessel, aircraft or hovercraft and any other place whatsoever.

(2)-(4) *****

(5) Nothing in sections 34, 35, 36 or 37 prejudices the operation of a provision of any enactment which provides (in whatever words) that any answer or evidence given by a person in specified circumstances shall not be admissible in evidence against him

or some other person in any proceedings or class of proceedings (however described, and whether civil or criminal).

In this subsection, the reference to giving evidence is a reference to giving evidence in any manner, whether by furnishing information, making discovery, producing documents or otherwise.

(6) Nothing in sections 34, 35, 36 or 37 prejudices any power of a court, in any proceedings, to exclude evidence (whether by preventing questions being put or otherwise) at its discretion.

39 * * * * *

Juries

40 Disqualification for jury service of persons on bail in criminal proceedings

(1) A person who is on bail in criminal proceedings shall not be qualified to serve as a juror in the Crown Court.

(2) In this section "bail in criminal proceedings" has the same meaning as in the Bail Act 1976.

41-47 * * * * *

Sentencing: guilty pleas

48 Reduction in sentences for guilty pleas

(1) In determining what sentence to pass on an offender who has pleaded guilty to an offence in proceedings before that or another court a court shall take into account—

(a) the stage in the proceedings for the offence at which the offender indicated his intention to plead guilty, and

(b) the circumstances in which this indication was given.

(2) If, as a result of taking into account any matter referred to in subsection (1) above, the court imposes a punishment on the offender which is less severe than the punishment it would otherwise have imposed, it shall state in open court that it has done so.

49-59 * * * * *

Powers of police to stop and search

60 Powers to stop and search in anticipation of violence

[(1) If a police officer of or above the rank of inspector reasonably believes—

(a) that incidents involving serious violence may take place in any locality in his police area, and that it is expedient to give an authorisation under this section to prevent their occurrence, or

(b) that persons are carrying dangerous instruments or offensive weapons in any locality in his police area without good reason,

he may give an authorisation that the powers conferred by this section are to be exercisable at any place within that locality for a specified period not exceeding 24 hours.]

(2) . . .

(3) If it appears to [an officer of or above the rank of] superintendent that it is expedient to do so, having regard to offences which have, or are reasonably suspected to have, been committed in connection with any [activity] falling within the authorisation, he may direct that the authorisation shall continue in being for a further [24] hours.

(3A) * * * * *

(4) This section confers on any constable in uniform power—

(a) to stop any pedestrian and search him or anything carried by him for offensive weapons or dangerous instruments.

(b) to stop any vehicle and search the vehicle, its driver and any passenger for offensive weapons or dangerous instruments.

(5) A constable may, in the exercise of those powers, stop any person or vehicle and make any search he thinks fit whether or not he has any grounds for suspecting that the person or vehicle is carrying weapons or articles of that kind.

(6) If in the course of a search under this section a constable discovers a dangerous instrument or an article which he has reasonable grounds for suspecting to be an offensive weapon, he may seize it.

(7), (8) *****

(9) Any authorisation under this section shall be in writing signed by the officer giving it and shall specify [the grounds on which it is given and] the locality in which and the period during which the powers conferred by this section are exercisable and a direction under subsection (3) above shall also be given in writing or, where that is not practicable, recorded in writing as soon as it is practicable to do so.

(10) Where a vehicle is stopped by a constable under this section, the driver shall be entitled to obtain a written statement that the vehicle was stopped under the powers conferred by this section if he applies for such a statement not later than the end of the period of twelve months from the day on which the vehicle was stopped . . .

[(10A) A person who is searched by a constable under this section shall be entitled to obtain a written statement that he was searched under the powers conferred by this section if he applies for such a statement not later than the end of the period of twelve months from the day on which he was searched.]

(11) In this section—

"dangerous instruments" means instruments which have a blade or are sharply pointed;

"offensive weapon" has the meaning given by section 1(9) of the Police and Criminal Evidence Act 1984 [or, in relation to Scotland, section 47(4) of the Criminal Law (Consolidation) (Scotland) Act 1995]; and

"vehicle" includes a caravan as defined in section 29(1) of the Caravan Sites and Control of Development Act 1960.

[(11A) For the purposes of this section, a person carries a dangerous instrument or an offensive weapon if he has it in his possession.]

(12) *****

PART V
PUBLIC ORDER: COLLECTIVE TRESPASS OR NUISANCE ON LAND

Powers to remove trespassers on land

61 Power to remove trespassers on land

(1) If the senior police officer present at the scene reasonably believes that two or more persons are trespassing on land and are present there with the common purpose of residing there for any period, that reasonable steps have been taken by or on behalf of the occupier to ask them to leave and—

(a) that any of those persons has caused damage to the land or to property on the land or used threatening, abusive or insulting words or behaviour towards the occupier, a member of his family or an employee or agent of his, or

(b) that those persons have between them six or more vehicles on the land,

he may direct those persons, or any of them, to leave the land and to remove any vehicles or other property they have with them on the land.

(2) Where the persons in question are reasonably believed by the senior police officer to be persons who were not originally trespassers but have become trespassers on the land, the officer must reasonably believe that the other conditions specified in subsection (1) are satisfied after those persons become trespassers before he can exercise the power conferred by that subsection.

(3) A direction under subsection (1) above, if not communicated to the persons referred to in subsection (1) by the police officer giving the direction, may be communicated to them by any constable at the scene.

(4) If a person knowing that a direction under subsection (1) above has been given which applies to him—

(a) fails to leave the land as soon as reasonably practicable, or

(b) having left again enters the land as a trespasser within the period of three months beginning with the day on which the direction was given,

he commits an offence and is liable on summary conviction to imprisonment for a term not exceeding three months or a fine not exceeding level 4 on the standard scale, or both.

(5) A constable in uniform who reasonably suspects that a person is committing an offence under this section may arrest him without a warrant.

(6) In proceedings for an offence under this section it is a defence for the accused to show—

(a) that he was not trespassing on the land, or

(b) that he had a reasonable excuse for failing to leave the land as soon as reasonably practicable or, as the case may be, for again entering the land as a trespasser.

(7) In its application in England and Wales to common land this section has effect as if in the preceding subsections of it—

(a) references to trespassing or trespassers were references to acts and persons doing acts which constitute either a trespass as against the occupier or an infringement of the commoners' rights; and

(b) references to "the occupier" included the commoners or any of them or, in the case of common land to which the public has access, the local authority as well as any commoner.

(8) Subsection (7) above does not—

(a) require action by more than one occupier; or

(b) constitute persons trespassers as against any commoner or the local authority if they are permitted to be there by the other occupier.

(9) ★★★★★

62 Supplementary powers of seizure

(1) If a direction has been given under section 61 and a constable reasonably suspects that any person to whom the direction applies has, without reasonable excuse—

(a) failed to remove any vehicle on the land which appears to the constable to belong to him or to be in his possession or under his control; or

(b) entered the land as a trespasser with a vehicle within the period of three months beginning with the day on which the direction was given,

the constable may seize and remove that vehicle.

(2) ★★★★★

Powers in relation to raves

63 Powers to remove persons attending or preparing for a rave

(1) This section applies to a gathering on land in the open air of 100 or more persons (whether or not trespassers) at which amplified music is played during the night (with or without intermissions) and is such as, by reason of its loudness and duration and the time at which it is played, is likely to cause serious distress to the inhabitants of the locality; and for this purpose—

(a) such a gathering continues during intermissions in the music and, where the gathering extends over several days, throughout the period during which amplified music is played at night (with or without intermissions); and

(b) "music" includes sounds wholly or predominantly characterised by the emission of a succession of repetitive beats.

(2) If, as respects any land in the open air, a police officer of at least the rank of superintendent reasonably believes that—

(a) two or more persons are making preparations for the holding there of a gathering to which this section applies,

(b) ten or more persons are waiting for such a gathering to begin there, or

(c) ten or more persons are attending such a gathering which is in progress,

he may give a direction that those persons and any other persons who came to prepare or wait for or to attend the gathering are to leave the land and remove any vehicles or other property which they have with them on the land.

(3) A direction under subsection (2) above, if not communicated to the persons referred to in subsection (2) by the police officer giving the direction, may be communicated to them by any constable at the scene.

(4) Persons shall be treated as having had a direction under subsection (2) above communicated to them if reasonable steps have been taken to bring it to their attention.

(5) ★★★★★

(6) If a person knowing that a direction has been given which applies to him—

(a) fails to leave the land as soon as reasonably practicable, or

(b) having left again enters the land within the period of 7 days beginning with the day on which the direction was given,

he commits an offence and is liable on a summary conviction to imprisonment for a term not exceeding three months or a fine not exceeding level 4 on the standard scale, or both.

(7) In proceedings for an offence under this section it is a defence for the accused to show that he had a reasonable excuse for failing to leave the land as soon as reasonably practicable or, as the case may be, for again entering the land.

(8) A constable in uniform who reasonably suspects that a person is committing an offence under this section may arrest him without a warrant.

(9) This section does not apply—

(a) in England and Wales, to a gathering licensed by an entertainment licence; or

(b) in Scotland, to a gathering in premises which, by virtue of section 41 of the Civic Government (Scotland) Act 1982, are licensed to be used as a place of public entertainment.

(10) ★★★★★

64 Supplementary powers of entry and seizure

(1) If a police officer of at least the rank of superintendent reasonably believes that circumstances exist in relation to any land which would justify the giving of a direction under section 63 in relation to a gathering to which that section applies he may authorise any constable to enter the land for any of the purposes specified in subsection (2) below.

(2) Those purposes are—

(a) to ascertain whether such circumstances exist; and

(b) to exercise any power conferred on a constable by section 63 or subsection (4) below.

(3) A constable who is so authorised to enter land for any purpose may enter the land without a warrant.

(4) If a direction has been given under section 63 and a constable reasonably suspects that any person to whom the direction applies has, without reasonable excuse—

(a) failed to remove any vehicle or sound equipment on the land which appear to the constable to belong to him or to be in his possession or under his control; or

(b) entered the land as a trespasser with a vehicle or sound equipment within the period of 7 days beginning with the day on which the direction was given,

the constable may seize and remove that vehicle or sound equipment.

(5), (6) ★★★★★

65 Raves: power to stop persons from proceeding

(1) If a constable in uniform reasonably believes that a person is on his way to a gathering to which section 63 applies in relation to which a direction under section 63(2) is in force, he may, subject to subsections (2) and (3) below—

(a) stop that person, and

(b) direct him not to proceed in the direction of the gathering.

(2) The power conferred by subsection (1) above may only be exercised at a place within 5 miles of the boundary of the site of the gathering.

(3)-(6) ★★★★★

66 Power of court to forfeit sound equipment

(1) Where a person is convicted of an offence under section 63 in relation to a gathering to which that section applies and the court is satisfied that any sound equipment which has been seized from him under section 64(4), or which was in his possession or under his control at the relevant time, has been used at the gathering the court may make an order for forfeiture under this subsection in respect of that property.

(2) The court may make an order under subsection (1) above whether or not it also deals with the offender in respect of the offence in any other way and without regard to any restrictions on forfeiture in any enactment.

(3) In considering whether to make an order under subsection (1) above in respect of any property a court shall have regard—

(a) to the value of the property; and

(b) to the likely financial and other effects on the offender of the making of the order (taken together with any other order that the court contemplates making).

(4) An order under subsection (1) above shall operate to deprive the offender of his rights, if any, in the property to which it relates, and the property shall (if not already in their possession) be taken into the possession of the police.

(5) Except in a case to which subsection (6) below applies, where any property has been forfeited under subsection (1) above, a magistrates' court may, on application by a claimant of the property, other than the offender from whom it was forfeited under subsection (1) above, make an order for delivery of the property to the applicant if it appears to the court that he is the owner of the property.

(6), (7) ★★★★★

(8) No such application shall succeed unless the claimant satisfies the court either that he had not consented to the offender having possession of the property or that he did not know, and had no reason to suspect, that the property was likely to be used at a gathering to which section 63 applies.

(9)-(13) ★★★★★

67 ★★★★★

Disruptive trespassers

68 Offence of aggravated trespass

(1) A person commits the offence of aggravated trespass if he trespasses on land in the open air and, in relation to any lawful activity which persons are engaging in or are about to engage in on that or adjoining land in the open air, does there anything which is intended by him to have the effect—

(a) of intimidating those persons or any of them so as to deter them or any of them from engaging in that activity,

(b) of obstructing that activity, or

(c) of disrupting that activity.

(2) Activity on any occasion on the part of a person or persons on land is "lawful" for the purposes of this section if he or they may engage in the activity on the land on that occasion without committing an offence or trespassing on the land.

(3) A person guilty of an offence under this section is liable on summary conviction to imprisonment for a term not exceeding three months or a fine not exceeding level 4 on the standard scale, or both.

(4) A constable in uniform who reasonably suspects that a person is committing an offence under this section may arrest him without a warrant.

(5) In this section "land" does not include—

(a) the highways and roads excluded from the application of section 61 by paragraph (b) of the definition of "land" in subsection (9) of that section; or

(b) a road within the meaning of the Roads (Northern Ireland) Order 1993.

69 Powers to remove persons committing or participating in aggravated trespass

(1) If the senior police officer present at the scene reasonably believes—

(a) that a person is committing, has committed or intends to commit the offence of aggravated trespass on land in the open air; or

(b) that two or more persons are trespassing on land in the open air and are present there with the common purpose of intimidating persons so as to deter them from engaging in a lawful activity or of obstructing or disrupting a lawful activity,

he may direct that person or (as the case may be) those persons (or any of them) to leave the land.

(2) A direction under subsection (1) above, if not communicated to the persons referred to in subsection (1) by the police officer giving the direction, may be communicated to them by any constable at the scene.

(3) If a person knowing that a direction under subsection (1) above has been given which applies to him—

(a) fails to leave the land as soon as practicable, or

(b) having left again enters the land as a trespasser within the period of three months beginning with the day on which the direction was given,

he commits an offence and is liable on summary conviction to imprisonment for a term not exceeding three months or a fine not exceeding level 4 on the standard scale, or both.

(4) In proceedings for an offence under subsection (3) it is a defence for the accused to show—

(a) that he was not trespassing on the land, or

(b) that he had a reasonable excuse for failing to leave the land as soon as practicable or, as the case may be, for again entering the land as a trespasser.

(5) A constable in uniform who reasonably suspects that a person is committing an offence under this section may arrest him without a warrant.

(6) In this section "lawful activity" and "land" have the same meaning as in section 68.

70-76 * * * * *

Powers to remove unauthorised campers

77 Power of local authority to direct unauthorised campers to leave land

(1) If it appears to a local authority that persons are for the time being residing in a vehicle or vehicles within that authority's area—

(a) on any land forming part of a highway;

(b) on any other unoccupied land; or

(c) on any occupied land without the consent of the occupier, the authority may give a direction that those persons and any others with them are to leave the land and remove the vehicle or vehicles and any other property they have with them on the land.

(2) Notice of a direction under subsection (1) must be served on the persons to whom the direction applies, but it shall be sufficient for this purpose for the direction to specify the land and (except where the direction applies to only one person) to be addressed to all occupants of the vehicles on the land, without naming them.

(3) If a person knowing that a direction under subsection (1) above has been given which applies to him—

(a) fails, as soon as practicable, to leave the land or remove from the land any vehicle or other property which is the subject of the direction, or

(b) having removed any such vehicle or property again enters the land with a vehicle within the period of three months begining with the day on which the direction was given,

he commits an offence and is liable on summary conviction to a fine not exceeding level 3 on the standard scale.

(4) A direction under subsection (1) operates to require persons who re-enter the land within the said period with vehicles or other property to leave and remove the vehicles or other property as it operates in relation to the persons and vehicles or other property on the land when the direction was given.

(5) In proceedings for an offence under this section it is a defence for the accused to show that his failure to leave or to remove the vehicle or other property as soon as practicable or his re-entry with a vehicle was due to illness, mechanical breakdown or other immediate emergency.

(6), (7) * * * * *

78 Orders for removal of persons and their vehicles unlawfully on land

(1) A magistrates' court may, on a complaint made by a local authority, if satisfied that persons and vehicles in which they are residing are present on land within that authority's area in contravention of a direction given under section 77, make an order requiring the removal of any vehicle or other property which is so present on the land and any person residing in it.

(2) An order under this section may authorise the local authority to take such steps as are reasonably necessary to ensure that the order is complied with and, in particular, may authorise the authority, by its officers and servants—

(a) to enter upon the land specified in the order; and

(b) to take, in relation to any vehicle or property to be removed in pursuance of the order, such steps for securing entry and rendering it suitable for removal as may be so specified.

(3) The local authority shall not enter upon any occupied land unless they have given to the owner and occupier at least 24 hours notice of their intention to do so, or unless after reasonable inquiries they are unable to ascertain their names and addresses.

(4) A person who wilfully obstructs any person in the exercise of any power conferred on him by an order under this section commits an offence and is liable on summary conviction to a fine not exceeding level 3 on the standard scale.

(5)-(7) * * * * *

79-162 * * * * *

Closed-circuit television by local authorities

163 Local authority powers to provide closed-circuit television

(1) Without prejudice to any power which they may exercise for those purposes under any other enactment, a local authority may take such of the following steps as they

consider will, in relation to their area, promote the prevention of crime or the welfare of the victims of crime—

(a) providing apparatus for recording visual images of events occurring on any land in their area;

(b) providing within their area a telecommunications system which, under Part II of the Telecommunictions Act 1984, may be run without a licence;

(c) arranging for the provision of any other description of telecommunications system within their area or between any land in their area and any building occupied by a public authority.

(2) Any power to provide, or to arrange for the provision of, any apparatus includes power to maintain, or operate, or, as the case may be, to arrange for the maintenance or operation of, that apparatus.

(3) Before taking such a step under this section, a local authority shall consult the chief officer of police for the police area in which the step is to be taken.

(4), (5) ★★★★★

★★★★★

DEREGULATION AND CONTRACTING OUT ACT 1994
(1994, c. 40)

An Act to amend, and make provision for the amendment of, statutory provisions and rules of law in order to remove or reduce certain burdens affecting persons in the carrying on of trades, businesses or professions or otherwise, and for other deregulatory purposes; to make future provision in connection with the licensing of operators of goods vehicles; to make provision for and in connection with the contracting out of certain functions vested in Ministers of the Crown, local authorities, certain governmental bodies and the holders of certain offices; and for purposes connected therewith. [3 November 1994]

Territorial extent United Kingdom (ss. 1-6), England and Wales, Scotland (remainder).

PART I
DEREGULATION

CHAPTER I
GENERAL

Removal or reduction of burdens

1 Power to remove or reduce certain statutory burdens on business, individuals etc.

(1) If, with respect to any provision made by an enactment, a Minister of the Crown is of the opinion—

(a) that the effect of the provision is such as to impose, or authorise or require the imposition of, a burden affecting any person in the carrying on of any trade, business or profession or otherwise, and

(b) that, by amending or repealing the enactment concerned and, where appropriate, by making such other provision as is referred to in subsection (4)(a) below, it would be possible, without removing any necessary protection, to remove or reduce the burden or, as the case may be, the authorisation or requirement by virtue of which the burden may be imposed,

he may, subject to the following provisions of this section and sections 2 to 4 below, by order amend or repeal that enactment.

(2) The reference in subsection (1)(b) above to reducing the authorisation or requirement by virtue of which a burden may be imposed includes a reference to shortening any period of time within which the burden may be so imposed.

(3) In this section and sections 2 to 4 below, in relation to an order under this section,—

(a) "the existing provision" means the provision by which the burden concerned is imposed or, as the case may be, is authorised or required to be imposed; and

(b) "the relevant enactment" means the enactment containing the existing provision.

(4) An order under this section shall be made by statutory instrument and may do all or any of the following—

(a) make provision (whether by amending any enactment or otherwise) creating a burden which relates to the subject matter of, but is less onerous than that imposed by, the existing provision;

(b) make such modifications of enactments as, in the opinion of the Minister concerned, are consequential upon, or incidental to, the amendment or repeal of the relevant enactment;

(c) contain such transitional provisions and savings as appear to the Minister to be appropriate;

(d) make different provision for different cases or different areas; but no order shall be made under this section unless a draft of the order has been laid before and approved by a resolution of each House of Parliament.

(5) In this section and sections 2 to 4 below—

(a) "Minister of the Crown" has the same meaing as in the Ministers of the Crown Act 1975 and "Minister" shall be construed accordingly;

(b) "burden" includes a restriction, requirement or condition (including one requiring the payment of fees), together with—

(i) any sanction (whether criminal or otherwise) for failure to observe the restriction or to comply with the requirement or condition; and

(ii) any procedural provisions (including provisions for appeal) relevant to that sanction; and

(c) "enactment", subject to subsection (6) below, means an enactment contained in this Act or in any other Act passed before or in the same Session as this Act, or any provision of an order under this section.

(6) In paragraph (c) of subsection (5) above—

(a) "Act" does not include anything contained in Northern Ireland legislation, within the meaning of section 24 of the Interpretation Act 1978; and

(b) the reference to an enactment is a reference to an enactment as for the time being amended, extended or applied by or under any Act mentioned in that paragraph.

(7) Where a restriction, requirement or condition is subject to a criminal sanction (as mentioned in subsection (5)(b)(i) above), nothing in this section shall authorise the making of an amendment which would have the effect of leaving the restriction, requirement or condition in place but producing a different criminal sanction or altering any procedural provisions relevant to the criminal sanction.

2 Limitations on the power under section 1

(1) If an order under section 1 creates a new criminal offence, then, subject to subsections (2) and (3) below, that offence shall not be punishable—

(a) on indictment with imprisonment for a term of more than two years; or

(b) on summary conviction with imprisonment for a term exceeding six months or a fine exceeding level 5 on the standard scale or both.

(2) In the case of an offence which, if committed by an adult, is triable either on indictment or summarily and is not an offence triable on indictment only by virtue of—

(a) Part V of the Criminal Justice Act 1988, or

(b) [section 292(6) and (7) of the Criminal Procedure (Scotland) Act 1995],

the reference in subsection (1)(b) above to level 5 on the standard scale shall be construed as a reference to the statutory maximum.

(3) If an order under section 1 above abolishes an offence contained in the relevant enactment and the maximum penalties for that offence are greater than those specified in subsection (1) above, the order may create a new criminal offence having maximum penalties not exceeding those applicable to the offence which is abolished.

(4) An order under section 1 above shall not contain any provision—

(a) providing for any forcible entry, search or seizure, or

(b) compelling the giving of evidence,

unless, and then only to the extent that, a provision to that effect is contained in the relevant enactment and is abolished by the order.

3 Preliminary consultation

(1) Before a Minister makes an order under section 1 above, he shall—

(a) consult such organisations as appear to him to be representative of interests substantially affected by his proposals; and

(b) consult such other persons as he considers appropriate.

(2) If it appears to the Minister, as a result of the consultation required by subsection (1) above, that it is appropriate to vary the whole or any part of his proposals, he shall undertake such further consultation with respect to the variations as appears to him to be appropriate.

(3) If, after the conclusion of—

(a) the consultations required by subsection (1) above, and

(b) any further consultation undertaken as mentioned in subsection (2) above,

the Minister considers it appropriate to proceed with the making of an order under section 1 above, he shall lay before Parliament a document containing his proposals in the form of a draft of the order, together with details of the matters specified in subsection (4) below.

(4) The matters referred to in subsection (3) above are—

(a) the burden, authorisation or requirement which it is proposed to remove or reduce;

(b) whether the existing provision affords any necessary protection and, if so, how that protection is to be continued if the burden, authorisation or requirement is removed or reduced;

(c) whether any savings in cost are estimated to result from the proposals and, if so, either the estimated amount or the reasons why savings should be expected;

(d) any other benefits which are expected to flow from the removal or reduction of the burden, authorisation or requirement;

(e) any consultation undertaken as required by subsection (1) or subsection (2) above;

(f) any representations received as a result of that consultation; and

(g) the changes (if any) which the Minister has made to his original proposals in the light of those representations.

(5) In giving details of the representations referred to in subsection (4)(f) above, the Minister shall not disclose any information relating to a particular person or business except—

(a) with the consent of that person or of the person carrying on that business; or

(b) in such a manner as not to identify that person or business.

(6) If, before the day on which this section comes into force, any consultation was undertaken which, had it been undertaken after that day, would to any extent have satisfied the requirements of subsection (1) above, those requirements shall to that extent be taken to have been satisfied.

4 Parliamentary consideration of proposals

(1) Where a document has been laid before Parliament under section 3(3) above, no draft of an order under section 1 above to give effect (with or without variations) to

proposals in that document shall be laid before Parliament until after the expiry of the period for Parliamentary consideration, as defined in subsection (2) below.

(2) In this section "the period for Parliamentary consideration", in relation to a document, means the period of sixty days beginning on the day on which it was laid before Parliament.

(3) In reckoning the period of sixty days referred to in subsection (2) above, no account shall be taken of any time during which Parliament is dissolved or prorogued or during which either House is adjourned for more than four days.

(4) In preparing a draft of an order under section 1 above to give effect, with or without variations, to proposals in a document laid before Parliament under section 3(3) above, the Minister concerned shall have regard to any representations made during the period for Parliamentary consideration and, in particular, to any resolution or report of, or of any committee of, either House of Parliament with regard to the document.

(5) Together with a draft of an order laid before Parliament under section 1(4) above, the Minister concerned shall lay a statement giving details of—

(a) any representations, resolution or report falling within subsection (4) above; and

(b) the changes (if any) which, in the light of any such representations, resolution or report, the Minister has made to his proposals as contained in the document previously laid before Parliament under section 3(3) above.

(6) Subsection (5) of section 3 above shall apply in relation to the representations referred to in subsection (5)(a) above as it applies in relation to the representations referred to in subsection (4)(f) of that section.

Enforcement procedures and appeals

5 Powers to improve enforcement procedures

(1) If, with respect to any provision made by an enactment, a Minister of the Crown is of the opinion—

(a) that the effect of the provision is such as to impose, or authorise or require the imposition of, a restriction, requirement or condition affecting any person in the carrying on of any trade, business or profession or otherwise, and

(b) that, by exercising any one or more of the powers conferred by Schedule 1 to this Act, it would be possible, without jeopardising any necessary protection, to improve (so far as fairness, transparency and consistency are concerned) the procedures for enforcing the restriction, requirement or condition,

he may, subject to the following provisions of this section, by order exercise the power or powers accordingly.

(2) No order shall be made under this section in any case where the sole or main effect which the restriction, requirement or condition may be expected to have on each person on whom it is imposed is an effect on him in his personal capacity, and not as a person carrying on a trade, business or profession.

(3) Where the relevant enactment—

(a) contains a power for the Minister to make regulations or orders; and

(b) provides for the power to be exercisable so as to give effect, with or without modifications, to proposals submitted by some other person,

the Minister shall consult with that person before he makes an order under this section.

(4) An order under this section shall be made by statutory instrument and may do all or any of the following—

(a) make provision as to the consequences of any failure to comply with a provision made by the order;

(b) contain provisions (including provisions modifying enactments relating to the periods within which proceedings must be brought) which are consequential upon, or supplemental or incidental to, the provisions made by the order;

(c) contain such transitional provisions and savings as appear to the Minister to be appropriate;

(d) make different provision for different cases or different areas;

and a statutory instrument containing an order under the section shall be subject to annulment in pursuance of a resolution of either House of Parliament.

(5) * * * * *

(6) In this section and Schedule 1 to this Act—

"enactment" means an enactment within the meaning of section 1 above, and any subordinate legislation made under such an enactment;

"enforcement action"—

(a) in relation to any restriction, requirement or condition, means any action taken with a view to or in connection with imposing any sanction (whether criminal or otherwise) for failure to observe or comply with it; and

(b) in relation to a restriction, requirement or condition relating to the grant or renewal of licences, include any refusal to grant, renew or vary a licence, the imposition of any condition on the grant or renewal of a licence and any variation or revocation of a licence;

* * * * *

6 Model provisions with respect to appeals

(1) The Secretary of State shall by order prescribe model provisions with respect to appeals against enforcement action with a view to their being incorporated, if thought fit and with or without modifications, in enactments to which subsection (2) below applies.

(2) This subsection applies to enactments which include provision the effect of which is to impose, or authorise or require the imposition of, a restriction, requirement or condition affecting any person in the carrying on of any trade, business or profession or otherwise.

(3) The Secretary of State shall perform his duty under this section in the manner which he considers is best calculated to secure—

(a) that appeals determined in accordance with the model provisions are determined without unnecessary delay; and

(b) that the costs or expenses incurred by the parties to appeals so determined are kept to the minimum.

(4) Model provisions prescribed by an order under this section may provide for the appointment of persons to hear and determine appeals and confer powers on persons so appointed, including in particular—

(a) power to appoint experts and their own counsel or solicitor;

(b) power to require respondents to disclose documents and other material;

(c) power to summon or, in Scotland, to cite witnesses;

(d) power to make interim orders, including orders staying or, in Scotland, suspending enforcement action; and

(e) power to award costs or expenses to appellants and, in certain cases, against them.

(5) Model provisions so prescribed may also—

(a) confer a right for interested persons to make representations before enforcement action is taken;

(b) require the giving of reasons to such persons for any decision to take such action;

(c) require appellants to state their ground of appeal and respondents to furnish statements by way of answer;

(d) enable appellants to amend their grounds of appeal before the hearing;

(e) require appeals to be determined on the merits rather than by way of review; and

(f) provide for further appeals to courts on points of law.

(6) An order under this section shall be made by statutory instrument which shall be subject to annulment in pursuance of a resolution of either House of Parliament.

(7) * * * * *

* * * * *

PART II
CONTRACTING OUT

Contracting out of functions

69 Functions of Ministers and office-holders

(1) This section applies to any function of a Minister or office-holder—

(a) which is conferred by or under any enactment; and

(b) which, by virtue of any enactment or rule of law, may be exercised by an officer of his; and

(c) which is not excluded by section 71 below.

(2) If a Minister by order so provides, a function to which this section applies may be exercised by, or by employees of, such person (if any) as may be authorised in that behalf by the office-holder or Minister whose function it is.

(3) A Minister shall not make an order under this section in relation to an office-holder without first consulting him.

(4) An order under this section may provide that a function to which this section applies may be exercised, and an authorisation given by virtue of such an order may (subject to the provisions of the order) authorise the exercise of such a function—

(a) either wholly or to such extent as may be specified in the order or authorisation;

(b) either generally or in such cases or areas as may be so specified; and

(c) either unconditionally or subject to the fulfilment of such conditions as may be so specified.

(5) An authorisation given by virtue of an order under this section—

(a) shall be for such period, not exceeding 10 years, as is specified in the authorisation;

(b) may be revoked at any time by the Minister or office-holder by whom the authorisation is given; and

(c) shall not prevent the Minister or office-holder or any other person from exercising the function to which the authorisation relates.

70 Functions of local authorities

(1) This section applies to any function of a local authority—

(a) which is conferred by or under any enactment; and

(b) which, by virtue of section 101 of the Local Government Act 1972 or section 56 of the Local Government (Scotland) Act 1973 (arrangements for discharge of functions by local authorities), may be exercised by an officer of the authority; and

(c) which is not excluded by section 71 below.

(2) If a Minister by order so provides, a function to which this section applies may be exercised by, or by employees of, such person (if any) as may be authorised in that behalf by the local authority whose function it is.

(3) A Minister shall not make an order under this section in relation to a local authority without first consulting—

(a) in the case of an authority in England or Wales, such representatives of local government;

(b) in the case of an authority in Scotland, such associations of local authorities, as he considers appropriate.

(4) Subsections (4) and (5) of section 69 above shall apply for the purposes of this section as they apply for the purposes of that section; and in subsection (5) of that section as so applied any reference to the Minister or office-holder by whom the authorisation is given shall be construed as a reference to the local authority by which the authorisation is given.

(5) * * * * *

71 Functions excluded from sections 69 and 70

(1) Subject to subections (2) and (3) below, a function is excluded from sections 69 and 70 above if—

(a) its exercise would constitute the exercise of jurisdiction of any court or of any tribunal which exercises the judicial power of the State; or

(b) its exercise, or a failure to exercise it, would necessarily interfere with or otherwise affect the liberty of any individual; or

(c) it is a power or right of entry, search or seizure into or of any property; or

(d) it is a power or duty to make subordinate legislation.

(2), (3) * * * * *

72 Effect of contracting out

(1) This section applies where by virtue of an order made under section 69 or 70 above a person is authorised to exercise any function of a Minister, office-holder or local authority.

(2) Subject to subsection (3) below, anything done or omitted to be done by or in relation to the authorised person (or an employee of his) in, or in connection with, the exercise or purported exercise of the function shall be treated for all purposes as done or omitted to be done—

(a) in the case of a function of a Minister or office-holder, by or in relation to the Minister or office-holder in his capacity as such;

(b) in the case of a function of a local authority, by or in relation to that authority.

(3) Subsection (2) above shall not apply—

(a) for the purposes of so much of any contract made between the authorised person and the Minister, office-holder or local authority as relates to the exercise of the function, or

(b) for the purposes of any criminal proceedings brought in respect of anything done or omitted to be done by the authorised person (or an employee of his).

* * * * *

DRUG TRAFFICKING ACT 1994
(1994, c. 37)

An Act to consolidate the Drug Trafficking Offences Act 1986 and certain provisions of the Criminal Justice (International Co-operation) Act 1990 relating to drug trafficking.

[3 November 1994]

Territorial extent England and Wales

PART I
CONFISCATION ORDERS

Introductory

1 Meaning of "drug trafficking" and "drug trafficking offence"

(1) In this Act "drug trafficking" means, subject to subsection (2) below, doing or being concerned in any of the following, whether in England and Wales or elsewhere—

(a) producing or supplying a controlled drug where the production or supply contravenes section 4(1) of the Misuse of Drugs Act 1971 or a corresponding law;

(b) transporting or storing a controlled drug where possession of the drug contravenes section 5(1) of that Act or a corresponding law;

(c) importing or exporting a controlled drug where the importation or exportation is prohibited by section 3(1) of that Act or a corresponding law;

(d) manufacturing or supplying a scheduled substance within the meaning of section 12 of the Criminal Justice (International Co-operation) Act 1990 where the manufacture or supply is an offence under that section or would be such an offence if it took place in England and Wales;

(e) using any ship for illicit traffic in controlled drugs in circumstances which amount to the commission of an offence under section 19 of that Act;

(f) conduct which is an offence under section 49 of this Act or which would be such an offence if it took place in England and Wales;

(g) acquiring, having possession of or using property in circumstances which amount to the commission of an offence under section 51 of this Act or which would amount to such an offence if it took place in England and Wales.

(2) "Drug trafficking" also includes a person doing the following, whether in England and Wales or elsewhere, that is to say entering into or being otherwise concerned in an arrangement whereby—

(a) the retention or control by or on behalf of another person of the other person's proceeds of drug trafficking is facilitated; or

(b) the proceeds of drug trafficking by another person are used to secure that funds are placed at the other person's disposal or are used for the other person's benefit to acquire property by way of investment.

(3)-(5) * * * * *

PART IV
MISCELLANEOUS AND SUPPLEMENTAL

Investigations into drug trafficking

55 Order to make material available

(1) A constable may, for the purpose of an investigation into drug trafficking, apply to a Circuit judge for an order under subsection (2) below in relation to particular material or material of a particular description.

(2) If on such an application the judge is satisfied that the conditions in subsection (4) below are fulfilled, he may make an order that the person who appears to him to be in possession of the material to which the application relates shall—

(a) produce it to a constable for him to take away, or

(b) give a constable access to it,

within such period as the order may specify.

This subsection has effect subject to section 59(11) of this Act.

(3) The period to be specified in an order under subsection (2) above shall be seven days unless it appears to the judge that a longer or shorter period would be appropriate in the particular circumstances of the application.

(4) The conditions referred to in subsection (2) above are—

(a) that there are reasonable grounds for suspecting that a specified person has carried on or has benefitted from drug trafficking;

(b) that there are reasonable grounds for suspecting that the material to which the application relates—

(i) is likely to be of substantial value (whether by itself or together with other material) to the investigation for the purpose of which the application is made; and

(ii) does not consist of or include items subject to legal privilege or excluded material; and

(c) that there are reasonable grounds for believing that it is in the public interest, having regard—

(i) to the benefit likely to accrue to the investigation if the material is obtained, and

(ii) to the circumstances under which the person in possession of the material holds it,

that the material should be produced or that access to it should be given.

(5) Where the judge makes an order under subsection (2)(b) above in relation to material on any premises he may, on the application of a constable, order any person who appears to him to be entitled to grant entry to the premises to allow a constable to enter the premises to obtain access to the material.

(6) An application under subsection (1) or (5) above may be made ex parte to a judge in chambers.

(7)-(9) * * * * *

(10) An order under subsection (2) above—

(a) shall not confer any right to production of, or access to, items subject to legal privilege or excluded material;

(b) shall have effect notwithstanding any obligation as to secrecy or other restriction upon the disclosure of information imposed by statute or otherwise; and

(c) may be made in relation to material in the possession of an authorised government department;

and in this subsection "authorised government department" means a government department which is an authorised department for the purposes of the Crown Proceedings Act 1947.

56 Authority for search

(1) A constable may, for the purpose of an investigation into drug trafficking, apply to a Circuit judge for a warrant under this section in relation to specified premises.

(2) On such application the judge may issue a warrant authorising a constable to enter and search the premises if the judge is satisfied—

(a) that an order made under section 55 of this Act in relation to material on the premises has not been complied with;

(b) that the conditions in subsection (3) below are fulfilled; or

(c) that the conditions in subsection (4) below are fulfilled.

(3) The conditions referred to in subsection (2)(b) above are—

(a) that there are reasonable grounds for suspecting that a specified person has carried on or has benefited from drug trafficking;

(b) that the conditions in subsection (4)(b) and (c) of section 55 of this Act are fulfilled in relation to any material on the premises; and

(c) that it would not be appropriate to make an order under that section in relation to the material because—

(i) it is not practicable to communicate with any person entitled to produce the material;

(ii) it is not practicable to communicate with any person entitled to grant access to the material or entitled to grant entry to the premises on which the material is situated; or

(iii) the investigation for the purpose of which the application is made might be seriously prejudiced unless a constable could secure immediate access to the material.

(4) The conditions referred to in subsection (2)(c) above are—

(a) that there are reasonable grounds for suspecting that a specified person has carried on or has benefited from drug trafficking;

(b) that there are reasonable grounds for suspecting that there is on the premises material relating to the specified person or to drug trafficking which is likely to be of substantial value (whether by itself or together with other material) to the investigation for the purpose of which the application is made, but that the material cannot at the time of the application be particularised; and

(c) that—

(i) it is not practicable to communicate with any person entitled to grant entry to the premises;

(ii) entry to the premises will not be granted unless a warrant is produced; or

(iii) the investigation for the purpose of which the application is made might be seriously prejudiced unless a constable arriving at the premises could secure immediate entry to them.

(5) Where a constable has entered premises in the execution of a warrant issued under this section, he may seize and retain any material, other than items subject to legal privilege and excluded material, which is likely to be of substantial value (whether by itself or together with other material) to the investigation for the purpose of which the warrant was issued.

57 Provisions supplementary to sections 55 and 56

(1) For the purposes of sections 21 and 22 of the Police and Criminal Evidence Act 1984 (access to, and copying and retention of, seized material)—

(a) an investigation into drug trafficking shall be treated as if it were an investigation of or in connection with an offence; and

(b) material produced in pursuance of an order under section 55(2)(a) of this Act shall be treated as if it were material seized by a constable.

(2) In sections 55 and 56 of this Act "excluded material", "items subject to legal privilege" and "premises" have the same meaning as in the 1984 Act.

58 Offence of prejudicing investigation

(1) Where, in relation to an investigation into drug trafficking—

(a) an order under section 55 of this Act has been made or has been applied for and has not been refused, or

(b) a warrant under section 56 of this Act has been issued,

a person is guilty of an offence if, knowing or suspecting that the investigation is taking place, he makes any disclosure which is likely to prejudice the investigation.

(2) In proceedings against a person for an offence under this section, it is a defence to prove—

(a) that he did not know or suspect that the disclosure was likely to prejudice the investigation; or

(b) that he had lawful authority or reasonable excuse for making the disclosure.

(3) Nothing in subsection (1) above makes it an offence for a professional legal adviser to disclose any information or other matter—

(a) to, or to a representative of, a client of his in connection with the giving by the adviser of legal advice to the client; or

(b) to any person—

(i) in contemplation of, or in connection with, legal proceedings; and

(ii) for the purpose of those proceedings.

(4) Subsection (3) above does not apply in relation to any information or other matter which is disclosed with a view to furthering any criminal purpose.

(5) A person guilty of an offence under this section shall be liable—

(a) on summary conviction, to imprisonment for a term not exceeding six months or to a fine not exceeding the statutory maximum or to both; and

(b) on conviction on indictment, to imprisonment for a term not exceeding five years or to a fine or to both.

★ ★ ★ ★ ★

EDUCATION ACT 1994
(1994, c. 30)

An Act to make provision about teacher training and related matters; to make provision with respect to the conduct of students' unions; and for connected purposes. [21 July 1994]

Territorial extent England and Wales, Scotland

★ ★ ★ ★ ★

PART II
STUDENTS' UNIONS

20 Meaning of "students' union"

(1) In this part a "students' union" means—

(a) an association of the generality of students at an establishment to which this Part applies whose principal purposes include promoting the general interests of its members as students; or

(b) a representative body (whether an association or not) whose principal purposes include representing the generality of students at an estblishment to which this Part applies in academic, disciplinary or other matters relating to the government of the establishment.

(2) References in this Part to a students' union include an association or body which would fall within subsection (1) if for the references to the generality of students at the establishment there were substituted a reference to—

(a) the generality of undergraduate students, or graduate students, at the establishment; or

(b) the generality of students at a particular hall of residence of the establishment.

(3) References in this Part to a students' union include an association or body which consists wholly or mainly of—

(a) constituent or affiliated associations or bodies which are themselves students' unions within subsection (1) or (2), or

(b) representatives of such constituent or affiliated associations,

and which fulfils the functions of a student's union within subsection (1) or (2) in relation to students at an establishment to which this Part applies.

(4) An association or body may be a students' union within the meaning of this Part in relation to more than one establishment but not in relation to establishments generally in the United Kingdom or a part of the United Kingdom.

(5) References in this section to an association of the generality of students, or of any description of students, include—

(a) any association which the generality of students, or of students of that description, may join, whether or not it has in membership a majority of them, and

(b) any association which would fall within paragraph (a) if the references there to students were confined to full-time students;

and references to a representative body whose principal purposes include representing the generality of students, or of any description of students, shall be similarly construed.

21 Establishments to which Part II applies

(1) The establishments in England and Wales to which this Part applies are—

(a) any university receiving financial support under section 65 of the Further and Higher Education Act 1992;

(b) any institution conducted by a higher education corporation or further education corporation within the meaning of that Act;

(c) any institution designated under section 129 of the Education Reform Act 1988 as eligible to receive support from funds administered by a higher education funding council;

(d) any institution designated under section 28 of the Further and Higher Education Act 1992 as eligible to receive support from funds administered by a further education funding council;

(e) any institution substantially dependent on financial support under section 6(5) of that Act (certain institutions providing facilities for part-time, or adult, further education);

(f) any institution designated, or of a description designated, by order of the Secretary of State;

(g) any college, school or hall in an establishment within any of the above paragraphs.

(2) The establishments in Scotland to which this Part applies are—

(a) any institution within the higher education sector for the purposes of section 56(2) of the Further and Higher Education (Scotland) Act 1992;

(b) any college of further education (within the meaning of section 36(1) of that Act), the board of managment of which, or in respect of which an appropriate person, is in receipt of a grant, loan or other payment as mentioned in section 4(1) of that Act;

(c) any central institution within the meaning of section 135(1) of the Education (Scotland) Act 1980;

(d) any institution designated, or of a description designated, by order of the Secretary of State.

(3) For the purposes of subsection (1)(e) an institution is substantially dependent on financial support under section 6(5) of the Further and Higher Education Act 1992 in any year in which such support amounts to 25 per cent. or more of its income.

For this purpose "year" means an accounting year of the institution, and "income" means receipts of any description, including capital receipts.

(4) In subsection (1)(g) "college" includes any institution in the nature of a college.

(5) References in this Part to the governing body of an establishment are to the executive governing body which has responsibility for the conduct of affairs of the establishment and the management and administration of its revenue and property.

22 Requirements to be observed in relation to students' unions

(1) The governing body of every establishment to which this Part applies shall take such steps as are reasonably practicable to secure that any students' union for students at the establishment operates in a fair and democratic manner and is accountable for its finances.

(2) The governing body shall in particular take such steps as are reasonably practicable to secure that the following requirements are observed by or in relation to any students' union for students at the establishment—

(a) the union should have a written constitution;

(b) the provisions of the constitution should be subject to the approval of the governing body and to review by that body at intervals of not more than five years;

(c) a student should have the right—

(i) not to be a member of the union, or

(ii) in the case of a representative body which is not an association, to signify that he does not wish to be represented by it,

and students who exercise that right should not be unfairly disadvantaged, with regard to the provision of services or otherwise, by reason of their having done so;

(d) appointment to major union offices should be by election in a secret ballot in which all members are entitled to vote;

(e) the govering body should satisfy themselves that the elections are fairly and properly conducted;

(f) a person should not hold sabbatical union office, or paid elected union office, for more than two years in total at the establishment;

(g) the financial affairs of the union should be properly conducted and appropriate arrangements should exist for the approval of the union's budget, and the monitoring of its expenditure, by the governing body;

(h) financial reports of the union should be published annually or more frequently, and should be made available to the governing body and to all students, and each such report should contain, in particular—

(i) a list of the external organisations to which the union has made donations in the period to which the report relates, and

(ii) details of those donations;

(i) the procedure for allocating resources to groups or clubs should be fair and should be set down in writing and freely accessible to all students;

(j) if the union decides to affiliate to an external organisation, it should publish notice of its decision stating—

(i) the name of the organisation, and

(ii) details of any subscription or similar fee paid or proposed to be paid, and of any donation made or proposed to be made, to the organisation,

and any such notice should be made available to the govering body and to all students;

(k) where the union is affiliated to any external organisations, a report should be published annually or more frequently containing—

(i) a list of the external organisations to which the union is currently affiliated, and

(ii) details of subscriptions or similar fees paid, or donations made, to such organisations in the past year (or since the last report),

and such reports should be made available to the governing body and to all students;

(l) there should be procedures for the review of affiliations to external organisations under which—

(i) the current list of affiliations is submitted for approval by members annually or more frequently, and

(ii) at such intervals of not more than a year as the governing body may determine, a requisition may be made by such proportion of members (not exceeding 5 per cent.) as the governing body may determine, that the question of continued affiliation to any particular organisation be decided upon by a secret ballot in which all members are entitled to vote;

(m) there should be a complaints procedure available to all students or groups of students who—

(i) are dissatisfied in their dealings with the union, or

(ii) claim to be unfairly disadvantaged by reason of their having exercised the right referred to in paragraph (c)(i) or (ii) above,

which should include provision for an independent person appointed by the governing body to investigate and report on complaints;

(n) complaints should be dealt with promptly and fairly and where a complaint is upheld there should be an effective remedy.

(3) The governing body of every establishment to which this Part applies shall for the purposes of this section prepare and issue, and when necessary revise, a code of practice as to the manner in which the requirements set out above are to be carried into effect in relation to any students' union for students at the establishment, setting out in relation to each of the requirements details of the arrangements made to secure its observance.

(4) The governing body of every establishment to which this Part applies shall as regards any students' union for students at the establishment bring to the attention of all students, at least once a year—

(a) the code of practice currently in force under subsection (3),

(b) any restrictions imposed on the activities of the union by the law relating to charities, and

(c) where the establishment is one to which section 43 of the Education (No. 2) Act 1986 applies (freedom of speech in universities and colleges), the provisions of that section, and of any code of practice issued under it, relevant to the activities or conduct of the union.

(5) The governing body of every establishment to which this Part applies shall bring to the attention of all students, at least once a year, and shall include in any information which is generally made available to persons considering whether to become students at the establishment—

(a) information as to the right referred to in subsection (2)(c)(i) and (ii), and

(b) details of any arrangements it has made for services of a kind which a students' union at the establishment provides for its members to be provided for students who are not members of the union.

(6) In subsections (2), (4) and (5) the expression "all students" shall be construed as follows—

(a) in relation to an association or body which is a students' union by virtue of section 20(1), the reference is to all students at the establishment;

(b) in relation to an association or body which is a students' union by virtue of section 20(2), the reference is to all undergraduate, or all graduate, students at the establishment or to all students at the hall of residence in question, as the case may be;

(c) in relation to an association or body which is a students' union by virtue of section 20(3), the reference is to all the students who by virtue of section 20(1) or (2) are comprehended by that expression in relation to its constituent or affiliated associations or bodies.

(7) In this section the expression "members", in relation to a representative body which is not an association, means those whom it is the purpose of the union to represent, excluding any student who has exercised the right referred to in subsection (2)(c)(ii).

(8) In subsection (2)(j) to (l) the references to affiliation to an external organisation, in relation to a students' union for students at an establishment, include any form of membership of, or formal association with, an organisation whose purposes are not confined to purposes connected with that establishment.

(9) Subsection (2)(d) and (1)(ii) (elections and affiliations: requirements to hold secret ballot of all members) do not apply in the case of an open or distance learning establishment, that is, an establishment where the students, or the great majority of them, are provided with materials for private study and are not required to attend the establishment to any significant extent or at all.

★ ★ ★ ★ ★

EUROPEAN UNION (ACCESSIONS) ACT 1994
(1994, c. 38)

An Act to amend the definition of "the treaties" and "the Community Treaties" in section 1(2) of the European Communities Act 1972 so as to include the treaty concerning the accession of the Kingdom of Norway, the Republic of Austria, the Republic of Finland and the Kingdom of Sweden to the European Union; and to approve the treaty for the purposes of section 6 of the European Parliamentary Elections Act 1978. [3 November 1994]

Territorial extent United Kingdom

1 Extended meaning of "the Treaties" and "the Community Treaties"

In section 1(2) of the European Communities Act 1972, in the definition of "the Treaties" and "the Community Treaties", after paragraph (m) there shall be inserted the words "and

(n) the treaty concerning the accession of the Kingdom of Norway, the Republic of Austria, the Republic of Finland and the Kingdom of Sweden to the European Union, signed at Corfu on 24th June 1994;"

2 Powers of European Parliament
For the purposes of section 6 of the European Parliamentary Elections Act 1978 the treaty concerning the accession of the Kingdom of Norway, the Republic of Austria, the Republic of Finland and the Kingdom of Sweden to the European Union, signed at Corfu on 24th June 1994, is approved.

3 Short title
This Act may be cited as the European Union (Accessions) Act 1994.

INTELLIGENCE SERVICES ACT 1994
(1994, c. 13)

An Act to make provision about the Secret Intelligence Service and the Government Communications Headquarters, including provision for the issue of warrants and authorisations enabling certain actions to be taken and for the issue of such warrants and authorisations to be kept under review; to make further provision about warrants issued on applications by the Security Service; to establish a procedure for the investigation of complaints about the Secret Intelligence Service and the Government Communications Headquarters; to make provision for the establishment of an Intelligence and Security Committee to scrutinise all three of those bodies; and for connected purposes. [26 May 1994]

Territorial extent United Kingdom. Sections 5(1) and 11(1) also apply to the Colonies Listed in the Intelligence Services Act 1994 (Dependent Territories) Order 1995 (SI 1995/752).

The Secret Intelligence Service

1 The Secret Intelligence Service
(1) There shall continue to be a Secret Intelligence Service (in this Act referred to as "the Intelligence Service") under the authority of the Secretary of State; and, subject to subsection (2) below, its functions shall be—

(a) to obtain and provide information relating to the actions or intentions of persons outside the British Islands; and

(b) to perform other tasks relating to the actions or intentions of such persons.

(2) The functions of the Intelligence Service shall be exercisable only—

(a) in the interests of national security, with particular reference to the defence and foreign policies of Her Majesty's Government in the United Kingdom; or

(b) in the interests of the economic well-being of the United Kingdom; or

(c) in support of the prevention or detection of serious crime.

2 The Chief of the Intelligence Service
(1) The operations of the Intelligence Service shall continue to be under the control of a Chief of that Service appointed by the Secretary of State.

(2) The Chief of the Intelligence Service shall be responsible for the efficiency of that Service and it shall be his duty to ensure—

(a) that there are arrangements for securing that no information is obtained by the Intelligence Service except so far as necessary for the proper discharge of its functions and that no information is disclosed by it except so far as necessary—

(i) for that purpose;
(ii) in the interests of national security;
(iii) for the purpose of the prevention or detection of serious crime; or
(iv) for the purpose of any criminal proceedings; and

(b) that the Intelligence Service does not take any action to further the interests of any United Kingdom political party.

(3) Without prejudice to the generality of subsection (2)(a) above, the disclosure of information shall be regarded as necessary for the proper discharge of the functions of the Intelligence Service if it consists of—

(a) the disclosure of records subject to and in accordance with the Public Records Act 1958; or

(b) the disclosure, subject to and in accordance with arrangements approved by the Secretary of State, of information to the Comptroller and Auditor General for the purposes of his functions.

(4) The Chief of the Intelligence Service shall make an annual report on the work of the Intelligence Service to the Prime Minister and the Secretary of State and may at any time report to either of them on any matter relating to its work.

GCHQ

3 The Government Communications Headquarters

(1) There shall continue to be a Government Communications Headquarters under the authority of the Secretary of State; and, subject to subsection (2) below, its functions shall be—

(a) to monitor or interfere with electromagnetic, acoustic and other emissions and any equipment producing such emissions and to obtain and provide information derived from or related to such emissions or equipment and from encrypted material; and

(b) to provide advice and assistance about—

(i) languages, including terminology used for technical matters, and

(ii) cryptography and other matters relating to the protection of information and other material,

to the armed forces of the Crown, to Her Majesty's Government in the United Kingdom or to a Northern Ireland Department or to any other organisation which is determined for the purposes of this section in such manner as may be specified by the Prime Minister.

(2) The functions referred to in subsection (1)(a) above shall be exercisable only—

(a) in the interests of national security, with particular reference to the defence and foreign policies of Her Majesty's Government in the United Kingdom; or

(b) in the interests of the economic well-being of the United Kingdom in relation to the actions or intentions of persons outside the British Islands; or

(c) in support of the prevention or detection of serious crime.

(3) In this Act the expression "GCHQ" refers to the Government Communications Headquarters and to any unit or part of a unit of the armed forces of the Crown which is for the time being required by the Secretary of State to assist the Government Communications Headquarters in carrying out its functions.

4 The Director of GCHQ

(1) The operations of GCHQ shall continue to be under the control of a Director appointed by the Secretary of State.

(2) The Director shall be responsible for the efficiency of GCHQ and it shall be his duty to ensure—

(a) that there are arrangements for securing that no information is obtained by GCHQ except so far as necessary for the proper discharge of its functions and that no information is disclosed by it except so far as necessary for that purpose or for the purpose of any criminal proceedings; and

(b) that GCHQ does not take any action to further the interests of any United Kingdom political party.

(3) Without prejudice to the generality of subsection (2)(a) above, the disclosure of information shall be regarded as necessary for the proper discharge of the functions of GCHQ if it consists of—

(a) the disclosure of records subject to and in accordance with the Public Records Act 1958; or

(b) the disclosure, subject to and in accordance with arrangements approved by the Secretary of State, of information to the Comptroller and Auditor General for the purposes of his functions.

(4) The Director shall make an annual report on the work of GCHQ to the Prime Minister and the Secretary of State and may at any time report to either of them on any matter relating to its work.

Authorisation of certain actions

5 Warrants: general

(1) No entry on or interference with property or with wireless telegraphy shall be unlawful if it is authorised by a warrant issued by the Secretary of State under this section.

(2) The Secretary of State may, on an application made by the Security Service, the Intelligence Service or GCHQ, issue a warrant under this section authorising the taking, subject to subsection (3) below, of such action as is specified in the warrant in respect of any property so specified or in respect of wireless telegraphy so specified if the Secretary of State—

(a) thinks it necessary for the action to be taken on the ground that it is likely to be of substantial value in assisting, as the case may be,—

(i) the Security Service in carrying out any of its functions under the 1989 Act; or

(ii) the Intelligence Service in carrying out any of its functions under section 1 above; or

(iii) GCHQ in carrying out any function which falls within section 3(1)(a) above; and

(b) is satisfied that what the action seeks to achieve cannot reasonably be achieved by other means; and

(c) is satisfied that satisfactory arrangements are in force under section 2(2)(a) of the 1989 Act (duties of the Director-General of the Security Service), section 2(2)(a) above or section 4(2)(a) above with respect to the disclosure of information obtained by virtue of this section and that any information obtained under the warrant will be subject to those arrangements.

[(3) A warrant issued on the application of the Intelligence Service or GCHQ for the purposes of the exercise of their functions by virtue of section 1(2)(c) or 3(2)(c) above may not relate to property in the British Islands.

(3A) A warrant issued on the application of the Security Service for the purposes of the exercise of their function under section 1(4) of the Security Service Act 1989 may not relate to property in the British Islands unless it authorises the taking of action in relation to conduct within subsection (3B) below.

(3B) Conduct is within this subsection if it constitutes (or, if it took place in the United Kingdom, would constitute) one or more offences, and either—

(a) it involves the use of violence, results in substantial financial gain or is conduct by a large number of persons in pursuit of a common purpose; or

(b) the offence or one of the offences is an offence for which a person who has attained the age of twenty-one and has no previous convictions could reasonably be expected to be sentenced to imprisonment for a term of three years or more.]

(4) Subject to subsection (5) below, the Security Service may make an application under subsection (2) above for a warrant to be issued authorising that Service (or a

person acting on its behalf) to take such action as is specified in the warrant on behalf of the Intelligence Service or GCHQ and, where such a warrant is issued, the functions of the Security Service shall include the carrying out of the action so specified, whether or not it would otherwise be within its functions.

(5) The Security Service may not make an application for a warrant by virtue of subsection (4) above except where the action proposed to be authorised by the warrant—

(a) is action in respect of which the Intelligence Service or, as the case may be, GCHQ could make such an application; and

(b) is to be taken otherwise than in support of the prevention or detection of serious crime.

6 Warrants: procedure and duration, etc.

(1) A warrant shall not be issued except—

(a) under the hand of the Secretary of State; or

(b) in an urgent case where the Secretary of State has expressly authorised its issue and a statement of the fact is endorsed on it, under the hand of a senior official of his department.

(2) A warrant shall, unless renewed under subsection (3) below, cease to have effect—

(a) if the warrant was under the hand of the Secretary of State, at the end of the period of six months beginning with the day on which it was issued; and

(b) in any other case, at the end of the period ending with the second working day following that day.

(3) If at any time before the day on which a warrant would cease to have effect the Secretary of State considers it necessary for the warrant to continue to have effect for the purpose for which it was issued, he may by an instrument under his hand renew it for a period of six months beginning with that day.

(4) The Secretary of State shall cancel a warrant if he is satisfied that the action authorised by it is no longer necessary.

(5), (6) ★ ★ ★ ★ ★

7 Authorisation of acts outside the British Islands

(1) If, apart from this section, a person would be liable in the United Kingdom for any act done outside the British Islands, he shall not be so liable if the act is one which is authorised to be done by virtue of an authorisation given by the Secretary of State under this section.

(2) In subsection (1) above "liable in the United Kingdom" means liable under the criminal or civil law of any part of the United Kingdom.

(3) The Secretary of State shall not give an authorisation under this section unless he is satisfied—

(a) that any acts which may be done in reliance on the authorisation or, as the case may be, the operation in the course of which the acts may be done will be necessary for the proper discharge of a function of the Intelligence Service; and

(b) that there are satisfactory arrangements in force to secure—

(i) that nothing will be done in reliance on the authorisation beyond what is necessary for the proper discharge of a function of the Intelligence Service; and

(ii) that, in so far as any act may be done in reliance on the authorisation, their nature and likely consequences will be reasonable, having regard to the purposes for which they are carried out; and

(c) that there are satisfactory arrangements in force under section 2(2)(a) above with respect to the disclosure of information obtained by virtue of this section and that any information obtained by virtue of anything done in reliance on the authorisation will be subject to those arrangements.

(4) Without prejudice to the generality of the power of the Secretary of State to give an authorisation under this section, such an authorisation—

(a) may relate to a particular act or acts, to acts of a description specified in the authorisation or to acts undertaken in the course of an operation so specified;

(b) may be limited to a particular person or persons of a description so specified; and

(c) may be subject to conditions so specified.

(5) An authorisation shall not be given under this section except—

(a) under the hand of the Secretary of State; or

(b) in an urgent case where the Secretary of State has expressly authorised it to be given and a statement of that fact is endorsed on it, under the hand of a senior official of his department.

(6) An authorisation shall, unless renewed under subsection (7) below, cease to have effect—

(a) if the authorisation was given under the hand of the Secretary of State, at the end of the period of six months beginning with the day on which it was given;

(b) in any other case, at the end of the period ending with the second working day following the day on which it was given.

(7) If at any time before the day on which an authorisation would cease to have effect the Secretary of State considers it necessary for the authorisation to continue to have effect for the purpose for which it was given, he may by an instrument under his hand renew it for a period of six months beginning with that day.

(8) The Secretary of State shall cancel an authorisation if he is satisfied that any act authorised by it is no longer necessary.

The Commissioner, the Tribunal and the investigation of complaints

8 The Commissioner

(1) The Prime Minister shall appoint as a Commissioner for the purposes of this Act a person who holds or has held high judicial office within the meaning of the Appellate Jurisdiction Act 1876.

(2) The Commissioner shall hold office in accordance with the terms of his appointment and there shall be paid to him by the Secretary of State such allowances as the Treasury may determine.

(3) In addition to his functions under the subsequent provisions of this Act the Commissioner shall keep under review the exercise by the Secretary of State of his powers under sections 5 to 7 above, except in so far as the powers under sections 5 and 6 above relate to the Security Service.

(4) It shall be the duty of—

(a) every member of the Intelligence Service,

(b) every member of GCHQ, and

(c) every official of the department of the Secretary of State,

to disclose or give to the Commissioner such documents or information as he may require for the purpose of enabling him to discharge his functions.

(5) The Commissioner shall make an annual report on the discharge of his functions to the Prime Minister and may at any time report to him on any matter relating to his discharge of those functions.

(6) The Prime Minister shall lay before each House of Parliament a copy of each annual report made by the Commissioner under subsection (5) above together with a statement as to whether any matter has been excluded from that copy in pursuance of subsection (7) below.

(7) If it appears to the Prime Minister, after consultation with the Commissioner, that the publication of any matter in a report would be prejudicial to the continued discharge of the functions of the Intelligence Service or, as the case may be, GCHQ, the

Prime Minister may exclude that matter from the copy of the report as laid before each House of Parliament.

(8) The Secretary of State may, after consultation with the Commissioner and with the approval of the Treasury as to numbers, provide the Commissioner with such staff as the Secretary of State thinks necessary for the discharge of his functions.

9 Investigation of complaints

(1) There shall be a Tribunal for the purpose of investigating complaints about the Intelligence Service or GCHQ in the manner specified in Schedule 1 to this Act.

(2) The Commissioner shall have the functions conferred on him by Schedule 1 to this Act and give the Tribunal all such assistance in discharging their functions under that Schedule as they may require.

(3) Schedule 2 to this Act shall have effect with respect to the constitution, procedure and other matters relating to the Tribunal.

(4) The decisions of the Tribunal and the Commissioner under Schedule 1 to this Act (including decisions as to their jurisdictions) shall not be subject to appeal or liable to be questioned in any court.

10 The Intelligence and Security Committee

(1) There shall be a Committee, to be known as the Intelligence and Security Committee and in this section referred to as "the Committee", to examine the expenditure, administration and policy of—

(a) the Security Service;

(b) the Intelligence Service; and

(c) GCHQ.

(2) The Committee shall consist of nine members—

(a) who shall be drawn both from the members of the House of Commons and from the members of the House of Lords; and

(b) none of whom shall be a Minister of the Crown.

(3) The members of the Committee shall be appointed by the Prime Minister after consultation with the Leader of the Opposition, within the meaning of the Ministerial and other Salaries Act 1975; and one of those members shall be so appointed as Chairman of the Committee.

(4) Schedule 3 to this Act shall have effect with respect to the tenure of office of members of, the procedure of and other matters relating to, the Committee; and in that Schedule "the Committee" has the same meaning as in this section.

(5) The Committee shall make an annual report on the discharge of their functions to the Prime Minister and may at any time report to him on any matter relating to the discharge of those functions.

(6) The Prime Minsiter shall lay before each House of Parliament a copy of each annual report made by the Committee under subsection (5) above together with a statement as to whether any matter has been excluded from that copy in pursuance of subsection (7) below.

(7) If it appears to the Prime Minister, after consultation with the Committee, that the publication of any matter in a report would be prejudicial to the continued discharge of the functions of either of the Services or, as the case may be, GCHQ, the Prime Minister may exclude that matter from the copy of the report as laid before each House of Parliament.

11, 12 * * * * *

TRADE MARKS ACT 1994
(1994, c. 26)

An Act to make new provision for registered trade marks, implementing Council Directive No. 89/104/EEC of 21st December 1988 to approximate the laws of the Member States relating to trade marks; to make provision in connection with Council Regulation (EC) No. 40/94 of 20th December 1993 of the Community trade mark; to give effect to the Madrid Protocol Relating to the International Registration of Marks of 27th June 1989, and to certain provisions of the Paris Convention for the Protection of Industrial Property of 20th March 1883, as revised and amended; and for connected purposes. [21 July 1994]

Territorial extent United Kingdom and (subject to s. 108(2)) the Isle of Man.

★ ★ ★ ★ ★

4 Specially protected emblems

(1) A trade mark which consists of or contains—

(a) the Royal arms, or any of the principal armorial bearings of the Royal arms, or any insignia or device so nearly resembling the Royal arms or any such armorial bearing as to be likely to be mistaken for them or it,

(b) a representation of the Royal crown or any of the Royal flags,

(c) a representation of Her Majesty or any member of the Royal family, or any colourable imitation thereof, or

(d) words, letters or devices likely to lead persons to think that the applicant either has or recently has had Royal patronage or authorisation,

shall not be registered unless it appears to the registrar that consent has been given by or on behalf of Her Majesty or, as the case may be, the relevant member of the Royal family.

(2) A trade mark which consists of or contains a representation of—

(a) the national flag of the United Kingdom (commonly known as the Union Jack), or

(b) the flag of England, Wales, Scotland, Northern Ireland or the Isle of Man,

shall not be registered if it appears to the registrar that the use of the trade mark would be misleading or grossly offensive.

Provision may be made by rules identifying the flags to which paragraph (b) applies.

(3), (4), (5) ★ ★ ★ ★ ★

★ ★ ★ ★ ★

Unauthorised use of Royal arms, &c.

99.—(1) A person shall not without the authority of Her Majesty use in connection with any business the Royal arms (or arms so closely resembling the Royal arms as to be calculated to deceive) in such manner as to be calculated to lead to the belief that he is duly authorised to use the Royal arms.

(2) A person shall not without the authority of Her Majesty or of a member of the Royal family use in connection with any business any device, emblem or title in such a manner as to be calculated to lead to the belief that he is employed by, or supplies goods or services to, Her Majesty or that member of the Royal family.

(3) A person who contravenes subsection (1) commits an offence and is liable on summary conviction to a fine not exceeding level 2 on the standard scale.

(4) Contravention of subsection (1) or (2) may be restrained by injunction in proceedings brought by—

(a) any person who is authorised to use the arms, device, emblem or title in question, or

(b) any person authorised by the Lord Chamberlain to take such proceedings.

(5) Nothing in this section affects any right of the proprietor of a trade mark containing any such arms, device, emblem or title to use that trade mark.

* * * * *

CRIMINAL APPEAL ACT 1995
(1995, c. 35)

An Act to amend provisions relating to appeals and references to the Court of Appeal in criminal cases; to establish a Criminal Cases Review Commission and confer functions on, and make other provision in relation to, the Commission; to amend section 142 of the Magistrates' Courts Act 1980 and introduce in Northern Ireland provision similar to those of that section; to amend section 133 of the Criminal Justice Act 1988; and for connected purposes. [19th July 1995]

Territorial extent England and Wales, Northern Ireland (except ss. 9, 11)

Note: The "1968 Act" refers to the Criminal Appeal Act 1968 and the "1980 Act" refers to the Criminal Appeal (Northern Ireland) Act 1980.

* * * * *

PART II
THE CRIMINAL CASES REVIEW COMMISSION

The Commission

8 The Commission

(1) There shall be a body corporate to be known as the Criminal Cases Review Commission.

(2) The Commission shall not be regarded as the servant or agent of the Crown or as enjoying any status, immunity or privilege of the Crown; and the Commission's property shall not be regarded as property of, or held on behalf of, the Crown.

(3) The Commission shall consist of not fewer than eleven members.

(4) The members of the Commission shall be appointed by Her Majesty on the recommendation of the Prime Minister.

(5) At least one third of the members of the Commission shall be persons who are legally qualified; and for this purpose a person is legally qualified if—

(a) he has a ten year general qualification, within the meaning of section 71 of the Courts and Legal Services Act 1990, or

(b) he is a member of the Bar of Northern Ireland, or solicitor of the Supreme Court of Northern Ireland, of at least ten years' standing.

(6) At least two thirds of the members of the Commission shall be persons who appear to the Prime Minister to have knowledge or experience of any aspect of the criminal justice system and of them at least one shall be a person who appears to him to have knowledge or experience of any aspect of the criminal justice system in Northern Ireland; and for the purposes of this subsection the criminal justice system includes, in particular, the investigation of offences and the treatment of offenders.

(7) * * * * *

References to court

9 Cases dealt with on indictment in England and Wales

(1) Where a person has been convicted of an offence on indictment in England and Wales, the Commission—

(a) may at any time refer the conviction to the Court of Appeal, and

(b) (whether or not they refer the conviction) may at any time refer to the Court of Appeal any sentence (not being a sentence fixed by law) imposed on, or in subsequent proceedings relating to, the conviction.

(2) A reference under subsection (1) of a person's conviction shall be treated for all purposes as an appeal by the person under section 1 of the 1968 Act against the conviction.

(3) A reference under subsection (1) of a sentence imposed on, or in subsequent proceedings relating to, a person's conviction on an indictment shall be treated for all purposes as an appeal by the person under section 9 of the 1968 Act against—

(a) the sentence, and

(b) any other sentence (not being a sentence fixed by law) imposed on, or in subsequent proceedings relating to, the conviction or any other conviction on the indictment.

(4) On a reference under subsection (1) of a person's conviction on an indictment the Commission may give notice to the Court of Appeal that any other conviction on the indictment which is specified in the notice is to be treated as referred to the Court of Appeal under subsection (1).

(5), (6) * * * * *

10 * * * * *

11 Cases dealt with summarily in England and Wales

(1) Where a person has been convicted of an offence by a magistrates' court in England and Wales, the Commission—

(a) may at any time refer the conviction to the Crown Court, and

(b) (whether or not they refer the conviction) may at any time refer to the Crown Court any sentence imposed on, or in subsequent proceedings relating to, the conviction.

(2) A reference under subsection (1) of a person's conviction shall be treated for all purposes as an appeal by the person under section 108(1) of the Magistrates' Courts Act 1980 against the conviction (whether or not he pleaded guilty).

(3) A reference under subsection (1) of a sentence imposed on, or in subsequent proceedings relating to, a person's conviction shall be treated for all purposes as an appeal by the person under section 108(1) of the Magistrates' Courts Act 1980 against—

(a) the sentence, and

(b) any other sentence imposed on, or in subsequent proceedings relating to, the conviction or any related conviction.

(4) On a reference under subsection (1) of a person's conviction the Commission may give notice to the Crown Court that any related conviction which is specified in the notice is to be treated as referred to the Crown Court under subsection (1).

(5) For the purposes of this section convictions are related if they are convictions of the same person by the same court on the same day.

(6) On a reference under this section the Crown Court may not award any punishment more severe than that awarded by the court whose decision is referred.

(7) The Crown Court may grant bail to a person whose conviction or sentence has been referred under this section; and any time during which he is released on bail shall not count as part of any term of imprisonment or detention under his sentence.

13 Conditions for making of references

(1) A reference of a conviction, verdict, finding or sentence shall not be made under any of sections 9 to 12 unless—

(a) the Commission consider that there is a real possibility that the conviction, verdict, finding or sentence would not be upheld were the reference to be made,

(b) the Commission so consider—

(i) in the case of a conviction, verdict or finding, because of an argument, or evidence, not raised in the proceedings which led to it or on any appeal or application for leave to appeal against it, or

(ii) in the case of a sentence, because of an argument on a point of law, or information, not so raised, and

(c) an appeal against the conviction, verdict, finding or sentence has been determined or leave to appeal against it has been refused.

(2) Nothing in subsection (1)(b)(i) or (c) shall prevent the making of a reference if it appears to the Commission that there are exceptional circumstances which justify making it.

14 Further provisions about references

(1) A reference of a conviction, verdict, finding or sentence may be made under any of sections 9 to 12 either after an application has been made by or on behalf of the person to whom it relates or without an application having been so made.

(2) In considering whether to make a reference of a conviction, verdict, finding or sentence under any of sections 9 to 12 the Commission shall have regard to—

(a) any application or representations made to the Commission by or on behalf of the person to whom it relates,

(b) any other representations made to the Commission in relation to it, and

(c) any other matters which appear to the Commission to be relevant.

(3) In considering whether to make a reference under section 9 or 10 the Commission may at any time refer any point on which they desire the assistance of the Court of Appeal to that Court for the Court's opinion on it; and on a reference under this subsection the Court of Appeal shall consider the point referred and furnish the Commission with the Court's opinion on the point.

(4) Where the Commission make a reference under any of sections 9 to 12 the Commission shall—

(a) give to the court to which the reference is made a statement of the Commission's reasons for making the reference, and

(b) send a copy of the statement to every person who appears to the Commission to be likely to be a party to any proceedings on the appeal arising from the reference.

(5) Where a reference under any of sections 9 to 12 is treated as an appeal against any conviction, verdict, finding or sentence, the appeal may be on any ground relating to the conviction, verdict, finding or sentence (whether or not the ground is related to any reason given by the Commission for making the reference).

(6) In every case in which—

(a) an application has been made to the Commission by or on behalf of any person for the reference under any of sections 9 to 12 of any conviction, verdict, finding or sentence, but

(b) the Commission decide not to make a reference of the conviction, verdict, finding or sentence,

the Commission shall give a statement of the reasons for their decision to the person who made the application.

15 * * * * *

16 Assistance in connection with prerogative of mercy

(1) Where the Secretary of State refers to the Commission any matter which arises in the consideration of whether to recommend the exercise of Her Majesty's prerogative of mercy in relation to a conviction and on which he desires their assistance, the Commission shall—

(a) consider the matter referred, and

(b) give to the Secretary of State a statement of their conclusions on it;

and the Secretary of State shall, in considering whether so to recommend, treat the Commission's statement as conclusive of the matter referred.

(2) Where in any case the Commission are of the opinion that the Secretary of State should consider whether to recommend the exercise of Her Majesty's prerogative of mercy in relation to the case they shall give him the reasons for their opinion.

Supplementary powers

17 Power to obtain documents etc.

(1) This section applies where the Commission believe that a person serving in a public body has possession or control of a document or other material which may assist the Commission in the exercise of any of their functions.

(2) Where it is reasonable to do so, the Commission may require the person who is the appropriate person in relation to the public body—

(a) to produce the document or other material to the Commission or to give the Commission access to it, and

(b) to allow the Commission to take away the document or other material or to make and take away a copy of it in such form as they think appropriate,

and may direct that person that the document or other material must not be destroyed, damaged or altered before the direction is withdrawn by the Commission.

(3) The documents and other material covered by this section include, in particular, any document or other material obtained or created during any investigation or proceedings relating to—

(a) the case in relation to which the Commission's function is being or may be exercised, or

(b) any other case which may be in any way connected with that case (whether or not any function of the Commission could be exercised in relation to that other case).

(4) The duty to comply with a requirement under this section is not affected by any obligation of secrecy or other limitation on disclosure (including any such obligation or limitation imposed by or by virtue of an enactment) which would otherwise prevent the production of the document or other material to the Commission or the giving of access to it to the Commission.

18-22 ★ ★ ★ ★ ★

Disclosure of information

23 Offence of disclosure

(1) A person who is or has been a member or employee of the Commission shall not disclose any information obtained by the Commission in the exercise of any of their functions unless the disclosure of the information is excepted from this section by section 24.

(2) A person who is or has been an investigating officer shall not disclose any information obtained by him in his inquiries unless the disclosure of the information is excepted from this section by section 24.

(3) A member of the Commission shall not authorise—

(a) the disclosure by an employee of the Commission of any information obtained by the Commission in the exercise of any of their functions, or

(b) the disclosure by an investigating officer of any information obtained by him in his inquiries,

unless the authorisation of the disclosure of the information is excepted from this section by section 24.

(4) A person who contravenes this section is guilty of an offence and liable on summary conviction to a fine of an amount not exceeding level 5 on the standard scale.

24 Exceptions from obligations of non-disclosure

(1) The disclosure of information, or the authorisation of the disclosure of information, is excepted from section 23 by this section if the information is disclosed, or is authorised to be disclosed—

(a) for the purposes of any criminal, disciplinary or civil proceedings,

(b) in order to assist in dealing with an application made to the Secretary of State for compensation for a miscarriage of justice,

(c) by a person who is a member or an employee of the Commission either to another person who is a member or an employee of the Commission or to an investigating officer,

(d) by an investigating officer to a member or an employee of the Commission,

(e) in any statement or report required by this Act.

(f) in or in connection with the exercise of any function under this Act, or

(g) in any circumstances in which the disclosure of information is permitted by an order made by the Secretary of State.

(2) The disclosure of information is also excepted from section 23 by this section if the information is disclosed by an employee of the Commission, or an investigating officer, who is authorised to disclose the information by a member of the Commission.

(3) The disclosure of information, or the authorisation of the disclosure of information, is also excepted from section 23 by this section if the information is disclosed, or is authorised to be disclosed, for the purposes of—

(a) the investigation of an offence, or

(b) deciding whether to prosecute a person for an offence,

unless the disclosure is or would be prevented by an obligation of secrecy or other limitation on disclosure (including any such obligation or limitation imposed by or by virtue of an enactment) arising otherwise than under that section.

(4), (5) ★ ★ ★ ★ ★

★ ★ ★ ★ ★

CRIMINAL LAW (CONSOLIDATION) (SCOTLAND) ACT 1995
(1995, c. 39)

An Act to consolidate for Scotland certain enactments creating offences and relating to criminal law there.

[8 November 1995]

Territorial extent Scotland

★ ★ ★ ★ ★

[16A Conspiracy or incitement to commit certain sexual acts outside the United Kingdom

(1) This section applies to any act done by a person in Scotland which would amount to the offence of conspiracy or incitement to commit a listed sexual offence but for the fact that the criminal purpose or, as the case may be, what he had in view is intended to occur in a country or territory outside the United Kingdom.

(2) Where a person does an act to which this section applies, the criminal purpose or, as the case may be, what he had in view shall be treated as the listed sexual offence mentioned in subsection (1) above and he shall, accordingly, be guilty of conspiracy or, as the case may be, incitement to commit the listed sexual offence.

(3) A person is guilty of an offence by virtue of this section only if—

(a) in the case of proceedings charging conspiracy, the criminal purpose would involve at some stage—

(i) an act by him or another party to the conspiracy; or

(ii) the happening of some other event,

constituting an offence under the law in force in the country or territory where the act or other event was intended to take place; or

(b) in the case of proceedings charging incitement, what he had in view would involve the commission of an offence under the law in force in the country or territory where the whole or any part of it was intended to take place, and conduct punishable under the law in force in the country or territory is an offence under that law for the purposes of this section however it is described in that law.

(4)–(7) ★ ★ ★ ★ ★

(8) Any act of incitement by means of a message (however communicated) is to be treated as done in Scotland if the message is sent or received in Scotland.

(9) In this section "listed sexual offence" means any of the following—

(a) rape of a girl under the age of 16;

(b) indecent assault of a person under the age of 16;

(c) lewd and libidinous conduct;

(d) shamelessly indecent conduct involving a person under the age of 16;

(e) sodomy with or against a boy under the age of 16;

(f) an offence under section 5(1) or (2) of this act (unlawful sexual intercourse with a girl under the age of 13);

(g) an offence under section 5(3) of this Act (unlawful sexual intercourse with a girl under the age of 16);

(h) an offence under section 6 of this Act (indecent behaviour towards a girl between the age of 12 and 16);

(i) an offence under section 13(5) or (6) of this Act where the homosexual act involves a person under the age of 16 (prohibition on certain homosexual acts).]

★ ★ ★ ★ ★

47 Prohibition of the carrying of offensive weapons

(1) Any person who without lawful authority or reasonable excuse, the proof whereof shall lie on him, has with him in any public place any offensive weapon shall be guilty of an offence, and shall be liable—

(a) on summary conviction, to imprisonment for a term not exceeding six months or a fine not exceeding the statutory maximum, or both;

(b) on conviction on indictment, to imprisonment for a term not exceeding two years or a fine, or both.

(2) Where any person is convicted of an offence under subsection (1) above the court may make an order for the forfeiture or disposal of any weapon in respect of which the offence was committed.

(3) A constable may arrest without warrant any person whom he has reasonable cause to believe to be committing an offence under subsection (1) above, if the constable is not satisfied as to that person's identity or place of residence, or has reasonable cause to believe that it is necessary to arrest him in order to prevent the commission by him of any other offence in the course of committing which an offensive weapon might be used.

(4) In this section "public place" includes any road within the meaning of the Roads (Scotland) Act 1984 and any other premises or place to which at the material time the public have or are permitted to have access, whether on payment or otherwise; and "offensive weapon" means any article made or adapted for use for causing injury to the person, or intended by the person having it with him for such use by him [or by some other person].

48 Search for offensive weapons

(1) Where a constable has reasonable grounds for suspecting that any person is carrying an offensive weapon and has committed or is committing an offence under section 47 of this Act, the constable may search that person without warrant, and detain him for such time as is reasonably required to permit the search to be carried out; and he shall inform the person of the reason for such detention.

(2) Any person who—

(a) intentionally obstructs a constable in the exercise of the constable's powers under subsection (1) above; or

(b) conceals from a constable acting in the exercise of those powers an offensive weapon,

shall be guilty of an offence and liable on summary conviction to a fine not exceeding level 4 on the standard scale.

(3) A constable may arrest without warrant any person who he has reason to believe has committed an offence under subsection (2) above.

(4) In this section, "offensive weapon" has the same meaning as in the said section 47.

49 Offence of having in public place article with blade or point

(1) Subject to subsections (4) and (5) below, any person who has an article to which this section applies with him in a public place shall be guilty of an offence and liable—

(a) on summary conviction, to imprisonment for a term not exceeding six months or a fine not exceeding the statutory maximum or both; and

(b) on conviction on indictment, to imprisonment for a term not exceeding [four] years or a fine or both.

(2) Subject to subsection (3) below, this section applies to any article which has a blade or is sharply pointed.

(3) This section does not apply to a folding pocketknife if the cutting edge of its blade does not exceed three inches (7.62 centimetres).

(4) It shall be a defence for a person charged with an offence under subsection (1) above to prove that he had good reason or lawful authority for having the article with him in the public place.

(5) Without prejudice to the generality of subsection (4) above, it shall be a defence for a person charged with an offence under subsection (1) above to prove that he had the article with him—

(a) for use at work;

(b) for religious reasons; or

(c) as part of any national costume.

(6) Where a person is convicted of an offence under subsection (1) above the court may make an order for the forfeiture of any article to which the offence relates, and any article forfeited under this subsection shall (subject to section 193 of the Criminal Procedure (Scotland) Act 1995 (suspension of forfeiture etc., pending appeal)) be disposed of as the court may direct.

(7) In this section "public place" includes any place to which at the material time the public have or are permitted access, whether on payment or otherwise.

[49A Offence of having article with blade or point (or offensive weapon) on school premises

(1) Any person who has an article to which section 49 of this Act applies with him on school premises shall be guilty of an offence.

(2) Any person who has an offensive weapon within the meaning of section 47 of this Act with him on school premises shall be guilty of an offence.

(3) It shall be a defence for a person charged with an offence under subsection (1) or (2) above to prove that he had good reason or lawful authority for having the article or weapon with him on the premises in question.

(4) Without prejudice to the generality of subsection (3) above, it shall be a defence for a person charged with an offence under subsection (1) or (2) above to prove that he had the article or weapon in question with him—

(a) for use at work,

(b) for educational purposes,

(c) for religious reasons, or

(d) as part of any national costume.

(5) A person guilty of an offence—

(a) under subsection (1) above shall be liable—

(i) on summary conviction to imprisonment for a term not exceeding six months, or a fine not exceeding the statutory maximum, or both;

(ii) on conviction on indictment, to imprisonment for a term not exceeding two years, or a fine, or both;

(b) under subsection (2) above shall be liable—

(i) on summary conviction, to imprisonment for a term not exceeding six months, or a fine not exceeding the statutory maximum, or both;

(ii) on conviction on indictment, to imprisonment for a term not exceeding four years, or a fine, or both.

(6) ★ ★ ★ ★ ★]

[49B Power of entry to search for articles with a blade or point and offensive weapons

(1) A constable may enter school premises and search those premises and any person on those premises for—

(a) any article to which section 49 of this Act applies, or

(b) any offensive weapon within the meaning of section 47 of this Act,

if he has reasonable grounds for suspecting that an offence under section 49A of this Act is being, or has been, committed.

(2) If in the course of a search under this section a constable discovers an article or weapon which he has reasonable grounds for believing to be an article or weapon of a kind described in subsection (1) above, he may seize it.

(3) The constable may use reasonable force, if necessary, in the exercise of the power of entry conferred by this section.]

50 Extension of constable's power to stop, search and arrest without warrant

(1) Where a constable has reasonable grounds for suspecting that a person has with him an article to which section 49 of this Act applies and has committed or is committing an offence under subsection (1) of that section, the constable may search that person without warrant and detain him for such time as is reasonably required to permit the search to be carried out.

(2) A constable who detains a person under subsection (1) above shall inform him of the reason for his detention.

(3) Where a constable has reasonable cause to believe that a person has committed or is committing an offence under section 49(1) [or section 49A(1) or (2)] of this Act and the constable—

(a) having requested that person to give his name or address or both—

(i) is not given the information requested; or

(ii) is not satisfied that such information as is given is correct; or

(b) has reasonable cause to believe that it is necessary to arrest him in order to prevent the commission by him of any other offence in the course of committing which an article to which that section applies might be used,

he may arrest that person without warrant.

(4) Any person who—

(a) intentionally obstructs a constable in the exercise of the constable's powers under subsection (1) above; or

(b) conceals from a constable acting in the exercise of those powers an article to which section 49 of this Act applies,

shall be guilty of an offence and liable on summary conviction to a fine not exceeding level 3 on the standard scale.

(5) Where a constable has reasonable cause to believe that a person has committed or is committing an offence under subsection (4) above he may arrest that person without warrant.

★ ★ ★ ★ ★

CRIMINAL PROCEDURE (SCOTLAND) ACT 1995
(1995, c. 46)

An Act to consolidate certain enactments relating to criminal procedure in Scotland.

[8 November 1995]

Territorial extent Scotland

★ ★ ★ ★ ★

PART II
POLICE FUNCTIONS

Lord Advocate's instructions

12 Instructions by Lord Advocate as to reporting of offences

The Lord Advocate may, from time to time, issue instructions to a chief constable with regard to the reporting, for consideration of the question of prosecution, of offences alleged to have been committed within the area of such chief constable, and it shall be the duty of a chief constable to whom any such instruction is issued to secure compliance therewith.

13 Powers relating to suspects and potential witnesses

(1) Where a constable has reasonable grounds for suspecting that a person has committed or is committing an offence at any place, he may require—

(a) that person, if the constable finds him at that place or at any place where the constable is entitled to be, to give his name and address and may ask him for an explanation of the circumstances which have given rise to the constable's suspicion;

(b) any other person whom the constable finds at that place or at any place where the constable is entitled to be and who the constable believes has information relating to the offence, to give his name and address.

(2) The constable may require the person mentioned in paragraph (a) of subsection (1) above to remain with him while he (either or both)—

(a) subject to subsection (3) below, verifies any name and address given by the person;

(b) notes any explanation proffered by the person.

(3) The constable shall exercise his power under paragraph (a) of subsection (2) above only where it appears to him that such verification can be obtained quickly.

(4) A constable may use reasonable force to ensure that the person mentioned in paragraph (a) of subsection (1) above remains with him.

(5) A constable shall inform a person, when making a requirement of that person under—

(a) paragraph (a) of subsection (1) above, of his suspicion and of the general nature of the offence which he suspects that the person has committed or is committing;

(b) paragraph (b) of subsection (1) above, of his suspicion, of the general nature of the offence which he suspects has been or is being committed and that the reason for the requirement is that he believes the person has information relating to the offence;

(c) subsection (2) above, why the person is being required to remain with him;

(d) either of the said subsections, that failure to comply with the requirement may constitute an offence.

(6) A person mentioned in—

(a) paragraph (a) of subection (1) above who having been required—

(i) under that subsection to give his name and address; or

(ii) under subsection (2) above to remain with a constable,

fails, without reasonable excuse, to do so, shall be guilty of an offence and liable on summary conviction to a fine not exceeding level 3 on the standard scale;

(b) paragraph (b) of the said subsection (1) who having been required under that subsection to give his name and address fails, without reasonable excuse, to do so shall be guilty of an offence and liable on summary conviction to a fine not exceeding level 2 on the standard scale.

(7) A constable may arrest without warrant any person who he has reasonable grounds for suspecting has committed an offence under subsection (6) above.

14 Detention and questioning at police station

(1) Where a constable has reasonable grounds for suspecting that a person has committed or is committing an offence punishable by imprisonment, the constable may, for the purpose of facilitating the carrying out of investigations—

(a) into the offence; and

(b) as to whether criminal proceedings should be instigated against the person,

detain that person and take him as quickly as is reasonably practicable to a police station or other premises and may thereafter for that purpose take him to any other place and, subject to the following provisions of this section, the detention may continue at the police station or, as the case may be, the other premises or place.

(2) Detention under subsection (1) above shall be terminated not more than six hours after it begins or (if earlier)—

(a) when the person is arrested;

(b) when he is detained in pursuance of any other enactment; or

(c) where there are no longer such grounds as are mentioned in the said subsection (1),

and when a person has been detained under subsection (1) above, he shall be informed immediately upon the termination of his detention in accordance with this subsection that his detention has been terminated.

(3) Where a person has been released at the termination of a period of detention under subsection (1) above he shall not thereafter be detained, under that subsection, on the same grounds or on any grounds arising out of the same circumstances.

(4) Subject to subsection (5) below, where a person has previously been detained in pursuance of any other enactment, and is detained under subsection (1) above on the same grounds or on grounds arising from the same circumstances as those which led to his earlier detention, the period of six hours mentioned in subsection (2) above shall be reduced by the length of that earlier detention.

(5) Subsection (4) above shall not apply in relation to detention under section 41(3) of the Prisons (Scotland) Act 1989 (detention in relation to introduction etc. into prison of prohibited article), but where a person was detained under section 41(3) immediately prior to his detention under subsection (1) above the period of six hours mentioned in subsection (2) above shall be reduced by the length of that earlier detention.

(6) At the time when a constable detains a person under subsection (1) above, he shall inform the person of his suspicion, of the general nature of the offence which he suspects has been or is being committed and of the reason for the detention; and there shall be recorded—

(a) the place where detention begins and the police station or other premises to which the person is taken;

(b) any other place to which the person is, during the detention, thereafter taken;

(c) the general nature of the suspected offence;

(d) the time when detention under subsection (1) above begins and the time of the person's arrival at the police station or other premises;

(e) the time when the person is informed of his rights in terms of subsection (9) below and of subsection (1)(b) of section 15 of this Act and the identity of the constable so informing him;

(f) where the person requests such intimation to be sent as is specified in section 15(1)(b) of this Act, the time when such request is—

(i) made;

(ii) complied with; and

(g) the time of the person's release from detention or, where instead of being released he is arrested in respect of the alleged offence, the time of such arrest.

(7) Where a person is detained under subsection (1) above, a constable may—

(a) without prejudice to any relevant rule of law as regards the admissibility in evidence of any answer given, put questions to him in relation to the suspected offence;

(b) exercise the same powers of search as are available following an arrest.

(8) A constable may use reasonable force in exercising any power conferred by subsection (1), or by paragraph (b) of subsection (7), above.

(9) A person detained under subsection (1) above shall be under no obligation to answer any question other than to give his name and address, and a constable shall so inform him both on so detaining him and on arrival at the police station or other premises.

15 Rights of person arrested or detained

(1) Without prejudice to section 17 of this Act, a person who, not being a person in respect of whose custody or detention subsection (4) below applies—

(a) has been arrested and is in custody in a police station or other premises, shall be entitled to have intimation of his custody and of the place where he is being held sent to a person reasonably named by him;

(b) is being detained under section 14 of this Act and has been taken to a police station or other premises or place, shall be entitled to have intimation of his detention and of the police station or other premises or place sent to a solicitor and to one other person reasonably named by him,

without delay or, where some delay is necessary in the interest of the investigation or the prevention of crime or the apprehension of offenders, with no more delay than is so necessary.

(2) A person shall be informed of his entitlement under subsection (1) above—

(a) on arrival at the police station or other premises; or

(b) where he is not arrested, or as the case may be detained, until after such arrival, on such arrest or detention.

(3) Where the person mentioned in paragraph (a) of subsection (1) above requests such intimation to be sent as is specified in that paragraph there shall be recorded the time when such request is—

(a) made;

(b) complied with.

(4) Without prejudice to the said section 17, a constable shall, where a person who has been arrested and is in such custody as is mentioned in paragraph (a) of subsection (1) above or who is being detained as is mentioned in paragraph (b) of that subsection appears to him to be a child, send without delay such intimation as is mentioned in the said paragraph (a), or as the case may be paragraph (b), to that person's parent if known; and the parent—

(a) in a case where there is reasonable cause to suspect that he has been involved in the alleged offence in respect of which the person has been arrested or detained, may; and

(b) in any other case shall,

be permitted access to the person.

(5) The nature and extent of any access permitted under subsection (4) above shall be subject to any restriction essential for the furtherance of the investigation or the well-being of the person.

(6) In subsection (4) above—
(a) "child" means a person under 16 years of age; and
(b) "parent" includes guardian and any person who has the [care] of a child.

16 Drunken persons: power to take to designated place

(1) Where a constable has power to arrest a person without a warrant for any offence and the constable has reasonable grounds for suspecting that that person is drunk, the constable may, if he thinks fit, take him to any place designated by the Secretary of State for the purposes of this section as a place suitable for the care of drunken persons.

(2) A person shall not by virtue of this section be liable to be detained in any such place as is mentioned in subsection (1) above, but the exercise in his case of the power conferred by this section shall not preclude his being charged with any offence.

17 Right of accused to have access to solicitor

(1) Where an accused has been arrested on any criminal charge, he shall be entitled immediately upon such arrest—

(a) to have intimation sent to a solicitor that his professional assistance is required by the accused, and informing the solicitor—
(i) of the place where the person is being detained;
(ii) whether the person is to be liberated; and
(iii) if the person is not to be liberated, the court to which he is to be taken and the date when he is to be so taken; and

(b) to be told what rights there are under—
(i) paragraph (a) above;
(ii) subsection (2) below; and
(iii) section 35(1) and (2) of this Act.

(2) The accused and the solicitor shall be entitled to have a private interview before the examination or, as the case may be, first appearance.

18 Prints, samples etc. in criminal investigations

(1) This section applies where a person has been arrested and is in custody or is detained under section 14(1) of this Act.

(2) A constable may take from the person [, or require the person to provide him with, such relevant physical data] as the constable may, having regard to the circumstances of the suspected offence in respect of which the person has been arrested or detained, reasonably consider it appropriate to take [from him or require him to provide, and the person so required shall comply with that requirement.].

(3) Subject to subsection (4) below, all records of any [relevant physical data taken from or provided by a person] under subsection (2) above, all samples taken under subsection (6) below and all information derived from such samples shall be destroyed as soon as possible following a decision not to institute criminal proceedings against the person or on the conclusion of such proceedings otherwise than with a conviction or an order under section 246(3) of this Act.

(4) The duty under subsection (3) above to destroy samples taken under subsection (6) below and information derived from such samples shall not apply—

(a) where the destruction of the sample or the information could have the effect of destroying any sample, or any information derived therefrom, lawfully held in relation to a person other than the person from whom the sample was taken; or

(b) where the record, sample or information in question is of the same kind as a record, a sample or, as the case may be, information lawfully held by or on behalf of any police force in relation to the person.

(5) No sample, or information derived from a sample, retained by virtue of subsection (4) above shall be used—

(a) in evidence against the person from whom the sample was taken; or

(b) for the purposes of the investigation of any offence.

(6) A constable may, with the authority of an officer of a rank no lower than inspector, take from the person—

(a) from the hair of an external part of the body other than pubic hair, by means of cutting, combing or plucking, a sample of hair or other material;

(b) from a fingernail or toenail or from under any such nail, a sample of nail or other material;

(c) from an external part of the body, by means of swabbing or rubbing, a sample of blood or other body fluid, of body tissue or of other material;

(d) from the inside of the mouth, by means of swabbing, a sample of saliva or other material.

(7) . . .

[(7A) For the purposes of this section and sections 19 and 20 of this Act "relevant physical data" means any—

(a) fingerprint;

(b) palm print;

(c) print or impression other than those mentioned in paragraph (a) and (b) above, of an external part of the body;

(d) record of a person's skin on an external part of the body created by a device approved by the Secretary of State.

(7B) The Secretary of State by order made by Statutory Instrument may approve a device for the purpose of creating such records as are mentioned in paragraph (d) of subsection (7A) above.]

(8) Nothing in this section shall prejudice—

(a) any power of search;

(b) any power to take possession of evidence where there is imminent danger of its being lost or destroyed; or

(c) any power to take prints, impressions or samples under the authority of a warrant.

19 Prints, samples etc. in criminal investigations: supplementary provisions

(1) [Without prejudice to any power exercisable under section 19A of this Act, this] section applies where a person convicted of an offence—

(a) has not, since the conviction, had [taken from him, or been required to provide, any relevant physical data or had any impression or sample] taken from him; or

(b) has [at any time had—

(i) taken from him or been required (whether under paragraph (a) above or under section 18 or 19A of this Act or otherwise) to provide any physical data; or

(ii) any impression or sample taken from him,

which was not suitable for the means of analysis for which the data were taken or required or the impression or sample was taken] from him but it was not suitable for the means of analysis for which it was taken or, though suitable, was insufficient (either in quantity or in quality) to enable information to be obtained by that means of analysis.

(2) Where this section applies, a constable may, within the permitted period—

[(a) take from or require the convicted person to provide him with such relevant physical data as he reasonably considers it appropriate to take or, as the case may be, require the provision of;] and

(b) with the authority of an officer of a rank no lower than inspector, take from the person any sample mentioned in any of paragraphs (a) to (d) of subsection (6) of section 18 of this Act by the means specified in that paragraph in relation to that sample.

(3) A constable—

(a) may require the convicted person to attend a police station for the purposes of subsection (2) above;

(b) may, where the convicted person is in legal custody by virtue of section 295 of this Act, exercise the powers conferred by subsection (2) above in relation to the person in the place where he is for the time being.

(4) In subsection (2) above, "the permitted period" means—

(a) in a case to which paragraph (a) of subsection (1) above applies, the period of one month beginning with the date of the conviction;

(b) in a case to which paragraph (b) of that subsection applies, the period of one month beginning with the date on which a constable of the police force which instructed the analysis receives written intimation that [the relevant physical data were or] the sample ... was unsuitable or, as the case may be, insufficient as mentioned in that paragraph.

(5) A requirement under subsection (3)(a) above—

(a) shall give the person at least seven days' notice of the date on which he is required to attend;

(b) may direct him to attend at a specified time of day or between specified times of day.

(6) Any constable may arrest without warrant a person who fails to comply with a requirement under subsection (3)(a) above.

19A, 19B * * * * *

20 Use of prints, samples etc.

Without prejudice to any power to do so apart from this section, [relevant physical data,] impressions and samples lawfully held by or on behalf of any police force or in connection with or as a result of an investigation of an offence and information derived therefrom may be checked against other such [data], impressions, samples and information.

21 * * * * *

22 Liberation by police

(1) Where a person has been arrested and charged with an offence which may be tried summarily, the officer in charge of a police station may—

(a) liberate him upon a written undertaking, signed by him and certified by the officer, in terms of which the person undertakes to appear at a specified court at a specified time; or

(b) liberate him without any such undertaking; or

(c) refuse to liberate him;

(2) A person in breach of an undertaking given by him under subsection (1) above without reasonable excuse shall be guilty of an offence and liable on summary conviction to the following penalties—

(a) a fine not exceeding level 3 on the standard scale; and

(b) imprisonment for a period—

(i) where conviction is in the district court, not exceeding 60 days; or

(ii) where conviction is in the sheriff court, not exceeding 3 months.

(3) The refusal of the officer in charge to liberate a person under subsection (1)(c) above and the detention of that person until his case is tried in the usual form shall not subject the officer to any claim whatsoever.

(4) The penalties provided for in subsection (2) above may be imposed in addition to any other penalty which it is competent for the court to impose, notwithstanding that the total of penalties imposed may exceed the maximum penalty which it is competent to impose in respect of the original offence.

(5) In any proceedings relating to an offence under this section, a writing, purporting to be such an undertaking as is mentioned in subsection (1)(a) above and bearing to be signed and certified, shall be sufficient evidence of the terms of the undertaking given by the arrested person.

23-34 * * * * *

35 Judicial examination

(1) The accused's solicitor shall be entitled to be present at the examination.

(2) The sheriff may delay the examination for a period not exceeding 48 hours from and after the time of the accused's arrest, in order to allow time for the attendance of the solicitor.

(3) Where the accused is brought before the sheriff for examination on any charge and he or his solicitor intimates that he does not desire to emit a declaration in regard to such a charge, it shall be unnecessary to take a declaration, and, subject to section 36 of this Act, the accused may be committed for further examination or until liberated in due course of law without a declaration being taken.

(4) Nothing in subsection (3) above shall prejudice the right of the accused subsequently to emit a declaration on intimating to the prosecutor his desire to do so; and that declaration shall be taken in further examination.

(5) Where, subsequent to examination or further examination on any charge, the prosecutor desires to question the accused as regards an extrajudicial confession, whether or not a full admission, allegedly made by him to or in the hearing of a constable, which is relevant to the charge and as regards which he has not previously been examined, the accused may be brought before the sheriff for further examination.

(6) Where the accused is brought before the sheriff for further examination the sheriff may delay that examination for a period not exceeding 24 hours in order to allow time for the attendance of the accused's' solicitor.

(7) Any proceedings before the sheriff in examination or further examination shall be conducted in chambers and outwith the presence of any co-accused.

(8) This section applies to procedure on petition, without prejudice to the accused being tried summarily by the sheriff for any offence in respect of which he has been committed until liberated in due course of law.

36 Judicial examination: questioning by prosecutor

(1) Subject to the following provisions of this section, an accused on being brought before the sheriff for examination on any charge (whether the first or a further examination) may be questioned by the prosecutor in so far as such questioning is directed towards eliciting any admission, denial, explanation, justification or comment which the accused may have as regards anything to which subsections (2) to (4) below apply.

(2) This subsection applies to matters averred in the charge, and the particular aims of a line of questions under this subsection shall be to determine—

(a) whether any account which the accused can give ostensibly discloses a defence; and

(b) the nature and particulars of that defence.

(3) This subsection applies to the alleged making by the accused, to or in the hearing of a constable, of an extrajudicial confession (whether or not a full admission) relevant to the charge, and questions under this subsection may only be put if the accused has, before the examination, received from the prosecutor or from a constable a written record of the confession allegedly made.

(4) This subsection applies to what is said in any declaration emitted in regard to the charge by the accused at examination.

(5) The prosecutor shall, in framing questions in exercise of his power under subsection (1) above, have regard to the following principles—

(a) the question should not be designed to challenge the truth of anything said by the accused;

(b) there should be no reiteration of a question which the accused has refused to answer at the examination; and

(c) there should be no leading questions,
and the sheriff shall ensure that all questions are fairly put to, and understood by, the accused.

(6) The accused shall be told by the sheriff—

(a) where he is represented by a solicitor at the judicial examination, that he may consult that solicitor before answering any question; and

(b) that if he answers any question put to him at the examination under this section in such a way as to disclose an ostensible defence, the prosecutor shall be under the duty imposed by subsection (10) below.

(7) With the permission of the sheriff, the solicitor for the accused may ask the accused any question the purpose of which is to clarify any ambiguity in an answer given by the accused to the prosecutor at the examination or to give the accused an opportunity to answer any question which he has previously refused to answer.

(8) An accused may decline to answer a question under subsection (1) above; and, where he is subsequently tried on the charge mentioned in that subsection or on any other charge arising out of the circumstances which gave rise to the charge so mentioned, his having so declined may be commented upon by the prosecutor, the judge presiding at the trial, or any co-accused, only where and in so far as the accused (or any witness called on his behalf) in evidence avers something which could have been stated appropriately in answer to that question.

(9) The procedure in relation to examination under this section shall be prescribed by Act of Adjournal.

(10) Without prejudice to any rule of law, on the conclusion of an examination under this section the prosecutor shall secure the investigation, to such extent as is reasonably practicable, of any ostensible defence disclosed in the course of the examination.

(11) The duty imposed by subsection (10) above shall not apply as respects any ostensible defence which is not reasonably capable of being investigated.

37 Judicial examination: record of proceedings

(1) The prosecutor shall provide for a verbatim record to be made by means of shorthand notes or by mechanical means of all questions to and answers and declarations by the accused in examination, or further examination, under sections 35 and 36 of this Act.

(2) A shorthand writer shall—

(a) sign the shorthand notes taken by him of the questions, answers and declarations mentioned in subsection (1) above and certify the notes as being complete and correct; and

(b) retain the notes.

(3) A person recording the questions, answers and declarations mentioned in subsection (1) above by mechanical means shall—

(a) certify that the record is true and complete;

(b) specify in the certificate the proceedings to which the record relates; and

(c) retain the record.

(4) The prosecutor shall require the person who made the record mentioned in subsection (1) above, or such other competent person as he may specify, to make a transcript of the record in legible form; and that person shall—

(a) comply with the requirement;

(b) certify the transcript as being a complete and correct transcript of the record purporting to have been made and certified, and in the case of shorthand notes signed, by the person who made the record; and

(c) send the transcript to the prosecutor.

(5) A transcript certified under subsection (4)(b) above shall, subject to section 38(1) of this Act, be deemed for all purposes to be a complete and correct record of the questions, answers and declarations mentioned in subsection (1) above.

(6) Subject to subsections (7) to (9) below, within 14 days of the date of examination or further examination, the prosecutor shall—

(a) serve a copy of the transcript on the accused examined; and

(b) serve a further such copy on the solicitor (if any) for that accused.

(7) Where at the time of further examination a trial diet is already fixed and the interval between the further examination and that diet is not sufficient to allow of the time limits specified in subsection (6) above and subsection (1) of section 38 of this Act, the sheriff shall (either or both)—

(a) direct that those subsections shall apply in the case with such modifications as to time limits as he shall specify;

(b) subject to subsection (8) below, postpone the trial diet.

(8) Postponement under paragraph (b) of subsection (7) above alone shall only be competent where the sheriff considers that to proceed under paragraph (a) of that subsection alone, or paragraphs (a) and (b) together, would not be practicable.

(9) Any time limit mentioned in subsection (6) above and subsection (1) of section 38 of this Act (including any such time limit as modified by a direction under subsection (7) above) may be extended, in respect of the case, by the High Court.

(10) A copy of—

(a) a transcript required by paragraph (a) of subsection (6) above to be served on an accused or by paragraph (b) of that subsection to be served on his solicitor; or

(b) a notice required by paragraph (a) of section 38(1) of this Act to be served on an accused or on the prosecutor,

shall be served in such manner as may be prescribed by Act of Adjournal; and a written execution purporting to be signed by the person who served such transcript or notice, together with, where appropriate, the relevant post office receipt shall be sufficient evidence of service of such a copy.

38, 39 * * * * *

40 Committal until liberated in due course of law

(1) Every petition shall be signed and no accused shall be committed until liberated in due course of law for any crime or offence without a warrant in writing expressing the particular charge in respect of which he is committed.

(2) Any such warrant for imprisonment which either proceeds on an unsigned petition or does not express the particular charge shall be null and void.

(3) The accused shall immediately be given a true copy of the warrant for imprisonment signed by the constable or person executing the warrant before imprisonment or by the prison officer receiving the warrant.

41-286 * * * * *

PART XIII
MISCELLANEOUS

Lord Advocate

287 Demission of office by Lord Advocate

(1) All indictments which have been raised by a Lord Advocate shall remain effective notwithstanding his subsequently having died or demitted office and may be taken up and proceeded with by his successor.

(2) During any period when the office of Lord Advocate is vacant it shall be lawful to indict accused persons in name of the Solicitor General then in office.

(3) The advocates depute shall not demit office when a Lord Advocate dies or demits office but shall continue in office until their successors receive commissions.

(4) The advocates depute and procurators fiscal shall have power, notwithstanding any vacancy in the office of Lord Advocate, to take up and proceed with any indictment which—

(a) by virtue of subsection (1) above, remains effective; or

(b) by virtue of subsection (2) above, is in the name of the Solicitor General.

(5) For the purposes of this Act, where, but for this subsection, demission of office by one Law Officer would result in the offices of both being vacant, he or, where both demit office on the same day, the person demitting the office of Lord Advocate shall be deemed to continue in office until the warrant of appointment of the person succeeding to the office of Lord Advocate is granted.

(6) The Lord Advocate shall enter upon the duties of his office immediately upon the grant of his warrant of appointment; and he shall as soon as is practicable thereafter take the oaths of office before the Secretary of State or any Lord Commissioner of Justiciary.

288 Intimation of proceedings in High Court to Lord Advocate

(1) In any proceeding in the High Court (other than a proceeding to which the Lord Advocate or a procurator fiscal is a party) it shall be competent for the court to order intimation of such proceeding to the Lord Advocate.

(2) On intimation being made to the Lord Advocate under subsection (1) above, the Lord Advocate shall be entitled to appear and be heard in such proceeding.

289 ★ ★ ★ ★ ★

290 Accused's right to request identification parade

(1) Subject to subsection (2) below, the sheriff may, on an application by an accused at any time after the accused has been charged with an offence, order that, in relation to the alleged offence, the prosecutor shall hold an identification parade in which the accused shall be one of those constituting the parade.

(2) The sheriff shall make an order in accordance with subsection (1) above only after giving the prosecutor an opportunity to be heard and only if—

(a) an identification parade, such as is mentioned in subsesction (1) above, has not been held at the instance of the prosecutor;

(b) after a request by the accused, the prosecutor has refused to hold, or has unreasonably delayed holding, such an identification parade; and

(c) the sheriff considers the application under subsection (1) above to be reasonable.

★ ★ ★ ★ ★

ASYLUM AND IMMIGRATION ACT 1996
(1996, c. 49)

An Act to amend and supplement the Immigration Act 1971 and the Asylum and Immigration Appeals Act 1993; to make further provision with respect to persons subject to immigration control and the employment of such persons; and for connected purposes. [24 July 1996]

Territorial extent United Kingdom.

Note "The 1993 Act": Asylum and Immigration Appeals Act 1993.

★ ★ ★ ★ ★

2 Removal etc. of asylum claimants to safe third countries

(1) Nothing in section 6 of the 1993 Act (protection of claimants from deportation etc.) shall prevent a person who has made a claim for asylum being removed from the United Kingdom if—

(a) the Secretary of State has certified that, in his opinion, the conditions mentioned in subsection (2) below are fulfilled;

(b) the certificate has not been set aside on an appeal under section 3 below; and

(c) except in the case of a person who is to be sent to a country or territory to which subsection (3) below applies, the time for giving notice of such an appeal has expired and no such appeal is pending.

(2) The conditions are—

(a) that the person is not a national or citizen of the country or territory to which he is to be sent;

(b) that his life and liberty would not be threatened in that country or territory by reason of his race, religion, nationality, membership of a particular social group, or political opinion; and

(c) that the government of that country or territory would not send him to another country or territory otherwise than in accordance with the Convention.

(3) This subsection applies to any country or territory which is or forms part of a member State, or is designated for the purposes of this subsection in an order made by the Secretary of State by statutory instrument.

(4)–(7) ★★★★★

3 Appeals against certificates under section 2

(1) Where a certificate has been issued under section 2(1) above in respect of any person—

(a) that person may appeal against the certificate to a special adjudicator on the ground that any of the conditions mentioned in section 2(2) above was not fulfilled when the certificate was issued, or has since ceased to be fulfilled; but

(b) unless and until the certificate is set aside on such an appeal, he shall not be entitled to bring or pursue any appeal under—

(i) Part II of the 1971 Act (appeals: general); or

(ii) section 8 of the 1993 Act (appeals to special adjudicator on Convention grounds),

as respects matters arising before his removal from the United Kingdom.

(2) A person who has been, or is to be, sent to a country or territory to which section 2(3) above applies shall not be entitled to bring or pursue an appeal under this section so long as he is in the United Kingdom.

(3)–(6) ★★★★★

4–6 ★★★★★

7 Power of arrest and search warrants

(1) A constable or immigration officer may arrest without warrant anyone whom he has reasonable grounds for suspecting to have committed an offence to which this section applies.

(2) If—

(a) a justice of the peace is by written information on oath satisfied that there is reasonable ground for suspecting that a person who is liable to be arrested under subsection (1) above is to be found on any premises; or

(b) in Scotland, a sheriff, or a justice of the peace, having jurisdiction in the place where the premises are situated is by evidence on oath so satisfied,

he may grant a warrant authorising any constable to enter, if need be by force, the premises named in the warrant for the purposes of searching for and arresting that person.

(3) The following provisions, namely—

(a) section 8 of the Police and Criminal Evidence Act 1984 (power of justice to authorise entry and search of premises); and

(b) Article 10 of the Police and Criminal Evidence (Northern Ireland) Order 1989 (corresponding provision for Northern Ireland),
shall have effect as if the reference in subsection (1) of that section or, as the case may be, paragraph (1) of that Article to a serious arrestable offence included a reference to an offence to which this section applies.

(4), (5) ★★★★★

Persons subject to immigration control

8 Restrictions on employment

(1) Subject to subsection (2) below, if any person ("the employer") employs a person subject to immigration control ("the employee") who has attained the age of 16, the employer shall be guilty of an offence if—

(a) the employee has not been granted leave to enter or remain in the United Kingdom; or

(b) the employee's leave is not valid and subsisting, or is subject to a condition precluding him from taking up employment,

and (in either case) the employee does not satisfy such conditions as may be specified in an order made by the Secretary of State.

(2) Subject to subsection (3) below, in proceedings under this section, it shall be a defence to prove that—

(a) before the employment began, there was produced to the employer a document which appeared to him to relate to the employee and to be of a description specified in an order made by the Secretary of State; and

(b) either the document was retained by the employer, or a copy or other record of it was made by the employer in a manner specified in the order in relation to documents of that description.

(3) The defence afforded by subsection (2) above shall not be available in any case where the employer knew that his employment of the employee would constitute an offence under this section.

(4) A person guilty of an offence under this section shall be liable on summary conviction to a fine not exceeding level 5 on the standard scale.

(5) Where an offence under this section committed by a body corporate is proved to have been committed with the consent or connivance of, or to be attributable to any neglect on the part of—

(a) any director, manager, secretary or other similar officer of the body corporate; or

(b) any person who was purporting to act in any such capacity,

he as well as the body corporate shall be guilty of the offence and shall be liable to be proceeded against and punished accordingly.

(6)–(8) ★★★★★

9 Entitlement to housing accommodation and assistance

(1) Each [local housing authority within the meaning of the Housing Act 1985] shall secure that, so far as practicable, no tenancy of, or licence to occupy, housing accommodation provided under the accommodation Part is granted to a person subject to immigration control unless he is of a class specified in an order made by the Secretary of State.

(2) . . .

(3), (4) ★★★★★

★★★★★

BROADCASTING ACT 1996
(1996, c. 55)

An Act to make new provision about the broadcasting in digital form of television and sound programme services and the broadcasting in that form on television or radio frequencies of other services; to amend the Broadcasting Act 1990; to make provision about rights to televise sporting or other events of national interest; to amend in other respects the law relating to the provision of television and sound programme services; to provide for the establishment and functions of a Broadcasting Standards Commission and for the dissolution of the Broadcasting Complaints Commission and the Broadcasting Standards Council; to make provision for the transfer to other persons of property, rights and liabilities of the British Broadcasting Corporation relating to their transmission network; and for connected purposes.

[24 July 1996]

Territorial extent United Kingdom

PART I
DIGITAL TERRESTRIAL TELEVISION BROADCASTING

Introductory

1 Multiplex services and digital programme services

(1) In this Part "multiplex service" means a service provided by any person which consists in the broadcasting for general reception of two or more services specified in subsection (3) by combining the relevant information in digital form, together with any broadcasting in digital form of digital additional services (as defined by section 24(1)).

(2) A service in respect of which a licence under section 7 is in force is not prevented from being a multiplex service at a particular time merely because only one service specified in subsection (3) is being broadcast in digital form at that time.

(3) The services referred to in subsections (1) and (2) are—

(a) a digital programme service (as defined by subsection (4)), or

(b) a qualifying service (as defined by section 2(2)).

(4) In this Part "digital programme service" means a service consisting in the provision by any person of television programmes (together with any ancillary services, as defined by section 24(2)) with a view to their being broadcast in digital form for general reception, whether by him or by some other person, but does not include—

(a) a qualifying service,

(b) a teletext service, or

(c) any service in the case of which the visual images to be broadcast do not consist wholly or mainly of images capable of being seen as moving pictures,

except, in the case of a service falling within paragraph (b) or (c), to the extent that it is an ancillary service.

(5) The Secretary of State may, if having regard to developments in broadcasting technology he considers it appropriate to do so, by order amend the definition of "digital programme service" in subsection (4).

(6) No order under subsection (5) shall be made unless a draft of the order has been laid before and approved by a resolution of each House of Parliament.

(7) In this section—

"broadcast" means broadcast otherwise than—

(a) by satellite, or

(b) in the provision of a local delivery service (as defined by section 72(1) of the 1990 Act), and

"for general reception" means for general reception in, or in any area in, the United Kingdom.

2 *****

General provisions about licences

3 Licences under Part I

(1) Any licence granted by the Independent Television Commission (in this Part referred to as "the Commission") under this Part shall be in writing and (subject to the provisions of this Part) shall continue in force for such period as is provided, in relation to a licence of the kind in question, by the relevant provision of this Part.

(2) A licence may be so granted for the provision of such a service as is specified in the licence or for the provision of a service of such a description as is so specified.

(3) The Commission—

(a) shall not grant a licence to any person unless they are satisfied that he is a fit and proper person to hold it, and

(b) shall do all that they can to secure that, if they cease to be so satisfied in the case of any person holding a licence, that person does not remain the holder of the licence;

and nothing in this Part shall be construed as affecting the operation of this subsection or of section 5(1) or (2)(b) or (c).

(4) The Commission may vary a licence by a notice served on the licence holder if—

(a) in the case of a variation of the period for which a licence having effect for a specified period is to continue in force, the licence holder consents, or

(b) in the case of any other variation, the licence holder has been given a reasonable opportunity of making representations to the Commission about the variation.

(5) Paragraph (a) of subsection (4) does not affect the operation of section 17(1)(b); and that subsection shall not authorise the variation of any conditions included in a licence in pursuance of section 13(1).

(6) A licence granted to any person under this Part shall not be transferable to any other person without the previous consent in writing of the Commission.

(7) Without prejudice to the generality of subsection (6), the Commission shall not give their consent for the purposes of that subsection unless they are satisfied that any such other person would be in a position to comply with all of the conditions included in the licence which would have effect during the periods for which it is to be in force.

(8) The holding by any person of a licence to provide any service shall not relieve him of any requirement to hold a licence under section 1 of the Wireless Telegraphy Act 1949 or section 7 of the Telecommunications Act 1984 in connection with the provision of that service.

4–17 * * * * *

Digital programme services

18 Licensing of digital programme services

(1) An application for a licence to provide digital programme services (in this Part referred to as a "digital programme licence") shall—

(a) be made in such manner as the Commission may determine, and

(b) be accompanied by such fee (if any) as they may determine.

(2) At any time after receiving such an application and before determining it, the Commission may require the applicant to furnish such additional information as they may consider necessary for the purpose of considering the application.

(3) Any information to be furnished to the Commission under this section shall, if they so require, be in such form or verified in such manner as they may specify.

(4) Where an application for a digital programme licence is made to the Commission in accordance with the provisions of this section, they shall grant the licence unless precluded from doing so by section 3(3)(a) or 5(1).

(5) Subject to subsection (6), sections 6 to 12 of the 1990 Act (general provisions relating to services licensed under Part I of that Act) shall apply in relation to a digital programme service licensed under this Part as they apply in relation to a service licensed under that Part of that Act.

(6) In its application in relation to a digital programme service—

(a) section 6 of the 1990 Act shall have effect with the omission of subsection (8), and

(b) section 12(1)(b) of that Act shall have effect as if the reference to the Commission's functions under Chaper II of Part I of that Act included a reference to their functions under this Part.

19–33 * * * * *

34 Promotion of equal opportunities and fair treatment

(1) Any multiplex licence or digital programme licence shall include conditions requiring the licence holder—

(a) to make arrangements for promoting, in relation to employment by him, equality of opportunity between men and women and between persons of different racial groups,

(b) to make arrangements for promoting, in relation to employment by him, the fair treatment of disabled persons, and

(c) to review those arrangements from time to time.

(2) In subsection (1) "racial group" has the same meaning as in the Race Relations Act 1976, and "disabled person" has the same meaning as in the Disability Discrimination Act 1995.

35–39 * * * * *

PART II
DIGITAL TERRESTRIAL SOUND BROADCASTING

Introductory

40 Radio multiplex services

(1) In this Part "radio multiplex service" means a service provided by any person which consists in the broadcasting for general reception of two or more services specified in subsection (3) by combining the relevant information in digital form, together with any broadcasting in digital form of digital additional services (as defined by section 63(1)).

(2) A service in respect of which a licence under section 46 or 50 is in force is not prevented from being a radio multiplex service at a particular time merely because only one service specified in subsection (3) is being broadcast in digital form at that time.

(3) The services referred to in subsections (1) and (2) are—

(a) a digital sound programme service (as defined by subsection (5)), or

(b) a simulcast radio service (as defined by section 41(2)).

(4) A radio multiplex service provided on a frequency or frequencies assigned to the Authority under section 45(1) may be either—

(a) provided for a particular area or locality in the United Kingdom (a "local radio multiplex service"), or

(b) provided without any restriction by virtue of this Act to a particular area or locality in the United Kingdom (a "national radio multiplex service").

(5) In this Part "digital sound programme service" means a service consisting in the provision by any person of programmes consisting wholly of sound (together with any ancillary services, as defined by section 63(2)) with a view to their being broadcast in digital form for general reception, whether by him or by some other person, but does not include—

(a) a simulcast radio service (as defined by section 41(2)), or

(b) a service where the sounds are to be received through the use of coded reference to pre-defined phonetic elements of sounds.

(6) The Secretary of State may, if having regard to developments in broadcasting technology he considers it appropriate to do so, by order amend the definition of "digital sound programme service" in subsection (5).

(7) No order under subsection (6) shall be made unless a draft of the order has been laid before and approved by a resolution of each House of Parliament.

(8) In this section—

"broadcast" means broadcast otherwise than—

(a) by satellite, or

(b) in the provision of a local delivery service (as defined by section 72(1) of the 1990 Act), and

"for general reception" means for general reception in, or in any area in, the United Kingdom.

41 * * * * *

General provisions about licences

42 Licences under Part II

(1) Any licence granted by the Radio Authority (in this Part referred to as "the Authority") under this Part shall be in writing and (subject to the provisions of this Part) shall continue in force for such period as is provided, in relation to a licence of the kind in question, by the relevant provision of this Part.

(2) The Authority—

(a) shall not grant a licence to any person unless they are satisfied that he is a fit and proper person to hold it, and

(b) shall do all that they can to secure that, if they cease to be so satisfied in the case of any person holding a licence, that person does not remain the holder of the licence;

and nothing in this Part shall be construed as affecting the operation of this subsection or of section 44(1) or (2)(b) or (c).

(3) The Authority may vary a licence by a notice served on the licence holder if—

(a) in the case of a variation of the period for which a licence having effect for a specified period is to continue in force, the licence holder consents, or

(b) in the case of any other variation, the licence holder has been given a reasonable opportunity of making representations to the Authority about the variation.

(4) Paragraph (a) of subsection (3) does not affect the operation of section 59(1)(b); and that subsection shall not authorise the variation of any condition included in a licence in pursuance of section 55(1).

(5) A licence granted to any person under this Part shall not be transferable to any other person without the previous consent in writing of the Authority.

(6) Without prejudice to the generality of subsection (5), the Authority shall not give their consent for the purposes of that subsection unless they are satisfied that any such other person would be in a position to comply with all of the conditions included in the licence which would have effect during the period for which it is to be in force.

(7) The holding by any person of a licence to provide any service shall not relieve him of any requirement to hold a licence under section 1 of the Wireless Telegraphy Act 1949 or section 7 of the Telecommunications Act 1984 in connection with the provision of that service.

43, 44 * * * * *

Radio multiplex services

45 Assignment of frequencies by Secretary of State

(1) The Secretary of State may by notice assign to the Authority, for the purpose of the provision of radio multiplex services falling to be licensed by them under this Part, such frequencies as he may determine.

(2) Any frequency assigned by the Secretary of State under subsection (1) may be so assigned for use only in such area or areas as may be specified by the Secretary of State when making the assignment.

(3) When assigning a frequency under subsection (1), the Secretary of State shall specify whether the frequency is to be assigned for the purpose of the provision of a national radio multiplex service or for the purpose of the provision of a local radio multiplex service; and any frequency assigned under that subsection shall be taken to be so assigned only for that purpose.

(4) When assigning a frequency under subsection (1) for the purpose of the provision of a national radio multiplex service, the Secretary of State may also direct the Authority to secure that the holder of the licence to provide that service is required—

(a) to broadcast one or more digital sound programme services of a particular character, or

(b) not to broadcast more than a specified number of digital sound programme services of a particular character.

(5) References in subsection (4) to digital sound programme services of a particular character include references to digital sound programme services catering for the tastes and interests of persons living within a specified area or locality.

(6) The Secretary of State may by notice revoke the assignment under subsection (1) of any frequency specified in the notice, and may do so whether or not that frequency is for the time being one on which a radio multiplex service is being provided.

46–96 * * * * *

PART IV
SPORTING AND OTHER EVENTS OF NATIONAL INTEREST

97 Listed events

(1) For the purposes of this Part, a listed event is a sporting or other event of national interest which is for the time being included in a list drawn up by the Secretary of State for the purposes of this Part.

(2) The Secretary of State shall not at any time draw up, revise or cease to maintain such a list as is mentioned in subsection (1) unless he has first consulted—

(a) the BBC,

(b) the Welsh Authority,

(c) the Commission, and

(d) in relation to a relevant event, the person from whom the rights to televise that event may be acquired;

and for the purposes of this subsection a relevant event is a sporting or other event of national interest which the Secretary of State proposes to include in, or omit from, the list.

(3) As soon as he has drawn up or revised such a list as is mentioned in subsection (1), the Secretary of State shall publish the list in such manner as he considers appropriate for bringing it to the attention of—

(a) the persons mentioned in subsection (2), and

(b) every person who is the holder of a licence granted by the Commission under Part I of the 1990 Act or a digital programme licence granted by them under Part I of this Act.

(4) In this section "national interest" includes interest within England, Scotland, Wales or Northern Ireland.

(5) The addition of any relevant event to such a list as is mentioned in subsection (1) shall not affect—

(a) the validity of any contract entered into before the date on which the Secretary of State consulted the persons mentioned in subsection (2) in relation to the proposed addition, or

(b) the exercise of any rights acquired under such a contract.

(6) The list drawn up by the Secretary of State for the purposes of section 182 of the 1990 Act, as that list is in force immediately before the commencement of this section, shall be taken to have been drawn up for the purposes of this Part.

98–105 ★ ★ ★ ★ ★

PART V
THE BROADCASTING STANDARDS COMMISSION

Establishment of Broadcasting Standards Commission

106 The Broadcasting Standards Commission

(1) There shall be a commission, to be known as the Broadcasting Standards Commission (in this Part referred to as "the BSC").

(2) the BSC shall consist of—

(a) a chairman appointed by the Secretary of State,

(b) a deputy chairman or two deputy chairmen so appointed, and

(c) such number of other members appointed by the Secretary of State as he may from time to time determine,

but so that the total number of members does not exceed fifteen.

(3) Schedule 3 shall have effect with respect to the BSC.

Unjust or unfair treatment or unwarranted infringement of privacy

107 Preparation by BSC of code relating to avoidance of unjust or unfair treatment or interference with privacy

(1) It shall be the duty of the BSC to draw up, and from time to time review, a code giving guidance as to principles to be observed, and practices to be followed, in connection with the avoidance of—

(a) unjust or unfair treatment in programmes to which this section applies, or

(b) unwarranted infringement of privacy in, or in connection with the obtaining of material included in, such programmes.

(2) It shall be the duty of each broadcasting or regulatory body, when drawing up or revising any code relating to principles and practice in connection with programmes, or in connection with the obtaining of material to be included in programmes, to reflect the general effect of so much of the code referred to in subsection (1) (as for the time being in force) as is relevant to the programmes in question.

(3) The BSC shall from time to time publish the code (as for the time being in force).

(4) Before drawing up or revising the code, the BSC shall consult—

(a) each broadcasting or regulatory body, and

(b) such other persons as appear to the BSC to be appropriate.

(5) This section applies to—

(a) any programme broadcast by the BBC,

(b) any programme broadcast by the Welsh Authority or included in the service referred to in section 57(1A)(a) of the 1990 Act, and

(c) any programme included in a licensed service.

Portrayal of violence or sexual conduct etc.

108 Preparation by BSC of code relating to broadcasting standards generally

(1) It shall be the duty of the BSC to draw up, and from time to time review, a code giving guidance as to—

(a) practices to be followed in connection with the portrayal of violence in programmes to which this section applies,

(b) practices to be followed in connection with the portrayal of sexual conduct in such programmes, and

(c) standards of taste and decency for such programmes generally.

(2) It shall be the duty of each broadcasting or regulatory body, when drawing up or revising any code relating to standards and practice for programmes, to reflect the general effect of so much of the code referred to in subsection (1) (as for the time being in force) as is relevant to the programmes in question.

(3) The BSC shall from time to time publish the code referred to in subsection (1) (as for the time being in force).

(4) Before drawing up or revising the code the BSC shall consult—

(a) each broadcasting or regulatory body, and

(b) such other persons as appear to the BSC to be appropriate.

(5) This section applies to—

(a) any programme broadcast by the BBC,

(b) any programme broadcast by the Welsh Authority or included in the service referred to in section 57(1A)(a) of the 1990 Act,

(c) any programme included in a licensed service, and

(d) any programme included in so much of a local delivery service licensed under Part II of the 1990 Act as is, by virtue of section 79(2) or (4) of that Act, treated for certain purposes as the provision of a service licensed under Part I of that Act.

(6) The code drawn up by the Broadcasting Standards Council under section 152 of the 1990 Act, as that code is in force immediately before the commencement of this section, shall be taken to have been drawn up by the BSC under this section.

109 Monitoring by BSC of broadcasting standards

(1) It shall be the duty of the BSC to monitor programmes to which section 108 applies with a view to enabling the BSC to make reports on the portrayal of violence and sexual conduct in, and the standards of taste and decency attained by, such programmes generally.

(2) Subject to section 125(2), the BSC may make reports on the matters specified in subsection (1) on such occasions as they think fit; and any such report may include an assessment of either or both of the following, namely—

(a) the attitudes of the public at large towards the portrayal of violence or sexual conduct in, or towards the standards of taste and decency attained by, programmes to which section 108 applies, and

(b) any effects or potential effects on the attitudes or behaviour of particular categories of persons of the portrayal of violence or sexual conduct in such programmes or of any failure on the part of such programmes to attain standards of taste and decency.

(3) The BSC may publish any report made by them in pursuance of subsection (1).

(4) The BSC shall have the further duty of monitoring, so far as is reasonably practicable, all television and sound programmes which are transmitted or sent from outside the United Kingdom but are capable of being received there, with a view to ascertaining—

(a) how violence and sexual conduct are portrayed in those programmes, and

(b) the extent to which these programmes meet standards of taste and decency.

Complaints

110 General functions of BSC in relation to complaints

(1) Subject to the provisions of this Part, it shall be the duty of the BSC to consider and adjudicate on complaints which are made to them in accordance with sections 111 and 114 and relate—

(a) to unjust or unfair treatment in programmes to which section 107 applies, or

(b) to unwarranted infringement of privacy in, or in connection with the obtaining of material included in, such programmes.

(2) Subject to those provisions, it shall also be the duty of the BSC to consider, and make findings on, complaints which are made to them in accordance with sections 113 and 114 and relate—

(a) to the portrayal of violence or sexual conduct in programmes to which section 108 applies, or

(b) to alleged failures on the part of such programmes to attain standards of taste and decency.

(3) In exercising their functions under subsection (1), the BSC shall take into account any relevant provisions of the code maintained by them under section 107; and in exercising their functions under subsection (2) they shall take into account any relevant provisions of the code maintained by them under section 108.

(4) In this Part—

"a fairness complaint" means a complaint to the BSC in respect of any of the matters referred to in subsection (1)(a) and (b), and

"a standards complaint" means a complaint to the BSC in respect of any of the matters referred to in subsection (2)(a) and (b).

111 Complaints of unfair treatment etc.

(1) A fairness complaint may be made by an individual or by a body of persons, whether incorporated or not, but, subject to subsection (2), shall not be entertained by the BSC unless made by the person affected or by a person authorised by him to make the complaint for him.

(2) Where the person affected is an individual who has died, a fairness complaint may be made by his personal representative or by a member of the family of the person affected, or by some other person or body closely connected with him (whether as his employer, or as a body of which he was at his death a member, or in any other way).

(3) Where the person affected is an individual who is for any reason both unable to make a complaint himself and unable to authorise another person to do so for him, a fairness complaint may be made by a member of the family of the person affected, or by some other person or body closely connected with him (whether as his employer, or as a body of which he is a member, or in any other way).

(4) The BSC shall not entertain, or proceed with the consideration of, a fairness complaint if it appears to them that the complaint relates to the broadcasting of the relevant programme, or to its inclusion in a licensed service, on an occasion more than five years after the death of the person affected, unless it appears to them that in the particular circumstances it is appropriate to do so.

(5) The BSC may refuse to entertain a fairness complaint if it appears to them not to have been made within a reasonable time after the last occasion on which the relevant programme was broadcast or, as the case may be, included in a licensed service.

(6) Where, in the case of a fairness complaint, the relevant programme was broadcast or included in a licensed service after the death of the person affected, subsection (5) shall apply as if at the end there were added "within five years (or such longer period as may be allowed by the BSC in the particular case under subsection (4)) after the death of the person affected".

(7) The BSC may refuse to entertain—

(a) a fairness complaint which is a complaint of unjust or unfair treatment if the person named as the person affected was not himself the subject of the treatment complained of and it appears to the BSC that he did not have a sufficiently direct interest in the subject-matter of that treatment to justify the making of a complaint with him as the person affected, or

(b) a complaint made under subsection (2) or (3) by a person other than the person affected or a person authorised by him, if it appears to the BSC that the complainant's connection with the person affected is not sufficiently close to justify the making of the complaint by him.

112–116 * * * * *

117 Duty to retain recordings

For the purposes of sections 115 and 116 of this Act and of section 167 of the 1990 Act (power to make copies of recordings in connection with certain offences) it shall be the duty of each broadcasting body to retain a recording of every television or sound programme which is broadcast by that body—

(a) where it is of a television programme, during the period of 90 days beginning with the day of the broadcast, and

(b) where it is of a sound programme, during the period of 42 days beginning with the day of the broadcast.

118 * * * * *

119 Publication of BSC's findings

(1) Where the BSC have—

(a) considered and adjudicated upon a fairness complaint, or

(b) considered and made their findings on a standards complaint,

they may give directions of the kind specified in subsection (2).

(2) Those directions are—

(a) where the relevant programme was broadcast by a broadcasting body, directions requiring that body to publish the matters mentioned in subsection (3) in such manner, and within such period, as may be specified in the directions, and

(b) where the relevant programme was included in a licensed service, directions requiring the appropriate regulatory body to direct the licence holder to publish those matters in such manner, and within such period, as may be so specified.

(3) Those matters are—

(a) a summary of the complaint;

(b) the BSC's findings on the complaint or a summary of them;

(c) in the case of a standards complaint, any observations by the BSC on the complaint or a summary of any such observations.

(4) References in subsection (2) to the publication of any matter are references to the publication of that matter without its being accompanied by any observations made by a person other than the BSC and relating to the complaint.

(5) The form and content of any such summary as is mentioned in subsection (3)(a), (b) or (c) shall be such as may be approved by the BSC.

(6) A broadcasting or regulatory body shall comply with any directions given to them under this section.

(7) Any licence to provide a licensed service which is granted by a regulatory body under this Act shall include conditions requiring the licence holder to comply with such directions as may be given to him by that body for the purpose of enabling them to comply with any directions given to them under this section.

(8) The BSC shall publish, monthly or at such other intervals as they think fit and in such manner as they think fit, reports each containing, as regards every fairness

complaint or standards complaint which falls within this subsection and has been dealt with by them in the period covered by the report—

(a) a summary of the complaint and the action taken by them on it,

(b) where they have adjudicated on it, a summary of—

(i) their findings,

(ii) any direction given under subsection (1), or other action taken by them, in relation to the complaint, and

(c) where a direction has been given under subsection (1) in relation to the complaint, a summary of any action taken by a broadcasting body, a regulatory body or the holder of a licence to provide a licensed service in pursuance of the direction.

(9) A fairness complaint or standards complaint made to the BSC falls within subsection (8) unless it is one which under section 111(1), (4) or (5), 113(1) or 114(2) they have refused to entertain.

(10) The BSC may, if they think fit, omit from any summary which is included in a report under subsection (8) and relates to a fairness complaint any information which could lead to the disclosure of the identity of any person connected with the complaint in question other than—

(a) a broadcasting or regulatory body, or

(b) a person providing a licensed service.

(11), (12) * * * * *

120 * * * * *

121 Certain statements etc. protected by qualified privilege for purposes of defamation

(1) For the purposes of the law relating to defamation—

(a) publication of any statement in the course of the consideration by the BSC of, and their adjudication on, a fairness complaint,

(b) publication by the BSC of directions under section 119(1) relating to a fairness complaint, or

(c) publication of a report of the BSC, so far as the report relates to fairness complaints,

is privileged unless the publication is shown to be made with malice.

(2) Nothing in subsection (1) shall be construed as limiting any privilege subsisting apart from that subsection.

* * * * *

CRIMINAL PROCEDURE AND INVESTIGATIONS ACT 1996
(1996, c. 25)

An Act to make provision about criminal procedure and criminal investigations.

[4 July 1996]

Territorial extent England and Wales, Northern Ireland (ss. 22–24, 26, 58); England and Wales, Scotland (ss. 37, 38, 40, 41); England and Wales (s. 39); United Kingdom (ss. 59, 60).

Note The Code of Practice made under s. 23 is printed below at p. 503.

PART II
CRIMINAL INVESTIGATIONS

22 Introduction

(1) For the purposes of this Part a criminal investigation is an investigation conducted by police officers with a view to it being ascertained—

(a) whether a person should be charged with an offence, or
(b) whether a person charged with an offence is guilty of it.

(2) In this Part references to material are to material of all kinds, and in particular include references to—
(a) information, and
(b) objects of all descriptions.

(3) In this Part references to recording information are to putting it in a durable or retrievable form (such as writing or tape).

23 Code of practice

(1) The Secretary of State shall prepare a code of practice containing provisions designed to secure—

(a) that where a criminal investigation is conducted all reasonable steps are taken for the purposes of the investigation and, in particular, all reasonable lines of inquiry are pursued;

(b) that information which is obtained in the course of a criminal investigation and may be relevant to the investigation is recorded;

(c) that any record of such information is retained;

(d) that any other material which is obtained in the course of a criminal investigation and may be relevant to the investigation is retained;

(e) that information falling within paragraph (b) and material falling within paragraph (d) is revealed to a person who is involved in the prosecution of criminal proceedings arising out of or relating to the investigation and who is identified in accordance with prescribed provisions;

(f) that where such a person inspects information or other material in pursuance of a requirement that it be revealed to him, and he requests that it be disclosed to the accused, the accused is allowed to inspect it or is given a copy of it;

(g) that where such a person is given a document indicating the nature of information or other material in pursuance of a requirement that it be revealed to him, and he requests that it be disclosed to the accused, the accused is allowed to inspect it or is given a copy of it;

(h) that the person who is to allow the accused to inspect information or other material or to give him a copy of it shall decide which of those (inspecting or giving a copy) is appropriate;

(i) that where the accused is allowed to inspect material as mentioned in paragraph (f) or (g) and he requests a copy, he is given one unless the person allowing the inspection is of opinion that it is not practicable or not desirable to give him one;

(j) that a person mentioned in paragraph (e) is given a written statement that prescribed activities which the code requires have been carried out.

(2) The code may include provision—

(a) that a police officer identified in accordance with prescribed provisions must carry out a prescribed activity which the code requires;

(b) that a police officer so identified must take steps to secure the carrying out by a person (whether or not a police officer) of a prescribed activity which the code requires;

(c) that a duty must be discharged by different people in succession in prescribed circumstances (as where a person dies or retires).

(3) The code may include provision about the form in which information is to be recorded.

(4) The code may include provision about the manner in which and the period for which—
(a) a record of information is to be retained, and
(b) any other material is to be retained;

and if a person is charged with an offence the period may extend beyond a conviction or an acquittal.

(5) The code may include provision about the time when, the form in which, the way in which, and the extent to which, information or any other material is to be revealed to the person mentioned in subsection (1)(e).

(6) The code must be so framed that it does not apply to material intercepted in obedience to a warrant issued under section 2 of the Interception of Communications Act 1985.

(7) The code may—

(a) make different provision in relation to different cases or descriptions of case;

(b) contain exceptions as regards prescribed cases or descriptions of case.

(8) In this section "prescribed" means prescribed by the code.

24 Examples of disclosure provisions

(1) This section gives examples of the kinds of provision that may be included in the code by virtue of section 23(5).

(2) The code may provide that if the person required to reveal material has possession of material which he believes is sensitive he must give a document which—

(a) indicates the nature of that material, and

(b) states that he so believes.

(3) The code may provide that if the person required to reveal material has possession of material which is of a description prescribed under this subsection and which he does not believe is sensitive he must give a document which—

(a) indicates the nature of that material, and

(b) states that he does not so believe.

(4) The code may provide that if—

(a) a document is given in pursuance of provision contained in the code by virtue of subsection (2), and

(b) a person identified in accordance with prescribed provisions asks for any of the material,

the person giving the document must give a copy of the material asked for to the person asking for it or (depending on the circumstances) must allow him to inspect it.

(5)–(9) * * * * *

25 * * * * *

26 Effect of code

(1) A person other than a police officer who is charged with the duty of conducting an investigation with a view to it being ascertained—

(a) whether a person should be charged with an offence, or

(b) whether a person charged with an offence is guilty of it,

shall in discharging that duty have regard to any relevant provision of a code which would apply if the investigation were conducted by police officers.

(2) A failure—

(a) by a police officer to comply with any provision of a code for the time being in operation by virtue of an order under section 25, or

(b) by a person to comply with subsection (1),

shall not in itself render him liable to any criminal or civil proceedings.

(3) In all criminal and civil proceedings a code in operation at any time by virtue of an order under section 25 shall be admissible in evidence.

(4) If it appears to a court or tribunal conducting criminal or civil proceedings that—

(a) any provision of a code in operation at any time by virtue of an order under section 25, or

(b) any failure mentioned in subsection (2)(a) or (b),
is relevant to any question arising in the proceedings, the provision or failure shall be taken into account in deciding the question.

27–36 * * * * *

Reporting restrictions

37 Restrictions on reporting

(1) Except as provided by this section—

(a) no written report of proceedings falling within subsection (2) shall be published in Great Britain;

(b) no report of proceedings falling within subsection (2) shall be included in a relevant programme for reception in Great Britain.

(2) The following proceedings fall within this subsection—

(a) a preparatory hearing;

(b) an application for leave to appeal in relation to such a hearing;

(c) an appeal in relation to such a hearing.

(3) The judge dealing with a preparatory hearing may order that subsection (1) shall not apply, or shall not apply to a specified extent, to a report of—

(a) the preparatory hearing, or

(b) an application to the judge for leave to appeal to the Court of Appeal under section 35(1) in relation to the preparatory hearing.

(4)–(8) * * * * *

(9) Subsection (1) does not apply to a report which contains only one or more of the following matters—

(a) the identity of the court and the name of the judge;

(b) the names, ages, home addresses and occupations of the accused and witnesses;

(c) the offence or offences, or a summary of them, with which the accused is or are charged;

(d) the names of counsel and solicitors in the proceedings;

(e) where the proceedings are adjourned, the date and place to which they are adjourned;

(f) any arrangements as to bail;

(g) whether legal aid was granted to the accused or any of the accused.

(10) The addresses that may be published or included in a relevant programme under subsection (9) are addresses—

(a) at any relevant time, and

(b) at the time of their publication or inclusion in a relevant programme;

and "relevant time" here means a time when events giving rise to the charges to which the proceedings relate occurred.

(11) Nothing in this section affects any prohibition or restriction imposed by virtue of any other enactment on a publication or on matter included in a programme.

(12) In this section—

(a) "publish", in relation to a report, means publish the report, either by itself or as part of a newspaper or periodical, for distribution to the public;

(b) expressions cognate with "publish" shall be construed accordingly;

(c) "relevant programme" means a programme included in a programme service, within the meaning of the Broadcasting Act 1996.

38 Offences in connection with reporting

(1) If a report is published or included in a relevant programme in contravention of section 37 each of the following persons in guilty of an offence—

(a) in the case of a publication of a written report as part of a newspaper or periodical, any proprietor, editor or publisher of the newspaper or periodical;

(b) in the case of a publication of a written report otherwise than as part of a newspaper or periodical, the person who publishes it;

(c) in the case of the inclusion of a report in a relevant programme, any body corporate which is engaged in providing the service in which the programme is included and any person having functions in relation to the programme corresponding to those of an editor of a newspaper.

(2) A person guilty of an offence under this section is liable on summary conviction to a fine of an amount not exceeding level 5 on the standard scale.

(3) Proceedings for an offence under this section shall not be instituted in England and Wales otherwise than by or with the consent of the Attorney General.

(4) Subsection (12) of section 37 applies for the purposes of this section as it applies for the purposes of that.

PART IV
RULINGS

39 Meaning of pre-trial hearing

(1) For the purposes of this Part a hearing is a pre-trial hearing if it relates to a trial on indictment and it takes place—

(a) after the accused has been committed for trial for the offence concerned or after the proceedings for the trial have been transferred to the Crown Court, and

(b) before the start of the trial.

(2), (3) * * * * *

40 Power to make rulings

(1) A judge may make at a pre-trial hearing a ruling as to—

(a) any question as to the admissibility of evidence;

(b) any other question of law relating to the case concerned.

(2) A ruling may be made under this section—

(a) on an application by a party to the case, or

(b) of the judge's own motion.

(3) Subject to subsection (4), a ruling made under this section has binding effect from the time it is made until the case against the accused or, if there is more than one, against each of them is disposed of; and the case against an accused is disposed of if—

(a) he is acquitted or convicted, or

(b) the prosecutor decides not to proceed with the case against him.

(4)–(7) * * * * *

41 Restrictions on reporting

(1) Except as provided by this section—

(a) no written report of matters falling within subsection (2) shall be published in Great Britain;

(b) no report of matters falling within subsection (2) shall be included in a relevant programme for reception in Great Britain.

(2) The following matters fall within this subsection—

(a) a ruling made under section 40;

(b) proceedings on an application for a ruling to be made under section 40;

(c) an order that a ruling made under section 40 be discharged or varied or further varied;

(d) proceedings on an application for a ruling made under section 40 to be discharged or varied or further varied.

(3) The judge dealing with any matter falling within subsection (2) may order that subsection (1) shall not apply, or shall not apply to a specified extent, to a report of the matter.

(4) Where there is only one accused and he objects to the making of an order under subsection (3) the judge shall make the order if (and only if) satisfied after hearing the representations of the accused that it is in the interests of justice to do so; and if the order is made it shall not apply to the extent that a report deals with any such objection or representations.

(5) Where there are two or more accused and one or more of them objects to the making of an order under subsection (3) the judge shall make the order if (and only if) satisfied after hearing the representations of each of the accused that it is in the interests of justice to do so; and if the order is made it shall not apply to the extent that a report deals with any such objection or representations.

(6) Subsection (1) does not apply to—

(a) the publication of a report of matters, or

(b) the inclusion in a relevant programme of a report of matters,

at the conclusion of the trial of the accused or of the last of the accused to be tried.

(7), (8) * * * * *

42–57 * * * * *

Derogatory assertions

58 Orders in respect of certain assertions

(1) This section applies where a person has been convicted of an offence and a speech in mitigation is made by him or on his behalf before—

(a) a court determining what sentence should be passed on him in respect of the offence, or

(b) a magistrates' court determining whether he should be committed to the Crown Court for sentence.

(2) This section also applies where a sentence has been passed on a person in respect of an offence and a submission relating to the sentence is made by him or on his behalf before—

(a) a court hearing an appeal against or reviewing the sentence, or

(b) a court determining whether to grant leave to appeal against the sentence.

(3) Where it appears to the court that there is a real possibility that an order under subsection (8) will be made in relation to the assertion, the court may make an order under subsection (7) in relation to the assertion.

(4) Where there are substantial grounds for believing—

(a) that an assertion forming part of the speech or submission is derogatory to a person's character (for instance, because it suggests that his conduct is or has been criminal, immoral or improper), and

(b) that the assertion is false or that the facts asserted are irrelevant to the sentence,

the court may make an order under subsection (8) in relation to the assertion.

(5) An order under subsection (7) or (8) must not be made in relation to an assertion if it appears to the court that the assertion was previously made—

(a) at the trial at which the person was convicted of the offence, or

(b) during any other proceedings relating to the offence.

(6) Section 59 has effect where a court makes an order under subsection (7) or (8).

(7) An order under this subsection—

(a) may be made at any time before the court has made a determination with regard to sentencing;

(b) may be revoked at any time by the court;

(c) subject to paragraph (b), shall cease to have effect when the court makes a determination with regard to sentencing.

(8) An order under this subsection—

(a) may be made after the court has made a determination with regard to sentencing, but only if it is made as soon as is reasonably practicable after the making of the determination;

(b) may be revoked at any time by the court;

(c) subject to paragraph (b), shall cease to have effect at the end of the period of 12 months beginning with the day on which it is made;

(d) may be made whether or not an order has been made under subsection (7) with regard to the case concerned.

59 Restriction on reporting of assertions

(1) Where a court makes an order under section 58(7) or (8) in relation to any assertion, at any time when the order has effect the assertion must not—

(a) be published in Great Britain in a written publication available to the public, or

(b) be included in a relevant programme for reception in Great Britain.

(2) In this section—

"relevant programme" means a programme included in a programme service, within the meaning of the Broadcasting Act 1990;

"written publication" includes a film, a soundtrack and any other record in permanent form but does not include an indictment or other document prepared for use in particular legal proceedings.

(3) For the purposes of this section an assertion is published or included in a programme if the material published or included—

(a) names the person about whom the assertion is made or, without naming him, contains enough to make it likely that members of the public will identify him as the person about whom it is made, and

(b) reproduces the actual wording of the matter asserted or contains its substance.

60 Reporting of assertions: offences

(1) If an assertion is published or included in a relevant programme in contravention of section 59, each of the following persons is guilty of an offence—

(a) in the case of publication in a newspaper or periodical, any proprietor, any editor and any publisher of the newspaper or periodical;

(b) in the case of publication in any other form, the person publishing the assertion;

(c) in the case of an assertion included in a relevant programme, any body corporate engaged in providing the service in which the programme is included and any person having functions in relation to the programme corresponding to those of an editor of a newspaper.

(2) A person guilty of an offence under this section is liable on summary conviction to a fine of an amount not exceeding level 5 on the standard scale.

(3) Where a person is charged with an offence under this section it is a defence to prove that at the time of the alleged offence—

(a) he was not aware, and neither suspected nor had reason to suspect, that an order under section 58(7) or (8) had effect at that time, or

(b) he was not aware, and neither suspected nor had reason to suspect, that the publication or programme in question was of, or (as the case may be) included, the assertion in question.

(4)–(6) * * * * *

* * * * *

DEFAMATION ACT 1996
(1996, c. 31)

An Act to amend the law of defamation and to amend the law of limitation with respect to actions for defamation or malicious falsehood. [4 July 1996]

Territorial extent United Kingdom

★ ★ ★ ★ ★

Evidence concerning proceedings in Parliament

13 Evidence concerning proceedings in Parliament

(1) Where the conduct of a person in or in relation to proceedings in Parliament is in issue in defamation proceedings, he may waive for the purposes of those proceedings, so far as concerns him, the protection of any enactment or rule of law which prevents proceedings in Parliament being impeached or questioned in any court or place out of Parliament.

(2) Where a person waives that protection—

(a) any such enactment or rule of law shall not apply to prevent evidence being given, questions being asked or statements, submissions, comments or findings being made about his conduct, and

(b) none of those things shall be regarded as infringing the privilege of either House of Parliament.

(3) The waiver by one person of that protection does not affect its operation in relation to another person who has not waived it.

(4) Nothing in this section affects any enactment or rule of law so far as it protects a person (including a person who has waived the protection referred to above) from legal liability for words spoken or things done in the course of, or for the purposes of or incidental to, any proceedings in Parliament.

(5) Without prejudice to the generality of subsection (4), that subsection applies to—

(a) the giving of evidence before either House or a committee;

(b) the presentation or submission of a document to either House or a committee;

(c) the preparation of a document for the purposes of or incidental to the transacting of any such business;

(d) the formulation, making or publication of a document, including a report, by or pursuant to an order of either House or a committee; and

(e) any communication with the Parliamentary Commissioner for Standards or any person having functions in connection with the registration of members' interests.

In this subsection "a committee" means a committee of either House or a joint committee of both Houses of Parliament.

Statutory privilege

14 Reports of court proceedings absolutely privileged

(1) A fair and accurate report of proceedings in public before a court to which this section applies, if published contemporaneously with the proceedings, is absolutely privileged.

(2) A report of proceedings which by an order of the court, or as a consequence of any statutory provision, is required to be postponed shall be treated as published contemporaneously if it is published as soon as practicable after publication is permitted.

(3) This section applies to—

(a) any court in the United Kingdom,

(b) the European Court of Justice or any court attached to that court,

(c) the European Court of Human Rights, and

(d) any international criminal tribunal established by the Security Council of the United Nations or by an international agreement to which the United Kingdom is a party.

In paragraph (a) "court" includes any tribunal or body exercising the judicial power of the State.

(4) * * * * *

15 Reports, &c. protected by qualified privilege

(1) The publication of any report or other statement mentioned in Schedule 1 to this Act is privileged unless the publication is shown to be made with malice, subject as follows.

(2) In defamation proceedings in respect of the publication of a report or other statement mentioned in Part II of that Schedule, there is no defence under this section if the plaintiff shows that the defendant—

(a) was requested by him to publish in a suitable manner a reasonable letter or statement by way of explanation or contradiction, and

(b) refused or neglected to do so.

For this purpose "in a suitable manner" means in the same manner as the publication complained of or in a manner that is adequate and reasonable in the circumstances.

(3) This section does not apply to the publication to the public, or a section of the public, of matter which is not of public concern and the publication of which is not for the public benefit.

(4) Nothing in this section shall be construed—

(a) as protecting the publication of matter the publication of which is prohibited by law, or

(b) as limiting or abridging any privilege subsisting apart from this section.

16–19 * * * * *

20 Short title and saving

(1) This Act may be cited as the Defamation Act 1996.

(2) Nothing in this Act affects the law relating to criminal libel.

SCHEDULES

Section 15

SCHEDULE 1
QUALIFIED PRIVILEGE

PART I
STATEMENTS HAVING QUALIFIED PRIVILEGE WITHOUT EXPLANATION OR CONTRADICTION

1. A fair and accurate report of proceedings in public of a legislature anywhere in the world.

2. A fair and accurate report of proceedings in public before a court anywhere in the world.

3. A fair and accurate report of proceedings in public of a person appointed to hold a public inquiry by a government or legislature anywhere in the world.

4. A fair and accurate report of proceedings in public anywhere in the world of an international organisation or an international conference.

5. A fair and accurate copy of or extract from any register or other document required by law to be open to public inspection.

6. A notice or advertisement published by or on the authority of a court, or of a judge or officer of a court, anywhere in the world.

7. A fair and accurate copy of or extract from matter published by or on the authority of a government or legislature anywhere in the world.

8. A fair and accurate copy of or extract from matter published anywhere in the world by an international organisation or an international conference.

PART II
STATEMENTS PRIVILEGED SUBJECT TO EXPLANATION OR CONTRADICTION

9.—(1) A fair and accurate copy of or extract from a notice or other matter issued for the information of the public by or on behalf of—

(a) a legislature in any member State or the European parliament;

(b) the government of any member State, or any authority performing governmental functions in any member State or part of a member State, or the European Commission;

(c) an international organisation or international conference.

(2) In this paragraph "governmental functions" includes police functions.

10. A fair and accurate copy of or extract from a document made available by a court in any member State or the European Court of Justice (or any court attached to that court), or by a judge or officer of any such court.

11.—(1) A fair and accurate report of proceedings at any public meeting or sitting in the United Kingdom of—

(a) a local authority or local authority committee;

(b) a justice or justices of the peace acting otherwise than as a court exercising judicial authority;

(c) a commission, tribunal, committee or person appointed for the purposes of any inquiry by any statutory provision, by Her Majesty or by a Minister of the Crown or a Northern Ireland Department;

(d) a person appointed by a local authority to hold a local inquiry in pursuance of any statutory provision;

(e) any other tribunal, board, committee or body constituted by or under, and exercising functions under, any statutory provision.

★ ★ ★ ★ ★

EDUCATION ACT 1996
(1996, c. 56)

An Act to consolidate the Education Act 1944 and certain other enactments relating to education, with amendments to give effect to a recommendation of the Law Commission.

[24 July 1996]

Territorial extent England and Wales

★ ★ ★ ★ ★

Sex education

403 Sex education: manner of provision

(1) The local education authority, governing body and head teacher shall take such steps as are reasonably practicable to secure that where sex education is given to any registered pupils at a maintained school, it is given in such a manner as to encourage those pupils to have due regard to moral considerations and the value of family life.

(2) In subsection (1) "maintained school" includes a maintained special school established in a hospital.

404 Sex education: statements of policy

(1) The governing body of a maintained school shall—

(a) make, and keep up to date, a separate written statement of their policy with regard to the provision of sex education, and

(b) make copies of the statement available for inspection (at all reasonable times) by parents of registered pupils at the school and provide a copy of the statement free of charge to any such parent who asks for one.

(2), (3) ★★★★★

405 Exemption from sex education

If the parent of any pupil in attendance at a maintained school requests that he may be wholly or partly excused from receiving sex education at the school, the pupil shall, except so far as such education is comprised in the National Curriculum, be so excused accordingly until the request is withdrawn.

Politics

406 Political indoctrination

(1) The local education authority, governing body and head teacher shall forbid—

(a) the pursuit of partisan political activities by any of those registered pupils at a maintained school who are junior pupils, and

(b) the promotion of partisan political views in the teaching of any subject in the school.

(2) In the case of activities which take place otherwise than on the school premises, subsection (1)(a) applies only where arrangements for junior pupils to take part in the activities are made by—

(a) any member of the school's staff (in his capacity as such), or

(b) anyone acting on behalf of the school or of a member of the school's staff (in his capacity as such).

(3) In this section "maintained school" includes a maintained special school established in a hospital.

407 Duty to secure balanced treatment of political issues

(1) The local education authority, governing body and head teacher shall take such steps as are reasonably practicable to secure that where political issues are brought to the attention of pupils while they are—

(a) in attendance at a maintained school, or

(b) taking part in extra-curricular activities which are provided or organised for registered pupils at the school by or on behalf of the school, they are offered a balanced presentation of opposing views.

(2) In this section "maintained school" includes a maintained special school established in a hospital.

EMPLOYMENT RIGHTS ACT 1996
(1996, c. 18)

An Act to consolidate enactments relating to employment rights. [22 May 1996]

Territorial extent England and Wales, Scotland

Note: The sections which are printed here apply to the civil service, the armed forces and parliamentary staff the major provisions of the Act, of employment, time off and maternity rights. Note that s. 192 (armed forces) has not yet been brought into force.

★★★★★

PART XIII
MISCELLANEOUS

CHAPTER I
PARTICULAR TYPES OF EMPLOYMENT

Crown employment etc.

191 Crown Employment

(1) Subject to sections 192 and 193, the provisions of this Act to which this section applies have effect in relation to Crown employment and persons in Crown employment as they have effect in relation to other employment and other employees or workers.

(2) This section applies to—

(a) Parts I to III,

(b) Part V, apart from section 45,

(c) Parts VI to VIII,

(d) in Part IX, sections 92 and 93,

(e) Part X, apart from section 101, and

(f) this Part and Parts XIV and XV.

(3) In this Act "Crown employment" means employment under or for the purposes of a government department or any officer or body exercising on behalf of the Crown functions conferred by a statutory provision.

(4) For the purposes of the application of provisions of this Act in relation to Crown employment in accordance with subsection (1)—

(a) references to an employee or a worker shall be construed as references to a person in Crown employment,

(b) references to a contract of employment, or a worker's contract, shall be construed as references to the terms of employment of a person in Crown employment,

(c) references to dismissal, or to the termination of a worker's contract, shall be construed as references to the termination of Crown employment,

(d) references to redundancy shall be construed as references to the existence of such circumstances as are treated, in accordance with any arrangements falling within section 177(3) for the time being in force, as equivalent to redundancy in relation to Crown employment, and

(e) references to an undertaking shall be construed—

(i) in relation to a Minister of the Crown, as references to his functions or (as the context may require) to the department of which he is in charge, and

(ii) in relation to a government department, officer or body, as references to the functions of the department, officer or body or (as the context may require) to the department, officer or body.

(5) Where the terms of employment of a person in Crown employment restrict his right to take part in—

(a) certain political activities, or

(b) activities which may conflict with his official functions,

nothing in section 50 requires him to be allowed time off work for public duties connected with any such activities.

(6) * * * * *

192 Armed forces

(1) Section 191—

(a) applies to service as a member of the naval, military or air forces of the Crown but subject to the following provisions of this section, and

(b) applies to employment by an association established for the purposes of Part XI of the Reserve Forces Act 1996.

(2) The provisions of this Act which have effect by virtue of section 191 in relation to service as a member of the naval, military or air forces of the Crown are—

(a) Part I,

(b) in Part VI, sections 55 to 57,

(c) Parts VII and VIII,

(d) in Part IX, sections 92 and 93,

(e) Part X, apart from sections 100 to 103 and 134, and

(f) this Part and Parts XIV and XV.

(3) Her Majesty may by Order in Council—

(a) amend subsection (2) by making additions to, or omissions from, the provisions for the time being specified in that subsection, and

(b) make any provision for the time being so specified apply to service as a member of the naval, military or air forces of the Crown subject to such exceptions and modifications as may be specified in the Order in Council,

but no provision contained in Part II may be added to the provisions for the time being specified in subsection (2).

(4)-(8) * * * * *

193 National security

(1) The provisions of this Act to which this section applies do not have effect in relation to any Crown employment in respect of which there is in force a certificate issued by or on behalf of a Minister of the Crown certifying that employment of a description specified in the certificate, or the employment of a particular person so specified, is (or, at a time specified in the certificate, was) required to be excepted from those provisions for the purpose of safeguarding national security.

(2) This section applies to—

(a) Part I, so far as it relates to itemised pay statements,

(b) Part III,

(c) in Part VI, sections 50 to 54,

(d) in Part VII, sections 64 and 65, and sections 69 and 70 so far as relating to those sections,

(e) in Part IX, sections 92 and 93, except where they apply by virtue of section 92(4),

(f) Part X, except so far as relating to a dismissal which is treated as unfair—

(i) by section 99(1) to (3), 100 or 103, or

(ii) by subsection (1) of section 105 by reason of the application or subsection (2), (3) or (6) of that section, and

(g) this Part and Parts XIV and XV (so far as relating to any of the provisions specified in paragraphs (a) to (f)).

(3) Any document purporting to be a certificate issued as mentioned in subsection (1)—

(a) shall be received in evidence, and

(b) unless the contrary is proved, shall be deemed to be such a certificate.

Parliamentary staff

194 House of Lords staff

(1) The provisions of this Act to which this section applies have effect in relation to employment as a relevant member of the House of Lords staff as they have effect in relation to other employment.

(2) This section applies to—

(a) Part I,

(b) Part III,

(c) in Part V, sections 44 and 47, and sections 48 and 49 so far as relating to those sections,

(d) Part VI, apart from sections 58 to 60,

(e) Parts VII and VIII,

(f) in Part IX, sections 92 and 93,

(g) Part X, apart from sections 101 and 102, and

(h) this Part and Parts XIV and XV.

(3) For the purposes of the application of the provisions of this Act to which this section applies in relation to a relevant member of the House of Lords staff references to an undertaking shall be construed as references to the House of Lords.

(4) Nothing in any rule of law or the law or practice of Parliament prevents a relevant member of the House of Lords staff from bringing before the High Court or a county court—

(a) a claim arising out of or relating to a contract of employment or any other contract connected with employment, or

(b) a claim in tort arising in connection with employment.

(5) Where the terms of the contract of employment of a relevant member of the House of Lords staff restrict his right to take part in—

(a) certain political activities, or

(b) activities which may conflict with his official functions,

nothing in section 50 requires him to be allowed time off work for public duties connected with any such activities.

(6) In this section "relevant member of the House of Lords staff" means any person who is employed under a contract of employment with the Corporate Office of the House of Lords.

(7) For the purposes of the application of—

(a) the provisions of this Act to which this section applies, or

(b) a claim within subsection (4),

in relation to a person continuously employed in or for the purposes of the House of Lords up to the time when he became so employed under a contract of employment with the Corporate Officer of the House of Lords, his employment shall not be treated as having been terminated by reason only of a change in his employer before or at that time.

195 House of Commons staff

(1) The provisions of this Act to which this section applies have effect in relation to employment as a relevant member of the House of Commons staff as they have effect in relation to other employment.

(2) This section applies to—

(a) Part I,

(b) Part III,

(c) in Part V, sections 44 and 47, and sections 48 and 49 so for as relating to those sections,

(d) Part VI, apart from sections 58 to 60,

(e) Parts VII and VIII,

(f) in Part IX, sections 92 and 93,

(g) Part X, apart from sections 101 and 102, and

(h) this Part and Parts XIV and XV.

(3) For the purposes of the application of the provisions of this Act to which this section applies in relation to a relevant member of the House of Commons staff—

(a) references to an employee shall be construed as references to a relevant member of the House of Commons staff,

(b) references to a contract of employment shall be construed as including references to the terms of employment of a relevant member of the House of Commons staff,

(c) references to dismissal shall be construed as including references to the termination of the employment of a relevant member of the House of Commons staff, and

(d) references to an undertaking shall be construed as references to the House of Commons.

(4) Nothing in any rule of law or the law or practice of Parliament prevents a relevant member of the House of Commons staff from bringing before the High Court or a county court—

(a) a claim arising out of or relating to a contract of employment or any other contract connected with employment, or

(b) a claim in tort arising in connection with employment.

(5) In this section "relevant member of the House of Commons staff" means any person—

(a) who was appointed by the House of Commons Commission or is employed in the refreshment department, or

(b) who is a member of the Speaker's personal staff.

(6) Subject to subsection (7), for the purposes of—

(a) the provisions of this Act to which this section applies,

(b) Part XI (where applicable to relevant members of the House of Commons staff), and

(c) a claim within subsection (4),

the House of Commons Commission is the employer of staff appointed by the Commission and the Speaker is the employer of his personal staff and of any person employed in the refreshment department and not appointed by the Commission.

(7) Where the House of Commons Commission or the Speaker designates a person to be treated for all or any of the purposes mentioned in subsection (6) as the employer of any description of staff (other than the Speaker's personal staff), the person so designated shall be treated for those purposes as their employer.

(8) Where any proceedings are brought by virtue of this section against—

(a) the House of Commons Commission,

(b) the Speaker, or

(c) any person designated under subsection (7),

the person against whom the proceedings are brought may apply to the court or industrial tribunal concerned to have some other person against whom the proceedings could at the time of the application be properly brought substituted for him as a party to the proceedings.

(9) For the purposes mentioned in subsection (6)—

(a) a person's employment in or for the purposes of the House of Commons shall not (provided he continues to be employed in such employment) be treated as terminated by reason only of a change in his employer, and

(b) (provided he so continues) his first appointment to such employment shall be deemed after the change to have been made by his employer for the time being.

(10) In accordance with subsection (9)—

(a) an employee shall be treated for the purposes mentioned in subsection (6) as being continuously employed by his employer for the time being from the commencement of his employment until its termination, and

(b) anything done by or in relation to his employer for the time being in respect of his employment before the change shall be so treated as having been done by or in relation to the person who is his employer for the time being after the change.

(11) In subsections (9) and (10) "employer for the time being", in relation to a person who has ceased to be employed in or for the purposes of the House of Commons, means the person who was his employer immediately before he ceased to be so employed, except that where some other person would have been his employer for the time being if he had not ceased to be so employed it means that other person.

(12) If the House of Commons resolves at any time that any provision of subsections (5) to (8) should be amended in its application to any member of the staff of that House, Her Majesty may by Order in Council amend that provision accordingly.

INDUSTRIAL TRIBUNALS ACT 1996
(1996, c. 17)

An Act to consolidate enactments relating to industrial tribunals and the Employment Appeal Tribunal. [22 May 1996]

Territorial extent England and Wales, Scotland.

★ ★ ★ ★ ★

PART III
SUPPLEMENTARY

Crown employment and Parliamentary staff

38 Crown employment

(1) This Act has effect in relation to Crown employment and persons in Crown employment as it has effect in relation to other employment and other employees.

(2) In this Act "Crown employment" means employment under or for the purposes of a government department or any officer or body exercising on behalf of the Crown functions conferred by a statutory provision.

(3) For the purposes of the application of this Act in relation to Crown employment in accordance with subsection (1)—

(a) references to an employee shall be construed as references to a person in Crown employment, and

(b) references to a contract of employment shall be construed as references to the terms of employment of a person in Crown employment.

(4) Subsection (1) applies to—

(a) service as a member of the naval, military or air forces of the Crown, and

(b) employment by an association established for the purposes of Part XI of the Reserve Forces Act 1996;

but Her Majesty may by Order in Council make any provision of this Act apply to service as a member of the naval, military or air forces of the Crown subject to such exceptions and modifications as may be specified in the Order in Council.

39 Parliamentary staff

(1) This Act has effect in relation to employment as a relevant member of the House of Lords staff or a relevant member of the House of Commons staff as it has effect in relation to other employment.

(2) Nothing in any rule of law or the law or practice of Parliament prevents a relevant member of the House of Lords staff or a relevant member of the House of Commons staff from bringing before an industrial tribunal proceedings of any description which could be brought before such a tribunal by a person who is not a relevant member of the House of Lords staff or a relevant member of the House of Commons staff.

(3) For the purposes of the application of this Act in relation to a relevant member of the House of Commons staff—

(a) references to an employee shall be construed as references to a relevant member of the House of Commons staff, and

(b) references to a contract of employment shall be construed as including references to the terms of employment of a relevant member of the House of Commons staff.

(4) In this Act "relevant member of the House of Lords staff" means any person who is employed under a contract of employment with the Corporate Officer of the House of Lords.

(5) In this Act "relevant member of the House of Commons staff" has the same meaning as in section 195 of the Employment Rights Act 1996; and (subject to an Order in Council under subsection (12) of that section)—

(a) subsections (6) and (7) of that section have effect for determining who is the employer of a relevant member of the House of Commons staff for the purposes of this Act, and

(b) subsection (8) of that section applies in relation to proceedings brought by virtue of this section.

NORTHERN IRELAND (EMERGENCY PROVISIONS) ACT 1996
(1996, c. 22)

An Act to re-enact, with omissions and amendments, the Northern Ireland (Emergency Provisions) Act 1991; and for connected purposes. [17 June 1996]

Territorial extent Northern Ireland

1–17 ★★★★★

18 Constables' general power of arrest and seizure

(1) Any constable may arrest without warrant any person who he has reasonable grounds to suspect is committing, has committed or is about to commit a scheduled offence or an offence under this Act which is not a scheduled offence.

(2) For the purpose of arresting a person under this section a constable may enter and search any premises or other place where that person is or where the constable has reasonable grounds for suspecting him to be.

(3) A constable may seize anything which he has reasonable grounds to suspect is being, has been or is intended to be used in the commission of a scheduled offence or an offence under this Act which is not a scheduled offence.

19 Powers of arrest and seizure by members of Her Majesty's forces

(1) Any member of Her Majesty's forces on duty may arrest without warrant, and detain for not more than four hours, a person who he has reasonable grounds to suspect is committing, has committed or is about to commit any offence.

(2) A person effecting an arrest under this section complies with any rule of law requiring him to state the ground of arrest if he states that he is effecting the arrest as a member of Her Majesty's forces.

(3) For the purpose of arresting a person under this section a member of Her Majesty's forces may enter and search any premises or other place—

(a) where that person is, or

(b) if there are reasonable grounds for suspecting that that person is a terrorist or has committed an offence involving the use or possession of an explosive substance or firearm, where there are reasonable grounds for suspecting him to be.

(4) Any member of Her Majesty's forces may seize, and detain for not more than four hours, anything which he has reasonable grounds to suspect is being, has been or is intended to be used in the commission of an offence under section 26 or 27.

20–24 * * * * *

25 Power to stop and question

(1) Any member of Her Majesty's forces on duty or any constable may stop any person for so long as is necessary in order to question him for the purpose of ascertaining—

(a) that person's identity and movements;

(b) what he knows concerning any recent explosion or any other recent incident endangering life or concerning any person killed or injured in any such explosion or incident; or

(c) any one or more of the matters referred to in paragraphs (a) and (b).

(2) Any person who—

(a) fails to stop when required to do so under this section, or

(b) refuses to answer, or fails to answer to the best of his knowledge and ability, any question addressed to him under this section,

is guilty of an offence and liable on summary conviction to a fine not exceeding level 5 on the standard scale.

26 General powers of entry and interference with rights of property and with highways

(1) Any member of Her Majesty's forces on duty or any constable may enter any premises or other place—

(a) if he considers it necessary to do so in the course of operations for the preservation of the peace or the maintenance of order; or

(b) if authorised to do so by or on behalf of the Secretary of State.

(2) Any member of Her Majesty's forces on duty, any constable or any person specifically authorised to do so by or on behalf of the Secretary of State may, if authorised to do so by or on behalf of the Secretary of State—

(a) take possession of any land or other property;

(b) take steps to place buildings or other structures in a state of defence;

(c) detain any property or cause it to be destroyed or moved;

(d) do any other act interfering with any public right or with any private rights of property, including carrying out any works on any land of which possession has been taken under this subsection.

(3) Any member of Her Majesty's forces on duty, any constable or any person specifically authorised to do so by or on behalf of the Secretary of State may, so far as he considers it immediately necessary for the preservation of the peace or the maintenance of order—

(a) wholly or partly close a highway or divert or otherwise interfere with a highway or the use of a highway; or

(b) prohibit or restrict the exercise of any right of way or the use of any waterway.

(4) Any person who, without lawful authority or reasonable excuse (the proof of which lies on him), interferes with works executed, or any apparatus, equipment or any other thing used, in or in connection with the exercise of powers conferred by this section is guilty of an offence and liable on summary conviction to imprisonment for a term not exceeding six months or a fine not exceeding level 5 on the standard scale or both.

(5) Any authorisation to exercise any powers under any provision of this section may authorise the exercise of all those powers, or powers of any class or a particular power specified, either by all persons by whom they are capable of being exercised or by persons of any class or a particular person specified.

27 Power of Secretary of State to direct the closure, etc. of roads

(1) If the Secretary of State considers it necessary to do so for the preservation of the peace or the maintenance of order he may by order direct—

(a) that any highway specified in the order shall either be wholly closed or be closed to such extent, or diverted in such manner, as may be so specified;

(b) that any highway specified in the order, being a highway which has already been wholly or partly closed or diverted—

(i) under this section; or

(ii) in the exercise or purported exercise of any power conferred by or under a relevant enactment,

shall continue to be so closed or diverted by virtue of the order.

(2) A person is guilty of an offence if, without lawful authority or reasonable excuse (the proof of which lies on him), he interferes with—

(a) works executed in connection with the closure or diversion of any highway specified in an order under this section (whether executed in pursuance of any such order or in pursuance of the exercise or purported exercise of any such power as is mentioned in subsection (1)(b)(ii)); or

(b) apparatus, equipment or any other thing used in pursuance of any such order in connection with the closure or diversion of any such highway.

(3) A person is guilty of an offence if—

(a) within 200 metres of any road closure works—

(i) he executes any bypass works; or

(ii) without lawful authority or reasonable excuse (the proof of which lies on him) he has in his possession or under his control any materials or equipment suitable for executing bypass works; or

(b) he knowingly permits on land occupied by him the doing or occurrence of anything which is an offence under paragraph (a).

(4) A person guilty of an offence under this section is liable on summary conviction to imprisonment for a term not exceeding six months or a fine not exceeding level 5 on the standard scale or both.

(5), (6) ★ ★ ★ ★ ★

28 ★ ★ ★ ★ ★

PART III
OFFENCES AGAINST PUBLIC SECURITY AND PUBLIC ORDER

29 Directing terrorist organisation

Any person who directs, at any level, the activities of an organisation which is concerned in the commission of acts of terrorism is guilty of an offence and liable on conviction on indictment to imprisonment for life.

30 ★ ★ ★ ★ ★

31 Display of support in public for a proscribed organisation

Any person who in a public place—

(a) wears any item of dress; or

(b) wears, carries or displays any article,

in such a way or in such circumstances as to arouse reasonable apprehension that he is a member or supporter of a proscribed organisation is guilty of an offence and liable—

(i) on conviction on indictment, to imprisonment for a term not exceeding one year or a fine or both;

(ii) on summary conviction, to imprisonment for a term not exceeding six months or a fine not exceeding the statutory maximum or both.

32 Possession of items intended for terrorist purposes

(1) A person is guilty of an offence if he has any article in his possession in circumstances giving rise to a reasonable suspicion that the item is in his possession for a purpose connected with the commission, preparation or instigation of acts of terrorism connected with the affairs of Northern Ireland.

(2) It is a defence for a person charged with an offence under this section to prove that at the time of the alleged offence the article in question was not in his possession for such a purpose as is mentioned in subsection (1).

(3), (4) * * * * *

33, 34 * * * * *

35 Wearing of hoods, etc. in public places

Any person who, without lawful authority or reasonable excuse (the proof of which lies on him), wears in a public place or in the curtilage of a dwelling-house (other than one in which he is residing) any hood, mask or other article whatsoever made, adapted or used for concealing the identity or features is guilty of an offence and liable—

(a) on conviction on indictment, to imprisonment for a term not exceeding one year or a fine or both;

(b) on summary conviction, to imprisonment for a term not exceeding six months or a fine not exceeding the statutory maximum or both.

NORTHERN IRELAND (ENTRY INTO NEGOTIATIONS, ETC.) ACT 1996 (1996, c. 11)

An Act to make provision for elections in Northern Ireland for the purpose of providing delegates from among whom participants in negotiations may be drawn; for a forum constituted by those delegates; for referendums in Northern Ireland; and for connected purposes. [29 April 1996]

Territorial extent Northern Ireland

1 The elections

(1) Elections shall be held in Northern Ireland for the purpose of providing delegates from among whom participants in negotiations may be drawn.

(2) Schedule 1 (which makes provision as to the holding of the elections and the provision of delegates) shall have effect.

2 The negotiations

(1) The negotiations mentioned in section 1 are the negotiations referred to in Command Paper 3232 presented to Parliament on 16 April 1996.

(2) As soon as practicable after the elections, the Secretary of State shall invite the nominating representative of each party for which delegates have been returned in accordance with Schedule 1 to nominate, from among those delegates, a team to participate in the negotiations.

(3) The Secretary of State shall refrain from inviting nominations from the nominating representative of a party, and shall exclude delegates already nominated from entering into the negotiations, if and for as long as he considers that requirements set out in paragraphs 8 and 9 of Command Paper 3232 are not met in relation to the party.

(4) The nominating representative of a party may from time to time substitute for any member of the team nominated for that party another delegate returned for that party in accordance with Schedule 1.

3 The forum

(1) The delegates returned in accordance with Schedule 1 shall constitute a forum for the discussion of issues relevant to promoting dialogue and understanding within Northern Ireland.

(2) The functions of the forum shall be deliberative only.

(3) Accordingly the forum shall not have any legislative, executive or administrative functions, or any power to determine the conduct, course or outcome of the negotiations mentioned in section 1.

(4) But if, in accordance with any rule of procedure adopted by them, the participants in the negotiations refer any matter to the forum, subsection (3) shall not be taken to prevent the forum from considering that matter.

(5) ★★★★★

4 Referendums

(1) The Secretary of State may from time to time by order direct the holding of a referendum for the purpose of obtaining the views of the people of Northern Ireland on any matter relating to Northern Ireland.

(2) An order under subsection (1) shall be made by statutory instrument; but no order shall be made unless a draft has been laid before, and approved by resolution of, each House of Parliament.

(3) An order under subsection (1) may include such provision relating to the conduct of the referendum as appears to the Secretary of State expedient, including provision—

(a) setting out the wording of the question to be put;

(b) as to the persons entitled to vote;

(c) applying, with or without modifications, any enactment (and in particular any enactment relating to elections) or any provision made under an enactment.

(4) Nothing in this section shall be construed as authorising the Secretary of State to direct the holding of a poll otherwise than in accordance with Schedule 1 to the Northern Ireland Constitution Act 1973 in relation to the matters dealt with in section 1 of that Act (status of Northern Ireland as part of United Kingdom).

5 "Nominating representative" of a party

(1) In this Act "nominating representative" in relation to a party means the person who at any time appears to the Secretary of State to be the leader of the party or otherwise the most appropriate person to act on behalf of the party for the purposes of this Act.

(2) The Secretary of State shall cause to be published in the Belfast Gazette—

(a) an initial list of the nominating representatives of the parties listed in Part II of Schedule 1;

(b) notice of any change in the nominating representative of any of those parties.

6 ★★★★★

7 Duration of sections 3 and 4

(1) Section 3 shall cease to have effect at the end of May 1997.

(2) The Secretary of State may by order provide that section 3 shall—

(a) continue to have effect, or

(b) come into force again,

until a time, not later than the end of May 1998, specified in the order.

(3) The Secretary of State may by order provide that section 3 shall cease to have effect at a time specified in the order (being a time earlier than the time at which it would cease to have effect by virtue of subsection (1) or (2)).

(4) If it appears to the Secretary of State that the negotiations mentioned in section 1 are concluded or suspended, he shall by order under subsection (3) provide for section 3 to cease to have effect.

(5) Section 4 shall cease to have effect at the end of May 1999.

(6) An order under this section shall be made by statutory instrument; but no order shall be made unless a draft has been laid before, and approved by resolution of, each House of Parliament.

8 ★★★★★

POLICE ACT 1996
(1996, c. 16)

An Act to consolidate the Police Act 1964, Part IX of the Police and Criminal Evidence Act 1984, Chapter I of Part I of the Police and Magistrates' Courts Act 1994 and certain other enactments relating to the police. [22 May 1996]

Territorial extent England and Wales (and in the case of Part III (ss. 59-64) Scotland).

PART I
ORGANISATION OF POLICE FORCES

Police areas

1 Police areas

(1) England and Wales shall be divided into police areas.

(2) The police areas referred to in subsection (1) shall be—

(a) those listed in Schedule 1 (subject to any amendment made to that Schedule by an order under section 32 below, section 58 of the Local Government Act 1972, or section 17 of the Local Government Act 1992),

(b) the metropolitan police district, and

(c) the City of London police area.

(3) References in Schedule 1 to any local government area are to that area as it is for the time being, but excluding any part of it within the metropolitan police district.

Forces outside London

2 Maintenance of police forces

A police force shall be maintained for every police area for the time being listed in Schedule 1.

3 Establishment of police authorities

(1) There shall be a police authority for every police area for the time being listed in Schedule 1.

(2) A police authority established under this section for any area shall be a body corporate to be known by the name of the area with the adddition of the words "Police Authority".

4 Membership of police authorities etc.

(1) Subject to subsection (2), each police authority established under section 3 shall consist of seventeen members.

(2) The Secretary of State may by order provide in relation to a police authority specified in the order that the number of its members shall be a specified odd number greater than seventeen.

(3) A statutory instrument containing an order under subsection (2) shall be laid before Parliament after being made.

(4) Schedules 2 and 3 shall have effect in relation to police authorities established under section 3 and the appointment of their members.

5 Reduction in size of police authorities etc.

(1) This section applies to any order under section 4(2) which varies of revokes an earlier order so as to reduce the number of a police authority's members.

(2) Before making an order to which this section applies, the Secretary of State shall consult—

(a) the authority,

(b) the councils which are relevant councils in relation to the authority for the purposes of Schedule 2, and

(c) any selection panel, constituted under regulations made in accordance with section 21(1A) of the Justices of the Peace Act 1979, which is responsible, or is represented on a joint committee which is responsible, for the appointment of members of the authority.

(3) An order to which this section applies may include provision as to the termination of the appointment of the existing members of the authority and the making of new appointments or re-appointments.

6 General functions of police authorities

(1) Every police authority established under section 3 shall secure the maintenance of an efficient and effective police force for its area.

(2) In discharging its functions, every police authority established under section 3 shall have regard to—

(a) any objectives determined by the Secretary of State under section 37,

(b) any objectives determined by the authority under section 7,

(c) any performance targets established by the authority, whether in compliance with a direction under section 38 or otherwise, and

(d) any local policing plan issued by the authority under section 8.

(3) In discharging any function to which a code of practice issued under section 39 relates, a police authority established under section 3 shall have regard to the code.

(4) A police authority shall comply with any direction given to it by the Secretary of State under section 38 or 40.

7 Local policing objectives

(1) Every police authority established under section 3 shall, before the beginning of each financial year, determine objectives for the policing of the authority's area during that year.

(2) Objectives determined under this section may relate to matters to which objectives determined under section 37 also relate, or to other matters, but in any event shall be so framed as to be consistent with the objectives determined under that section.

(3) Before determining objectives under this section, a police authority shall—

(a) consult the chief constable for the area, and

(b) consider any views obtained by the authority in accordance with arrangements made under section 96.

8 Local policing plan

(1) Every police authority established under section 3 shall, before the beginning of each financial year, issue a plan setting out the proposed arrangements for the policing of the authority's area during the year ("the local policing plan").

(2) The local policing plan shall include a statement of the authority's priorities for the year, of the financial resources expected to be available and of the proposed allocation of those resources, and shall give particulars of—

(a) any objectives determined by the Secretary of State under section 37,

(b) any objectives determined by the authority under section 7, and

(c) any performance targets established by the authority, whether in compliance with a direction under section 38 or otherwise.

(3) A draft of the local policing plan shall be prepared by the chief constable for the area and submitted by him to the police authority for it to consider.

(4) Before issuing a local policing plan which differs from the draft submitted by the chief constable under subsection (3), a police authority shall consult the chief constable.

(5) A police authority shall arrange for every local policing plan issued by it under this section to be published in such manner as appears to it to be appropriate, and shall send a copy of the plan to the Secretary of State.

9 Annual reports by police authorities

(1) As soon as possible after the end of each financial year every police authority established under section 3 shall issue a report relating to the policing of the authority's area for the year.

(2) A report issued by a police authority under this section for any year shall include an assessment of the extent to which the local policing plan for that year issued under section 8 has been carried out.

(3) A police authority shall arrange for every report issued by it under this section to be published in such manner as appears to it to be appropriate, and shall send a copy of the report to the Secretary of State.

10 General functions of chief constables

(1) A police force maintained under section 2 shall be under the direction and control of the chief constable appointed under section 11.

(2) In discharging his functions, every chief constable shall have regard to the local policing plan issued by the police authority for his area under section 8.

11 Appointment and removal of chief constables

(1) The chief constable of a police force maintained under section 2 shall be appointed by the police authority responsible for maintaining the force, but subject to the approval of the Secretary of State and to regulations under section 50.

(2) Without prejudice to any regulations under section 50 or under the Police Pensions Act 1976, the police authority, acting with the approval of the Secretary of State, may call upon the chief constable to retire in the interests of efficiency or effectiveness.

(3) Before seeking the approval of the Secretary of State under subsection (2), the police authority shall give the chief constable an opportunity to make representations and shall consider any representations that he makes.

(4) A chief constable who is called upon to retire under subsection (2) shall retire on such date as the police authority may specify or on such earlier date as may be agreed upon between him and the authority.

12 Assistant chief constables

(1) The ranks that may be held in a police force maintained under section 2 shall include that of assistant chief constable; and in every such police force there shall be at least one person holding that rank.

(2) Appointments and promotions to the rank of assistant chief constable shall be made, in accordance with regulations under section 50, by the police authority after consultation with the chief constable and subject to the approval of the Secretary of State.

(3) Subsections (2), (3) and (4) of section 11 shall apply to an assistant chief constable as they apply to a chief constable.

(4) A chief constable shall, after consulting his police authority, designate a person holding the rank of assistant chief constable to exercise all the powers and duties of the chief constable—

(a) during any absence, incapacity or suspension from duty of the chief constable, or

(b) during any vacancy in the office of chief constable.

(5) No more than one person shall be authorised to act by virtue of a designation under subsection (4) at any one time; and a person so authorised shall not have power to act by virtue of that subsection for a continuous period exceeding three months except with the consent of the Secretary of State.

(6) The provisions of subsection (4) shall be in addition to, and not in substitution for, any other enactment which makes provision for the exercise by any other person of powers conferred on a chief constable.

13 Other members of police forces

(1) The ranks that may be held in a police force maintained under section 2 shall be such as may be prescribed by regulations under section 50 and the ranks so prescribed shall include, in addition to chief constable and assistant chief constable, the ranks of superintendent, chief inspector, inspector, sergeant and constable.

(2) The ranks prescribed by regulations under section 50 for the purposes of subsection (1) above shall not include that of deputy chief constable.

(3) Appointments and promotions to any rank below that of assistant chief constable in any police force maintained under section 2 shall be made, in accordance with regulations under section 50, by the chief constable.

14 Police fund

(1) Each police authority established under section 3 shall keep a fund to be known as the police fund.

(2) Subject to any regulations under the Police Pensions Act 1976, all receipts of the police authority shall be paid into the police fund and all expenditure of the authority shall be paid out of that fund.

(3) Accounts shall be kept by each police authority of payments made into or out of the police fund.

15-19 ★★★★★

20 Questions on police matters at council meetings

(1) Every relevant council shall make arrangements (whether by standing orders or otherwise) for enabling questions on the discharge of the functions of a police authority to be put by members of the council at a meeting of the council for answer by a person nominated by the authority for that purpose.

(2) On being given reasonable notice by a relevant council of a meeting of that council at which questions on the discharge of the police authority's functions are to be put, the police authority shall nominate one or more of its members to attend the meeting to answer those questions.

(3) In this section "relevant council" has the same meaning as in Schedule 2.

21 ★★★★★

General provisions

22 Reports by chief constables to police authorities

(1) Every chief constable shall, as soon as possible after the end of each financial year, submit to the police authority a general report on the policing during that year of the area for which his force is maintained.

(2) A chief constable shall arrange for a report submitted by him under subsection (1) to be published in such manner as appears to him to be appropriate.

(3) The chief constable of a police force shall, whenever so required by the police authority, submit to that authority a report on such matters as may be specified in the requirement, being matters connected with the policing of the area for which the force is maintained.

(4) A report submitted under subsection (3) shall be in such form as the police authority may specify.

(5) If it appears to the chief constable that a report in compliance with subsection (3) would contain information which in the public interest ought not to be disclosed, or is not needed for the discharge of the functions of the police authority, he may request that authority to refer the requirement to submit the report to the Secretary of State; and in any such case the requirement shall be of no effect unless it is confirmed by the Secretary of State.

(6) The police authority may arrange, or require the chief constable to arrange, for a report submitted under subsection (3) to be published in such manner as appears to the authority to be appropriate.

(7) This section shall apply in relation to the City of London police force as if for references to a chief constable there were substituted references to the Commissioner.

23 Collaboration agreements

(1) If it appears to the chief officers of police of two or more police forces that any police functions can more efficiently or effectively be discharged by members of those forces acting jointly, they may, with the approval of the police authorities which maintain those forces, make an agreement for that purpose.

(2) If it appears to any two or more police authorities that any premises, equipment or other material or facilities can with advantage be provided jointly for the police forces maintained by those authorities, they may make an agreement for that purpose.

(3) Any expenditure incurred under an agreement made under this section shall be borne by the police authorities in such proportions as they may agree or as may, in the absence of agreement, be determined by the Secretary of State.

(4)-(7) ★★★★★

24 Aid of one police force by another

(1) The chief officer of police of any police force may, on the application of the chief officer of police of any other police force, provide constables or other assistance for the purpose of enabling the other force to meet any special demand on its resources.

(2) If it appears to the Secretary of State to be expedient in the interests of public safety or order that any police force should be reinforced or should receive other assistance for the purpose of enabling it to meet any special demand on its resources, and that satisfactory arrangements under subsection (1) cannot be made, or cannot be made in time, he may direct the chief officer of police of any police force to provide such constables or other assistance for that purpose as may be specified in the direction.

(3) While a constable is provided under this section for the assistance of another police force he shall, notwithstanding section 10(1), be under the direction and control of the chief officer of police of that other force.

(4) The police authority maintaining a police force for which assistance is provided under this section shall pay to the police authority maintaining the force from which that assistance is provided such contribution as may be agreed upon between those authorities or, in the absence of any such agreement, as may be provided by any agreement subsisting at the time between all police authorities generally, or, in the absence of such general agreement, as may be determined by the Secretary of State.

25 Provision of special services

(1) The chief officer of police of a police force may provide, at the request of any person, special police services at any premises or in any locality in the police area for which the force is maintained, subject to the payment to the police authority of charges on such scales as may be determined by the authority.

(2) In the application of this section to the metropolitan police force, for the reference in subsection (1) to the police authority there shall be substituted a reference to the Receiver for the Metropolitan Police District.

26-28 ★★★★★

29 Attestation of constables

Every member of a police force maintained for a police area and every special constable appointed for a police area shall, on appointment, be attested as a constable by making a declaration in the form set out in Schedule 4—

(a) in the case of a member of the metropolitan police force or a special constable appointed for the metropolitan police district, before the Commissioner or an Assistant Commissioner of Police of the Metropolis, and

(b) in any other case, before a justice of the peace having jurisdiction within the police area.

30 Jurisdiction of constables

(1) A member of a police force shall have all the powers and privileges of a constable throughout England and Wales and the adjacent United Kingdom waters.

(2) A special constable shall have all the powers and privileges of a constable in the police area for which he is appointed and, where the boundary of that area includes the coast, in the adjacent United Kingdom waters.

(3)-(6) ★★★★★

31 ★★★★★

Alteration of police areas

32 Power to alter police areas by order

(1) The Secretary of State may by order make alterations in police areas in England and Wales other than the City of London police area.

(2) The alterations that may be made by an order under this section include alterations that result in a reduction or an increase in the number of police areas, but not alterations that result in the abolition of the metropolitan police district.

(3) The Secretary of State shall not exercise his power under this section to make alterations unless either—

(a) he has received a request to make the alterations from the police authority for each of the areas (other than the metropolitan police district) affected by them, or

(b) it appears to him to be expedient to make the alterations in the interests of efficiency or effectiveness.

(4), (5) ★★★★★

33-35 ★★★★★

PART II
CENTRAL SUPERVISION, DIRECTION AND FACILITIES

Functions of Secretary of State

36 General duty of Secretary of State

(1) The Secretary of State shall exercise his powers under the provisions of this Act referred to in subsection (2) in such manner and to such extent as appears to him to be best calculated to promote the efficiency and effectiveness of the police.

(2) The provisions of this Act mentioned in subsection (1) are—

(a) Part I;
(b) this Part;
(c) Part III (other than sections 61 and 62);
(d) in Chapter II of Part IV, section 85 and Schedule 6; and
(e) in Part V, section 95.

37 Setting of objectives for police authorities

(1) The Secretary of State may by order determine objectives for the policing of the areas of all police authorities established under section 3.

(2) Before making an order under this section the Secretary of State shall consult—

(a) persons whom he considers to represent the interests of police authorities established under section 3, and

(b) persons whom he considers to represent the interests of chief constables of forces maintained by those authorities.

(3) A statutory instrument containing an order under this section shall be laid before Parliament after being made.

38 Setting of performance targets

(1) Where an objective has been determined under section 37, the Secretary of State may direct police authorities to establish levels of performance ("performance targets") to be aimed at in seeking to achieve the objective.

(2) A direction under this section may be given to all police authorities established under section 3 or to one or more particular authorities.

(3) A direction given under this section may impose conditions with which the performance targets must conform, and different conditions may be imposed for different authorities.

(4) The Secretary of State shall arrange for any direction given under this section to be published in such manner as appears to him to be appropriate.

39 Codes of practice

(1) The Secretary of State may issue codes of practice relating to the discharge by police authorities established under section 3 of any of their functions.

(2) The Secretary of State may from time to time revise the whole or part of any code of practice issued under this section.

(3) The Secretary of State shall lay before Parliament a copy of any code of practice, and of any revision of a code of practice, issued by him under this section.

40 Power to give directions to police authorities after adverse reports

(1) The Secretary of State may at any time require the inspectors of constabulary to carry out, for the purposes of this section, an inspection under section 54 of any police force maintained under section 2.

(2) Where a report made to the Secretary of State under section 54 on an inspection carried out for the purposes of this section states—

(a) that, in the opinion of the person making the report, the force inspected is not efficient or not effective, or

(b) that in his opinion, unless remedial measures are taken, the force will cease to be efficient or will cease to be effective,

the Secretary of State may direct the police authority responsible for maintaining the force to take such measures as may be specified in the direction.

41 Directions as to minimum budget

(1) The power of the Secretary of State to give directions under section 40 to a police authority established under section 3 shall include power to direct the authority that the amount of its budget requirement for any financial year (under section 43 of the Local Government Finance Act 1992) shall not be less than an amount specified in the direction.

(2) The power exercisable by virtue of subsection (1), and any direction given under that power, are subject to any limitation imposed under Chapter V of Part I of the Local Government Finance Act 1992.

(3) A direction shall not be given by virtue of subsection (1) in relation to a financial year at any time after the end of the preceding December.

(4) Where the Secretary of State gives a direction to a police authority by virtue of subsection (1), any precept issued or calculation made by the authority under Part I of the Local Government Finance Act 1992 which is inconsistent with the direction shall be void.

42 Removal of chief constables, etc.

(1) The Secretary of State may require a police authority to exercise its power under section 11 to call upon the chief constable to retire in the interests of efficiency or effectiveness.

(2) Before requiring the exercise of that power or approving the exercise of that or the similar power exercisable with respect to an assistant chief constable, the Secretary of State shall give the chief constable or assistant chief constable an opportunity to make representations to him and shall consider any representations so made.

(3) Where representations are made under this section the Secretary of State may, and in a case where he proposes to require the exercise of the power mentioned in subsection (1) shall, appoint one or more persons (one at least of whom shall be a person who is not an officer of police or of a Government department) to hold an inquiry and report to him and shall consider any report made under this subsection.

(4) The costs incurred by a chief constable or assistant chief constable in respect of an inquiry under this section, taxed in such manner as the Secretary of State may direct, shall be defrayed out of the police fund.

43 Reports from police authorities

(1) A police authority shall, whenever so required by the Secretary of State, submit to the Secretary of State a report on such matters connected with the discharge of the authority's functions, or otherwise with the policing of its area, as may be specified in the requirement.

(2) A requirement under subsection (1) may specify the form in which a report is to be given.

(3) The Secretary of State may arrange, or require the police authority to arrange, for a report under this section to be published in such manner as appears to him to be appropriate.

44 Reports from chief constables

(1) The Secretary of State may require a chief constable to submit to him a report on such matters as may be specified in the requirement, being matters connected with the policing of the chief constable's police area.

(2) A requirement under subsection (1) may specify the form in which a report is to be given.

(3) The Secretary of State may arrange, or require the chief constable to arrange, for a report under this section to be published in such manner as appears to the Secretary of State to be appropriate.

(4) Every chief constable shall, as soon as possible after the end of each financial year, submit to the Secretary of State the like report as is required by section 22(1) to be submitted to the police authority.

(5) This section shall apply in relation to the City of London police force as if for references to a chief constable there were substituted references to the Commissioner.

45 * * * * *

46 Police grant

(1) Subject to the following provisions of this section, the Secretary of State shall for each financial year make grants for police purposes to—

(a) police authorities for areas other than the metropolitan police district, and

(b) the Receiver for the Metropolitan Police District;

and in those provisions references to police authorities shall be taken as including references to the Receiver.

(2) For each financial year the Secretary of State shall with the approval of the Treasury determine—

(a) the aggregate amount of grants to be made under this section, and

(b) the amount of the grant to be made to each authority;
and any determination may be varied by further determinations under this subsection.

(3) The Secretary of State shall prepare a report setting out any determination under subsection (2), and stating the considerations which he took into account in making the determination.

(4) In determining the allocation among police authorities of the whole or any part of the aggregate amount of grants, the Secretary of State may exercise his discretion by applying such formulae or other rules as he considers appropriate.

(5) The considerations which the Secretary of State takes into account in making a determination under subsection (2), and the formulae and other rules referred to in subsection (4), may be different for different authorities or different classes of authority.

(6)-(8) ★★★★★

47-49 ★★★★★

50 Regulations for police forces

(1) Subject to the provisions of this section, the Secretary of State may make regulations as to the government, administration and conditions or service of police forces.

(2) Without prejudice to the generality of subsection (1), regulations under this section may make provision with respect to—

(a) the ranks to be held by members of police forces;

(b) the qualifications for appointment and promotion of members of police forces;

(c) periods of service on probation;

(d) voluntary retirement of members of police forces;

(e) the conduct, efficiency and effectiveness of members of police forces and the maintenance of discipline;

(f) the suspension of members of a police force from membership of that force and from their office as constable;

(g) the maintenance of personal records of members of police forces;

(h) the duties which are or are not to be performed by members of police forces;

(i) the treatment as occasions of police duty of attendance at meetings of the Police Federations and of any body recognised by the Secretary of State for the purposes of section 64;

(j) the hours of duty, leave, pay and allowances of members of police forces; and

(k) the issue, use and return of police clothing, personal equipment and accoutrements.

(3) Without prejudice to the powers conferred by this section, regulations under this section shall—

(a) establish, or make provision for the establishment of, procedures for cases in which a member of a police force may be dealt with by dismissal, requirement to resign, reduction in rank, reduction in rate of pay, fine, reprimand or caution, and

(b) make provision for securing that any case in which a senior officer may be dismissed or dealt with in any of the other ways mentioned in paragraph (a) is decided—

(i) where he is a member of the metropolitan police force, by the Commissioner of Police of the Metropolis, and

(ii) where he is a member of any other force, by the police authority which maintains the force or by a committee of that authority.

For the purposes of this subsection "senior officer" means a member of a police force holding a rank above that of superintendent.

(4) In relation to any matter as to which provision may be made by regulations under this section, the regulations may, subject to subsection (3)(b),—

(a) authorise or require provision to be made by, or confer discretionary powers on, the Secretary of State, police authorities, chief officers of police or other persons, or

(b) authorise or require the delegation by any person of functions conferred on that person by or under the regulations.

(5) Regulations under this section for regulating pay and allowances may be made with retrospective effect to any date specified in the regulations, but nothing in this subsection shall be construed as authorising pay or allowances payable to any person to be reduced retrospectively.

(6) Regulations under this section as to conditions of service shall secure that appointments for fixed terms are not made except where the person appointed holds the rank of superintendent or a higher rank.

(7), (8) * * * * *

51-53 * * * * *

Inspectors of constabulary

54 Appointment and functions of inspectors of constabulary

(1) Her Majesty may appoint such number of inspectors (to be known as "Her Majesty's Inspectors of Constabulary") as the Secretary of State may with the consent of the Treasury determine, and of the persons so appointed one may be appointed as chief inspector of constabulary.

(2) The inspectors of constabulary shall inspect, and report to the Secretary of State on the efficiency and effectiveness of, every police force maintained for a police area.

(3) The inspectors of constabulary shall carry out such other duties for the purpose of furthering police efficiency and effectiveness as the Secretary of State may from time to time direct.

(4) The chief inspector of constabulary shall in each year submit to the Secretary of State a report in such form as the Secretary of State may direct, and the Secretary of State shall lay a copy of that report before Parliament.

(5) The inspectors of constabulary shall be paid such salary and allowances as the Secretary of State may with the consent of the Treasury determine.

55 Publication of reports

(1) Subject to subsection (2), the Secretary of State shall arrange for any report received by him under section 54(2) to be published in such manner as appears to him to be appropriate.

(2) The Secretary of State may exclude from publication under subsection (1) any part of a report if, in his opinion, the publication of that part—

(a) would be against the interests of national security, or

(b) might jeopardise the safety of any person.

(3) The Secretary of State shall send a copy of the published report—

(a) (except where he is himself the police authority) to the police authority maintaining the police force to which the report relates, and

(b) to the chief officer of police of that police force.

(4) The police authority shall invite the chief officer of police to submit comments on the published report to the authority before such date as it may specify.

(5) The police authority shall prepare comments on the published report and shall arrange for—

(a) its comments,

(b) any comments submitted by the chief officer of police in accordance with subsection (4), and

(c) any response which the authority has to the comments submitted by the chief officer of police,

to be published in such manner as appears to the authority to be appropriate.

(6) The police authority (except where it is the Secretary of State) shall send a copy of any document published under subsection (5) to the Secretary of State.

56-58 * * * * *

PART III
POLICE REPRESENTATIVE INSTITUTIONS

59 Police Federation

(1) There shall continue to be a Police Federation for England and Wales and a Police Federation of Scotland for the purpose of representing members of the police forces in those countries respectively in all matters affecting their welfare and efficiency, except for—

(a) questions of promotion affecting individuals, and

(b) (subject to subsection (2)) questions of discipline affecting individuals.

(2) A Police Federation may represent a member of a police force at any proceedings brought under regulations made in accordance with section 50(3) above or section 26(2A) of the Police (Scotland) Act 1967 or on an appeal from any such proceedings.

(3) Except on an appeal to a police appeals tribunal or as provided by section 84, a member of a police force may only be represented under subsection (2) by another member of a police force.

(4) The Police Federations shall act through local and central representative bodies.

(5) The Police Federations and every branch of a Federation shall be entirely independent of, and subject to subsection (6) unassociated with, any body or person outside the police service, but may employ persons outside the police service in an administrative or advisory capacity.

(6) The Secretary of State—

(a) may authorise a Police Federation or a branch of a Federation to be associated with a person or body outside the police service in such cases and manner, and subject to such conditions and restrictions, as he may specify, and

(b) may vary or withdraw an authorisation previously given;

and anything for the time being so authorised shall not be precluded by subsection (5).

(7) This section applies to police cadets as it applies to members of police forces, and references to the police service shall be construed accordingly.

60 Regulations for Police Federation

(1) The Secretary of State may by regulations—

(a) prescribe the constitution and proceedings of the Police Federations, or

(b) authorise the Federations to make rules concerning such matters relating to their constitution and proceedings as may be specified in the regulations.

(2) Without prejudice to the generality of subsection (1), regulations under this section may make provision—

(a) with respect to the membership of the Federations;

(b) with respect to the raising of funds by the Federations by voluntary subscription and the use and management of funds derived from such subscriptions;

(c) with respect to the manner in which representations may be made by committees or bodies of the Federations to police authorities, chief officers of police and the Secretary of State;

(d) for the payment by the Secretary of State of expenses incurred in connection with the Federations and for the use by the Federations of premises provided by police authorities for police purposes; and

(e) for modifying any regulations under the Police Pensions Act 1976, section 50 above or section 26 of the Police (Scotland) Act 1967 in relation to any member of a police force who is the secretary or an officer of a Police Federation and for requiring the appropriate Federation to make contributions in respect of the pay, pension or allowances payable to or in respect of any such person.

(3)-(6) * * * * *

61 The Police Negotiating Board for the United Kingdom

(1) There shall continue to be a Police Negotiation Board for the United Kingdom for the consideration by persons representing the interests of—

(a) the authorities who between them maintain the police forces in Great Britain and the Royal Ulster Constabulary,

(b) the persons who are members of those police forces or of that Constabulary or are police cadets,

(c) the Commissioner of Police of the Metropolis, and

(d) the Secretary of State,

of questions relating to hours of duty, leave, pay and allowances, pensions or the issue, use and return of police clothing, personal equipment and accoutrements.

(2) The Chairman and any deputy chairman or chairmen of the Board shall be appointed by the Prime Minister.

(3) Subject to subsection (2), the Board shall continue to be constituted in accordance with such arrangements, made after consultations between the Secretary of State and organisations representing the interests of the persons referred to in paragraphs (a), (b) and (c) of subsection (1), as appear to the Secretary of State to be satisfactory.

(4) The Secretary of State may—

(a) pay to the Chairman and to any deputy chairman or chairmen of the Board such fees as the Secretary of State may, with the approval of the Treasury, determine, and

(b) defray any expenses incurred by the Board.

62, 63 * * * * *

64 Membership of trade unions

(1) Subject to the following provisions of this section, a member of a police force shall not be a member of any trade union, or of any association having for its objects, or one of its objects, to control or influence the pay, pensions or conditions of service of any police force.

(2) Where a person was a member of a trade union before becoming a member of a police force, he may, with the consent of the chief officer of police, continue to be a member of that union during the time of his service in the police force.

(3) If any question arises whether any body is a trade union or an association to which this section applies, the question shall be determined by the chief registrar of friendly societies.

(4) This section applies to police cadets as it applies to members of a police force, and references to a police force or to service in a police force shall be construed accordingly.

(3) Nothing in this section applies to membership of the Police Federations, or of any body recognised by the Secretary of State for the purposes of this section as representing members of police forces who are not members of those Federations.

PART IV
COMPLAINTS, DISCIPLINARY PROCEEDINGS ETC.

CHAPTER I
COMPLAINTS

Interpretation

65 Interpretation of Chapter I

In this Chapter—

"the appropriate authority" means—

(a) in relation to a member of the metropolitan police force, the Commissioner of Police of the Metropolis, and

(b) in relation to a member of any other police force—

(i) if he is a senior officer, the police authority for the force's area, and

(ii) if he is not a senior officer, the chief officer of police of the force;

"the Authority" means the Police Complaints Authority;

"complaint" means a complaint about the conduct of a member of a police force which is submitted—

(a) by a member of the public, or

(b) on behalf of a member of the public and with his written consent;

"disciplinary proceedings" means proceedings identified as such by regulations under section 50;

"investigating officer" means a member of a police force appointed under section 68(3) or, as the case may be, section 69(5) or (6) to investigate a complaint;

"senior officer" means a member of a police force holding a rank above that of superintendent;

"serious injury" means a fracture, damage to an internal organ, impairment of bodily function, a deep cut or a deep laceration.

The Police Complaints Authority

66 The Police Complaints Authority

(1) The authority known as "the Police Complaints Authority" shall continue in existence as a body corporate.

(2) Schedule 5 shall have effect in relation to the Authority.

Handling of Complaints etc.

67 Preliminary

(1) Where a complaint is submitted to the chief officer of police for a police area, he shall take any steps that appear to him to be desirable for the purpose of obtaining or preserving evidence relating to the conduct complained of.

(2) After complying with subsection (1), the chief officer shall determine whether he is the appropriate authority in relation to the member of a police force whose conduct is the subject of the complaint.

(3) If the chief officer determines that he is not the appropriate authority, he shall—

(a) send the complaint or, if it was submitted orally, particulars of it, to the appropriate authority, and

(b) give notice that he has done so to the person by whom or on whose behalf the complaint was submitted.

(4) Nothing in this Chapter shall have effect in relation to a complaint in so far as it relates to the direction or control of a police force by the chief officer of police or the person performing the functions of the chief officer of police.

(5) If any conduct to which a complaint wholly or partly relates is or has been the subject of criminal or disciplinary proceedings, none of the provisions of this Chapter which relate to the recording and investigation of complaints shall have effect in relation to the complaint in so far as it relates to that conduct.

68 Investigation of complaints: senior officers

(1) Where a complaint about the conduct of a senior officer—

(a) is submitted to the appropriate authority, or

(b) is sent to the appropriate authority under section 67(3),

the appropriate authority shall record and, subject to subsection (2), investigate it.

(2) If satisfied that the conduct complained of, even if proved, would not justify criminal or disciplinary proceedings, the appropriate authority may deal with the complaint according to the appropriate authority's discretion.

(3) In any other case, the appropriate authority shall appoint a member of the appropriate authority's force or of some other force to investigate the complaint.

(4) If the appropriate authority requests the chief officer of police of a police force to provide a member of his force for appointment under subsection (3), the chief officer shall comply with the request.

(5) No member of a police force of a rank lower than that of the member whose conduct is the subject of the complaint may be appointed under subsection (3).

(6) Unless an investigation under this section is supervised by the Authority under section 72, the investigating officer shall submit his report on it to the appropriate authority.

69 Investigation of complaints: standard procedure

(1) If a chief officer of police determines that he is the appropriate authority in relation to a member of a police force—

(a) whose conduct is the subject of a complaint, and

(b) who is not a senior officer,

he shall record the complaint.

(2) After recording a complaint under subsection (1), the chief officer of police shall consider whether the complaint is suitable for informal resolution and may appoint a member of his force to assist him.

(3) A complaint is not suitable for informal resolution unless—

(a) the member of the public concerned gives his consent, and

(b) the chief officer of police is satisfied that the conduct complained of, even if proved, would not justify criminal or disciplinary proceedings.

(4) If it appears to the chief officer of police that the complaint is suitable for informal resolution, he shall seek to resolve it informally and may appoint a member of his force to do so on his behalf.

(5) If it appears to the chief officer of police that the complaint is not suitable for informal resolution, he shall appoint a member of his own or some other force to investigate it formally.

(6) If, after attempts have been made to resolve a complaint informally, it appears to the chief officer of police—

(a) that informal resolution of the complaint is impossible, or

(b) that the complaint is for any other reason not suitable for informal resolution,

he shall appoint a member of his own or some other force to investigate it formally.

(7) A member of a police force may not be appointed to investigate a complaint formally if he has previously been appointed to act in relation to it under subsection (4).

(8) If a chief officer of police requests the chief officer of police of some other force to provide a member of that other force for appointment under subsection (5) or (6), that chief officer shall comply with the request.

(9) Unless the investigation is supervised by the Authority under section 72, the investigating officer shall submit his report on it to the chief officer of police who appointed him.

70 References of complaints to Authority

(1) The appropriate authority—

(a) shall refer to the Authority—

(i) any complaint alleging that the conduct complained of resulted in the death of, or serious injury to, some other person, and

(ii) any complaint of a description specified for the purposes of this section in regulations made by the Secretary of State, and

(b) may refer to the Authority any complaint which is not required to be referred to them.

(2) The Authority may require the submission to them for consideration of any complaint not referred to them by the appropriate authority; and the appropriate authority shall comply with any such requirement not later than the end of the period specified for the purposes of this subsection in regulations made by the Secretary of State.

(3) Where a complaint falls to be referred to the Authority under subsection (1)(a), the appropriate authority shall refer it to them not later than the end of the period specified for the purposes of sub-paragraph (i) or, as the case may be, (ii) of that subsection in regulations made by the Secretary of State.

71 References of other matters to Authority

(1) The appropriate authority may refer to the Authority any matter to which this section applies, if it appears to the appropriate authority that the matter ought to be referred by reason—

(a) of its gravity, or

(b) of exceptional circumstances.

(2) This section applies to any matter which—

(a) appears to the appropriate authority to indicate that a member of a police force may have committed a criminal offence or behaved in a manner which would justify disciplinary proceedings, and

(b) is not the subject of a complaint.

72 Supervision of investigations by Authority

(1) The Authority shall supervise the investigation of—

(a) any complaint alleging that the conduct of a member of a police force resulted in the death of, or serious injury to, some other person,

(b) any other description of complaint specified for the purposes of this section in regulations made by the Secretary of State, and

(c) any complaint which is not within paragraph (a) or (b), and any matter referred to the Authority under section 71, if the Authority determine that it is desirable in the public interest that they should do so.

(2) Where the Authority have made a determination under subsection (1)(c), they shall notify it to the appropriate authority.

(3) Where an investigation is to be supervised by the Authority, they may require—

(a) that no appointment is made under section 68(3) or 69(5) unless they have given notice to the appropriate authority that they approve the person whom that authority propose to appoint, or

(b) if such an appointment has already been made and the Authority are not satisfied with the person appointed, that—

(i) the appropriate authority, as soon as is reasonably practicable, select another member of a police force and notify the Authority that it proposes to appoint him, and

(ii) the appointment is not made unless the Authority give notice to the appropriate authority that they approve that person.

(4) The Secretary of State shall by regulations authorise the Authority, subject to any restrictions or conditions specified in the regulations, to impose requirements as to a particular investigation additional to any requirements imposed by virtue of subsection (3).

(5) A member of a police force shall comply with any requirement imposed on him by virtue of regulations under subsection (4).

73 Reports on investigations etc.

(1) At the end of an investigation which the Authority have supervised, the investigating officer shall—

(a) submit a report on the investigation to the Authority, and

(b) send a copy of the report to the appropriate authority.

(2) After considering a report submitted to them under subsection (1), the Authority shall submit an appropriate statement to the appropriate authority.

(3) If it is practicable to do so, the Authority, when submitting the appropriate statement under subsection (2), shall send a copy of it to the member of a police force whose conduct has been investigated.

(4) If—

(a) the investigation related to a complaint, and

(b) it is practicable to do so,

the Authority shall also send a copy of the appropriate statement to the person by or on behalf of whom the complaint was submitted.

(5) The power to issue an appropriate statement includes power to issue separate statements in respect of the disciplinary and criminal aspects of an investigation.

(6) No disciplinary proceedings shall be brought before the appropriate statement is submitted to the appropriate authority.

(7) Subject to subsection (8), neither the appropriate authority nor the Director of Public Prosecutions shall bring criminal proceedings before the appropriate statement is submitted to the appropriate authority.

(8) The restriction imposed by subsection (7) does not apply if it appears to the Director that there are exceptional circumstances which make it undesirable to wait for the submission of the appropriate statement.

(9) In this section "appropriate statement" means a statement—

(a) as to whether the investigation was or was not conducted to the Authority's satisfaction,

(b) specifying any respect in which it was not so conducted, and

(c) dealing with any such other matters as the Secretary of State may by regulations provide.

74 Steps to be taken after investigation: senior officers

On receiving—

(a) a report concerning the conduct of a senior officer which is submitted to it under section 68(6), or

(b) a copy of a report concerning the conduct of a senior officer which is sent to it under section 73(1),

the appropriate authority shall send a copy of the report to the Director of Public Prosecutions unless the report satisfies the appropriate authority that no criminal offence has been committed.

75 Steps to be taken after investigation: standard procedure

(1) Nothing in this section or section 76 has effect in relation to senior officers.

(2) On receiving—

(a) a report concerning the conduct of a member of a police force who is not a senior officer which is submitted to him under section 69(9), or

(b) a copy of a report concering the conduct of such a member which is sent to him under section 73(1),

a chief officer of police shall determine whether the report indicates that a criminal offence may have been committed by a member of the police force for his area.

(3) If the chief officer determines that the report indicates that a criminal offence may have been committed by a member of the police force for his area, he shall send a copy of the report to the Director of Public Prosecutions.

(4) After the Director has dealt with the question of criminal proceedings, the chief officer shall, in such cases as may be prescribed by regulations made by the Secretary of State, send the Authority a memorandum which—

(a) is signed by the chief officer,

(b) states whether he has brought (or proposes to bring) disciplinary proceedings in respect of the conduct which was the subject of the investigation, and

(c) if he has not brought (or does not propose to bring) such proceedings, gives his reasons.

(5) If the chief officer considers that the report does not indicate that a criminal offence may have been committed by a member of the police force for his area, he shall, in such cases as may be prescribed by regulations made by the Secretary of State, send the Authority a memorandum to the effect which—

(a) is signed by the chief officer,

(b) states whether he has brought (or proposes to bring) disciplinary proceedings in respect of the conduct which was the subject of the investigation, and

(c) if he has not brought (or does not propose to bring) such proceedings, gives his reasons.

(6) Where the investigation—

(a) related to conduct which was the subject of a complaint, and

(b) was not supervised by the Authority,

the chief officer shall, if he is required by virtue of regulations under subsection (4) or (5) to send the Authority a memorandum, at the same time send them a copy of the complaint, or of the record of the complaint, and a copy of the report of the investigation.

(7) Where a chief officer has sent the Authority a memorandum under subsection (4) or (5), he shall—

(a) if the memorandum states that he proposes to bring disciplinary proceedings, bring and proceed with them, and

(b) if the memorandum states that he has brought such proceedings, proceed with them.

76 Powers of Authority as to disciplinary proceedings

(1) Where a memorandum under section 75 states that a chief officer of police has not brought disciplinary proceedings or does not propose to bring such proceedings, the Authority may recommend him to bring such proceedings.

(2) Where a chief officer has brought disciplinary proceedings in accordance with a recommendation under subsection (1), he shall proceed with them.

(3) If after the Authority have made a recommendation under this section and consulted the chief officer he is still unwilling to bring disciplinary proceedings, they may direct him to do so.

(4) Where the Authority give a chief officer a direction under this section, they shall supply him with a written statement of their reasons for doing so.

(5) Subject to subsection (6), it shall be the duty of a chief officer to comply with such a direction.

(6) The Authority may withdraw a direction given under this section.

(7) A chief officer shall—

(a) advise the Authority of what action he has taken in response to a recommendation or direction under this section, and

(b) supply the Authority with such other information as they may reasonably require for the purposes of discharging their functions under this section.

77 Information as to the manner of dealing with complaints etc.

Every police authority in carrying out its duty with respect to the maintenance of an efficient and effective police force, and inspectors of constabulary in carrying out their duties with respect to the efficiency and effectiveness of any police force, shall keep themselves informed as to the working of sections 67 to 76 in relation to the force.

78 Constabularies maintained by authorities other than police authorities

(1) An agreement for the establishment in relation to any body of constables maintained by an authority, other than a police authority, of procedures corresponding or similar to any of those established by or by virtue of this Chapter may, with the approval of the Secretary of State, be made between the Authority and the authority maintaining the body of constables.

(2) Where no such procedures are in force in relation to a body of constables, the Secretary of State may by order establish such procedures.

(3) An agreement under this section may at any time be varied or terminated with the approval of the Secretary of State.

(4)-(7) ★★★★★

79 Reports

(1) The Authority shall, at the request of the Secretary of State, report to him on such matters relating generally to their functions as the Secretary of State may specify, and the Authority may for that purpose carry out research into any such matters.

(2) The Authority may make a report to the Secretary of State on any matters coming to their notice under this Chapter to which they consider that his attention should be drawn by reason of their gravity or of other exceptional circumstances.

(3) The Authority shall send a copy of any report under subsection (2)—

(a) to the police authority and the chief officer of police of any police force which appears to the Authority to be concerned, or

(b) if the report concerns a body of constables such as is mentioned in section 78, to the authority maintaining it and the officer having the direction and the control of it.

(4) As soon as practicable after the end of each calendar year the Authority shall make to the Secretary of State a report on the discharge of their functions during that year.

(5) The Secretary of State shall lay before Parliament a copy of every report received by him under this section and shall cause every such report to be published.

(6) ★★★★★

80 Restriction on disclosure of information

(1) No information received by the Authority in connection with any of their functions under sections 67 to 79 or regulations made by virtue of section 81 shall be disclosed by any person who is or has been a member, officer or servant of the Authority except—

(a) to the Secretary of State or to a member, officer or servant of the Authority or, so far as may be necessary for the proper discharge of the functions of the Authority to other persons,

(b) for the purposes of any criminal, civil or disciplinary proceedings, or

(c) in the form of a summary or other general statement made by the Authority which does not identify the person from whom the information was received or any person to whom it relates.

(2) Any person who discloses information in contravention of this section shall be guilty of an offence and liable on summary conviction to a fine of an amount not exceeding level 5 on the standard scale.

81-83 ★★★★★

CHAPTER II
DISCIPLINARY AND OTHER PROCEEDINGS

84 Representation at disciplinary and other proceedings

(1) A member of a police force of the rank of superintendent or below may not be dismissed, required to resign or reduced in rank by a decision taken in proceedings under regulations made in accordance with section 50(3)(a) unless he has been given an opportunity to elect to be legally represented at any hearing held in the course of those proceedings.

(2) Where a member of a police force makes an election to which subsection (1) refers, he may be represented at the hearing, at his option, either by counsel or by a solicitor.

(3) Except in a case where a member of a police force of the rank of superintendent or below has been given an opportunity to elect to be legally represented and has so elected, he may be represented at the hearing only by another member of a police force.

(4) Regulations under section 50 shall specify—

(a) a procedure for notifying a member of a police force of the effect of subsections (1) to (3) above,

(b) when he is to be notified of the effect of those subsections, and

(c) when he is to give notice whether he wishes to be legally represented at the hearing.

(5) If a member of a police force—

(a) fails without reasonable cause to give notice in accordance with the regulations that he wishes to be legally represented, or

(b) gives notice in accordance with the regulations that he does not wish to be legally represented,

he may be dismissed, required to resign or reduced in rank without his being legally represented.

(6) If a member of a police force has given notice in accordance with the regulations that he wishes to be legally represented, the case against him may be presented by counsel or a solicitor whether or not he is actually so represented.

85 Appeals against dismissal etc.

(1) A member of a police force who is dismissed, required to resign or reduced in rank by a decision taken in proceedings under regulations made in accordance with section 50(3) may appeal to a police appeals tribunal against the decision except where he has a right of appeal to some other person; and in that case he may appeal to a police appeals tribunal from any decision of that other person as a result of which he is dismissed, required to resign or reduced in rank.

(2) Where a police appeals tribunal allows an appeal it may, if it considers that it is appropriate to do so, make an order dealing with the appellant in a way—

(a) which appears to the tribunal to be less severe than the way in which he was dealt with by the decision appealed against, and

(b) in which he could have been dealt with by the person who made that decision.

(3) The Secretary of State may make rules as to the procedure on appeals to police appeals tribunals under this section.

(4)-(6) ★ ★ ★ ★ ★

86 Admissibility of statements in subsequent proceedings

(1) Subject to subsection (2), no statement made by a person for the purpose of the informal resolution of a complaint shall be admissible in any subsequent criminal, civil or disciplinary proceedings.

(2) A statement is not rendered inadmissible by subsection (1) if it consists of or includes an admission relating to a matter which does not fall to be resolved informally.

(3) In this section "complaint" and "disciplinary proceedings" have the meanings given in section 65.

87 * * * * *

88 Liability for wrongful acts of constables

(1) The chief officer of police for a police area shall be liable in respect of torts committed by constables under his direction and control in the performance or purported performance of their functions in like manner as a master is liable in respect of torts committed by his servants in the course of their employment, and accordingly shall in respect of any such tort be treated for all purposes as a joint tortfeasor.

(2) There shall be paid out of the police fund—

(a) any damages or costs awarded against the chief officer of police in any proceedings brought against him by virtue of this section and any costs incurred by him in any such proceedings so far as not recovered by him in the proceedings; and

(b) any sum required in connection with the settlement of any claim made against the chief officer of police by virtue of this section, if the settlement is approved by the police authority.

(3) Any proceedings in respect of a claim made by virtue of this section shall be brought against the chief officer of police for the time being or, in the case of a vacancy in that office, against the person for the time being performing the functions of the chief officer of police; and references in subsections (1) and (2) to the chief officer of police shall be construed accordingly.

(4) A police authority may, in such cases and to such extent as appear to it to be appropriate, pay out of the police fund—

(a) any damages or costs awarded against a person to whom this subsection applies in proceedings for a tort committed by that person,

(b) any costs incurred and not recovered by such a person in such proceedings, and

(c) any sum required in connection with the settlement of a claim that has or might have given rise to such proceedings.

(5) Subsection (4) applies to a person who is—

(a) a member of the police force maintained by the police authority,

(b) a constable for the time being required to serve with that force by virtue of section 24 or 98, or

(c) a special constable appointed for the authority's police area.

PART V
MISCELLANEOUS AND GENERAL

Offences

89 Assaults on constables

(1) Any person who assaults a constable in the execution of his duty, or a person assisting a constable in the execution of his duty, shall be guilty of an offence and liable on summary conviction to imprisonment for a term not exceeding six months or to a fine not exceeding level 5 on the standard scale, or to both.

(2) Any person who resists or wilfully obstructs a constable in the execution of his duty, or a person assisting a constable in the execution of his duty, shall be guilty of an offence and liable on summary conviction to imprisonment for a term not exceeding one month or to a fine not exceeding level 3 on the standard scale, or to both.

(3) This section also applies to a constable who is a member of a police force maintained in Scotland or Northern Ireland when he is executing a warrant, or otherwise acting in England and Wales, by virtue of any enactment conferring powers on him in England and Wales.

90 Impersonation, etc.

(1) Any person who with intent to deceive impersonates a member of a police force or special constable, or makes any statement or does any act calculated falsely to suggest that he is such a member or constable, shall be guilty of an offence and liable on summary conviction to imprisonment for a term not exceeding six months or to a fine not exceeding level 5 on the standard scale, or to both.

(2) Any person who, not being a constable, wears any article of police uniform in circumstances where it gives him an appearance so nearly resembling that of a member of a police force as to be calculated to deceive shall be guilty of an offence and liable on summary conviction to a fine not exceeding level 3 on the standard scale.

(3) Any person who, not being a member of a police force or special constable, has in his possession any article of police uniform shall, unless he proves that he obtained possession of that article lawfully and has possession of it for a lawful purpose, be guilty of an offence and liable on summary conviction to a fine not exceeding level 1 on the standard scale.

(4) In this section—

(a) "article of police uniform" means any article of uniform or any distinctive badge or mark or document of identification usually issued to members of police forces or special constables, or anything having the appearance of such an article, badge, mark or document, and

(b) "special constable" means a special constable appointed for a police area.

91 Causing disaffection

(1) Any person who causes, or attempts to cause, or does any act calculated to cause, disaffection amongst the members of any police force, or induces or attempts to induce, or does any act calculated to induce, any member of a police force to withhold his services, shall be guilty of an offence and liable—

(a) on summary conviction, to imprisonment for a term not exceeding six months or to a fine not exceeding the statutory maximum, or to both;

(b) on conviction on indictment, to imprisonment for a term not exceeding two years or to a fine, or to both.

(2) This section applies to special constables appointed for a police area as it applies to members of a police force.

92 * * * * *

93 Acceptance of gifts and loans

(1) A police authority may, in connection with the discharge of any of its functions, accept gifts of money, and gifts or loans of other property, on such terms as appear to the authority to be appropriate.

(2) The terms on which gifts or loans are accepted under subsection (1) may include terms providing for the commercial sponsorship of any activity of the police authority or of the police force maintained by it.

(3) In the application of this section in relation to the metropolitan police force, for the references to the police authority there shall be substituted references to the Receiver for the Metropolitan Police District.

94, 95 * * * * *

96 Arrangements for obtaining the views of the community on policing

(1) Arrangements shall be made for each police area for obtaining—

(a) the views of people in that area about matters concerning the policing of the area, and

(b) their co-operation with the police in preventing crime in that area.

(2) Except as provided by subsections (3) to (6), arrangements for each police area shall be made by the police authority after consulting the chief constable as to the arrangements that would be appropriate.

(3) The Secretary of State shall issue guidance to the Commissioner of Police of the Metropolis concerning arrangements for the metropolitan police district; and the Commissioner shall make arrangements under this section after taking account of that guidance.

(4) The Commissioner shall make separate arrangements—

(a) for each London borough;

(b) for each district which falls wholly within the metropolitan police district; and

(c) in the case of districts which fall partly within the metropolitan police district, for each part of such a district which falls within that police district.

(5) The Commissioner shall—

(a) consult the council of each London borough as to the arrangements that would be appropriate for the borough,

(b) consult the council of each district mentioned in subsection (4)(b) as to the arrangements that would be appropriate for the district, and

(c) consult the council of each district mentioned in subsection (4)(c) as to the arrangements that would be appropriate for the part of the district which falls within the metropolitan police district.

(6) The Common Council of the City of London shall issue guidance to the Commissioner of Police for the City of London concerning arrangements for the City of London police area; and the Commissioner shall make arrangements under this section after taking account of that guidance.

(7)-(10) ★★★★★

★★★★★

SCHEDULE 2
POLICE AUTHORITIES ESTABLISHED UNDER SECTION 3

Membership of police authorities

1.—(1) Where, by virtue of section 4, a police authority is to consist of seventeen members—

(a) nine of those members shall be members of a relevant council appointed under paragraph 2,

(b) five shall be persons appointed under paragraph 5, and

(c) three shall be magistrates appointed under paragraph 8.

(2) Where, by virtue of an order under subsection (2) of that section, a police authority is to consist of more than seventeen members—

(a) a number which is greater by one than the number of members provided for in paragraphs (b) and (c) below shall be members of a relevant council appointed under paragraph 2,

(b) such number as may be prescribed by the order, not exceeding one third of the total membership, shall be persons appointed under paragraph 5, and

(c) the remainder shall be magistrates appointed under paragraph 8.

Appointment of members by relevant councils

2.—(1) In the case of a police authority in relation to which there is only one relevant council, the members of the police authority referred to in paragraph 1(1)(a) or (2)(a) shall be appointed by that council.

(2) In any other case, those members shall be appointed by a joint committee consisting of persons appointed by the relevant councils from among their own members.

3. The number of members of the joint committee, and the number of those members to be appointed by each relevant council, shall be such as the councils may agree or, in the absence of agreement, as may be determined by the Secretary of State.

4.—(1) A council or joint committee shall exercise its power to appoint members of a police authority under paragraph 2 so as to ensure that, so far as practicable, the members for whose appointment it is responsible reflect—

(a) in the case of appointments by a council, the balance of parties for the time being prevailing among the members of the council, and

(b) in the case of appointments by a joint committee, the balance of parties for the time being prevailing among the members of the relevant councils taken as a whole.

(2) The members referred to in sub-paragraph (1)(a) and (b) do not include any member of a relevant council who is disqualified for being appointed as or being a member of the police authority under paragraph 12.

Appointment of independent members

5. The members of a police authority referred to in paragraph 1(1)(b) or (2)(b) shall be appointed—

(a) by the members of the police authority appointed under paragraph 2 or 8,

(b) from among persons on a short-list prepared by the Secretary of State in accordance with Schedule 3.

6.—(1) Every police authority shall arrange for a notice stating—

(a) the name of each of its members appointed under paragraph 5, and

(b) such other information relating to him as the authority considers appropriate,

to be published in such manner as appears to it to be appropriate.

(2) A police authority shall send to the Secretary of State a copy of any notice which it has arranged to be published under sub-paragraph (1).

Appointment of magistrates

7. The members of a police authority referred to in paragraph 1(1)(c) or (2)(c)—

(a) must be magistrates for an area all or part of which constitutes or forms part of the authority's area, and

(b) shall be appointed in accordance with paragraph 8;

and in that paragraph references to a panel are references to a selection panel constituted under regulations made in accordance with section 21(1A) of the Justices of the Peace Act 1979.

8.—(1) Where there is a panel for an area which constitutes or includes the police authority's area, that panel shall make the appointment.

(2) Where the area of more than one panel falls wholly or partly within the police authority's area, the appointment shall be made by a joint committee consisting of representatives from the panels concerned.

(3) The number of members of a joint committee, and the number of those members to be appointed by each panel, shall be such as the panels may agree or, in the absence of agreement, as may be determined by the Lord Chancellor.

★ ★ ★ ★ ★

SCHEDULE 4
FORM OF DECLARATION

I, ... of .... do solemnly and sincerely declare and affirm that I will well and truly serve Our Sovereign Lady the Queen in the office of constable, without favour or affection, malice or ill will; and that I will to the best of my power cause the peace to be kept and preserved, and prevent all offences against the persons and properties of Her

Majesty's subjects; and that while I continue to hold the said office I will to the best of my skill and knowledge discharge all the duties thereof faithfully according to law.

SCHEDULE 5
THE POLICE COMPLAINTS AUTHORITY

Constitution of Authority

1.—(1) The Police Complaints Authority shall consist of a chairman and not less than eight other members.

(2) The chairman shall be appointed by Her Majesty.

(3) The other members shall be appointed by the Secretary of State.

(4) The members of the Authority shall not include any person who is or has been a constable in any part of the United Kingdom.

(5) Persons may be appointed as whole-time or part-time members of the Authority.

(6) The Secretary of State may appoint not more than two of the members of the Authority to be deputy chairmen.

Status of Authority

2. The Authority shall not be regarded as the servant or agent of the Crown or as enjoying any status, privilege or immunity of the Crown; and the Authority's property shall not be regarded as property of or property held on behalf of the Crown.

★ ★ ★ ★ ★

PREVENTION OF TERRORISM (ADDITIONAL PROVISIONS) ACT 1996
(1996, c. 7)

An Act to extend powers of search in connection with acts of terrorism and terrorist investigations; confer powers on constables in relation to areas on which police cordons are imposed in connection with terrorist investigations; and confer powers in connection with the prevention of acts of terrorism to impose prohibitions and restrictions in relation to vehicles on roads. [3 April 1996]

Territorial extent United Kingdom

Note: This Act amends the Prevention of Terrorism (Temporary Provisions) Act 1989 by providing additional powers. These provisions are incorporated into the text of the 1989 Act (above).

SEXUAL OFFENCES (CONSPIRACY AND INCITEMENT) ACT 1996
(1996, c. 29)

An Act to make provision about conspiracy, or incitement, to commit certain sexual acts outside the United Kingdom. [4 July 1996]

Territorial extent England and Wales, Northern Ireland. Equivalent provisions for Scotland are in s. 16A Criminal Law (Consolidation) (Scotland) Act 1995 (above), as inserted by s. 6 of this Act.

1 Conspiracy to commit certain sexual acts outside the United Kingdom

(1) Where each of the following conditions is satisfied in the case of any agreement, Part I of the Criminal Law Act 1977 (conspiracy) has effect in relation to the agreement as it has effect in relation to an agreement falling within section 1(1) of that Act.

(2) The first condition is that the pursuit of the agreed course of conduct would at some stage involve—

(a) an act by one or more of the parties, or
(b) the happening of some other event,
intended to take place in a country or territory outside the United Kingdom.

(3) The second condition is that that act or other event constitutes an offence under the law in force in that country or territory.

(4) The third condition is that the agreement would fall within section 1(1) of that Act as an agreement relating to the commission of a listed sexual offence but for the fact that the offence would not be an offence triable in England and Wales if committed in accordance with the parties' intentions.

(5) The fourth condition is that—

(a) a party to the agreement, or a party's agent, did anything in England and Wales in relation to the agreement before its formation, or

(b) a party to the agreement became a party in England and Wales (by joining it either in person or through an agent), or

(c) a party to the agreement, or a party's agent, did or omitted anything in England and Wales in pursuance of the agreement.

(6) * * * * *

2 Incitement to commit certain sexual acts outside the United Kingdom

(1) This section applies where—

(a) any act done by a person in England and Wales would amount to the offence of incitement to commit a listed sexual offence but for the fact that what he had in view would not be an offence triable in England and Wales,

(b) the whole or part of what he had in view was intended to take place in a country or territory outside the United Kingdom, and

(c) what he had in view would involve the commission of an offence under the law in force in that country or territory.

(2) Where this section applies—

(a) what he had in view is to be treated as that listed sexual offence for the purposes of any charge of incitement brought in respect of that act, and

(b) any such charge is accordingly triable in England and Wales.

(3) Any act of incitement by means of a message (however communicated) is to be treated as done in England and Wales if the message is sent or received in England and Wales.

3, 4 * * * * *

5 Interpretation

In this Act "listed sexual offence" has the meaning given by the Schedule.

6, 7 * * * * *

Section 5

SCHEDULE

LISTED SEXUAL OFFENCES

England and Wales

1.—(1) In relation to England and Wales, the following are listed sexual offences;

(a) offences under the following provisions of the Sexual Offences Act 1956—
(i) section 1 (rape),
(ii) section 5 (intercourse with girl under the age of thirteen),
(iii) section 6 (intercourse with girl under the age of sixteen),
(iv) section 12 (buggery),
(v) section 14 (indecent assault on a boy),
(vi) section 15 (indecent assault on a boy).

(b) an offence under section 1 of the Indecency with Children Act 1960 (indecent conduct towards young child).

(2) In sub-paragraph (1)(a), sub-paragraphs (i), (iv), (v) and (vi) do not apply where the victim of the offence has attained the age of sixteen years.

★ ★ ★ ★ ★

BRITISH NATIONALITY (HONG KONG) ACT 1997
(1997, c. 20)

An Act to provide for the acquisition of British citizenship by certain British nationals in Hong Kong. [19 March 1997]

Territorial extent United Kingdom

1 Acquisition of British citzenship

(1) Subject to the provisions of this section, the Secretary of State shall, on an application made for the purpose, register as a British citizen any person who—

(a) is ordinarily resident in Hong Kong at the time of the application; and

(b) satisfies the requirements of subsection (2) or (3) below.

(2) The requirements of this subsection are that, immediately before 4 February 1997 ("the relevant date"), the person—

(a) was ordinarily resident in Hong Kong;

(b) was a British Dependent Territories citizen by virtue only of his having a connection with Hong Kong (within the meaning given by the Schedule to this Act); and

(c) would have been a stateless person if he had not been such a citizen, or such a citizen and a British National (Overseas).

(3) The requirements of this subsection are that, immediately before the relevant date, the person—

(a) was ordinarily resident in Hong Kong;

(b) was a British Overseas citizen, a British subject or a British protected person; and

(c) would have been a stateless person if he had not been such a citizen, subject or person.

(4) Subsections (2) and (3) above shall each have effect, in relation to a person who is or was born at any time on or after the relevant date, as if the reference to immediately before that date were a reference to that time.

(5)–(8) ★ ★ ★ ★ ★

2, 3 ★ ★ ★ ★ ★

Schedule ★ ★ ★ ★ ★

CONFISCATION OF ALCOHOL (YOUNG PERSONS) ACT 1997
(1997, c. 33)

An Act to permit the confiscation of intoxicating liquor held by or for use by young persons in public and certain other places; and for connected purposes. [21 March 1997]

Territorial extent England and Wales, Northern Ireland. Similar powers are conferred in Scotland by s. 61 Crime and Punishment (Scotland) Act 1997.

1 Confiscation of intoxicating liquor

(1) Where a constable reasonably suspects that a person in a relevant place is in possession of intoxicating liquor and that either—

(a) he is under the age of 18; or

(b) he intends that any of the liquor should be consumed by a person under the age of 18 in that or any other relevant place; or

(c) a person under the age of 18 who is, or has recently been, with him has recently consumed intoxicating liquor in that or any other relevant place,

the constable may require him to surrender anything in his possession which is, or which the constable reasonably believes to be, intoxicating liquor and to state his name and address.

(2) A constable may dispose of anything surrendered to him under subsection (1) in such manner as he considers appropriate.

(3) A person who fails without reasonable excuse to comply with a requirement imposed on him under subsection (1) commits an offence and is liable on summary conviction to a fine not exceeding level 2 on the standard scale.

(4) A constable who imposes a requirement on a person under subsection (1) shall inform him of his suspicion and that failing without reasonable excuse to comply with a requirement imposed under that subsection is an offence.

(5) A constable may arrest without warrant a person who fails to comply with a requirement imposed on him under subsection (1).

(6) In subsection (1) "relevant place", in relation to a person, means—

(a) any public place, other than licensed premises; or

(b) any place, other than a public place, to which the person has unlawfully gained access;

and for this purpose a place is a public place if at the material time the public or any section of the public has access to it, on payment or otherwise, as of right or by virtue of express or implied permission.

(7) * * * * *

2 * * * * *

JUSTICES OF THE PEACE ACT 1997
(1997, c. 25)

An Act to consolidate the Justices of the Peace Act 1979 and provisions of Part IV of the Police and Magistrates' Courts Act 1994. [19 March 1997]

Territorial extent England and Wales

PART V
PROTECTION AND INDEMNIFICATION OF JUSTICES AND JUSTICES' CLERKS

51 Immunity for acts within jurisdiction

No action shall lie against any justice of the peace or justices' clerk in respect of any act or omission of his—

(a) in the execution of his duty—

(i) as such a justice; or

(ii) as such a clerk exercising, by virtue of any statutory provision, any of the functions of a single justice; and

(b) with respect to any matter within his jurisdiction.

52 Immunity for certain acts beyond jurisdiction

An action shall lie against any justice of the peace or justices' clerk in respect of any act or omission of his—

(a) in the purported execution of his duty—

(i) as such a justice; or

(ii) as such a clerk exercising, by virtue of any statutory provision, any of the functions of a single justice; but

(b) with respect to a matter which is not within his jurisdiction,
if, but only if, it is proved that he acted in bad faith.

53 Where action prohibited, proceedings may be set aside

If any action is brought in circumstances in which this Part of this Act provides that no action is to lie, a judge of the court in which the action is brought may, on the application of the defendant and upon an affidavit as to the facts, set aside the proceedings in the action, with or without costs, as the judge thinks fit.

54 Indemnification of justices and justices' clerks

(1) For the purposes of subsection (2) below, the following amounts are "relevant amounts" in relation to a justice of the peace or justices' clerk—

(a) any costs which he reasonably incurs—

(i) in or in connection with proceedings against him in respect of anything done or omitted in the exercise (or purported exercise) of his duty as a justice of the peace or justices' clerk; or

(ii) in taking steps to dispute any claim which might be made in such proceedings;

(b) any damages awarded against him or costs ordered to be paid by him in any such proceedings; and

(c) any sums payable by him in connection with a reasonable settlement of any such proceedings or claim,

and relevant amounts relate to criminal matters if the duty mentioned in paragraph (a)(i) above relates to criminal matters.

(2) Subject to the provisions of this section, a justice of the peace or justices' clerk—

(a) shall be indemnified out of local funds in respect of relevant amounts which relate to criminal matters unless it is proved, in respect of the matters giving rise to the proceedings or claim, that he acted in bad faith; and

(b) in respect of other relevant amounts—

(i) may be indemnified out of local funds; and

(ii) shall be so indemnified if, in respect of the matters giving rise to the proceedings or claim, he acted reasonably and in good faith.

(3) Any question whether, or to what extent, a person is to be indemnified under this section shall be determined by the magistrates' courts committee for the area for which he acted at the material time.

(4) A determination under subsection (3) above with respect to any such costs or sums as are mentioned in subsection (1)(a) or (c) above may, if the person claiming to be indemnified so requests, be made in advance before those costs are incurred or the settlement made, as the case may be.

(5) Any such determination in advance for indemnity in respect of costs to be incurred shall be subject to such limitations, if any, as the committee think proper and to the subsequent determination of the amount of the costs reasonably incurred and shall not affect any other determination which may fail to be made in connection with the proceedings or claim in question.

(6) An appeal shall lie to a person appointed for the purpose by the Lord Chancellor—

(a) on the part of the person claiming to be indemnified, from any decision of the magistrates' courts committee under subsection (3) or (4) above, other than a decision to postpone until after the conclusion of the proceedings any determination with respect to his own costs or to impose limitations on making a determination in advance for indemnity in respect of such costs;

(b) on the part of any paying authority, from any determination of the magistrates' courts committee under subsection (3) above other than a determination in advance for indemnity in respect of costs to be incurred by the person claiming to be indemnified.

(7)–(9) * * * * *

* * * * *

KNIVES ACT 1997
(1997, c. 21)

An Act to create new criminal offences in relation to the possession or marketing of, and publications relating to, knives; to confer powers on the police to stop and search people or vehicles for knives and other offensive weapons and to seize items found; and for connected purposes. [19 March 1997]

The offences

1 Unlawful marketing of knives

(1) A person is guilty of an offence if he markets a knife in a way which—

(a) indicates, or suggests, that it is suitable for combat; or

(b) is otherwise likely to stimulate or encourage violent behaviour involving the use of the knife as a weapon.

(2) "Suitable for combat" and "violent behaviour" are defined in section 10.

(3) For the purposes of this Act, an indication or suggestion that a knife is suitable for combat may, in particular, be given or made by a name or description—

(a) applied to the knife;

(b) on the knife or on any packaging in which it is contained; or

(c) included in any advertisement which, expressly or by implication, relates to the knife.

(4) For the purposes of this Act, a person markets a knife if—

(a) he sells or hires it;

(b) he offers, or exposes, it for sale or hire; or

(c) he has it in his possession for the purpose of sale or hire.

(5) A person who is guilty of an offence under this section is liable—

(a) on summary conviction to imprisonment for a term not exceeding six months or to a fine not exceeding the statutory maximum, or to both;

(b) on conviction on indictment to imprisonment for a term not exceeding two years or to a fine, or to both.

2 Publications

(1) A person is guilty of an offence if he publishes any written, pictorial or other material in connection with the marketing of any knife and that material—

(a) indicates, or suggests, that the knife is suitable for combat; or

(b) is otherwise likely to stimulate or encourage violent behaviour involving the use of the knife as a weapon.

(2) A person who is guilty of an offence under this section is liable—

(a) on summary conviction to imprisonment for a term not exceeding six months or to a fine not exceeding the statutory maximum, or to both;

(b) on conviction on indictment to imprisonment for a term not exceeding two years or to a fine, or to both.

The defences

3 Exempt trades

(1) It is a defence for a person charged with an offence under section 1 to prove that—

(a) the knife was marketed—

(i) for use by the armed forces of any country;

(ii) as an antique or curio; or
(iii) as falling within such other category (if any) as may be prescribed;
(b) it was reasonable for the knife to be marketed in that way; and
(c) there were no reasonable grounds for suspecting that a person into whose possession the knife might come in consequence of the way in which it was marketed would use it for an unlawful purpose.

(2) It is a defence for a person charged with an offence under section 2 to prove that—
(a) the material was published in connection with marketing a knife—
(i) for use by the armed forces of any country;
(ii) as an antique or curio; or
(iii) as falling within such other category (if any) as may be prescribed;
(b) it was reasonable for the knife to be marketed in that way; and
(c) there were no reasonable grounds for suspecting that a person into whose possession the knife might come in consequence of the publishing of the material would use it for an unlawful purpose.

(3) In this section "prescribed" means prescribed by regulations made by the Secretary of State.

4 * * * * *

Supplementary powers

5 Supplementary powers of entry, seizure and retention

(1) If, on an application made by a constable, a justice of the peace or sheriff is satisfied that there are reasonable grounds for suspecting—
(a) that a person ("the suspect") has committed an offence under section 1 in relation to knives of a particular description, and
(b) that knives of that description and in the suspect's possession or under his control are to be found on particular premises,
the justice or sheriff may issue a warrant authorising a constable to enter those premises, search for the knives and seize and remove any that he finds.

(2) If, on an application made by a constable, a justice of the peace or sheriff is satisfied that there are reasonable grounds for suspecting—
(a) that a person ("the suspect") has committed an offence under section 2 in relation to particular material, and
(b) that publications consisting of or containing that material and in the suspect's possession or under his control are to be found on particular premises,
the justice or sheriff may issue a warrant authorising a constable to enter those premises, search for the publications and seize and remove any that he finds.

(3) A constable, in the exercise of his powers under a warrant issued under this section, may if necessary use reasonable force.

(4) Any knives or publications which have been seized and removed by a constable under a warrant issued under this section may be retained until the conclusion of proceedings against the suspect.

(5) For the purposes of this section, proceedings in relation to a suspect are concluded if—
(a) he is found guilty and sentenced or otherwise dealt with for the offence;
(b) he is acquitted;
(c) proceedings for the offence are discontinued; or
(d) it is decided not to prosecute him.

(6) In this section "premises" includes any place and, in particular, any vehicle, vessel, aircraft or hovercraft and any tent or movable structure.

6 Forfeiture of knives and publications

(1) If a person is convicted of an offence under section 1 in relation to a knife of a particular description, the court may make an order for forfeiture in respect of any knives of that description—

(a) seized under a warrant issued under section 5; or

(b) in the offender's possession or under his control at the relevant time.

(2) If a person is convicted of an offence under section 2 in relation to particular material, the court may make an order for forfeiture in respect of any publications consisting of or containing that material which—

(a) have been seized under a warrant issued under section 5; or

(b) were in the offender's possession or under his control at the relevant time.

(3) The court may make an order under subsection (1) or (2)—

(a) whether or not it also deals with the offender in respect of the offence in any other way; and

(b) without regard to any restrictions on forfeiture in any enactment.

(4) In considering whether to make an order, the court must have regard—

(a) to the value of the property; and

(b) to the likely financial and other effects on the offender of the making of the order (taken together with any other order that the court contemplates making).

(5) ★ ★ ★ ★ ★

7–9 ★ ★ ★ ★ ★

10 Interpretation

In this Act—

★ ★ ★ ★ ★

"knife" means an instrument which has a blade or is sharply pointed;

"suitable for combat" means suitable for use as a weapon for inflicting injury on a person or causing a person to fear injury;

"violent behaviour" means an unlawful act inflicting injury on a person or causing a person to fear injury;

11 ★ ★ ★ ★ ★

NORTHERN IRELAND ARMS DECOMMISSIONING ACT 1997
(1997, c. 7)

An Act to make provision connected with Northern Ireland about the decommissioning of firearms, ammunition and explosives; and for connected purposes. [27 February 1997]

Territorial extent United Kingdom

1 Decommissioning scheme

(1) In this Act a "decommissioning scheme" is any scheme which—

(a) is made by the Secretary of State to facilitate the decommissioning of firearms, ammunition and explosives in Northern Ireland, and

(b) includes provisions satisfying the requirements of sections 2 and 3 (whether or not it also includes other provisions).

(2) ★ ★ ★ ★ ★

2 Duration of decommissioning scheme

(1) A decommissioning scheme must identify a period during which firearms, ammunition and explosives may be dealt with in accordance with the scheme ("the amnesty period").

(2) The amnesty period must end before—

(a) the first anniversary of the day on which this Act is passed, or

(b) such later day as the Secretary of State may by order from time to time appoint.

(3) A day appointed by an order under subsection (2)(b) must not be—

(a) more than twelve months after the day on which the order is made, or

(b) more than five years after the day on which this Act is passed.

(4) An order under subsection (2)(b) shall be made by statutory instrument; and no order shall be made unless a draft has been laid before, and approved by resolution of, each House of Parliament.

3 Methods of decommissioning

(1) A decommissioning scheme must make provision for one or more of the following ways of dealing with firearms, ammunition and explosives (and may make provision for others)—

(a) transfer to the Commission mentioned in section 7, or to a designated person, for destruction;

(b) depositing for collection and destruction by the Commission or a designated person;

(c) provision of information for the purpose of collection and destruction by the Commission or a designated person;

(d) destruction by persons in unlawful possession.

(2) In subsection (1) "designated person" means a person designated by the Secretary of State or, in the case of firearms, ammunition or explosives transferred or collected in the Republic of Ireland, a person designated by the Minister for Justice of the Republic.

4 Amnesty

(1) No proceedings shall be brought for an offence listed in the Schedule to this Act in respect of anything done in accordance with a decommissioning scheme.

(2)–(4) ★ ★ ★ ★ ★

5 Evidence

(1) A decommissioned article, or information derived from it, shall not be admissible in evidence in criminal proceedings.

(2) Evidence of anything done, and of any information obtained, in accordance with a decommissioning scheme shall not be admissible in criminal proceedings.

(3) Subsections (1) and (2) shall not apply to the admission of evidence adduced in criminal proceedings on behalf of the accused.

(4) Subsection (1) shall not apply to proceedings for an offence alleged to have been committed by the use of, or in relation to, something which was a decommissioned article at the time when the offence is alleged to have been committed.

6 Testing decommissioned articles

(1) A person who has received a decommissioned article shall not carry out, or cause or permit anyone else to carry out, a test or procedure in relation to the article the purpose of which is—

(a) to discover information about anything done with or in relation to any decommissioned article,

(b) to discover who has been in contact with, or near to, any decommissioned article,

(c) to discover where any decommissioned article was at any time (including the conditions under which it was kept),

(d) to discover when any decommissioned article was in contact with, or near to, a particular person or when it was in a particular place or kept under particular conditions,

(e) to discover when or where any decommissioned article was made, or
(f) to discover the composition of any decommissioned article.
(2), (3) ★★★★★

7 The Commission

(1) In this section "the Commission" means an independent organisation established by an agreement, made in connection with the affairs of Northern Ireland between Her Majesty's Government in the United Kingdom and the Government of the Republic of Ireland, to facilitate the decommissioning of firearms, ammunition and explosives.

(2) The Secretary of State may by order—

(a) confer on the Commission the legal capacities of a body corporate;

(b) confer on the Commission, in such cases, to such extent and with such modifications as the order may specify, any of the privileges and immunities set out in Part I of Schedule 1 to the International Organisations Act 1968;

(c) confer on members and servants of the Commission and members of their families who form part of their households, in such cases, to such extent and with such modifications as the order may specify any of the privileges and immunities set out in Parts II, III and V of that Schedule;

(d) make provision about the waiver of privileges and immunities.

In this subsection "servants of the Commission" includes agents of, and persons carrying out work for or giving advice to, the Commission.

(3)–(6) ★★★★★

8 Arms in England and Wales and Scotland

(1) This section applies to any scheme which—

(a) is made by the Secretary of State, for purposes relating to the affairs of Northern Ireland, to facilitate the decommissioning of firearms, ammunition and explosives in England and Wales or in Scotland, and

(b) includes provisions satisfying the requirement of sections 2 and 3 (whether or not it also includes other provisions).

(2) The Secretary of State may by order provide that a scheme to which this section applies shall be a decommissioning scheme for the purposes of this Act.

(3) In relation to a scheme which is a decommissioning scheme by virtue of subsection (2), the Schedule to this Act shall have effect with the substitution for any offence under the law of Northern Ireland of such similar offence under the law of England and Wales, or as the case may be of Scotland, as the Secretary of State may specify by order.

(4) An order under this section shall be made by statutory instrument; and no order shall be made unless a draft has been laid before, and approved by resolution of, each House of Parliament.

9–11 ★★★★★

Schedule ★★★★★

POLICE ACT 1997
(1997, c. 50)

An Act to make provision for the National Criminal Intelligence Service and the National Crime Squad; to make provision about entry on and interference with property and with wireless telegraphy in the course of the prevention or detection of serious crime; to make provision for the Police Information Technology Organisation; to provide for the issue of certificates about criminal records; to make provision about the administration and organisation of the police; to repeal certain enactments about rehabilitation of offenders; and for connected purposes.

[21 March 1997]

Territorial extent United Kingdom (sections printed).

PART III
AUTHORISATION OF ACTION IN RESPECT OF PROPERTY

The Commissioners

91 The Commissioners

(1) The Prime Minister shall appoint for the purposes of this Part—

(a) a Chief Commissioner, and

(b) such number of other Commissioners as the Prime Minister thinks fit.

(2) The persons appointed under subsection (1) shall be persons who hold or have held high judicial office within the meaning of the Appellate Jurisdiction Act 1876.

(3) Subject to subsections (4) to (7), each Commissioner shall hold and vacate office in accordance with the terms of his appointment.

(4) Each Commissioner shall be appointed for a term of three years.

(5) A person who ceases to be a Commissioner (otherwise than under subsection (7)) may be reappointed under this section.

(6) Subject to subsection (7), a Commissioner shall not be removed from office before the end of the term for which he is appointed unless a resolution approving his removal has been passed by each House of Parliament.

(7) ★★★★★

(8) The Secretary of State shall pay to each Commissioner such allowances as the Secretary of State considers appropriate.

(9) The Secretary of State shall, after consultation with the Chief Commissioner, provide the Commissioners with such staff as the Secretary of State considers necessary for the discharge of their functions.

(10) The decisions of the Chief Commissioner or, subject to sections 104 and 106, any other Commissioner (including decisions as to his jurisdiction) shall not be subject to appeal or liable to be questioned in any court.

Authorisations

92 Effect of authorisation under Part III

No entry on or interference with property or with wireless telegraphy shall be unlawful if it is authorised by an authorisation having effect under this Part.

93 Authorisations to interfere with property etc.

(1) Where subsection (2) applies, an authorising officer may authorise—

(a) the taking of such action, in respect of such property in the relevant area, as he may specify, or

(b) the taking of such action in the relevant area as he may specify, in respect of wireless telegraphy.

(2) This subsection applies where the authorising officer believes—

(a) that it is necessary for the action specified to be taken on the ground that it is likely to be of substantial value in the prevention or detection of serious crime, and

(b) that what the action seeks to achieve cannot reasonably be achieved by other means.

(3) An authorising officer shall not give an authorisation under this section except on an application made—

(a) if the authorising officer is within subsection (5)(a) to (e), by a member of his police force,

(b) if the authorising officer is within subsection (5)(f), by a member of the National Criminal Intelligence Service,

(c) if the authorising officer is within subsection (5)(g), by a member of the National Crime Squad, or

(d) if the authorising officer is within subsection (5)(h), by a customs officer.

(4) For the purposes of subsection (2), conduct which constitutes one or more offences shall be regarded as serious crime if, and only if,—

(a) it involves the use of violence, results in substantial financial gain or is conduct by a large number of persons in pursuit of a common purpose, or

(b) the offence or one of the offences is an offence for which a person who has attained the age of twenty-one and has no previous convictions could reasonably be expected to be sentenced to imprisonment for a term of three years or more,

and, where the authorising officer is within subsection (5)(h), it relates to an assigned matter within the meaning of section 1(1) of the Customs and Excise Management Act 1979.

(5) In this section "authorising officer" means—

(a) the chief constable of a police force maintained under section 2 of the Police Act 1996 (maintenance of police forces for areas in England and Wales except London);

(b) the Commissioner, or an Assistant Commissioner, of Police of the Metropolis;

(c) the Commissioner of Police for the City of London;

(d) the chief constable of a police force maintained under or by virtue of section 1 of the Police (Scotland) Act 1967 (maintenance of police forces for areas in Scotland);

(e) the Chief Constable or a Deputy Chief Constable of the Royal Ulster Constabulary;

(f) the Director General of the National Criminal Intelligence Service;

(g) the Director General of the National Crime Squad; or

(h) the customs officer designated by the Commissioners of Customs and Excise for the purposes of this paragraph.

(6) * * * * *

(7) The powers conferred by, or by virtue of, this section are additional to any other powers which a person has as a constable either at common law or under or by virtue of any other enactment and are not to be taken to affect any of those other powers.

94 * * * * *

95 Authorisations: form and duration etc.

(1) An authorisation shall be in writing, except that in an urgent case an authorisation (other than one given by virtue of section 94) may be given orally.

(2) An authorisation shall, unless renewed under subsection (3), cease to have effect—

(a) if given orally or by virtue of section 94, at the end of the period of 72 hours beginning with the time when it took effect;

(b) in any other case, at the end of the period of three months beginning with the day on which it took effect.

(3) If at any time before an authorisation would cease to have effect the authorising officer who gave the authorisation, or in whose absence it was given, considers it necessary for the authorisation to continue to have effect for the purpose for which it was issued, he may, in writing, renew it for a period of three months beginning with the day on which it would cease to have effect.

(4) A person shall cancel an authorisation given by him if satisfied that the action authorised by it is no longer necessary.

(5)–(7) * * * * *

96 Notification of authorisations etc.

(1) Where a person gives, renews or cancels an authorisation, he shall, as soon as is reasonably practicable and in accordance with arrangements made by the Chief Commissioner, give notice in writing that he has done so to a Commissioner appointed under section 91(1)(b).

(2) Subject to subsection (3), a notice under this section shall specify such matters as the Secretary of State may by order prescribe.

(3) A notice under this section of the giving or renewal of an authorisation shall specify—

(a) whether section 97 applies to the authorisation or renewal, and

(b) where that section does not apply by virtue of subsection (3) of that section, the grounds on which the case is believed to be one of urgency.

(4) Where a notice is given to a Commissioner under this section, he shall, as soon as is reasonably practicable, scrutinise the notice.

(5), (6) * * * * *

Authorisations requiring approval

97 Authorisations requiring approval

(1) An authorisation to which this section applies shall not take effect until—

(a) it has been approved in accordance with this section by a Commissioner appointed under section 91(1)(b), and

(b) the person who gave the authorisation has been notified under subsection (4).

(2) Subject to subsection (3), this section applies to an authorisation if, at the time it is given, the person who gives it believes—

(a) that any of the property specified in the authorisation—

(i) is used wholly or mainly as a dwelling or as a bedroom in a hotel, or

(ii) constitutes office premises, or

(b) that the action authorised by it is likely to result in any person acquiring knowledge of—

(i) matters subject to legal privilege,

(ii) confidential personal information, or

(iii) confidential journalistic material.

(3) This section does not apply to an authorisation where the person who gives it believes that the case is one of urgency.

(4) Where a Commissioner receives a notice under section 96 which specifies that this section applies to the authorisation, he shall as soon as is reasonably practicable—

(a) decide whether to approve the authorisation or refuse approval, and

(b) give written notice of his decision to the person who gave the authorisation.

(5) A Commissioner shall approve an authorisation if, and only if, he is satisfied that there are reasonable grounds for believing the matters specified in section 93(2).

(6)–(8) * * * * *

98 Matters subject to legal privilege

(1) Subject to subsection (5) below, in section 97 "matters subject to legal privilege" means matters to which subsection (2), (3) or (4) below applies.

(2) This subsection applies to communications between a professional legal adviser and—

(a) his client, or

(b) any person representing his client,

which are made in connection with the giving of legal advice to the client.

(3) This subsection applies to communications—

(a) between a professional legal adviser and his client or any person representing his client, or

(b) between a professional legal adviser or his client or any such representative and any other person,

which are made in connection with or in contemplation of legal proceedings and for the purposes of such proceedings.

(4) This subsection applies to items enclosed with or referred to in communications of the kind mentioned in subsection (2) or (3) and made—

(a) in connection with the giving of legal advice, or

(b) in connection with or in contemplation of legal proceedings and for the purposes of such proceedings.

(5) For the purposes of section 97—

(a) communications and items are not matters subject to legal privilege when they are in the possession of a person who is not entitled to possession of them, and

(b) communications and items held, or oral communications made, with the intention of furthering a criminal purpose are not matters subject to legal privilege.

99 Confidential personal information

(1) In section 97 "confidential personal information" means—

(a) personal information which a person has acquired or created in the course of any trade, business, profession or other occupation or for the purposes of any paid or unpaid office, and which he holds in confidence, and

(b) communications as a result of which personal information—

(i) is acquired or created as mentioned in paragraph (a), and

(ii) is held in confidence.

(2) For the purposes of this section "personal information" means information concerning an individual (whether living or dead) who can be identified from it and relating—

(a) to his physical or mental health, or

(b) to spiritual counselling or assistance given or to be given to him.

(3) A person holds information in confidence for the purposes of this section if he holds it subject—

(a) to an express or implied undertaking to hold it in confidence, or

(b) to a restriction on disclosure or an obligation of secrecy contained in any enactment (including an enactment contained in an Act passed after this Act).

100 Confidential journalistic material

(1) In section 97 "confidential journalistic material" means—

(a) material acquired or created for the purposes of journalism which—

(i) is in the possession of persons who acquired or created it for those purposes,

(ii) is held subject to an undertaking, restriction or obligation of the kind mentioned in section 99(3), and

(iii) has been continuously held (by one or more persons) subject to such an undertaking, restriction or obligation since it was first acquired or created for the purposes of journalism, and

(b) communications as a result of which information is acquired for the purposes of journalism and held as mentioned in paragraph (a)(ii).

(2) For the purposes of subsection (1), a person who receives material, or acquires information, from someone who intends that the recipient shall use it for the purposes of journalism is to be taken to have acquired it for those purposes.

Code of Practice

101 Code of practice

(1) The Secretary of State shall issue a code of practice in connection with the performance of functions under this Part by persons other than Commissioners appointed under section 91.

(2) Before issuing a code of practice under subsection (1), the Secretary of State shall prepare and publish a draft of that code, shall consider any representations made to him about the draft and may modify the draft accordingly.

(3) The Secretary of State shall lay before both Houses of Parliament a draft of the code of practice prepared by him under this section.

(4) The code of practice laid before Parliament in draft under subsection (3) shall not be brought into operation except in accordance with an order made by the Secretary of State by statutory instrument.

(5) A statutory instrument which contains an order under subsection (4) shall not be made unless a draft has been laid before, and approved by a resolution of, each House of Parliament.

(6) An order bringing the code into operation may contain such transitional provisions or savings as appear to the Secretary of State to be necessary or expedient in connection with the bringing into operation of that code.

(7) The Secretary of State may from time to time revise the whole or any part of a code to which this section applies and issue that revised code; and the foregoing provision of this section shall apply (with appropriate modifications) to such a revised code as they apply to the first issue of the code.

(8) Persons, other than Commissioners appointed under section 91, shall have regard to any code of practice issued under this section in the performance of their functions under this Part.

(9) A failure on the part of any person to comply with any provision of a code of practice issued under this section shall not of itself render him liable to any criminal or civil proceedings.

(10) A code issued under this section shall be admissible in evidence in criminal and civil proceedings; and if any provision of such a code appears to the court or tribunal conducting the proceedings to be relevant to any question arising in the proceedings it shall be taken into account in determining that question.

Complaints etc.

102 Complaints

(1) Where a complaint is made, in accordance with arrangements made by the Chief Commissioner, to a Commissioner appointed under section 91(1)(b), the Commissioner shall investigate the complaint if and so far as it alleges that anything has been done in relation to any property of the complainant in pursuance of an authorisation under section 93(1)(a) or (b).

(2) For the purposes of subsection (1), a place where the complainant works or resides shall be treated as property of the complainant.

(3) A Commissioner's duty under this section does not extend to a complaint if he considers that it is frivolous or vexatious.

(4) Schedule 7 makes further provision in relation to the investigation of complaints by a Commissioner.

103 Quashing of authorisations etc.

(1) Where, at any time, a Commissioner appointed under section 91(1)(b) is satisfied that, at the time an authorisation was given or renewed, there were no reasonable grounds for believing the matters specified in section 93(2), he may quash the authorisation or, as the case may be, renewal.

(2) Where, in the case of an authorisation or renewal to which section 97 does not apply, a Commissioner appointed under section 91(1)(b) is at any time satisfied that, at the time the authorisation was given or, as the case may be, renewed,—

(a) there were reasonable grounds for believing any of the matters specified in subsection (2) of section 97, and

(b) there were no reasonable grounds for believing the case to be one of urgency for the purposes of subsection (3) of that section,

he may quash the authorisation or, as the case may be, renewal.

(3) Where a Commissioner quashes an authorisation or renewal under subsection (1) or (2), he may order the destruction of any records relating to information obtained by virtue of the authorisation (or, in the case of a renewal, relating wholly or partly to information so obtained after the renewal) other than records required for pending criminal or civil proceedings.

(4)–(9) * * * * *

Appeals

104 Appeals by authorising officers

(1) An authorising officer who gives an authorisation, or in whose absence it is given, may, within the prescribed period, appeal to the Chief Commissioner against—

(a) any refusal to approve the authorisation or any renewal of it under section 97;

(b) any decision to quash the authorisation, or any renewal of it, under subsection (1) of section 103;

(c) any decision to quash the authorisation, or any renewal of it, under subsection (2) of that section;

(d) any decision to cancel the authorisation under subsection (4) of that section;

(e) any decision to order the destruction of records under subsection (5) of that section;

(f) any refusal to make an order under subsection (6) of that section;

(g) any determination in favour of a complainant under Schedule 7.

(2) In subsection (1), "the prescribed period" means the period of seven days beginning with the day on which the refusal, decision or, as the case may be, determination appealed against is reported to the authorising officer.

(3) In determining an appeal within subsection (1)(a), the Chief Commissioner shall, if he is satisfied that there are reasonable grounds for believing the matters specified in section 93(2), allow the appeal and direct the Commissioner to approve the authorisation or renewal under that section.

(4)–(8) * * * * *

105 * * * * *

106 Appeals by complainants

(1) Where a complainant is notified under paragraph 3(2) of Schedule 7 that no determination in his favour has been made on a complaint, he may, within the period of seven days beginning with the day on which he receives the notice, appeal to the Chief Commissioner against the decision.

(2) Where a complainant appeals under this section, the Chief Commissioner shall have—

(a) all the powers and duties conferred by Schedule 7 on a Commissioner appointed under section 91(1)(b) who is required to investigate a complaint, and

(b) where the Chief Commissioner makes a determination in favour of the complainant by virtue of paragraph (a), all the powers and duties conferred by section 103.

(3) Where, by virtue of subsection (2), the Chief Commissioner makes an order to destroy records under section 103 or directs the payment of compensation under Schedule 7, subsection (8) of that section and paragraph 5(2) of that Schedule shall not apply.

(4) * * * * *

General

107 Supplementary provisions relating to Commissioners

(1) The Chief Commissioner shall keep under review the performance of functions under this Part.

(2) The Chief Commissioner shall make an annual report on the discharge of functions under this Part to the Prime Minister and may at any time report to him on any matter relating to those functions.

(3) The Prime Minister shall lay before each House of Parliament a copy of each annual report made by the Chief Commissioner under subsection (2) together with a statement as to whether any matter has been excluded from that copy in pursuance of subsection (4) below.

(4) The Prime Minister may exclude a matter from the copy of a report as laid before each House of Parliament, if it appears to him, after consultation with the Chief Commissioner, that the publication of that matter in the report would be prejudicial to the prevention or detection of serious crime or otherwise to the discharge of—

(a) the functions of any police authority,

(b) the functions of the Service Authority for the National Criminal Intelligence Service or the Service Authority for the National Crime Squad, or

(c) the duties of the Commissioners of Customs and Excise,

(5), (6) ★ ★ ★ ★ ★

108 ★ ★ ★ ★ ★

PROTECTION FROM HARASSMENT ACT 1997
(1997, c. 40)

An Act to make provision for protecting persons from harassment and similar conduct.

[21 March 1997]

Territorial extent England and Wales (sections printed). Sections 8–11 make corresponding provisions for Scotland; s. 13 provides for equivalent legislation by Order for Northern Ireland.

England and Wales

1 Prohibition of harassment

(1) A person must not pursue a course of conduct—

(a) which amounts to harassment of another, and

(b) which he knows or ought to know amounts to harassment of the other.

(2) For the purposes of this section, the person whose course of conduct is in question ought to know that it amounts to harassment of another if a reasonable person in possession of the same information would think the course of conduct amounted to harassment of the other.

(3) Subsection (1) does not apply to a course of conduct if the person who pursued it shows—

(a) that it was pursued for the purpose of preventing or detecting crime,

(b) that it was pursued under any enactment or rule of law or to comply with any condition or requirement imposed by any person under any enactment, or

(c) that in the particular circumstances the pursuit of the course of conduct was reasonable.

2 Offence of harassment

(1) A person who pursues a course of conduct in breach of section 1 is guilty of an offence.

(2) A person guilty of an offence under this section is liable on summary conviction to imprisonment for a term not exceeding six months, or a fine not exceeding level 5 on the standard scale, or both.

(3) In section 24(2) of the Police and Criminal Evidence Act 1984 (arrestable offences), after paragraph (m) there is inserted—

"(n) An offence under section 2 of the Protection from Harassment Act 1997 (harassment)."

3 Civil remedy

(1) An actual or apprehended breach of section 1 may be the subject of a claim in civil proceedings by the person who is or may be the victim of the course of conduct in question.

(2) On such a claim, damages may be awarded for (among other things) any anxiety caused by the harassment and any financial loss resulting from the harassment.

(3) Where—

(a) in such proceedings the High Court or a county court grants an injunction for the purpose of restraining the defendant from pursuing any conduct which amounts to harassment, and

(b) the plaintiff considers that the defendant has done anything which he is prohibited from doing by the injunction,

the plaintiff may apply for the issue of a warrant for the arrest of the defendant.

(4) An application under subsection (3) may be made—

(a) where the injunction was granted by the High Court, to a judge of that court, and

(b) where the injunction was granted by a county court, to a judge or district judge of that or any other county court.

(5) The judge or district judge to whom an application under subsection (3) is made may only issue a warrant if—

(a) the application is substantiated on oath, and

(b) the judge or district judge has reasonable grounds for believing that the defendant has done anything which he is prohibited from doing by the injunction.

(6) Where—

(a) the High Court or a county court grants an injunction for the purpose mentioned in subsection (3)(a), and

(b) without reasonable excuse the defendant does anything which he is prohibited from doing by the injunction,

he is guilty of an offence.

(7) Where a person is convicted of an offence under subsection (6) in respect of any conduct, that conduct is not punishable as a contempt of court.

(8) A person cannot be convicted of an offence under subsection (6) in respect of any conduct which has been punished as a contempt of court.

(9) A person guilty of an offence under subsection (6) is liable—

(a) on conviction on indictment, to imprisonment for a term not exceeding five years, or a fine, or both, or

(b) on summary conviction, to imprisonment for a term not exceeding six months, or a fine not exceeding the statutory maximum, or both.

4 Putting people in fear of violence

(1) A person whose course of conduct causes another to fear, on at least two occasions, that violence will be used against him is guilty of an offence if he knows or ought to know that his course of conduct will cause the other so to fear on each of those occasions.

(2) For the purposes of this section, the person whose course of conduct is in question ought to know that it will cause another to fear that violence will be used against him on any occasion if a reasonable person in possession of the same information would think the course of conduct would cause the other so to fear on that occasion.

(3) It is a defence for a person charged with an offence under this section to show that—

(a) his course of conduct was pursued for the purpose of preventing or detecting crime,

(b) his course of conduct was pursued under any enactment or rule of law or to comply with any condition or requirement imposed by any person under any enactment, or

(c) the pursuit of his course of conduct was reasonable for the protection of himself or another or for the protection of his or another's property.

(4) A person guilty of an offence under this section is liable—

(a) on conviction on indictment, to imprisonment for a term not exceeding five years, or a fine, or both, or

(b) on summary conviction, to imprisonment for a term not exceeding six months, or a fine not exceeding the statutory maximum, or both.

(5), (6) ★★★★★

5 Restraining orders

(1) A court sentencing or otherwise dealing with a person ("the defendant") convicted of an offence under section 2 or 4 may (as well as sentencing him or dealing with him in any other way) make an order under this section.

(2) The order may, for the purpose of protecting the victim of the offence, or any other person mentioned in the order, from further conduct which—

(a) amounts to harassment, or

(b) will cause a fear of violence,

prohibit the defendant from doing anything described in the order.

(4)–(6) ★★★★★

6 ★★★★★

7 Interpretation of this group of sections

(1) This section applies for the interpretation of sections 1 to 5.

(2) References to harassing a person include alarming the person or causing the person distress.

(3) A "course of conduct" must involve conduct on at least two occasions.

(4) "Conduct" includes speech.

8–16 ★★★★★

UNITED NATIONS PERSONNEL ACT 1997
(1997, c. 13)

An Act to enable effect to be given to certain provisions of the Convention on the Safety of United Nations and Associated Personnel adopted by the General Assembly of the United Nations on 9 December 1994. [27 February 1997]

Territorial extent Worldwide (for purposes relating to ss. 1 and 2); United Kingdom (for purposes relating to s. 3).

1 Attacks on UN workers

(1) If a person does outside the United Kingdom any act to or in relation to a UN worker which, if he had done it in any part of the United Kingdom, would have made him guilty of any of the offences mentioned in subsection (2), he shall in that part of the United Kingdom be guilty of that offence.

(2) The offences referred to in subsection (1) are—

(a) murder, manslaughter, culpable homicide, rape, assault causing injury, kidnapping, abduction and false imprisonment;

(b) an offence under section 18, 20, 21, 22, 23, 24, 28, 29, 30 or 47 of the Offences Against the Person Act 1861; and

(c) an offence under section 2 of the Explosive Substances Act 1883.

2 Attacks in connection with premises and vehicles

(1) If a person does outside the United Kingdom any act, in connection with an attack on relevant premises or on a vehicle ordinarily used by a UN worker which is made when a UN worker is on or in the premises or vehicle, which, if he had done it in any part of the United Kingdom, would have made him guilty of any of the offences mentioned in subsection (2), he shall in that part of the United Kingdom be guilty of that offence.

(2) The offences referred to in subsection (1) are—

(a) an offence under section 2 of the Explosive Substances Act 1883;

(b) an offence under section 1 of the Criminal Damage Act 1971;

(c) an offence under article 3 of the Criminal Damage (Northern Ireland) Order 1977; and

(d) wilful fire-raising.

(3) In this section—

"relevant premises" means premises at which a UN worker resides or is staying or which a UN worker uses for the purpose of carrying out his functions as such a worker; and

"vehicle" includes any means of conveyance.

3 Threats of attacks on UN workers

(1) If a person in the United Kingdom or elsewhere contravenes subsection (2) he shall be guilty of an offence.

(2) A person contravenes this subsection if, in order to compel a person to do or abstain from doing any act, he—

(a) makes to a person a threat that any person will do an act which is—

(i) an offence mentioned in section 1(2) against a UN worker, or

(ii) an offence mentioned in subsection (2) of section 2 in connection with such an attack as is mentioned in subsection (1) of that section, and

(b) intends that the person to whom he makes the threat shall fear that it will be carried out.

(3) A person guilty of an offence under this section shall be liable on conviction on indictment to imprisonment for a term—

(a) not exceeding ten years, and

(b) not exceeding the term of imprisonment to which a person would be liable for the offence constituted by doing the act threatened at the place where the conviction occurs and at the time of the offence to which the conviction relates.

4 Meaning of UN worker

(1) For the purposes of this Act a person is a UN worker, in relation to an alleged offence, if at the time of the alleged offence—

(a) he is engaged or deployed by the Secretary-General of the United Nations as a member of the military, police or civilian component of a UN operation,

(b) he is, in his capacity as an official or expert on mission of the United Nations, a specialised agency of the United Nations or the International Atomic Energy Agency, present in an area where a UN operation is being conducted,

(c) he is assigned, with the agreement of an organ of the United Nations, by the Government of any State or by an international governmental organisation to carry out activities in support of the fulfilment of the mandate of a UN operation,

(d) he is engaged by the Secretary-General of the United Nations, a specialised agency or the International Atomic Energy Agency to carry out such activities, or

(e) he is deployed by a humanitarian non-governmental organisation or agency under an agreement with the Secretary-General of the United Nations, with a specialised agency or with the International Atomic Energy Agency to carry out such activities.

(2) Subject to subsection (3), in this section "UN operation" means an operation—

(a) which is established, in accordance with the Charter of the United Nations, by an organ of the United Nations,

(b) which is conducted under the authority and control of the United Nations, and

(c) which—

(i) has as its purpose the maintenance or restoration of international peace and security, or

(ii) has, for the purposes of the Convention, been declared by the Security Council or the General Assembly of the United Nations to be an operation where there exists an exceptional risk to the safety of the participating personnel.

(3) In this section "UN operation" does not include any operation—

(a) which is authorised by the Security Council of the United Nations as an enforcement action under Chaper VII of the Charter of the United Nations,

(b) in which UN workers are engaged as combatants against organised armed forces, and

(c) to which the law of international armed conflict applies.

(4), (5) ★★★★★

5 Provisions supplementary to sections 1 to 3

(1) Proceedings for an offence which (disregarding the provisions of the Internationally Protected Persons Act 1978, the Suppression of Terrorism Act 1978 and the Nuclear Material (Offences) Act 1983) would not be an offence apart from section 1, 2 or 3 above shall not be begun—

(a) in England and Wales, except by or with the consent of the Attorney General;

(b) in Northern Ireland, except by or with the consent of the Attorney General for Northern Ireland.

(2) ★★★★★

(3) A person is guilty of an offence under, or by virtue of, section 1, 2 or 3 regardless of his nationality.

(4) For the purposes of those sections, it is immaterial whether a person knows that another person is a UN worker.

6–10 ★★★★★

Schedule ★★★★★

PART II
OTHER CONSTITUTIONAL MATERIALS

THE CONSTITUTION OF THE UNITED STATES

We the People of the United States, in order to form a more perfect Union, establish Justice, ensure Domestic Tranquillity, provide for the common Defence, promote the general Welfare, and secure the Blessings of Liberty to ourselves and our Posterity, do ordain and establish this CONSTITUTION for the United States of America.

Articles I-VII
★ ★ ★ ★ ★

AMENDMENTS TO THE CONSTITUTION

Article I
Congress shall make no law respecting an establishment of religion, or prohibiting the free exercise thereof; or abridging the freedom of speech or of the press; or the right of the people peaceably to assemble, and to petition the government for a redress of grievances.

Article II
A well-regulated militia being necessary to the security of a free state, the right of the people to keep and bear arms shall not be infringed.

Article III
No soldier shall, in time of peace, be quartered in any house without the consent of the owner, nor in time of war but in a manner to be prescribed by law.

Article IV
The right of the people to be secure in their persons, houses, papers, and effects, against unreasonable searches and seizures, shall not be violated, and no warrants shall issue but upon probable cause, supported by oath or affirmation, and particularly describing the place to be searched, and the persons or things to be seized.

Article V
No person shall be held to answer for a capital or other infamous crime unless on a presentment or indictment of a grand jury, except in cases arising in the land or naval forces, or in the militia, when in actual service, in time of war or public danger; nor shall any person be subject for the same offence to be twice put in jeopardy of life or limb; nor shall be compelled in any criminal case to be a witness against himself, nor be deprived of life, liberty, or property, without due process of law; nor shall private property be taken for public use without just compensation.

Article VI
In all criminal prosecutions, the accused shall enjoy the right to a speedy and public trial, by an impartial jury of the state and district wherein the crime shall have been committed, which district shall have been previously ascertained by law, and to be informed of the nature and cause of the accusation; to be confronted with the witnesses against him; to have compulsory process for obtaining witnesses in his favor, and to have the assistance of counsel for his defence.

Article VII
In suits at common law, where the value in controversy shall exceed twenty dollars, the right of trial by jury shall be preserved, and no fact tried by a jury shall be otherwise re-examined in any court of the United States than according to the rules of the common law.

Article VIII
Excessive bail shall not be required, nor excessive fines imposed, nor cruel and unusual punishments inflicted.

Article IX
The enumeration in the constitution of certain rights shall not be construed to deny or disparage others retained by the people.

Article X
The powers not delegated to the United States by the constitution, nor prohibited by it to the states, are reserved to the states respectively, or to the people.

[*The foregoing ten amendments were adopted at the first session of Congress, and were declared to be in force, December 15, 1791.*]

Articles XI-XIII
★ ★ ★ ★ ★

Article XIV
1. All persons born or naturalized in the United States, and subject to the jurisdiction thereof, are citizens of the United States and of the state wherein they reside. No state shall make or enforce any law which shall abridge the privileges or immunities of citizens of the United States; nor shall any state deprive any person of life, liberty, or property without due process of law; nor deny to any person within its jurisdiction the equal protection of the law.

2.-4. ★ ★ ★ ★ ★

5. The Congress shall have power to enforce, by appropriate legislation, the provisions of this article.

[*Declared in force, July 28, 1868.*]

★ ★ ★ ★ ★

EUROPEAN CONVENTION FOR THE PROTECTION OF HUMAN RIGHTS AND FUNDAMENTAL FREEDOMS (1950)

[*The European Convention on Human Rights*]

The Governments signatory hereto, being Members of the Council of Europe,

Considering the Universal Declaration of Human Rights proclaimed by the General Assembly of the United Nations on 10 December 1948;

Considering that this Declaration aims at securing the universal and effective recognition and observance of the Rights therein declared;

Considering that the aim of the Council of Europe is the achievement of greater unity between its Members and that one of the methods by which the aim is to be pursued is the maintenance and further realization of Human Rights and Fundamental Freedoms;

Reaffirming their profound belief in those Fundamental Freedoms which are the foundation of justice and peace in the world and are best maintained on the one hand by an effective political democracy and on the other by a common understanding and observance of the Human Rights upon which they depend;

Being resolved, as the Governments of European countries which are like-minded and have a common heritage of political traditions, ideals, freedom and the rule of law to take the first steps for the collective enforcement of certain of the Rights stated in the Universal Declaration;

Have agreed as follows:

Article 1

The High Contracting Parties shall secure to everyone within their jurisdiction the rights and freedoms defined in Section I of this Convention.

SECTION I

Article 2

1. Everyone's right to life shall be protected by law. No one shall be deprived of his life intentionally save in the execution of a sentence of a court following his conviction of a crime for which this penalty is provided by law.

2. Deprivation of life shall not regarded as inflicted in contravention of this article when it results from the use of force which is no more than absolutely necessary:

(a) in defence of any person from unlawful violence;

(b) in order to effect a lawful arrest or to prevent the escape of a person lawfully detained;

(c) in action lawfully taken for the purpose of quelling a riot or insurrection.

Article 3

No one shall be subjected to torture or to inhuman or degrading treatment or punishment.

Article 4

1. No one shall be held in slavery or servitude.

2. No one shall be required to perform forced or compulsory labour.

3. For the purpose of this article the term "forced or compulsory labour' shall not include:

(a) any work required to be done in the ordinary course of detention imposed according to the provisions of Article 5 of this Convention or during conditional release from such detention;

(b) any service of a military character or, in case of conscientious objectors in countries where they are recognized, service exacted instead of compulsory military service;

(c) any service exacted in case of an emergency or calamity threatening the life or well-being of the community;

(d) any work or service which forms part of normal civic obligations.

Article 5

1. Everyone has the right to liberty and security of person.

No one shall be deprived of his liberty save in the following cases and in accordance with a procedure prescribed by law:

(a) the lawful detention of a person after conviction by a competent court;

(b) the lawful arrest or detention of a person for non-compliance with the lawful order of a court or in order to secure the fulfilment of any obligation prescribed by law;

(c) the lawful arrest or detention of a person effected for the purpose of bringing him before the competent legal authority on reasonable suspicion of having committed an offence or when it is reasonably considered necessary to prevent his committing an offence or fleeing after having done so;

(d) the detention of a minor by lawful order for the purpose of educational supervision or his lawful detention for the purpose of bringing him before the competent legal authority;

(e) the lawful detention of persons for the prevention of the spreading of infectious diseases, of persons of unsound mind, alcoholics or drug addicts, or vagrants;

(f) the lawful arrest or detention of a person to prevent his effecting an unauthorized entry into the country or of a person against whom action is being taken with a view to deportation or extradition.

2. Everyone who is arrested shall be informed promptly, in a language which he understands, of the reasons for his arrest and of any charge against him.

3. Everyone arrested or detained in accordance with the provisions of paragraph 1(c) of this article shall be brought promptly before a judge or other officer authorized by law to exercise judicial power and shall be entitled to trial within a reasonable time or to release pending trial. Release may be conditioned by guarantees to appear for trial.

4. Everyone who is deprived of his liberty by arrest or detention shall be entitled to take proceedings by which the lawfulness of his detention shall be decided speedily by a court and his release ordered if the detention is not lawful.

5. Everyone who has been the victim of arrest or detention in contravention of the provisions of this article shall have an enforceable right to compensation.

Article 6

1. In the determination of his civil rights and obligations or of any criminal charge against him, everyone is entitled to a fair and public hearing within a reasonable time by an independent and impartial tribunal established by law. Judgment shall be pronounced publicly but the press and public may be excluded from all or part of the trial in the interest of morals, public order or national security in a democratic society, where the interests of juveniles or the protection of the private life of the parties so require, or to the extent strictly necessary in the opinion of the court in special circumstances where publicity would prejudice the interests of justice.

2. Everyone charged with a criminal offence shall be presumed innocent until proved guilty according to law.

3. Everyone charged with a criminal offence has the following minimum rights:

(a) to be informed promptly, in a language which he understands and in detail, of the nature and cause of the accusation against him;

(b) to have adequate time and facilities for the preparation of his defence;

(c) to defend himself in person or through legal assistance of his own choosing or, if he has not sufficient means to pay for legal assistance, to be given it free when the interests of justice so require;

(d) to examine or have examined witnesses against him and to obtain the attendance and examination of witnesses on his behalf under the same conditions as witnesses against him;

(e) to have the free assistance of an interpreter if he cannot understand or speak the language used in court.

Article 7

1. No one shall be held guilty of any criminal offence on account of any act or omission which did not constitute a criminal offence under national or international law at the time when it was committed. Nor shall a heavier penalty be imposed than the one that was applicable at the time the criminal offence was committed.

2. This article shall not prejudice the trial and punishment of any person for any act or omission which, at the time when it was committed, was criminal according to the general principles of law recognized by civilized nations.

Article 8

1. Everyone has the right to respect for his private and family life, his home and his correspondence.

2. There shall be no interference by a public authority with the exercise of this right except such as is in accordance with the law and is necessary in a democratic society in the interests of national security, public safety or the economic well-being of the country, for the prevention of disorder or crime, for the protection of health or morals, or for the protection of the rights and freedoms of others.

Article 9

1. Everyone has the right to freedom of thought, conscience and religion; this right includes freedom to change his religion or belief, and freedom, either alone or in community with others and in public or private, to manifest his religion or belief, in worship, teaching, practice and observance.

2. Freedom to manifest one's religion or beliefs shall be subject only to such limitations as are prescribed by law and are necessary in a democratic society in the interests of public safety, for the protection of public order, health or morals, or for the protection of the rights and freedoms of others.

Article 10

1. Everyone has the right to freedom of expression. This right shall include freedom to hold opinions and to receive and impart information and ideas without interference by public authority and regardless of frontiers. This article shall not prevent States from requiring the licensing of broadcasting, television or cinema enterprises.

2. The exercise of these freedoms, since it carries with it duties and responsibilities, may be subject to such formalities, conditions, restrictions or penalties as are prescribed by law and are necessary in a democratic society, in the interests of national security, territorial integrity or public safety, for the prevention of disorder or crime, for the protection of health or morals, for the protection of the reputation or rights of others, for preventing the disclosure of information received in confidence, or for maintaining the authority and impartiality of the judiciary.

Article 11

1. Everyone has the right to freedom of peaceful assembly and to freedom of association with others, including the right to form and to join trade unions for the protection of his interests.

2. No restrictions shall be placed on the exercise of these rights other than such as are prescribed by law and are necessary in a democratic society in the interests of national security or public safety, for the prevention of disorder or crime, of the protection of health or morals or for the protection of the rights and freedoms of others. This article shall not prevent the imposition of lawful restrictions on the exercise of these rights by members of the armed forces, of the police or of the administration of the State.

Article 12

Men and women of marriageable age have the right to marry and to found a family, according to the national laws governing the exercise of this right.

Article 13

Everyone whose rights and freedoms as set forth in this Convention are violated shall have an effective remedy before a national authority notwithstanding that the violation has been committed by persons acting in an official capacity.

Article 14

The enjoyment of the rights and freedoms set forth in this Convention shall be secured without discrimination on any ground such as sex, race, colour, language, religion, political or other opinion, national or social origin, association with a national minority, property, birth or other status.

Article 15

1. In time of war or other public emergency threatening the life of the nation any High Contracting Party may take measures derogating from its obligations under this Convention to the extent strictly required by the exigencies of the situation, provided that such measures are not inconsistent with its other obligations under international law.

2. No derogation from Article 2, except in respect of deaths resulting from lawful acts of war, or from Articles 3, 4 (paragraph 1) and 7 shall be made under this provision.

3. Any High Contracting Party availing itself of this right of derogation shall keep the Secretary-General of the Council of Europe fully informed of the measures which it has taken and the reasons therefor. It shall also inform the Secretary-General of the Council of Europe when such measures have ceased to operate and the provisions of the Convention are again being fully executed.

Article 16

Nothing in Articles 10, 11, and 14 shall be regarded as preventing the High Contracting Parties from imposing restrictions on the political activity of aliens.

Article 17

Nothing in this Convention may be interpreted as implying for any State, group or person any right to engage in any activity or perform any act aimed at the destruction of any of the rights and freedoms set forth herein or at their limitation to a greater extent than is provided for in the Convention.

Article 18

The restrictions permitted under this Convention to the said rights and freedoms shall not be applied for any purpose other than those for which they have been prescribed.

SECTION II

Article 19

To ensure the observance of the engagements undertaken by the High Contracting Parties in the present Convention, there shall be set up:

1. A European Commission of Human Rights hereinafter referred to as 'the Commission';

2. A European Court of Human Rights, hereinafter referred to as 'the Court'.

SECTION III

Article 20

1. The Commission shall consist of a number of members equal to that of the High Contracting Parties. No two members of the Commission may be nationals of the same State.

[2. The Commission shall sit in plenary session. It may, however, set up Chambers, each composed of at least seven members. The Chambers may examine petitions submitted under Article 25 of this Convention which can be dealt with on the basis of established case law or which raise no serious question affecting the interpretation or application of the Convention. Subjects to this restriction and to the provisions of paragraph 5 of this Article, the Chambers shall exercise all the powers conferred on the Commission by the Convention.

The member of the Commission elected in respect of a High Contracting Party against which a petition has been lodged shall have the right to sit on a Chamber to which that petition has been referred.

3. The Commission may set up committees, each composed of at least three members, with the power, exercisable by a unanimous vote, to declare inadmissible or strike from its list of cases a petition submitted under Article 25, when such a decision can be taken without further examination.

4. A Chamber or committee may at any time relinquish jurisdiction in favour of the plenary Commission, which may also order the transfer to it of any petition referred to a Chamber or committee.

5. Only the examination of applications submitted under Article 24;
(a) the examination of applications submitted under Article 24;
(b) the bringing of a case before the Court in accordance with Article 48a;
(c) the drawing up of rules of procedure in accordance with Article 36.]

Article 21

1. The members of the Commission shall be elected by the Committee of Ministers by an absolute majority of votes, from a list of names drawn up by the Bureau of the Consultative Assembly; each group of the Representatives of the High Contracting Parties in the Consultative Assembly shall put forward three candidates, of whom two at least shall be its nationals.

2. As far as applicable, the same procedure shall be followed to complete the Commission in the event of other States subsequently becoming Parties to this Convention, and in filling casual vacancies.

[3. The candidates shall be of high moral character and must either possess the qualifications required for appointment to high judicial office or be persons of recognised competence in national or international law.]

Article 22

1. The members of the Commission shall be elected for a period of six years. They may be re-elected. However, of the members elected at the first election, the terms of seven members shall expire at the end of three years.

2. The members whose terms are to expire at the end of the initial period of three years shall be chosen by lot by the Secretary-General of the Council of Europe immediately after the first election has been completed.

3.-6. * * * * *

Article 23

The members of the Commission shall sit on the Commission in their individual capacity.

[During their term of office they shall not hold any position which is incompatible with their independence and impartiality as members of the Commission as the demands of this office.]

Article 24

Any High Contracting Party may refer to the Commission, through the Secretary-General of the Council of Europe, any alleged breach of the provisions of the Convention by another High Contracting Party.

Article 25

1. The Commission may receive petitions addressed to the Secretary-General of the Council of Europe from any person, non-governmental organization or group of individuals claiming to be the victim of a violation by one of the High Contracting Parties of the rights set forth in this Convention, provided that the High Contracting Party against which the complaint has been lodged has declared that it recognizes the competence of the Commission to receive such petitions. Those of the High Contracting Parties who have made such a declaration undertake not to hinder in any way the effective exercise of this right.

2. Such declarations may be made for a specific period.

3. The declarations shall be deposited with the Secretary-General of the Council of Europe who shall transmit copies thereof to the High Contracting Parties and publish them.

4. The Commission shall only exercise the powers provided for in this article when at least six High Contracting Parties are bound by declarations made in accordance with the preceding paragraphs.

Article 26

The Commission may only deal with the matter after all domestic remedies have been exhausted, according to the generally recognized rules of international law, and within a period of six months from the date on which the final decision was taken.

Article 27

1. The Commission shall not deal with any petition submitted under Article 25 which

(a) is anonymous, or

(b) is substantially the same as a matter which has already been examined by the Commission or has already been submitted to another procedure or international investigation or settlement and if it contains no relevant new information.

2. The Commission shall consider inadmissible any petition submitted under Article 25 which it considers incompatible with the provisions of the present Convention, manifestly ill-founded, or an abuse of the right of petition.

3. The Commission shall reject any petition referred to it which it considers inadmissible under Article 26.

Article 28

1. In the event of the Commission accepting a petition referred to it:

(a) it shall, with a view to ascertaining the facts undertake together with the representatives of the parties an examination of the petition and, if need be, an investigation, for the effective conduct of which the States concerned shall furnish all necessary facilities, after an exchange of views with the Commission:

(b) it shall place itself at the disposal of the parties concerned with a view to securing a friendly settlement of the matter on the basis of respect for Human Rights as defined in this Convention.

[2. If the Commission succeeds in effecting a friendly settlement, it shall be sent to the States concerned, to the Committee of Ministers and to the Secretary General of the Council of Europe for publication. This Report shall be confined to a brief statement of the facts and of the solution reached.]

Article 29

[After it has accepted a petition submitted under Article 25, the Commission may nevertheless decide [by a majority of two thirds of its members] to reject the petition if, in the course of its examination, it finds that the existence of one of the grounds for non-acceptance provided for in Article 27 has been established.

In such a case, the decision shall be communicated to the parties.]

Article 30

[1. The Commission may at any stage of the proceedings decide to strike a petition out of its list of cases where the circumstances lead to the conclusion that:

(a) the applicant does not intend to pursue his petition, or

(b) the matter has been resolved, or

(c) for any other reason established by the Commission, it is no longer justified to continue the examination of the petition.

However, the Commission shall continue the examination of a petition if respect for Human Rights as defined in this Convention so requires.

2. If the Commission decides to strike a petition out of its list after having accepted it, it shall draw up a Report which shall contain a statement of the facts and the decision striking out the petition together with the reasons therefore. The Report shall be transmitted to the parties, as well as to the Committee of Ministers for information. The Commission may publish it.

3. The Commission may decide to restore a petition to its list of cases if it considers that the circumstances justify such a course.]

Article 31

[1. If the examination of a petition has not been completed in accordance with Article 28 (paragraph 2), 29 or 30, the Commission shall draw up a Report on the facts and state its opinion as to whether the facts found disclose a breach by the State concerned of its obligations under the Convention. The individual opinions of members of the Commission on this point may be stated in the Report.]

2. The Report shall be transmitted to the Committee of Ministers. It shall also be transmitted to the States concerned, who shall not be at liberty to publish it.

3. In transmitting the Report to the Committee of Ministers the Commission may make such proposals as it thinks fit.

Article 32

1. If the question is not referred to the Court in accordance with Article 48 of this Convention within a period of three months from the date of the transmission of the Report to the Committee of Ministers, the Committee of Ministers shall decide by a majority of two-thirds of the members entitled to sit on the Committee whether there has been a violation of the Convention.

2. In the affirmative case the Committee of Ministers shall prescribe a period during which the Contracting Party concerned must take the measures required by the decision of the Committee of Ministers.

3. If the High Contracting Party concerned has not taken satisfactory measures within the prescribed period, the Committee of Ministers shall decide by the majority provided for in paragraph 1 above what effect shall be given to its original decision and shall publish the Report.

4. The High Contracting Parties undertake to regard as binding on them any decision which the Committee of Ministers may take in application of the preceding paragraphs.

Article 33

The Commission shall meet *in camera*.

Article 34

[Subject to the provisions of Articles 20 (paragraph 3) and 29, the] Commission shall take its decision by a majority of the Members present and voting; . . .

Article 35

The Commission shall meet as the circumstances require. The meetings shall be convened by the Secretary-General of the Council of Europe.

Article 36

The Commission shall draw up its own rules of procedure.

Article 37

★★★★★

SECTION IV

Article 38
The European Court of Human Rights shall consist of a number of judges equal to that of the Members of the Council of Europe. No two judges may be nationals of the same State.

Article 39
1. The members of the Court shall be elected by the Consultative Assembly by a majority of the votes cast from a list of persons nominated by the Members of the Council of Europe; each Member shall nominate three candidates, of whom two at least shall be its nationals.
2. As far as applicable, the same procedure shall be followed to complete the Court in the event of the admission of new members of the Council of Europe, and in filling casual vacancies.
3. The candidates shall be of high moral character and must either possess the qualifications required for appointment to high judicial office or be jurisconsults of recognized competence.

Article 40
1. The members of the Court shall be elected for a period of nine years. They may be re-elected. However, of the members elected at the first election the terms of four members shall expire at the end of three years, and the terms of four more members shall expire at the end of six years.
2. The members whose terms are to expire at the end of the initial periods of three and six years shall be chosen by lot by the Secretary-General immediately after the first election has been completed.
3.-7. ★★★★★

Article 41
The Court shall elect its President and [one or two] Vice-President for a period of three years. They may be re-elected.

Articles 42, 43
★★★★★

Article 44
Only the High Contracting Parties and the Commission shall have the right to bring a case before the Court.

Article 45
The jurisdiction of the Court shall extend to all cases concerning the interpretation and application of the present Convention which the High Contracting Parties or the Commission shall refer to it in accordance with Article 48.

Article 46
1. Any of the High Contracting Parties may at any time declare that it recognizes as compulsory *ipso facto* and without special agreement the jurisdiction of the Court in all matters concerning the interpretation and application of the present Convention.
2. The declarations referred to above may be made unconditionally or on condition of reciprocity on the part of several or certain other High Contracting Parties or for a specified period.
3. These declarations shall be deposited with the Secretary-General of the Council of Europe who shall transmit copies thereof to the High Contracting Parties.

Article 47
The Court may only deal with a case after the Commission has acknowledged the failure of efforts for a friendly settlement and within the period of three months provided for in Article 32.

Article 48
The following may bring a case before the Court, provided that the High Contracting Party concerned, if there is only one, or the High Contracting Parties concerned, if there is more than one, are subject to the compulsory jurisdiction of the Court or, failing that, with the consent of the High Contracting Party concerned, if there is only one, or of the High Contracting Parties concerned if there is more than one:

(a) the Commission;
(b) a High Contracting Party whose national is alleged to be a victim;
(c) a High Contracting Party which referred the case to the Commission;
(d) a High Contracting Party against which the complaint has been lodged.

Article 49
In the event of dispute as to whether the Court has jurisdiction, the matter shall be settled by the decision of the Court.

Article 50
If the Court finds that a decision or a measure taken by a legal authority or any other authority of a High Contracting Party, is completely or partially in conflict with the obligations arising from the present Convention, and if the internal law of the said Party allows only partial reparation to be made for the consequences of this decision or measure, the decision of the Court shall, if necessary, afford just satisfaction to the injured party.

Article 51
1. Reasons shall be given for the judgment of the Court.
2. If the judgment does not represent in whole or in part the unanimous opinion of the judges, any judge shall be entitled to deliver a separate opinion.

Article 52
The judgment of the Court shall be final.

Article 53
The High Contracting Parties undertake to abide by the decision of the Court in any case to which they are parties.

Articles 54-56
★ ★ ★ ★ ★

Articles 57-59
★ ★ ★ ★ ★

SECTION V

Article 60
Nothing in this Convention shall be construed as limiting or derogating from any of the human rights and fundamental freedoms which may be ensured under the laws of any High Contracting Party or under any other agreement to which it is a Party.

Articles 61-63
★ ★ ★ ★ ★

Article 64

1. Any State may, when signing this Convention or when depositing its instrument of ratification, make a reservation in respect of any particular provision of the Convention to the extent that any law then in force in its territory is not in conformity with the provision. Reservations of a general character shall not be permitted under this article.

2. Any reservation made under this article shall contain a brief statement of the law concerned.

* * * * *

Protocols

1. Enforcement of certain Rights and Freedoms not included in Section I of the Convention

The Governments signatory hereto, being Members of the Council of Europe,

Being resolved to take steps to ensure the collective enforcement of certain rights and freedoms other than those already included in Section I of the Convention for the Protection of Human Rights and Fundamental Freedoms signed at Rome on 4th November 1950 (hereinafter referred to as 'the Convention'),

Have agreed as follows:

Article 1

Every natural or legal person is entitled to the peaceful enjoyment of his possessions. No one shall be deprived of his possessions except in the public interest and subject to the conditions provided for by law and by the general principles of international law.

The preceding provisions shall not, however, in any way impair the right of a State to enforce such laws as it deems necessary to control the use of property in accordance with the general interest or to secure the payment of taxes or other contributions or penalties.

Article 2

No person shall be denied the right to education. In the exercise of any functions which it assumes in relation to education and to teaching, the State shall respect the right of parents to ensure such education and teaching in conformity with their own religious and philosophical convictions.

Article 3

The High Contracting Parties undertake to hold free elections at reasonable intervals by secret ballot, under conditions which will ensure the free expression of the opinion of the people in the choice of the legislature.

* * * * *

4. Protecting certain Additional Rights

The Governments signatory hereto, being Members of the Council of Europe.

Being resolved to take steps to ensure the collective enforcement of certain rights and freedoms other than those already included in Section I of the Convention for the Protection of Human Rights and Fundamental Freedoms signed at Rome on 4 November 1950 (hereinafter referred to as 'the Convention') and in Articles 1 to 3 of the First Protocol to the Convention, signed at Paris on 20 March 1952,

Have agreed as follows:

Article 1

No one shall be deprived of his liberty merely on the ground of inability to fulfil a contractual obligation.

Article 2

1. Everyone lawfully within the territory of a State shall, within that territory, have the right to liberty of movement and freedom to choose his residence.

2. Everyone shall be free to leave any country, including his own.

3. No restrictions shall be placed on the exercise of these rights other than such as are in accordance with law and are necessary in a democratic society in the interests of national security or public safety, for the maintenance of 'order public', for the prevention of crime, for the protection of the rights and freedoms of others.

4. The rights set forth in paragraph 1 may also be subject, in particular areas, to restrictions imposed in accordance with law and justified by the public interest in a democratic society.

Article 3

1. No one shall be expelled, by means either of an individual or of a collective measure, from the territory of the State of which he is a national.

2. No one shall be deprived of the right to enter the territory of the State of which he is a national.

Article 4

Collective expulsion of aliens is prohibited.

★ ★ ★ ★ ★

Note This Protocol has not yet been ratified by the United Kingdom.

6. *Concerning the Abolition of the Death Penalty*

The member States of the Council of Europe, signatory to this Protocol to the Convention for the Protection of Human Rights and Fundamental Freedoms, signed at Rome on 4 November 1950 (hereinafter referred to as 'the Convention').

Considering that the evolution that has occurred in several member States of the Council of Europe expresses a general tendency in favour of abolition of the death penalty.

Have agreed as follows:

Article 1

The death penalty shall be abolished. No one shall be condemned to such penalty or executed.

Article 2

A state may make provision in its law for the death penalty in respect of acts committed in time of war or of imminent threat of war; such penalty shall be applied only in the instance laid down in the law and in accordance with its provisions. The State shall communicate to the Secretary General of the Council of Europe the relevant provisions of that law.

Article 3

No derogation from the provision of this Protocol shall be made under Article 15 of the Convention.

Article 4

No reservation may be made under Article 64 of the Convention in respect of the provisions of this Protocol.

Note Not ratified by the United Kingdom. Protocol 7 is not included as it is not yet in force and has not been ratified by the UK. Protocol 11 which extensively amends the Convention by replacing the existing European Commission and European Court of Human Rights with a new permanent Court, though ratified by the UK, is not included as it is not yet in force.

TREATY ESTABLISHING THE EUROPEAN COMMUNITY (TREATY OF ROME)

(25 March 1957)

Note The Treaty is printed as amended with effect from 1 November 1993 by the Maastricht Treaty. The EEC is now the EU (European Union). Further amendments to the Treaty to accommodate the admission of Austria, Finland, Norway and Sweden were made by the Act of Accession of 24 June 1994 and are incorporated in the text; these came into force on 1 January 1995 (except in relation to Norway, which decided in a referendum not to join the EU), and are incorporated into the UK by the European Community (Accessions) Act 1994.

EC TREATY (MAASTRICHT VERSION)
PART ONE
(PRINCIPLES)

Article 1
By this Treaty, the High Contracting Parties establish among themselves a EUROPEAN COMMUNITY.

Article 2
The Community shall have as its task, by establishing a common market and an economic and monetary union and by implementing the common policies or activities referred to in Articles 3 and 3a, to promote throughout the Community a harmonious and balanced development of economic activities, sustainable and non-inflationary growth respecting the environment, a high degree of convergence of economic performance, a high level of employment and of social protection, the raising of the standard of living and quality of life, and economic and social cohesion and solidarity among Member States.

Article 3
For the purposes set out in Article 2, the activities of the Community shall include, as provided in this Treaty and in accordance with the timetable set out therein:

(a) the elimination, as between Member States, of customs duties and quantitative restrictions on the import and export of goods, and of all other measures having equivalent effect;

(b) a common commercial policy;

(c) an internal market characterised by the abolition, as between Member States, of obstacles to the free movement of goods, persons, services and capital;

(d) measures concerning the entry and movement of persons in the internal market as provided for in Article 100c;

(e) a common policy in the sphere of agriculture and fisheries;

(f) a common policy in the sphere of transport;

(g) a system ensuring that competition in the internal market is not distorted;

(h) the approximation of the laws of Member States to the extent required for the functioning of the common market;

(i) a policy in the social sphere comprising a European Social Fund;

(j) the strengthening of economic and social cohesion;

(k) a policy in the sphere of the environment;

(l) the strengthening of the competitiveness of Community industry;

(m) the promotion of research and technological development;

(n) encouragement for the establishment and development of trans-European networks;

(o) a contribution to the attainment of a high level of health protection;

(p) a contribution to education and training of quality and to the flowering of the cultures of the Member States;

(q) a policy in the sphere of development cooperation;

(r) the association of the overseas countries and territories in order to increase trade and promote jointly economic and social development;

(s) a contribution to the strengthening of consumer protection;

(t) measures in the spheres of energy, civil protection and tourism.

Article 3a

1. For the purposes set out in Article 2, the activities of the Member States and the Community shall include, as provided in this Treaty and in accordance with the timetable set out therein, the adoption of an economic policy which is based on the close coordination of Member States' economic policies, on the internal market and on the definition of common objectives, and conducted in accordance with the principle of an open market economy with free competition.

2. Concurrently with the foregoing, and as provided in this Treaty and in accordance with the timetable and the procedures set out therein, these activities shall include the irrevocable fixing of exchange rates leading to the introduction of a single currency, the ECU, and the definition and conduct of a single monetary policy and exchange-rate policy the primary objective of both of which shall be to maintain price stability and, without prejudice to this objective, to support the general economic policies in the Community, in accordance with the principle of an open market economy with free competition.

3. These activities of the Member States and the Community shall entail compliance with the following guiding principles: stable prices, sound public finances and monetary conditions and a sustainable balance of payments.

Article 3b

The Community shall act within the limits of the powers conferred upon it by this Treaty and of the objectives assigned to it therein.

In areas which do not fall within its exclusive competence, the Community shall take action, in accordance with the principle of subsidiarity, only if and in so far as the objectives of the proposed action cannot be sufficiently achieved by the Member States and can therefore, by reason of the scale or effects of the proposed action, be better achieved by the Community.

Any action by the Community shall not go beyond what is necessary to achieve the objectives of this Treaty.

Article 4

1. The tasks entrusted to the Community shall be carried out by the following institutions:

— a EUROPEAN PARLIAMENT,
— a COUNCIL,
— a COMMISSION,
— a COURT OF JUSTICE,
— a COURT OF AUDITORS.

Each institution shall act within the limits of the powers conferred upon it by this Treaty.

2. The Council and the Commission shall be assisted by an Economic and Social Committee and a Committee of the Regions acting in an advisory capacity.

Articles 4a, 4b * * * * *

Article 5

Member States shall take all appropriate measures, whether general or particular, to ensure fulfilment of the obligations arising out of this Treaty or resulting from action taken by the institutions of the Community. They shall facilitate the achievement of the Community's tasks.

They shall abstain from any measure which could jeopardise the attainment of the objectives of this Treaty.

Article 6
Within the scope of application of this Treaty, and without prejudice to any special provisions contained therein, any discrimination on grounds of nationality shall be prohibited.

The Council, acting in accordance with the procedure referred to in Article 189c, may adopt rules designed to prohibit such discrimination.

Article 7 * * * * *

Article 7a
The Community shall adopt measures with the aim of progressively establishing the internal market over a period expiring on 31 December 1992, in accordance with the provisions of this Article and of Articles 7b, 7c, 28, 57(2), 59, 70(1), 84, 99, 100a and 100b and without prejudice to the other provisions of this Treaty.

The internal market shall comprise an area without internal frontiers in which the free movement of goods, persons, services and capital is ensured in accordance with the provisions of this Treaty.

Article 7b
The Commission shall report to the Council before 31 December 1988 and again before 31 December 1990 on the progress made towards achieving the internal market within the time limit fixed in Article 7a.

The Council, acting by a qualified majority on a proposal from the Commission, shall determine the guidelines and conditions necessary to ensure balanced progress in all the sectors concerned.

Article 7c
When drawing up its proposals with a view to achieving the objectives set out in Article 7a, the Commission shall take into account the extent of the effort that certain economies showing differences in development will have to sustain during the period of establishment of the internal market and it may propose appropriate provisions.

If these provisions take the form of derogations, they must be of a temporary nature and must cause the least possible disturbance to the functioning of the common market.

PART TWO
(CITIZENSHIP OF THE UNION)

Article 8
1. Citizenship of the Union is hereby established.

Every person holding the nationality of a Member State shall be a citizen of the Union.

2. Citizens of the Union shall enjoy the rights conferred by this Treaty and shall be subject to the duties imposed thereby.

* * * * *

CHAPTER 2—(ELIMINATION OF QUANTITATIVE RESTRICTIONS BETWEEN MEMBER STATES)

Article 30
Quantitative restrictions on imports and all measures having equivalent effect shall, without prejudice to the following provisions, be prohibited between Member States.

* * * * *

Article 36
The provisions of Articles 30 to 34 shall not preclude prohibitions or restrictions on imports, exports or goods in transit justified on grounds of public morality, public policy or public security; the protection of health and life of humans, animals or plants; the protection of national treasures possessing artistic, historic or archaeological value; or the protection of industrial and commercial property. Such prohibitions or restrictions shall not, however, constitute a means of arbitrary discrimination or a disguised restriction on trade between Member States.

★ ★ ★ ★ ★

TITLE III
FREE MOVEMENT OF PERSONS, SERVICES AND CAPITAL

CHAPTER 1—(WORKERS)

Article 48
1. Freedom of movement for workers shall be secured within the Community by the end of the transitional period at the latest.
2. Such freedom of movement shall entail the abolition of any discrimination based on nationality between workers of the Member States as regards employment, remuneration and other conditions of work and employment.
3. It shall entail the right, subject to limitations justified on grounds of public policy, public security or public health:
   (a) to accept offers of employment actually made;
   (b) to move freely within the territory of Member States for this purpose;
   (c) to stay in a Member State for the purpose of employment in accordance with the provisions governing the employment of nationals of that State laid down by law, regulation or administrative action;
   (d) to remain in the territory of a Member State after having been employed in that State, subject to conditions which shall be embodied in implementing regulations to be drawn up by the Commission.
4. The provisions of this Article shall not apply to employment in the public service.

★ ★ ★ ★ ★

CHAPTER 2—(RIGHT OF ESTABLISHMENT)

Article 52
Within the framework of the provisions set out below, restrictions on the freedom of establishment of nationals of a Member State in the territory of another Member State shall be abolished by progressive stages in the course of the transitional period. Such progressive abolition shall also apply to restrictions on the setting up of agencies, branches or subsidiaries by nationals of any Member State established in the territory of any Member State.

Freedom of establishment shall include the right to take up and pursue activities as self-employed persons and to set up and manage undertakings, in particular companies or firms within the meaning of the second paragraph of Article 58, under the conditions laid down for its own nationals by the law of the country where such establishment is effected, subject to the provisions of the Chapter relating to capital.

★ ★ ★ ★ ★

Article 58
Companies or firms formed in accordance with the law of a Member State and having their registered office, central administration or principal place of business within the

Community shall, for the purposes of this Chapter, be treated in the same way as natural persons who are nationals of Member States.

"Companies or firms" means companies or firms constituted under civil or commercial law, including co-operative societies, and other legal persons governed by public or private law, save for those which are non-profit-making.

CHAPTER 3—(SERVICES)

Article 59

Within the framework of the provisions set out below, restrictions on freedom to provide services within the Community shall be progressively abolished during the transitional period in respect of nationals of Member States who are established in a State of the Community other than that of the person for whom the services are intended.

The Council may, acting by a qualified majority on a proposal from the Commission, extend the provisions of the Chapter to nationals of a third country who provide services and who are established within the Community.

Article 60

Services shall be considered to be "services" within the meaning of this Treaty where they are normally provided for remuneration, in so far as they are not governed by the provisions relating to freedom of movement for goods, capital and persons.

"Services" shall in particular include:

(a) activities of an industrial character;

(b) activities of a commercial character;

(c) activities of craftsmen;

(d) activities of the professions.

Without prejudice to the provisions of the Chapter relating to the right of establishment, the person providing a service may, in order to do so, temporarily pursue his activity in the State where the service is provided, under the same conditions as are imposed by that State on its own nationals.

★★★★★

TITLE V
COMMON RULES ON COMPETITION, TAXATION AND APPROXIMATION OF LAWS

CHAPTER 1—(RULES ON COMPETITION)

Section 1—Rules applying to undertakings

Article 85

1. The following shall be prohibited as incompatible with the common market: all agreements between undertakings, decisions by associations of undertakings and concerted practices which may affect trade between Member States and which have as their object or effect the prevention, restriction or distortion of competition within the common market, and in particular those which:

(a) directly or indirectly fix purchase or selling prices or any other trading conditions;

(b) limit or control production, markets, technical development, or investment;

(c) share markets or sources of supply;

(d) apply dissimilar conditions to equivalent transactions with other trading parties, thereby placing them at a competitive disadvantage;

(e) make the conclusion of contracts subject to acceptance by the other parties of supplementary obligations which, by their nature or according to commercial usage, have no connection with the subject of such contracts.

2. Any agreements or decisions prohibited pursuant to this Article shall be automatically void.

3. The provisions of paragraph 1 may, however, be declared inapplicable in the case of:

— any agreement or category of agreements between undertakings;
— any decision or category of decisions by associations of undertakings;
— any concerted practice or category of concerted practices;

which contributes to improving the production or distribution of goods or to promoting technical or economic progress, while allowing consumers a fair share of the resulting benefit, and which does not:

(a) impose on the undertakings concerned restrictions which are not indispensable to the attainment of these objectives;

(b) afford such undertakings the possibility of eliminating competition in respect of a substantial part of the products in question.

Article 86

Any abuse by one or more undertakings of a dominant position within the common market or in a substantial part of it shall be prohibited as incompatible with the common market in so far as it may affect trade between Member States.

Such abuse may, in particular, consist in:

(a) directly or indirectly imposing unfair purchase or selling prices or other unfair trading conditions;

(b) limiting production, markets or technical development to the prejudice of consumers;

(c) applying dissimilar conditions to equivalent transactions with other trading parties, thereby placing them at a competitive disadvantage;

(d) making the conclusion of contracts subject to acceptance by the other parties of supplementary obligations which, by their nature or according to commercial usage, have no connection with the subject of such contracts.

★ ★ ★ ★ ★

CHAPTER 3—(APPROXIMATION OF LAWS)

Article 100

The Council shall, acting unanimously on a proposal from the Commission and after consulting the European Parliament and the Economic and Social Committee, issue directives for the approximation of such laws, regulations or administrative provisions of the Member States as directly affect the establishment or functioning of the common market.

Article 100a

1. By way of derogation from Article 100 and save where otherwise provided in this Treaty, the following provisions shall apply for the achievement of the objectives set out in Article 7a. The Council shall, acting in accordance with the procedure referred to in Article 189b and after consulting the Economic and Social Committee, adopt the measures for the approximation of the provisions laid down by law, regulation or administrative action in Member States which have as their object the establishment and functioning of the internal market.

2. Paragraph 1 shall not apply to fiscal provisions, to those relating to the free movement of persons nor to those relating to the rights and interests of employed persons.

3. The Commission, in its proposals envisaged in paragraph 1 concerning health, safety, environmental protection and consumer protection, will take as a base a high level of protection.

4. If, after the adoption of a harmonisation measure by the Council acting by a qualified majority, a Member State deems it necessary to apply national provisions on grounds of major needs referred to in Article 36, or relating to protection of the environment or the working environment, it shall notify the Commission of these provisions.

The Commission shall confirm the provisions involved after having verified that they are not a means of arbitrary discrimination or a disguised restriction on trade between Member States.

★ ★ ★ ★ ★

TITLE VIII
SOCIAL POLICY, EDUCATION, VOCATIONAL TRAINING AND YOUTH

Note This part of the Treaty (Arts. 117 to 122) is supplemented in relation to all Member States except the UK by the Protocol on Social Policy (below). This part remains in force as between all 15 Member States.

CHAPTER 1—(SOCIAL PROVISIONS)

Article 117

Member States agree upon the need to promote improved working conditions and an improved standard of living for workers, so as to make possible their harmonisation while the improvement is being maintained.

They believe that such a development will ensue not only from the functioning of the common market, which will favour the harmonisation of social systems, but also from the procedures provided for in this Treaty and from the approximation of provisions laid down by law, regulation or administrative action.

Article 118

Without prejudice to the other provisions of this Treaty and in conformity with its general objectives, the Commission shall have the task of promoting close co-operation between Member States in the social field, particularly in matters relating to:

— employment;
— labour law and working conditions;
— basic and advanced vocational training;
— social security;
— prevention of occupational accidents and diseases;
— occupational hygiene;
— the right of association, and collective bargaining between employers and workers.

To this end, the Commission shall act in close contact with Member States by making studies, delivering opinions and arranging consultations both on problems arising at national level and on those of concern to international organisations.

Before delivering the opinions provided for in this Article, the Commission shall consult the Economic and Social Committee.

Article 118a

1. Member States shall pay particular attention to encouraging improvements, especially in the working environment, as regards the health and safety of workers, and shall set as their objective the harmonisation of conditions in this area, while maintaining the improvements made.

2. In order to help achieve the objective laid down in the first paragraph, the Council, acting in accordance with the procedure referred to in Article 189c and after consulting the Economic and Social Committee, shall adopt, by means of directives, minimum requirements for gradual implementation, having regard to the conditions and technical rules obtaining in each of the Member States.

Such directives shall avoid imposing administrative, financial and legal contraints in a way which would hold back the creation and development of small and medium-sized undertakings.

3. The provisions adopted pursuant to this Article shall not prevent any Member State from maintaining or introducing more stringent measures for the protection of working conditions compatible with this Treaty.

Article 118b

The Commission shall endeavour to develop the dialogue between management and labour at European level which could, if the two sides consider it desirable, lead to relations based on agreement.

Article 119

Each Member State shall during the first stage ensure and subsequently maintain the application of the principle that men and women should receive equal pay for equal work.

For the purpose of this Article, "pay" means the ordinary basic or minimum wage or salary and any other consideration, whether in cash or in kind, which the worker receives, directly or indirectly, in respect of his employment from his employer.

Equal pay without discrimination based on sex means:

(a) that pay for the same work at piece rates shall be calculated on the basis of the same unit of measurement;

(b) that pay for work at time rates shall be the same for the same job.

Arts. 120-122 ★★★★★

TITLE XIII INDUSTRY

Article 130

1. The Community and the Member States shall ensure that the conditions necessary for the competitiveness of the Community's industry exist.

For that purpose, in accordance with a system of open and competitive markets, their action shall be aimed at:

—speeding up the adjustment of industry to structural changes;

—encouraging an environment favourable to initiative and to the development of undertakings throughout the Community, particularly small and medium-sized undertakings;

—encouraging an environment favourable to co-operation between undertakings;

—fostering better exploitation of the industrial potential of policies of innovation, research and technological development.

2. The Member States shall consult each other in liaison with the Commission and, where necessary, shall co-ordinate their action. The Commission may take any useful initiative to promote such co-ordination.

3. The Community shall contribute to the achievement of the objectives set out in paragraph 1 through the policies and activities it pursues under other provisions of this Treaty. The Council, acting unanimously on a proposal from the Commission, after consulting the European Parliament and the Economic and Social Committee, may decide on specific measures in support of action taken in the Member States to achieve the objectives set out in paragraph 1.

This Title shall not provide a basis for the introduction by the Community of any measure which could lead to a distortion of competition.

★★★★★

PART FIVE
(INSTITUTIONS OF THE COMMUNITY)
TITLE I: PROVISIONS GOVERNING THE INSTITUTIONS

CHAPTER 1—(THE INSTITUTIONS)

Section 1—The European Parliament

Article 137

The European Parliament, which shall consist of representatives of the peoples of the States brought together in the Community, shall exercise the powers conferred upon it by this Treaty.

Article 138

1. The representatives in the European Parliament of the peoples of the States brought together in the Community shall be elected by direct universal suffrage.
2. The number of representatives elected in each Member State is as follows:

[Belgium	25
Denmark	16
Germany	99
Greece	25
Spain	64
France	87
Ireland	15
Italy	87
Luxembourg	6
Netherlands	31
[Austria	21]
Portugal	25
[Finland	16
Sweden	22]
United Kingdom	87]

3. The European Parliament shall draw up proposals for elections by direct universal suffrage in accordance with a uniform procedure in all Member States.

The Council shall, acting unanimously after obtaining the assent of the European Parliament, which shall act by a majority of its component members, lay down the appropriate provisions, which it shall recommend to Member States for adoption in accordance with their respective constitutional requirements.

Article 138a

Political parties at European level are important as a factor for integration within the Union. They contribute to forming a European awareness and to expressing the political will of the citizens of the Union.

Article 138b

In so far as provided in this Treaty, the European Parliament shall participate in the process leading up to the adoption of Community acts by exercising its powers under the procedures laid down in Articles 189b and 189c and by giving its assent or delivering advisory opinions. The European Parliament may, acting by a majority of its members, request the Commission to submit any appropriate proposal on matters on which it considers that a Community act is required for the purpose of implementing this Treaty.

Article 138c

In the course of its duties, the European Parliament may, at the request of a quarter of its members, set up a temporary Committee of Inquiry to investigate, without prejudice to the powers conferred by this Treaty on other institutions or bodies, alleged contraventions or maladministration in the implementation of Community law, except where the alleged facts are being examined before a court and while the case is still subject to legal proceedings.

The temporary Committee of Inquiry shall cease to exist on the submission of its report.

The detailed provisions governing the exercise of the right of inquiry shall be determined by common accord of the European Parliament, the Council and the Commission.

Article 138d

Any citizen of the Union, and any natural or legal person residing or having its registered office in a Member State, shall have the right to address, individually or in association with other citizens or persons, a petition to the European Parliament on a matter which comes within the Community's fields of activity and which affects him, her or it directly.

Article 138e

1. The European Parliament shall appoint an Ombudsman empowered to receive complaints from any citizen of the Union or any natural or legal person residing or having its registered office in a Member State concerning instances of maladministration in the activities of the Community institutions or bodies, with the exception of the Court of Justice and the Court of First Instance acting in their judicial role.

In accordance with his duties, the Ombudsman shall conduct inquiries for which he finds grounds, either on his own initiative or on the basis of complaints submitted to him direct or through a member of the European Parliament, except where the alleged facts are or have been the subject of legal proceedings. Where the Ombudsman establishes an instance of maladministration, he shall refer the matter to the institution concerned, which shall have a period of three months in which to inform him of its views.

The Ombudsman shall then forward a report to the European Parliament and the institution concerned. The person lodging the complaint shall be informed of the outcome of such inquiries.

The Ombudsman shall submit an annual report to the European Parliament on the outcome of his inquiries.

2. The Ombudsman shall be appointed after each election of the European Parliament for the duration of its term of office. The Ombudsman shall be eligible for re-appointment.

The Ombudsman may be dismissed by the Court of Justice at the request of the European Parliament if he no longer fulfils the conditions required for the performance of his duties or if he is guilty of serious misconduct.

3. The Ombudsman shall be completely independent in the performance of his duties. In the performance of those duties he shall neither seek nor take instructions from any body.

The Ombudsman may not, during his term of office, engage in any other occupation, whether gainful or not.

4. The European Parliament shall, after seeking an opinion from the Commission and with the approval of the Council acting by a qualified majority, lay down the regulation and general conditions governing the performance of the Ombudsman's duties.

Article 139

The European Parliament shall hold an annual session. It shall meet, without requiring to be convened, on the second Tuesday in March.

The European Parliament may meet in extraordinary session at the request of a majority of its members or at the request of the Council or of the Commission.

Article 140

The European Parliament shall elect its President and its officers from among its members.

Members of the Commission may attend all meetings and shall, at their request, be heard on behalf of the Commission.

The Commission shall reply orally or in writing to questions put to it by the European Parliament or by its members.

The Council shall be heard by the European Parliament in accordance with the conditions laid down by the Council in its rules of procedure.

Article 141

Save as otherwise provided in this Treaty, the European Parliament shall act by an absolute majority of the votes cast.

The rules of procedure shall determine the quorum.

Article 142

The European Parliament shall adopt its rules of procedure, acting by a majority of its members.

The proceedings of the European Parliament shall be published in the manner laid down in its rules of procedure.

Article 143

The European Parliament shall discuss in open session the annual general report submitted to it by the Commission.

Article 144

If a motion of censure on the activities of the Commission is tabled before it, the European Parliament shall not vote thereon until at least three days after the motion has been tabled and only by open vote.

If the motion of censure is carried by a two-third majority of the votes cast, representing a majority of the members of the European Parliament, the members of the Commission shall resign as a body. They shall continue to deal with current business until they are replaced in accordance with Article 158. In this case, the term of office of the members of the Commission appointed to replace them shall expire on the date on which the term of office of the members of the Commission obliged to resign as a body would have expired.

Section 2—The Council

Article 145

To ensure that the objectives set out in the Treaty are attained, the Council shall, in accordance with the provisions of this Treaty:

—ensure co-ordination of the general economic policies of the Member States;

—have power to take decisions;

—confer on the Commission, in the acts which the Council adopts, powers for the implementation of the rules which the Council lays down. The Council may impose certain requirements in respect of the exercise of these powers. The Council may also reserve the right, in specific cases, to exercise directly implementing powers itself. The procedures referred to above must be consonant with principles and rules to be laid down in advance by the Council, acting unanimously on a proposal from the Commission and after obtaining the Opinion of the European Parliament.

★ ★ ★ ★ ★

Article 148

1. Save as otherwise provided in this Treaty, the Council shall act by a majority of its members.

2. Where the Council is required to act by a qualified majority, the votes of its members shall be weighted as follows:

Belgium	5
Denmark	3
Germany	10
Greece	5
Spain	8
France	10
Ireland	3
Italy	10
Luxembourg	2
Netherlands	5
[Austria	4]
Portugal	5
[Finland	3
Sweden	4]
United Kingdom	10

For their adoption, acts of the Council shall require at least:

— [62] votes in favour where this Treaty requires them to be adopted on a proposal from the Commission,

— [62] votes in favour, cast by at least [10] members, in other cases.

3. Abstentions by members present in person or represented shall not prevent the adoption by the Council of acts which require unanimity.

* * * * *

Section 3—The Commission

Article 155

In order to ensure the proper functioning and development of the common market, the Commission shall:

— ensure that the provisions of this Treaty and the measures taken by the institutions pursuant thereto are applied;

— formulate recommendations or deliver opinions on matters dealt with in this Treaty, if it expressly so provides or if the Commission considers it necessary;

— have its own power of decision and participate in the shaping of measures taken by the Council and by the European Parliament in the manner provided for in this Treaty;

— exercise the powers conferred on it by the Council for the implementation of the rules laid down by the latter.

* * * * *

Section 4—The Court of Justice

Article 164

The Court of Justice shall ensure that in the interpretation and application of this Treaty the law is observed.

Article 165

The Court of Justice shall consist of [15] Judges.

The Court of Justice shall sit in plenary session. It may, however, form chambers, each consisting of three [, five or seven] Judges, either to undertake certain preparatory inquiries or to adjudicate on particular categories of cases in accordance with rules laid down for these purposes.

The Court of Justice shall sit in plenary session when a Member State or a Community institution that is a party to the proceedings so requests. Should the Court of Justice so request, the Council may, acting unanimously, increase the number of Judges and make the necessary adjustments to the second and third paragraphs of this Article and to the second paragraph of Article 167.

Article 166

[The Court of Justice shall be assisted by eight Advocates General. However a ninth Advocate-General shall be appointed as from the date of accession until 6 October 2000.]

It shall be the duty of the Advocate-General, acting with complete impartiality and independence, to make, in open court, reasoned submissions on cases brought before the Court of Justice, in order to assist the Court in the performance of the task assigned to it in Article 164.

Should the Court of Justice so request, the Council may, acting unanimously, increase the number of Advocates General and make the necessary adjustments to the third paragraph of Article 167.

Article 167

The Judges and Advocates General shall be chosen from persons whose independence is beyond doubt and who possess the qualifications required for appointment to the highest judicial offices in their respective countries or who are jurisconsults of recognised competence; they shall be appointed by common accord of the Governments of the Member States for a term of six years.

Every three years there shall be a partial replacement of the Judges. [Eight and seven Judges shall be replaced alternately.]

Every three years there shall be a partial replacement of the Advocates General. [Four] Advocates General shall be replaced on each occasion.

Retiring Judges and Advocates General shall be eligible for reappointment.

The Judges shall elect the President of the Court of Justice from among their number for a term of three years. He may be re-elected.

Article 168

The Court of Justice shall appoint its Registrar and lay down the rules governing his service.

Article 168a

1. A Court of First Instance shall be attached to the Court of Justice with jurisdiction to hear and determine at first instance, subject to a right of appeal to the Court of Justice on points of law only and in accordance with the conditions laid down by the Statute, certain classes of action or proceedings defined in accordance with the conditions laid down in paragraph 2. The Court of First Instance shall not be competent to hear and determine questions referred for a preliminary ruling under Article 177.

2. At the request of the Court of Justice and after consulting the European Parliament and the Commission, the Council, acting unanimously, shall determine the classes of action or proceeding referred to in paragraph 1 and the composition of the Court of First Instance and shall adopt the necessary adjustments and additional provisions to the Statute of the Court of Justice. Unless the Council decides otherwise, the provisions of this Treaty relating to the Court of Justice, in particular the provisions of the Protocol on the Statute of the Court of Justice, shall apply to the Court of First Instance.

3. The members of the Court of First Instance shall be chosen from persons whose independence is beyond doubt and who possess the ability required for appointment to judicial office; they shall be appointed by common accord of the governments of the Member States for a term of six years. The membership shall be partially renewed every three years. Retiring members shall be eligible for re-appointment.

4. The Court of First Instance shall establish its rules of procedure in agreement with the Court of Justice. Those rules shall require the unanimous approval of the Council.

Article 169

If the Commission considers that a Member State has failed to fulfil an obligation under this Treaty, it shall deliver a reasoned opinion on the matter after giving the State concerned the opportunity to submit its observations.

If the State concerned does not comply with the opinion within the period laid down by the Commission, the latter may bring the matter before the Court of Justice.

Article 170

A Member State which considers that another Member State has failed to fulfil an obligation under this Treaty may bring the matter before the Court of Justice.

Before a Member State brings an action against another Member State for an alleged infringement of an obligation under this Treaty, it shall bring the matter before the Commission.

The Commission shall deliver a reasoned opinion after each of the States concerned has been given the opportunity to submit its own case and its observations on the other party's case both orally and in writing.

If the Commission has not delivered an opinion within three months of the date on which the matter was brought before it, the absence of such opinion shall not prevent the matter from being brought before the Court of Justice.

Article 171

1. If the Court of Justice finds that a Member State has failed to fulfil an obligation under this Treaty, the State shall be required to take the necessary measures to comply with the judgment of the Court of Justice.

2. If the Commission considers that the Member State concerned has not taken such measures it shall, after giving that State the opportunity to submit its observations, issue a reasoned opinion specifying the points on which the Member State concerned has not complied with the judgment of the Court of Justice. If the Member State concerned fails to take the necessary measures to comply with the Court's judgment within the time-limit laid down by the Commission, the latter may bring the case before the Court of Justice. In so doing it shall specify the amount of the lump sum or penalty payment to be paid by the Member State concerned which it considers appropriate in the circumstances. If the Court of Justice finds that the Member State concerned has not complied with its judgment it may impose a lump sum or penalty payment on it. This procedure shall be without prejudice to Article 170.

Article 172

Regulations adopted jointly by the European Parliament and the Council, and by the Council, pursuant to the provisions of this Treaty, may give the Court of Justice unlimited jurisdiction with regard to the penalties provided for in such regulations.

Article 173

The Court of Justice shall review the legality of acts adopted jointly by the European Parliament and the Council, of acts of the Council, of the Commission and of the ECB, other than recommendations and opinions, and of acts of the European Parliament intended to produce legal effects *vis-à-vis* third parties.

It shall for this purpose have jurisdiction in actions brought by a Member State, the Council or the Commission on grounds of lack of competence, infringement of an essential procedural requirement, infringement of this Treaty or of any rule of law relating to its application, or misuse of powers.

The Court shall have jurisdiction under the same conditions in actions brought by the European Parliament and by the ECB for the purpose of protecting their prerogatives.

Any natural or legal person may, under the same conditions, institute proceedings against a decision addressed to that person or against a decision which, although in the form of a regulation or a decision addressed to another person, is of direct and individual concern to the former.

The proceedings provided for in this Article shall be instituted within two months of the publication of the measure, or of its notification to the plaintiff, or, in the absence thereof, of the day on which it came to the knowledge of the latter, as the case may be.

Article 174

If the action is well founded, the Court of Justice shall declare the act concerned to be void.

In the case of a regulation, however, the Court of Justice shall, if it considers this necessary, state which of the effects of the regulation which it has declared void shall be considered as definitive.

★ ★ ★ ★ ★

Article 177

The Court of Justice shall have jurisdiction to give preliminary rulings concerning:

(a) the interpretation of this Treaty;

(b) the validity and interpretation of acts of the institutions of the Community and of the ECB;

(c) the interpretation of the statutes of bodies established by an act of the Council, where those statutes so provide.

Where such a question is raised before any court or tribunal of a Member State, that court or tribunal may, if it considers that a decision on the question is necessary to enable it to give judgment, request the Court of Justice to give a ruling thereon.

Where any such question is raised in a case pending before a court or tribunal of a Member State against whose decisions there is no judicial remedy under national law, that court or tribunal shall bring the matter before the Court of Justice.

★ ★ ★ ★ ★

CHAPTER 2—(PROVISIONS COMMON TO SEVERAL INSTITUTIONS)

Article 189

In order to carry out their task and in accordance with the provisions of this Treaty, the European Parliament acting jointly with the Council, the Council and the Commission shall make regulations and issue directives, take decisions, make recommendations or deliver opinions.

A regulation shall have general application. It shall be binding in its entirety and directly applicable in all Member States.

A directive shall be binding, as to the result to be achieved, upon each Member State to which it is addressed, but shall leave to the national authorities the choice of form and methods.

A decision shall be binding in its entirety upon those to whom it is addressed.

Recommendations and opinions shall have no binding force.

Article 189a

1. Where, in pursuance of this Treaty, the Council acts on a proposal from the Commission, unanimity shall be required for an act constituting an amendment to that proposal, subject to Article 189b(4) and (5).

2. As long as the Council has not acted, the Commission may alter its proposal at any time during the procedures leading to the adoption of a Community act.

Article 189b

1. Where reference is made in this Treaty to this Article for the adoption of an act, the following procedure shall apply.

2. The Commission shall submit a proposal to the European Parliament and the Council.

The Council, acting by a qualified majority after obtaining the Opinion of the European Parliament, shall adopt a common position. The common position shall be communicated to the European Parliament. The Council shall inform the European Parliament fully of the reasons which led it to adopt its common position. The Commission shall inform the European Parliament fully of its position.

If, within three months of such communication, the European Parliament:

(a) approves the common position, the Council shall definitively adopt the act in question in accordance with that common position;

(b) has not taken a decision, the Council shall adopt the act in question in accordance with its common position;

(c) indicates, by an absolute majority of its component members, that it intends to reject the common position, it shall immediately inform the Council. The Council may convene a meeting of the Conciliation Committee referred to in paragraph 3 to explain further its position. The European Parliament shall thereafter either confirm, by an absolute majority of its component members, its rejection of the common position, in which event the proposed act shall be deemed not to have been adopted, or propose amendments in accordance with subparagraph (d) of this paragraph;

(d) proposes amendments to the common position by an absolute majority of its component members, the amended text shall be forwarded to the Council and to the Commission, which shall deliver an opinion on those amendments.

3. If, within three months of the matter being referred to it, the Council, acting by a qualified majority, approves all the amendments of the European Parliament, it shall amend its common position accordingly and adopt the act in question; however, the Council shall act unanimously on the amendments on which the Commission has delivered a negative opinion. If the Council does not approve the act in question, the President of the Council, in agreement with the President of the European Parliament, shall forthwith convene a meeting of the Conciliation Committee.

4. The Conciliation Committee, which shall be composed of the members of the Council or their representatives and an equal number of representatives of the European Parliament, shall have the task of reaching agreement on a joint text, by a qualified majority of the members of the Council or their representatives and by a majority of the representatives of the European Parliament. The Commission shall take part in the Conciliation Committee's proceedings and shall take all the necessary initiatives with a view to reconciling the positions of the European Parliament and the Council.

5. If, within six weeks of its being convened, the Conciliation Committee approves a joint text, the European Parliament, acting by an absolute majority of the votes cast, and the Council, acting by a qualified majority, shall have a period of six weeks from that approval in which to adopt the act in question in accordance with the joint text. If one of the two institutions fails to approve the proposed act, it shall be deemed not to have been adopted.

6. Where the Conciliation Committee does not approve a joint text, the proposed act shall be deemed not to have been adopted unless the Council, acting by a qualified majority within six weeks of expiry of the period granted to the Conciliation Committee, confirms the common position to which it agreed before the conciliation procedure was initiated, possibly with amendments proposed by the European Parliament. In this case, the act in question shall be finally adopted unless the European Parliament, within six weeks of the date of confirmation by the Council, rejects the text by an absolute majority of its component members, in which case the proposed act shall be deemed not to have been adopted.

7. The periods of three months and six weeks referred to in this Article may be extended by a maximum of one month and two weeks respectively by common accord of the European Parliament and the Council. The period of three months referred to in

paragraph 2 shall be automatically extended by two months where paragraph 2(c) applies.

8. The scope of the procedure under this Article may be widened, in accordance with the procedure provided for in Article N(2) of the Treaty on European Union, on the basis of a report to be submitted to the Council by the Commission by 1996 at the latest.

Article 189c

Where reference is made in this Treaty to this Article for the adoption of an act, the following procedure shall apply:

(a) The Council, acting by a qualified majority on a proposal from the Commission and after obtaining the Opinion of the European Parliament, shall adopt a common position.

(b) The Council's common position shall be communicated to the European Parliament. The Council and the Commission shall inform the European Parliament fully of the reasons which led the Council to adopt its common position and also of the Commission's position.

If, within three months of such communication, the European Parliament approves this common position or has not taken a decision within that period, the Council shall definitively adopt the act in question in accordance with the common position.

(c) The European Parliament may, within the period of three months referred to in point (b), by an absolute majority of its component members, propose amendments to the Council's common position.

The European Parliament may also, by the same majority, reject the Council's common position. The result of the proceedings shall be transmitted to the Council and the Commission.

If the European Parliament has rejected the Council's common position, unanimity shall be required for the Council to act on a second reading.

(d) The Commission shall, within a period of one month, re-examine the proposal on the basis of which the Council adopted its common position, by taking into account the amendments proposed by the European Parliament.

The Commission shall forward to the Council, at the same time as its re-examined proposal, the amendments of the European Parliament which it has not accepted, and shall express its opinion on them. The Council may adopt these amendments unanimously.

(e) The Council, acting by a qualified majority, shall adopt the proposal as re-examined by the Commission.

Unanimity shall be required for the Council to amend the proposal as re-examined by the Commission.

(f) In the cases referred to in points (c), (d) and (e), the Council shall be required to act within a period of three months. If no decision is taken within this period, the Commission proposal shall be deemed not to have been adopted.

(g) The periods referred to in points (b) and (f) may be extended by a maximum of one month by common accord between the Council and the European Parliament.

★ ★ ★ ★ ★

CHAPTER 3—(THE ECONOMIC AND SOCIAL COMMITTEE)

Article 193

An Economic and Social Committee is hereby established. It shall have advisory status.

The Committee shall consist of representatives of the various categories of economic and social activity, in particular, representatives of producers, farmers, carriers, workers, dealers, craftsmen, professional occupations and representatives of the general public.

Article 194
The number of members of the Committee shall be as follows:

Belgium	12
Denmark	9
Germany	24
Greece	12
Spain	21
France	24
Ireland	9
Italy	24
Luxembourg	6
Netherlands	12
[Austria	12]
Portugal	12
[Finland	9
Sweden	12]
United Kingdom	24

The members of the Committee shall be appointed by the Council, acting unanimously, for four years. Their appointments shall be renewable. The members of the Committee may not be bound by any mandatory instructions. They shall be completely independent in the performance of their duties, in the general interest of the Community. The Council, acting by a qualified majority, shall determine the allowances of members of the Committee.

★ ★ ★ ★ ★

Article 235
If action by the Community should prove necessary to attain, in the course of the operation of the common market, one of the objectives of the Community and this Treaty has not provided the necessary powers, the Council shall, acting unanimously on a proposal from the Commission and after consulting the European Parliament, take the appropriate measures.

★ ★ ★ ★ ★

Article 239
The Protocols annexed to this Treaty by common accord of the Member States shall form an integral part thereof.

Article 240
This Treaty is concluded for an unlimited period.

TREATY ON EUROPEAN UNION

ADOPTED BY THE EU MEMBER STATES

(Done at Maastricht) 7 February 1992

Entry into force: 1 November 1993

Territorial application: EU Member States

TITLE I
COMMON PROVISIONS

Article A
By this Treaty, the High Contracting Parties establish among themselves a European Union, hereinafter called "the Union".

This Treaty marks a new stage in the process of creating an ever closer union among the peoples of Europe, in which decisions are taken as closely as possible to the citizen.

The Union shall be founded on the European Communities, supplemented by the policies and forms of co-operation established by this Treaty. Its task shall be to organise, in a manner demonstrating consistency and solidarity, relations between the Member States and between their peoples.

Article B

The Union shall set itself the following objectives:

—to promote economic and social progress which is balanced and sustainable, in particular through the creation of an area without internal frontiers, through the strengthening of economic and social cohesion and through the establishment of economic and monetary union, ultimately including a single currency in accordance with the provisions of this Treaty;

—to assert its identity on the international scene, in particular through the implementation of a common foreign and security policy including the eventual framing of a common defence policy, which might in time lead to a common defence;

—to strengthen the protection of the rights and interests of the nationals of its Member States through the introduction of a citizenship of the Union;

—to develop close co-operation on justice and home affairs;

—to maintain in full the "*acquis communautaire*" and build on it with a view to considering, through the procedure referred to in Article N(2), to what extent the policies and forms of co-operation introduced by this Treaty may need to be revised with the aim of ensuring the effectiveness of the mechanisms and the institutions of the Community.

The objectives of the Union shall be achieved as provided in this Treaty and in accordance with the conditions and the timetable set out therein while respecting the principle of subsidiarity as defined in Article 3b of the Treaty establishing the European Community.

Article C

The Union shall be served by a single institutional framework which shall ensure the consistency and the continuity of the activities carried out in order to attain its objectives while respecting and building upon the "*acquis communautaire*".

The Union shall in particular ensure the consistency of its external activities as a whole in the context of its external relations, security, economic and development policies. The Council and the Commission shall be responsible for ensuring such consistency. They shall ensure the implementation of these policies, each in accordance with its respective powers.

Article D

The European Council shall provide the Union with the necessary impetus for its development and shall define the general political guidelines thereof.

The European Council shall bring together the Heads of State or of Government of the Member States and the President of the Commission.

They shall be assisted by the Ministers for Foreign Affairs of the Member States and by a Member of the Commission. The European Council shall meet at least twice a year, under the chairmanship of the Head of State or of Government of the Member State which holds the Presidency of the Council.

The European Council shall submit to the European Parliament a report after each of its meetings and a yearly written report on the progress achieved by the Union.

Article E

The European Parliament, the Council, the Commission and the Court of Justice shall exercise their powers under the conditions and for the purposes provided for, on the one hand, by the provisions of the Treaties establishing the European Communities and of the subsequent Treaties and Acts modifying and supplementing them and, on the other hand, by the other provisions of this Treaty.

Article F

1. The Union shall respect the national identities of its Member States, whose systems of government are founded on the principles of democracy.

2. The Union shall respect fundamental rights, as guaranteed by the European Convention for the Protection of Human Rights and Fundamental Freedoms signed in Rome on 4 November 1950 and as they result from the constitutional traditions common to the Member States, as general principles of Community law.

3. The Union shall provide itself with the means necessary to attain its objectives and carry through its policies.

★ ★ ★ ★ ★

TITLE VI
PROVISIONS ON CO-OPERATION IN THE FIELDS OF JUSTICE AND HOME AFFAIRS

Article K

Co-operation in the fields of justice and home affairs shall be governed by the following provisions.

Article K.1

For the purposes of achieving the objectives of the Union, in particular the free movement of persons, and without prejudice to the powers of the European Community, Member States shall regard the following areas as matters of common interest:

1. asylum policy;
2. rules governing the crossing by persons of the external borders of the Member States and the exercise of controls thereon;
3. immigration policy and policy regarding nationals of third countries:
   (a) conditions of entry and movement by nationals of third countries to the territory of Member States;
   (b) conditions of residence by nationals of third countries on the territory of Member States, including family reunion and access to employment;
   (c) combating unauthorised immigration, residence and work by nationals of third countries on the territory of Member States;
4. combating drug addiction in so far as this is not covered by 7 to 9;
5. combating fraud on an international scale in so far as this is not covered by 7 to 9;
6. judicial co-operation in civil matters;
7. judicial co-operation in criminal matters;
8. customs co-operation;
9. police co-operation for the purposes of preventing and combating terrorism, unlawful drug trafficking and other serious forms of international crime, including if necessary certain aspects of customs co-operation, in connection with the organisation of a Union-wide system for exchanging information within a European Policy Office (Europol).

Article K.2

1. The matters referred to in Article K.1 shall be dealt with in compliance with the European Convention for the Protection of Human Rights and Fundamental Freedoms of 4 November 1950 and the Convention relating to the Status of Refugees of 28 July 1951 and having regard to the protection afforded by Member States to persons persecuted on political grounds.

2. This Title shall not affect the exercise of the responsibilities incumbent upon Member States with regard to the maintenance of law and order and the safeguarding of internal security.

★ ★ ★ ★ ★

PROTOCOLS

PROTOCOL ON CERTAIN PROVISIONS RELATING TO THE UNITED KINGDOM OF GREAT BRITAIN AND NORTHERN IRELAND

(Annexed to EC Treaty)

Note This Protocol has been adopted by the 3 new member States, Austria, Finland and Sweden

THE HIGH CONTRACTING PARTIES,

RECOGNISING that the United Kingdom shall not be obliged or committed to move to the third stage of Economic and Monetary Union without a separate decision to do so by its government and Parliament,

NOTING the practice of the government of the United Kingdom to fund its borrowing requirement by the sale of debt to the private sector,

HAVE AGREED the following provisions,

1. The United Kingdom shall notify the Council whether it intends to move to the third stage before the Council makes its assessment under Article 109j(2) of this Treaty. Unless the United Kingdom notifies the Council that it intends to move to the third stage, it shall be under no obligation to do so.

If no date is set for the beginning of the third stage under Article 109j(3) of this Treaty, the United Kingdom may notify its intention to move to the third stage before 1 January 1998.

2. Paragraphs 3 to 9 shall have effect if the United Kingdom notifies the Council that it does not intend to move to the third stage.

3. The United Kingdom shall not be included among the majority of Member States which fulfil the necessary conditions referred to in the second indent of Article 109j(2) and the first indent of Article 109j(3) of this Treaty.

4. The United Kingdom shall retain its powers in the field of monetary policy according to national law.

5.-9. ★ ★ ★ ★ ★

10. If the United Kingdom does not move to the third stage, it may change its notification at any time after the beginning of that stage. In that event:

(a) The United Kingdom shall have the right to move to the third stage provided only that it satisfies the necessary conditions. The Council, acting at the request of the United Kingdom and under the conditions and in accordance with the procedure laid down in Article 109k(2) of this Treaty, shall decide whether it fulfils the necessary conditions.

(b) The Bank of England shall pay up its subscribed capital, transfer to the ECB foreign reserve assets and contribute to its reserves on the same basis as the national central bank of a Member State whose derogation has been abrogated.

(c) The Council, acting under the conditions and in accordance with the procedure laid down in Article 109l(5) of this Treaty, shall take all other necessary decisions to enable the United Kingdom to move to the third stage.

If the United Kingdom moves to the third stage pursuant to the provisions of this protocol, paragraphs 3 to 9 shall cease to have effect.

11. ★ ★ ★ ★ ★

PROTOCOL ON SOCIAL POLICY

(Annexed to EC Treaty)

Note This Protocol has been adopted by the 3 new member States, Austria, Finland and Sweden.

THE HIGH CONTRACTING PARTIES,

NOTING that 11 Member States, that is to say the Kingdom of Belgium, the Kingdom of Denmark, the Federal Republic of Germany, the Hellenic Republic, the Kingdom of Spain, the French Republic, Ireland, the Italian Republic, the Grand Duchy of Luxembourg, the Kingdom of the Netherlands, the Portuguese Republic, wish to continue along the path laid down in the 1989 Social Charter; that they have adopted among themselves an Agreement to this end; that this Agreement is annexed to this Protocol; that this Protocol and the said Agreement are without prejudice to the provisions of this Treaty, particularly those which relate to social policy which constitute an integral part of the "*acquis communautaire*":

1. Agree to authorise those 11 Member States to have recourse to the institutions, procedures and mechanisms of the Treaty for the purposes of taking among themselves and applying as far as they are concerned the acts and decisions required for giving effect to the above-mentioned Agreement.

2. The United Kingdom of Great Britain and Northern Ireland shall not take part in the deliberations and the adoption by the Council of Commission proposals made on the basis of this Protocol and the above-mentioned Agreement.

[By way of derogation from Article 148(2) of the Treaty, acts of the Council which are made pursuant to this Protocol and which must be adopted by a qualified majority shall be deemed to be so adopted if they have received at least 52 votes in favour.]

The unanimity of the members of the Council, with the exception of the United Kingdom of Great Britain and Northern Ireland, shall be necessary for acts of the Council which must be adopted unanimously and for those amending the Commission proposal.

Acts adopted by the Council and any financial consequences other than administrative costs entailed for the institutions shall not be applicable to the United Kingdom of Great Britain and Northern Ireland.

AGREEMENT ON SOCIAL POLICY CONCLUDED BETWEEN THE MEMBER STATES OF THE EUROPEAN COMMUNITY WITH THE EXCEPTION OFTHE UNITED KINGDOM OF GREAT BRITAIN AND NORTHERN IRELAND

The undersigned 11 HIGH CONTRACTING PARTIES, that is to say the Kingdom of Belgium, the Kingdom of Denmark, the Federal Republic of Germany, the Hellenic Republic, the Kingdom of Spain, the French Republic, Ireland, the Italian Republic, the Grand Duchy of Luxembourg, the Kingdom of the Netherlands and the Portuguese Republic (hereinafter referred to as "the Member States"),

WISHING to implement the 1989 Social Charter on the basis of the "*acquis communautaire*",

CONSIDERING the Protocol on social policy,

HAVE AGREED as follows:

Article 1

The Community and the Member States shall have as their objectives the promotion of employment, improved living and working conditions, proper social protection, dialogue between management and labour, the development of human resources with a view to lasting high employment and the combating of exclusion. To this end the Community and the Member States shall implement measures which take account of the diverse forms of national practice, in particular in the field of contractual relations, and the need to maintain the competitiveness of the Community economy.

Article 2

1. With a view to achieving the objectives of Article 1, the Community shall support and complement the activities of the Member States in the following fields:

— improvement in particular of the working environment to protect workers' health and safety;

— working conditions;

— the information and consultation of workers;

— equality between men and women with regard to labour market opportunities and treatment at work;

— the integration of persons excluded from the labour market, without prejudice to Article 127 of the Treaty establishing the European Community (hereinafter referred to as "the Treaty".

2. To this end, the Council may adopt, by means of directives, minimum requirements for gradual implementation, having regard to the conditions and technical rules obtaining in each of the Member States. Such directives shall avoid imposing administrative, financial and legal constraints in a way which would hold back the creation and development of small and medium-sized undertakings.

The Council shall act in accordance with the procedure referred to in Article 189c of the Treaty after consulting the Economic and Social Committee.

3. However, the Council shall act unanimously on a proposal from the Commission, after consulting the European Parliament and the Economic and Social Committee, in the following areas:

— social security and social protection of workers;

— protection of workers where their employment contract is terminated;

— representation and collective defence of the interests of workers and employers, including co-determination, subject to paragraph 6;

— conditions of employment for third-country nationals legally residing in Community territory;

— financial contributions for promotion of employment and job-creation, without prejudice to the provisions relating to the Social Fund.

★★★★★

Article 6

1. Each Member State shall ensure that the principle of equal pay for male and female workers for equal work is applied.

2. For the purpose of this Article, "pay" means the ordinary basic or minimum wage or salary and any other consideration, whether in cash or in kind, which the worker receives directly or indirectly, in respect of his employment, from his employer.

Equal pay without discrimination based on sex means:

(a) that pay for the same work at piece rates shall be calculated on the basis of the same unit of measurement;

(b) that pay for work at time rates shall be the same for the same job.

3. This Article shall not prevent any Member State from maintaining or adopting measures providing for specific advantages in order to make it easier for women to pursue a vocational activity or to prevent or compensate for disadvantage is their professional careers.

REGULATION (EC) No 1612/68 OF THE COUNCIL of 15 October 1968

on freedom of movement for workers within the Community

THE COUNCIL OF THE EUROPEAN COMMUNITIES.

Having regard to the Treaty establishing the European Economic Community, and in particular Article 49 thereof;

Having regard to the proposal from the Commission;
Having regard to the Opinion of the European Parliament;
Having regard to the Opinion of the Economic and Social Committee;

Whereas freedom of movement for workers should be secured within the Community by the end of the transitional period at the latest; whereas the attainment of this objective entails the abolition of any discrimination based on nationality between workers of the Member States as regards employment, remuneration and other conditions of work and employment, as well as the right of such workers to move freely within the Community in order to pursue activities as employed persons subject to any limitations justified on grounds of public policy, public security or public health;

Whereas by reason in particular of the early establishment of the customs union and in order to ensure the simultaneous completion of the principal foundations of the Community, provisions should be adopted to enable the objectives laid down in Articles 48 and 49 of the Treaty in the field of freedom of movement to be achieved and to perfect measures adopted successively under Regulation No 15 on the first steps for attainment of freedom of movement and under Council Regulation No 38/64/EEC of 25 March 1964 on freedom of movement for workers within the Community;

Whereas freedom of movement constitutes a fundamental right of workers and their families; whereas mobility of labour within the Community must be one of the means by which the worker is guaranteed the possibility of improving his living and working conditions and promoting his social advancement, while helping to satisfy the requirements of the economies of the Member States; whereas the right of all workers in the Member States to pursue the activity of their choice within the Community should be affirmed;

Whereas such right must be enjoyed without discrimination by permanent, seasonal and frontier workers and by those who pursue their activities for the purpose of providing services;

Whereas the right of freedom of movement, in order that it may be exercised, by objective standards, in freedom and dignity, requires that equality of treatment shall be ensured in fact and in law in respect of all matters relating to the actual pursuit of activities as employed persons and to eligibility for housing, and also that obstacles to the mobility of workers shall be eliminated, in particular as regards the worker's right to be joined by his family and the conditions for the integration of that family into the host country;

Whereas the principle of non-discrimination between Community workers entails that all nationals of Member States have the same priority as regards employment as is enjoyed by national workers;

★ ★ ★ ★ ★

Note Parts of the Preamble relating to those parts of the Regulation not reproduced herein are omitted.

HAS ADOPTED THIS REGULATION:

PART 1: EMPLOYMENT AND WORKERS' FAMILIES
TITLE I—ELIGIBILITY FOR EMPLOYMENT

Article 1

1. Any national of a Member State, shall, irrespective of his place of residence, have the right to take up an activity as an employed person, and to pursue such activity, within the territory of another Member State in accordance with the provisions laid down by law, regulation or administrative action governing the employment of nationals of that State.

2. He shall, in particular, have the right to take up available employment in the territory of another Member State with the same priority as nationals of that State.

Article 2
Any national of a Member State and any employer pursuing an activity in the territory of a Member State may exchange their applications for and offers of employment, and may conclude and perform contracts of employment in accordance with the provisions in force laid down by law, regulation or administrative action, without any discrimination resulting therefrom.

Article 3
1. Under this Regulation, provisions laid down by law, regulation or administrative action or administrative practices of a Member State shall not apply:
—where they limit application for and offers of employment, or the right of foreign nationals to take up and pursue employment or subject these to conditions not applicable in respect of their own nationals; or
—where, though applicable irrespective of nationality, their exclusive or principal aim or effect is to keep nationals of other Member States away from the employment offered.

This provision shall not apply to conditions relating to linguistic knowledge required by reason of the nature of the post to be filled.

2. * * * * *

Article 4
* * * * *

Article 5
A national of a Member State who seeks employment in the territory of another Member State shall receive the same assistance there as that afforded by the employment offices in that State to their own nationals seeking employment.

Article 6
* * * * *

TITLE II—EMPLOYMENT AND EQUALITY OF TREATMENT

Article 7
1. A worker who is a national of a Member State may not, in the territory of another Member State, be treated differently from national workers by reason of his nationality in respect of any conditions of employment and work, in particular as regards remuneration, dismissal, and should he become unemployed, reinstatement or re-employment.

2. He shall enjoy the same social and tax advantages as national workers.

3. He shall also, by virtue of the same right and under the same conditions as national workers, have access to training in vocational schools and retraining centres.

4. Any clause of a collective or individual agreement or of any other collective regulation concerning eligibility for employment, employment, remuneration and other conditions of work or dismissal shall be null and void in so far as it lays down or authorises discriminatory conditions in respect of workers who are nationals of the other Member States.

Article 8
1. A worker who is a national of a Member State and who is employed in the territory of another Member State shall enjoy equality of treatment as regards membership of trade unions and the exercise of rights attaching thereto, including the right to vote; he may be excluded from taking part in the management of bodies governed by public law and from holding an office governed by public law. Further-

more, he shall have the right of eligibility for workers' representative bodies in the undertaking. The provisions of this Article shall not affect laws or regulations in certain Member States which grant more extensive rights to workers coming from the other Member States.

2. ...

Article 9

★★★★★

TITLE III—WORKERS' FAMILIES

Article 10

1. The following shall, irrespective of their nationality, have the right to install themselves with a worker who is a national of one Member State and who is employed in the territory of another Member State:

(a) his spouse and their descendants who are under the age of 21 years or are dependants;

(b) dependent relatives in the ascending line of the worker and his spouse.

2. Member States shall facilitate the admission of any member of the family not coming within the provisions of paragraph 1 if dependent on the worker referred to above or living under his roof in the country whence he comes.

3. For the purposes of paragraphs 1 and 2, the worker must have available for his family housing considered as normal for national workers in the region where he is employed; this provision, however must not give rise to discrimination between national workers and workers from the other Member States.

EC COUNCIL DIRECTIVE 64/221 of 25 February 1964

On the Co-ordination of Special Measures concerning the movement and residence of Foreign Nationals which are justified on Grounds of Public Policy, Public Security or Public Health

THE COUNCIL OF THE EUROPEAN COMMUNITIES,

Having regard to the Treaty establishing the European Economic Community, and in particular Article 56(2) thereof;

Having regard to Council Regulation 15 of August 16, 1961 (J.O. 1961, 1073), on initial measures to bring about free movement of workers within the Community, and in particular Article 47 thereof;

Having regard to Council directive of August 16, 1961 (J.O. 1961, 1513), on administrative procedures and practices governing the entry into and employment and residence in a Member State of workers and their families from other Member States of the Community;

Having regard to the General Programmes for the abolition of restrictions on freedom of establishment and on freedom to provide services, and in particular Title II of each such programme;

Having regard to the Council directive of February 25, 1964 (J.O. 1964, 845), on the abolition of restrictions on movement and residence within the Community for nationals of Member States with regard to establishment and the provision of services;

Having regard to the proposal from the Commission;

Having regard to the Opinion of the European Parliament;

Having regard to the Opinion of the Economic and Social Committee;

Whereas co-ordination of provisions laid down by law, regulation or administrative action which provide for special treatment for foreign nationals on grounds of public policy, public security or public health should in the first place deal with the conditions for entry and residence of nationals of Member States moving within the Community either in order to pursue activities as employed or self-employed persons, or as recipients of services;

Whereas such co-ordination presupposes in particular an approximation of the procedures followed in each Member State when invoking grounds of public policy, public security or public health in matters connected with the movement or residence of foreign nationals;

Whereas, in each Member State, nationals of other Member States should have adequate remedies available to them in respect of the decisions of the administration in such matters;

Whereas it would be of little practical use to compile a list of diseases and disabilities which might endanger public health, public policy or public security and it would be difficult to make such a list exhaustive; whereas it is sufficient to classify such diseases and disabilities in groups;

HAS ADOPTED THIS DIRECTIVE:

Article 1

1. The provisions of this directive shall apply to any national of a Member State who resides in or travels to another Member State of the Community, either in order to pursue an activity as an employed or self-employed person, or as a recipient of services.

2. These provisions shall apply also to the spouse and to members of the family who come within the provisions of the regulations and directives adopted in this field in pursuance of the Treaty.

Article 2

1. This directive relates to all measures concerning entry into their territory, issue or renewal of residence permits, or expulsion from their territory, taken by Member States on grounds of public policy, public security or public health.

2. Such grounds shall not be invoked to service economic ends.

Article 3

1. Measures taken on grounds of public policy or of public security shall be based exclusively on the personal conduct of the individual concerned.

2. Previous criminal convictions shall not in themselves constitute grounds for the taking of such measures.

3. Expiry of the identity card or passport used by the person concerned to enter the host country and to obtain a residence permit shall not justify expulsion from the territory.

4. The State which issued the identity card or passport shall allow the holder of such document to re-enter its territory without any formality even if the document is no longer valid or the nationality of the holder is in dispute.

Article 4

1. The only diseases or disabilities justifying refusal of entry into a territory or refusal to issue a first residence permit shall be those listed in the Annex to this directive. [*Not printed.*]

2. Diseases or disabilities occurring after a first residence permit has been issued shall not justify refusal to renew the residence permit or expulsion from the territory.

3. Member States shall not introduce new provisions or practices which are more restrictive than those in force at the date of notification of this directive.

Article 5

1. A decision to grant or to refuse a first residence permit shall be taken as soon as possible and in any event not later than six months from the date of application for the permit.

The person concerned shall be allowed to remain temporarily in the territory pending a decision either to grant or to refuse a residence permit.

2. The host country may, in cases where this is considered essential, request the Member State of origin of the applicant, and if need be other Member States, to provide information concerning any previous police record. Such enquiries shall not be made as a matter of routine. The Member State consulted shall give its reply within two months.

Article 6
The person concerned shall be informed of the grounds of public policy, public security, or public health upon which the decision taken in his case is based, unless this is contrary to the interests of the security of the State involved.

Article 7
The person concerned shall be officially notified of any decision to refuse the issue or renewal of a residence permit or to expel him from the territory. The period allowed for leaving the territory shall be stated in this notification. Save in cases of urgency, this period shall be not less than 15 days if the person concerned has not yet been granted a residence permit and not less than one month in all other cases.

Article 8
The person concerned shall have the same legal remedies in respect of any decision concerning entry, or refusing the issue or renewal of a residence permit, or ordering expulsion from the territory, as are available to nationals of the State concerned in respect of acts of the administration.

Articles 9-11
★ ★ ★ ★ ★

POLICE AND CRIMINAL EVIDENCE ACT 1984 REVISED CODES OF PRACTICE A-C

Note For the legal status of the Codes and other issues relating to them, see ss. 66 and 67 of the Police and Criminal Evidence Act 1984 (*supra*). The Codes were revised in accordance with s. 67(7) of the Act with effect from 9 April 1995. A further revised Code A was approved to come into effect from 15 May 1997. The most recent revised version of each Code is printed below (except for Codes D and E which are not reproduced).

CODE OF PRACTICE FOR THE EXERCISE BY POLICE OFFICERS OF STATUTORY POWERS OF STOP AND SEARCH (CODE A)

1 General

1.1-1.4 ★ ★ ★ ★ ★

1.5 This code applies to stops and searches under powers:

(a) requiring reasonable grounds for suspicion that articles unlawfully obtained or possessed are being carried;

(b) authorised under section 60 of the Criminal Justice and Public Order Act 1994 based upon a reasonable belief that incidents involving serious violence may take place within a locality;

(c) authorised under section 13A of the Prevention of Terrorism (Temporary Provisions) Act 1989 as amended by section 81 of the Criminal Justice and Public Order Act 1994;

(d) exercised under paragraph 4(2) of Schedule 5 to the Prevention of Terrorism (Temporary Provisions) Act 1989.

(a) Powers requiring reasonable suspicion

1.6 Whether reasonable grounds for suspicion exist will depend on the circumstances in each case, but there must be some objective basis for it. An officer will need to consider the nature of the article suspected of being carried in the context of other factors such as the time and the place, and the behaviour of the person concerned or those with him. Reasonable suspicion may exist, for example, where information has been received such as a description of an article being carried or of a suspected offender; a person is seen acting covertly or warily or attempting to hide something; or a person is carrying a certain type of article at an unusual time or in a place where a number of burglaries or thefts are known to have taken place recently. But the decision to stop and search must be based on all the facts which bear on the likelihood that an article of a certain kind will be found.

1.6A For example, reasonable suspicion may be based upon reliable information or intelligence which indicates that members of a particular group or gang, or their associates, habitually carry knives unlawfully or weapons or controlled drugs.

1.7 Subject to the provision in paragraph 1.7AA below, reasonable suspicion can never be supported on the basis of personal factors alone without supporting intelligence or information. For example, a person's colour, age, hairstyle or manner of dress, or the fact that he is known to have a previous conviction for possession of an unlawful article, cannot be used alone or in combination with each other as the sole basis on which to search that person. Nor may it be founded on the basis of stereotyped images of certain persons or groups as more likely to be committing offences.

1.7AA However, where there is reliable information or intelligence that members of a group or gang who habitually carry knives unlawfully or weapons or controlled drugs, and wear a distinctive item of clothing or other means of identification to indicate membership of it, the members may be identified by means of that distinctive item of clothing or other means of identification.

1.7A Where a police officer has reasonable grounds to suspect that a person is in innocent possession of a stolen or prohibited article or other item for which he is empowered to search, the power to stop and search exists notwithstanding that there would be no power of arrest. However every effort should be made to secure the person's co-operation in the production of the article before resorting to the use of force.

(b) Authorisation under section 60 of the Criminal Justice and Public Order Act 1994

1.8 Authority to exercise the powers of stop and search under section 60 of the Criminal Justice and Public Order Act 1994 may be given where it is reasonably believed that incidents involving serious violence may take place in a locality, and it is expedient to use these powers to prevent their occurrence. Authorisation should normally be given by an officer of the rank of superintendent or above, in writing, specifying the locality in which the powers may be exercised and the period of time for which they are in force. Authorisation may be given by an inspector or chief inspector if he reasonably believes that violence is imminent and no superintendent is available. In either case the period authorised shall be no longer than appears reasonably necessary to prevent, or try to prevent incidents of serious violence, and it may not exceed 24 hours. A superintendent or the authorising officer may direct that the period shall be extended for a further six hours if violence has occurred or is suspected to have occurred and the continued use of the powers is considered necessary to prevent further violence. That direction must also be given in writing at the time or as soon as practicable afterwards.

(c) Authorisation under section 13A of the Prevention of Terrorism (Temporary Provisions) Act 1989, as amended by section 81 of the Criminal Justice and Public Order Act 1994

1.8A Authority to exercise the powers of stop and search under section 13A of the Prevention of Terrorism (Temporary Provisions) Act 1989 may be given where it appears expedient to do so to prevent acts of terrorism. Authorisation must be given by an officer of the rank of assistant chief constable (or equivalent) or above, in writing, specifying where the powers may be exercised and the period of time for which they are to remain in force. The period authorised may not exceed 28 days. Further periods of up to 28 days may be authorised.

2 Action before a search is carried out

(a) Searches requiring reasonable suspicion

2.1 Where an officer has the reasonable grounds for suspicion necessary to exercise a power of stop and search he may detain the person concerned for the purposes of and with a view to searching him. There is no power to stop or detain a person against his will in order to find grounds for a search.

2.2 Before carrying out a search the officer may question the person about his behaviour or his presence in circumstances which gave rise to the suspicion, since he may have a satisfactory explanation which will make a search unnecessary. If, as a result of any questioning preparatory to a search, or other circumstances which come to the attention of the officer, there cease to be reasonable grounds for suspecting that an article is being carried of a kind for which there is a power of stop and search, no search may take place.

2.3 The reasonable grounds for suspicion which are necessary for the exercise of the initial power to detain may be confirmed or eliminated as a result of the questioning of a person detained for the purposes of a search (or such questioning may reveal reasonable grounds to suspect the possession of a different kind of unlawful article from that originally suspected); but the reasonable grounds for suspicion without which any search or detention for the purposes of a search is unlawful cannot be retrospectively provided by such questioning during his detention or by his refusal to answer any question put to him.

(b) All searches

2.4 Before any search of a detained person or attended vehicle takes place the officer must take reasonable steps to give the person to be searched or in charge of the vehicle the following information:

(i) his name (except in the case of enquiries linked to the investigation of terrorism, in which case he shall give his warrant or other identification number) and the name of the police station to which he is attached;
(ii) the object of the search; and
(iii) his grounds or authorisation for undertaking it.

2.5 If the officer is not in uniform he must show his warrant card. In doing so in the case of enquiries linked to the investigation of terrorism, the officer need not reveal his name. Stops and searches under the powers mentioned in paragraphs 1.5 (b) and (c) may be undertaken only by a constable in uniform.

2.6 Unless it appears to the officer that it will not be practicable to make a record of the search, he must also inform the person to be searched (or the owner or person in charge of a vehicle that is to be searched, as the case may be) that he is entitled to a copy of the record of the search if he asks for it within a year. If the person wishes to have a copy and is not given one on the spot, he should be advised to which police station he should apply.

2.7 If the person to be searched, or in charge of a vehicle to be searched, does not appear to understand what is being said, or there is any doubt about his ability to understand English, the officer must take reasonable steps to bring the information in paragraphs 2.4 and 2.6 to his attention. If the person is deaf or cannot understand English and has someone with him then the officer must try to establish whether the person can interpret or otherwise help him to give the required information.

3 Conduct of the search

3.1 Every reasonable effort must be made to reduce to the minimum the embarrassment that a person being searched may experience.

3.2 The co-operation of the person to be searched should be sought in every case, even if he initially objects to the search. A forcible search may be made only if it has been established that the person is unwilling to co-operate (e.g., by opening a bag) or resists. Although force may only be used as a last resort, reasonable force may be used if necessary to conduct a search or to detain a person or vehicle for the purposes of a search.

3.3 The length of time for which a person or vehicle may be detained will depend on the circumstances, but must in all circumstances be reasonable and not extend beyond the time taken for the search. Where the exercise of the power requires reasonable suspicion, the thoroughness and extent of a search must depend on what is suspected of being carried, and by whom. If the suspicion relates to a particular article which is seen to be slipped into a person's pocket, then, in the absence of other grounds for suspicion or an opportunity for the article to be moved elsewhere, the search must be confined to that pocket. In the case of a small article which can readily be concealed, such as a drug, and which might be concealed anywhere on the person, a more extensive search may be necessary. In the case of searches mentioned in paragraph 1.5(b), (c) and (d), which do not require reasonable grounds for suspicion, the officer may make any reasonable search to find what he is empowered to search for.

3.4 The search must be conducted at the place where the person or vehicle was first detained or nearby.

3.5 Searches in public must be restricted to superficial examination of outer clothing. There is no power to require a person to remove any clothing in public other than an outer coat, jacket or gloves. Where on reasonable grounds it is considered necessary to conduct a more thorough search (e.g., by requiring a person to take off a T-shirt or headgear), this should be done out of public view, for example in a police van or police station if there is one nearby. Any search involving the removal of more than an outer coat, jacket, gloves, headgear or footwear may only be made by an officer of the same sex as the person searched and may not be made in the presence of anyone of the opposite sex unless the person being searched specifically requests it.

3.5A Where a pedestrian is stopped under section 13A of the Prevention of Terrorism (Temporary Provisions) Act 1989, a search may be made of anything carried by him. The pedestrian himself must not be searched under this power. This would not prevent a search being carried out under other powers if, in the course of a search of anything carried by the pedestrian, the police officer formed reasonable grounds for suspicion.

4 ★★★★★

CODE OF PRACTICE FOR THE SEARCHING OF PREMISES BY POLICE OFFICERS AND THE SEIZURE OF PROPERTY FOUND BY POLICE OFFICERS ON PERSONS OR PREMISES (CODE B)

Note See note to Code A (*supra*). The Notes for Guidance are not reproduced.

1 General

1.1 This code of practice must be readily available at all police stations for consultation by police officers, detained persons and members of the public.

1.2 The notes for guidance included are not provisions of this code, but are guidance to police officers and others about its application and interpretation.

1.3 This code applies to the following searches of premises:

(a) undertaken for the purposes of an investigation into an alleged offence, with the occupier's consent, other than searches made in the following circumstances:

—routine scenes of crime searches

—calls to a fire or a burglary made by or on behalf of an occupier or searches following the activation of fire or burglar alarms

—searches to which paragraph 4.4 applies

—bomb threat calls;

(b) under powers conferred by sections 17, 18 and 32 of the Police and Criminal Evidence Act 1984;

(c) undertaken in pursuance of a search warrant issued in accordance with section 15 of, or Schedule 1 to the Police and Criminal Evidence Act 1984, or section 15 of, or Schedule 7 to the Prevention of Terrorism (Temporary Provisions) Act 1989.

★★★★★

1.3A Any search of a person who has not been arrested which is carried out during a search of premises shall be carried out in accordance with Code A.

1.3B This code does not apply to the exercise of a statutory power to enter premises or to inspect goods, equipment or procedures if the exercise of that power is not dependent on the existence of grounds for suspecting that an offence may have been committed and the person exercising the power has no reasonable grounds for such suspicion.

2 Search warrants and production orders

(a) Action to be taken before an application is made

2.1 Where information is received which appears to justify an application, the officer concerned must take reasonable steps to check that the information is accurate, recent and has not been provided maliciously or irresponsibly. An application may not be made on the basis of information from an anonymous source where corroboration has not been sought.

2.2 The officer shall ascertain as specifically as is possible in the circumstances the nature of the articles concerned and their location.

2.3 The officer shall also make reasonable enquiries to establish what, if anything, is known about the likely occupier of the premises and the nature of the premises themselves; and whether they have been previously searched and if so how recently; and to obtain any other information relevant to the application.

2.4 No application for a search warrant may be made without the authority of an officer of at least the rank of inspector (or, in a case of urgency where no officer of this rank is readily available, the senior officer on duty). No application for a production order or warrant under Schedule 1 to the Police and Criminal Evidence Act 1984, or under Schedule 7 to the Prevention of Terrorism (Temporary Provisions) Act 1989, may be made without the authority of an officer of at least the rank of superintendent.

2.5 Except in a case of urgency, if there is reason to believe that a search might have an adverse effect on relations between the police and the community then the local police community liaison officer shall be consulted before it takes place. In urgent cases, the local police community liaison officer should be informed of the search as soon as practicable after it has been made.

(b) Making an application

2.6 An application for a search warrant must be supported by an information in writing, specifying:

(i) the enactment under which the application is made;

(ii) as specifically as is reasonably practicable the premises to be searched and the object of the search; and

(iii) the grounds on which the application is made (including, where the purpose of the proposed search is to find evidence of an alleged offence, an indication of how the evidence relates to the investigation).

2.7 An application for a search warrant under paragraph 12(a) of Schedule 1 to the Police and Criminal Evidence Act 1984, or under Schedule 7 to the Prevention of Terrorism (Temporary Provisions) Act 1989, shall also, where appropriate, indicate why it is believed that service of notice of an application for a production order may seriously prejudice the investigation.

2.8 If an application is refused, no further application may be made for a warrant to search those premises unless supported by additional grounds.

3 ★★★★★

4 Search with consent

4.1 Subject to paragraph 4.4 below, if it is proposed to search premises with the consent of a person entitled to grant entry to the premises the consent must, if practicable, be given in writing on the notice of Powers and Rights before the search takes place. The officer must make enquiries to satisfy himself that the person is in a position to give such consent.

4.2 ★★★★★

4.3 An officer cannot enter and search premises or continue to search premises under 4.1 above if the consent has been given under duress or is withdrawn before the search is completed.

4.4 ★★★★★

5 Searching of premises: general considerations

(a) Time of searches

5.1 Searches made under warrant must be made within one calendar month from the date of issue of the warrant.

5.2 Searches must be made at a reasonable hour unless this might frustrate the purpose of the search.

5.3 A warrant authorises an entry on one occasion only.

(b) Entry other than with consent

5.4-5.6 * * * * *

(c) Notice of powers and rights

5.7 If an officer conducts a search to which this code applies he shall, unless it is impracticable to do so, provide the occupier with a copy of a notice in a standard format:

(i) specifying whether the search is made under warrant, or with consent, or in the exercise of the powers described in 3.1 to 3.3 above (the format of the notice shall provide for authority or consent to be indicated where appropriate — see 3.3 and 4.1 above);

(ii) summarising the extent of the powers of search and seizure conferred in the Act;

(iii) explaining the rights of the occupier, and of the owner of property seized in accordance with the provisions of 6.1 to 6.5 and 6.8 below, set out in the Act and in this code;

(iv) explaining that compensation may be payable in appropriate cases for damage caused in entering and searching premises, and giving the address to which an application for compensation should be directed; and

(v) stating that a copy of this code is available to be consulted at any police station.

5.8 If the occupier is present, copies of the notice mentioned above, and of the warrant (if the search is made under warrant) should if practicable be given to the occupier before the search begins, unless the officer in charge of the search reasonably believes that to do so would frustrate the object of the search or endanger the officers concerned or other persons. If the occupier is not present, copies of the notice, and of the warrant where appropriate, should be left in a prominent place on the premises or appropriate part of the premises and endorsed with the name of the officer in charge of the search (except in the case of inquiries linked to the investigation of terrorism, in which case the officer's warrant or other identification number should be given), the name of the police station to which he is attached and the date and time of the search. The warrant itself should be endorsed to show that this has been done.

5.9-5.14 * * * * *

6 Seizure and retention of property

(a) Seizure

6.1 Subject to paragraph 6.2 below, an officer who is searching any premises under any statutory power or with the consent of the occupier may seize:

(a) anything covered by a warrant; and

(b) anything which he has reasonable grounds for believing is evidence of an offence or has been obtained in consequence of the commission of an offence.

Items under (b) may only be seized where this is necessary to prevent their concealment, alteration, loss, damage or destruction.

6.2 No item may be seized which is subject to legal privilege (as defined in section 10 of the Police and Criminal Evidence Act 1984).

6.3 An officer who decides that it is not appropriate to seize property because of an explanation given by the person holding it, but who has reasonable grounds for believing that it has been obtained in consequence of the commission of an offence by some person, shall inform the holder of his suspicions and shall explain that, if he disposes of the property, he may be liable to civil or criminal proceedings.

6.4 An officer may photograph or copy, or have photographed or copied, any document or other article which he has power to seize in accordance with paragraph 6.1 above.

6.5 Where an officer considers that a computer may contain information that could be used in evidence, he may require the information to be produced in a form that can be taken away and in which it is visible and legible.

(b) Retention

6.6 Subject to paragraph 6.7 below, anything which has been seized in accordance with the above provisions may be retained only for as long as is necessary in the circumstances. It may be retained, among other purposes:

(i) for use as evidence at a trial for an offence;

(ii) for forensic examination or for other investigation in connection with an offence; or

(iii) where there are reasonable grounds for believing that it has been stolen or obtained by the commission of an offence, in order to establish its lawful owner.

6.7 Property shall not be retained in accordance with 6.6 (i) and (ii) (i.e., for use as evidence or for the purposes of investigation) if a photograph or copy would suffice for those purposes.

6.8-6.9 ★ ★ ★ ★ ★

7 Action to be taken after searches

7.1 Where premises have been searched in circumstances to which this code applies, other than in the circumstances covered by paragraph 1.3(a), the officer in charge of the search shall, on arrival at a police station, make or have made a record of the search. The record shall include:

(i) the address of the premises searched;

(ii) the date, time and duration of the search;

(iii) the authority under which the search was made. Where the search was made in the exercise of a statutory power to search premises without warrant, the record shall include the power under which the search was made; and where the search was made under warrant, or with written consent, a copy of the warrant or consent shall be appended to the record or kept in a place identified in the record;

(iv) the names of all the officers who conducted the search (except in the case of enquiries linked to the investigation of terrorism, in which case the record shall state the warrant or other identification number and duty station of each officer concerned);

(v) the names of any persons on the premises if they are known;

(vi) either a list of any articles seized or a note of where such a list is kept and, if not covered by a warrant, the reason for their seizure;

(vii) whether force was used, and, if so, the reason why it was used;

(viii) details of any damage caused during the search, and the circumstances in which it was caused.

7.2 Where premises have been searched under warrant, the warrant shall be endorsed to show:

(i) whether any articles specified in the warrant were found;

(ii) whether any other articles were seized;

(iii) the date and time at which it was executed;

(iv) the names of the officers who executed it (except in the case of enquiries linked to the investigation of terrorism, in which case the warrant or other identification number and duty station of each officer concerned shall be shown);

(v) whether a copy, together with a copy of the notice of powers and rights was handed to the occupier; or whether it was endorsed as requested by paragraph 5.8, and left on the premises together with the copy notice and, if so, where.

7.3 Any warrant which has been executed or which has not been executed within one calendar month of its issue shall be returned, if it was issued by a justice of the peace, to the clerk to the justices for the petty sessions area concerned or, if issued by a judge, to the appropriate officer of the court from which he issued it.

8 ★★★★★

CODE OF PRACTICE FOR THE DETENTION, TREATMENT AND QUESTIONING OF PERSONS BY POLICE OFFICERS (CODE C)

Note See note to Code A (*supra*). The Notes for Guidance are not reproduced.

1 General

1.1 All persons in custody must be dealt with expeditiously, and released as soon as the need for detention has ceased to apply.

1.1A A custody officer is required to perform the functions specified in this code as soon as is practicable. A custody officer shall not be in breach of this code in the event of delay provided that the delay is justifiable and that every reasonable step is taken to prevent unnecessary delay. The custody record shall indicate where a delay has occurred and the reason why.

1.2 This code of practice must be readily available at all police stations for consultation by police officers, detained persons and members of the public.

1.3 The notes for guidance included are not provisions of this code, but are guidance to police officers and others about its application and interpretation. Provisions in the annexes to this code are provisions of this code.

1.4 If an officer has any suspicion, or is told in good faith, that a person of any age may be mentally disordered or mentally handicapped, or mentally incapable of understanding the significance of questions put to him or his replies, then that person shall be treated as a mentally disordered or mentally handicapped person for the purposes of this code.

1.5 If anyone appears to be under the age of 17 then he shall be treated as a juvenile for the purposes of this code in the absence of clear evidence to show that he is older.

1.6 If a person appears to be blind or seriously visually handicapped, deaf, unable to read, unable to speak or has difficulty orally because of a speech impediment, he should be treated as such for the purposes of this code in the absence of clear evidence to the contrary.

1.7 In this code "the appropriate adult" means:

(a) in the case of a juvenile:

(i) his parent or guardian (or, if he is in care, the care authority or voluntary organisation. The term "in care" is used in this code to cover all cases in which a juvenile is "looked after" by a local authority under the terms of the Children Act 1989);

(ii) a social worker; or

(iii) failing either of the above, another responsible adult aged 18 or over who is not a police officer or employed by the police.

(b) in the case of a person who is mentally disordered or mentally handicapped:

(i) a relative, guardian or other person responsible for his care or custody;

(ii) someone who has experience of dealing with mentally disordered or mentally handicapped persons but is not a police officer or employed by the police (such as an approved social worker as defined by the Mental Health Act 1983 or a specialist social worker); or

(iii) failing either of the above, some other responsible adult aged 18 or over who is not a police officer or employed by the police.

1.8 Whenever this code requires a person to be given certain information he does not have to be given it if he is incapable at the time of understanding what is said to him or is violent or likely to become violent or is in urgent need of medical attention, but he must be given it as soon as practicable.

1.9 Any reference to a custody officer in this code includes an officer who is performing the functions of a custody officer.

1.10 Subject to paragraph 1.12, this code applies to people who are in custody at police stations in England and Wales whether or not they have been arrested for an offence and to those who have been removed to a police station as a place of safety under section 135 and 136 of the Mental Health Act 1983. Section 15 (reviews and extensions of detention) however applies solely to people in police detention, for example those who have been brought to a police station under arrest for an offence or have been arrested at a police station for an offence after attending there voluntarily.

1.11-1.12 ★★★★★

2 Custody records

2.1 A separate custody record must be opened as soon as practicable for each person who is brought to a police station under arrest or is arrested at the police station having attended there voluntarily. All information which has to be recorded under this code must be recorded as soon as practicable in the custody record unless otherwise specified. Any audio or video recording made in the custody area is not part of the custody record.

2.2 In the case of any action requiring the authority of an officer of a specified rank, his name and rank must be noted in the custody record. The recording of names does not apply to officers dealing with persons detained under the Prevention of Terrorism (Temporary Provisions) Act 1989. Instead the record shall state the warrant or other identification number and duty station of such officers.

2.3 The custody officer is responsible for the accuracy and completeness of the custody record and for ensuring that the record or a copy of the record accompanies a detained person if he is transferred to another police station. The record shall show the time of and reason for transfer and the time a person is released from detention.

2.4 A solicitor or appropriate adult must be permitted to consult the custody record of a person detained as soon as practicable after their arrival at the police station. When a person leaves police detention or is taken before a court, he or his legal representative or his appropriate adult shall be supplied on request with a copy of the custody record as soon as practicable. This entitlement lasts for 12 months after his release.

2.5 ★★★★★

2.6 All entries in custody records must be timed and signed by the maker. In the case of a record entered on a computer this shall be timed and contain the operator's identification. Warrant or other identification numbers shall be used rather than names in the case of detention under the Prevention of Terrorism (Temporary Provisions) Act 1989.

2.7 The fact and time of any refusal by a person to sign a custody record when asked to do so in accordance with the provisions of this code must itself be recorded.

3 Initial action

(a) Detained persons: normal procedure

3.1 When a person is brought to a police station under arrest or is arrested at the police station having attended there voluntarily the custody officer must tell him clearly of the following rights and of the fact that they are continuing rights which may be exercised at any stage during the period in custody.

(i) the right to have someone informed of his arrest in accordance with section 5 below;

(ii) the right to consult privately with a solicitor in accordance with section 6 below, and the fact that independent legal advice is available free of charge; and

(iii) the right to consult this and the other codes of practice.

3.2 In addition the custody officer must give the person a written notice setting out the above three rights, the right to a copy of the custody record in accordance with paragraph 2.4 above and the caution in the terms prescribed in section 10 below. The notice must also explain the arrangements for obtaining legal advice. The custody officer must also give the person an additional written notice briefly setting out his entitlements while in custody. The custody officer shall ask the person to sign the custody record to acknowledge receipt of these notices and any refusal to sign must be recorded on the custody record.

3.3 ★★★★★

3.4 The custody officer shall note on the custody record any comment the person may make in relation to the arresting officer's account but shall not invite comment. If the custody officer authorises a person's detention he must inform him of the grounds as soon as practicable and in any case before that person is then questioned about any offence. The custody officer shall note any comment the person may make in respect of the decision to detain him but, again, shall not invite comment. The custody officer shall not put specific questions to the person regarding his involvement in any offence, nor in respect of any comments he may make in response to the arresting officer's account or the decision to place him in detention. . . .

3.5 The custody officer shall ask the detained person whether at this time he would like legal advice (see paragraph 6.5). The person shall be asked to sign the custody record to confirm his decision. The custody officer is responsible for ensuring that in confirming any decision the person signs in the correct place.

3.5A If video cameras are installed in the custody area, notices which indicate that cameras are in use shall be prominently displayed. Any request by a detained person or other person to have video cameras switched off shall be refused.

(b) Detained persons: special groups

3.6 If the person appears to be deaf or there is doubt about his hearing or speaking ability or ability to understand English, and the custody officer cannot establish effective communication, the custody officer must as soon as practicable call an interpreter, and ask him to provide the information required above. [See Section 13]

3.7 If the person is a juvenile, the custody officer must, if it is practicable, ascertain the identity of a person responsible for his welfare. That person may be his parent or guardian (or, if he is in care, the care authority or voluntary organisation) or any other person who has, for the time being, assumed responsibility for his welfare. That person must be informed as soon as practicable that the juvenile has been arrested, why he has been arrested and where he is detained. This right is in addition to the juvenile's right in section 5 of the code not to be held incommunicado.

3.8 In the case of a juvenile who is known to be subject to a supervision order, reasonable steps must also be taken to notify the person supervising him.

3.9 If the person is a juvenile, is mentally handicapped or appears to be suffering from a mental disorder, then the custody officer must, as soon as practicable, inform the appropriate adult (who in the case of a juvenile may or may not be a person responsible for his welfare, in accordance with paragraph 3.7 above) of the grounds for his detention and his whereabouts, and ask the adult to come to the police station to see the person.

3.10 It is imperative that a mentally disordered or mentally handicapped person who has been detained under section 136 of the Mental Health Act 1983 should be assessed as soon as possible. If that assessment is to take place at the police station, an approved social worker and a registered medical practitioner should be called to the police station as soon as possible in order to interview and examine the person. Once the person has been interviewed and examined and suitable arrangements have been made for his treatment or care, he can no longer be detained under section 136. The person should not be released until he has been seen by both the approved social worker and the registered medical practitioner.

3.11 If the appropriate adult is already at the police station, then the provisions of paragraphs 3.1 to 3.5 above must be complied with in his presence. If the appropriate adult is not at the police station when the provisions of paragraphs 3.1 to 3.5 above are complied with, then these provisions must be complied with again in the presence of the appropriate adult once that person arrives.

3.12 The person should be advised by the custody officer that the appropriate adult (where applicable) is there to assist and advise him and that he can consult privately with the appropriate adult at any time.

3.13 If, having been informed of the right to legal advice under paragraph 3.11 above, either the appropriate adult or the person detained wishes legal advice to be taken, then the provisions of section 6 of this code apply.

3.14 If the person is blind or seriously visually handicapped or is unable to read, the custody officer should ensure that his solicitor, relative, the appropriate adult or some other person likely to take an interest in him (and not involved in the investigation) is available to help in checking any documentation. Where this code requires written consent or signification, then the person who is assisting may be asked to sign instead if the detained person so wishes.

(c) Persons attending a police station voluntarily

3.15 Any person attending a police station voluntarily for the purpose of assisting with an investigation may leave at will unless placed under arrest. If it is decided that he should not be allowed to do so then he must be informed at once that he is under arrest and brought before the custody officer, who is responsible for ensuring that he is notified of his rights in the same way as other detained persons. If he is not placed under arrest but is cautioned in accordance with section 10 below, the officer who gives the caution must at the same time inform him that he is not under arrest, that he is not obliged to remain at the police station but that if he remains at the police station he may obtain free legal advice if he wishes. The officer shall point out that the right to legal advice includes the right to speak with a solicitor on the telephone and ask him if he wishes to do so.

3.16 If a person who is attending the police station voluntarily (in accordance with paragraph 3.15) asks about his entitlement to legal advice, he should be given a copy of the notice explaining the arrangements for obtaining legal advice.

(d) Documentation

3.17 The grounds for a person's detention shall be recorded, in his presence if practicable.

3.18 Action taken under paragraphs 3.6 to 3.14 shall be recorded.

4 Detained persons' property

(a) Action

4.1 The custody officer is responsible for:

(a) ascertaining:

(i) what property a detained person has with him when he comes to the police station (whether on arrest, re-detention on answering to bail, commitment to prison custody on the order or sentence of a court, on lodgement at the police station with a view to his production in court from such custody, on arrival at a police station on transfer from detention at another station or from hospital or on detention under section 135 or 136 of the Mental Health Act 1983);

(ii) what property he might have acquired for an unlawful or harmful purpose while in custody.

(b) the safekeeping of any property which is taken from him and which remains at the police station.

To these ends the custody officer may search him or authorise his being searched to the extent that he considers necessary (provided that a search of intimate parts of the body or involving the removal of more than outer clothing may only be made in accordance with Annex A to this code). A search may only be carried out by an officer of the same sex as the person searched.

4.2 A detained person may retain clothing and personal effects at his own risk unless the custody officer considers that he may use them to cause harm to himself or others, interfere with evidence, damage property or effect an escape or they are needed as evidence. In this event the custody officer may withhold such articles as he considers necessary. If he does so he must tell the person why.

4.3 Personal effects are those items which a person may lawfully need or use or refer to while in detention but do not include cash and other items of value.

(b) Documentation

4.4 The custody officer is responsible for recording all property brought to the police station that a detained person had with him, or had taken from him on arrest. The detained person shall be allowed to check and sign the record of property as correct. Any refusal to sign should be recorded.

4.5 If a detained person is not allowed to keep any article of clothing or personal effects the reason must be recorded.

5 Right not to be held incommunicado

(a) Action

5.1 Any person arrested and held in custody at a police station or other premises may on request have one person known to him or who is likely to take an interest in his welfare informed at public expense as soon as practicable of his whereabouts. If the person cannot be contacted the person who has made the request may choose up to two alternatives. If they too cannot be contacted the person in charge of detention or of the investigation has discretion to allow further attempts until the information has been conveyed.

5.2 * * * * *

5.3 The above right may be exercised on each occasion that a person is taken to another police station.

5.4 The person may receive visits at the custody officer's discretion.

5.5 Where an enquiry as to the whereabouts of the person is made by a friend, relative or person with an interest in his welfare, this information shall be given, if he agrees and if Annex B does not apply.

5.6 Subject to the following condition, the person should be supplied with writing materials on request and allowed to speak on the telephone for a reasonable time to one person. Where an officer of the rank of inspector or above considers that the sending of a letter or the making of a telephone call may result in:

(a) any of the consequences set out in the first and second paragraph of Annex B and the person is detained in connection with an arrestable or a serious arrestable offence, for which purpose, any reference to a serious arrestable offence in Annex B includes an arrestable offence; or

(b) either of the consequences set out in paragraph 8 of Annex B and the person is detained under the Prevention of Terrorism (Temporary Provisions) Act 1989,

that officer can deny or delay the exercise of either or both these privileges. However, nothing in this section permits the restriction or denial of the rights set out in sections 5.1 and 6.1.

5.7 Before any letter or message is sent, or telephone call made, the person shall be informed that what he says in any letter, call or message (other than in the case of a communication to a solicitor) may be read or listened to as appropriate and may be given in evidence. A telephone call may be terminated if it is being abused. The costs can be at public expense at the discretion of the custody officer.

(b) Documentation

5.8 A record must be kept of:

(a) any request made under this section and the action taken on it;

(b) any letters, messages or telephone calls made or received or visits received; and

(c) any refusal on the part of the person to have information about himself or his whereabouts given to an outside enquirer. The person must be asked to countersign the record accordingly and any refusal to sign should be recorded.

6 Right to legal advice

(a) Action

6.1 Subject to the provisos in Annex B all people in police detention must be informed that they may at any time consult and communicate privately, whether in person, in writing or by telephone with a solicitor, and that independent legal advice is available free of charge from the duty solicitor.

6.2-6.5 * * * * *

6.6 A person who wants legal advice may not be interviewed or continue to be interviewed until he has received it unless:

(a) Annex B applies; or

(b) an officer of the rank of superintendent or above has reasonable grounds for believing that:

(i) delay will involve an immediate risk of harm to persons or serious loss of, or damage to, property; or

(ii) where a solicitor, including a duty solicitor, has been contacted and has agreed to attend, awaiting his arrival would cause unreasonable delay to the process of investigation; or

(c) the solicitor nominated by the person, or selected by him from a list:

(i) cannot be contacted; or

(ii) has previously indicated that he does not wish to be contacted; or

(iii) having been contacted, has declined to attend;

and the person has been advised of the Duty Solicitor Scheme (where one is in operation) but has declined to ask for the duty solicitor, or the duty solicitor is unavailable. (In these circumstances the interview may be started or continued without further delay provided that an officer of the rank of inspector or above has given agreement for the interview to proceed in those circumstances.)

(d) the person who wanted legal advice changes his mind.

In these circumstances the interview may be started or continued without further delay provided that the person has given his agreement in writing or on tape to being interviewed without receiving legal advice and that an officer of the rank of Inspector or above, having inquired into the person's reasons for his change of mind, has given authority for the interview to proceed. Confirmation of the person's agreement, his change of mind, his reasons where given and the name of the authorising officer shall be recorded in the taped or written interview record at the beginning or recommencement of interview.

6.7 Where 6.6(b)(i) applies, once sufficient information to avert the risk has been obtained, questioning must cease until the person has received legal advice or 6.6(a), (b)(ii), (c) or (d) apply.

6.8 Where a person has been permitted to consult a solicitor and the solicitor is available (i.e., present at the station or on his way to the station or easily contactable by telephone) at the time the interview begins or is in progress, he must be allowed to have his solicitor present while he is interviewed.

6.9 The solicitor may only be required to leave the interview if his conduct is such that the investigating officer is unable properly to put questions to the suspect.

6.10 If the investigating officer considers that a solicitor is acting in such a way, he will stop the interview and consult an officer not below the rank of superintendent, if one is readily available, and otherwise an officer not below the rank of inspector who is not connected with the investigation. After speaking to the solicitor, the officer who has been consulted will decide whether or not the interview should continue in the presence of that solicitor. If he decides that it should not, the suspect will be given the opportunity to consult another solicitor before the interview continues and that solicitor will be given an opportunity to be present at the interview.

6.11 The removal of a solicitor from an interview is a serious step and, if it occurs, the officer of superintendent rank or above who took the decision will consider whether the incident should be reported to the Law Society. If the decision to remove the solicitor has been taken by an officer below the rank of superintendent, the facts must be reported to an officer of superintendent rank or above who will similarly consider whether a report to the Law Society would be appropriate. Where the solicitor concerned is a duty solicitor, the report should be both to the Law Society and to the Legal Aid Board.

6.12-6.15 ★ ★ ★ ★ ★

(b) Documentation

6.16 Any request for legal advice and the action taken on it shall be recorded.

6.17 If a person has asked for legal advice and an interview is begun in the absence of a solicitor or his representative (or the solicitor or his representative has been required to leave an interview), a record shall be made in the interview record.

7 * * * * *

8 Conditions of Detention

(a) Action

8.1 So far as is practicable, not more than one person shall be detained in each cell.

8.2 Cells in use must be adequately heated, cleaned and ventilated. They must be adequately lit, subject to such dimming as is compatible with safety and security to allow people detained overnight to sleep. No additional restraints shall be used within a locked cell unless absolutely necessary, and then only suitable handcuffs. In the case of a mentally handicapped or mentally disordered person, particular care must be taken when deciding whether to use handcuffs.

8.3 Blankets, mattresses, pillows and other bedding supplied should be of a reasonable standard and in a clean and sanitary condition.

8.4 Access to toilet and washing facilities must be provided.

8.5 If it is necessary to remove a person's clothes for the purposes of investigation, for hygiene or health reasons or for cleaning, replacement clothing of a reasonable standard of comfort and cleanliness shall be provided. A person may not be interviewed unless adequate clothing has been offered to him.

8.6 At least two light meals and one main meal shall be offered in any period of 24 hours. Drinks should be provided at mealtimes and upon reasonable request between mealtimes. Whenever necessary, advice shall be sought from the police surgeon on medical or dietary matters. As far as practicable, meals provided shall offer a varied diet and meet any special dietary needs or religious beliefs that the person may have; he may also have meals supplied by his family or friends at his or their own expense.

8.7 Brief outdoor exercise shall be offered daily if practicable.

8.8 A juvenile shall not be placed in a police cell unless no other secure accommodation is available and the custody officer considers that it is not practicable to supervise him if he is not placed in a cell or the custody officer considers that a cell provides more comfortable accommodation than other secure accommodation in the police station. He may not be placed in a cell with a detained adult.

8.9 Reasonable force may be used if necessary for the following purposes:

(i) to secure compliance with reasonable instructions, including instructions given in pursuance of the provisions of a code of practice; or

(ii) to prevent escape, injury, damage to property or the destruction of evidence.

8.10 People detained shall be visited every hour, and those who are drunk, at least every half hour. A person who is drunk shall be roused and spoken to on each visit. Should the custody officer feel in any way concerned about the person's condition, for example because he fails to respond adequately when roused, then the officer shall arrange for medical treatment in accordance with paragraph 9.2 of this code.

(b) Documentation

8.11 A record must be kept of replacement clothing and meals offered.

8.12 If a juvenile is placed in a cell, the reason must be recorded.

9 Treatment of Detained Persons

(a) General

9.1 If a complaint is made by or on behalf of a detained person about his treatment since his arrest, or it comes to the notice of any officer that he may have been treated improperly, a report must be made as soon as practicable to an officer of the rank of inspector or above who is not connected with the investigation. If the matter concerns a possible assault or the possibility of the unnecessary or unreasonable use of force then the police surgeon must also be called as soon as practicable.

(b) Medical Treatment

9.2 The custody officer must immediately call the police surgeon (or, in urgent cases, — for example, where a person does not show signs of sensibility or awareness, — must send the person to hospital or call the nearest available medical practitioner) if a person brought to a police station or already detained there:

(a) appears to be suffering from physical illness or a mental disorder; or
(b) is injured; or
(c) [Not Used]
(d) fails to respond normally to questions or conversation (other than through drunkenness alone); or
(e) otherwise appears to need medical attention.

This applies even if the person makes no request for medical attention and whether or not he has recently had medical treatment elsewhere (unless brought to the police station direct from hospital).

9.3 If it appears to the custody officer, or he is told, that a person brought to the police station under arrest may be suffering from an infectious disease of any significance he must take steps to isolate the person and his property until he has obtained medical directions as to where the person should be taken, whether fumigation should take place and what precautions should be taken by officers who have been or will be in contact with him.

9.4 If a detained person requests a medical examination the police surgeon must be called as soon as practicable. He may in addition be examined by a medical practitioner of his own choice at his own expense.

9.5-9.9 ★★★★★

10 Cautions

(a) When a caution must be given

10.1 A person whom there are grounds to suspect of an offence must be cautioned before any questions about it (or further questions if it is his answers to previous questions which provide the grounds for suspicion) are put to him regarding his involvement or suspected involvement in that offence if his answers or his silence (i.e., failure or refusal to answer a question or to answer satisfactorily) may be given in evidence to a court in a prosecution. He therefore need not be cautioned if questions are put for other purposes, for example, solely to establish his identity or his ownership of any vehicle or to obtain information in accordance with any relevant statutory requirement (see paragraph 10.5C) or in furtherance of the proper and effective conduct of a search (for example to determine the need to search in the exercise of powers of stop and search or to seek co-operation while carrying out a search), or to seek verification of a written record in accordance with paragraph 11.13.

10.2 Whenever a person who is not under arrest is initially cautioned or is reminded that he is under caution (see paragraph 10.5) he must at the same time be told that he is not under arrest and is not obliged to remain with the officer (see paragraph 3.15).

10.3 A person must be cautioned upon arrest for an offence unless:
(a) it is impracticable to do so by reason of his condition or behaviour at the time; or
(b) he has already been cautioned immediately prior to arrest in accordance with paragraph 10.1 above.

(b) Action: general

10.4 The caution shall be in the following terms:

> You do not have to say anything. But it may harm your defence if you do not mention when questioned something which you later rely on in court. Anything you do say may be given in evidence.

10.5 When there is a break in questioning under caution the interviewing officer must ensure that the person being questioned is aware that he remains under caution. If there is any doubt the caution should be given again in full when the interview resumes.

Special warnings under sections 36 and 37 of the Criminal Justice and Public Order Act 1994

10.5A When a suspect who is interviewed after arrest fails or refuses to answer certain questions, or to answer them satisfactorily, after due warning, a court or jury may draw such inferences as appear proper under sections 36 and 37 of the Criminal Justice and Public Order Act 1994. This applies when:
(a) a suspect is arrested by a constable and there is found on his person, or in or on his clothing or footwear, or otherwise in his possession, or in the place where he was arrested, any objects, marks or substances, or marks on such objects, and the person fails or refuses to account for the objects, marks or substances found; or
(b) an arrested person was found by a constable at a place at or about the time the offence for which he was arrested, is alleged to have been committed, and the person fails or refuses to account for his presence at that place.

10.5B For an inference to be drawn from a suspect's failure or refusal to answer a question about one of these matters or to answer it satisfactorily, the interviewing officer must first tell him in ordinary language:
(a) what offence he is investigating;
(b) what fact he is asking the suspect to account for;
(c) that he believes this fact may be due to the suspect's taking part in the commission of the offence in question;
(d) that a court may draw a proper inference if he fails or refuses to account for the fact about which he is being questioned;
(e) that a record is being made of the interview and that it may be given in evidence if he is brought to trial.

10.5C Where, despite the fact that a person has been cautioned, failure to co-operate may have an effect on his immediate treatment, he should be informed of any relevant consequences and that they are not affected by the caution. Examples are when his refusal to provide his name and address when charged may render him liable to detention, or when his refusal to provide particulars and information in accordance with a statutory requirement, for example, under the Road Traffic Act 1988, may amount to an offence or may make him liable to arrest.

(c) Juveniles, the mentally disordered and the mentally handicapped

10.6 If a juvenile or a person who is mentally disordered or mentally handicapped is cautioned in the absence of the appropriate adult, the caution must be repeated in the adult's presence.

(d) Documentation

10.7 A record shall be made when a caution is given under this section, either in the officer's pocket book or in the interview record as appropriate.

11 Interviews: general

11.1A, 11.1, 11.2 * * * * *

11.2A At the beginning of an interview carried out in a police station, the interviewing officer, after cautioning the suspect, shall put to him any significant statement or silence which occurred before his arrival at the police station, and shall ask him whether he confirms or denies that earlier statement or silence and whether he wishes to add anything. A 'significant' statement or silence is one which appears capable of being used in evidence against the suspect, in particular a direct admission of guilt, or failure or refusal to answer a question or to answer it satisfactorily, which might give rise to an inference under Part III of the Criminal Justice and Public Order Act 1994.

11.3 No police officer may try to obtain answers to questions or to elicit a statement by the use of oppression. Except as provided for in paragraph 10.5C, no police officer shall indicate, except in answer to a direct question, what action will be taken on the part of the police if the person being interviewed answers questions, makes a statement or refuses to do either. If the person asks the officer directly what action will be taken in the event of his answering questions, making a statement or refusing to do either, then the officer may inform the person what action the police propose to take in that event provided that action is itself proper and warranted.

11.4 As soon as a police officer who is making enquiries of any person about an offence believes that a prosecution should be brought against him and that there is sufficient evidence for it to succeed, he should ask the person if he has anything further to say. If the person indicates that he has nothing more to say the officer shall without delay cease to question him about that offence. This should not, however, be taken to prevent officers in revenue cases or acting under the confiscation provisions of the Criminal Justice Act 1988 or the Drug Trafficking Offences Act 1986 from inviting suspects to complete a formal question and answer record after the interview is concluded.

(b) Interview records

11.5 (a) An accurate record must be made of each interview with a person suspected of an offence, whether or not the interview takes place at a police station.

(b) The record must state the place of the interview, the time it begins and ends, the time the record is made (if different), any breaks in the interview and the names of all those present; and must be made on the forms provided for this purpose or in the officer's pocket-book or in accordance with the code of practice for the tape-recording of police interviews with suspects.

(c) The record must be made during the course of the interview, unless in the investigating officer's view this would not be practicable or would interfere with the conduct of the interview, and must constitute either a verbatim record of what has been said or, failing this, an account of the interview which adequately and accurately summarises it.

11.6 ★★★★★

11.7 If an interview record is not made during the course of the interview it must be made as soon as practicable after its completion.

11.8 Written interview records must be timed and signed by the maker.

11.9 If an interview record is not completed in the course of the interview the reason must be recorded in the officer's pocket book.

11.10 Unless it is impracticable the person interviewed shall be given the opportunity to read the interview record and to sign it as correct or to indicate the respects in which he considers it inaccurate. If the interview is tape-recorded the arrangements set out in the relevant code of practice apply. If the person concerned cannot read or refuses to read the record or to sign it, the senior police officer present shall read it over to him and ask him whether he would like to sign it as correct (or make his mark) or to indicate the respects in which he considers it inaccurate. The police officer shall then certify on the interview record itself what has occurred.

11.11 If the appropriate adult or the person's solicitor is present during the interview, he should also be given an opportunity to read and sign the interview record (or any written statement taken down by a police officer).

11.12 Any refusal by a person to sign an interview record when asked to do so in accordance with the provisions of this code must itself be recorded.

11.13-11.16 ★★★★★

12 Interviews in police stations

(a) Action

12.1 If a police officer wishes to interview, or conduct enquiries which require the presence of a detained person the custody officer is responsible for deciding whether to deliver him into his custody.

12.2 In any period of 24 hours a detained person must be allowed a continuous period of at least 8 hours for rest, free from questioning, travel or any interruption by police officers in connection with the investigation concerned. This period should normally be at night. The period of rest may not be interrupted or delayed, except at the request of the person, his appropriate adult or his legal representative, unless there are reasonable grounds for believing that it would:

(i) involve a risk of harm to persons or serious loss of, or damage to, property;
(ii) delay unnecessarily the person's release from custody; or
(iii) otherwise prejudice the outcome of the investigation.

If a person is arrested at a police station after going there voluntarily, the period of 24 hours runs from the time of his arrest and not the time of arrival at the police station. Any action which is required to be taken in accordance with section 8 of this code, or in accordance with medical advice or at the request of the detained person, his appropriate adult or his legal representative, does not constitute an interruption to the rest period such that a fresh period must be allowed.

12.3 A detained person may not be supplied with intoxicating liquor except on medical directions. No person who is unfit through drink or drugs to the extent that he is unable to appreciate the significance of questions put to him and his answers may be questioned about an alleged offence in that condition except in accordance with Annex C.

12.4 As far as practicable interviews shall take place in interview rooms which must be adequately heated, lit and ventilated.

12.5 Persons being questioned or making statements shall not be required to stand.

12.6 Before the commencement of an interview each interviewing officer shall identify himself and any other officers present by name and rank to the person being interviewed, except in the case of persons detained under the Prevention of Terrorism (Temporary Provisions) Act 1989 when each officer shall identify himself by his warrant or other identification number and rank rather than his name.

12.7 Breaks from interviewing shall be made at recognised meal times. Short breaks for refreshment shall also be provided at intervals of approximately two hours, subject to the interviewing officer's discretion to delay a break if there are reasonable grounds for believing that it would:

(i) involve a risk of harm to persons or serious loss of, or damage to, property;
(ii) delay unnecessarily the person's release from custody; or
(iii) otherwise prejudice the outcome of the investigation.

12.8 If in the course of the interview a complaint is made by the person being questioned or on his behalf concerning the provisions of this code then the interviewing officer shall:

(i) record it in the interview record; and
(ii) inform the custody officer, who is then responsible for dealing with it in accordance with section 9 of this code.

(b) Documentation

12.9-12.13 ★★★★★

13-15 ★★★★★

16 Charging of detained persons

(a) Action

16.1 When an officer considers that there is sufficient evidence to prosecute a detained person, and that there is sufficient evidence for a prosecution to succeed, and that the person has said all that he wishes to say about the offence, he should without delay (and subject to the following qualification) bring him before the custody officer who shall then be responsible for considering whether or not he should be charged. When a person is detained in respect of more than one offence it is permissible to delay bringing him before the custody officer until the above conditions are satisfied in respect of all the offences (but see paragraph 11.4). Any resulting action should be taken in the presence of the appropriate adult if the person is a juvenile or mentally disordered or mentally handicapped.

16.2 When a detained person is charged with or informed that he may be prosecuted for an offence he shall be cautioned in the terms:

> You do not have to say anything. But it may harm your defence if you do not mention now something which you later rely on in court. Anything you do say may be given in evidence.

16.3 At the time a person is charged he shall be given a written notice showing particulars of the offence with which he is charged and including the name of the officer in the case (in terrorist cases, the officer's warrant or other identification number instead), his police station and the reference number for the case. So far as possible the particulars of the charge shall be stated in simple terms, but they shall also show the precise offence in law with which he is charged. The notice shall begin with the following words:

> You are charged with the offence(s) shown below. You do not have to say anything. But it may harm your defence if you do not mention now something which you later rely on in court. Anything you do say may be given in evidence.

If the person is a juvenile or is mentally disordered or mentally handicapped the notice shall be given to the appropriate adult.

16.4 If at any time after a person has been charged with or informed he may be prosecuted for an offence, a police officer wishes to bring to the notice of the person any written statement made by another person or the content of an interview with another person, he shall hand to that person a true copy of any such written statement or bring to his attention the content of the interview record, but shall say or do nothing to invite any reply or comment save to warn him that he does not have to say anything but that anything he does say may be given in evidence and to remind him of his right to legal advice in accordance with paragraph 6.5 above. If the person cannot read then the officer may read it to him. If the person is a juvenile or mentally disordered or mentally handicapped the copy shall also be given to, or the interview record brought to the attention of, the appropriate adult.

16.5 Questions relating to an offence may not be put to a person after he has been charged with that offence, or informed that he may be prosecuted for it, unless they are necessary for the purpose of preventing or minimising harm or loss to some other person or to the public or for clearing up an ambiguity in a previous answer or statement, or where it is in the interests of justice that the person should have put to him and have an opportunity to comment on information concerning the offence which has come to light since he was charged or informed that he might be prosecuted. Before any such questions are put to him, he shall be warned that he does not have to say anything but that anything he does say may be given in evidence and reminded of his right to legal advice in accordance with paragraph 6.5 above.

16.6 Where a juvenile is charged with an offence and the custody officer authorises his continued detention he must try to make arrangements for the juvenile to be taken into the care of a local authority to be detained pending appearance in court unless he certifies that it is impracticable to do so, or, in the case of a juvenile of at least 12 years of age, no secure accommodation is available and there is a risk to the public of serious harm from that juvenile, in accordance with section 38(6) of the Police and Criminal Evidence Act 1984, as amended by Section 59 of the Criminal Justice Act 1991 and section 24 of the Criminal Justice and Public Order Act 1994.

(b) Documentation

16.7 A record shall be made of anything a detained person says when charged.

16.8 Any questions put after charge and answers given relating to the offence shall be contemporaneously recorded in full on the forms provided and the record signed by that person or, if he refuses, by the interviewing officer and any third parties present. If the questions are tape-recorded the arrangements set out in Code E apply.

16.9 If it is not practicable to make arrangements for the transfer of a juvenile into local authority care in accordance with paragraph 16.6 above the custody officer must record the reasons and make out a certificate to be produced before the court together with the juvenile.

ANNEX A ★★★★★

ANNEX B
DELAY IN NOTIFYING ARREST OR ALLOWING ACCESS TO LEGAL ADVICE

A Persons detained under the Police and Criminal Evidence Act 1984

(a) Action

1. The rights set out in sections 5 or 6 of the code or both may be delayed if the person is in police detention in connection with a serious arrestable offence, has not yet been charged with an offence and an officer of the rank of superintendent or above has reasonable grounds for believing that the exercise of either right:

(i) will lead to interference with or harm to evidence connected with a serious arrestable offence or interference with or physical injury to other persons; or

(ii) will lead to the alerting of other persons suspected of having committed such an offence but not yet arrested for it; or

(iii) will hinder the recovery of property obtained as a result of such an offence.

2. These rights may also be delayed where the serious arrestable offence is either:

(i) a drug trafficking offence and the officer has reasonable grounds for believing that the detained person has benefited from drug trafficking, and that the recovery of the value of that person's proceeds of drug trafficking will be hindered by the exercise of either right; or

(ii) an offence to which Part VI of the Criminal Justice Act 1988 (covering confiscation orders) applies and the officer has reasonable grounds for believing that the detained person has benefited from the offence, and that the recovery of the value of the property obtained by that person from or in connection with the offence or if the pecuniary advantage derived by him from or in connection with it will be hindered by the exercise of either right.

3. Access to a solicitor may not be delayed on the grounds that he might advise the person not to answer any questions or that the solicitor was initially asked to attend the police station by someone else, provided that the person himself then wishes to see the solicitor. In the latter case the detained person must be told that the solicitor has come to the police station at another person's request, and must be asked to sign the custody record to signify whether or not he wishes to see the solicitor.

4. These rights may be delayed only for as long as is necessary and, subject to paragraph 9 below, in no case beyond 36 hours after the relevant time as defined in section 41 of the Police and Criminal Evidence Act 1984. If the above grounds cease to apply within this time, the person must as soon as practicable be asked if he wishes to exercise either right, the custody record must be noted accordingly, and action must be taken in accordance with the relevant section of the code.

5. A detained person must be permitted to consult a solicitor for a reasonable time before any court hearing.

(b) Documentation

6. The grounds for action under this Annex shall be recorded and the person informed of them as soon as practicable.

7. Any reply given by a person under paragraphs 4 or 9 must be recorded and the person asked to endorse the record in relation to whether he wishes to receive legal advice at this point.

8.-11. ★★★★★

ANNEX C-E ★★★★★

Note Codes D (identification) and E (tape recording) are not reproduced.

CRIMINAL PROCEDURE AND INVESTIGATIONS ACT 1996 CODE OF PRACTICE UNDER PART II

Note This Code came into effect on 1 April 1997 and applies to England and Wales and Northern Ireland.

1 Introduction

1.1 This code of practice is issued under Part II of the Criminal Procedure and Investigations Act 1996 ("the Act"). It applies in respect of criminal investigations conducted by police officers which begin on or after the day on which this code comes into effect. Persons other than police officers who are charged with the duty of conducting an investigation as defined in the Act are to have regard to the relevant provisions of the code, and should take these into account in applying their own operating procedures.

1.2 This code does not apply to persons who are not charged with the duty of conducting an investigation as defined in the Act.

1.3 Nothing in this code applies to material intercepted in obedience to a warrant issued under section 2 of the Interception of Communications Act 1985, or to any copy of that material as defined in section 10 of that Act.

2 Definitions

2.1 In this code:

—a *criminal investigation* is an investigation conducted by police officers with a view to it being ascertained whether a person should be charged with an offence, or whether a person charged with an offence is guilty of it. This will include

—investigations into crimes that have been committed;

—investigations whose purpose is to ascertain whether a crime has been committed, with a view to the possible institution of criminal proceedings; and

—investigations which begin in the belief that a crime may be committed, for example when the police keep premises or individuals under observation for a period of time, with a view to the possible institution of criminal proceedings;

—*charging* a person with an offence includes prosecution by way of summons;

—an *investigator* is any police officer involved in the conduct of a criminal investigation. All investigators have a responsibility for carrying out the duties imposed on them under this code, including in particular recording information, and retaining records of information and other material;

—the *officer in charge of an investigation* is the police officer responsible for directing a criminal investigation. He is also responsible for ensuring that proper procedures are in place for recording information, and retaining records of information and other material, in the investigation;

—the *disclosure officer* is the person responsible for examining material retained by the police during the investigation; revealing material to the prosecutor during the investigation and any criminal proceedings resulting from it, and certifying that he has done this; and disclosing material to the accused at the request of the prosecutor;

—the *prosecutor* is the authority responsible for the conduct of criminal proceedings on behalf of the Crown. Particular duties may in practice fall to individuals acting on behalf of the prosecuting authority;

—*material* is material of any kind, including information and objects, which is obtained in the course of a criminal investigation and which may be relevant to the investigation;

—material may be *relevant to an investigation* if it appears to an investigator, or to the officer in charge of an investigation, or to the disclosure officer, that it has some bearing on any offence under investigation or any person being investigated, or on the surrounding circumstances of the case, unless it is incapable of having any impact on the case;

—*sensitive material* is material which the disclosure officer believes, after consulting the officer in charge of the investigation, it is not in the public interest to disclose;

—references to *primary prosecution disclosure* are to the duty of the prosecutor under section 3 of the Act to disclose material which is in his possession or which he has inspected in pursuance of this code, and which in his opinion might undermine the case against the accused;

—references to *secondary prosecution disclosure* are to the duty of the prosecutor under section 7 of the Act to disclose material which is in his possession or which he has inspected in pursuance of this code, and which might reasonably be expected to assist the defence disclosed by the accused in a defence statement given under the Act;

—references to the disclosure of material to a person accused of an offence include references to the disclosure of material to his legal representative;

—references to police officers and to the chief officer of police include those employed in a police force as defined in section 3(3) of the Prosecution of Offences Act 1985.

3 General responsibilities

3.1 The functions of the investigator, the officer in charge of an investigation and the disclosure officer are separate. Whether they are undertaken by one, two or more persons will depend on the complexity of the case and the administrative arrangements within each police force. Where they are undertaken by more than one person, close consultation between them is essential to the effective performance of the duties imposed by this code.

3.2 The chief officer of police for each police force is responsible for putting in place arrangements to ensure that in every investigation the identity of the officer in charge of an investigation and the disclosure officer is recorded.

3.3 The officer in charge of an investigation may delegate tasks to another investigator or to civilians employed by the police force, but he remains responsible for ensuring that these have been carried out and for accounting for any general policies followed in the investigation. In particular, it is an essential part of his duties to ensure that all material which may be relevant to an investigation is retained, and either made available to the disclosure officer or (in exceptional circumstances) revealed directly to the prosecutor.

3.4 In conducting an investigation, the investigator should pursue all reasonable lines of inquiry, whether these point towards or away from the suspect. What is reasonable in each case will depend on the particular circumstances.

3.5 If the officer in charge of an investigation believes that other persons may be in possession of material that may be relevant to the investigation, and if this has not been obtained under paragraph 3.4 above, he should ask the disclosure officer to inform them of the existence of the investigation and to invite them to retain the material in case they receive a request for its disclosure. The disclosure officer should inform the prosecutor that they may have such material. However, the officer in charge of an investigation is not required to make speculative enquiries of other persons: there must be some reason to believe that they may have relevant material. That reason may come from information provided to the police by the accused or from other inquiries made or from some other source.

3.6 If, during a criminal investigation, the officer in charge of an investigation or disclosure officer for any reason no longer has responsibility for the functions falling to him, either his supervisor or the police officer in charge of criminal investigations for the police force concerned must assign someone else to assume that responsibility. That person's identity must be recorded, as with those initially responsible for these functions in each investigation.

4 Recording of information

4.1 If material which may be relevant to the investigation consists of information which is not recorded in any form, the officer in charge of an investigation must ensure that it is recorded in a durable or retrievable form (whether in writing, on video or audio tape, or on computer disk).

4.2 Where it is not practicable to retain the initial record of information because it forms part of a larger record which is to be destroyed, its contents should be transferred as a true record to a durable and more easily-stored form before that happens.

4.3 Negative information is often relevant to an investigation. If it may be relevant it must be recorded. An example might be a number of people present in a particular place at a particular time who state that they saw nothing unusual.

4.4 Where information which may be relevant is obtained, it must be recorded at the time it is obtained or as soon as practicable after that time. This includes, for example, information obtained in house-to-house enquiries, although the requirement to record information promptly does not require an investigator to take a statement from a potential witness where it would not otherwise be taken.

5 Retention of material

(a) Duty to retain material

5.1 The investigator must retain material obtained in a criminal investigation which may be relevant to the investigation. This includes not only material coming into the possession of the investigator (such as documents seized in the course of searching premises) but also material generated by him (such as interview records). Material may be photographed, or retained in the form of a copy rather than the original, if the original is perishable, or was supplied to the investigator rather than generated by him and is to be returned to its owner.

5.2 Where material has been seized in the exercise of the powers of seizure conferred by the Police and Criminal Evidence Act 1984, the duty to retain it under this code is subject to the provisions on the retention of seized material in section 22 of that Act.

5.3 If the officer in charge of an investigation becomes aware as a result of developments in the case that material previously examined but not retained (because it was not thought to be relevant) may now be relevant to the investigation, he should, wherever practicable, take steps to obtain it or ensure that it is retained for further inspection or for production in court if required.

5.4 The duty to retain material includes in particular the duty to retain material falling into the following categories, where it may be relevant to the investigation:

—crime reports (including crime report forms, relevant parts of incident report books or police officers' notebooks);

—custody records;

—records which are derived from tapes of telephone messages (for example, 999 calls) containing descriptions of an alleged offence or offender;

—final versions of witness statements (and draft versions where their content differs from the final version), including any exhibits mentioned (unless these have been returned to their owner on the understanding that they will be produced in court if required);

—interview records (written records, or audio or video tapes, of interviews with actual or potential witnesses or suspects);

—communications between the police and experts such as forensic scientists, reports of work carried out by experts, and schedules of scientific material prepared by the expert for the investigator, for the purposes of criminal proceedings;

—any material casting doubt on the reliability of a confession;

—any material casting doubt on the reliability of a witness;

—any other material which may fall within the test for primary prosecution disclosure in the Act.

5.5 The duty to retain material falling into these categories does not extend to items which are purely ancillary to such material and possess no independent significance (for example, duplicate copies of records or reports).

(b) Length of time for which material is to be retained

5.6 All material which may be relevant to the investigation must be retained until a decision is taken whether to institute proceedings against a person for an offence.

5.7 If a criminal investigation results in proceedings being instituted, all material which may be relevant must be retained at least until the accused is acquitted or convicted or the prosecutor decides not to proceed with the case.

5.8 Where the accused is convicted, all material which may be relevant must be retained at least until:

—the convicted person is released from custody, or discharged from hospital, in cases where the court imposes a custodial sentence or a hospital order;

—six months from the date of conviction, in all other cases.

If the court imposes a custodial sentence or hospital order and the convicted person is released from custody or discharged from hospital earlier than six months from the date of conviction, all material which may be relevant must be retained at least until six months from the date of conviction.

5.9 If an appeal against conviction is in progress when the release or discharge occurs, or at the end of the period of six months specified in paragraph 5.8, all material which may be relevant must be retained until the appeal is determined. Similarly, if the Criminal Cases Review Commission is considering an application at that point in time, all material which may be relevant must be retained at least until the Commission decides not to refer the case to the Court of Appeal, or until the Court determines the appeal resulting from the reference by the Commission.

5.10 Material need not be retained by the police as required in paragraph 5.8 if it was seized and is to be returned to its owner.

6 Preparation of material for prosecutor

(a) Introduction

6.1 The officer in charge of the investigation, the disclosure officer or an investigator may seek advice from the prosecutor about whether any particular item of material may be relevant to the investigation.

6.2 Material which may be relevant to an investigation, which has been retained in accordance with this code, and which the disclosure officer believes will not form part of the prosecution case, must be listed on a schedule.

6.3 Material which the disclosure officer does not believe is sensitive must be listed on a schedule of non-sensitive material. The schedule must include a statement that the disclosure officer does not believe the material is sensitive.

6.4 Any material which is believed to be sensitive must be either listed on a schedule of sensitive material or, in exceptional circumstances, revealed to the prosecutor separately.

6.5 Paragraphs 6.6 to 6.11 below apply to both sensitive and non-sensitive material. Paragraphs 6.12 to 6.14 apply to sensitive material only.

(b) Circumstances in which a schedule is to be prepared

6.6 The disclosure officer must ensure that a schedule is prepared in the following circumstances:

—the accused is charged with an offence which is triable only on indictment;

—the accused is charged with an offence which is triable either way, and it is considered either that the case is likely to be tried on indictment or that the accused is likely to plead not guilty at a summary trial;

—the accused is charged with a summary offence, and it is considered that he is likely to plead not guilty.

6.7 In respect of either way and summary offences, a schedule may not be needed if a person has admitted the offence, or if a police officer witnessed the offence and that person has not denied it.

6.8 If it is believed that the accused is likely to plead guilty at a summary trial, it is not necessary to prepare a schedule in advance. If, contrary to this belief, the accused pleads not guilty at a summary trial, or the offence is to be tried on indictment, the disclosure officer must ensure that a schedule is prepared as soon as is reasonably practicable after that happens.

(c) Way in which material is to be listed on schedule

6.9 The disclosure officer should ensure that each item of material is listed separately on the schedule, and is numbered consecutively. The description of each item should make clear the nature of the item and should contain sufficient detail to enable the prosecutor to decide whether he needs to inspect the material before deciding whether or not it should be disclosed.

6.10 In some enquiries it may not be practicable to list each item of material separately. For example, there may be many items of a similar or repetitive nature. These may be listed in a block and described by quantity and generic title.

6.11 Even if some material is listed in a block, the disclosure officer must ensure that any items among that material which might meet the test for primary prosecution disclosure are listed and described individually.

(d) Treatment of sensitive material

6.12 Subject to paragraph 6.13 below, the disclosure officer must list on a sensitive schedule any material which he believes it is not in the public interest to disclose, and the reason for that belief. The schedule must include a statement that the disclosure officer believes the material is sensitive. Depending on the circumstances, examples of such material may include the following among others:

—material relating to national security;
—material received from the intelligence and security agencies;
—material relating to intelligence from foreign sources which reveals sensitive intelligence gathering methods;
—material given in confidence;
—material which relates to the use of a telephone system and which is supplied to an investigator for intelligence purposes only;
—material relating to the identity or activities of informants, or under-cover police officers, or other persons supplying information to the police who may be in danger if their identities are revealed;
—material revealing the location of any premises or other place used for police surveillance, or the identity of any person allowing a police officer to use them for surveillance;
—material revealing, either directly or indirectly, techniques and methods relied upon by a police officer in the course of a criminal investigation, for example covert surveillance techniques, or other methods of detecting crime;
—material whose disclosure might facilitate the commission of other offences or hinder the prevention and detection of crime;
—internal police communications such as management minutes;
—material upon the strength of which search warrants were obtained;
—material containing details of persons taking part in identification parades;
—material supplied to an investigator during a criminal investigation which has been generated by an official of a body concerned with the regulation or supervision of bodies corporate or of persons engaged in financial activities, or which has been generated by a person retained by such a body;
—material supplied to an investigator during a criminal investigation which relates to a child or young person and which has been generated by a local authority social services department, an Area Child Protection Committee or other party contacted by an investigator during the investigation.

6.13 In exceptional circumstances, where an investigator considers that material is so sensitive that its revelation to the prosecutor by means of an entry on the sensitive schedule is inappropriate, the existence of the material must be revealed to the prosecutor separately. This will apply where compromising the material would be likely to lead directly to the loss of life, or directly threaten national security.

6.14 In such circumstances, the responsibility for informing the prosecutor lies with the investigator who knows the detail of the sensitive material. The investigator should act as soon as is reasonably practicable after the file containing the prosecution case is sent to the prosecutor. The investigator must also ensure that the prosecutor is able to inspect the material so that he can assess whether it needs to be brought before a court for a ruling on disclosure.

7 Revelation of material to prosecutor

7.1 The disclosure officer must give the schedules to the prosecutor. Wherever practicable this should be at the same time as he gives him the file containing the material for the prosecution case (or as soon as is reasonably practicable after the decision on mode of trial or the plea, in cases to which paragraph 6.8 applies).

7.2 The disclosure officer should draw the attention of the prosecutor to any material an investigator has retained (whether or not listed on a schedule) which may fall within the test for primary prosecution disclosure in the Act, and should explain why he has come to that view.

7.3 At the same time as complying with the duties in paragraphs 7.1 and 7.2, the disclosure officer must give the prosecutor a copy of any material which falls into the following categories (unless such material has already been given to the prosecutor as part of the file containing the material for the prosecution case):

—records of the first description of a suspect given to the police by a potential witness, whether or not the description differs from that of the alleged offender;

—information provided by an accused person which indicates an explanation for the offence with which he has been charged;

—any material casting doubt on the reliability of a confession;

—any material casting doubt on the reliability of a witness;

—any other material which the investigator believes may fall within the test for primary prosecution disclosure in the Act.

7.4 If the prosecutor asks to inspect material which has not already been copied to him, the disclosure officer must allow him to inspect it. If the prosecutor asks for a copy of material which has not already been copied to him, the disclosure officer must give him a copy. However, this does not apply where the disclosure officer believes, having consulted the officer in charge of the investigation, that the material is too sensitive to be copied and can only be inspected.

7.5 If material consists of information which is recorded other than in writing, whether it should be given to the prosecutor in its original form as a whole, or by way of relevant extracts recorded in the same form, or in the form of a transcript, is a matter for agreement between the disclosure officer and the prosecutor.

8 Subsequent action by disclosure officer

8.1 At the time a schedule of non-sensitive material is prepared, the disclosure officer may not know exactly what material will form the case against the accused, and the prosecutor may not have given advice about the likely relevance of particular items of material. Once these matters have been determined, the disclosure officer must give the prosecutor, where necessary, an amended schedule listing any additional material:

—which may be relevant to the investigation,

—which does not form part of the case against the accused,

—which is not already listed on the schedule, and

—which he believes is not sensitive,

unless he is informed in writing by the prosecutor that the prosecutor intends to disclose the material to the defence.

8.2 After a defence statement has been given, the disclosure officer must look again at the material which has been retained and must draw the attention of the prosecutor to any material which might reasonably be expected to assist the defence disclosed by the accused; and he must reveal it to him in accordance with paragraphs 7.4 and 7.5 above.

8.3 Section 9 of the Act imposes a continuing duty on the prosecutor, for the duration of criminal proceedings against the accused, to disclose material which meets the tests for disclosure (subject to public interest considerations). To enable him to do this, any new material coming to light should be treated in the same way as the earlier material.

9 Certification by disclosure officer

9.1 The disclosure officer must certify to the prosecutor that, to the best of his knowledge and belief, all material which has been retained and made available to him has been revealed to the prosecutor in accordance with this code. He must sign and date the certificate. It will be necessary to certify not only at the time when the schedule and accompanying material is submitted to the prosecutor, but also when material which has been retained is reconsidered after the accused has given a defence statement.

10 Disclosure of material to accused

10.1 If material has not already been copied to the prosecutor, and he requests its disclosure to the accused on the ground that:

—it falls within the test for primary or secondary prosecution disclosure, or

—the court has ordered its disclosure after considering an application from the accused,

the disclosure officer must disclose it to the accused.

10.2 If material has been copied to the prosecutor, and it is to be disclosed, whether it is disclosed by the prosecutor or the disclosure officer is a matter for agreement between the two of them.

10.3 The disclosure officer must disclose material to the accused either by giving him a copy or by allowing him to inspect it. If the accused person asks for a copy of any material which he has been allowed to inspect, the disclosure officer must give it to him, unless in the opinion of the disclosure officer that is either not practicable (for example because the material consists of an object which cannot be copied, or because the volume of material is so great), or not desirable (for example because the material is a statement by a child witness in relation to a sexual offence).

10.4 If material which the accused has been allowed to inspect consists of information which is recorded other than in writing, whether it should be given to the accused in its original form or in the form of a transcript is a matter for the discretion of the disclosure officer. If the material is transcribed, the disclosure officer must ensure that the transcript is certified to the accused as a true record of the material which has been transcribed.

10.5 If a court concludes that it is in the public interest that an item of sensitive material must be disclosed to the accused, it will be necessary to disclose the material if the case is to proceed. This does not mean that sensitive documents must always be disclosed in their original form: for example, the court may agree that sensitive details still requiring protection should be blocked out, or that documents may be summarised, or that the prosecutor may make an admission about the substance of the material under section 10 of the Criminal Justice Act 1967.

RULES OF THE SUPREME COURT 1965

Order 53: Applications for judicial review

1 Cases appropriate for application for judicial review

(1) An application for—

(a) an order of mandamus, prohibition or certiorarti, or

(b) an injunction under section 30 of the Act restraining a person from acting in any office in which he is not entitled to act,

shall be made by way of an application for judicial review in accordance with the provisions of this Order.

(2) An application for a declaration or an injunction (not being an injunction mentioned in paragraph (1)(b)) may be made by way of an application for judicial review, and on such an application the Court may grant the declaration or injunction claimed if it considers that, having regard to—

(a) the nature of the matters in respect of which relief may be granted by way of an order of mandamus, prohibition or certiorari,

(b) the nature of the persons and bodies against whom relief may be granted by way of such an order, and

(c) all the circumstances of the case,
it would be just and convenient for the declaration or injunction to be granted on an application for judicial review.

2 Joinder of claims for relief
On an application for judicial review any relief mentioned in rule 1(1) or (2) may be claimed as an alternative or in addition to any other relief so mentioned if it arises out of or relates to or is connected with the same matter.

3 Grant of leave to apply for judicial review
(1) No application for judicial review shall be made unless the leave of the Court has been obtained in accordance with this rule.
(2) An application for leave must be made *ex parte* to a Judge by filing in the Crown Office—
(a) a notice in Form No. 86A containing a statement of
(i) the name and description of the applicant,
(ii) the relief sought and the grounds upon which it is sought,
(iii) the name and address of the applicant's solicitors (if any) and
(iv) the applicant's address for service; and
(b) an affidavit verifying the facts relied on.
(3) The Judge may determine the application without a hearing, unless a hearing is requested in the notice of application, and need not sit in open Court; in any case, the Crown Office shall serve a copy of the Judge's order on the applicant.
(4) Where the application for leave is refused by the Judge, or is granted on terms, the applicant may renew it by applying—
(a) in any criminal cause or matter, to a Divisional Court of the Queen's Bench Division;
(b) in any other case, to a single Judge sitting in open Court or, if the Court so directs, to a Divisional Court of the Queen's Bench Division:
Provided that no application for leave may be renewed in any non-criminal cause or matter in which the Judge has refused leave under paragraph (3) after a hearing.
(5) In order to renew his application for leave the applicant must, within 10 days of being served with notice of the Judge's refusal, lodge in the Crown Office notice of his intention in Form No. 86B.
(6) Without prejudice to its powers under Order 20, rule 8, the Court hearing an application for leave may allow the applicant's statement to be amended, whether by specifying different or additional grounds or relief or otherwise, on such terms, if any, as it thinks fit.
(7) The Court shall not grant leave unless it considers that the applicant has a sufficient interest in the matter to which the application relates.
(8) Where leave is sought to apply for an order of certiorari to remove for the purpose of its being quashed any judgment, order, conviction or other proceeding which is subject to appeal and a time is limited for the bringing of the appeal, the Court may adjourn the application for leave until the appeal is determined or the time for appealing has expired.
(9) If the Court grants leave, it may impose such terms as to costs and as to giving security as it thinks fit.
(10) Where leave to apply for judicial review is granted, then—
(a) if the relief sought is an order of prohibition or certiorari and the Court so directs, the grant shall operate as a stay of the proceedings to which the application relates until the determination of the application or until the Court otherwise orders;
(b) if any other relief is sought, the Court may at any time grant in the proceedings such interim relief as could be granted in an action begun by writ.

4 Delay in applying for relief

(1) An application for leave to apply for judicial review shall be made promptly and in any event within three months from the date when grounds for the application first arose unless the Court considers that there is good reason for extending the period within which the application shall be made.

(2) Where the relief sought is an order of certiorari in respect of any judgment, order, conviction or other proceeding, the date when grounds for the application first arose shall be taken to be the date of that judgment, order, conviction or proceeding.

(3) Paragraph (1) is without prejudice to any statutory provision which has the effect of limiting the time within which an application for judicial review may be made.

5 Mode of applying for judicial review

(1) In any criminal cause or matter, where leave has been granted to make an application for judicial review, the application shall be made by originating motion to a Divisional Court of the Queen's Bench Division.

(2) In any other such cause or matter, the application shall be made by originating motion to a judge sitting in open Court, unless the Court directs that it shall be made—

(a) by originating summons to a Judge in Chambers; or

(b) by originating motion to a Divisional Court of the Queen's Bench Division.

Any direction under sub-paragraph (a) shall be without prejudice to the Judge's powers under Order 32, rule 13.

(3) The notice of motion or summons must be served on all persons directly affected and where it relates to any proceedings in or before a Court and the object of the application is either to compel the Court or an officer of the Court to do any act in relation to the proceedings or to quash them or any order made therein, the notice or summons must also be served on the Clerk or Registrar of the Court and, where any objection to the conduct of the Judge is to be made, on the Judge.

(4) Unless the Court granting leave has otherwise directed, there must be at least 10 days between the service of the notice of motion or summons and the hearing.

(5) A motion must be entered for hearing within 14 days after the grant of leave.

(6), (7) * * * * *

6 Statements and affidavits

(1) Copies of the statement in support of an application for leave under rule 3 must be served with the notice of motion or summons and, subject to paragraph (2) no grounds shall be relied upon or any relief sought at the hearing except the grounds and relief set out in the statement.

(2) The Court may on hearing of the motion or summons allow the applicant to amend his statement, whether by specifying different or additional grounds of relief or otherwise, on such terms, if any, as it thinks fit and may allow further affidavits to be used by him.

(3) Where the applicant intends to ask to be allowed to amend his statement or to use further affidavits, he shall give notice of his intention and of any proposed amendment to every other party.

(4), (5) * * * * *

7 Claim for damages

(1) On an application for judicial review the Court may, subject to paragraph (2) award damages to the applicant if—

(a) he has included in the statement in support of his application for leave under rule 3 a claim for damages arising from any matter to which the application relates, and

(b) the Court is satisfied that, if the claim had been made in an action begun by the applicant at the time of making his application, he could have been awarded damages.

(2) Order 18, rule 12, shall apply to a statement relating to a claim for damages as it applies to a pleading.

8 ★★★★★

9 Hearing of application for judicial review

(1) On the hearing of any motion or summons under rule 5, any person who desires to be heard in opposition to the motion or summons, and appears to the Court to be a proper person to be heard, shall be heard, notwithstanding that he has not been served with notice of the motion or the summons.

(2) Where the relief sought is or includes an order of certiorari to remove any proceedings for the purpose of quashing them, the applicant may not question the validity of any order, warrant, commitment, conviction, inquisition or record unless before the hearing of the motion or summons he has lodged in the Crown Office a copy thereof verified by affidavit or accounts for his failure to do so to the satisfaction of the Court hearing the motion or summons.

(3) Where an order of certiorari is made in any such case as is referred to in paragraph (2) the order shall, subject to paragraph (4) direct that the proceedings shall be quashed forthwith on their removal into the Queen's Bench Division.

(4) Where the relief sought is an order of certiorari and the Court is satisfied that there are grounds for quashing the decision to which the application relates, the Court may, in addition to quashing it, remit the matter to the Court, tribunal or authority concerned with a direction to reconsider it and reach a decision in accordance with the findings of the Court.

(5) Where the relief sought is a declaration, an injunction or damages and the Court considers that it should not be granted on an application for judicial review but might have been granted if it had been sought in an action begun by writ by the applicant at the time of making his application, the Court may, instead of refusing the application, order the proceedings to continue as if they had been begun by writ; and Order 28, rule 8, shall apply as if, in the case of an application made by motion, it had been made by summons.

10–14 ★★★★★

INDEX

BLACKSTONE'S STATUTES
TITLES IN THE SERIES

Company Law
Contract, Tort and Restitution Statutes
Public Law Statutes
Employment Law Statutes
Criminal Law Statutes
Evidence Statutes
Family Law Statutes
Property Law Statutes
Commercial and Consumer Law Statutes
English Legal System Statutes
EC Legislation
International Law Documents
Landlord and Tenant Statutes
Medical Law Statutes
Planning Law Statutes
Intellectual Property Statutes
Environmental Law Statutes
International Human Rights Documents